THE BOOK OF

American Values and Virtues

THE BOOK OF

American Values
and Virtues

OUR TRADITION OF FREEDOM, LIBERTY & TOLERANCE

Edited by Erik A. Bruun and Robin Getzen

BLACK DOG
& LEVENTHAL
PUBLISHERS
NEW YORK

Copyright © 1996 Black Dog & Leventhal Publishers, Inc.

Published by

Black Dog & Leventhal Publishers, Inc.
151 West 19th Street
New York, NY 10011

Distributed by

Workman Publishing Company
708 Broadway
New York, NY 10003

Pages 605–612 are a continuation of the copyright page.

Designed by Martin Lubin Graphic Design

Typeset by Brad Walrod/High Text Graphics

Manufactured in the United States of America

ISBN: 1-884822-77-0

h g f e d c b a

Library of Congress Cataloging-in-Publication Data
The book of American values and virtues: our tradition of freedom, liberty & tolerance/
    edited by Erik A. Bruun and Robin Getzen.
        p.   cm.
    Includes index.
    ISBN 1-884822-77-0
    1. United States—Civilization—Quotations, maxims, etc.   2. United States—Politics
and government—Philosophy—Quotations, maxims, etc.   3. Civil rights—United
States—Quotations, maxims, etc.   4. National characteristics, American—Quotations,
maxims, etc.   5. Social values—United States—Quotations, maxims, etc.   I. Bruun,
Erik A., 1961–   . II. Getzen, Robin.
E169.1.B736   1996   96-34292
973—dc20   CIP

CONTENTS

INTRODUCTION

The United States of America was the first nation, and is, arguably, still today the only nation to be founded on and "dedicated" to, throughout its history, the *values* and *virtues* of Freedom, Liberty, and Tolerance.

Our Founding Fathers—Jefferson, Franklin, Adams, and Washington—"conceived" of a nation where every man and every woman could live a life, seek an opportunity, practice a creed, or assert an idea without fear of intervention, restraint, or retribution from the government or from the popular plurality.

Keeping to these principles has not been without challenge. America has survived civil war, civil strife, hatred, greed, and bigotry. Our commitment to Freedom, Liberty, and Tolerance has evolved and adapted to an increasingly complex society. These principles, these values, and these virtues, from which America began, endure.

No matter where you go in this world people think that their culture, tribe, or nation is special. Many communities think of themselves as being the center of the world, holding a superior lifestyle. We in the United States are not entirely immune from this phenomenon. At a time when the United States is the most prosperous nation in the world, as it dominates the international scene, and is the only global superpower, it easy to think of our American lifestyle as somehow better than everyone else's—'might makes right', and all that sort of thing.

But this pronouncement would be a mistake; it is an attitude contrary to the fundamental virtues and values that make America beautiful. The strength of America is based on the priority that we as a nation place on embracing diversity and on the rights of an individual to think and act as he or she pleases. At its best, America does not look down upon people, nations, and cultures that are different from its own. The virtue of the American system is that it finds ways to embrace diversity and to allow people to try to become who they envision themselves to be.

This is no simple task. It is and has been a struggle to balance the freedom of an individual with the rights of others and at the same time keep the trains running on schedule. Life, Liberty, and the Pursuit of Happiness are not easy concepts to understand or practice on a national scale. New nations across the globe freed from the chains of authoritarian government rush into the democratic forms of government under the misconception that liberty means being able to do, to think, and to act the way they want. Were it that simple all nations would have been drenched many years ago in the blessings of liberty.

Liberty involves self-sacrifice. It doesn't simply mean taking rights, it also means giving some up. It is time-consuming, taxing, and at times outright difficult. Liberty means not taking your ball home if the rest of the team wants to play by different rules. It involves patience, hard work, and respect, but the burdens are borne with the understanding that one's own liberty lies in the hands of other people's liberty.

The history of the United States is in large measure about the struggle to keep the virtues and values of Liberty, Freedom, and Tolerance alive and vibrant. Some of the most eloquent passages in American history and literature are on this subject. The patriotic contributors to this book have been able to articulate what it is that makes the United States of America special. It is up to Americans ourselves to fulfill the vision and the dream that has been so well described in the following chapters.

We, The People

WILLA CATHER
O Pioneers!

The history of every country begins in the heart of a man or woman.

THE MAYFLOWER COMPACT

Having undertaken for the Glory of God, and Advancement of the Christian Faith, and the Honour of our King and Country, a voyage to plant the first colony in the northern Parts of Virginia; do by these Presents, solemnly and mutually in the Presence of God and of one another, convenant and combine ourselves together into a civil Body Politick, for our better Ordering and Preservation, and Furtherance of the Ends aforesaid; And by Virtue hereof to enact, constitute, and frame, such just and equal Laws, Ordinances, Acts, Constitutions and Offices, from time to time, as shall be thought most meet and convenient for the General good of the Colony; unto which we promise all due Submission and Obedience.

THOMAS PAINE
Common Sense

O! ye that love Mankind! Ye that dare oppose not only the tyranny but the tyrant, stand forth! Every spot of the Old World is overrun with oppression. Freedom hath been hunted round the globe. Asia and Africa have long expelled her. Europe regards her like a stranger and England hath given her warning to depart. O! receive the fugitive and prepare in time an asylum for mankind.

SAMUEL ADAMS

Driven from every other corner of the earth, freedom of thought and the right of private judgment in matters of conscience direct their course to this happy country as their last asylum.

OLIVER WENDELL HOLMES

Urania: A Rhymed Lesson

The Angel spake: "This threefold hill shall be
The home of Arts, the nurse of Liberty!"

RALPH WALDO EMERSON

Journals

The office of America is to liberate, to abolish kingcraft, priestcraft, caste, monopoly, to pull down the gallows, to burn up the bloody statute-book, to take in the immigrant, to open the doors of the sea and the fields of the earth.

ADLAI E. STEVENSON

Call to Greatness

Throughout its history, America has given hope, comfort and inspiration to freedom's cause in all lands. The reservoir of good will and respect for America was not built up by American arms or intrigue; it was built upon our deep dedication to the cause of human liberty and welfare.

HUBERT H. HUMPHREY

The Cause is Mankind

We are the standard-bearers in the only really authentic revolution, the democratic revolution against tyrannies. Our strength is not to be measured by our military capacity alone, by our industry, or by our technology. We will be remembered, not for the power of our weapons, but for the power of our compassion, our dedication to human welfare.

JOHN QUINCY ADAMS

Wherever the standard of freedom and independence has been or shall be unfurled, there will be America's heart, her benedictions and her prayers.

F. SCOTT FITZGERALD
The Crack-Up

France was a land, England was a people, but America, having about it still that quality of the idea, was harder to utter—it was the graves at Shiloh, and the tired, drawn, nervous faces of its great men, and the country boys dying in the Argonne for a phrase that was empty before their bodies withered. It was a willingness of the heart.

WILLIAM JENNINGS BRYAN
"American Mission" speech

Great has been the Greek, the Latin, the Slav, the Celt, the Teuton, and the Anglo-Saxon, but greater than any of these is the American, in which are blended the virtues of them all.

JOSEPH G. CANNON
Speech in Congress

By descent, I am one-fourth German, one-fourth Irish, one-fourth English, and another quarter French. My god! If my ancestors are permitted to look down upon me, they might perhaps upbraid me. But I am also an American!

"America means…"

ROBERT FROST
Interview, New York Times Book Review

America means certain things to the people who come here. It means the Declaration of Independence, it means Washington, it means Lincoln, it means Emerson—never forget Emerson—it means the English language, which is not the language that is spoken in England or her provinces. Just as soon as the alien gets all that—and it may take two or three generations—he is as much an American as is the man who can boast of nine generations of American forebears. He gets the tone of America, and as soon as there is tone there is poetry.

People do me the honor to say that I am truly a poet of America. They point to my New England background, to the fact that my paternal ancestor came here some time in the sixteen hundreds. So much is true, but what they either do not know or do not say is that my mother was an immigrant. She came to these shores from Edinburgh in an old vessel that docked at Philadelphia. But she felt the spirit of America and became part of it before she even set her foot off the boat.

She used to tell about it when I was a child. She was sitting on the deck of the boat waiting for orders to come ashore. Near her some workmen were loading Delaware peaches onto the ship. One of them picked out one of them and dropped it into her lap.

"Here, take that," he said. The way he said it and the spirit in which he gave it left an indelible impression on her mind.

"It was a bonny peach," she used to say, "and I didn't eat it. I kept it to show my friends."

Looking back would I say that she was less American than my father? No. America meant something live and real and virile to her. He took it for granted. He was a Fourth-of-July American, by which I mean that he rarely failed to celebrate in the way considered proper and appropriate. She, however, was a year-around American.

I had an aunt in New England who used to talk long and loud about the foreigners who were taking over this country. Across the way from her house stood a French Catholic church which the new people of the village had put up.

Every Sunday my aunt would stand at her window, behind the curtain, and watch the steady stream of men and women pouring into church. Her mouth would twist in the way that seems peculiar to dried-up New Englanders, and she would say, "My soul!" Just that: "My soul!"

All the disapproval and indignation and disgust were concentrated in these two words. She never could see why I laughed at her, but it did strike me very funny for her to be calling upon her soul for help when this mass of industrious people were going to church to save theirs.

New England is constantly going through periods of change. In my own state (in Vermont, I mean) there have been three distinct changes of population. First came the Irish, then the French, and now the Poles.

There are those among us who raise their hands in horror at this, but what does it matter? All these people are becoming, have become, Americans.

If soil is sacred, then I would say that they are more godly in their attitude to it. The Pole today in New England gets much more out of his plot of ground than does his Yankee neighbor. He knows how to cultivate it so that each inch produces, so that each grain is alive. Today the Pole may not be aware of the beauty of the old Colonial house he buys...but three generations from now, two generations, his children will be proud of it and may even boast of Yankee heritage. It has been done before; it will be done in the future.

And if there are poets among these children, theirs will be the poetry of America. They will be part of the soil of America as their cousins may be part of the city life of America.

I am [im]patient with this jealousy of the old for the young. It is change, this constant flow of new blood, which will make America eternally young, which will make her poets sing the songs of a young country—virile songs, strong songs, individual songs. The old cannot keep them back.

HAROLD ICKES
"I am an American" *speech*

What constitutes an American? Not color nor race nor religion. Not the pedigree of his family nor the place of his birth. Not the coincidence of his citizenship. Not his social status nor his bank account. Not his trade nor his profession. An American is one who loves justice and believes in the dignity of man. An American is one who will fight for his freedom and that of his neighbor. An American is one who will sacrifice property, ease, and security in order that he and his children may retain the rights of free men.

WOODROW WILSON

America was established not to create wealth but to realize a vision, to realize an ideal—to discover and maintain liberty among men.

BENJAMIN HARRISON
Cited in Clifton Fadiman, The American Treasury

Have you not learned that not stocks or bonds or stately homes, or products of mill or field are our country? It is the splendid thought that is in our minds.

MAX LERNER
"The United States as Exclusive Hotel," *Actions and Passions*

America is a passionate idea or it is nothing. America is a human brotherhood or it is a chaos.

JAMES RUSSELL LOWELL
On a Certain Condescension in Foreigners

To Americans America is something more than a promise and an expectation. It has a past and traditions of its own. A descent from men who sacrificed everything and came hither, not to better their fortunes, but to plant their idea in virgin soil, should be a good pedigree. There was never colony save this that went forth, not to seek gold, but God.

ARCHIBALD MACLEISH
"America was Promises"

O my America for whom?
For whom the promises? For whom the river?
"It flows west! Look at the ripple of it!"
The grass "So that it was wonderful to see

And endless without end with wind wonderful!"
The Great Lakes: landless as oceans: their beaches
Coarse sand: clean gravel: pebbles:
Their bluffs smelling of sunflowers: smelling of surf:
Of fresh water: of wild sunflowers...wilderness.
For whom the evening mountains on the sky:
The night wind from the west: the moon descending?
Tom Paine knew.
Tom Paine knew the People.
The promises were spoken to the People.
History was voyages toward the People.
Americas were landfalls of the People.
Stars and expectations were the signals of the People.
Whatever was truly built the People had built it.
Whatever was taken down they had taken down.
Whatever was worn they had worn—ax-handles: fiddle-bows:
Sills of doorways: names for children: for mountains...
The People had the promises: they'd keep them.

JAMES BALDWIN
"Many Thousands Gone"

The making of an American begins at that point where he himself rejects all other ties, any other history, and himself adopts the vesture of his adopted land.

JAMES RUSSELL LOWELL
Letter to Charles Eliot Norton

There is something magnificent in having a country to love. It is almost like what one feels for a woman. Not so tender, perhaps, but to the full as self-forgetful.

CHARLES GOODNIGHT
Cited in Daniel J. Boorstin, The Americans: The Democratic Experience

Most of the time we were solitary adventurers in a great land as fresh and new as a spring morning, and we were free and full of the zest of darers.

HERMAN MELVILLE
Mardi

That voyager steered his bark through seas, untracked before; ploughed his own path mid jeers; though with a heart that oft was heavy with the thought, that he might only be too bold, and grope where land was none.

ROBERT FROST
"The Gift Outright"

The land was ours before we were the land's.
She was our land more than a hundred years
Before we were her people. She was ours
In Massachusetts, in Virginia,
But we were England's still colonials,
Possessing what we still were unpossessed by,
Possessed by what we now no more possessed.
Something we were withholding made us weak
Until we found out that it was ourselves
We were withholding from our land of living,
And forthwith found salvation in surrender.
Such as we were we gave ourselves outright
(The deed of gift was many deeds of war)
To the land vaguely realizing westward,
But still unstoried, artless, unenhanced,
Such as she was, such as she would become.

WOODROW WILSON

America lives in the heart of every man everywhere who wishes to find a region where he will be free to work out his destiny as he chooses.

ARCHIBALD MACLEISH
Freedom is the Right to Choose

The whole history of our continent is a history of the imagination. Men imagined land beyond the sea and found it. Men imagined the forests, the great plains, the rivers, the mountains— and found these plains, these mountains. They came, as the great explorers crossed the Atlantic, because of the imagination of their minds—because they imagined a better, a more beautiful, a freer, happier world.

MARK TWAIN
The Adventures of Tom Sawyer

They came back to camp wonderfully refreshed, glad-hearted, and ravenous; and they soon had the camp-fire blazing up again. Huck found a spring of clear cold water close by, and the boys made cups of broad oak or hickory leaves, and felt that water, sweetened with such a wild-wood charm as that, would be a good enough substitute for coffee. While Joe was slicing bacon for breakfast, Tom and Huck asked him to hold on a minute; they stepped to a promising nook in the river-bank and threw in their lines; almost immediately they had reward.

CARL SANDBURG
"The People, Yes"

This is the tale of the Howdeehow powpow,
One of a thousand drolls the people tell of themselves,
Of tall corn, of wide rivers, of big snakes,
Of giants and dwarfs, heroes and clowns,
Grown in the soil of the mass of the people.

CHIEF SEATTLE

Every part of this country is sacred to my people. Every hillside, every valley, every plain and grove, has been hallowed by some fond memory or some sad experience of my tribe. Even the rocks that seem to lie dumb as they swelter in the sun along the silent seashore in solemn grandeur thrill with memories of past events connected with the fate of my people, and the very dust under your feet responds more lovingly to our footsteps than to yours, because it is the ashes of our ancestors, and our bare feet are conscious of the sympathetic touch, for the soil is rich with the life of our kindred.

GERTRUDE STEIN
The Geographical History of America

In the United States there is more space where nobody is than where anybody is. That is what makes America what it is.

AMERICAN FOLKSONG

Oh, give me a home where the buffalo roam,
Where the deer and the antelope play;
Where seldom is heard a discouraging word,
And the skies are not cloudy all day.

ARTHUR GUITERMAN

What joy to see, what joy to win
So fair a land for his kith and kin
Of streams unstained and woods unhewn!
"Elbowroom!" laughed Daniel Boone.

RALPH WALDO EMERSON
"The Young American," *Nature; Addresses and Lectures*

Any relation to the land, the habit of tilling it, or mining it, or even hunting on it, generates the feeling of patriotism.

JOSEPH CONRAD
Lord Jim

Each blade of grass has its spot on earth whence it draws its life, its strength; and so is man rooted to the land from which he draws his faith together with his life.

WILLIAM CULLEN BRYANT
"The Prairies"

These are the gardens of the Desert, these
The unshorn fields, boundless and beautiful,
For which the speech of England has no name—
The Prairies. I behold them for the first,
And my heart swells, while the dilated sight
Takes in the encircling vastness. Lo! they stretch,
In airy undulations, far away,

As if the ocean, in his gentlest swell,
Stood still, with all his rounded billows fixed,
And motionless forever.—Motionless?—
No—they are all unchained again. The clouds
Sweep over with their shadows, and, beneath,
The surface rolls and fluctuates to the eye;
Dark hollows seem to glide along and chase
The sunny ridges. Breezes of the South!
Who toss the golden and the flame-like flowers,
And pass the prairie-hawk that, poised on high,
Flaps his broad wings, yet moves not—ye have played
Among the palms of Mexico and vines
Of Texas, and have crisped the limpid brooks
That from the fountains of Sonora glide
Into the calm Pacific—have ye fanned
A nobler or a lovelier scene than this?

LORENA ALICE HICKOK

To me those wide, treeless spaces offered the promise of the infinite and intoxicating freedom. You could run all the way to the very rim of the world if you wanted to! If I close my eyes, I can still feel the wind on my face and feel again the exhilaration, the sense of physical well-being it used to give me.

WALLACE STEGNER
Wolf Willow

How does one know in his bones what this continent has meant to Western man unless he has, though briefly and in the midst of failure, belatedly and in the wrong place, made trails and paths on an untouched country and built human living places, however transitory, at the edge of a field that he helped break from prairie sod? How does one know what wilderness has meant to Americans unless he has shared the guilt of wastefully and ignorantly tampering with it in the name of Progress?

One who has lived the dream, the temporary fulfillment, and the disappointment has had the full course. He may lack a thousand things that the rest of the world takes for granted, and because his experience is belated he may feel like an anachronism all his life. But he will know one thing about what it means to be an American, because he has known the raw continent, and not as a tourist but as denizen. Some of the beauty, the innocence, and the callousness must stick to him, and some of the regret.

ANNIE DILLARD
Pilgrim at Tinker Creek

I live by a creek, Tinker Creek, in a valley in Virginia's Blue Ridge.... It's a good place to live; there's a lot to think about. The creeks—Tinker and Carvin's—are an active mystery, fresh every minute. Theirs is the mystery of the continuous creation and all that providence implies: the uncertainty of vision, the horror of the fixed, the dissolution of the present, the intricacy of beauty, the pressure of fecundity, the elusiveness of the free, and the flawed nature of perfection.

STEPHEN VINCENT BENET
"American Names"

I have fallen in love with American names,
The sharp names that never get fat,
The snakeskin-titles of mining-claims,
The plumed war-bonnet of Medicine Hat,
Tucson and Deadwood and Lost Mule Flat.

Seine and Piave are silver spoons,
But the spoonbowl-metal is thin and worn,
There are English counties like hunting-tunes
Played on the keys of a postboy's horn,
But I will remember where I was born.

I will remember Carquinez Straits,
Little French Lick and Lundy's Lane,
The Yankee ships and the Yankee dates
and the bullet-towns of Calamity Jane.
I will remember Skunktown Plain...

I shall not rest quiet in Montparnasse.
I shall not lie easy at Winchelsea.
You may bury my body in Sussex grass,
You may bury my tongue at Champmédy.
I shall not be there. I shall rise and pass.
Bury my heart at Wounded Knee.

Blue Highways, A Journey Into America

WILLIAM LEAST HEAT MOON
(WILLIAM TROGDON)

Dime Box, Texas, is not the funniest town in America. Traditionally, that honor belongs to Intercourse, Pennsylvania. I prefer Scratch Ankle, Alabama, Gnawbone, Indiana, or even Humptulips, Washington. Nevertheless, Dime Box, as a name, caught my ear, so that's where I headed the next morning out of College Station.

In the humid night, the inside windows had dripped like cavern walls: Along state 21, I opened up and let warm air blow out the damp. West of the Brazos, the land unfolded even farther to the blue sky. Now the horizon wasn't ten or fifteen miles away, it was thirty or forty. On telephone wires sat scissor-tailed flycatchers, their oddly long tails hanging under them like stilts. Roadside wildflowers—bluebonnets, purple winecups, evening primroses, and more —were abundant as crops, and where wide reaches of bluebonnets (once called buffalo clover, wolf flower, and, by the Spanish, "the rabbit") covered the slopes, their scent filled the highway. To all the land was an intense clarity as the little things gave off light.

Across the Yegua River a sign pointed south to Dime Box. Over broad hills, over the green expansion spreading under cedars and live oaks, on into a valley where I found Dime Box, essentially a three-street town. Vegetable gardens and flowerbeds lay to the side, behind, and in front of the houses. Perpendicular to the highway, two streets ran east and west: one of worn brick buildings facing the South Pacific tracks, the other a double row of false-front stores and wooden sidewalks. Disregarding a jarring new bank, Dime Box could have been an M-G-M backlot set for a Western.

You can't walk down a board sidewalk without clomping, so I clomped down to Ovcarik's Cafe and through the screendoor, which banged shut as they always do. An aroma of ham and beans. Four calendars. From long cords three naked bulbs burned, and still the place was dim. Everthing was wood except a heating stove and the Coca-Cola cooler. Near the door, a sign tacked above the flyswatter and next to the machete explained the ten-year prison term for carrying a weapon into premises where liquor is served.

At the counter I drank a Royal Crown; the waitress dropped my quarter into the cash register, a King Edward cigarbox. Forks and knives clinked on plates behind a partition in the rear. It was too much. I ordered a dinner.

She set down a long plate of ham, beans, beets, and brown gravy. I seasoned everything with hot peppers in vinegar. From the partition came a *thump-thump* like an empty beer bottle rapping on a table. The waitress pulled two Lone Stars from the faded cooler, foam trickling over her fingers as she carried them back. In all the time I was there, I heard a voice from the rear only once: "I'm tellin' you, he can flat out throw that ball."

A man came from the kitchen, sat beside me, and began dropping toothpicks through the small openings of Tabasco sauce bottles used as dispensers. Down the counter, a fellow with tarnished eyes said, "Is it Tuesday?" The waitress nodded, and everything fell quiet again but the clinking of forks. After a while, a single *thump,* and she carried back a Lone Star. The screendoor opened: a woman, old and tall, stepped into the dimness cane first, thwacking it to and fro. Loudly she croaked, "Cain't see, damn it!"

A middle-aged woman said, "Straight on, Mother. It isn't that dark." She helped the crone sit at one of the tables. They ordered the meal.

"Ain't no use," the waitress said. "Just sold the last plate to him."

Him was me. They turned and looked. "Let's go, Mother." The tall woman rose, breaking wind as she did. "Easy, Mother."

"You don't feed me proper!" she croaked and thwacked out the door.

The man with the Tabasco bottles said to no one in particular, "Don't believe the old gal needed any beans."

Again a long quiet. Then the one who had ascertained the day said to the waitress, "Saw a cat runned over on the highway. Was it yourn?"

She shifted the toothpick with her tongue. "What color?" He couldn't remember. "Lost me an orange cat. Ain't seen Peewee in a week."

"I got me too many cats," he said. "I'll pay anybody a quarter each to kill my spares."

That stirred a conversation on methods of putting away kittens, and that led to methods of killing fire ants. The man beside me put down a toothpick bottle. It had taken some time to fill. He said, "I got the best way to kill far ants, and it ain't by diggin' or poison." No one paid attetion. Finally he muttered, "Pour gasoline on the hive." No one said anything.

"Do you light it?" I asked.

"Light what?"

"The gasoline."

"Hell no, you don't light it." He held out a big, gullied palm and pointed to a tiny lump. "Got nipped there last year by a far ant. If you don't pick the poisosn out, it leaves a knot for two or three years."

The other man talked of an uncle who once kept sugar ants in his pantry and fed them molasses. "When they fattened up, he put them on a butter sandwich. Butter kept them from runnin' off the bread." The place was so quiet you could almost hear the heat on the tin roof. If anyone was listening to him, I couldn't tell. "Claimed molasses gave them ants real flavor," he said.

Thump-thump. The woman turned from the small window, her eyes vacant, and went to the cooler for two more bottles of Lone Star.

I walked to the post office for stamps. The postmistress explained the town name. A century ago the custom was to drop a letter and ten cents for postage into the pickup box. That was in Old Dime Box up on the San Antonio road, now Texas 21. "What happened to Old Dime Box?"

"A couple houses there yet," she said, "but the railroad came through in nineteen thirteen, three miles south, so they moved the town to the tracks—to here. Now the train's about gone. Some freights, but that's it."

"I see Czech names on stores."

"We're between Giddings and Caldwell. Giddings is mostly German and Caldwell's mostly Czech. We're close to fifty-fifty. Whites, that is. A third of Dime Box is black people."

"How do the different groups get along?"

"Pretty well. We had a to-do in the sixties over integration, but it was mostly between white groups arguing about who had the right to run the schools. Some parents bussed kids away for a spell, but that was just anger."

"Bussing in Dime Box?"

"City people don't think anything important happens in a place like Dime Box. And usually it doesn't, unless you call conflict important. Or love or babies or dying."

HENRY VAN DYKE
America for Me

So it's home again, and home again, America for me!
My heart is turning home again, and there I long to be
In the land of youth and freedom beyond the ocean bars,
Where the air is full of sunlight, and the flag is full of stars.

ELIAS LIEBERMAN
I Am An American

The history of my ancestors is a trail of blood to the palace-gate of the Great White Czar. But then the dream came—the dream of America. In the light of the Liberty torch the atom of dust became a man and the straw in the wind became a woman for the first time. 'See,' said my father, pointing to the flag that fluttered near, 'that flag of stars and stripes is yours; it is the emblem of the promised land. It means, my son, the hope of humanity. Live for it . . . die for it!' Under the open sky of my new country I swore to do so; and every drop of blood in me will keep that vow. I am proud of my future. I am an American.

FLAG DAY
The New York Times *editorial*

What's a flag? What's the love of country for which it stands? Maybe it begins with love of the land itself. It is the fog rolling in with the tide at Eastport, or through the Golden Gate and among the towers of San Francisco. It is the sun coming up behind the White Mountains, over the Green, throwing a shiny glory on Lake Champlain and above the Adirondacks. It is the storied Mississippi rolling swift and muddy past St. Louis, rolling past Cairo, pouring down past the levees of New Orleans. It is lazy noontide in the pines of Carolina, it is a sea of wheat rippling in Western Kansas, it is the San Francisco peaks far north across the glowing nakedness of Arizona, it is the Grand Canyon and a little stream coming down out of a New England ridge, in which are trout.

It is men at work. It is the storm-tossed fishermen coming into Gloucester and Providence and Astoria. It is the farmer riding his great machine in the dust of harvest, the dairyman going to the barn before sunrise, the lineman mending the broken wire, the miner drilling for the blast. It is the servants of fire in the murky splendor of Pittsburgh, between the Allegheny and the Monongahela, the trucks rumbling through the night, the locomotive engineer bringing the train in on time, the pilot in the clouds, the riveter running along the beam a hundred feet in air. It is the clerk in the office, the housewife doing the dishes and sending the children off to school. It is the teacher, doctor, and parson tending and helping, body and soul, for small reward.

It is small things remembered, the little corners of the land, the houses, the people that each one loves. We love our country because there was a little tree on a hill, and grass thereon, and a sweet valley below; because the hurdy-gurdy man came along on a sunny morning in a city street; because a beach or a farm or a lane or a house that might not seem much to others were once, for each of us, made magic. It is voices that are remembered only, no longer heard. It is parents, friends, the lazy chat of street and store and office, and the ease of mind that makes life tranquil. It is summer and winter, rain and sun and storm. These are flesh of our flesh, bone of our bone, blood of our blood, a lasting part of what we are, each of us and all of us together.

It is stories told. It is the Pilgrims dying in their first dreadful winter. It is the minuteman standing his ground at Concord Bridge, and dying there. It is the army in rags, sick, freezing, starving at Valley Forge. It is the wagons and the men on foot going westward over Cumberland Gap, floating down the great rivers, rolling over the great plains. It is the settler hacking fiercely at the primeval forest on his new, his own lands. It is Thoreau at Walden Pond, Lincoln at Cooper Union, and Lee riding home from Appomattox. It is corruption and disgrace, answered always by men who would not let the flag lie in the dust, who have stood up in every generation to fight for the old ideals and the old rights, at risk of ruin or of life itself.

It is a great multitude of people on pilgrimage, common and ordinary people, charged with the usual human failings, yet filled with such a hope as never caught the imaginations and the hearts of any nation on earth before. The hope of liberty. The hope of justice. The hope of a land in which a man can stand straight, without fear, without rancor.

The land and the people and the flag—the land a continent, the people of every race, the flag a symbol of what humanity may aspire to when the wars are over and the barriers are down; to these each generation must be dedicated and consecrated anew, to defend with life itself, if need be, but, above all, in friendliness, in hope, in courage, to live for.

HOPI ELDERS OF SHONGOPOVI
Cited in Lee Miller, *From the Heart, Voices of the American Indian*

Our land, our religion, and our life are one. . . . It is from the land that each true Hopi gathers the rocks, the plants, the different woods, roots, and his life, and each in the authority of his rightful obligation brings to our ceremonies proof of our ties to this land. Our footprints mark well the trails to these sacred places. It is here on this land that we are bringing up our younger generation and through preserving the ceremonies are teaching them proper human behavior and strength of character to make them true citizens among all people. It is upon this land that we wish to live in peace and harmony with our friends and with our neighbors.

CARL SANDBURG
"Ever A Seeker"

The fingers turn the pages.
The pages unfold as a scroll.
There was the time there was no America.
Then came on the scroll an early
    America, a land of beginnings,
    an America being born.
Then came a later America, seeker
    and finder, yet ever more seeker
    than finder, ever seeking its way
    amid storm and dream.

WALDO FRANK
Our America

We go forth all to seek America. And in the seeking we create her. In the quality of our search shall be the nature of the America that we created.

PEARL S. BUCK
Speech

When I first came here, then, I endeavored to find a recognizable country of my own. I looked for Americans. But I could not find them. It seemed to me the country was full of foreigners. I found delightful people, for I came home under the best possible circumstances, having done a sort of work of my own which somehow made me friends. The people were wonderfully kind to me, but they seemed to me like English people, or Europeans. I kept thinking, "Where are the Americans?" It was very puzzling. I couldn't find Americans even in Boston. In fact, I bored everybody by asking confidently, "Where does one find the real Americans? What would *you* consider the typical American?" To my bewilderment everyone replied the same way...that is, *he* was the typical American if there ever was one. So after repetitions of this sort of thing, I decided there never was one, at least that I could find. I hurried then to American literature, reading every book praised by critics as being American and endeavoring to find out in this way what was American. But the books varied even more than the people and each might have been written about a totally different country and people...I came to see that these true Americans I had been looking for didn't exist at all, and there were not typical Americans. I have come indeed to feel that if there is a typical American it is the one least typical of anyone except himself. The one-hundred-percent American, for instance, is one hundred percent nothing except himself. And America is wherever you happen to find yourself between Canada and the Rio Grande and the great oceans east and west, and American food is codfish and baked beans and Hungarian goulash or scrapple, and beaten biscuit and fried chicken, or cornpone and salt pork, or hot tamales, or whatever is put on the table before you wherever you happen to be. And the American religion is to be found in little Pentecostal chapels or in great Fifth Avenue churches or in Catholic cathedrals or nowhere at all. The only thing you can be sure of is that if you keep going, you'll not eat the same American food two days alike, or hear the same God preached two Sundays the same, and you will certainly hear—in English, nasal with New England winter, in English, German-tinged or Italian-haunted, or dying with the fading inflections of a slave-ridden past in southern swamps—the conviction that whatever is fed you or preached to you is the real American article.

THOMAS PAINE
The American Crisis

Our citizenship in the United States is our national character. Our citizenship in any particular state is only our local distinction. By the latter we are known at home, by the former to the world. Our great title is AMERICANS. . . .

GEORGE WASHINGTON
Farewell address

The name of American, which belongs to you in your national capacity, must always exalt the just pride of patriotism more than any appellation derived from local discriminations. With slight shades of difference, you have the same religion, manners, habits and political principles. You have in common cause fought and triumphed together. The independence and liberty you possess are the work of joint councils and joint efforts, of common dangers, sufferings, and successes.

THOMAS JEFFERSON
Letter to Thomas Law

My affections were first for my own country, and then, generally, for all mankind.

WILLIAM LLOYD GARRISON
Motto of the abolitionist journal The Liberator

Our country is the world—our countrymen are mankind.

STEPHEN DECATUR
Toast at a dinner in his honor at Norfolk, Virginia

Our country! In her intercourse with foreign nations may she always be in the right; but our country, right or wrong!

GOUVERNEUR MORRIS
Speech in Senate

I anticipate the day when to command respect in the remotest regions it will be sufficient to say, "I am an American." Our flag shall then wave in glory over the ocean and our commerce feel no restraint but what our own government may impose. Happy, thrice happy day. Thank God, to reach this envied state we need only to will. Yes, my countrymen, our destiny depends on our will. But if we would stand high on the record of time, that will must be inflexible.

DANIEL WEBSTER

I shall know but one country. The ends I aim at shall be my country's, my God's, and Truth's. I was born an American; I live an American; I shall die an American.

DANIEL WEBSTER

One country, one constitution, one destiny.

OLIVER WENDELL HOLMES
Voyage of the Good Ship Union

One flag, one land, one heart, one hand,
One Nation, evermore!

JAMES GILLESPIE BLAINE

There is no "Republican," no "Democrat," on the Fourth of July,—all are Americans. All feel that their country is greater than party.

EDMUND VANCE COOKE
"Each for All"

The North! the South! the West! the East!
No one the most and none the least,
But each with its own heart and mind,
Each of its own distinctive kind,
Yet each a part and none the whole,
But all together form one soul;
That soul Our Country at its best,
No North, no South, no East, no West,
No yours, no mine, but always Ours,
Merged in one Power our lesser powers,
For no one's favor great or small,
But all for Each and each for All.

RALPH ELLISON
Invisible Man

America is woven of many strands; I would recognize them and let it so remain. Our fate is to become one, and yet many—This is not prophecy, but description.

FRANKLIN D. ROOSEVELT
Campaign speech

We are a nation of many nationalities, many races, many religions—bound together by a single unity, the unity of freedom and equality. Whoever seeks to set one nationality against another, seeks to degrade all nationalities. Whoever seeks to set one race against another seeks to enslave all races. Whoever seeks to set one religion against another seeks to destroy all religion. I am fighting for a free America—for a country in which *all* men and women have equal rights to liberty and justice. I am fighting, as I always have fought, for the right of the little man as well as the big man—for the weak as well as the strong, for those who are helpless as well as for those who can help themselves.

WOODROW WILSON

Sometimes people call me an idealist. Well, that is the way I know I am an American. America is the only idealistic nation in the world.

SINCLAIR LEWIS
Interview in Berlin

Intellectually I know that America is no better than any other country; emotionally I know she is better than every other country.

ADLAI E. STEVENSON

When an American says that he loves his country, he . . . means that he loves an inner air, an inner light in which freedom lives and in which a man can draw the breath of self-respect.

JIMMY CARTER
Speech in the California State Senate

All I want is the same thing you want. To have a nation with a government that is as good and honest and decent and competent and compassionate and as filled with love as are the American people.

AMBROSE BIERCE
The Devil's Dictionary

Un-American, *adj*. Wicked, intolerable, heathenish.

EDWARD EVERETT HALE
"Ten Times One is Ten"

To look up and not down,
To look forward and not back,
To look out and not in—and
To lend a hand.

H.L. MENCKEN
Prejudices: Fifth Series

A home is not a mere transient shelter: its essence lies in its permanence, in its capacity for accretion and solidification, in its quality of representing, in all its details, the personalities of the people who live in it.

RALPH WALDO EMERSON
Society and Solitude

The true test of civilization is, not the census, nor the size of cities, nor the crops—no, but the kind of man the country turns out.

JOHN DICKINSON
Letters of Fabius

Let us assert and maintain *our true character—sincerity* of thought, and *rectitude* of action; and convince the world, that *no man*, or *body of men*, whatever advantages may for a while be taken of our *unsuspecting confidence*, shall ever be able to draw this nation out of the direct road of an honest, candid, and generous conduct.

THEODORE ROOSEVELT
Address, Syracuse

Our average fellow-citizen is a sane and healthy man who believes in decency and has a wholesome mind.

FREDERICK DOUGLASS
Speech on the 23rd anniversary of Emancipation

The life of the nation is secure only while the nation is honest, truthful, and virtuous.

RALPH WALDO EMERSON
Journals

The head of Washington hangs in my dining room for a few days past, and I cannot keep my eyes off of it. It has a certain Appalachian strength, as if it were truly the first-fruits of America, and expressed the Country. The heavy, leaden eyes turn on you, as the eyes of an ox in a pasture. And the mouth has gravity and depth of quiet, as if this MAN has absorbed all the serenity of America, and left none for his restless, rickety, hysterical countrymen.

HENRY JAMES
The American

The gentleman on the divan was the superlative American; to which affirmation of character he was partly helped by the general easy magnificence of his manhood. He appeared to possess that kind of health and strength which, when found in perfection, are the most impressive—the physical tone which the owner does nothing to "keep up..." He was by inclination a temperate man; but he had supped the night before his visit to the Louvre at the Cafe Anglais —some one had told him it was an experience not to be omitted—and he had slept none the less the sleep of the just. His usual attitude and carriage had a liberal looseness, but when, under a special inspiration, he straightened himself, he looked a grenadier on parade. . . . His complexion was brown and the arch of his nose bold and well-marked. . . . He had the flat jaw and the firm, dry neck which are frequent in the American type. . . .

Tales, Sketches and Other Papers

NATHANIEL HAWTHORNE

Unquestionably, western man though he be and Kentuckian by birth, President Lincoln is the essential representative of all Yankees and the veritable specimen, physically, of what the world seems determined to regard as our characteristic qualities. It is the strangest and yet the fittest thing in the jumble of human vicissitudes that he, out of so many millions, unlooked for, uns-elected by any intelligible process that could be based upon his genuine qualities, unknown to those who chose him, and unsuspected of what endowments may adapt him for his tremen-dous responsibility, should have found the way open for him to fling his lank personality into the chair of state—where, I presume, it was his first impulse to throw his legs on the council table and tell the cabinet ministers a story. There is no describing his lengthy awkwardness nor the uncouthness of his movement, and yet it seemed as if I had been in the habit of seeing him daily and had shaken hands with him a thousand times in some village street; so true was he to the aspect of the pattern American, though with a certain extravagance which, possibly, I exaggerated still further by the delighted eagerness with which I took it in. If put to guess his calling and livelihood, I should have taken him for a country schoolmaster as soon as anything else. He was dressed in a rusty black frock coat and pantaloons, unbrushed, and worn so faith-fully that the suit had adapted itself to the curves and angularities of his figure and had grown to be an outer skin of the man. He had shabby slippers on his feet. His hair was black, still unmixed with gray, stiff, somewhat bushy, and had apparently been acquainted with neither brush nor comb that morning, after the disarrangement of the pillow; and as to a night-cap, Uncle Abe probably knows nothing of such effeminacies. His complexion is dark and sallow, betokening, I fear, an insalubrious atmosphere around the White House; he has thick black eye-brows and an impending brow; his nose is large, and the lines about his mouth are very strongly defined.

The whole physiognomy is as coarse a one as you would meet anywhere in the length and breadth of the states, but withal it is redeemed, illuminated, softened, and brightened by a kindly though serious look out of the eyes and an expression of homely sagacity that seems weighted with rich results of village experience. A great deal of native sense; no bookish cultivation, no refinement; honest at heart, and thoroughly so, and yet, in some sort, sly—at least, endowed with a sort of tact and wisdom that are akin to craft, and would impel him, I think, to take an antagonist in flank, rather than to make a bull run at him right on front. But, on the whole, I like this sallow, queer, sagacious visage, with the homely human sympathies that warmed it and, for my small share in the matter, would as lief have Uncle Abe for a ruler as any man whom it would have been practicable to put in his place.

KATE SIMON
Bronx Primitive

Instead of a city of silver rivers and golden bridges, America turned out to be Uncle David's flat on Avenue C in which my father had first lived when he came to America. . . . [Uncle David] had a long white beard and puffs of white hair leaping from the edge of his skullcap and a magical skill of putting his finger inside his cheek and pulling it out to make a big popping sound. He laughed a lot, told incomprehensible stories about Italians whose only English was "sonnomabitz," drank great quantities of tea, sipped from a saucer and drained through a cube of sugar held in his teeth. Everything about him was wonderful: the black straps and boxes he wrapped on his arms and forehead and the rhythmic bowing of his prayers when he was God; the fluttering old fingers and light touch of his gray carpet slippers as he paced a Chassidic dance when he was Old King Cole.

GEORGE SANTAYANA
Character and Opinion in the United States

The American is wonderfully alive; and his vitality, not having often found a suitable outlet, makes him appear agitated on the surface; he is always letting off an unnecessarily loud blast of incidental steam. Yet his vitality is not superficial; it is inwardly prompted, and as sensitive and quick as a magnetic needle. He is inquisitive, and ready with an answer to any question that he may put to himself of his own accord; but if you try to pour instruction into him, on matters that do not touch his own spontaneous life, he shows the most extraordinary powers of resistance and oblivescence; so that he often is remarkably expert in some directions and surprisingly obtuse in others. He seems to bear lightly the sorrowful burden of human knowledge. In a word, he is young.

JOHN UPDIKE

Anywhere is Where You Hang Your Hat, Assorted Prose

What is it that distinguishes the American Man from his counterparts in other climes; what *is* it that makes him so special? He is quietly affirmative. He is trustworthy, loyal, helpful, friendly, courteous, kind, obedient, cheerful, thrifty, brave, clean, and reverent.

THE BOY SCOUT LAW

A Scout is Trustworthy   A Scout is Obedient

A Scout is Loyal   A Scout is Cheerful

A Scout is Helpful   A Scout is Thrifty

A Scout is Friendly   A Scout is Brave

A Scout is Courteous   A Scout is Clean

A Scout is Kind   A Scout is Reverent

THE GIRL SCOUT LAW

I will do my best:
- to be honest
- to be fair
- to help where I am needed
- to be cheerful
- to be friendly and considerate
- to be a sister to every Girl Scout
- to respect authority
- to use resources wisely
- to protect and improve the world around me
- to show respect for myself and others through my words and actions

WILLIAM JAMES

Letter to Mrs. Henry Whitman

One loves America above all things, for her youth, her greenness, her plasticity, innocence, good intentions, friends, everything.

WALT WHITMAN
Preface to Leaves of Grass

The genius of the United States is not best or most in its executives or legislatures, nor in its ambassadors or authors or colleges or churches or parlors, nor even in its newspapers or inventors . . . but always most in the common people. Their manners speech dress friendships—the freshness and candor of their physiognomy—the picturesque looseness of their carriage . . . their deathless attachment to freedom—their aversion to anything indecorous or soft or mean—the practical acknowledgment of the citizens of one state by the citizens of all other states—the fierceness of their roused resentment—their curiosity and welcome of novelty—their self-esteem and wonderful sympathy—their susceptibility to a slight—the air they have of persons who never knew how it felt to stand in the presence of superiors—the fluency of their speech—their delight in music, the sure symptom of manly tenderness and native elegance of soul . . . their good temper and openhandedness—the terrible significance of their elections—the President's taking off his hat to them not they to him—these too are unrhymed poetry.

H.L. MENCKEN
On Being an American

All our cities are full of aristocrats whose grandfathers were day laborers, and clerks whose grandfathers were aristocrats.

THOMAS JEFFERSON
Letter to Martha Jefferson

It is part of the American character to consider nothing as desperate, to surmount every difficulty by resolution and contrivance.

FRANKLIN D. ROOSEVELT

The saving grace of America lies in the fact that the overwhelming majority of Americans are possessed of two great qualities—a sense of humor and a sense of proportion.

MARY MCCARTHY
"America the Beautiful: The Humanist in the Bathtub,"
On the Contrary

The happy ending is our national belief.

ALFRED E. SMITH

The American people never carry an umbrella. They prepare to walk in eternal sunshine.

BROOKS ATKINSON
"January," *Once Around the Sun*

We cheerfully assume that in some mystic way love conquers all, that good outweighs evil in the just balances of the universe and that at the eleventh hour something gloriously triumphant will prevent the worst before it happens.

JOHN F. KENNEDY
Address, Washington, D.C.

The American, by nature, is optimistic. He is experimental, an inventor and a builder who builds best when called upon to build greatly.

WILL ROGERS
The Autobiography of Will Rogers

We don't know what we want, but we are ready to bite somebody to get it.

RALPH WALDO EMERSON

The Yankee is one who, if he once gets his teeth set on a thing, all creation can't make him let go.

FRANCES FITZGERALD
Fire in the Lake

Americans see history as a straight line and themselves standing at the cutting edge of it as representatives for all mankind. They believe in the future as if it were a religion; they believe that there is nothing they cannot accomplish, that solutions wait somewhere for all problems, like a bride.

HELEN KELLER

Optimism is the faith that leads to achievement. Nothing can be done without hope or confidence.

E. B. WHITE
Letter to Mr. Nadeau

As long as there is one upright man, as long as there is one compassionate woman, the contagion may spread and the scene is not desolate. Hope is the thing that is left us in a bad time.

MARK TWAIN

Lord save us all from . . . a hope tree that has lost the faculty of putting out blossoms.

PEARL S. BUCK

What is America? What makes our country more than any other piece of land and water on the globe? Nothing—except our ideal of human freedom, freedom for the individual! Because we have this ideal we, almost alone among the peoples today, have *hope*. We still dare to hope.

You can easily see that ideals are the most important things in the world. Indeed they are. They are the food of the soul, which nourishes the spirit with faith and with hope. When hope and faith are gone, when we say, "ideals are only talk," the soul dies and the spirit grows weak and then the tyrants take over. We must keep our ideals alive, we cannot let them die, for they alone give us the strength to keep our own freedom and spread the strength of hope and faith to other peoples.

SHIRLEY CHISHOLM
Speech at Federal City College, Washington, D.C.

We will build a democratic America in spite of undemocratic Americans. We have rarely worried about the odds or the obstacles before—we will not start worrying now. We will have both of our goals—Peace and Power!

CARL SANDBURG
I Am the People, the Mob

I am the people—the mob—the crowd—the mass.
Do you know that all the great work of the world is done
      through me?

HERMAN MELVILLE
White Jacket

We are the pioneers of the world; the advance guard sent on through the wilderness of untried things to break a new path in the New World that is ours. In our youth is our strength; in our inexperience, our wisdom.

JAMES RUSSELL LOWELL
"Ode for the Fourth of July"

Her children shall rise up to bless her name,
And wish her harmless length of days,
The mighty mother of a mighty brood,
Blessed in all tongues and dear to every
    blood,
The beautiful, the strong, and, best of all,
    the good.

E.B. WHITE
Writings from the New Yorker

Dr. Sockman, the Methodist pastor, says the American city is more like a sand pile than a melting pot. "People are heaped together, but they do not hold together." Well, we have a letter telling us of an incident when Americans held together beautifully. The writer of the letter went, during his lunch hour, to buy stamps at the small post office in Bloomingdale's basement. Ahead of him in line was a lady who brought things to a standstill by changing her mind about what kind of stamps and envelopes she wanted, by running up a bill of more than thirty dollars, and by discovering that she didn't have thirty dollars and could she pay the balance by check? The line grew and grew. After a while, someone ventured to hope, out loud, that she wouldn't change her mind again, because he was on his lunch hour. At this, the woman turned on him and said, "You aren't even American, are you?" The man was quite shaken by this, but the others in the line weren't, and they came to his aid instantly. "We're all Americans," shouted one of them, "and we are all on the lunchhour."

That was no sand pile. People hold together and will continue to hold together, even in the face of abrupt and unfounded charges calculated to destroy.

AMY LOWELL
"The Congressional Liberty"

This is America,
This vast, confused beauty,
This staring, restless speed of loveliness,
Mighty, overwhelming, crude, of all forms,
Making grandeur out of profusion,
Afraid of no incongruities,
Sublime in its audacity,
Bizarre breaker of moulds.

DANIEL J. BOORSTIN
The Image

Never has a people expected so much more than the world could offer.

FRANKLIN D. ROOSEVELT

Democracy is not a static thing. It is an everlasting march.

MARTIN LUTHER KING, JR.
"The American Dream," *speech*

America is essentially a dream, a dream as yet unfulfilled. It is a dream of a land where men of all races, of all nationalities and of all creeds can live together as brothers.

LYNDON B. JOHNSON
Inaugural Address

For this is what America is all about. It is the uncrossed desert and the unclimbed ridge. It is the star that is not reached and the harvest that is sleeping in the unplowed ground.

THOMAS WOLFE

The place where miracles not only happen, but where they happen all the time.

LANGSTON HUGHES
"Let America Be America Again," *The Poetry of the Negro*

O, yes,
I say it plain,
America never was America to me.
And yet I swear this oath—
America will be!

LAWRENCE FERLINGHETTI
"I am waiting"

I am waiting for my case to come up
and I am waiting
for a rebirth of wonder
and I am waiting for someone
to really discover America...

THOMAS PAINE

The cause of America is, in a great measure, the cause of all mankind.

THOMAS JEFFERSON
Letter to John Adams

I do believe we shall continue to grow, to multiply and prosper until we exhibit an association powerful, wise, and happy beyond what has yet been seen by men.

ANDREW JACKSON
First message to Congress

Turning our eyes to other nations, our great desire is to see our brethren of the human race secured in the blessings enjoyed by ourselves, and advancing in knowledge, in freedom, and in social happiness.

BERNARD BARUCH
Address on accepting The Churchman Award, New York

America has never forgotten—and will never forget—the nobler things that brought her into being and that light her path—the path that was entered upon only one hundred and fifty years ago.... How young she is!

ARCHIBALD MACLEISH

The American journey has not ended. America is never accomplished, America is always still to build.... West is a country in the mind, and so eternal.

A More Perfect Union

BILL MOYERS
Broadcast on Public Broadcasting System

America is the longest argument in the world.

PREAMBLE TO THE CONSTITUTION OF THE UNITED STATES

We, the people of the United States, in order to form a more perfect union, establish justice, insure domestic tranquillity, provide for the common defense, promote the general welfare, and secure the blessings of liberty to ourselves and our posterity, do ordain and establish this Constitution for the United States of America.

E.B. WHITE

... Thomas Jefferson pointed out that there was nothing sacred about constitutions, and that they were useful only if changed frequently to fit the changing needs of the people. Reverence for our Constitution is going to reach droll new heights this year; yet the Constitution, far from being a sacred document, isn't even a grammatical one. "We, the people of the United States, in order to form a more perfect union..." has turned many a grammarian's stomach, perfection being a state which does not admit of degree. A meticulous draughtsman would have written simply "in order to form a perfect union"—a thing our forefathers didn't dare predict, even for the sake of grammar.

THURGOOD MARSHALL
"The Real Meaning of the Constitutional Bicentennial," Ebony

I do not believe that the meaning of the Constitution was forever "fixed" at the Philadephia Convention....The government they devised was defective from the start, requiring several amendments, a civil war, and momentous social transformation to attain the system of constitutional government, and its respect for individual freedoms and human rights, we hold as fundamental today.

THE DECLARATION OF INDEPENDENCE

...Whenever any form of government becomes destructive of these ends, it is the right of the people to alter or to abolish it, and to institute a new government, laying its foundation on such principles, and organising its powers in such form, as to them shall seem most likely to effect their safety and happiness.

THOMAS JEFFERSON
Message to the citizens of Washington County, Maryland

The care of human life and happiness, and not their destruction, is the first and only legitimate object of good government.

WILLIAM ELLERY CHANNING
In a review in the Christian Examiner

The office of government is not to confer happiness, but to give men opportunity to work out happiness for themselves.

THOMAS JEFFERSON

Every man wishes to pursue his occupation and to enjoy the fruits of his labours and the produce of his property in peace and safety, and with the least possible expense. When these things are accomplished, all the objects for which government ought to be established are answered.

JEANE J. KIRKPATRICK

Governments can encourage the cultivation of private virtue. They can provide a framework in which we may pursue virtue (or happiness), but they cannot make us virtuous (or happy), and the effort to use the coercive power of government for that purpose not only fails to produce private morality, it undermines public morality as well.

ABRAHAM LINCOLN
"Fragment on Government"

The legitimate object of government is to do for a community of people whatever they need to have done, but cannot do at all, or cannot so well do, for themselves, in their separate and individual capacities.

JIMMY CARTER
Inaugural Address as Governor of Georgia

Government is a contrivance of human wisdom to provide for human wants.

MARK TWAIN
Notebook

That government is not best which best secures mere life and property—there is a more valuable thing—manhood.

GROVER CLEVELAND
Second Annual Message to Congress

Good government, and especially the government of which every American citizen boasts, has for its objects the protection of every person within its care in the greatest liberty consistent with the good order of society, and his perfect security in the enjoyment of his earnings with the least possible diminution for public needs.

THOMAS JEFFERSON

A wise and frugal government, which shall restrain men from injuring one another, shall leave them otherwise free to regulate their own pursuits of industry and improvement, and shall not take from the mouth of labor the bread it has earned. This is the sum of good government, and this is necessary to close the circle of our felicities.

First Inaugural Address

THOMAS JEFFERSON

About to enter, fellow-citizens, on the exercise of duties which comprehend everything dear and valuable to you, it is proper you should understand what I deem the essential principles of our Government, and consequently those which ought to shape its Administration. I will compress them within the narrowest compass they will bear, stating the general principle, but not all its limitations. Equal and exact justice to all men, of whatever state or persuasion, religious or political; peace, commerce, and honest friendship with all nations, entangling alliances with none; the support of the State governments in all their rights, as the most competent administrations for our domestic concerns and the surest bulwarks against antirepublican tendencies; the preservation of the General Government in its whole constitutional vigor, as the sheer anchor of our peace at home and safety abroad; a jealous care of the right of election by the people—a mild and safe corrective of abuses which are lopped by the sword of revolution where peaceable remedies are unprovided; absolute acquiescence in the decisions of the majority, the vital principle of republics, from which is no appeal but to force, the vital principle and immediate parent of despotism; a well-disciplined militia, our best reliance in peace and for the first moments of war, till regulars may relive them; the supremacy of the civil over the military authority; economy in the public expense, that labor may be lightly burthened; the honest payment of our debts and sacred preservation of the public faith; encouragement of agriculture, and of commerce as its handmaid; the diffusion of information and arraignment of all abuses at the bar of the public reason; freedom of religion, freedom of the press, and freedom of person under the protection of habeas corpus, and trial by juries impartially selected. These principles form the bright constellation which has gone before us and guided our steps through an age of revolution and formation. The wisdom of our sages and blood of our heroes have been devoted to their attainment. They should be the creed of our political faith, the text of civic instruction, the touchstone by which to try the services of those we trust; and should we wander from them in moments of error or of alarm, let us hasten to retrace our steps and to regain the road which alone leads to peace, liberty, and safety.

JAMES MADISON
Letter to Thomas Ritchie

All power in human hands is liable to be abused. In Governments independent of the people, the rights and interests of the whole may be sacrificed to the views of the Government. In Republics, where . . . the majority govern, a danger to the minority arises from . . . a sacrifice of their rights to the interests . . . of the majority. No form of government, therefore, can be a perfect guard against the abuse of power.

Ralph Waldo Emerson
Essays, Second Series

The less government we have the better—the fewer laws, and the less confided power. The antidote to this abuse of formal government is the influence of private character, the growth of the Individual; the appearance of the principal to supersede the proxy; the appearance of the wise man; of whom the existing government is, it must be owned, but a shabby imitation.

Walter Lippmann
"The Red Herring," *A Preface to Politics*

It is perfectly true that that government is best which governs least. It is equally true that that government is best which provides most.

John C. Calhoun

The very essence of a free government consists in considering offices as public trusts, bestowed for the good of the country, and not for the benefit of an individual or a party.

Henry Clay

Government is a trust, and the officers of the government are trustees; and both the trust and the trustees are created for the benefit of the people.

Grover Cleveland
Speech in accepting the mayoralty nomination of Buffalo, New York

Public office is a public trust.

Louis D. Brandeis

The most important office is that of private citizen.

Woodrow Wilson

The machinery of political control must be put in the hands of the people ... for the purpose of recovering what seems to have been lost—their right to exercise a free and constant choice in the management of their own affairs....The service rendered the people by the national government must be of a more extended sort and of a kind not only to protect it against monopoly, but also to facilitate its life....We do not mean to strike at any essential economic arrangement; but we do mean to drive all beneficiaries of governmental policy into the open and demand of them by what principle of national advantage, as contrasted with selfish privilege, they enjoy the extraordinary assistance extended to them. The great monopoly in this country is the money monopoly. So long as that exists our old variety and freedom and individual energy of development are out of the question. . . . The growth of the nation, therefore, and all our activities are in the hands of a few men . . . who necessarily, by very reason of their own limitations, chill and check and destroy genuine economic freedom. This is the greatest question of all. . . . What do we stand for here tonight and what shall we stand for as long as we live? We stand for setting the Government of this country free and the business of this country free. . . . Now, the real difficulty in the United States . . . is not the existence of great individual combinations—that is dangerous enough in all countries—but the real danger is the combination of the combinations, the real danger is that the same groups of men control chains of banks, systems of railways, whole manufacturing enterprises, great mining projects, great enterprises for the developing of the natural water power of this country, and that threaded together in the personnel of a series of boards of directors is a community of interest more formidable than any conceivable combination in the United States. . . . What we have got to do . . . is to disentangle this colossal community of interest . . . to pull apart, and gently, but firmly and persistently, dissect. When I think over what we are engaged in doing in the field of politics, I conceive it this way, men who are behind any interest always unite in organization, and the danger in every country is that these special interests will be the only things organized, and that the common interest will be unorganized against them. The business of government is to organize the common interest against the special interests.

LYNDON B. JOHNSON
Speech, University of New Mexico

Government is not an enemy of the people. Government is the people themselves.

DANIEL WEBSTER

The people's government made for the people, made by the people, and answerable to the people.

RALPH ELLISON
"Perspective of Literature"

Democracy is a collectivity of individuals.

WILLIAM TYLER PAGE
The American Creed

I believe in the United States of America as a government of the people, by the people, for the people; whose just powers are derived from the consent of the governed; a democracy in a republic; a sovereign Nation of many sovereign States; a perfect union, one and inseparable; established upon those principles of freedom, equality, justice, and humanity for which American patriots sacrificed their lives and fortunes. I therefore believe it is my duty to my country to love it, to support its Constitution, to obey its laws, to respect its flag, and to defend it against all enemies.

THEODORE ROOSEVELT
Speech in Asheville, North Carolina

The government is us; we are the government, you and I.

THEODORE PARKER
The American Idea

A democracy—that is a government of all the people, by all the people, for all the people; of course, a government of the principles of eternal justice, the unchanging law of God, for shortness' sake I will call it the idea of Freedom.

JAMES MADISON
Federalist LXIII

It is essential to liberty that the government in general should have a common interest with the people.

FRANKLIN D. ROOSEVELT
Radio address

The only sure bulwark of continuing liberty is a government strong enough to protect the interests of the people, and a people strong enough and well enough informed to maintain its sovereign control over its government.

FRANKLIN D. ROOSEVELT

Our government is not the master but the creature of the people. The duty of the State toward the citizens is the duty of a servant to its master. The people have created it; the people, by common consent, permit its continual existence.

ADLAI E. STEVENSON

As citizens of this democracy, you are the rulers and the ruled, the lawgivers and the law-abiding, the beginning and the end.

MARTIN VAN BUREN
Inquiry into the Origin and Course of Political Parties

The people under our system, like the king in a monarchy, never die.

ANDREW JACKSON
Letter to General John Coffee

The people are the sovereigns, they can alter and amend.

THOMAS JEFFERSON
Letter to John Cartwright

The constitutions of most of our States assert that all power is inherent in the people.

THOMAS JEFFERSON
Letter to William C. Jarvis

I know no safe depository of the ultimate powers of the society but the people themselves; and if we think them not enlightened enough to exercise their control with a wholesome discretion, the remedy is not to take it from them, but to inform their discretion by education.

ELEANOR ROOSEVELT
"Let Us Have Faith in Democracy," Department of Agriculture Land Policy

A democratic form of government, a democratic way of life, presupposes free public education over a long period; it presupposes also an education for personal responsibility that too often is neglected.

THOMAS JEFFERSON
Letter to H.D. Tiffin

That government is the strongest of which every man feels himself a part.

WOODROW WILSON

Just what is it that America stands for? If she stands for one thing more than another, it is for the sovereignty of self-governing people.

HENRY CLAY
Speech, House of Representatives

Self-government is the natural government of man.

JOHN ADAMS
Proclamation adopted by the Council of Massachusetts Bay

As the happiness of the people is the sole end of government, so the consent of the people is the only foundation of it, in reason, morality, and the natural fitness of things.

ADLAI E. STEVENSON
"War, Weakness, and Ourselves," Look magazine

By "America," I suppose we all think of not *just* the real estate or inhabitants of the United States, but also of the idea that we who live here share and cherish in common—the concept of government by the free consent of the governed as the only tolerable system of management of human affairs.

JAMES RUSSELL LOWELL
The Biglow papers

Democracy gives every man
The right to be his own oppressor.

Civil Disobedience

HENRY DAVID THOREAU

The authority of government, even such as I am willing to submit to—for I will cheerfully obey those who know and can do better than I, and in many things even those who neither know nor can do so well—is still an impure one: to be strictly just, it must have the sanction and consent of the governed. It can have no pure right over my person and property but what I concede to it. The progress from an absolute to a limited monarchy, from a limited monarchy to a democracy, is a progress toward a true respect for the individual. Even the Chinese philosopher was wise enough to regard the individual as the basis of the empire. Is a democracy, such as we know it, the last improvement possible in government? Is it not possible to take a step further towards recognizing and organizing the rights of man? There will never be a really free and enlightened State, until the State comes to recognize the individual as a higher and independent power, from which all its own power and authority are derived, and treats him accordingly. I please myself with imagining a State at last which can afford to be just to all men, and to treat the individual with respect as a neighbor; which even would not think it inconsistent with its own repose, if a few were to live aloof from it, not meddling with it, nor embraced by it, who fulfilled all the duties of neighbors and fellowmen. A State which bore this kind of fruit, and suffered it to drop off as fast as it ripened, would prepare the way for a still more perfect and glorious State, which also I have imagined, but not yet anywhere seen.

Harry S Truman

Democracy is based on the conviction that man has the moral and intellectual capacity, as well as the inalienable right, to govern himself with reason and justice.

Milton Friedman
Capitalism and Freedom

To the free man, the country is the collection of individuals who compose it, not something over and above them. He is proud of a common heritage and loyal to common traditions. But he regards government as a means, an instrumentality, neither a grantor of favors and gifts, nor a master or god to be blindly worshipped and served. He recognizes no national goal except as it is the consensus of the goals the citizens severally serve. He recognizes no national purpose except as it is the consensus of the purposes for which the citizens severally strive.

Woodrow Wilson

No government has ever been beneficent when the attitude of government was that it was taking care of the people. The only freedom consists in the people taking care of the government.

Thomas Jefferson
Letter to Benjamin Waring

The will of the people is the only legitimate foundation of any government, and to protect its free expression should be our first object.

ANDREW JACKSON
First Inaugural Address

As long as our Government is administered for the good of the people, and is regulated by their will; as long as it secures to us the rights of persons and of property, liberty of conscience, and of the press, it will be worth defending.

JAMES MADISON
National Gazette

A government deriving its energy from the will of the society... is the government for which philosophy has been searching, and humanity been fighting, from the most remote ages. Such are republican governments which it is the glory of America to have invented, and her unrivalled happiness to possess.

JOHN ADAMS
Letter to E. C. E. Genet

All governments depend upon the good will of the people.

THOMAS JEFFERSON.
Letter to Henry Lee

Men by their constitutions are naturally divided into two parties: 1. Those who fear and distrust the people, and wish to draw all powers from them into the hands of the higher classes. 2. Those who identify themselves with the people, have confidence in them, cherish and consider them as the most honest and safe, although not the most wise, depository of the public interests. In every country these two parties exist; and in every one where they are free to think, speak, and write, they will declare themselves.

ABRAHAM LINCOLN
First Inaugural Address

Why should there not be a patient confidence in the ultimate justice of the people? Is there any better or equal hope in the world?

ABRAHAM LINCOLN

With public sentiment, nothing can fail; without it, nothing can succeed. Consequently he who molds public sentiment goes deeper than he who enacts statutes or pronounces decisions.

Grover Cleveland
Fourth annual message to Congress

To lose faith in the intelligence of the people is a surrender and an abandonment of the struggle. To arouse their intelligence, and free it from darkness and delusion, gives assurance of speedy and complete victory.

Eleanor Roosevelt

The outstanding issue today is much as it was in Jefferson's day—trust in the people or fear the people. . . . Is the Government to be in the hands of the aristocrats . . . or shall it again be in the hands of the people who may make more mistakes but who will be free, responsible citizens?

Thomas Jefferson
Letter to Samuel Kercheval

I am not among those who fear the people. They, and not the rich, are our dependence for continued freedom.

William Allen White
Emporia Gazette

Put fear out of your heart. This nation will survive, this state will prosper, the orderly business of life will go forward if only men can speak in whatever way given them to utter what their hearts hold—by voice, by posted card, by letter, or by press. Reason never has failed men. Only force and oppression have made the wrecks in the world.

Andrew Jackson
Letter to James Hamilton

I for one do not despair of the republic; I have great confidence in the virtue of the great majority of the people, and I cannot fear the result.

James Madison

The people of this country, by their conduct and example, will decide the important question, whether societies of men are really capable or not of establishing good government from reflection and choice, or whether they are forever destined to depend for their political constitutions on accident and force.

NATHANIEL HAWTHORNE
The Gray Champion

[Oppression] is the deformity of any government that does not grow out of the nature of things and the character of the people.

JAMES A. GARFIELD

All free governments are managed by the combined wisdom and folly of the people.

ADLAI E. STEVENSON

Democracy cannot be saved by supermen, but only by the unswerving devotion and goodness of millions of little men.

WOODROW WILSON

I am all kinds of a democrat, so far as I can discover—but the root of the whole business is this, that I believe in the patriotism and energy and initiative of the average man.

JOHN F. KENNEDY
Why England Slept

Democracy is the superior form of government, because it is based on a respect for man as a reasonable human being.

Democratic Vistas

WALT WHITMAN

The ulterior object of political and all other government (having, of course, provided for the police, the safety of life, property, and for the basic statute and common law, and their administration, always first in order), to be among the rest, not merely to rule, to repress disorder, etc., but to develop, to open up to cultivation, to encourage the possibilities of all beneficent and manly outcroppage, and of that aspiration for independence, and the pride and self-respect latent in all characters.

I say the mission of government, henceforth, in civilized lands, is not repression alone, and not authority alone, not even of law, nor by that favorite standard of the eminent writer the rule of the best men, the born heroes and captains of the race (as if such ever, or one time out of a hundred, get into the big places, elective or dynastic), but higher than the highest arbitrary rule, to train communities through all their grades, beginning with individuals and ending there again, to rule themselves....

We do not (at any rate I do not) put it either on the ground that the People, the masses, even the best of them, are, in their latent or exhibited qualities, essentially sensible and good —nor on the ground of their rights; but that good or bad, rights or no rights, the democratic formula is the only safe and preservative one for coming times. We endow the masses with the suffrage for their own sake, no doubt; then, perhaps still more, from another point of view, for community's sake.

E.B. White

For ourselves, we shall resolve not to overwrite in the New Year, and to defend and exalt those principles and quirks that have carried the nation slowly up the long hill since it started: its gaiety, its resilience, its diversity, its tolerance of the divergent or the harassing idea, its respect for all men. Who is to say we are not greatly ascendant still?

Ralph Ellison
"What America Would Be Like Without Blacks," *Going to the Territory*

Democracy is not simply material well-being but the extension of the democratic process in the direction of perfecting itself.

Alexis de Tocqueville
Democracy in America

I confess that in America I saw more than America; I sought there the image of democracy itself, with its inclinations, its character, its prejudices, and its passions, in order to learn what we have to fear or to hope from its progress.

Harry Emerson Fosdick

Democracy is based upon the conviction that there are extraordinary possibilities in ordinary people.

Woodrow Wilson

I believe in Democracy because it releases the energies of every human being.

WALT WHITMAN
Song of Myself

I speak the pass-word primeval, I give the sign of democracy,
By God! I will accept nothing which all cannot have their
counterpart of on the same terms.

THOMAS JEFFERSON
Letter to Edward Carrington

But with all the imperfections of our present government, it is without comparison the best existing, or that ever did exist.

ELDRIDGE CLEAVER
"Why I Left the U.S. and Why I am Returning"

With all of its faults, the American political system is the freest and most democratic in the world.

MICHAEL HARRINGTON
Toward a Democratic Left

Democracy, it must be emphasized, is a practical necessity and not just a philosophic value.

FRANKLIN D. ROOSEVELT

The democratic aspiration is no mere recent phase of human history. It is human history.

HARRY S TRUMAN

Hitler learned that efficiency without justice is a vain thing. Democracy does not work that way. Democracy is a matter of faith—a faith in the soul of man—a faith in human rights.

REINHOLD NIEBUHR

Man's capacity for evil makes democracy necessary and man's capacity for good makes democracy possible.

E.B. WHITE
The Wild Flag

Democracy is the recurrent suspicion that more than half of the people are right more than half of the time.

CLAUDE BOWERS
Keynote address, Democratic National Convention

Ladies and Gentlemen of the Convention:

The American Democracy has mobilized today to wage a war of extermination against privilege and pillage. We prime our guns against autocracy and bureaucracy. We march against that centralization which threatens the liberties of the people. We fight for the republic of the fathers, and for the recovery of the covenant from the keeping of a caste and class. We battle for the honor of the nation, besmirched and bedraggled by the most brazen and shameless carnival of corruption that ever blackened the reputation of a decent and self-respecting people.

We stand for the spirit of the preamble of the Declaration that is made a mockery; for the Bill of Rights that is ignored; for the social and economic justice which is refused; for the sovereign right of states that are denied; and for a return to the old-fashioned civic integrity of a Jackson, a Tilden, a Cleveland, and a Wilson. We stand for the restoration of the government to the people who built it by their bravery and cemented it with their blood.

JOHN F. KENNEDY
State of the Union Address

Any system of government will work well when everything is going well. It's the system that functions in the pinches that survives.

HARRY S TRUMAN
Lecture, Columbia University

If you want an efficient government why then go someplace where they have a dictatorship and you'll get it.

JOHN HANCOCK

Some boast of being friends to government; I am a friend to righteous government, to a government founded upon the principles of reason and justice; but I glory in publicly avowing my eternal enmity to tyranny.

OLIVER WENDELL HOLMES, JR.
Speech, Harvard Law School Association

Modesty and reverence are no less virtues of freemen than the democratic feeling which will submit neither to arrogance nor to servility.

HARRY S TRUMAN
Address to Congress

No government is perfect. One of the chief virtues of a democracy, however, is that its defects are always visible and under democratic processes can be pointed out and corrected.

FRANCIS WRIGHT
Independence Day address

It is for Americans, more especially, to nourish a nobler sentiment, one more consistent with their origin, and more conducive to their future improvement. It is for them more especially to know why they love their country; and to feel that they love it, not because it is their country, but because it is the palladium of human liberty—the favored scene of human improvement. It is for them, more especially, to examine their institutions; and to feel that they honor them because they are based on just principles. It is for them, more especially, to examine their institutions, because they have the means of improving them; to examine their laws, because at will they can alter them.

ADLAI E. STEVENSON, ADDRESS
Democratic National Convention

Self-criticism is the secret weapon of democracy, and candor and confession are good for the political soul.

MARTIN LUTHER KING, JR.
Where Do We Go From Here?

It is not a sign of weakness, but a sign of high maturity, to rise to the level of self-criticism.

JAMES BALDWIN
Notes of a Native Son

I love America more than any other country in the world, and, exactly for this reason, I insist on the right to criticize her perpetually.

HUBERT H. HUMPHREY
Beyond Civil Rights: A New Day of Equality

What we need are critical lovers of America—patriots who express their faith in their country by working to improve it.

W.E.B. DuBois
The Autobiography of W.E.B. DuBois:
A Soliloquy on Viewing My Life from the last Decade of Its First Century

Honest men may and must criticize America.

JOHN F. KENNEDY
Speech in praise of Robert Frost, Amherst College

The men who create power make an indispensable contribution to the nation's greatness. But the men who question power make a contribution just as indispensable, especially when that questioning is disinterested.

For they determine whether we use power or power uses us. Our national strength matters; but the spirit which informs and controls our strength matters just as much.

MARK TWAIN
Inscription beneath his bust in the Hall of Fame

Loyalty to petrified opinion never yet broke a chain or freed a human soul.

WALTER LIPPMANN
Address at the International Press Institute Assembly

Without criticism and reliable and intelligent reporting, the government cannot govern.

W.E.B. Du Bois

If we expect to gain our rights by nerveless acquiescence in wrong then we expect to do what no other nation ever did. What must we do then? We must complain. Yes, plain, blunt, complain, ceaseless agitation, unfailing exposure of dishonesty and wrong—this is the ancient, unerring way to liberty, and we must follow it.

WILLIAM HENRY HARRISON

A decent and manly examination of the acts of Government should be not only tolerated, but encouraged.

Martin Luther King, Jr.

We must encourage creative dissenters. We must demonstrate, teach, and preach, until the foundations of our nation are secure.

Dwight D. Eisenhower
Speech at Columbia University Bicentennial

Here in America we are descended in blood and in spirit from revolutionaries and rebels—men and women who dared to dissent from accepted doctrine. As their heirs, may we never confuse honest dissent with disloyal subversion.

Arthur Schlesinger

What we need is a rebirth of satire, of dissent, of irreverence, of uncompromising insistence that phoniness is phony and platitudes platitudinous.

Wole Soyinka

The greatest threat to freedom is the absence of criticism.

Henry Steele Commager
Freedom, Loyalty, Dissent

If our democracy is to flourish, it must have criticism; if our government is to function it must have dissent.

Edward Roscoe Murrow
See It Now (broadcast). Report on Senator Joseph R. McCarthy

We must not confuse dissent with disloyalty.

Walter Lippmann

In a democracy, the opposition is not only tolerated as constitutional, but must be maintained because it is indispensable.

Will Rogers

A difference of opinion is what makes horse racing and missionaries.

ALEXANDER HAMILTON

In the legislature, promptitude of decision is oftener an evil than a benefit. The differences of opinion, and the jarrings of parties in that department of the government, though they may sometimes obstruct salutary plans, yet often promote deliberation and circumspection; and serve to check excesses in the majority.

LEARNED HAND
Speech to the Board of Regents, University of the State of New York

The mutual confidence on which all else depends can be maintained only by an open mind and a brave reliance upon free discussion.

ADLAI E. STEVENSON
Speech in Detroit

My definition of a free society is a society where it is safe to be unpopular.

EDWARD ROSCOE MURROW
"See It Now" (broadcast). Report on Senator Joseph R. McCarthy

We will not be driven by fear into an age of unreason if we...remember that we are not descended from fearful men, not from men who feared to write, to speak, to associate and to defend causes which were, for the moment, unpopular.

RALPH WALDO EMERSON
Essays, First Series

Who so would be a man must be a nonconformist.

THOMAS JEFFERSON
Letter to John Taylor

An association of men who will not quarrel with one another is a thing which never yet existed, from the greatest confederacy of nations down to a town-meeting or a vestry.

ALEXIS DE TOCQUEVILLE

In politics a community of hatred is almost always the foundation of friendships.

WILLIAM MCKINLEY

Our differences are policies, our agreements principles.

ROBERT FROST

"The Future of Man," *a symposium held at New York City*

The certainty of conflict is originality, that's all—the bursting power, the bursting energy and daring of man. And it's always there, always there. You can't hope for anything that doesn't include that.

FRANKLIN D. ROOSEVELT

The country needs and, unless I mistake its temper, the country demands bold, persistent experimentation. It is common sense to take a method and try it. If it fails, admit it frankly and try another. But above all, try something.

WILLIAM JOHNSON

Supreme Court opinion, Anderson v. Dunn

The science of government is ... the science of experiment.

ERNEST J. GAINES

The Sky is Gray

Question everything. Every stripe, every star, every word spoken. Everything.

ARCHIBALD MACLEISH

Reflections

I really wasn't very aware of the Republic. I took it entirely for granted. I'd come from a home which was intelligent and orderly. My father was a Scotsman with very deep feelings about Scotland, but even deeper feelings about the United States, which he'd come to at the age of eighteen. And my mother was the daughter of a Congregational clergyman whose ancestry was straight Connecticut, right back to Elder Brewster, who landed somewhere else as you recall. Between the two of them, my mother took Connecticut totally for granted; she took New England for granted. She moved to Illinois and Illinois was a new experience. She went to work in Hull House and thereabouts as soon as her children were old enough to learn. But she had three hundred years of the United States back of her; and she had no serious questions about the Republic at all. Her assumptions were assumptions of total acceptance. She realized its faults. She didn't talk about them much, although she fought them like a tiger when they met her, when they got in the way of what she cared about. A swastika on the church in Glencoe, Illinois, put Mother, at the age of ninety, on a war horse. She had that whole town turned upside down by five o'clock in the afternoon.

With this kind of a background and going to a very establishment preparatory school, Hotchkiss, and going to Yale and Harvard Law School, I was interested in the intellectual world as I began to learn about it, but I was not much concerned about the United States; I simply accepted that situation. And the question didn't really arise for me until, first of all, my year during the war and then my wife's and my return to Paris five or six years later and the six or seven years we stopped there.

I came back from that with a very sharp realization that to be an American was a question, not an answer.

RALPH WALDO EMERSON
Essays

Every revolution was first a thought in one man's mind.

HENRY DAVID THOREAU
Civil Disobedience

Unjust laws exist: shall we be content to obey them, or shall we endeavor to amend them, and obey them until we have succeeded, or shall we transgress them at once? Men generally, under such a government as this, think that they ought to wait until they have persuaded the majority to alter them. They think that, if they should resist, the remedy would be worse than the evil. But it is the fault of the government itself that the remedy *is* worse than the evil. *It* makes it worse. Why is it not more apt to anticipate and provide for reform? Why does it not cherish its wise minority? Why does it cry and resist before it is hurt?

JAMES WELDON JOHNSON
"Africa at the Peace Table and the Descendants of Africans in our American Democracy,"
speech given at NAACP Annual Conference

It is our intention to carry on an intelligent, persistent and aggressive agitation until we educate this nation, more than educate it, until we whip and sting its conscience, until we awaken it, until we startle it into a realization that we know what we want, we know what we are entitled to, and that we are determined by all that is sacred to have it and be satisfied with nothing less.

FREDERICK DOUGLASS
"What to the Slave is the Fourth of July?"

For it is not light that is needed, but fire; it is not the gentle shower, but thunder. We need the storm, the whirlwind, and the earthquake. The feeling in the nation must be quickened, the conscience of the nation must be roused, the propriety of the nation must be startled, the hypocrisy of the nation must be exposed; and its crimes against God and man must be denounced.

WENDELL PHILLIPS
Cited in The American Political Tradition by Richard Hofstadter

Republics exist only on the tenure of being constantly agitated. The antislavery agitation is an important, nay, an essential part of the machinery of the state. . . . Every government is always growing corrupt. Every Secretary of State . . . is an enemy to the people of necessity, because the moment he joins the government, he gravitates against that popular agitation which is the life of a republic. A republic is nothing but a constant overflow of lava. . . . The republic which sinks to sleep, trusting to constitutions and machinery, to politicians and statesmen, for the safety of its liberties, never will have any.

ALBERT EINSTEIN

The world is a dangerous place to live—not because of the people who are evil but because of the people who don't do anything about it.

MARY ELIZABETH LEASE

What you farmers need to do is raise less corn and more Hell!

RALPH WALDO EMERSON
Journals

Sometimes a scream is better than a thesis.

HENRY WARD BEECHER
Proverbs from Plymouth Pulpit

When a nation's young men are conservative, its funeral bell is already rung.

THOMAS JEFFERSON
Letter to James Madison

I hold that a little rebellion now and then is a good thing, and as necessary in the political world as storms in the physical. Unsuccessful rebellions indeed generally establish the incroachments on the rights of the people which have produced them. An observation of this truth should render honest republican governors so mild in their punishment of rebellions, as not to discourage them too much. It is a medicine necessary for the sound health of government.

JAMES GARFIELD
Diary

I love agitation and investigation and glory in defending unpopular truth against popular error.

JOHN F. KENNEDY
Campaign Address

I want every American free to stand up for his rights, even if sometimes he has to sit down for them.

MALCOLM X

You're not supposed to be so blind with patriotism that you can't face reality. Wrong is wrong, no matter who does it or who says it.

GORE VIDAL
Rocking the Boat

I am a correctionist. If something is wrong in society, it must be fixed. At least one should try to fix it.

NATHANIEL HAWTHORNE
The House of Seven Gables

There is nothing wrong with America that together we can't fix.

The world owes all its onward impulses to men ill at ease. The happy man inevitably confines himself within ancient limits.

LYNDON B. JOHNSON

We will have differences. Men of different ancestries, men of different tongues, men of different environments, men of different geographies do not see everything alike. If we did we would all want the same wife—and that would be a problem, wouldn't it!

HEYWOOD BROUN
"Whims," *New York World*

Nobody expects to find comfort and companionability in reformers.

WENDELL PHILLIPS

The reformer is careless of numbers, disregards popularity, and deals only with ideas, conscience, and common sense. He feels, with Copernicus, that as God waited long for an interpreter, so he can wait for his followers.

J.K. GALBRAITH

If you can't comfort the afflicted then afflict the comfortable.

BERTRAND RUSSELL
"The Place of Sex Among Human Values," *Marriage and Morals*

The desire to understand the world and the desire to reform it are the two great engines of progress, without which human society would stand still or retrogress.

ROBERT FROST

I never dared be radical when young
for fear it would make me conservative when old.

JOHN KILLENS
Beyond the Angry Black

Every time I sit down to the typewriter, with every line I put on paper I am out to change the world, to capture reality, to melt it down and forge it into something entirely different.

FRANTZ FANON
Black Skin, White Masks

What matters is not to know the world but to change it.

ULYSSES S. GRANT
Second Inaugural Address

The Theory of government changes with general progress.

THEODORE ROOSEVELT
Cited by Franklin D. Roosevelt at the dedication of the Theodore Roosevelt Memorial

A great democracy must be progressive or it will soon cease to be a great democracy.

H.L. MENCKEN
Prejudices: Third Series

Human progress is furthered, not by conformity, but by aberration.

HENRY MILLER
"Reflections on Writing," *The Wisdom of the Heart*

Whatever there be of progress in life comes not through adaptation but through daring, through obeying the blind urge.

MARTIN LUTHER KING, JR.
Strength to Love

All progress is precarious, and the solution of one problem brings us face to face with another problem.

ROBERT F. KENNEDY
"Federal Power and Local Poverty," *The Pursuit of Justice*

Progress is a nice word. But change is its motivator. And change has its enemies.

SENATOR EVERETT M. DIRKSEN

Life is not a static thing. The only people who do not change their minds are incompetents in asylums, who can't, and those in cemeteries.

HENRY WARD BEECHER
Proverbs from Plymouth Pulpit

When a man says that he is perfect already, there is only one of two places for him, and that is heaven or the lunatic asylum.

WILLIAM CULLEN BRYANT
Mutation

Weep not that the world changes—did it keep
A stable, changeless state, 'twere cause indeed to weep.

THOMAS JEFFERSON

Laws and institutions must go hand in hand with the progress of the human mind. As that becomes more developed, more enlightened, as new discoveries are made, new truths disclosed, and manners and opinions change with the change of circumstances, institutions must advance also, and keep pace with the times. We might as well require a man to wear still the coat which fitted him as a boy, as a civilized society to remain ever under the regimen of their barbarous ancestors.

JOHN C. CALHOUN
A Disquisition on Government

The interval between the decay of the old and the establishment of the new constitutes a period of transition, which must always necessarily be one of uncertainty, confusion, error, and wild and fierce fanaticism.

TENNESSEE WILLIAMS
Camino Real

There is a time for departure even when there's no certain place to go.

LYNDON B. JOHNSON
State of the Union Message

When a great ship cuts through the sea, the waters are always stirred and troubled. And our ship is moving—moving through troubled new waters, toward new and better shores.

MARGARET MEAD

Never doubt that a small group of committed citizens can change the world. Indeed, it is the only thing that ever has.

MARTIN LUTHER KING, JR.
"The Death of Evil upon the Seashore,"
sermon given at the Cathedral of St. John the Divine, New York City

Change does not roll in on the wheels of inevitability, but comes through continuous struggle. And so we must straighten our back and work for our freedom. A man can't ride you unless your back is bent.

JOHN F. KENNEDY

With a good conscience our only sure reward, with history the final judge of our deeds, let us go forth to lead the land we love asking His Blessing and His help, but knowing that here on earth God's work must truly be our own.

ADLAI E. STEVENSON

I venture to suggest that patriotism is not a short and frenzied outburst of emotion but the tranquil and steady dedication of a lifetime.

FREDERICK DOUGLASS
Cited in John W. Blassingame, Frederick Douglass: The Clarion Voice

The whole history of the progress of human liberty shows that all concessions yet made to her august claims have been born of earnest struggle. . . . If there is no struggle, there is no progress. Those who profess to favor freedom, and yet deprecate agitation, are men who want crops without plowing up the ground, they want rain without thunder and lightning. They want the ocean without the awful roar of its many waters.

ADLAI E. STEVENSON
Democratic Acceptance Speech

What does concern me, in common with thinking partisans of both parties, is not just winning the election, but how it is won, how well we can take advantage of this great quadrennial opportunity to debate issues sensibly and soberly. I hope and pray that we Democrats, win or lose, can campaign not as a crusade to exterminate the opposing party, as our opponents seem to prefer, but as a great opportunity to educate and elevate a people whose destiny is leadership, not alone of a rich and prosperous, contented country as in the past, but of a world in ferment.

And, my friends, more important than winning the election is governing the nation. That is the test of a political party—the acid, final test. When the tumult and the shouting die, when the bands are gone and the lights are dimmed, there is the stark reality of responsibility in an hour of history haunted with those gaunt, grim specters of strife, dissension and materialism at home, and ruthless, inscrutable and hostile powers abroad.

The ordeal of the twentieth century—the bloodiest, most turbulent era of the Christian age—is far from over. Sacrifice, patience, understanding and implacable purpose may be our lot for years to come. Let's face it. Let's talk sense to the American people. Let's tell them the truth, that there are no gains without pains, that we are now on the eve of great decisions, not easy decisions, like resistance when you're attacked, but a long, patient, costly struggle which alone can assure triumph over the great enemies of man—war, poverty and tyranny—and the assaults upon human dignity which are the most grievous consequences of each.

Let's tell them that the victory to be won in the twentieth century, this portal to the Golden Age, mocks the pretensions of individual acumen and ingenuity. For it is a citadel guarded by thick walls of ignorance and of mistrust which do not fall before the trumpets' blast or the politicians' imprecations or even a general's baton. They are, my friends, walls that must be directly stormed by the hosts of courage, of morality and of vision, standing shoulder to shoulder, unafraid of ugly truth, contemptuous of lies, half truths, circuses and demagoguery.

WALTER LIPPMANN
"Some Necessary Iconoclasm," *A Preface to Politics*

The best servants of the people, like the best valets, must whisper unpleasant truths in the master's ear. It is the court fool, not the foolish courtier, whom the king can least afford to lose.

WALT WHITMAN
Democratic Vistas

Political democracy, as it exists and practically works in America, with all its threatening evils, supplies a training school for making first-class men. It is life's gymnasium, not of good only, but of all.

WALT WHITMAN
From C.J. Furness, Walt Whitman's Workshop

There is no week nor day nor hour, when tyranny may not enter upon this country, if the people lose their supreme confidence in themselves—and lose their roughness and spirit of defiance—tyranny may always enter—there is no charm, no bar against it—the only bar against it is a large resolute breed of men.

JOHN ADAMS
Letter to Mercy Warren

Public virtue cannot exist in a nation without private, and public virtue is the only foundation of republics.

FREDERICK DOUGLASS
Speech on the twenty-third anniversary of Emancipation

The life of the nation is secure only while the nation is honest, truthful, and virtuous.

The New Nationalism

THEODORE ROOSEVELT

One of the fundamental necessities in a representative government such as ours is to make certain that the men to whom the people delegate their power shall serve the people by whom they are elected, and not the special interests. I believe that every national officer, elected or appointed, should be forbidden to perform any service or receive any compensation, directly or indirectly, from interstate corporations, and a similar provision could not fail to be useful within the States.

The object of government is the welfare of the people. The material progress and prosperity of a nation are desirable chiefly so far as they lead to the moral and material welfare of all good citizens. Just in proportion as the average man and woman are honest, capable of sound judgment and high ideals, active in public affairs—but, first of all, sound in their home life, and the father and mother of healthy children whom they bring up well—just so far, and no farther, we may count our civilization a success. We must have—I believe we have already—a genuine and permanent moral awakening, without which no wisdom of legislation or administration really means anything; and, on the other hand, we must try to secure the social and economic legislation without which any improvement due to purely moral agitation is necessarily evanescent.... No matter how honest and decent we are in our private lives, if we do not have the right kind of law and the right kind of administration of the law, we cannot go forward as a nation. That is imperative; but it must be an addition to, and not a substitution for, the qualities that make us good citizens. In the last analysis, the most important elements in any man's career must be the sum of those qualities which, in the aggregate, we speak of as character. If he has not got it, then no law that the wit of man can devise, no administration of the law by the boldest and strongest executive, will avail to help him. We must have the right kind of character—character that makes a man, first of all, a good man in the home, a good father, a good husband—that makes a man a good neighbor. You must have that, and, then, in addition, you must have the kind of law and the kind of administration of the law which will give to those qualities in the private citizen the best possible chance for development. The prime problem of our nation is to get the right type of good citizenship, and, to get it, we must have progress, and our public men must be genuinely progressive.

ROBERT G. INGERSOLL

He loves his country best who strives to make it best.

CALVIN COOLIDGE

No person was ever honored for what he received. Honor has been the reward for what he gave.

GEORGE WASHINGTON

I shall never ask, never refuse, nor ever resign an office.

ABRAHAM LINCOLN
Speech, Lawrenceburg, Indiana

I have been selected to fill an important office for a brief period, and am now, in your eyes, invested with an influence which will soon pass away, but should my administration prove to be a very wicked one, or what is more probable, a very foolish one, if you, the people, are true to yourselves and the Constitution, there is but little harm I can do, thank God.

ABRAHAM LINCOLN

I have been driven many times to my knees by the overwhelming conviction that I had nowhere else to go. My own wisdom, and that of all about me seemed insufficient for the day.

HUBERT H. HUMPHREY

If I believe in something, I will fight for it with all I have. But I do not demand all or nothing. I would rather get something than nothing. Professional liberals want the fiery debate. They glory in defeat. The hardest job for a politician today is to have the courage to be a moderate. It's easy to take an extreme position.

DWIGHT D. EISENHOWER
Letter to Mamie Doud Eisenhower

As men and women of character and of faith in the soundness of democratic methods, we must work like dogs to justify that faith.

ADLAI E. STEVENSON

I have said what I meant and meant what I said. I have not done as well as I should like to have done. But I have done my best, frankly and forthrightly; no man can do more, and you are entitled to no less.

NORMAN MAILER
Miami and the Siege of Chicago

Politics is the hard dealing of hard men over properties; their strength is in dealing and their virility.

JOHN F. KENNEDY

If we are strong, our strength will speak for itself. If we are weak, words will be no help.

HENRY DAVID THOREAU

Politics is the gizzard of society, full of gut and gravel.

WILLIAM JAMES
Memories and Studies

The deadliest enemies of nations are not their foreign foes; they always dwell within their borders. And from these internal enemies civilization is always in need of being saved. The nation blessed above all nations is she in whom the civic genius of the people does the saving day by day, by acts without external picturesqueness; by speaking, writing, voting reasonably; by smiting corruption swiftly; by good temper between parties; by the people knowing true men when they see them, and preferring them as leaders to rabid partisans or empty quacks.

The Glory and the Dream

WILLIAM MANCHESTER

He was the American Isaiah,
the nation's conscience,
the voice of the mute,
the advocate of the dispossessed,
the patrician rebel.

He ran for the Presidency six times and never came close to a single electoral vote. Yet he refused to yield his idealism to despair, declined to quit the system, and in the end he found he had won as much as the winners—and without the loss of integrity.

Norman Thomas was an evangelist. It was in his blood, in the bone of his bone. His father and both his grandfathers had been Presbyterian ministers, and as a boy in Ohio, delivering copies of the Marion Star, owned by Warren G. Harding, he practiced intonation alone until he had developed the spellbinding delivery of a Bryan, a Debs, a Theodore Roosevelt.

He had the style. What he needed now was something to say. A trip around the world after leaving Princeton—he was class valedictorian—persuaded him that colonialism was evil. Back in New York, he became a social worker in Manhattan's blighted Spring Street neighborhood. The misery and want there tore at him, he looked for answers, and found some from Walter Rauschenbusch at the Union Theological Seminary. Later he said: "Life and work in a wretchedly poor district in New York City drove me steadily toward Socialism, and the coming of the war completed the process. In it there was a large element of ethical compulsion."

That war came in 1917. He campaigned against it, was stoned, and founded with Roger N. Baldwin the American Civil Liberties Bureau, later League. In 1918 he wrote Gene Debs:

> I am sending you an application for membership in the Socialist
> party. I am doing this because I think these are the days when
> radicals ought to stand up and be counted. I believe in the
> necessity of establishing a cooperative commonwealth and
> the abolition of our present unjust economic institutions and
> class distinctions based thereon.

He was moved by:

> grotesque inequalities, conspicuous waste, gross exploitation and
> unnecessary poverty all around me.

Debs died in 1926; Thomas became the party's new leader. He was now forty-two, six-foot-two, 185 pounds, with merry blue eyes—a gentle moralist, a good-humored Puritan. His health was oddly affected by the human condition. If the world was peaceful and prosperous, he glowed with vitality; if world conditions deteriorated, so did he. But he never let illnesses stop him.

In 1932 he knew he could not be elected, and warned his young followers to prepare for defeat. But, "Vote your hopes and not your fears," he told them, and, "Don't vote for what you won't want and get it."

The planks in his presidential platform were public works, unemployment insurance, minimum wage laws, low-cost housing, slum clearance, the five-day week, abolition of child labor, health insurance for the aged, anti-Communism, civil liberties, civil rights for Negroes, and old age pensions. Nearly every one of these proposals was then considered radical.

The program was approved by 728,860 voters and by the man from New York who won the election.

In 1936 Thomas's vote dwindled to 187,342 and he knew why: "... the Socialists watched with some eagerness as Democrats adopted policies they had long recommended in such fields as tariffs and trade barriers, labor legislation, social legislation, social security, and ... farm policy, such as the Resettlement Administration."

He would join almost any picket line, mount any stump, whatever the danger. In March 1935, in a Mississippi county called Birdsong, he spoke out for black sharecroppers, and a drunken mob of whites dragged him from the platform, beat him bloody, and threw him across the county line. One said, "We don't need no goddam Yankee bastard to tell us what to do with our niggers."

Three years later he went into Jersey City to speak against Mayor Frank ("I am the law") Hague. Hague forbade the rally and warned Thomas to stay away. Thomas came. Hague's police slugged him, drove him across the Hudson, and ordered him never to enter Jersey again. He returned to it an hour later. The cops mauled him again and again threw him, hemorrhaging, on a Manhattan sidewalk. This time he went to a federal court. A judge issued an injunction against the major and his heavies, and Thomas, bandaged but upright, denounced "Hagueism" to an enormous throng in Jersey City's Journal Square.

Communists hated him. He visited Moscow during the purge trials and later declared:

> For the believer in the dignity of the individual, there is
> only one standard by which to judge a given society and that
> is the degree to which it approaches the ideal of a fellowship of
> free men. Unless one can believe in the practicability of some
> sort of anarchy, or find evidence there exists a superior and
> recognizable governing caste to which men should by nature
> cheerfully submit, there is no approach to a good society save
> by democracy. The alternative is tyranny.

Leon Trotsky hooted, "Norman Thomas called himself a Socialist as the result of a mis-understanding." But Thomas was firm: one must work within the system. He believed the New Deal should have nationalized the steel industry, but he became convinced that Roo-sevelt's election had brought "the salvation of America...the welfare state and almost a revolution."

In World War II he battled against the internment of Japanese-Americans and Roosevelt's demand for unconditional surrender. He believed "the lowest circle of hell" would be a Nazi victory, but thought a call for a statement of democratic peace terms would be more reasonable.

Almost alone in 1945 he condemned America's use of atomic bombs: "We shall pay for this in a horrible hatred of millions of people which goes deeper and farther than we think."

His last campaign was in 1948; he entered only because he saw how the Communist party was manipulating Henry Wallace. The day after the election an eminent New York Democrat said, "The wrong man lost." "Dewey?" asked a friend. "No," said the Democrat, "Thomas."

In later years he spoke not as a candidate, but as the evangelist he had always been. In 1960 he anticipated the ecological crisis and the need for disarmament. He was convinced that ultimate disaster lay in military aid to other nations, and he believed in the wisdom of the Marshall Plan.

Along the way he wrote twenty books. His energy was unbelievable. In his eighties, crip-pled by arthritis, this old man deformed by sickness criss-crossed the country by auto or in trains—sleeping in upper berths to save money—speaking out against the Vietnam war. And college students, who had sworn to distrust everyone else of his generation, crowded halls to hear his indictment of the war. But he never counseled them to violence:

> The secret of a good life is to have the right loyalties and to hold them in the right scale of values. The value of dissent and dissenters is to make us reappraise those val-ues with supreme concern for truth. Rebellion per se is not a virtue. If it were, we should have some heroes on very low levels.

A reporter once asked him what he considered to be his achievements over the years. He replied in part:

> I suppose it is an achievement to live to my years and feel that
> one has kept the faith, or tried to...to be able to sleep at night with
> reasonable satisfaction...to have had a part...in some of the things
> that have been accomplished in the field of civil liberties, in the
> field of better race relations, and the rest of it. It is something of
> an achievement, I think, to keep the idea of socialism before a
> rather indifferent or even hostile American public.

When he died in his sleep in December 1968, President Johnson, Vice President Humphrey, Governor Nelson Rockefeller, United Nations ambassador Arthur Goldberg, and

New York Mayor John Lindsay issued shining tributes to him. Everyone agreed he had kept the faith.

They omitted the end of Norman Thomas's answer to the reporter's question: "That's the kind of achievement that I have to my credit. As the world counts achievement, I have not got much."

Not much. Only a beam of immortality.

ISAAC BASHEVIS SINGER

Every creator painfully experiences a chasm between his inner vision and its ultimate expression. The chasm is never completely bridged. We all have the conviction, perhaps illusory, that we have much more to say than appears on the paper.

JOHN F. KENNEDY

All this will not be finished in the first one hundred days. Nor will it be finished in the first one thousand days, nor in the life of this administration, nor even perhaps in our lifetime on this planet.

A Busy Place

E.B. WHITE

Our Misfortunes in Canada are enough to melt an Heart
of Stone. The Small Pox is ten times more terrible than
Britons, Canadians and Indians together... there has been Want,
approaching to Famine, as well as Pestilence... But these
Reverses of Fortune don't discourage me. It was natural to
expect them, and We ought to be prepared in our Minds for
greater Changes, and more melancholly Scenes still.

So wrote John Adams to Abigail, in one of his mercurial moments, June 26, 1776. We don't know how far into the future he was gazing, but if he were around today, celebrating our two-hundredth, he would not lack for melancholy scenes. As far as the eye can see in any direction, corruption and wrongdoing, our rivers and lakes poisoned, our flying machines arriving before the hour of their departure, our ozone layer threatened, our sea gasping for breath, our fish inedible, our national bird laying defective eggs, our economy inflated, our food adulterated, our children weaned on ugly plastic toys, our diversions stained with pornography and obscenity, violence everywhere, venery in Congress, cheating at West Point, the elms sick and dying, our youth barely able to read and write, the Postal Service buckling under the crushing burden of the mails and terrified by gloom of night, our sources of energy depleted, our railroads in decline, our small farms disappearing, our small businesses driven against the wall by bureaucratic edicts, and our nuclear power plants hard at work on plans to evacuate the countryside the minute something goes wrong. It is indeed a melancholy scene.

There is one thing, though, that can be said for this beleaguered and beloved country—it is alive and busy. It was busy in Philadelphia in 1776, trying to get squared away on a sensible course; it is busy in New York and Chillicothe today, trying to straighten out its incredible mess.

The world "patriot" is commonly used for Adams and for those other early geniuses. Today, the word is out of favor. Patriotism is unfashionable, having picked up the taint of chauvinism, jingoism, and demagoguery. A man is not expected to love his country, lest he make an ass of himself. Yet our country, seen through the mists of smog, is curiously lovable, in somewhat the way an individual who has got himself into an unconscionable scrape often seems lovable—or at least deserving of support. What other country is so appalled by its own shortcomings, so eager to atone for its own bad conduct? What other country ever issued an invitation like the one on the statue in New York's harbor? Wrongdoing, debauchery, decadence, decline—these are no more apparent in America today than are the myriad attempts to correct them and the myriad devices for doing it. The elms may be dying, but someone has developed a chemical compound that can be injected into the base of an elm tree to inhibit the progress of the disease. The Hudson River may be loaded with polychlorinated biophenyls, but there is an organization whose whole purpose is to defend and restore the Hudson River. It isn't as powerful as General Electric, but it is there, and it even gets out a little newspaper. Our food is loaded with carcinogens, while lights burn all night in laboratories where people are probing the mysteries of cancer. Everywhere you look, at the desolation and the melancholy scene, you find somebody busy with an antidote to melancholy, a cure for disease, a correction for misconduct. Sometimes there seems almost too much duplication of good works and therapeutic enterprise; but at least it suggests great business—a tremendous desire to carry on, against odds that, in July of 1976, as in June of 1776, often seem insuperable.

> But these Reverses of Fortune don't discourage me.... It is an animating
> Cause, and brave Spirits are not subdued with Difficulties.

Let us, on this important day when the tall ships move up the poisoned river, take heart from good John Adams. We might even for a day assume the role of patriot, with neither apology nor shame. It would be pleasant if we could confront the future with confidence, it would be relaxing if we could pursue happiness without worrying about a bad fish. But we are stuck with our chemistry, our spraymongers, our raunchy and corrupt public servants, just as Adams was stuck with the Britons, the Canadians, the Indians, and the shadow of Small Pox. Let not the reverses discourage us—liberty is an animating Cause (and there's not much smallpox around, either). If the land does not unfold fair and serene before our eyes, neither is this a bad place to be. It is unquestionably a busy one. Bang the bell! Touch off the fuse! Send up the rocket! On to the next hundred years of melancholy scene, splendid deeds, and urgent business!

Establish Justice

JOHN ADAMS
Boston Gazette

A government of laws, and not of men.

THEODORE ROOSEVELT

No man is above the law and no man is below it; nor do we ask any man's permission when we ask him to obey it.

THOMAS PAINE
Common Sense

Where, say some, is the king of America? I'll tell you, Friend, he reigns above, and doth not make havoc of mankind like the royal brute of Great Britain. Yet that we may not appear to be defective even in earthly honors, let a day be solemnly set apart for proclaiming the charter; let it be brought forth placed on the divine law, the Word of God; let a crown be placed thereon, by which the world may know, that so far as we approve of monarchy, that in America the law is king. For as absolute governments the king is law, so in free countries the law ought to be king; and there ought to be no other. But lest any ill use should afterwards arise, let the crown at the conclusion of the ceremony be demolished, and scattered among the People whose right it is.

CHIEF JOSEPH
An Indian's Views of Indian Affairs

Our fathers gave us many laws, which they had learned from their fathers. These laws were good. They told us to treat all men as they treated us; that we should never be the first to break a bargain; that it was a disgrace to tell a lie; that we should speak only the truth; that it was a shame for one man to take from another his wife, or his property without paying for it. We were taught to believe that the Great Spirit sees and hears everything, and that he never forgets; that hereafter he will give every man a spirit-home according to his deserts: if he has been a good man, he will have a good home; if he has been a bad man, he will have a bad home. This I believe, and all my people believe the same.

ALEXANDER HAMILTON

The sacred rights of mankind are not to be rummaged for among old parchments, or musty records. They are written, as with a sunbeam, in the whole volume of human nature by the hand of the divinity itself; and can never be erased or obscured by mortal power.

JAMES MADISON

Justice is the end of government. It is the end of civil society. It ever has been and ever will be pursued until it be obtained, or until liberty be lost in the pursuit.

JAMES MADISON

But what is government itself, but the greatest of all reflections on human nature? If men were angels, no government would be necessary. If angels were to govern men, neither external nor internal controls on government would be necessary.

GEORGE WASHINGTON

The administration of justice is the firmest pillar of government.

WOODROW WILSON

Speech concerning the League of Nations, Mount Vernon

What we seek is the reign of law, based upon the consent of the governed and sustained by the organized opinion of mankind.

ALBERT EINSTEIN

The New York Times

Our defense is not in armaments, nor in science, nor in going underground. Our defense is in law and order.

WILLIAM J. BRENNAN
Roth v. United States

The law is not an end in itself, not does it provide ends. It is preeminently a means to serve what we think is right.

GEORGE WASHINGTON
Letter to Colonel Vanneter

Laws made by common consent must not be trampled on by individuals.

ABRAHAM LINCOLN
Speech at Springfield, Illinois

Let every man remember that to violate the law is to trample on the blood of his father, and to tear the charter of his own and his children's liberty.

JAMES BUCHANAN

I acknowledge no master but the law.

AMERICAN BAR ASSOCIATION OATH

I will not counsel or maintain any suit or proceeding which shall appear to be unjust, nor any defense except such as I believe to be honestly debatable under the law of the land.

BENJAMIN HARRISON
Speech at Topeka, Kansas

The law, the will of the majority expressed in orderly, constitutional methods, is the only king to which we bow.

EARL WARREN
The Memoirs of Chief Justice Earl Warren

The Court then has the choice of doing what Mr. Dooley said ("The Supreme Court follows the election returns") or removing itself as far as possible from the political tumult of the times and dedicating its efforts to: "...a more perfect Union, establish justice, insure domestic tranquility, provide for the common defense, promote the general welfare, and secure the blessings of liberty to ourselves and our posterity..." as provided in the Preamble to the Constitution. Every man in the Court must choose for himself which course he should take. Conformity to the wishes of the powerful would be the easiest by far. To habitually ride the crests of the waves through the constantly recurring storms that arise in a free government, always agreeing with the dominant interests, would be a serene way of life. It is comforting to be liked, and it would be pleasant to bask in the sunshine of perpetual public favor. As tempting as that might be, I could not go that way. Of necessity, I chose the latter course because that is the only means by which I could find satisfaction in my work. So many times in life the only permanent satisfaction one can find comes from bucking an adverse tide or swimming upstream to reach a goal. The fulfillment of that goal, according to my lights, rested in the discharge of my constitutional oath of office to "support and defend the Constitution against all enemies, foreign, and domestic," and the judicial oath to "administer justice without respect to persons, and do equal right to the poor and to the rich."

"Limited and Unlimited Power..."

JOHN MARSHALL
Madison v. Marbury

The question, whether an act, repugnant to the constitution, can become the law of the land, is a question deeply interesting to the United States; but, happily, not of an intricacy proportionate to its interest. It seems only necessary to recognize certain principles, supposed to have been long and well established, to decide it. That the people have an original right to establish, for their future government, such principles as, in their opinion, shall most conduce to their own happiness, is the basis on which the whole American fabric has been erected. The exercise of this original right is a very great exertion; nor can it, nor ought it, to be frequently repeated. The principles, therefore, so established, are deemed fundamental: and as the authority from which they proceed is supreme, and can seldom act, they are designed to be permanent. This original and supreme will organizes the government, and assigns to different departments their respective powers. It may either stop here, or establish certain limits not to be transcended by those departments. The government of the United States is of the latter description. The powers of the legislature are defined and limited; and those limits may not be mistaken or forgotten, the constitution is written. To what purpose are powers limited, and to what purpose is that limitation committed to writing, if these limits may, at any time, be passed by those intended to be restrained? The distinction between a government with limited and unlimited powers is abolished, if those limits do not confine the persons on whom they are imposed, and if acts prohibited and acts allowed, are of equal obligation. It is a proposition too plain to be contested, that the constitution controls any legislative act repugnant to it; or that the legislature may later alter the constitution by an ordinary act.

Between these alternatives, there is no middle ground. The constitution is either superior paramount law, unchangeable by ordinary means, or it is on a level with ordinary legislative acts, and, like other acts, is alterable when the legislature shall please to alter it. If the former part of the alternative be true, then a legislative act, contrary to the Constitution, is not law: if the latter part be true, then written constitutions are absurd attempts, on the part of the people, to limit a power, in its own nature, illimitable.

Certainly, all those who have framed written constitutions contemplate them as forming the fundamental and paramount law of the nation, and consequently, the theory of every such government must be, that an act of the legislature, repugnant to the constitution, is void. This theory is essentially attached to a written constitution, and is, consequently to be considered, by this court, as one of the fundamental principles of our society. It is not, therefore, to be lost sight of, in the further consideration of this subject.

If an act of the legislature, repugnant to the constitution, is void, does it, notwithstanding its invalidity, bind the courts, and oblige them to give it effect? Or, in other words, though it be not law, does it constitute a rule as operative as if it was a law? This would be to overthrow, in fact, what was established in theory; and would seem, at first view, an absurdity too gross to be insisted on. It shall, however, receive a more attentive consideration.

It is, emphatically, the province and duty of the judicial department, to say what the law is. Those who apply the rule to particular cases, must of necessity expound and interpret that rule. If two laws conflict with each other, the courts must decide on the operation of each. So, if a law be in opposition to the constitution; if both the law and the constitution apply to a particular case, so that the court must either decide that case, conformable to the law, disregarding the constitution; or conformable to the constitution, disregarding the law; the court must determine which of these conflicting rules governs the case: this is of the very essence of judicial duty. If then, the courts are to regard the constitution, and the constitution is the superior to any ordinary act of the legislature, the constitution, and not such ordinary act, must govern the case to which they both apply.

Those, then, who controvert the principle, that the constitution is to be considered, in court, as a paramount law, are reduced to the necessity of maintaining that courts must close their eyes on the constitution, and see only the law. This doctrine would subvert the very foundation of all written constitutions. It would declare that an act which, according to the principles and theory of our government, is entirely void, is yet, in practice, completely obligatory. It would declare, that if the legislature shall do what is expressly forbidden, such act, notwithstanding the express prohibition, is in reality effectual. It would be giving to the legislature a practical and real omnipotence, with the same breath which professes to restrict their powers within narrow limits. It is prescribing limits, and declaring that those limits may be passed at pleasure. That it thus reduces to nothing, what we have deemed the greatest improvement on political institutions, a written constitution, would, of itself, be sufficient, in America, where written constitutions have been viewed with so much reverence, for rejecting the construction. But the peculiar expressions of the constitution of the United States furnish additional arguments in favor of its rejection. The judicial power of the United States is extended to all cases arising under the constitution. Could it be the intention of those who gave this power, to say, that in using it, the constitution should not be looked into? That a case arising under the constitution should be decided, without examining the instrument under which it arises? This is too extravagant to be maintained. In some cases, then, the constitution must be looked into by the judges. And if they can open it at all, what part of it are they forbidden to read or to obey?

There are many other parts of the constitution which serve to illustrate this subject....

[The phraseology] of the constitution of the United States confirms and strengthens the principle, supposed to be essential to all written constitutions, that a law repugnant to the constitution is void; and that courts, as well as other departments, are bound by that instrument.

FRANKLIN D. ROOSEVELT

You see, unfortunately, in spite of what some people say, the President of the United States is more or less bound by the law.

CALVIN COOLIDGE
Republican Convention speech

One with the law is a majority.

DWIGHT D. EISENHOWER

We cannot subscribe one law for the weak, another law for the strong; one law for those opposing us, another for those allied with us. There can be only one law—or there shall be no peace.

WOODROW WILSON

The only thing that ever distinguished America among the nations is that she has shown that all men are entitled to the benefits of the law.

HARRY S TRUMAN

The friendless, the weak, the victims of prejudice and public excitement are entitled to the same quality of justice and fair play that the rich, the powerful, the well-connected, and the fellow with pull, thinks he can get.

ULYSSES S. GRANT
Message to Congress regarding the Fifteenth Amendment

To the race more favored by our laws I would say, withhold no legal privilege of advancement to the new citizen.

RUTHERFORD B. HAYES

I must make a clear, firm and accurate statement of the facts as to Southern outrages, and reiterate the sound opinions I have long held on the subject. What good people demand is exact justice, equality before the law, perfect freedom of political speech and action and no denial of rights to any citizen on account of color or race—the same to colored as to whites.

LYNDON B. JOHNSON
State of the Union Address

Justice means a man's hope should not be limited by the color of his skin.

GROVER CLEVELAND
Message to Congress

The equal and exact justice of which we boast, as the underlying principle of our institutions, should not be confined to the relations of our citizens to each other. The government itself is under bond to the American people that, in the exercise of its functions and powers, it will deal with the body of citizens in a manner scrupulously fair, and absolutely just.

OLIVER WENDELL HOLMES, JR.
Frank v. Mangum, dissenting opinion

It is our duty to declare lynch law as little valid when practiced by a regularly drawn jury as when administered by one elected by a mob intent on death.

HENRY GEORGE
Progress and Poverty

The law of society is, each for all, as well as all for each.

WOODROW WILSON

Justice has nothing to do with expediency. It has nothing to do with any temporary standard whatever. It is rooted and grounded in the fundamental instincts of humanity.

To Kill a Mockingbird

HARPER LEE

Atticus paused and took out his handkerchief. Then he took off his glasses and wiped them, and we saw another "first"; we had never seen him sweat—he was one of those men whose faces never perspired, but now it was shining tan.

"One more thing, gentlemen, before I quit. Thomas Jefferson once said that all men are created equal, a phrase that the Yankees and the distaff side of the Executive branch in Washington are fond of hurling at us. There is a tendency in this year of grace, 1935, for certain people to use this phrase out of context, to satisfy all conditions. The most ridiculous example I can think of is that the people who run public education promote the stupid and idle along with the industrious—because all men are created equal, educators will gravely tell you, the children left behind suffer terrible feelings of inferiority. We know all men are not created equal in the sense that some people would have us believe—some people are smarter than others, some people have more opportunity because they're born with it, some men make more money than others, some ladies make better cakes than others—some people are born gifted beyond the normal scope of most men.

"But there is one way in this country in which all men are created equal—there is one human institution that makes a pauper the equal of a Rockefeller, the stupid man the equal of an Einstein, and the ignorant man the equal of any college president. That institution, gentleman, is a court. It can be the Supreme Court of the United States or the humblest J.P. court in the land, or this honorable court which you serve. Our courts have their faults, as does any human institution, but in this country our courts are the great levelers, and in our courts all men are created equal.

"I'm no idealist to believe firmly in the integrity of our courts and in the jury system—that is no ideal to me, it is a living, working reality. Gentlemen, a court is no better than each man of you sitting before me on this jury. A court is only as sound as its jury, and a jury is only as sound as the men who make it up. I am confident that you gentlemen will review without passion the evidence you have heard, come to a decision, and restore this defendant to his family. In the name of God, do your duty."

JAMES RUSSELL LOWELL
Among My Books

Exact justice is commonly more merciful in the long run than pity, for it tends to foster in men those stronger qualities which make them good citizens.

ANDREW JACKSON
Letter to John Quincy Adams

I did believe, and ever will believe, that just laws can make no distinction of privilege between the rich and poor, and that when men of high standing attempt to trample upon the rights of the weak, they are the fittest objects for example and punishment. In general, the great can protect themselves, but the poor and humble require the arm and shield of the law.

JUSTICE HUGO L. BLACK
Gideon v. Wainwright

Governments, both state and federal, quite properly spend vast sums of money to establish machinery to try defendants accused of crime. Lawyers to prosecute are everywhere deemed essential to protect the public's interest in an orderly society. Similarly, there are few defendants charged with crime, few indeed who fail to hire the best lawyers they can get to prepare and present their defenses. That government hires lawyers to prosecute and defendants who have the money hire lawyers to defend are the strongest indications of the widespread belief that lawyers in criminal courts are necessities, not luxuries. The right of one charged with crime to counsel may not be deemed fundamental and essential to fair trials in some countries, but it is in ours. From the very beginning, our state and national constitutions and laws have laid great emphasis on procedural and substantive safeguards designed to assure fair trials before impartial tribunals in which every defendant stands equal before the law. This noble ideal cannot be realized if the poor man charged with crime has to face his accusers without a lawyer to assist him.

NATHANIEL HAWTHORNE
American Notebooks

Generosity is the flower of justice.

WILLIAM O. DOUGLAS
An Almanac of Liberty

The Fifth Amendment is an old friend and a good friend. It is one of the great landmarks of man's struggle to be free of tyranny, to be decent and civilized.

THE SUPREME COURT
Fuentes v. Shevin

The Constitution recognizes higher values than speed and efficiency. Indeed, one might fairly say of the Bill of Rights in general, and the Due Process Clause in particular, that they were designed to protect the fragile values of a vulnerable citizenry from the overbearing concern for efficiency and efficacy that may characterize praiseworthy government officials.

EARL WARREN
Miranda v. Arizona

We hold that when an individual is taken into custody or otherwise deprived of his freedom by the authorities in any significant way and is subjected to questioning, the privilege against self-incrimination is jeopardized. Procedural safeguards must be employed to protect the privilege, and unless other fully effective means are adopted to notify the person of his right of silence and to assure that the exercise of the right will be scrupulously honored, the following measures are required. He must be warned prior to any questioning that he has the right to remain silent, that anything he says can be used against him in a court of law, that he has the right to the presence of an attorney, and that if he cannot afford an attorney one will be appointed for him prior to any questioning if he so desires. Opportunity to exercise these rights must be afforded to him throughout the interrogation. After such warnings have been given, and such opportunity afforded him, the individual may knowingly and intelligently waive these rights and agree to answer questions or make a statement. But unless and until such warnings and waiver are demonstrated by the prosecution at trial, no evidence obtained as a result of interrogation can be used against him.

LILLIAN HELLMAN

Since when do you have to agree with people to defend them from injustice?

ROGER BALDWIN

I always felt from the beginning that you had to defend people you disliked and feared as well as those you admired.

CLARENCE S. DARROW

True patriotism hates injustice in its own land more than anywhere else.

OLIVER WENDELL HOLMES, JR.
Law and the Court

I do not think the United States would come to an end if we lost our power to declare an Act of Congress void. I do think the Union would be imperiled if we could not make that declaration as to the laws of the several states.

HENRY GEORGE
Social Problems

That justice is the highest quality in the moral hierarchy I do not say, but that it is the first. That which is above justice must be based on justice, and include justice, and be reached through justice.

REINHOLD NIEBUHR
The Irony of American History

Man's capacity for justice makes democracy possible, but man's inclination to injustice makes democracy necessary.

OLIVER WENDELL HOMES, JR.
Adkins v. Children's Hospital, dissenting opinion

Pretty much all law consists in forbidding men to do some things they want to do.

JOHN JAY

Justice is always the same, whether it be due from one man to a million, or from a million to one man.

JAMES CONE
Black Theology and Black Power

To demand freedom is to demand justice. When there is no justice in the land, a man's freedom is threatened. Freedom and justice are interdependent. When a man has no protection under the law it is difficult for him to make others recognize him.

DANIEL WEBSTER
Mr. Justice Story

Justice, sir, is the great interest of man on earth. It is the ligament which holds civilized beings and civilized nations together.

RALPH WALDO EMERSON
Essays

Let a man keep the law, any law, and his way will be strewn with satisfactions.

DANIEL WEBSTER
New York City speech

There is no happiness, there is no liberty, there is no enjoyment of life, unless a man can say, when he rises in the morning, I shall be subject to the decision of no unwise judge today.

RALPH WALDO EMERSON
The Conduct of Life

The judge weighs the argument and puts a brave face on the matter, and, since there must be a decision, decides as he can, and hopes he has done justice and given satisfaction to the community.

The Renowned Wouter Van Twiller

WASHINGTON IRVING
(From Knickerbocker's History of New York)

It was in the year of our Lord 1629 that Mynheer Wouter Van Twiller was appointed governor of the province of Nieuw Nederlandts, under the commission and control of their High Mightinesses the Lords States General of the United Netherlands, and the privileged West India Company.

The renowned old gentleman arrived at New Amsterdam in the merry month of June, the sweetest month in all the year; when dan Apollo seems to dance up the transparent firmament,—when the robin, the thrush, and a thousand other wanton songsters, make the woods to resound with amorous ditties, and the luxurious little boblincon revels among the clover-blossoms of the meadows,—all which happy coincidence persuaded the old dames of New Amsterdam, who were skilled in the art of foretelling events, that this was to be a happy and prosperous administration.

The renowned Wouter (or Walter) Van Twiller was descended from a long line of Dutch burgomasters, who had successively dozed away their lives, and grown fat upon the bench of magistracy in Rotterdam; and who had comported themselves with such singular wisdom and propriety, that they were never either heard or talked of—which, next to being universally applauded, should be the object of ambition of all magistrates and rulers. There are two opposite ways by which some men make a figure in the world: one, by talking faster than they think, and the other, by holding their tongues and not thinking at all. By the first, many a smatterer acquires the reputation of a man of quick parts; by the other, many a dunderpate, like the owl, the stupidest of birds, comes to be considered the very type of wisdom. This, by the way, is a casual remark, which I would not, for the universe, have it thought I apply to Governor Van Twiller. It is true he was a man shut up within himself, like an oyster, and rarely spoke, except in monosyllables; but then it was allowed he seldom said a foolish thing. So invincible was his gravity that he was never known to laugh or even to smile through the whole course of a long and prosperous life. Nay, if a joke were uttered in his presence that set lightminded hearers in a roar, it was observed to throw him into a state of perplexity. Sometimes he would deign to inquire into the matter, and when, after much explanation, the joke was made as plain as a pike-staff, he would continue to smoke his pipe in silence, and at length, knocking out the ashes, would exclaim, "Well! I see nothing in all that to laugh about."

With all his reflective habits, he never made up his mind on a subject. His adherents accounted for this by the astonishing magnitude of his ideas. He conceived on every subject on so grand a scale that he had not room in his head to turn it over and examine both sides of it. Certain it is, that, if any matter were propounded to him on which ordinary mortals would rashly determine at first glance, he would put on a vague, mysterious look, shake his capacious head, smoke some time in profound silence, and at length observe, that "he had his doubts about the matter"; which gained him the reputation of a man slow of belief and not easily imposed upon. What is more, it gained him a lasting name; for to this habit of the mind has been attributed his surname of Twiller; which is said to be a corruption of the original Twijfler, or, in plain English, Doubter.

The person of this illustrious old gentleman was formed and proportioned, as though it had been moulded by the hands of some cunning Dutch statuary, as a model of majesty and lordly grandeur. He was exactly five feet six inches in height, and six feet five inches in cir-cumference. His head was a perfect sphere, and of such stupendous dimensions, that dame Nature, with all her sex's ingenuity, would have been puzzled to construct a neck capable of sup-porting it; wherefore she wisely declined the attempt, and settled it firmly on top of his back-bone, just between the shoulders. His body was oblong and particularly capacious at bottom; which was wisely ordered by Providence, seeing that he was a man of sedentary habits, and very adverse to the idle labor of walking. His legs were short, but sturdy in proportion to the weight they had to sustain; so that when erect he had not a little the appearance of a beer-barrel on skids. His face, that infallible index of the mind, presented a vast expanse, unfurrowed by any of those lines and angles which disfigure the human countenance with what is termed expres-sion. Two small gray eyes twinkled feebly in the midst, like two stars of lesser magnitude in a hazy firmament, and his full-fed cheecks, which seemed to have taken toll of everything that went into his mouth, were curiously mottled and streaked with dusky red, like a spitzenberg apple.

His habits were as regular as his person. He daily took his four stated meals, appropriat-ing exactly an hour to each; he smoked and doubted eight hours, and he slept the remaining twelve of the four-and-twenty. Such was the renowned Wouter Van Twiller,—a true philosopher, for his mind was either elevated above, or tranquilly settled below, the cares and perplexities of this world. He had lived in it for years, without feeling the least curiosity to know whether the sun revolved round it, or it round the sun; and he had watched, for at least half a century, the smoke curling from his pipe to the ceiling, without once troubling his head with any of those numerous theories by which a philosopher would have perplexed his brain, in accounting for its rising above the surrounding atmosphere.

In his council he presided with great state and solemnity. He sat in a huge chair of solid oak, hewn in the celebrated forest of the Hague, fabricated by an experienced carpenter of Amsterdam, and curiously carved about the arms and feet, into exact imitations of gigantic eagle's claws. Instead of a spectre, he swayed a long Turkish pipe, wrought with jasmine and amber, which had been presented to a stadtholder of Holland at the conclusion of a treaty with one of the petty Barbary powers. In this stately chair would he sit, and this magnificent pipe would he smoke, shaking his right knee with a constant motion, and fixing his eye for hours together upon a little print of Amsterdam, which hung in a black frame against the opposite wall of the council-chamber. Nay, it has even been said, that when any deliberation of extraordinary length and intricacy was on the carpet, the renowned Wouter would shut his eyes for full two hours at a time, that he might not be disturbed by external objects; and at such times the internal commotion of his mind was evinced by certain regular guttural sounds, which his admirers declared were merely the noise of conflict, made by his contending doubts and opinions.

It is with infinite difficulty I have been enabled to collect these biographical anecdotes of the great man under consideration. The facts respecting him were so scattered and vague, and divers of them so questionable in point of authenticity, that I have had to give up the search after many, and decline the admission of still more, which would have tended to heighten the coloring of his portrait.

I have been the more anxious to delineate fully the person and habits of Wouter Van Twiller, from the consideration that he was not only the first, but also the best governor that ever presided over this ancient and respectable province; and so tranquil and benevolent was his reign, that I do not find throughout the whole of it a single instance of any offender being brought to punishment,—a most indubitable sign of a merciful governor, and a case unparalleled, excepting the reign of the illustrious King Log, from whom, it is hinted, the renowned Van Twiller was a lineal descendant.

The very outset of the career of this excellent magistrate was distinguished by an example of legal acumen, that gave flattering presage of a wise and equitable administration. The morning after he had been installed in office, and at the moment that he was making his breakfast from a prodigious earthen dish, filled with milk and Indian pudding, he was interrupted by the appearance of Wandle Schoonhoven, a very important old burgher of New Amsterdam, who complained bitterly of one Barent Bleecker, inasmuch as he refused to come to a settlement of accounts, seeing that there was a heavy balance in favor of the said Wandle. Governor Van Twiller, as I have already observed, was a man of few words; he was likewise a mortal enemy to multiplying writings—or being disturbed at his breakfast. Having listened attentively to the statement of Wandle Schoonhoven, giving an occasional grunt, as he shovelled a spoonful of Indian pudding into his mouth,—either as a sign that he relished the dish, or comprehended the story,—he called unto him his constable, and pulling out of his breeches-pocket a huge jack-knife, dispatched it after the defendant as a summons, accompanied by his tobacco-box as a warrant.

This summary process was as effectual in those simple days as was the seal-ring of the great Haroun Alraschid among the true believers. The two parties, being confronted before him, each produced a book of accounts, written in a language and character that would have puzzled any but a High-Dutch commentator, or a learned decipherer of Egyptian obelisks. The sage Wouter took them one after the other, and having poised them in his hands, and attentively counted over the number of leaves, fell straightaway into a very great doubt, and smoked for half an hour without saying a word; at length, laying his finger beside his nose, and shutting his eyes for a moment, with the air of a man who has just caught a subtle idea by the tail, he slowly took his pipe from his mouth, puffed forth a column of tobacco-smoke, and with marvelous gravity and solemnity pronounced, that, having carefully counted over the leaves and weighed the books, it was found, that one was just as thick and as heavy as the other: therefore, it was the final opinion of the court, that the accounts were equally balanced: therefore, Wandle should give Barent a receipt, and Barent should give Wandle a receipt, and the constable should pay the costs.

This decision, being straightaway made known, diffused general joy throughout New Amsterdam, for the people immediately perceived that they had a very wise and equitable magistrate to rule over them. But its happiest effect was, that not another lawsuit took place throughout the whole of his administration; and the office of constable fell into such decay, that there was not one of those losel scouts known in the province for many years. I am the more particular in dwelling on this transaction, not only because I deem it one of the most sage and righteous judgments on record, and well worthy the attention of modern magistrates, but because it was a miraculous event in the history of the renowned Wouter—being the only time he was ever known to come to a decision in the whole course of his life.

THEODORE ROOSEVELT
Speech in Santiago, Chile

Our judges have been, on the whole, both able and upright public servants...But their whole training and the aloofness of their position on the bench prevent their having, as a rule, any real knowledge, or understanding sympathy with, the lives and needs of the ordinary hardworking toiler.

GERHART HUSSERL
Journal of Social Philosophy

Law is what a judge dispenses. The judge, however, is no representative of the average man's common sense. A certain remoteness from the experiences of everyday life and a certain rigidity of viewpoint are essential to his role as judge.

WOODROW WILSON

No man can be just who is not free.

WILLIAM ALLEN WHITE

Peace without justice is tyranny.

ROBERT F. KENNEDY
The Pursuit of Justice

Justice delayed is democracy denied.

Mumbet: The Story of Elizabeth Freeman
HAROLD W. FELTON

On an August day in 1781, Bet and Brom, with Theodore Sedgwick and Tapping Reeve from Litchfield, went to the court in Great Barrington. There, before the judge, they met Colonel John Ashley and his lawyers.

Bet seemed calm as the lawyers went about their affairs in the conduct of the trial, but a great turmoil was within her as the jury was selected and Jonathan Holcomb was named foreman.

Bet had lived on the western frontier all her life. She knew people often disagreed with each other. Sometimes disagreement led to fights and warfare. The Indian wars and the Revolutionary War were fought because people could not agree. As the August sun, shining through the windows, spread neat patterns of light on the floor of the courtroom, she was moved with the simplicity and the beauty of this peaceful way of settling disputes. She wondered why all men at all times could not find the answer to their problems in law instead of conflict.

"I am troubled, Bet," Mr. Sedgwick whispered.

"About my trial?" Bet asked.

"Yes."

"There's no reason for that," Bet replied.

Mr. Sedgwick looked at her curiously. "Why do you say that?" he asked.

If Mr. Sedgwick was troubled about legal points, Bet was not. "The Constitution says all people are free and equal. If that is so, how can I, how can anybody, be a slave?" she said.

Mr. Sedgwick smiled and nodded. Here was a remarkable woman. She would have made a good lawyer, he thought.

"There is no law that makes me a slave. You told me that."

"That's right. But there are laws about slaves. And there is custom, and custom is sometimes stronger than law," he said.

"There's nothin' about custom in the Constitution. Jes' you tell those things to the judge and jury in lawyer words. Then everything will be all right."

She heard the evidence and the arguments of the lawyers and no outward sign betrayed the tension that filled her. Her future was at stake. She lived in Massachusetts and she was testing the law of the land she lived in. As the trial went on a great feeling of serenity replaced all the disturbing emotions of the past months.

The judge listened. The jury leaned forward in their seats so that no word would escape them.

Bet sighed with soft contentment when she heard the verdict. She was not the servant of John Ashley for her lifetime. She was awarded thirty shillings lawful silver money as damages, and for costs, five pounds, fourteen shillings, and four pence.

Soon she was alone with Mr. Sedgwick in the silent courtroom. "You have been given damages for your services since you were twenty-one years old, and costs. What shall I do with the money?" Mr. Sedgwick asked with a smile.

"Pay Mr. Reeve and pay yourself for your lawyers' fees. Pay well because now I have the dearest thing on earth—my freedom. Then, I'd be obliged to you if you will keep what may be left for me. Keep it so I can use it if I need it."

No one was waiting to cheer her for her great victory. There was only Brom to grasp her hand in friendship. But Massachusetts and the County of Berkshire had done their part. They had fulfilled the promise of the Constitution. Bet was a free person!

There was no doubt what she would do now. She was so much needed, so completely capable. She, with Little Bet, remained in the Sedgwick household. To the satisfaction of everyone, she became the gentle intelligent force behind its daily organization . . .

The months became years and the Sedgwick family moved to Stockbridge. Theodore Sedgwick's law practice grew rapidly after his success in handling Bet's case. More and more clients sought his services as a lawyer. The size of the family increased.

To the children who depended on the black woman so much, the one who cared for them so tenderly, she became Mumbet, or Mama Bet. Soon she was Mumbet not only to the children, but to the parents, friends, and neighbors. It was a name that fixed Bet's position in the family, a name created of honor, of respect, of love.

RALPH WALDO EMERSON
"Voluntaries"

Whoever fights, whoever falls,
Justice conquers evermore, . . .
And he who battles on her side,
God, though he were ten times slain,
Crowns him victor glorified
Victor over death and pain.

CLARENCE S. DARROW
Speaking to a jury in Chicago

As long as the world shall last there will be wrongs, and if no man objected and no man rebelled, those wrongs would last forever.

ABRAHAM LINCOLN
First Inaugural Address

Why should there not be a patient confidence in the ultimate justice of the people? Is there any better or equal hope in the world?

ABE FORTAS
Concerning Dissent and Civil Disobedience

The story of man is the history, first, of the acceptance and imposition of restraints necessary to permit communal life; and second, of the emancipation of the individual within that system of necessary restraints.

THOMAS JEFFERSON
Notes on Virginia

It is better to toss up cross and pile in a cause than to refer it to a judge whose mind is warped by any motive whatever, in that particular case. But the common sense of twelve honest men gives a still better chance of just decision than the hazard of cross and pile.

HENRY DAVID THOREAU
Slavery in Massachusetts

The law will never make men free; it is men who have got to make the law free. They are the lovers of law and order who observe the law when the government breaks it.

WILLIAM J. BRENNAN, JR.
The New York Times

The task of nurturing the constitutional ideal of dignity does not rest solely with the nine Justices, or even the cadre of Federal and state judges. We all share the burden.

HERBERT HOOVER
Message to Congress

If the law is upheld only by government officials, then all law is at an end.

CALVIN COOLIDGE
Message to Congress

Free government has no greater menace than disrespect for authority and continual violation of law. It is the duty of a citizen not only to observe the law but to let it be known that he is opposed to its violation.

LEARNED HAND
The Spirit of Liberty

The profession of the law of which he [a judge] is a part is charged with the articulation and final incidence of the successive efforts towards justice; it must feel the circulation of the communal blood or it will wither and drop off, a useless member.

LEARNED HAND
Washington, D.C., speech

The language of the law must not be foreign to the ears of those who are to obey it.

THOMAS JEFFERSON
Letter to William Johnson

Laws are made for men of ordinary understanding, and should therefore be constructed by the ordinary rules of common sense. Their meaning is not to be sought for in metaphysical subtleties, which may make anything mean everything or nothing, at pleasure.

Learned Hand
The Spirit of Liberty

Our common law is the stock instance of a combination of custom and its successive adaptations.

Wendell Phillips

Law is nothing unless close behind it stands a warm, living public opinion.

Elbert Hubard
The Roycroft Dictionary and Book of Epigrams

Laws that do not embody public opinion can never be enforced.

Oliver Wendell Holmes, Jr.

The law is the witness and external deposit of our moral life. Its history is the history of the moral development of the race.

Roscoe Pound
Introduction to the Philosophy of Law

The law must be stable, but it must not stand still.

Thurgood Marshall
Quoted in Dream Makers, Dream Breakers *by Carl Rowan*

[The Constitution] is the greatest body of laws set out ever, and what to me, and to many people, is so extraordinary about it is that at this late date you find that it works. And when you dig down into it, I don't know of any better job that could have been done. I have studied it considerably, along with constitutions of other countries, and compared it with Britain, which has no constitution, and I think we've just got a great body of laws.

There's hardly anything it doesn't cover. I mean, it's just unbelievable that a Constitution written in the horse and buggy days will cover outer space.

We are celebrating a Constitution that didn't do what you and I would want it to do. It did not free all men. It didn't say that all men were free. It didn't say that all men were equal. It said all except slaves. And we have to recognize that they deliberately left out the slaves and that, to that extent, the Constitution was not as good as it could, or should, have been.

Somebody months ago made the suggestion that this present Court should sit in Philadelphia like it did two hundred years ago, and I made the point, "Well, if you're gonna do what you did two hundred years ago, somebody's going to give me short pants and a tray so I can serve coffee."

I don't back off that [criticism of the Constitution] at all. I think we have a great Constitution today. I've defended it all over the world and I'll continue to defend it, but it didn't start out that way. It has become a great Constitution by considering it as a living document. And the legislature passing amendments, and this Court issuing judgments. That's what made it a great Constitution.

BROOKS ADAMS
The Laws of Civilization and Decay

Law is merely the expression of the will of the strongest for the time being, and therefore laws have no fixity, but shift from generation to generation.

JAMES BRYCE
The American Commonwealth

Law will never be strong or respected unless it has the sentiment of the people behind it. If the people of a state make bad laws, they will suffer for it. They will be the first to suffer. Suffering, and nothing else, will implant that sentiment of responsibility which is the first step to reform.

JAMES M. LAWSON
"From a Lunch-Counter Stool" speech

Law is always nullified by practice and disdain, unless the minds and hearts of a people sustain law.

HENRY WARD BEECHER
Life Thoughts

Laws and institutions are constantly tending to gravitate. Like clocks, they must be occasionally cleansed, and wound up, and set to true time.

MICHAEL HARRINGTON
The Accidental Century

With the appearance of the modern working class, driven to economic and political organization by the necessities of daily life, a social force had come into being that would be impelled toward the theory and practice of justice.

WILLIAM J. BRENNAN
Roth v. United States

Law cannot stand aside from the social changes around it.

HUBERT H. HUMPHREY

There are not enough jails, not enough policemen, not enough courts to enforce a law not supported by the people.

THOMAS JEFFERSON
Letter to Samuel Kercheval

Laws and institutions must go hand in hand with the progress of the human mind.

WALTER LIPPMANN
A Preface to Politics

Ignore what a man desires and you ignore the very source of his power; run against the grain of a nation's genius and see where you get with your laws.

OLIVER WENDELL HOLMES, JR.

The life of the law has not been logic; it has been experience.

EARL WARREN
The Memoirs of Chief Justice Earl Warren

In more than fifty years of public service, I have been exposed to both processes, the political and the judicial, and to the interrelationship between the two, until I have what I believe is a clear concept of each in the administration of justice. In those official positions I have held, I have tried to carry this distinction in mind, and to honor both sides as essential ingredients of our governmental system. One is not born with such a concept, nor is it acquired overnight. It is an evolving thing that stems from one's experiences in life and from interpretations he or she gives them, particularly when the paths of the two processes cross.

ROSCOE POUND

Law is experience developed by reason and applied continually to further experience.

FREDERICK DOUGLASS
"Reconstruction"

To change the character of the government at this point is neither possible nor desirable. All that is necessary to be done is to make the government consistent with itself, and render the rights of the states compatible with the sacred rights of human nature.

E.L. DOCTOROW
"A Citizen Reads the Constitution"

The voice of the Constitution is the inescapably solemn self-consciousness of the people giving the law unto themselves.

Democracy in America
ALEXIS DE TOCQUEVILLE
"Respect for the Law"

It is not always feasible to consult the whole people, either directly or indirectly, in the formation of the law; but it cannot be denied that, when this is possible, the authority of the law is much augmented. This popular origin, which impairs the excellence and the wisdom of legislation, contributes much to increase its power. There is an amazing strength in the expression of the will of a whole people; and when it declares itself, even the imagination of those who would wish to contest it is overawed. The truth of this fact is well known by parties; and they consequently strive to make out a majority whenever they can. If they have not the greater number of votes on their side, they assert that the true majority abstained from voting; and if they are foiled even there, they have recourse to those who had no right to vote.

In the United States, except slaves, servants, and paupers supported by the townships, there is no class of persons who do not exercise the elective franchise, and who do not indirectly contribute to make the laws. Those who wish to attack the laws must consequently either change the opinion of the nation, or trample upon its decision.

A second reason, which is still more direct and weighty, may be adduced: in the United States, every one is personally interested in enforcing the obedience of the whole community to the law; for as the minority may shortly rally the majority to its principles, it is interested in professing that respect for the decrees of the legislator which it may soon have occasion to claim for its own. However irksome an enactment may be, the citizen of the United States complies with it, not only because it is the work of the majority, but because it is his own, and he regards it as a contract to which he is himself a party.

In the United States, then, that numerous and turbulent multitude does not exist, who, regarding the law as their natural enemy, look upon it with fear and distrust. It is impossible, on the contrary, not to perceive that all classes display the utmost reliance upon the legislation of their country, and are attached to it by a kind of parental affection.

I am wrong, however, in saying all classes; for as, in America, the European scale of authority is inverted, the wealthy are there placed in a position analogous to that of the poor in the Old World, and it is the opulent classes who frequently look upon the law with suspicion. I have already observed that the advantage of democracy is not, as has been sometimes asserted, that it protects those of the majority. In the United States, where the poor rule, the rich have always something to fear from the abuse of their power. This natural anxiety of the rich may produce a secret dissatisfaction; but society is not disturbed by it, for the same reason, which withholds the confidence of the rich from the legislative authority, makes them obey its mandates: their wealth, which prevents them from making the law, prevents them from withstanding it. Amongst civilized nations, only those who have nothing to lose ever revolt; and if the laws of a democracy are not always worthy of respect, they are always respected; for those who usually infringe the laws cannot fail to obey those which they have themselves made, and by which they are benefited, whilst the citizens who might be interested in the infraction of them are induced, by their character and station, to submit to the decisions of the legislature, whatever they may be. Besides, the people in America obey the law, not only because it is their work, but because, first, it is a self-imposed evil, and secondly, it is an evil of transient duration.

HARRY S TRUMAN

Democracy is based on the conviction that man has the moral and intellectual capacity, as well as the inalienable right, to govern himself with reason and justice.

PROGRESSIVE PARTY PLATFORM

The conscience of the people, in a time of grave national problems, has called into being a new party, born of the nation's sense of justice.

FRANCES E.W. HARPER
Washington, D.C., address

A government which has power to tax a man in peace, draft him in war, should have power to defend his life in the hour of peril. A government which can protect and defend its citizens from wrong and outrage and does not is vicious. A government which would do it and and cannot is weak; and where human life is insecure through either weakness or viciousness in the administration of law, there must be a lack of justice and where this is wanting, nothing can make up the deficiency.

THOMAS JEFFERSON
Letter to F. W. Gilmor

No man has a natural right to commit aggression on the equal rights of another, and this is all from which the laws ought to restrict him; every man is under the natural duty of contributing to the necessities of society, and this is all the laws should enforce on him; and no man having a natural right to be the judge between himself and another, it is his natural duty to submit to the umpirage of an impartial third.

THOMAS JEFFERSON
Letter to Abbé Arnoud

The execution of the laws is more important than the making them.

MARK TWAIN

No country can be well governed unless its citizens as a body keep religiously before their minds that they are the guardians of the law, and that the law officers are only the machinery for its execution, no more.

THOMAS JEFFERSON
Letter to Sarah Mease

The sword of the law should never fall but on those whose guilt is so apparent as to be pronounced by their friends as well as foes.

OLIVER WENDELL HOLMES, JR.
Olmstead v. United States

For my part I think it a less evil that some criminals should escape than that the government should play an ignoble part... If the existing code does not permit district attorneys to have a hand in such dirty business [wiretapping], it does not permit the judge to allow such iniquities to succeed.

THOMAS JEFFERSON
Letter to William Carmichael

[It is] more dangerous that even a guilty person should be punished without the forms of law than that he should escape.

Doonesbury

G.B. TRUDEAU

Then and There the Child Independence Was Born

RICHARD MORRIS

Few freedoms are more fundamental to our way of life—and few so clearly differentiate our democracy from the rival system which seeks to bury it—than the freedom from the midnight knock on the door, from the arbitrary invasion of a man's home by soldiery or police. Enshrined in the Fourth Amendment to the Constitution, the right is nevertheless still a matter of contention: almost every year that passes sees cases based upon it coming before the United States Supreme Court. Given the almost inevitable conflict between the legitimate demands of civil authority and the equally legitimate demands of the individual freedom, it is likely that the controversy will be always with us.

What one famous Supreme Court justice called "the right most valued by civilized man," the right to be let alone, is a venerable one in America: long before the Revolution, violation of it by representatives of the king rankled deeply in the hearts of his American subjects; it was, indeed, one of the major reasons they eventually decided they could no longer serve him.

The issue was first expounded in the course of an extraordinary forensic argument made in the year 1761 before five scarlet-robed judges in the council chamber of the Town-house in Boston. The speaker was James Otis, Jr., then thirty-six years old, born in nearby West Barnstable and considered the ablest young lawyer at the Boston bar.

His plea for the fight of privacy was at once significant and poignant. It was significant because without the burning moral issue thus precipitated, it might have been possible for the cynical to dismiss the forthcoming Revolution as a mere squabble between colonies and mother country over taxation....

The specific occasion of Otis's appearance was an application to the Superior Court of Massachusetts Bay by Charles Paxton, Surveyor of Customs for the Port of Boston, for writs of assistance. These were general warrants which, as they were commonly interpreted, empowered customs officers under police protection to enter—if necessary, to break into—warehouses, stores, or homes to search for smuggled goods. The intruders were not even required to present any grounds for suspecting the presence of the illicit items. Such writs had been authorized in England—where they were issued by the Court of Exchequer—since the time of Charles II, but nothing like them had been used in the colonies prior to the French and Indian War. The only writs theretofore procurable had been specific search warrants issued by the regular common-law courts; but these had authorized search only in places specified in the warrants and only upon specific information, supported by oath, that smuggled goods were hidden there. True, an act of King William III regulating colonial trade had given the customs officers in America the same rights of search as their opposite numbers in England enjoyed. But it was a new question whether the royal order extended to colonial courts the same authority to issue the writs that the Court of Exchequer exercised in the mother country.

During the final phase of the Second Hundred Years' War between Britain and France, however, the writs of assistance had been issued in Massachusetts to facilitate the feverish if futile efforts of customs officers to stamp out illegal trade between the colonists and the enemy —in Canada and the French West Indies. These writs had been issued in the name of King George II, but that monarch died in October, 1760, and his grandson succeeded to the throne as George III. According to law, the old writs expired six months after the death of a sovereign, and new ones had to be issued in the name of his successor. Now, in February of 1761, while the issue hung in the balance—George III would not be crowned until September—Surveyor Paxton's case came to trial.

Sixty-three prominent Boston merchants joined to oppose him, retaining the brilliant, impassioned, unstable Otis—and his amiable and temperate associate, Oxbridge Thacher—

to represent them. In order to take their case, Otis resigned his office as Advocate General of the Vice-Admiralty Court, in which capacity he would have been expected to represent the Crown and present the other side of the argument. That task was now assigned to Jeremiah Gridley, a leader of the Boston bar, who appeared as counsel for the customs officers....

[Chief Justice Thomas] Hutchinson, attired in his new judicial robes, took his seat in the great Town-house council chamber as the trial opened on February 24. With him on the bench were Justices Lynde, Cushing, Oliver, and Russell. Gridley opened for the Crown. He argued that such general writs were being issued in England by the Court of Exchequer, which had the statutory authority to issue them; the province law of 1699, he continued, had granted the Superior Court jurisdiction in Massachusetts "generally" over matters which the courts of King's Bench, Common Pleas, and Exchequer "Have or ought to have."

Thatcher replied first. Addressing himself largely to technical issues, he denied that the Superior Court could exercise the right of the Court of Exchequer in England to issue such writs. Then Otis arose to speak. One contemporary critic described him as "a plump, round-faced, smooth-skinned, short-necked, eagle-eyed politician," but to John Adams—who attended the trial, reported it in his diary, and was to write an account of it more than fifty years later—"Otis was a flame of fire."

He had prepared his argument with care. Although his oration covered some four or five hours and was not taken down stenographically, it left on Adams an indelible impression. With a "profusion of legal authorities," Adams tells us, "a prophetic glance of his eye into futurity, and a torrent of impetuous eloquence, he hurried away everything before him." Adams continued: "Every man of a crowded audience appeared to me to go away, as I did, ready to take arms against writs of assistance." And he concluded: "Then and there the child Independence was born."

More important than the electrifying effect of Otis's argument upon his auditors was its revolutionary tenor. Anticipating ideas that would be set forth in the Declaration of Independence fifteen years later, Otis argued that the rights to life, liberty, and property were derived from nature and implied the guarantee of privacy, without which individual liberty could not survive. (Venturing beyond the immediate issue, Otis declared that liberty should be granted to all men regardless of color—an abolitionist note that startled even the sympathetic Adams.)

Relying on English lawbooks to prove that only special warrants were legal, Otis attacked the writs as "instruments of slavery," which he swore to oppose to his dying day with all the powers and faculties God had given him. Defending the right of privacy, he pointed out that the power to issue general search warrants placed "the liberty of every man in the hands of every petty officer." The freedom of one's house, he contended, was "one of the most essential branches of English liberty." In perhaps his most moving passage he was reported to have declared: "A man's house is his castle, and whilst he is quiet he is as well guarded as a prince in his castle. This writ, if it should be declared legal, would totally annihilate this privilege.

Custom-house officers may enter our houses when they please; we are commanded to permit their entry. Their menial servants may enter, may break locks, bars, and everything in their way; and whether they break through malice or revenge, no man, no court, can inquire. Bare suspicion without oath is sufficient. This wanton exercise of this power is not a chimerical suggestion of a heated brain...What a scene does this open! Every man, prompted by revenge, ill humor, or wantonness to inspect the inside of a neighbor's house, may get a writ of assistance. Others will ask it from self-defense; one arbitrary exertion will provoke another, until society be involved in tumult and blood." With remarkable prescience Otis's words captured the mood of the midnight visitation by totalitarian police which would terrify a later era less sensitive to individual freedom....

Measured by its effect on its auditors and its immediate impact on the majority of the court, Otis's speech ranks among the most memorable in American history...Had a decision been rendered on the spot, Otis and Thacher would have won, for all the judges save Thomas Hutchinson were against the writs; even from *his* opinion, carefully worded, opponents of the writs could take comfort: "The Court has considered the subject of writs of assistance," the chief justice announced, "and can see no foundation for such a writ; but as the practice in England is not known, it has been thought best to continue the question to the next term, and that in the meantime opportunity may be given to know the result." But the crafty chief justice, aware that he stood alone among his colleagues, was merely buying precious time... [The court eventually ruled in favor of the writs of assistance.]

The attack against the writs, initiated by Otis, developed into a notable series of legal battles, fought not only in Massachusetts but throughout the colonies. Local justices of the peace in the Bay Colony refused in 1765 to grant them on the ground that they were repugnant to the common law. They continued to be issued by that province's Superior Court, but individuals sometimes managed to defy them: in 1766 a merchant named Daniel Malcolm, presumably on the advice if not at the instigation of Otis, refused to admit the customs officials into part of his cellar, even though they were armed with writs of assistance, and warned them that he would take legal action against them if they entered. The customs men backed down.

Meantime opposition to the writs was spreading to other colonies. In 1766 the customs collector of New London, Connecticut, sought legal advice as to his power of search and seizure, but the judges at New Haven felt that in the absence of a colonial statute they could make no determination. The collector referred the matter to the Commissioner of Customs in England, who in turn asked the advice of Attorney General William de Grey. His opinion came as a shock to the customs officials, for he found that the Courts of Exchequer in England "do not send their Processes into the Plantations, nor is there any Process in the plantations that corresponds with the description in the act of [King William]."

Aware that the ground was now cut from under them, the Lords of Treasury saw to it that the Townsend Acts passed in 1767 contained a clause specifically authorizing superior or supreme courts in the colonies to grant writs of assistance. Significantly, the American Board of Commissioners of Customs set up under the act sought between 1767 and 1773 to obtain writs in each of the thirteen colonies, but succeeded fully only in Massachusetts and New Hampshire. But as late as 1772 charges were made in Boston that "our houses and even our bed chambers are exposed to be ransacked, our boxes, chests, and trunks broke open, ravaged and plundered by wretches, whom no prudent man would venture to employ as menial servants."

In other colonies the issue was stubbornly fought out in the courts. New York's Supreme Court granted the writs when the customs officers first applied for them in 1768, though not in the form of the applications demanded; finally, the court flatly refused to issue the writs at all. In Pennsylvania the Tory Chief Justice, William Allen, refused also on the ground that it would be "of dangerous consequence and was not warranted by law." The writs were denied, too, in every southern colony save South Carolina, which finally capitulated and issued them in 1773. Significantly, the courts, though often manned by royal appointees, based their denials on the grounds advanced by Otis in the original Paxton case, going so far as to stigmatize the writs as unconstitutional.

What is important to remember throughout the controversy in which Otis played so large a part is that the colonists were seeking to define personal liberties—freedom of speech, the press, and religion—which even in England, right up to the eve of the American Revolution, were not firmly enshrined in law. Indeed, the issues of whether a person could be arrested under a general warrant or committed to prison on any charge by a privy councillor were not settled until the 1760s. Then Lord Camden took a strong stand for freedom from police intrusion. Less dramatically perhaps than in the colonies, similar issues of civil liberties were being thrashed out in the mother country, but in the colonies this struggle laid the groundwork upon which the new Revolutionary states, and later the federal government, built their safeguards for civil liberties.

In Virginia, where the issue was contested most bitterly, writs of assistance were condemned in the Bill of Rights of June 12, 1776, as "grievous and oppressive." Condemnation was also reflected in the clauses in the Declaration of Independence denouncing the King because he had made judges dependent for their tenure and their salaries upon his will alone. Five other states soon followed Virginia in outlawing the writs. Of these, Massachusetts in her constitution of 1780 provided the most explicit safeguards. The relevant section of the state constitution, notable because it served as the basis for Madison's later incorporation of such a guarantee in the federal Bill of Rights, reads as follows: "XIV. Every subject has a right to be secure from all unreasonable searches and seizures of his person, his houses, his papers and all his possessions. All warrants, therefore, are contrary to this right, if the cause or foundation of them be not previously supported by oath or affirmation; and if the order in the warrant to a civil officer, to make search in suspected places, or to arrest one or more suspected persons, or to seize their property, be not accompanied with a special designation of the persons or objects of search, arrest, or seizure; and no warrant ought to be issued but in cases, and with the formalities prescribed in the laws." John Adams, who wrote that constitution, had remembered his lessons very well indeed.

More succinctly than the guarantee in the Massachusetts constitution, the Fourth Amendment to the federal Constitution affirmed "the right of the people to be secure in their persons, houses, papers, and effects, against unreasonable searches and seizures," and declared that "no warrants shall issue, but upon probable cause, supported by oath or affirmation, and particularly describing the place to be searched, and the persons or things to be seized."

In our own day, several members of a Supreme Court heavily preoccupied with safeguarding personal liberty have conspicuously defended the guarantees of the Fourth Amendment. It was the late Justice Louis Brandeis who, in his dissenting opinion in a wiretapping decision of 1928 (Olmstead v. U.S.) opposing police intrusion without a search warrant, championed "the right to be left alone"–the most comprehensive of rights and the right most valued by civilized man...."To protect that right," he asserted, "every unjustifiable intrusion by the Government upon the privacy of the individual, whatever the means employed, must be deemed a violation of the Fourth Amendment."

More recently Justice Felix Frankfurter has opposed searches conducted as an incident to a warrant of arrest. In a notable dissent (Harris v. U. S., 1946) he pointed out that the decision turned "on whether one gives the [Fourth] Amendment a place second to none in the Bill of Rights, or considers it on the whole a kind of nuisance, a serious impediment in the war against crime... How can there be freedom of thought or freedom of speech or freedom of religion," he asked, "if the police can, without warrant, search your house and mine from garret to cellar merely because they are executing a warrant of arrest?" He went on to warn: "Yesterday the justifying document was an illicit ration book, tomorrow it may be some suspect piece of literature." Again, in a more recent case (United States v. Rabinowitz, 1950), Justice Frankfurter dissented from a decision authorizing federal officers to seize forged postage stamps without a search warrant but as incident to arrest. He said pointedly: "It makes all the difference in the world whether one recognizes the central fact about the Fourth Amendment, namely that it was a safeguard against recurrence of abuses so deeply felt by the Colonies as to be one of the potent causes of the Revolution, or whether one thinks of it as merely a requirement for a piece of paper."

Once it was a powerful monarch concerned about securing every shilling of customs revenue. Today it is a great republic legitimately concerned about the nation's security. Once it was a knock on the door. Today it is wiretapping or other electronic devices. The circumstances and techniques may differ. As the tragic James Otis would have realized, the issue remains the same.

FELIX FRANKFURTER
Felix Frankfurter's Reminiscences

Fragile as reason is and limited as law is as the institutionalized medium of reason, that's all we have standing between us and the tyranny of mere will and the cruelty of unbridled, undisciplined feeling.

MARTIN LUTHER KING, JR.
Strength to Love

Morality cannot be legislated, but behavior can be regulated. Judicial decrees may not change the heart, but they can restrain the heartless.

RALPH W. SOCKMAN
Sermon at Riverside Church, New York City

Government laws are needed to give us civil rights, and God is needed to make us civil.

PHILIP K. DICK
A Scanner Darkly

How can justice fall victim, ever, to what is right?

HENRY GEORGE
The Irish Land Question

That which is unjust can really profit no one; that which is just can really harm no one.

JAMES A. GARFIELD
Letter accepting nomination for presidency

Justice and goodwill will outlast passion.

OLIVER WENDELL HOLMES, JR.
Schenek v. United States

The most stringent protection of free speech would not protect a man in falsely shouting fire in a theater and causing a panic...The question in every case is whether the words are used in such circumstances and are of such a nature as to create a clear and present danger that they will bring about the substantive evils that Congress has a right to prevent.

CARRIE CHAPMAN CATT
Speech in Stockholm, Sweden

When a just cause reaches its flood tide . . . whatever stands in the way must fall before its overwhelming power.

HAROLD FABER
The New York Times Magazine

If there isn't a law, there will be.

ALEXANDER HAMILTON
The Federalist

It is essential to the idea of a law that it be attended with a sanction; or, in other words, a penalty or punishment for disobedience.

NATHANIEL HAWTHORNE
The Scarlet Letter

The founders of a new colony, whatever Utopia of human virtue and happiness they might originally project, have invariably recognized it among their earliest practical necessities to allot a portion of virgin soil as a cemetery, and another portion as the site of a prison.

SHIRLEY CHISHOLM
Unbought and Unbossed

Law will not eliminate prejudice from the hearts of human beings. But that is no reason to allow prejudice to continue to be enshrined in our laws to perpetuate injustice through inaction.

HENRY WARD BEECHER
Proverbs from the Plymouth Pulpit

Take all the robes of all the good judges that have ever lived on the face of the earth, and they would not be large enough to cover the iniquity of one corrupt judge.

OLIVER WENDELL HOLMES, JR.
Law and the Court

Judges are apt to be [naive], simple-minded men, and they need something of the Mephistopheles. We too need education in the obvious—to learn to transcend our own convictions and to leave room for much that we hold dear to be done away with short of revolution by the orderly change of law.

ROBERT G. INGERSOLL
Speech in Washington, D.C.

We must remember that we have to make judges out of men, and that by being made judges their prejudices are not diminished and their intelligence is not increased.

BENJAMIN FRANKLIN
Poor Richard's Almanack

Laws too gentle are seldom obeyed; too severe, seldom executed.

LAURENCE H. TRIBE

An excess of law inescapably weakens the rule of law.

THOMAS JEFFERSON
Notes on the State of Virginia

Were it made a question, whether no law, as among the savage Americans, or too much law, as among the civilized Europeans, submits man to the greatest evil, one who has seen both conditions of existence would pronounce it to be the last; and that the sheep are happier of themselves, than under the care of wolves.

ABRAHAM LINCOLN
Message to Congress

The severest justice may not always be the best policy.

ABRAHAM LINCOLN

I have always found that mercy bears richer fruits than strict justice.

GERALD FORD
Proclamation upon pardoning Richard M. Nixon

The law, whether human or divine, is no respecter of persons, but the law is a respecter of reality.

ROBERT TAFT
Kenyon College speech

I believe that most Americans view with discomfort the war trials which have just been concluded in Germany and are proceeding in Japan. They violate that fundamental principle of American law that a man cannot be tried under an ex post facto statute. The trial of the vanquished by the victors cannot be impartial, no matter how it is hedged about with the forms of justice.

MARY McCARTHY
"My Confession"

Anybody who has ever tried to rectify an injustice or set a record straight comes to feel that he is going mad.

OLIVER WENDELL HOLMES, JR.

This is a court of law, young man, not a court of justice.

CLARENCE S. DARROW
The New York Times

There is no such thing as justice—in or out of court.

LEARNED HAND
Guiseppi v. Walling

There is no surer way to misread any document than to read it literally...As nearly as we can, we must put ourselves in the place of those who uttered the words, and try to divine how they would have dealt with the unforeseen situation; and, although their words are by far the most decisive evidence of what they would have done, they are by no means final.

REINHOLD NIEBUHR
The Irony of American History

Any modern community which establishes a tolerable justice is the beneficiary of the ironic triumph of the wisdom of common sense over the foolishness of its wise men.

RALPH WALDO EMERSON
The Conduct of Life

The good lawyer is not the man who has an eye on every side and angle of contingency, and qualifies all his qualifications, but who throws himself on your part so heartily that he can get you out of a scrape.

Letter to William Harrison Dunbar

LOUIS D. BRANDEIS

My Dear Dunbar: For some time I have intended to lay before you my views in regard to your professional [legal] life—and what it is necessary for you to do in order to attain that degree of success to which your abilities and character clearly entitle you. . . .

Cultivate the society of men—particularly men of affairs. This is essential to your professional success. Pursue that study as heretofore you have devoted yourself to books. Lose no opportunity of becoming acquainted with men of learning, to feel instinctively their inclinations, of familiarizing yourself with their personal and business habits, use you ability in making opportunities to do this. This is for you the indispensable study—as for another the study of law—or good habits of work are the missing desideratum.

The knowledge of men, the ability to handle, to impress them is needed by you—not only in order that clients may appreciate your advice and that you may be able to apply the law to human affairs—but also that you may more accurately and surely determine what the rules of law are, that is, what the courts will adopt. You are prone to legal investigation to be controlled by logic and to underestimate the logic of facts. Knowledge of the decided cases and of the rules of logic cannot alone make a great lawyer...

If you will recall [Sir George] Jessel's opinion you will see what I mean. Knowledge of decisions and powers of logic are mere handmaidens—they are servants not masters. The controlling force is the deep knowledge of human necessities. It was this which made Jessel the great lawyer and the greater judge. The man who does not know intimately human affairs is apt to make of the law a bed of Procrustes. No hermit can be a great lawyer, least of all a commercial lawyer. When from a knowledge of the law, you pass to its application, the need of a full knowledge of men and of their affairs becomes even more apparent... The great physicians are those who in addition to that knowledge of therapeutics which is opened to all, know not merely the human body but the human mind and emotions, so as to make themselves the proper diagnosis—to know the truth which their patients fail to disclose and who add to this an influence over the patients which is apt to spring from a real understanding of him. . . .

Your law may be perfect, your knowledge of human affairs may be such as to enable you to apply it with wisdom and skill, and yet without individual acquaintance with men, their haunts and habits, the pursuit of the profession becomes difficult, slow and expensive. A lawyer who does not know men is handicapped. It is like practicing in a strange city. Every man that you know makes it to that extent easier to practice, to accomplish what you have in hand. You know him, know how to talk, how to treat him; he knows you and the transaction of business is simplified.

WILLIAM HITZ
Letter to Felix Frankfurter

I have just heard Mr. Brandeis make one of the greatest arguments I have ever listened to . . . He spoke on the minimum wage cases in the Supreme Court, and the reception which he wrested from that citadel of the past was very moving and impressive to one who knows the Court . . . When Brandeis began to speak, the Court showed all the inertia and elemental hostility which courts cherish for a new thought, or a new right, or even a new remedy for an old wrong, but he visibly lifted all this burden, and without orationizing or chewing of the rag he reached them all and held even Pitney quiet.

He not only reached the Court, but he dwarfed the Court, because it was clear that here stood a man who knew infinitely more, and who cared infinitely more, for the vital daily rights of the people than the men who sat there sworn to protect them. It was so clear that something had happened in the court today that even Charles Henry Butler saw it and he stopped me afterwards on the coldest corner in town to say that no man this winter had received such close attention from the Court as Brandeis got today, while one of the oldest members of the Clerk's office remarked to me that "that fellow Brandeez has got the impudence of the Devil to bring his socialism into the Supreme Court."

ROBERT G. INGERSOLL
Speech in Chicago

There is but one blasphemy and that is injustice.

PAUL ROBESON
"The Constitutional Right to Travel"

The answer to injustice is not to silence the critic but to end the injustice.

NORMAN DOUGLAS

Justice is too good for some people, and not good enough for the rest.

HENRY DAVID THOREAU
Journals

Somehow strangely the vice of men gets well represented and protected but their virtue has none to plead its cause—nor any charter of immunities and rights. The Magna Charta is not chartered rights—but chartered wrongs.

BENJAMIN N. CARDOZO
Snyder v. Commonwealth of Massachusetts

Justice, though due to the accused, is due to the accuser also. The concept of fairness must not be strained till it is narrowed to a filament. We are to keep the balance true.

RALPH WALDO EMERSON
Essays

One man's justice is another's injustice; one man's beauty is another's ugliness; one man's wisdom another's folly as one beholds the same objects from a higher point. One man thinks justice consists in paying debts, and has no measure in his abhorrence of another who is very remiss in his duty and makes the creditor wait tediously. But the second man has his own way of looking at things; asks himself Which debt must I pay first, the debt to the rich, or the debt to the poor? the debt of money, or the debt of thought to mankind, of genius to nature?

"Pretty Boy Floyd"
WOODY GUTHRIE

If you'll gather round me children,
A story I will tell
About Pretty Boy Floyd, the outlaw,
Oklahoma knew him well.

It was in the town of Shawnee,
It was Saturday afternoon,
His wife beside him in the wagon
As into town they rode.

There a deputy Sheriff approached him,
In a manner rather rude,
Using vulgar words of language,
And his wife she overheard.

Pretty Boy grabbed a log chain,
And the deputy grabbed a gun,
And in the fight that followed
He laid that deputy down.

He took to the trees and timbers,
And he lived a life of shame,
Every crime in Oklahoma
Was added to his name.

Yes, he took to the trees and timbers,
On that Canadian River's shore,
And Pretty Boy found a welcome
At many a farmer's door.

There's many a starvin' farmer,
The same old story told,
How this outlaw paid their mortgage,
And saved their little home.

Others tell you 'bout a stranger,
That come to beg a meal,
And underneath his napkin
Left a thousand dollar bill.

It was in Oklahoma City
It was on Christmas Day,
There came a whole car load of groceries,
With a letter that did say:

"You say that I'm an outlaw,
You say that I'm a thief,
Here's a Christmas dinner
For the families on relief."

Now as through this world I ramble,
I see lots of funny men,
Some will rob you with a six-gun,
And some with a fountain pen.

But as through this life you travel,
As through your life you roam,
You won't never see an outlaw,
Drive a family from their home.

MALCOLM X
Malcolm X Speaks

I am willing by any means necessary to bring an end to the injustices our people suffer.

THURGOOD MARSHALL

The battle for racial and economic justice is not yet won; indeed, it has barely begun.

WALT WHITMAN
Democratic Vistas

Judging from the main portions of the history of the world, so far, justice is always in jeopardy.

HENRY DAVID THOREAU
Civil Disobedience

I think that we should be men first, and subjects afterward. It is not desirable to cultivate a respect for the law, so much as for the right.

HENRY DAVID THOREAU
Civil Disobedience

A government in which the majority rule in all cases cannot be based on justice, even as far as men understand it.

WENDELL PHILLIPS

The best use of good laws is to teach men to trample bad laws under their feet.

ROBERT G. INGERSOLL
Prose-Poems and Selections

Justice should remove the bandage from her eyes long enough to distinguish between the vicious and the unfortunate.

WILLIAM H. SEWARD
Speech in the U.S. Senate

There is a higher law than the Constitution.

THOMAS JEFFERSON
Letter to John B. Colvin

A strict observance of the written law is doubtless one of the high duties of a good citizen, but it is not the highest. The laws of necessity, of self-preservation, of saving our country when in danger, are of higher obligation.

HENRY DAVID THOREAU

The man for whom law exists—the man of forms, the conservative—is a tame man.

GROVER CLEVELAND

No man has ever yet been hanged for breaking the spirit of a law.

MAE WEST
Every Day's a Holiday

It ain't no sin if you crack a few laws now and then, just so long as you don't break any.

HENRY DAVID THOREAU
A Plea for Captain John Brown

Is it not possible that an individual may be right and a government wrong? Are laws to be enforced simply because they are made? Or declared by any number of men to be good, if they are not good?

ADLAI E. STEVENSON
Speech in Alton, Illinois

Man may burn his brother at the stake, but he cannot reduce truth to ashes; he may murder his fellow man with a shot in the back, but he does not murder justice; he may slay armies of men, but as it is written, "Truth Beareth off the victory."

HENRY WADSWORTH LONGFELLOW
Evangeline

Man is unjust, but God is just; and finally justice triumphs.

Domestic Tranquillity

WALT WHITMAN
"The Sleepers"

Peace is always beautiful.

JOHN FOSTER DULLES
War or Peace

A peaceful world is a world in which differences are tolerated, and are not eliminated by violence.

RALPH WALDO EMERSON
"Self-Reliance," *Essays*

Nothing can bring you peace but yourself. Nothing can bring you peace but the triumph of principles.

THOMAS JEFFERSON
Letter to William Frederick Dumas

Peace and friendship with all mankind is our wisest policy, and I wish we may be permitted to pursue it.

ELEANOR ROOSEVELT
Voice of America broadcast

It isn't enough to talk about peace. One must believe in it. And it isn't enough to believe in it. One must work at it.

ADLAI E. STEVENSON
Speech in New Orleans

Peace is not the work of a single day, nor will it be the consequence of a single act. Yet every constructive act contributes to its growth; every omission impedes it. Peace will come, in the end, if it comes at all, as a child grows to maturity—slowly, imperceptibly, until we realize one day in incredulous surprise that the child is almost grown.

LYNDON B. JOHNSON
The Vantage Point: Perspectives of the Presidency, 1963–1969

No man should think that peace comes easily. Peace does not come by merely wanting it, or shouting for it, or marching down Main Street for it. Peace is built brick by brick, mortared by the stubborn effort and the total energy and imagination of able and dedicated men. And it is built in the living faith that, in the end, man can and will master his own destiny.

ALBERT EINSTEIN
Out of My Later Years

Laws alone cannot secure freedom of expression: in order that every man present his views without penalty there must be a spirit of tolerance in the entire population.

FRANKLIN D. ROOSEVELT
Message to Congress

The driving force of a nation lies in its spiritual purpose, made effective by free, tolerant but unremitting national will.

RENÉ DUBOS
Celebrations of Life

Human diversity makes tolerance more than a virtue; it makes it a requirement for survival.

American Tolerance

WILLIAM ALLEN WHITE

Commencement address at Northwestern University

...The thing that has bound America into one nation is tolerance—tolerance and patience; indeed, tolerance and patience upheld by a sense of duty.

At this point, dearly beloved members of the class of '37, I propose to reveal the screw loose in my mental processes, also to show you something of the aberration of your forebears. You have this dementia in your blood, and you might as well know it. Your fathers, mothers, and remote ancestors for several thousand years believed in the reality of duty. Upon that madness they built the world. Not that I wish to brag about it—this sense of duty—but I still hug the delirium of my generation to my heart and believe there is something in those old-fashioned eccentricities known as Christian virtues. Don't get excited. I am not preaching piety. I have no plan of salvation to offer you, no theology to defend. But I feel, and my generation has believed in a general way, that democracy with its freedom, with its patience, with its tolerance, with its altruism, is a sort of rough attempt to institutionalize the Christian philosophy. And when I say rough, I mean rough, something like 20 percent realization of a noble ideal. Our American Constitution, for instance, is a national compact of our individual and of our social duties. It has worked in this country after a fashion. Yet the same Constitution, or nearly the same, has been adopted in a dozen other lands and has failed. Why has it held us to an essential unity? I am satisfied that our Constitution has stood up because Americans actually have established here a sort of code of duties. That has been the crystallizing principle that has held us together—duty of man to man, of region to region, of class to class, of race to race, of faith to faith. That duty has bred something more than neighborly tolerance. It has engendered a profound desire in every American's heart to make life as pleasant as it may be made—not merely for himself, indeed not chiefly for himself, but for others. Thus we have found and cherished true liberty.

Liberty, if it shall cement man into political unity, must be something more than a man's conception of his rights, much more than his desire to fight for his own rights. True liberty is founded upon a lively sense of the rights of others and a fighting conviction that the rights of others must be maintained. Only when a people have this love of liberty, this militant belief in the sacredness of another man's self-respect, do races and nations possess the catalyzer in their political and social organism which produces the chemical miracle of crystallized national unity and strength. We Americans have had it for three hundred years on this continent. It was in the blood of our fathers. It was the basis of our faith in humanity when we wrote our Constitution. It has been with us a long time on this continent—this capacity for compromise, this practical passion for social justice and for altruistic equality in settling the genuine differences of men. This high quality of mutual respect is no slight gift. It is a heroic spiritual endowment, this knack of getting along together on a continental scale.

We have set as a national custom the habit of majority rule. This custom is maintained not by arms but by a saving sense in the heart of every minority that any majority will not be puffed up, will not infringe upon the rights of the minority. Matching this duty of the majority to be fair, we have set up the component duty of the minority to be patient, but to agitate until the justice of a losing cause has convinced the winning majority. This American tradition of political adjustment cuts through every line of cleavage and all differences in our social organization—regions, classes, races, creeds. Here is the way it has worked. As our country has expanded geographically, this political genius for unity has tapped our store of certain basic virtues: neighborly forbearance, meekness, unselfishness, and that belief in the essential decency of one's neighbors which for want of a better word we have called love. Now, in our land abideth these three—faith in our fellows, hope in the triumph of reason, and love for humanity. With all the grievous faults and glaring weaknesses of our federal union, these things are the centripetal forces which have solidified America.

These commonsense qualities which have grown out of the Beatitudes have helped to preserve the American Union for the last century and a half. Now, what are you going to do about it, you who stand here at the threshold of the reality of your past, looking into the evanescent horizon of your future? We who shall soon be petrified into pedestaled ghosts as your ancestors have a notion that you, our descendants, don't have much use for duty, for patience, and for tolerance. We get the general idea that you have no sort of faith in the strength of the humble. Yet it is out of this lack of faith that a new challenge has appeared in the world, a challenge aimed at democracy, a challenge which scorns these lowly neighborly virtues that have held our world together. This challenge is finding its way into our American life. We are being told that the majority sometimes has emergency mandates to ignore the rights of the minorities. We have set up rulers all over the earth who preach against the virtue of patience. It is a new thing in our America to hear men defending the tyrannies of Europe—communism, fascism, and the Nazis—declaring that the minority may oppress the majority if the minority happens to be convinced that it is right. It is even a stranger doctrine in America, which holds that a passing majority, by reason of its being a ballot box majority at one or two elections, has an inherent right immediately to suppress and ruthlessly destroy an honest minority.

Now, as an ancestor, let me caution you, my heirs and assigns, that these new political attitudes are symptoms of greed for power. They will fool you if you channel your thinking into narrow dialectics. Don't take your logical premise from your class self-interest. Don't build your logic upon a purely selfish structure. Don't think as plutocrats. Don't reason as members of the middle class or as proletarians. Such thinking is too sure of its own syllogisms ever to be just. Such thinking rejects the possibility that there is truth and that there may be reason in the contention of another class of society. This same discord that has torn asunder so many peoples in Europe, where fifty years ago democracy seemed to be taking root, today is seeding in our land. Capitalists are scorning labor leaders. Labor leaders are preaching distrust and hatred of capitalists. The revelations of the La Follette committee in the United States Senate now investigating the infringement of civil liberties certainly lay bare the cancer of hatred in our economic body that is poisoning our national blood. The class-conscious arrogance of wealth is creating its own class morals. Proletarian logic is justifying the use of force in class conflict and condoning cunning. The industrial enterpriser shuts his eyes to the tragedy of the farmer's economic plight. Then the farmer envies the financier.

But I feel sure the tide will turn. You who stand here, chisel in hand, about to hew out the future, have something in you; humanity's most precious mental gift—the eternal resilience, the everlasting bounce in man. You may love for the moment the indolent sense of futility that comes with the grand cynicism of youth. But life, experience, the hazards of your day, and time will bring out of you the courage bred into you. You will find that you have the urge that we had. You will want to believe in something in spite of yourselves. You will want to construct something. For you are the sons and daughters of creative people, inventive, resourceful, daring. And above all, in spite of the many unpleasant things you have learned in this cloister, in spite of the hard realities that have molded your youth, you are mystics, you are crusaders, you are incorrigible visionaries in the noblest sense of these words. The eternal verities of your inheritance, the organizing brains, the industry, the noble purpose that during the nineteenth century made America a kindlier and more beautiful land than ever before was brought forth on this planet, will be beckoning you, urging you, indeed, sternly commanding you to follow whatever is fine and just in the achievement of your country....

The residuum of what I am trying to say is this: you must reorganize life in your America and point your achievement toward a fairer distributive system. Abundance is here for the taking. Don't bemoan your lost frontier. It is even now flashing on your horizon. A gorgeous land lies before you fair and more beautiful than man before has ever known. Out of the laboratories will come new processes to multiply material things for your America, to multiply them almost infinitely; but only if you will hold open the channels of free science, unfettered thought, and the right of a man to use his talents to the utmost provided he gives honest social returns for the rewards he takes. Don't delude yourselves about your new frontier. For on that frontier which will rise over the laboratories you will find the same struggle, the same hardships, the same inequities that your forefathers have found on every frontier since the beginning of time. You will find rapacious men trying to grab more than their share of the common bounties of the new frontier. You will find human greeds and human perfidies there as we found them fifty years ago and as our fathers found them generations upon generations before. Energetic buccaneers always thrive wherever men are pioneering. In every one of the ten long generations during which our ancestors have been conquering this continent and building a proud civilization here, they have struggled as you will struggle against the injustices of life which are bred out of the lust for power in unsocial men. But don't let that discourage you. . . .

And now, in closing, on behalf of your fathers who are bequeathing to you their choicest gifts, let me say that your heritage is not in these great lovely cities, not this wide and fertile land, not the mountains full of undreamed-of riches. These you may find in other continents. What we leave you that is precious are the few simple virtues which have stood us in good stead in the struggle of our generation. We will and bequeath to you our enthusiasm, our diligence, our zeal for a better world, that were the lodestars of our fathers. As our legatees we assign you our tolerance, our patience, our kindness, our faith, hope, and love, which make for the self-respect of man. These qualities of heart and mind grow out of a conviction that the democratic philosophy as mode of thinking will lead mankind into a nobler way of life.

The Great Gatsby
F. SCOTT FITZGERALD
Chapter I

In my younger and more vulnerable years my father gave me some advice that I've been turning over in my mind ever since.

"Whenever you feel like criticizing anyone," he told me, "just remember that all the people in this world haven't had the advantages that you've had."

He didn't say any more but we've always been unusually communicative in a reserved way, and I understood that he meant a great deal more than that. In consequence, I'm inclined to reserve all judgments, a habit that has opened up many curious natures to me and also made me the victim of not a few veteran bores. The abnormal mind is quick to detect and attach itself to this quality when it appears in a normal person, and so it came about that in college I was unjustly accused of being a politician, because I was privy to the secret griefs of wild, unknown men. Most of the confidences were unsought—frequently I have feigned sleep, preoccupation or a hostile levity when I realized by some unmistakable sign that an intimate revelation was quivering on the horizon—for the intimate revelations of young men or at least the terms in which they express them are usually plagiaristic and marred by obvious suppressions. Reserving judgments is a matter of infinite hope. I am still a little afraid of missing something if I forget that, as my father snobbishly suggested and I snobbishly repeat, a sense of fundamental decencies is parceled out unequally at birth.

And, after boasting this way of my tolerance, I come to the admission that it has a limit. Conduct may be founded on the hard rock or the wet marshes but after a certain point I don't care what it is founded on. When I came back from the East last autumn I felt that I wanted the world to be in uniform and at a sort of moral attention forever; I wanted no more riotous excursions with privileged glimpses into the human heart. Only Gatsby, the man who gives his name to this book, was exempt from my reaction—Gatsby, who represented everything for which I have unaffected scorn. If personality is an unbroken series of successful gestures, then there was something gorgeous about him, some heightened sensitivity to the promises of life, as if he were related to one of those intricate machines that register earthquakes ten thousand miles away. This responsiveness had nothing to do with that flabby impressionability which is dignified under the name of the "creative temperament"—it was an extraordinary gift for hope, a romantic readiness such as I have never found in any other person and which it is not likely I shall ever find again. No—Gatsby turned out all right at the end; it is what preyed on Gatsby, what foul dust floated in the wake of his dreams that temporarily closed out my interest in the abortive sorrows and short-winded elations of men.

HENRY WADSWORTH LONGFELLOW
Driftwood

If we could read the secret history of our enemies, we should find in each man's life sorrow and suffering enough to disarm hostility.

ROBERT FROST

A Liberal is a man too broadminded to take his own side in a quarrel.

RALPH WALDO EMERSON
Journals

The doctrine of Necessity or Destiny is the doctrine of Toleration.

HELEN KELLER
Optimism

The highest result of education is tolerance.

OGDEN NASH
"I'm a Stranger Here Myself"

Sometimes with secret pride I sigh
To think how tolerant am I;
Then wonder which is really mine:
Tolerance or a rubber spine?

MARIANNE MOORE
"Blessed Is the Man"

who does not sit in the seat of the scoffer—
    the man who does not denigrate, depreciate, denunciate;
      who is not "characteristically intemperate,"
who does not "excuse, retreat, equivocate; and will be heard."

(Ah, Giorgione! there are those who mongrelize
    and those who heighten anything they touch; although it
                    may well be
    that if Giorgione's self-portrait were not said to be he,
it might not take my fancy. Blessed the geniuses who know

that egomania is not a duty.)
    "Diversity, controversy; tolerance"—in that "citadel
      of learning" we have a fort that ought to armor us well.
Blessed is the man who "takes the risk of a decision"—asks

himself the right question: "Would it solve the problem?
    Is it right as I see it? Is it in the best interests of all?"
      Alas, Ulysses' companions are now political—
living self-indulgently until the moral sense is drowned,

having lost all power of comparison,
    thinking license emancipates one, "slaves whom they
             themselves have bound."
      Brazen authors, downright soiled and downright spoiled, as
              if sound
and exceptional, are the old quasi-modish counterfeit,

mitin-proofing conscience against character.
    Affronted by "private lies and public shame," blessed is the
             author
    Who favors what the supercilious do *not* favor—
who will not comply. Blessed, the unaccommodating man.

Blessed the man whose faith is different
    from possessiveness—of a kind not framed by "things which
           do appear"—
    who will not visualize defeat, too intent to cover;
whose illumined eye has seen the shaft that gilds Nesultan's tower.

GROVER CLEVELAND
Speech to Evangelical Alliance

If you seek to teach your countrymen toleration you yourself must be tolerant; if you would teach them liberality for the opinions of others, you yourselves must be liberal; and if you would teach them unselfish patriotism, you yourselves must be unselfish and patriotic.

The True Meaning of Patriotism
ADLAI E. STEVENSON

...True patriotism, it seems to me, is based on tolerance and a large measure of humility.

There are men among us who use "patriotism" as a club for attacking other Americans. What can we say for the self-styled patriot who thinks that a Negro, a Jew, a Catholic, or a Japanese-American is less an American than he? That betrays the deepest article of our faith, the belief in individual liberty and equality which has always been the heart and soul of the American idea.

What can we say for the man who proclaims himself a patriot—and then for political or personal reasons attacks the patriotism of faithful public servants? I give you, as a shocking example, the attacks which have been made on the loyalty and the motives of our great wartime chief of staff, General Marshall. To me this is the type of "patriotism" which is, in Dr. Johnson's phrase, "the last refuge of scoundrels."

The anatomy of patriotism is complex. But surely intolerance and public irresponsibility cannot be cloaked in the shining armor of rectitude and righteousness. Nor can the denial of the right to hold ideas that are different—the freedom of man to think as he pleases. To strike freedom of the mind with the fist of patriotism is an old and ugly subtlety....

Men who have offered their lives for their country know that patriotism is not the fear of something; it is the love of something. Patriotism with us is not the hatred of Russia; it is the love of this Republic and of the ideal of liberty of man and mind in which it was born, and to which the Republic is dedicated.

With this patriotism—patriotism in its large and wholesome meaning—Americans can master its power and turn it to the noble cause of peace. We can maintain military power without militarism; political power without oppression; and moral power without compulsion or complacency.

The road we travel is long, but at the end lies the grail of peace. And in the valley of peace we see the faint outlines of a new world, fertile and strong. It is odd that one of the keys to abundance should have been handed to civilization on a platter of destruction. But the power of the atom to work evil gives only the merest hint of its power for good.

I believe that man stands on the eve of his greatest day. I know, too, that that day is not a gift but a prize—that we shall not reach its until we have won it.

JAMES MADISON
The Federalist LI

If men were angels, no government would be necessary. If angels were to govern men, neither external nor internal controls on government would be necessary. In framing a government which is to be administered by men over men, the greatest difficulty lies in this: You must first enable the government to control the governed; and in the next place, oblige it to control itself. A dependence on the people is no doubt the primary control on the government; but experience has taught mankind the necessity of auxiliary precautions.

A Talk for Students
ROBERT FROST
Commencement address at Sarah Lawrence College

Now there is a word we've had that goes wrong. I don't know whether you have encountered it or not. The word is, "the dream." I wonder how much you have encountered it? I have it thrown in my face every little while, and always by somebody who thinks the dream has come true. And then the next time I pick it up to knit I wonder what the dream is, or why. And the next time I pick it up, I wonder who dreamed it. Did Tom Paine dream it, did Thomas Jefferson dream it, did George Washington dream it? Gouverneur Morris? And lately I've decided the best dreamer of it was Madison. I have been reading the Federalist papers.

But anyway I am always concerned with the question, is it a dream that goes by? Each age is a dream that is dying, they say, or one that is coming to birth. It depends on what you mean by an age. Is the age over in which that dream had its existence—has it gone by? Can we treat the Constitution as if it were something gone by? Can we interpret it out of existence? By calling it a living document, it means something different every day, something new every day, until it doesn't mean anything that it meant to Madison. And this thought occurred to me the other day when I picked it up. Has the dream, instead of having come true, has it done something that the witches talk about? Has it simply materialized?

Young writers that I know—novelists that I know—began as poets, most of them. They began more ethereal than substantial, and have ended up more substantial than ethereal. And is that what has happened to our country? Has the ethereal idealism of the founders materialized into something too material? In South America last year at a convention I heard everybody regretting or fearing or worrying about our materialism. Not for our own sake, but for their sake, because we were misleading them into a material future for the whole world, and anxiety for us. I told them we were anxious about that too. We had scales in our bathrooms to see how material we were getting...

Now I know—I think I know, as of today—what Madison's dream was. It was just a dream of new land to fulfill with people in self-control. In self-control. That is all through his thinking. And let me say that again to you. To fulfill this land—a new land—with people in self-control. And do I think that dream has failed? Has come to nothing, or has materialized too much? It is always the fear. We live in constant fear, of course. To cross the road we live in fear of cars. But we can live in fear, if we want to, of too much education, too little education, too much of this, too little of that. The thing is, the measure.

I am always pleased when I see someone making motions like this [gesture of conducting a chorus]—like a metronome. Seeing the music measured. Measure always reassures me. Measure in love, in government, measure in selfishness, measure in unselfishness.

To Break and Control the Violence of Faction

JAMES MADISON ("PUBLIUS")

The Federalist X

Among the numerous advantages promised by a well constructed Union, none deserves to be more accurately developed than its tendency to break and control the violence of faction. The friend of popular governments never finds himself so much alarmed for their character and fate as when he contemplates their propensity to this dangerous vice. He will not fail therefore to set a due value on any plan which, without violating the principles to which he is attached, provides a proper cure for it. The instability, injustice and confusion introduced into the public councils have in truth been the mortal diseases under which popular governments have everywhere perished; as they continue to be the favorite and fruitful topics from which the adversaries to liberty derive their most specious declamations....

There are two methods of curing the mischiefs of faction: the one, by removing its causes; the other, by controlling its effects.

There are again two methods of removing the causes of faction: the one by destroying the liberty which is essential to its existence; the other, by giving to every citizen the same opinions, the same passions, and the same interests.

It could never be more truly said than of the first remedy, that it is worse than the disease. Liberty is to faction, what air is to fire, an aliment without which it instantly expires. But it could not be a less folly to abolish liberty, which is essential to political life, because it nourishes faction, than it would be to wish the annihilation of air, which is essential to animal life, because it imparts to fire its destructive agency.

The second expedient is as impracticable, as the first would be unwise. As long as the reason of man continues to be fallible, and he is at liberty to exercise it, different opinions will be formed. As long as the connection subsists between his reason and his self-love, his opinions and his passions will have a reciprocal influence on each other; and the former will be objects to which the latter will attach themselves. The diversity in the faculties of men, from which the rights of property originate, is not less an insuperable obstacle to a uniformity of interests. The protection of these faculties is the first object of Government. From the protection of different and unequal faculties of acquiring property, the possession of different degrees and kinds of property immediately results: and from the influence of these on the sentiments and views of the respective proprietors, ensues a division of the society into different interests and parties.

The latent causes of faction are thus sown in the nature of man; and we see them everywhere brought into different degrees of activity, according to the different circumstances of civil society. A zeal for different opinions concerning religion, concerning Government, and many other points, as well of speculation as of practice; an attachment to different leaders ambitiously contending for pre-eminence and power; or to persons of other descriptions whose fortunes have been interesting to the human passions, have in turn divided mankind into parties, inflamed them with mutual animosity, and rendered them much more disposed to vex and oppress each other, than to cooperate for their common good. So strong is this propensity of mankind to fall into mutual animosities, that where no substantial occasion presents itself, the most frivolous and fanciful distinctions have been sufficient to kindle their unfriendly passions, and excite their most violent conflicts. But the most common and durable source of factions has been the various and unequal distribution of property. Those who hold, and those who are without property, have ever formed distinct interests in society. Those who are creditors, and those who are debtors, fall under a like discrimination. A landed interest, a manufacturing interest, a mercantile interest, a monied interest, with many lesser interests, grow up of necessity in civilized nations, and divide them into different classes, actuated by different sentiments and views. The regulation of these various and interfering interests forms the principal task of modern Legislation, and involves the spirit of party and faction in the necessary and ordinary operations of Government.

No man is allowed to be a judge in his own cause; because his interest would certainly bias his judgment, and, not improbably, corrupt his integrity. With equal, nay with greater reason, a body of men are unfit to be both judges and parties at the same time; yet, what are many of the most important acts of legislation, but so many judicial determinations, not indeed concerning the rights of single persons, but concerning the rights of large bodies of citizens; and what are the different classes of legislators, but advocates and parties to the causes which they determine? Is a law proposed concerning private debts? It is a question to which the creditors are parties on one side, and the debtors on the other. Justice ought to hold the balance between them. Yet the parties are and must be themselves the judges; and the most numerous party, or, in other words, the most powerful faction must be expected to prevail. Shall domestic manufactures be encouraged, and in what degree, by restriction on foreign manufactures are questions which would be differently decided by the landed and the manufacturing classes; and probably by neither, with a sole regard to justice and the public good. The apportionment of taxes on the various descriptions of property is an act which seems to require the most exact impartiality; yet there is perhaps no legislative act in which greater opportunity and temptation are given to a predominant party, to trample on the rules of justice. Every shilling, with which they overburden the inferior number, is a shilling saved to their own pockets.

It is in vain to say, that enlightened statesmen will be able to adjust these clashing interests, and render them all subservient to the public good. Enlightened statesmen will not always be at the helm: Nor, in many cases, can such an adjustment be made at all, without taking into view indirect and remote considerations, which will rarely prevail over the immediate interest which one party may find in disregarding the rights of another, or the good of the whole.

The inference to which we are brought is that the causes of faction cannot be removed; and that relief is only to be sought in the means of controlling its effects.

If a faction consists of less than a majority, relief is supplied by the republican principle, which enables the majority to defeat its sinister views by regular vote: It may clog the administration, it may convulse the society; but it will be unable to execute and mask its violence under the forms of the Constitution. When a majority is included in a faction, the form of popular government on the other hand enables it to sacrifice to its ruling passion or interest both the public good and the rights of other citizens. To secure the public good, and private rights, against the danger of such a faction, and at the same time to preserve the spirit and the form of popular government, is then the great object to which our enquiries are directed: Let me add that it is the great desideratum, by which alone this form of government can be rescued from the opprobrium under which it has so long labored, and be recommended to the esteem and adoption of mankind.

By what means is this object attainable? Evidently by one of two only. Either the existence of the same passion or interest in a majority at the same time must be prevented; or the majority, having such co-existent passion or interest, must be rendered, by their number and local situation, unable to concert and carry into effect schemes of oppression. If the impulse and the opportunity be suffered to coincide, we well know that neither moral nor religious motives can be relied on as an adequate control. They are not found to be such on the injustice and violence of individuals, and lose their efficacy in proportion to the number combined together; that is, in proportion as their efficacy becomes needful.

From this view of the subject, it may be concluded, that a pure Democracy, by which I mean, a Society, consisting of a small number of citizens, who assemble and administer the

Government in person, can admit of no cure for the mischiefs of faction. A common passion or interest will, in almost every case, be felt by a majority of the whole; a communication and concert results from the form of Government itself; and there is nothing to check the inducements to sacrifice the weaker party, or an obnoxious individual. Hence it is, that such Democracies have ever been spectacles of turbulence and contention; have ever been found incompatible with personal security, or the rights of property; and have in general been as short in their lives, as they have been violent in their deaths. Theoretic politicians, who have patronized this species of Government, have erroneously supposed, that by reducing mankind to a perfect equality in their political rights, they would, at the same time, be perfectly equalized and assimilated in their possessions, their opinions, and their passions.

A Republic, by which I mean a Government in which the scheme of representation takes place, opens a different prospect, and promises the cure for which we are seeking. Let us examine the points in which it varies from pure Democracy, and we shall comprehend both the nature of the cure, and the efficacy which it must derive from the Union.

The two great points of difference between a Democracy and a Republic are, first, the delegation of the Government, in the latter, to a small number of citizens elected by the rest: secondly, the greater number of citizens, and greater sphere of country, over which the latter may be extended.

The effect of the first difference is, on the one hand to refine and enlarge the public views, by passing them through the medium of a chosen body of citizens, whose wisdom may best discern the true interest of their country, and whose patriotism and love of justice, will be least likely to sacrifice it to temporary or partial considerations. Under such a regulation, it may well happen that the public voice pronounced by the representatives of the people will be more consonant to the public good than if pronounced by the people themselves convened for the purpose. On the other hand, the effect may be inverted. Men of factious tempers, of local prejudices, or of sinister designs, may by intrigue, by corruption or by other means, first obtain the suffrages, and then betray the interests of the people. The question resulting is, whether small or extensive Republics are most favorable to the election of proper guardians of the public weal; and it is clearly decided in favor of the latter by two obvious considerations.

In the first place it is to be remarked that however small the Republic may be, the Representatives must be raised to a certain number, in order to guard against the cabals of a few; and that however large it may be, they must be limited to a certain number, in order to guard against the confusion of the multitude. Hence the number of Representatives in the two cases, not being in proportion to that of the Constituents, and being proportionally greatest in the small Republic, it follows, that if the proportion of fit characters be not less, in the large than in the small Republic, the former will present a greater option, and consequently a greater probability of a fit choice.

In the next place, as each Representative will be chosen by a greater number of citizens in the large than in the small Republic, it will be more difficult for unworthy candidates to practice with success the vicious arts, by which elections are too often carried; and the suffrages of the people, being more free, will be more likely to center on men who possess the most attractive merit, and most diffusive and established characters.

It must be confessed, that in this, as in most other cases, there is a mean, on both sides of which inconveniences will be found to lie. By enlarging too much the number of citizens and extent of territory which may be brought within the compass of Republican, than of Democratic Government; and it is this circumstance principally which renders factious combinations less to be dreaded in the former than in the latter. The smaller the society the fewer probably will be the distinct parties and interests, the more frequently will a majority be found of the same party; and the smaller the number of individuals composing a majority, and the smaller the compass within which they are placed, the more easily will they concert and execute their plans of oppression. Extend the sphere, and you take in a greater variety of parties and interests; you make it less probable that a majority of the whole will have a common motive to invade the rights of other citizens; or if such a common motive exists, it will be more difficult for all who feel it to discover their own strength, and to act in unison with each other. Besides other impediments, it may be remarked, that where there is a consciousness of unjust or dishonorable purposes, communication is always checked by distrust, in proportion to the number whose concurrence is necessary.

Hence it clearly appears, that the same advantage, which a Republic has over a Democracy in controlling the effects of faction, and is enjoyed by a large over a small Republic—is enjoyed by the Union over the States composing it. Does this advantage consist in the substitution of Representatives, whose enlightened views and virtuous sentiments render them superior to local prejudices, and to schemes of injustice? It will not be denied, that the Representation of the Union will be most likely to possess these requisite endowments. Does it consist in the greater security afforded by a greater variety of parties, against the event of any one party being able to outnumber and oppress the rest? In an equal degree does the increased variety of parties, comprised within the Union, increase this security. Does it, in fine, consist in the greater obstacles opposed to the concert and accomplishment of the secret wishes of an unjust and interested majority? Here, again, the extent of the Union gives it the most palpable advantage.

The influence of factious leaders may kindle a flame within their particular States, but will be unable to spread a general conflagration through the other States: a religious sect may degenerate into a political faction in a part of the Confederacy; but the variety of sects, dispersed over the entire face of it, must secure the national Councils against any danger from that source: a rage for paper money, for an abolition of debts, for an equal division of property, or for any other improper or wicked project, will be less apt to pervade the whole body of the Union than a particular member of it; in the same proportion as such a malady is more likely to taint a particular county or district than an entire State.

In the extent and proper structure of the Union, therefore, we behold a Republican remedy for the diseases most incident to Republican Government. And according to the degree of pleasure and pride we feel in being Republicans, ought to be our zeal in cherishing the spirit, and supporting the character of Federalists.

On the safety of multiple interests: Ambition will counter ambition

JAMES MADISON ("PUBLIUS")
The Federalist LI

. . . It is of great importance, not only to guard the society against the oppression of its rulers; but to guard one part of the society against the injustice of the other part. Different interests necessarily exist in different classes of citizens. If a majority be united by a common interest, the rights of the minority will be insecure. There are but two methods of providing against this evil: The one by creating a will in the community independent of the majority, that is, of the society itself; the other by comprehending in the society so many separate descriptions of citizens as will render an unjust combination of a majority of the whole, very improbable, if not impracticable. The first method prevails in all governments possessing an hereditary or self-appointed authority. This at best is but a precarious security; because a power independent of the society may as well espouse the unjust views of the major, as the rightful interests of the minor party, and may possibly be turned against both parties. The second method will be exemplified in the federal republic of the United States. Whilst all authority in it will be derived from and dependent on the society, the society itself will be broken into so many parts, interests and classes of citizens, that the rights of individuals, or of the minority, will be in little danger from interested combinations of the majority. In a free government, the security of civil rights must be the same as that for religious rights. It consists in the one case in the multiplicity of sects. The degree of security in both cases will depend on the number of interests and sects; and this may be presumed to depend on the extent of country and number of people comprehended under the same government. This view of the subject must particularly recommend a proper federal system to all the sincere and considerate friends of republican government: Since it shows that in exact proportion as the territory of the union may be formed into more circumscribed confederacies or states, oppressive combinations of a majority will be facilitated, the best security under the republican form, for the rights of every class of citizens, will be diminished; and consequently, the stability and independence of some member of the government, the only other security, must be proportionally increased. Justice is the end of government. It is the end of civil society. It ever has been, and ever will be pursued, until it be obtained, or until liberty be lost in the pursuit. In a society under the forms of which the stronger faction can readily unite and oppress the weaker, anarchy may as truly be said to reign, as in a state of nature where the weaker individual is not secured against the violence of the stronger: And as in the latter state even the stronger individuals are prompted by the uncertainty of their condition, to submit to a government which may protect the weak as well as themselves: So in the former state, will the more powerful factions or parties be gradually induced by a like motive, to wish for a government which will protect all parties, the weaker as well as the more powerful? It can be little doubted, that if the state of Rhode Island was separated from the confederacy, and left to itself, the insecurity of rights, under the popular form of government within such narrow limits, would be displayed by such reiterated oppressions of factious majorities, that some power altogether independent of the people would soon be called for by the voice of the very factions whose misrule had proved the necessity of it. In the extended republic of the United States, and among the great variety of interests, parties, and sects which it embraces, a coalition of a majority of the whole society could seldom take place on any other principles than those of justice and the general good; and there being thus less danger to a minor from the will of the major party, there must be less pretext, also, to provide for the security of the former by introducing into the government a will not dependent on the latter; or, in other words, a will independent of the society itself. It is no less certain than it is important, notwithstanding the contrary opinions which have been entertained, that the larger the society, provided it lie within a practicable sphere, the more duly capable it will be of self government. And happily for the republican cause, the practicable sphere may be carried to a very great extent by a judicious modification and mixture of the federal principle.

RALPH WALDO EMERSON

Shall we judge a country by the majority, or by the minority? By the minority, surely.

WENDELL PHILLIPS

Governments exist to protect the rights of minorities. The loved and the rich need no protection—they have many friends and few enemies.

JAMES K. POLK
Message to Congress

One great object of the Constitution in conferring upon the President a qualified negative upon the legislation of Congress was to protect minorities from injustice and oppression by majorities.

FRANKLIN D. ROOSEVELT
Letter to the National Association for the Advancement of Colored People

No democracy can long survive which does not accept as fundamental to its very existence the recognition of the rights of minorities.

FRANKLIN D. ROOSEVELT
Radio broadcast

The moment a mere numerical superiority by either states or voters in this country proceeds to ignore the needs and desires of the minority, and, for their own selfish purpose or advancement, hamper or oppress that minority, or debar them in any way from equal privileges and equal rights—that moment will mark the failure of our constitutional system.

WILLIAM HOWARD TAFT
Veto of Arizona Enabling Act

Constitutions are checks upon the hasty action of the majority. They are the self-imposed restraints of a whole people upon a majority of them to secure sober action and a respect for the rights of the minority.

JOHN C. CALHOUN

Property is in its nature timid and seeks protection, and nothing is more gratifying to government than to become a protector.

GEORGE WASHINGTON
Farewell Address

Let me now...warn you in the most solemn manner against the baneful effects of the spirit of party.

ALFRED E. SMITH

The thing we have to fear in this country, to my way of thinking, is the influence of organized minorities, because somehow or other the great majority does not seem to organize. They seem to feel that they are going to be effective because of their own strength, but they give no expression of it.

JOHN DICKINSON

For who are free people? Not those, over whom government is reasonably and equitably exercised, but those who live under a government so constitutionally checked and controlled, that proper provision is made against its being otherwise exercised.

Observations on the Constitution
Proposed by the Federal Convention

JOHN DICKINSON
1788

The Writer of this Address hopes that he will now be thought so disengaged from the objections against the part of the principle assumed, concerning the power of the people, that he may be excused for recurring to his assertion, that the power of the people pervading the proposed system, together with the strong confederation of the states, will form an adequate security against every danger that has been apprehended.

It is a mournful, but may be a useful truth, that the liberty of single republics has generally been destroyed by some of the citizens, and of confederated republics, by some of the associated states.

It is more pleasing, and may be more profitable to reflect, that their tranquillity and prosperity have commonly been promoted, in proportion to the strength of their government for protecting the worthy against the licentious.

As in forming a political society, each individual contributes some of his rights, in order that he may, from a common stock of rights, derive greater benefits than he could from merely his own; so, in forming a confederation, each political society should contribute such a share of their rights as will, from a common stock of rights, produce the largest quantity of benefits for them.

But, what is that share? and, how to be managed? Momentous questions! Here, flattery is treason; and error, destruction.

Are they unanswerable? No. Our most gracious Creator does not condemn us to sigh for unattainable blessedness: But one thing he demands—that we should seek for it in his way, and not in our own.

Humility and benevolence must take place of pride and overweening selfishness. Reason, then rising above these mists, will discover to us, that we cannot be true to ourselves, without being true to others—that to be solitary, is to be wretched—that to love our neighbors as ourselves is to love ourselves in the best manner—that to give is to gain—and, that we never consult our own happiness more effectually than when we most endeavor to correspond with the

Divine designs, by communicating happiness, as much as we can, to our fellow-creatures. INES-TIMABLE TRUTH! sufficient, if they do not barely ask what it is, to melt tyrants into men, and to sooth the inflamed minds of a multitude into mildness—sufficient to overflow this earth with unknown felicity—INESTIMABLE TRUTH! which our Maker, in his providence, enables us not only to talk and write about, but to adopt in practice of vast extent, and of instructive example.

Let us now enquire, if there be not some principle, simple as the laws of nature in other instances, from which, as from a source, the many benefits of society are deduced.

We may with reverence say, that our Creator designed men for society, because otherwise they cannot be happy. They cannot be happy without freedom; nor free without security; that is, without the absence of fear; nor thus secure, without society. The conclusion is strictly syl-logistic—that men cannot be free without society, which freedom produces the greatest happiness.

As these premises are invincible, we have advanced a considerable way in our inquiry upon this deeply interesting subject. If we can determine what share of his rights every individual must contribute to the common stock of rights in forming a society, for obtaining equal free-dom, we determine at the same time, what share of their rights each political society must con-tribute to the common stock of rights in forming a confederation, which is only a larger society, for obtaining equal freedom: For, if the deposit be not proportioned to the magnitude of the association in the latter case, it will generate the same mischief among the component parts of it, from their inequality, that would result from a defective contribution to association in the former case, among the component parts of it, from their inequality.

Each individual then must contribute such a share of his rights as is necessary for attain-ing that SECURITY that is essential freedom; and he is bound to make this contribution by the law of his nature; that is, by the command of his creator; therefore, he must submit his will, in what concerns all, to the will of the whole society. What does he lose by this submission? The power of doing injuries to others—the dread of suffering injuries from them—and the incommodities of mental or bodily weakness. What does he gain by it? The aid of those asso-ciated with him—protection against injuries from them or others—a capacity of enjoying his undelegated rights to the best advantage—a repeal of his fears—and tranquillity of mind—or, in other words, that perfect liberty better described in the Holy Scriptures, than any where else, in these expressions—"When every man shall sit under his vine, and under his fig tree, and NONE SHALL MAKE HIM AFRAID."

The like submission, with a correspondent expansion and accommodation, must be made between states, for the like benefits in a confederation. . . .

If, as some persons seem to think, a bill of rights is the best security of rights, the sover-eignties of the several states have this best security, for they are not barely declared to be rights, but are taken into it as component parts for their perpetual preservation by themselves. In short, the government of each state is, and is to be, sovereign and supreme in all matters that relate to each state only. It is to be subordinate barely in those matters that relate to the whole; and it will be their own faults, if the several states suffer the federal sovereignty to interfere in things of their respective jurisdictions. An instance of such interference with regard to any single state will be a dangerous precedent as to all, and therefore will be guarded against by all, as the trustees or servants of the several states will not dare, if they retain their senses, so to violate the independent sovereignty of their respective states, that justly darling object of American affections, to which they are responsible, besides being endeared by all the charities of life.

The common sense of mankind agrees to the devolution of individual wills in society; and if it has not been as universally assented to in confederation, the reasons are evident, and worthy of being retained in remembrance by Americans....

How beautifully and forcibly does the inspired Apostle Saint Paul, argue upon a sublimer subject, with a train of reasoning strictly applicable to the present? His words are—"If the foot shall say, because I am not the hand, I am not of the body; is it therefore not of the body? and if the ear shall say, because I am not the eye, I am not of the body; is it therefore not of the body?" As plainly inferring, as could be done in that allegorical manner, the strongest censure of such partial discontents, especially, as his meaning is enforced by his description of the benefits of union in these expressions—"But, now they are many members, yet but one body: and the eye cannot say to the hand, I have no need of thee again; nor again, the head to the feet, I have no need of you."

THOMAS JEFFERSON
Letter to Joseph Priestley

Though written constitutions may be violated in moments of passion or delusion, yet they furnish a text to which those who are watchful may again rally and recall the people; they fix too for the people the principles of their political creed.

SAMUEL ELIOT MORISON
The Wisdom of Benjamin Franklin

Franklin may...be considered one of the founding fathers of American democracy, since no democratic government can last long without conciliation and compromise.

Address in Favor of the Constitution

BENJAMIN FRANKLIN

Mr. President, I confess that I do not entirely approve of this Constitution at present, but Sir, I am not sure I shall never approve it: For having lived long, I have experienced many Instances of being oblig'd, by better Information or fuller Consideration, to change Opinions even on important Subjects, which I once thought right, but found to be otherwise. It is therefore that the older I grow the more apt I am to doubt my own Judgment, and to pay more Respect to the Judgment of others. Most Men indeed, as well as most Sects in Religion, think themselves in Possession of all Truth, and that wherever others differ from them it is far Error. Steele, a Protestant in a Dedication, tells the Pope, that the only Difference between our two Churches, in their Opinions of the Certainty of their Doctrine, is, the Romish Church is infallible, and the Church of England is never in the Wrong. But tho' many private Persons think almost as highly of their own infallibility, as of that of their Sect, few express it so naturally as a certain French Lady, who, in a little Dispute with her Sister, said, I don't know how it happens, Sister, but I meet with nobody but myself that's always in the right. *Il n'y a que moi qui a toujours raison.*

In these Sentiments, Sir, I agree to this Constitution, with all its Faults, if they are such; because I think a General Government necessary for us, and there is no Form of Government but what may be a Blessing to the People if well administered; and I believe farther that this is likely to be well administered for a Course of Years, and can only end in Despotism as other Forms have done before it when the People shall become so corrupted as to need Despotic Government, being incapable of any other. I doubt too whether any other Convention we can obtain may be able to make a better Constitution: For when you assemble a Number of Men to have the Advantage of their joint Wisdom, you inevitably assemble with those Men all their Prejudices, their Passions, their Errors of Opinion, their local Interests, and their selfish Views. From such an Assembly can a perfect Production be expected? It therefore astonishes me, Sir, to find this System approaching so near to Perfection as it does; and I think it will astonish our Enemies, who are waiting with Confidence to hear that our Councils are confounded, like those of the Builders of Babel, and that our States are on the Point of Separation, only to meet hereafter for the Purpose of cutting one another's Throats. Thus I consent, Sir, to this Constitution because I expect no better, and because I am sure that it is not the best. The Opinions I have had of its Errors, I sacrifice to the Public Good. I have never whisper'd a Syllable of them abroad. Within these Walls they were born, and here they shall die. If every one of us in returning to our Constituents were to report the Objections he has had to it, and use his Influence to gain partizans in support of them, we might prevent its being generally received, and thereby lose all the salutary Effects and great Advantages resulting naturally in our favor among foreign Nations, as well as among ourselves, from our real or apparent Unanimity. Much of the

Strength and Efficiency of any Government, in procuring and securing Happiness to the People, depends on Opinion, on the general Opinion of the Goodness of that Government as well as of the Wisdom and Integrity of its Governors. I hope therefore that for our own Sakes, as a part of the People, and for the sake of our Posterity, we shall act heartily and unanimously in recommending this Constitution, wherever our Influence may extend, and turn our future Thoughts and Endeavours to the Means of having it well administered.

On the whole, Sir, I cannot help expressing a Wish, that every Member of the Convention, who may still have Objections to it, would with me on this Occasion doubt a little of his own Infallibility, and to make manifest our Unanimity, put his Name to this Instrument.

AMBROSE BIERCE
The Devil's Dictionary

Compromise, n. Such an adjustment of conflicting interests as gives each adversary the satisfaction of thinking he has got what he ought not to have, and is deprived of nothing except what was justly his due.

JOHN F. KENNEDY
Profiles in Courage

Some of my colleagues who are criticized today for lack of forthright principles—or who are looked upon with scorn as compromising "politicians"—are simply engaged in the fine art of conciliating, balancing and interpreting the forces and factions of public opinion, an art essential to keeping our nation united and enabling our Government to function.

Inaugural Address
THOMAS JEFFERSON

Let us then, fellow citizens, unite with one heart and one mind; let us restore to social intercourse that harmony and affection without which liberty and even life itself are but dreary things. And let us reflect that, having banished from our land that religious intolerance under which mankind so long bled and suffered, we have yet gained little, if we countenance a political intolerance, as despotic, as wicked, and as capable of bitter and bloody persecutions. During the throes and convulsions of the ancient world, during the agonizing spasms of infuriated man, seeking through blood and slaughter his long-lost liberty, it was not wonderful that the agitation of the billows should reach even this distant and peaceful shore; that this should be more felt and feared by some, and less by others, and should divide opinions as to measures of safety; but every difference of opinion is not a difference of principle. We have called by different names brethren of the same principle. We are all Republicans; we are all Federalists. If there be any among us who wish to dissolve this Union, or to change its republican form, let them stand undisturbed as monuments of the safety with which error of opinion may be tolerated, where reason is left free to combat it. I know, indeed, that some honest men fear that a republican government cannot be strong, that this government is not strong enough. But would the honest patriot, in the full tide of successful experiment, abandon a government which has so far kept us free and firm, on the theoretic and visionary fear, that this government, the world's best hope, may, by possibility, want energy to preserve itself? I trust not. I believe this, on the contrary, the strongest government on earth. I believe it the only one where every man, at the call of the law, would fly to the standard of the law, and would meet invasion of the public order as his own personal concern. Sometimes it is said that man cannot be trusted with the government of himself. Can he, then, be trusted with the government of others? Or have we found angels, in the form of kings, to govern him? Let history answer this question.

Let us, then, with courage and confidence, pursue our own federal and republican principles, our attachment to union and representative government. Kindly separated by nature and a wide ocean from the exterminating havoc of one quarter of the globe; too high-minded to endure the degradation of the others, possessing a chosen country, with room enough for our descendants to the thousandth and thousandth generation, entertaining a due sense of our equal right to the use of our own facilities, to the acquisition of our own industry, to honor and confidence from our fellow citizens, resulting not from birth but from our actions and their sense of them, enlightened by a benign religion, professed in deed and practiced in various forms, yet all of them inculcating honesty, truth, temperance, gratitude, and the love of man, acknowledging and adorning an overruling Providence, which, by all its dispensations, proves that it delights in the happiness of man here, and his greater happiness hereafter—with all these blessings, what more is necessary to make us a happy and prosperous people? Still one thing more, fellow citizens, a wise and frugal government, which shall restrain men from injuring one another, shall leave them otherwise free to regulate their own pursuits of industry and improvement, and shall not take from the mouth of labor the bread it has earned. This is the sum of good government; and this is necessary to close the circle of our felicities.

Lincoln's Faith

ADLAI E. STEVENSON

In the near-century since his death, Abraham Lincoln has become a symbol and much more, not only to Americans, but to all men everywhere, a symbol of many facets, many meanings.

To Americans at large he is the President who saved the Union of States from self-destruction and freed a whole race of men from human bondage. To the informed student of history, he is the foremost defender of constitutional law. At home and abroad he is proof incontrovertible of the dream that brought the first settlers to our shores and has beckoned folk from other lands ever since, the core of the American philosophy—that in a free society a man can pull himself up by his own bootstraps. Lincoln did it. And so it can be done.

But the universality of his appeal is more than that, and is found in the character of the man himself. Other statesmen have become remote in greatness—Lincoln never did. He has lived on for the people as a man—a flesh and blood and bone human being, whose greatness they can accept because they can understand his origin, his ways, his talk and his laughter.

Perhaps it is his gift for language that has kept the image clear. An avid student of Shakespeare, Byron, Burns, Lincoln spoke oftenest in parables, illustrating a point with a homely story of frontier life, or even of animals in the manner of Aesop. "God tells the truth in parables," he is quoted as saying, "they are easier for the common folk to understand and recollect." And yet his great speeches—the farewell to his townfolk when he left Springfield, Illinois, for Washington, the Gettysburg address, the inaugurals and some of his messages to the United States Congress—soared to heights seldom approached by any other statesman in history.

However, Lincoln was more than a writer, a spokesman. What endears him in the minds of all freedom-loving people as the greatest democrat in our history—or any history—was his own faith in democracy, in the ability of the people to govern themselves. He based this faith in the Declaration of Independence, and spoke of it time and again, perhaps most succinctly on his way to Washington in February, 1861, before the New Jersey Senate. He recalled the revolutionary struggle and said:

"I am exceedingly anxious that that thing which they struggled for; that something even more than national independence; that something that held out a great promise to all people of the world for all time to come . . . shall be perpetuated in accordance with the original ideal for which the struggle was made, and I shall be most happy indeed if I shall be an humble instrument in the hands of the Almighty, and of this His almost chosen people, for perpetuating the object of that great struggle."

Lincoln regarded democracy as "the last, best hope of earth," as that form of government which promised "that in due time the weight would be lifted from the shoulders of all men."

He saw America as the trustee for humanity, and the terrible civil war, more costly in human lives than any other war in [our] history, as a testing of that trusteeship. The Union of

States was bound together by an idea—the idea that men are fit to govern themselves—and if the Union perished, the idea would perish with it. Slavery was only part of the issue—the excuse, but not the whole reason, for the war.

Very early in the conflict he explained his feeling to his young secretary, John Hay, saying, "For my part, I consider the central idea pervading this struggle is for the necessity that is upon us of proving that popular government is not an absurdity. We must settle this question now, whether in a free government the minority have the right to break up the government whenever they choose. If we fail it will go far to prove the incapability of the people to govern themselves." He expressed his faith most forcibly in the ringing closing of his speech at Gettysburg: "this nation, under God, shall have a new birth of freedom—and that government of the people, by the people, for the people, shall not perish from the earth."

Lincoln believed firmly in social evolution, a kind of inevitability for human development, and saw the democratic form of government as the most promising environment for that evolution. "We propose to give all a chance," he said, "and we expect the weak to grow stronger, the ignorant to grow wiser; and all better and happier together."

Lincoln, by his own acknowledgment, derived his political beliefs mostly from Thomas Jefferson. His own contributions to democratic thought consist solely of amplifications, extensions, and masterly expressions of it. Yet it is to Lincoln rather than to Jefferson that people in general look today as democracy's foremost spokesman and exemplar. If the supreme test of a democratic leader is his democratic faith, Lincoln stands pre-eminent. How did Lincoln arrive at this deep faith in mankind? Because he was one of them. He knew nothing of privilege; born in poverty, schooling himself, working incredibly hard for every personal advancement, he knew the people good and bad, ridiculous and sublime, and he believed there was more good than bad in most of them. He believed it so completely that he was willing to risk war to prove it.

And so we see ourselves in Lincoln, as he saw himself in people. That greatness in him—is there not some of it in my neighbor, myself, my son? Of course there is, we tell ourselves, for Lincoln was all of us—the spokesman for all that went before him in the building of America and everything we have fought since to preserve. And so, while statesmen come and statesmen go, Lincoln in his person and in his life work remains the greatest democrat of us all, and a continuing inspiration to all mankind.

THOMAS JEFFERSON
Letter to John Taylor

An association of men who will not quarrel with one another is a thing which never existed, from the greatest confederacy of nations down to a town meeting or a vestry.

"With Malice Toward None"
ABRAHAM LINCOLN'S SECOND INAUGURAL ADDRESS

Fellow Countrymen:

At this second appearing to take the oath of the presidential office, there is less occasion for an extended address than there was at the first. Then a statement, somewhat in detail, of a course to be pursued, seemed fitting and proper. Now, at the expiration of four years, during which public declarations have been constantly called forth on every point and phase of the great contest which still absorbs the attention, and engrosses the energies of the nation, little that is new could be presented. The progress of our arms, upon which all else chiefly depends, is as well known to the public as to myself; and it is, I trust, reasonably satisfactory and encouraging to all. With high hope for the future, no prediction in regard to it is ventured.

On the occasion corresponding to this four years ago, all thoughts were anxiously directed to an impending civil war. All dreaded it—all sought to avert it. While the inaugural address was being delivered from this place, devoted altogether to *saving* the Union without war, insurgent agents were in the city seeking to *destroy* it without war—seeking to dissolve the Union, and divide effects, by negotiation. Both parties deprecated war; but one of them would *make* war rather than let the nation survive; and the other would *accept* war rather than let it perish. And the war came.

One-eighth of the whole population were colored slaves, not distributed generally over the Union, but localized in the Southern part of it. These slaves constituted a peculiar and powerful interest. All knew that this interest was, somehow, the cause of the war. To strengthen, perpetuate, and extend this interest was the object for which the insurgents would rend the Union, even by war; while the government claimed no right to do more than to restrict the territorial enlargement of it. Neither party expected for the war the magnitude, or the duration, which it has already attained. Neither anticipated that the *cause* of the conflict might cease with, or even before, the conflict itself should cease. Each looked for an easier triumph, and a result less fundamental and astounding. Both read the same Bible, and pray to the same God; and each invokes His aid against the other. It may seem strange that any men should dare to ask a just God's assistance in wringing their bread from the sweat of other men's faces; but let us judge not that we be not judged. The prayers of both could not be answered; that of neither has been answered fully. The Almighty has His own purposes. "Woe unto the world because of offences! For it must needs be that offences come; but woe to that man by whom the offence cometh!" If we shall suppose that American Slavery is one of those offenses which, in the providence of God, must needs come, but which, having continued through His appointed time, He now wills to remove, and that He gives to both North and South, this terrible war, as the woe due to those by whom the offense came, shall we discern therein any departure from those divine attributes which the believers in a Living God always ascribe to

Him? Fondly do we hope—fervently do we pray—that this mighty scourge of war may speedily pass away. Yet, if God wills that it continue, until all the wealth plied by the bondman's two hundred and fifty years of unrequited toil shall be sunk, and until every drop of blood drawn with the lash, shall be paid by another drawn with the sword, as was said three thousand years ago, so still it must be said, "the judgments of the Lord, are true and righteous altogether."

With malice toward none; with charity for all; with firmness in the right, as God gives us to see the right, let us strive on to finish the work we are in; to bind up the nation's wounds; to care for him who shall have borne the battle, and for his widow, and his orphan—to do all which may achieve and cherish a just, and a lasting peace, among ourselves, and with all nations.

ULYSSES S. GRANT
Address to men after Lee's surrender

The war is over—the rebels are our countrymen again.

RANDOLPH RAY
New York World Telegram & Sun

I say, when there are spats, kiss and make up before the day is done and live to fight another day.

ABRAHAM LINCOLN
Message to Congress

Ballots are the rightful and peaceful successors to bullets.

LEARNED HAND
Speech, Federal Bar Association

Even though counting heads is not an ideal way to govern, at least it is better than breaking them.

H.L. MENCKEN
Minority Report

Voting is simply a way of determining which side is the stronger without putting it to the test of fighting.

LYNDON B. JOHNSON
Address on signing the voting-rights bill

The vote is the most powerful instrument ever devised by man for breaking down injustice and destroying the terrible walls which imprison men because they are different from other men.

HENRY WARD BEECHER
Proverbs from Plymouth Pulpit

A man without a vote is in this land like a man without a hand.

LOUIS L'AMOUR
Education of a Wandering Man

To make democracy work, we must be a nation of participants, not simply observers. One who does not vote has no right to complain.

SHIRLEY CHISOLM
Address to Congress

I believe that women have a special contribution to make to help bring order out of chaos in our nation because they have special qualities of leadership which are greatly needed today. And these qualities are the patience, tolerance, and perseverance which have developed in many women because of suppression. And if we can add to these qualities a reservoir of information about the techniques of community action, we can indeed become effective harbingers for change.

BARBARA EHRENREICH
"Teach Diversity with a Smile"

Racist, sexist, and homophobic thoughts cannot, alas, be abolished by fiat but only by the time-honored methods of persuasion, education and exposure to the other guy's—or excuse me, woman's—point of view.

JIMMY CARTER
Speech at Tuscumbia, Alabama

As a Southerner, it makes me feel angry when I see them [the Ku Klux Klan] with a Confederate battle flag, because I remember Judah P. Benjamin, who was Secretary of State; he was a Jew. And I remember General Pat Cleburne of Arkansas, who died in battle not far from this very spot, and General Beauregard of Louisiana—brave men. Both were Catholics.... And sometimes when I see the raising of a cross, and I remember that the One who was crucified taught us to have faith, to hope, and not to hate but to love one another.

H.L. Mencken
Minority Report

We must accept the other fellow's religion, but only in the sense and to the extent that we respect his theory that his wife is beautiful and his children smart.

Emily Dickinson

Some keep the Sabbath going to church;
I keep it staying at home,
With a bobolink for a chorister,
And an orchard for a dome.

Some keep the Sabbath in surplice;
I just wear my wings,
And instead of tolling the bell for church,
Our little sexton sings.

God preaches,—a noted clergyman,—
And the sermon is never long;
So instead of getting to heaven at last,
I'm going all along!

Thomas Jefferson
Letter to William Canby

He who steadily observes the moral precepts in which all religions concur, will never be questioned at the gates of heaven as to the dogmas in which they all differ.

On Religion

From Thomas Jefferson's Notes on Virginia

The legitimate powers of government extend to such acts only as are injurious to others. But it does me no injury for my neighbor to say there are twenty gods, or no God. It neither picks my pocket nor breaks my leg. If it be said, his testimony in a court of justice cannot be relied on, reject it then, and be the stigma on him. Constraint may make him worse by making him a hypocrite, but it will never make him a truer man. It may fix him obstinately in his errors, but will not cure them. Reason and free inquiry are the only effectual agents against error. Give a loose to them, they will support the true religion by bringing every false one to their tribunal, to the test of their investigation. They are the natural enemies of error and of error only. Had not the Roman government permitted free inquiry, Christianity could never have been introduced. Had not free inquiry been indulged at the era of the Reformation, the corruptions of Christianity could not have been purged away. If it be restrained now, the present corruptions will be protected, and new ones encouraged.

Was the government to prescribe to us our medicine and diet, our bodies would be in such keeping as our souls are now. Thus in France the emetic was once forbidden as a medicine, and the potato as an article of food. Government is just as infallible, too, when it fixed systems in physics. Galileo was sent to the Inquisition for affirming that the earth was a sphere; the government had declared it to be as flat as a trencher, and Galileo was obliged to abjure his error. This error, however, at length prevailed, the earth became a globe, and Descartes declared it was whirled round its axis by a vortex. The government in which he lived was wise enough to see that this was no question of civil jurisdiction, or we should all have been involved by authority in vortices. In fact, the vortices have been exploded, and the Newtonian principle of gravitation is now more firmly established, on the basis of reason, than it would be were the government to step in, and to make it an article of necessary faith.

Reason and experiment have been indulged, and error has fled before them. It is error alone which needs the support of government. Truth can stand by itself. Subject opinion to coercion: whom will you make your inquisitors? Fallible men; men governed by bad passions, by private as well as public reasons. And why subject it to coercion? To produce uniformity. But is uniformity of opinion desirable? No more than of face and stature. Introduce the bed of Procustes then, and as there is danger that the large men may beat the small, make us all of a size, by lopping the former and stretching the latter. Difference of opinion is advantageous to religion. The several sects perform the office of a *censor morum* over such other. Is uniformity attainable? Millions of innocent men, women, and children, since the introduction of Christianity, have been burnt, tortured, fined, imprisoned; yet we have not advanced one inch toward uniformity. What has been the effect of coercion? To make one-half the world fools, and the other half hypocrites, to support roguery and error all over the earth. Let us reflect that it is inhabited by a thousand millions of people. That these profess probably a thousand different systems of religion. That ours is but one of that thousand. That if there be but one right, and ours that one, we should wish to see the 999 wandering sects gathered into the fold of truth. But against such a majority we cannot effect this by force. Reason and persuasion are the only practicable instruments. To make way for these, free inquiry must be indulged; and how can we wish others to indulge it while we refuse it ourselves. No two, say I, have established the same. Is this a proof of the infallibility of establishments? Our sister states of Pennsylvania and

New York, however, have long subsisted without any establishment at all. The experiment was new and doubtful when they made it. It has answered beyond conception. They flourished infinitely. Religion is well supported to preserve peace and order; or if a sect arises, whose tenets should subvert morals, good sense has fair play, and reasons and laughs it out of doors, without suffering the state to be troubled with it. They do not hang more malefactors than we do. They are not more disturbed with religious dissensions. On the contrary, their harmony is unparalleled, and can be ascribed to nothing but their unbounded tolerance, because there is is no other circumstance in which they differ from every nation on earth. They have made the happy discovery that the way to silence religious disputes is to take no notice of them.

GEORGE WASHINGTON
Letter to United Baptist Chamber of Virginia

Every man, conducting himself as a good citizen, and being accountable to God alone for his religious opinions, ought to be protected in worshiping the Deity according to the dictates of his own conscience.

JOHN ADAMS
Letter to Benjamin Rush

The government of the United States of America is not in any sense founded on the Christian religion, as it has itself no character of enmity against the law, religion or tranquility of Musselmen.

The Bill for Establishing Religious Freedom
THOMAS JEFFERSON

Well aware that the opinions and belief of men depend not on their own will, but follow involuntarily the evidence proposed to their minds; that Almighty God hath created the mind free, and manifested his supreme will that free it shall remain by making it altogether insusceptible of restraint; that all attempts to influence it by temporal punishments, or burthens, or by civil incapacitations, tend only to beget habits of hypocrisy and meanness, and are a departure from the plan of the holy author of our religion, who being lord both of body and mind, yet chose not to propagate it by coercions on either, as was in his Almighty power to do, but to extend it by its influence on reason alone; that the impious presumption of legislators and rulers, civil as well as ecclesiastical, who, being themselves but fallible and uninspired men, have assumed dominion over the faith of others, setting up their own opinions and modes of thinking as the only true and infallible, and as such endeavoring to impose them on others, hath established and maintained false religions over the greatest part of the world and through all time: That to compel a man to furnish contributions of money for the propagation of opinions which he disbelieves and abhors, is sinful and tyrannical; that even the forcing him to support this or that teacher of his own religious persuasion, is depriving him of the comfortable liberty of giving his contributions to the particular pastor whose morals he would make his pattern, and whose power he feels most persuasive to righteousness; and is withdrawing from the ministry those temporary rewards, which proceeding from an approbation of their personal conduct, are an additional incitement to earnest and unremitting labors for the instruction of mankind; that our civil rights have no dependence on our religious opinions, any more than our opinions in physics or geometry; that therefore the proscribing of any citizen as unworthy of public confidence by laying upon him an incapacity of being called to offices of trust and emolument, unless he profess or renounce this or that religious opinion, is depriving him injuriously of those privileges and advantages to which, in common with his fellow citizens, he has a natural right; that it tends also to corrupt the principles of that very religion it is meant to encourage, by bribing, with a monopoly of worldly honors and emoluments, those who will externally profess and conform to it; that though indeed these are criminal who do not withstand such temptation, yet neither are those innocent who lay the bait in their way; that the opinions of men are not the object of civil government, nor under its jurisdiction; that to suffer the civil magistrate to intrude his powers into the field of opinion and to restrain the profession of propagation of principles on supposition of their ill tendency is a dangerous fallacy, which at once destroys all religious liberty, because he being of course judge of that tendency will make his opinions the rule of judgment, and approve or condemn the sentiments of others only as they shall square with or differ from his own; that is time enough for the rightful purposes of civil government for its officers to interfere when principles break out into overt acts against peace and good order; and finally, that truth is great and will prevail if left to herself; that she is the proper and sufficient antagonist to error, and has nothing to fear from conflict unless by human interposition disarmed of her natural weapons, free argument and debate; errors ceasing to be dangerous when it is permitted freely to contradict them.

We the General Assembly of Virginia do enact that no man shall be compelled to frequent or support any religious worship, place, or ministry whatsoever, nor shall be enforced, restrained, molested, or burthened in his body or goods, nor shall otherwise suffer, on account of his religious opinions or belief; but that all men shall be free to profess, and by argument to maintain, their opinions in matters of religion, and that the same shall in no wise diminish, enlarge, or affect their civil capacities.

And though we well know that this assembly, elected by the people for the ordinary purposes of legislation only, have no power to restrain the acts of succeeding Assemblies, constituted with powers equal to our own, and that therefore to declare this act irrevocable would be of no effect in law; yet we are free to declare, and do declare, that the rights hereby asserted are of the natural rights of mankind, and that if any act shall be hereafter passed to repeal the present or to narrow its operation, such act will be an infringement of natural right.

JAMES MADISON
Letter to Mordecai M. Noah

I have ever regarded the freedom of religious opinions and worship as equally belonging to every sect & the secure enjoyment of it as the best human provision for bringing all either into the same way of thinking, or into . . . mutual charity.

JAMES MADISON
Letter to F.L. Schaeffer

The experience of the United States is a happy disproof of the error so long rooted in the unenlightened minds of well-meaning Christians, as well as in the corrupt hearts of the persecuting usurpers, that without a legal incorporation of religious and civil polity, neither could be supported. A mutual independence is found most friendly to practical Religion, to social harmony, and to political prosperity.

"We also have a religion"
CHIEF RED JACKET SPEAKS

Brother, our seats were once large and yours were small. You have now become a great people, and we have scarcely a place left to spread our blankets. You have got your country, but are not satisfied; you want to force your religion upon us.

Brother, continue to listen.

You say that you are sent to instruct us how to worship the Great Spirit agreeably to his mind; and, if we do not take hold of the religion which you white people teach, we shall be unhappy hereafter. You say that you are right and we are lost. How do we know this to be true?

We understand that your religion is written in a book. If it was intended for us, as well as you, why has not the Great Spirit given it to us, and not only to us, but why did he not give to our forefathers the knowledge of that book, with the means of understanding it rightly. We only know what you tell us about it. How shall we know when to believe, being so often deceived by the white people?

Brother, you say there is but one way to worship the Great Spirit. If there is but one religion, why do you white people differ so much about it? Why do not all agree, as you can all read the book?

Brother, we do not understand these things. We are told that your religion was given to your forefathers and has been handed down from father to son. We also have a religion which was given to our forefathers and has been handed down to us, their children. We worship in that way. It teaches us to be thankful for all the favors we receive, to love each other, and to be united. We never quarrel about religion.

Brother, we do not wish to destroy your religion and take it from you. We only want to enjoy our own.

ROBERT H. JACKSON
Zorach v. Clausor, dissenting opinion

The day that this country ceases to be free for irreligion, it will cease to be free for religion.

SUPREME COURT JUSTICE TOM C. CLARK
Abington School District vs. Schempp

It is no defense to urge that the religious practices here may be relatively minor encroachments on the First Amendment. The breach of neutrality that is today a trickling stream may all too soon become a raging torrent.

The place of religion in our society is an exalted one, achieved through a long tradition of reliance on the home, the church and the inviolable citadel of the individual heart and mind. We have come to recognize through bitter experience that it is not within the power of government to invade that citadel, whether its purpose or effect be to aid or oppose, to advance or retard. In the relationship between man and religion, the State is firmly committed to a position of neutrality. Though the application of that rule requires interpretation of a delicate sort, the rule itself is clearly and concisely stated in the words of the First Amendment.

ULYSSES S. GRANT
Seventh annual message to Congress

Declare the church and state forever separate and distinct, but each free within their proper spheres.

THOMAS PAINE

As to religion, I hold it to be the indispensable duty of all government, to protect all conscientious professors thereof, and I know of no other business which government hath to do therewith. Let a man throw aside that narrowness of soul, that selfishness of principle, which the niggards of all professions are so unwilling to part with, and he will be at once delivered of his fears on that head. Suspicion is the companion of mean souls, and the bane of all good society. For myself I fully and conscientiously believe, that it is the will of the Almighty, that there should be diversity of religious opinions among us: It affords a larger field for our Christian kindness. Were we all of one way of thinking, our religious dispositions would want matter for probation; and on this liberal principle, I look on the various denominations among us, to be like children of the same family, differing only, in what is called their Christian names.

BARRY GOLDWATER

Religious factions will go on imposing their will on others unless the decent people connected to them recognize that religion has no place in public policy.

WILLIAM HOWARD TAFT

Anti-semitism is a noxious weed that should be cut out. It has no place in America.

ALFRED E. SMITH
Atlantic Monthly

I am unable to understand how anything I was taught to believe as a Catholic could possibly be in conflict with what is good citizenship. The essence of my faith is built upon the Commandments of God. The law of the land is built upon the Commandments of God. There can be no conflict between them.

What is the conflict about which you talk? It may exist in some lands which do not guarantee religious freedom. But in the wildest dreams of your imagination you cannot conjure up a possible conflict between religious principle and political duty in the United States except on the unthinkable hypothesis that some law were to be passed which violated the common morality of all God-fearing men. And if you can conjure up such a conflict, how would a Protestant resolve it? Obviously by the dictates of his conscience. That is exactly what a Catholic would do. There is no ecclesiastical tribunal which would have the slightest claim upon the obedience of Catholic communicants in the resolution of such a conflict.

HARRY S TRUMAN

All my life I have fought against prejudice and intolerance.

HARRY S TRUMAN
Speech, National Association for the Advancement of Colored People

We can no longer afford the luxury of a leisurely attack upon prejudice and discrimination. There is much that state and local governments can do in providing positive safeguards for civil rights. But we cannot any longer await the growth of a will to action in the slowest state or the most backward community. Our national government must show the way.

BERTOLT BRECHT
"To Posterity"

Even hatred of vileness
Distorts a man's features

HELEN KELLER
Optimism

No loss by flood and lightning, no destruction of cities and temples by the hostile forces of nature, has deprived man of so many noble lives and impulses as those which intolerance has destroyed.

AMBROSE BIERCE
The Devil's Dictionary

Prejudice, n. A vagrant opinion without visible means of support.

GROUCHO MARX
Comment while applying for membership in a country club

Since my little daughter is only half Jewish, would it be alright if she went into the pool only up to her waist.

MARK TWAIN

Travel is fatal to prejudice, bigotry and narrow-mindedness.

OLIVER WENDELL HOLMES, JR.

The mind of a bigot is like the pupil of the eye; the more light you pour upon it, the more it will contract.

EDWARD R. MURROW

Everyone is a prisoner of his own experiences. No one can eliminate prejudices—just recognize them.

BOB GIBSON

From Ghetto to Glory: The story of Bob Gibson

In a world filled with hate, prejudice, and protest, I find that I too am filled with hate, prejudice, and protest.

RUBIN HURRICANE CARTER

If I have learned anything in my life, it is that bitterness consumes the vessel that contains it.

BENJAMIN FRANKLIN

Search others for their Virtues, thyself for thy Vices.

WALT WHITMAN

In all people I see myself—none more, and not one a
  barleycorn less,
And the good or bad I say of myself, I say of them.

E.B. WHITE

"Coon Hunt," *One Man's Meat*

There would never be a moment, in war or in peace, when I wouldn't trade all the patriots in the country for one tolerant man. Or when I wouldn't swap the vitamins in a child's lunchbox for a jelly glass of magnanimity.

ISAAC BASHEVIS SINGER

Kindness, I've discovered, is everything in life.

RALPH WALDO EMERSON

You cannot do a kindness too soon, for you never know how soon it will be too late.

THOMAS PAINE
The American Crisis

If there must be trouble let it be in my day, that my child may have peace.

LYNDON B. JOHNSON

I do not want to be the President who built empires or sought grandeur or extended dominion. I want to be the President who helped the poor find their own way and who protected the right of every citizen to vote in every election. I want to be the President who helped end hatred among his fellow men.

MARTIN LUTHER KING, JR.
Speech accepting Nobel Peace Prize, Stockholm, Sweden

Nonviolence is the answer to the crucial political and moral questions of our time; the need for man to overcome oppression and violence without resorting to oppression and violence. Man must evolve for all human conflict a method which rejects revenge, aggression and retaliation. The foundation of such a method is love.

POWATAN
Speech to John Smith, Jamestown, Virginia

Why will you take by force what you may have quietly by love? Why will you destroy us who supply you with food? What can you get by war?...Take away your guns and swords, the cause of all our jealousy, or you may all die in the same manner.

GEORGE WASHINGTON
Letter to the Rev. Jonathan Boucher

Peace with all the world is my sincere wish. I am sure it is our true policy, and am persuaded it is the ardent desire of the government.

HENRY WADSWORTH LONGFELLOW
"The Song of Hiawatha"

Buried was the bloody hatchet,
Buried was the dreadful war-club,
Buried were all warlike weapons,
And the war-cry was forgotten,
There was peace among the nations.

Benjamin Harvey Hill
Tribute to Robert E. Lee

He [Lee] was a foe without hate, a friend without treachery, a soldier without cruelty, and a victim without murmuring. He was a public officer without vices, a private citizen without wrong, a neighbor without reproach, a Christian without hypocrisy, and man without guile. He was a Caesar without his ambition, a Frederick without his tyranny, a Napoleon without his selfishness, and a Washington without his reward.

Ulysses S. Grant
Speech accepting presidential nomination

Let us have peace.

Dwight D. Eisenhower
Speech in Frankfurt-am-Main, Germany

I say we are going to have peace even if we have to fight for it.

Harry S Truman

I want peace and I'm willing to fight for it.

Adlai E. Stevenson

Our first, our greatest, our most relentless purpose is peace. For without peace there is nothing.

Ralph Waldo Emerson
"Worship," *The Conduct of Life*

The real and lasting victories are those of peace, and not of war.

Alice Walker
Living by the Word

I remember when I used to dismiss the bumper sticker "Pray for Peace." I realize now that I did not understand it, since I also did not understand prayer; which I know now to be the active affirmation in the physical world of our inseparableness from the divine; and everything, especially the physical world, is divine. War will stop when we no longer praise it, or give it any attention at all. Peace will come wherever it is sincerely invited. Love will overflow every sanctuary given it. Truth will grow where the fertilizer that nourishes it is also truth. Faith will be its own reward.

A Prayer for Peace

WILLIAM SLOANE COFFIN

The Courage to Love

O God, who hast created a world beautiful beyond any singing of it, gratefully we acknowledge that of thy fullness have we received, grace upon grace. Grant now that we may be responsible in the measure that we have received.

Keep us eager to pursue truth beyond the outermost limits of human thought, scornful of the cowardice that dares not face new truth, the laziness content with half-truth, and the arrogance that thinks it knows all truth.

Strengthen our resolve to see fulfilled, the world around and in our time, all hopes for justice so long deferred, and keep us on the stony, long, and lonely road that leads to peace. May we think for peace, struggle for peace, suffer for peace. Fill our hearts with courage that we not give in to bitterness and self-pity, but learn rather to count pain and disappointment, humiliation and setback, as but straws on the tide of life.

So may we run and not grow weary, walk and not faint, until that day when by thy grace faith and hope will be outdistanced by sight and possession, and love will be all in all in this wonderful, terrible, beautiful world.

ABRAHAM LINCOLN

First Inaugural Address

I am loath to close. We are not enemies but friends. We must not be enemies. Though passion may have strained, it must not break our bonds of affection. The mystic chords of memory, stretching from every battlefield and patriot grave to every living heart and hearthstone all over this broad land, will yet swell the chorus of Union, when again touched, as surely they will be, by the better angels of our nature.

Provide for the Common Defense

INSCRIPTION ON THE TOMB OF THE UNKNOWN SOLDIER

Here Rests in
Honored Glory
An American
Soldier
Known But to God.

GENERAL DOUGLAS MACARTHUR
Speech to Congress

Their story is known to all of you. It is the story of the American man-at-arms. My estimate of him was formed on the battlefields many, many years ago, and has never changed. I regarded him then, as I regard him now, as one of the world's noblest figures—not only as one of the finest military characters, but also as one of the most stainless.

His name and fame are the birthright of every American citizen. In his youth and strength, his love and loyalty, he gave all that mortality can give. He needs no eulogy from me, or from any other man. He has written his own history and written it in red on his enemy's breast.

In twenty campaigns, on a hundred battlefields, around a thousand campfires, I have witnessed that enduring fortitude, that patriotic self-abnegation, and that invincible determination which have carved his statue in the hearts of his people.

From one end of the world to the other, he has drained deep the chalice of courage. As I listened to those songs in memory's eye, I could see those staggering columns of the First World War, bending under soggy packs on many a weary march, from dripping dusk to drizzling dawn, slogging ankle deep through mire of shell-pocked roads; to form grimly for the attack, blue-lipped, covered with sludge and mud, chilled by the wind and rain, driving home to their objective, and for many, to the judgment seat of God.

I do not know the dignity of their birth, but I do know the glory of their death. They died unquestioning, uncomplaining, with faith in their hearts, and on their lips the hope that we would go on to victory.

Always for them: duty, honor, country. Always their blood, and sweat, and tears, as they saw the way and the light. And twenty years after, on the other side of the globe, against the filth of dirty foxholes, the stench of ghostly trenches, the slime of dripping dugouts, those boiling suns of the relentless heat, those torrential rains of devastating storms, the loneliness and utter desolation of jungle trails, the bitterness of long separation of those they loved and cherished, the deadly pestilence of tropic disease, the horror of stricken areas of war.

HENRY DAVID THOREAU

Where there is a brave man, in the thickest of the fight, there is the post of honor.

PATRICK S. GILMORE
"When Johnny Comes Marching Home"

When Johnny comes marching home again,
Hurrah, Hurrah!
We'll give him a hearty welcome then,
Hurrah, Hurrah!
The men will cheer, and the boys will shout,
The ladies they will all turn out,
And we'll all feel gay,
When Johnny comes marching home!

The old church bell will peal with joy,
Hurrah! Hurrah!
To welcome home our darling boy,
Hurrah! Hurrah!
The village lads and lassies say
With roses they will strew the way,
And we'll all feel gay
When Johnny comes marching home.

Get ready for the Jubilee,
Hurrah! Hurrah!
We'll give the hero three times three,
Hurrah! Hurrah!
The laurel wreath is ready now

To place upon his loyal brow
And we'll all feel gay
When Johnny comes marching home.

HERBERT HOOVER
Speech at the Republican Party National Convention

Older men declare war. But it is youth that must fight and die. And it is youth who must inherit the tribulation, the sorrow, and the triumphs that are the aftermath of war.

GENERAL DOUGLAS MACARTHUR
Address, U.S. Military Academy, West Point, New York

The soldier, above all other people, prays for peace, for he must suffer and bear the deepest wounds and scars of war.

STEPHEN CRANE
"War is Kind"

Do not weep, maiden, for war is kind.
Because your lover threw wild hands toward the sky
And the affrighted steed ran on alone,
Do not weep.
War is kind.

    Hoarse, booming drums of the regiment,
    Little souls who thirst for fight,
    These men were born to drill and die.
    The unexplained glory flies above them,
    Great is the battle god, great, and his kingdom—
    A field where a thousand corpses lie.

Do not weep, babe, for war is kind.
Because your father tumbled in the yellow trenches,
Raged at his breast, gulped and died,
Do not weep.
War is kind.

    Swift blazing flag of the regiment,
    Eagle with crest of red and gold,
    These men were born to drill and die.

Point for them the virtue of slaughter,
Make plain to them the excellence of killing
And a field where a thousand corpses lie.

Mother whose heart hung humble as a button
On the bright splendid shroud of your son,
Do not weep.
War is kind.

ABRAHAM LINCOLN
First Inaugural Address

The mystic chords of memory, stretching from every battlefield and patriot grave to every living heart and hearthstone all over this broad land.

THEODORE O'HARA
"The Bivouac of the Dead"

The muffled drum's sad roll has beat
    The soldier's last tattoo;
No more on Life's parade shall meet
    That brave and fallen few.
On Fame's eternal camping-ground
    Their silent tents are spread,
And Glory guards with solemn round,
    The bivouac of the dead.

EMILY DICKINSON

That such have died enable us
The tranquiller to die;
That such have lived, certificate
For immortality.

Ernie's War

ERNIE PYLE

At the Front Lines in Italy, January 10, 1944—In this war I have known a lot of officers who were loved and respected by the soldiers under them. But never have I crossed the trail of any man as beloved as Capt. Henry T. Waskow of Belton, Texas.

Capt. Waskow was a company commander in the 36th Division. He had led his company since long before it left the States. He was very young, only in his middle twenties, but he carried in him a sincerity and gentleness that made people want to be guided by him.

"After my own father, he came next," a sergeant told me.

"He always looked after us," a soldier said. "He'd go to bat for us every time."

"I've never known him to do anything unfair," another one said.

I was at the foot of the mule trail the night they brought Capt. Waskow's body down. The moon was nearly full at the time, and you could see far up the trail and even part way across the valley below. Soldiers made shadows in the moonlight as they walked.

Dead men had been coming down the mountain all evening, lashed onto the backs of mules. They came lying belly-down across the wooden pack-saddles, their heads hanging down on the left side of the mule, their stiffened legs sticking out awkwardly from the other side, bobbing up and down as the mule walked.

The Italian mule-skinners were afraid to walk beside dead men, so Americans had to lead the mules down that night. Even the Americans were reluctant to unlash and lift the bodies at the bottom, so an officer had to do it himself, and ask others to help.

The first one came early in the morning. They slid him down from the mule and stood him on his feet for a moment, while they got a new grip. In the half light he might have been merely a sick man standing there, leaning on the others. Then they laid him on the ground in the shadow of the low stone wall alongside the road.

I don't know who that first one was. You feel small in the presence of dead men, and ashamed at being alive, and you don't ask silly questions.

We left him there beside the road, that first one, and we all went back into the cowshed and sat on water cans or lay on the straw, waiting for the next batch of mules.

Somebody said the dead soldier had been dead for four days, and then nobody said anything more about it. We talked soldier talk for an hour or more. The dead man lay all alone outside in the shadow of the low stone wall.

Then a soldier came into the cowshed and said there were some more bodies outside. We went out into the road. Four mules stood there, in the moonlight, in the road where the trail came down off the mountain. The soldiers who led them stood there waiting. "This one is Captain Waskow," one of them said quietly.

Two men unlashed his body from the mule and lifted it off and laid it in the shadow beside the low stone wall. Other men took the other bodies off. Finally there were five lying end to end in a long row, alongside the road. You don't cover up dead men in the combat zone. They just lie there in the shadows until somebody else comes after them.

The unburdened mules moved off to their olive orchard. The men in the road seemed reluctant to leave. They stood around, and gradually one by one I could sense them moving close to Capt. Waskow's body. Not so much to look, I think, as to say something in finality to him, and to themselves. I stood close by and I could hear.

One soldier came and looked down, and he said out loud, "God damn it." That's all he said, and then he walked away. Another one came. He said, "God damn it to hell anyway." He looked down for a few last moments, and then he turned and left.

Another man came; I think he was an officer. It was hard to tell officers from men in the half light, for all were bearded and grimy dirty. The man looked down into the dead captain's face, and then he spoke directly to him, as though he were alive. He said: "I'm sorry, old man."

Then a soldier came and stood beside the officer, and bent over, and he too spoke to his dead captain, not in a whisper but awfully tenderly, and he said:

"I sure am sorry, sir."

Then the first man squatted down, and he reached down and took the dead hand, and he sat there for a full five minutes, holding the dead hand in his own and looking intently into the dead face, and he never uttered a sound all the time he sat there.

And finally he put the hand down, and then reached up and gently straightened the points of the captain's shirt collar, and then he sort of rearranged the tattered edges of his uniform around the wound. And then he got up and walked away down the road in the moonlight, all alone.

WALT WHITMAN
"Vigil Strange I Kept on the Field One Night"

Vigil strange I kept on the field one night;
When you my son and my comrade dropt at my side that day,
One look I but gave which your dear eyes return'd with a look I
    shall never forget,
One touch of your hand to mine O boy, reach'd up as you lay on the
    ground,
Then onward I sped in the battle, the even-contested battle,
Till late in the night reliev'd to the place at last again I made my way,
Found you in death so cold, dear comrade, found your body son of
    responding kisses, (never again on earth responding,)

Bared your face in the starlight, curious the scene, cool blew the
    moderate night-wind,
Long there and then in vigil I stood, dimly around me the battle-field
    spreading,
Vigil wondrous and vigil sweet there in the fragrant silent night,
But not a tear fell, not even a long-drawn sigh, long, long I gazed,
Then on the earth partially reclining sat by your side leaning my
    chin in my hands,
Passing sweet hours, immortal and mystic hours with you dearest
    comrade—not a tear, not a word,
Vigil of silence, love and death, vigil for you my son and my soldier,
As onward silently stars aloft, eastward new ones upward stole,
Vigil final for you brave boy, (I could not save you, swift was your
    death,
I faithfully loved you and cared for you living, I think we shall surely
    meet again,)
Till at latest lingering of the night, indeed just as the dawn appear'd,
My comrade I wrapt in his blanket, envelop'd well his form,
Folded the blanket well, tucking it carefully over head and carefully
    under feet,
And there and then and bathed by the rising sun, my son in his
    grave, in his rude-dug grave I deposited,
Ending my vigil strange with that, vigil of night and battle-field dim,
Vigil for comrade swiftly slain, vigil I never forget, how as day
    brighten'd,
I rose from the chill ground and folded my soldier well in his
    blanket,
And buried him where he fell.

EUGENE V. DEBS

The master class has always declared the wars; the subject class has always fought the battles. The master class has had all to gain and nothing to lose, while the subject class has had nothing to gain and all to lose—especially their lives.

DICK GREGORY
Dick Gregory's Political Primer

I think it is reasonable that if we must continue to fight wars, they ought to be fought by those people who really want to fight them. Since it seems to be the top half of the generation gap that is the most enthusiastic about going to war, why not send the Old Folks Brigade to Vietnam—with John Wayne leading them?

SLOGAN USED DURING THE CONSCRIPTION RIOTS IN NEW YORK CITY
A rich man's war and a poor man's fight.

MARTIN LUTHER KING, JR.
Address given at Riverside Church

Perhaps the more tragic recognition of reality took place when it became clear to me that the war was doing far more than devastating the hopes of the poor at home. It was sending their sons and their brothers and their husbands to fight and to die in extraordinarily high proportions relative to the rest of the population. We were taking the black young men who had been crippled by our society and sending them 8,000 miles away to guarantee liberties in Southeast Asia which they had not found in Southwest Georgia and East Harlem. So we have been repeatedly faced with the cruel irony of watching Negro and white boys on TV screens as they kill and die together for a nation that has been unable to seat them together in the same schools. So we watch them in brutal solidarity burning the huts of a poor village but we realize that they would never live on the same block in Detroit.

BILL MAULDIN
Up Front, cartoon caption

He's right, Joe, when we ain't fightin we should act like sojers.

TRADITIONAL ARMY SONG
You're in the Army now
You're not behind a plow;
You'll never get rich,
A diggin' a ditch,
You're in the Army now.

You're in the Army now,
You're in the Army now,
You'll never get rich
On the salary which
You get in the Army now.

Ernie's War

ERNIE PYLE

Normandy Beachhead, June 17, 1944—In the preceding column we told about the D-day wreckage among our machines of war that were expended in taking one of the Normandy beaches.

But there is another and more human litter. It extends in a thin little line, just like a high-water mark, for miles along the beach. This is the strewn personal gear, gear that will never be needed again, of those who fought and died to give us our entrance into Europe.

Here in a jumbled row for mile on mile are soldiers' packs. Here are socks and shoe polish, sewing kits, diaries, Bibles and hand grenades. Here are the latest letters from home, with the address on each one neatly razored out—one of the security precautions enforced before the boys embarked.

Here are toothbrushes and razors, and snapshots of families back home staring up at you from the sand. Here are pocketbooks, metal mirrors, extra trousers, and bloody, abandoned shoes. Here are broken-handled shovels, and portable radios smashed almost beyond recognition, and mine detectors twisted and ruined.

Here are torn pistol belts and canvas water buckets, first-aid kits and jumbled heaps of lifebelts. I picked up a pocket Bible with a soldier's name in it, and put it in my jacket. I carried it half a mile or so and then put it back down on the beach. I don't know why I picked it up, or why I put it back down.

Soldiers carry strange things ashore with them. In every invasion you'll find at least one soldier hitting the beach at H-hour with a banjo slung over his shoulder. The most ironic piece of equipment marking our beach—this beach of first despair, then victory—is a tennis racket that some soldier had brought along. It lies lonesomely on the sand, clamped in its rack, not a string broken.

Two of the most dominant items in the beach refuse are cigarets and writing paper. Each soldier was issued a carton of cigarets just before he started. Today these cartons by the thousand, water-soaked and spilled out, mark the line of our first savage blow.

Writing paper and air-mail envelopes came second. The boys had intended to do a lot of writing in France. Letters that would have filled those blank, abandoned pages.

Always there are dogs in every invasion. There is a dog still on the beach today, still piti-fully looking for his masters.

He stays at the water's edge, near a boat that lies twisted and half sunk at the water line. He barks appealingly to every soldier who approaches, trots eagerly along with him for a few feet, and then, sensing himself unwanted in all this haste, runs back to wait in vain for his own people at his own empty boat.

Over and around this long thin line of personal anguish, fresh men today are rushing vast supplies to keep our armies pushing on into France. Other squads of men pick amidst the wreckage to salvage ammunition and equipment that are still usable.

Men worked and slept on the beach for days before the last D-day victim was taken away for burial.

I stepped over the form of one youngster whom I thought dead. But when I looked down I saw he was only sleeping. He was very young, and very tired. He lay on one elbow, his hand suspended in the air about six inches from the ground. And in the palm of his hand he held a large, smooth rock.

I stood and looked at him a long time. He seemed in his sleep to hold that rock lovingly, as though it were his last link with a vanishing world. I have no idea at all why he went to sleep with the rock in his hand, or what kept him from dropping it once he was asleep. It was just one of those little things without explanation that a person remembers for a long time.

The strong, swirling tides of the Normandy coastline shift the contours of the sandy beach as they move in and out. They carry soldiers' bodies out to sea, and later they return them. They cover the corpses of heroes with sand, and then in their whims they uncover them.

As I plowed out over the wet sand of the beach on that first day ashore, I walked around what seemed to be a couple of pieces of driftwood sticking out of the sand. But they weren't driftwood.

They were a soldier's two feet. He was completely covered by the shifting sands except for his feet. The toes of his GI shoes pointed toward the land he had come so far to see, and which he saw so briefly.

JOYCE KILMER
Rouge Bouquet

In a wood they call the Rouge Bouquet,
There is a new-made grave today,
Built by never a spade nor pick,
Yet covered with earth ten meters thick.

There lie many fighting men,
Dead in their youthful prime.
Never to laugh nor love again
Nor taste the Summertime.

The Things They Carried

TIM O'BRIEN

First Lieutenant Jimmy Cross carried letters from a girl named Martha, a junior at Mount Sebastian College in New Jersey. They were not love letters, but Lieutenant Cross was hoping, so he kept them folded in plastic at the bottom of his rucksack. In the late afternoon, after a day's march, he would dig his foxhole, wash his hands under a canteen, unwrap the letters, hold them with the tips of his fingers, and spend the last hour of light pretending. He would imagine romantic camping trips into the White Mountains in New Hampshire. He would sometimes taste the envelope flaps, knowing her tongue had been there. More than anything, he wanted Martha to love him as he loved her, but the letters were mostly chatty, elusive on the matter of love. She was a virgin, he was almost sure. She was an English major at Mount Sebastian, and she wrote beautifully about her professors and roommates and midterm exams, about her respect for Chaucer and her great affection for Virginia Woolf. She often quoted lines of poetry; she never mentioned the war except to say, Jimmy, take care of yourself. The letters weighed 10 ounces. They were signed Love, Martha, but Lieutenant Cross understood that Love was only a way of signing and did not mean what he sometimes pretended it meant. At dusk, he would carefully return the letters to his rucksack. Slowly, a bit distracted, he would get up and move among his men, checking the perimeter, then at full dark he would return to his hole and watch the night and wonder if Martha was a virgin.

The things they carried were largely determined by necessity. Among the necessities or near-necessities were P-38 can openers, pocket knives, heat tabs, wristwatches, dog tags, mosquito repellent, chewing gum, candy, cigarettes, salt tablets, packets of Kool-Aid, lighters, matches, sewing kits, Military Payment Certificates, C rations, and two or three canteens of water. Together, these items weighed between 15 and 20 pounds, depending upon a man's habit or rate of metabolism. Henry Dobbins, who was a big man, carried extra rations; he was especially fond of canned peaches in heavy syrup over pound cake. Dave Jensen, who practiced field hygiene, carried a toothbrush, dental floss, and several hotel-sized bars of soap he'd stolen on R&R in Sydney, Australia. Ted Lavender, who was scared, carried tranquilizers until he was shot in the head outside the village of Than Khe in mid-April. By necessity, and because it was SOP, they all carried steel helmets that weighed 5 pounds including the liner and camouflage cover. They carried the standard fatigue jackets and trousers. Very few carried underwear. On their feet they carried jungle boots—2.1 pounds—and David Jensen carried three pairs of socks and a can of Dr. Scholl's foot powder as a precaution against trench foot. Until he was shot, Ted Lavender carried six or seven ounces of premium dope, which for him was a necessity. Mitchell Sanders, the RTO, carried condoms. Norman Bowker carried a diary. Rat Kiley carried comic books. Kiowa, a devout Baptist, carried an illustrated New Testament that had been presented to him by his father, who taught Sunday school in Oklahoma City, Oklahoma. As a hedge against bad times, however, Kiowa also carried his grandmother's distrust of the white man, his grandfather's old hunting hatchet. Necessity dictated. Because the land was mined and booby-trapped, it was SOP for each man to carry a steel-centered, nylon-covered flask jacket, which weighed 6.7 pounds, but which on hot days seemed much heavier. Because you could die so quickly, each man carried at least one large compress bandage, usually in the helmet band for easy access. Because the nights were cold, and because the monsoons were wet, each carried a green plastic poncho that could be used as a raincoat or groundsheet or makeshift tent. With its quilted liner, the poncho weighed almost two pounds, but it was worth every ounce. In April, for instance, when Ted Lavender was shot, they used his poncho to wrap him up, then to carry him across the paddy, then to lift him into the chopper that took him away.

They were called legs or grunts.

To carry something was to hump it, as when Lieutenant Jimmy Cross humped his love for Martha up the hills and through the swamps. In its intransitive form, to hump meant to walk, or to march, but it implied burdens far beyond the intransitive.

Almost everyone humped photographs. In his wallet, Lieutenant Cross carried two photographs of Martha. The first was a Kodacolor snapshot signed Love, though he knew better. She stood against a brick wall. Her eyes were gray and neutral, her lips slightly open as she stared straight-on at the camera. At night, sometimes, Lieutenant Cross wondered who had taken the picture, because he knew she had boyfriends, because he loved her so much, and because he could see the shadow of the picture-taker spreading out against the brick wall. . . .

LOUIS UNTERMEYER
Reveille

What sudden bugle calls us in the night
And wakes us from a dream that we had shaped;
Flinging us sharply up against a fight
We thought we had escaped?

It is no easy waking, and we win
No final peace; our victories are few.
But still imperative forces pull us in
And sweep us somehow through.

Summoned by a supreme and confident power
That wakes our sleeping courage like a blow,
We rise, half-shaken, to the challenging hour,
And answer it—and go...

EDMUND WILSON
Patriotic Gore

Having myself lived through a couple of world wars and having read a certain amount of history, I am no longer disposed to take very seriously the professions of "war aims" that nations make. I think that it is a serious deficiency on the part of historians and political writers that they so rarely interest themselves in biological and zoological phenomena. In a recent Walt Disney film showing life at the bottom of the sea, a primitive organism called a sea slug is seen gobbling up smaller organisms through a large orifice at one end of its body; confronted with another sea slug of an only lightly lesser size, it ingurgitates that, too. Now, the wars fought by human beings are stimulated as a rule primarily by the same instincts as the voracity of the sea slug. It is true that among the animals other than man it is hard to find organized aggression of the kind that has been developed by humanity. There are perhaps only the army ants which have mastered a comparable technique. But baboons travel in gangs; small birds will gang up on an owl; bees will defend a hive. The anthropoid gorilla, it seems, is now one of the least pugnacious of mammals: he lives in a family tree and does not molest the homes of others; but there is evidence that primitive man had to fight to defend his home. In any case, all animals must prey on some form of life that they can capture, and all will eat as much as they can. The difference in this respect between man and the other forms of life is that man has succeeded in cultivating enough of what he calls "morality" and "reason" to justify what he is doing in terms of what he calls "virtue" and "civilization."

GEORGE WASHINGTON
Letter to George Mason

That no man should scruple, or hesitate a moment to use arms in defense of so valuable a blessing [as freedom], on which all the good and evil of life depends, is clearly my opinion; yet arms...should be the last resource.

THOMAS JEFFERSON
Letter to Thomas Barclay

[We] prefer war in all cases to tribute under any form, and to any people whatever.

JAMES A. GARFIELD
Speech in the House of Representatives

A nation is not worthy to be saved if, in the hour of its fate, it will not gather up all its jewels of manhood and life, and go down into the conflict, however bloody and doubtful, resolved on measureless ruin or complete success.

THEODORE ROOSEVELT
Annual message to Congress

War is not merely justifiable, but imperative, upon honorable men, upon an honorable nation, where peace can only be obtained by the sacrifice of conscientious conviction or of national welfare.

THEODORE ROOSEVELT

We are fighting in the quarrel of civilization against barbarism, of liberty against tyranny. Germany has become a menace to the whole world. She is the most dangerous enemy of liberty now existing.

THEODORE ROOSEVELT
Annual message to Congress

A just war is in the long run far better for a nation's soul than the most prosperous peace obtained by acquiescence in wrong or injustice. Moreover, though it is criminal for a nation not to prepare for war, so that it may escape the dreadful consequences of being defeated in war, yet it must always be remembered that even to be defeated in war may be better than not to have fought at all.

WILLIAM GRAHAM SUMNER
"War," War and Other Essays

The four great motives which move men to social activity are hunger, love, vanity, and fear of superior powers. If we search out the causes which have moved men to war we find them under each of these motives or interests.

WOODROW WILSON
Address to Congress

The world must be made safe for democracy.

WOODROW WILSON
Versailles Peace Conference

Tell me what's right and I'll fight for it.

H.L. MENCKEN
Prejudices, Fifth Series

There is no record in history of a nation that ever gained anything valuable by being unable to defend itself.

FRANKLIN D. ROOSEVELT

The core of our defense is the faith we have in the institutions we defend.

FRANKLIN D. ROOSEVELT
Fireside chat

We must be the great arsenal of democracy.

FRANKLIN D. ROOSEVELT
Message to Young Democrats Convention

Against naked force the only possible defense is naked force. The aggressor makes the rules for such a war; the defenders have no alternative but matching destruction with more destruction, slaughter with greater slaughter.

MAX LERNER
"The Negroes and the Draft," Actions and Passions

It is not the armed forces which can protect our democracy. It is the moral strength of democracy which alone can give any meaning to the efforts at military security.

JOHN F. KENNEDY
Address at El Boxque housing project, Costa Rica

Democracy is never a final achievement. It is a call to untiring effort, to continual sacrifice and to the willingness, if necessary, to die in its defense.

LYNDON B. JOHNSON

In short...we must be constantly prepared for the worst, and constantly acting for the best...strong enough to win a war and...wise enough to prevent one.

CALVIN COOLIDGE

No nation ever had an army large enough to guarantee it against attack in time of peace or ensure it victory in time of war.

YANKEE DOODLE DANDY

Fath'r and I went down to camp,
Along with Captain Goodin',
And there we saw the men and boys,
As thick as hasty puddin'.

Yankee Doodle keep it up,
Yankee Doodle Dandy,
Mind the music and the step,
And with the girls be handy.

And there we saw a thousand men,
As rich as Squire David;
And what they wasted ev'ry day,
I wish it could be saved.

And there was Captain Washington
Upon a slapping stallion,
A-giving orders to his men;
I guess there was a million.

And then the feathers on his hat,
They looked so 'tarnal fine, ah!
I wanted peskily to get
To give to my Jemima.

And there I saw a little keg,
Its heads were made of leather,
They knocked upon't with little sticks,
To call the folks together.

And there they'd fife away like fun,
And play on cornstalk fiddles,
And some had ribbons red as blood,
All bound about their middles.

The troopers, too, would gallop up
And fire right in our faces;
It scared me almost half to death
To see them run such races.

Uncle Sam came there to change
Some pancakes and some onions,
For 'lasses cake to carry home
To give his wife and young ones.

But I can't tell half I see,
They kept up such a smother;
So I took my hat off, made a bow,
And scampered home to mother.

Yankee Doodle keep it up,
Yankee Doodle Dandy,
Mind the music and the step,
And with the girls be handy.

GEORGE WASHINGTON
Letter to Martha Washington

My Dearest: I am now set down to write to you on a subject which fills me with inexpressible concern, and this concern is greatly aggravated and increased when I reflect upon the uneasiness I know it will give you. It has been determined in Congress that the whole army raised for the defense of the American cause shall be put under my care, and that it is necessary for me to proceed immediately to Boston to take upon me the command of it.

You may believe me, my dear Patsy, when I assure you, in the most solemn manner, that, so far from seeking this appointment, I have used every endeavor in my power to avoid it, not only from my unwillingness to part with you and the family, but from a consciousness of its being a trust too great for my capacity...But as it has been a kind of destiny that has thrown me upon this service, I shall hope that my undertaking is designed to answer some good purpose.

GEORGE WASHINGTON
Letter to regimental commanders

Put none but Americans on guard to-night.

HENRY WADSWORTH LONGFELLOW
Tales of a Wayside Inn, pt. I, The Landlord's Tale: Paul Revere's Ride

> It was one by the village clock,
> When he galloped into Lexington.
> He saw the gilded weathercock
> Swim in the moonlight as he passed,
> And the meeting-house windows, blank and bare,
> Gaze at him with a spectral glare,
> As if they already stood aghast
> At the bloody work they would look upon.
>
> It was two by the village clock,
> When he came to the bridge in Concord town.
> He heard the bleating of the flock,
> And the twitter of birds among the trees,
> and felt the breath of the morning breeze
> Blowing over the meadows brown.
> And one was safe and asleep in his bed
> Who at the bridge would be first to fall,
> Who that day would be lying dead,
> Pierced by a British musket-ball.
>
> You know the rest. In the books you have read,
> How the British Regulars fired and fled—
> How the farmers gave them ball for ball,
> From behind each fence and farmyard wall,
> Chasing the redcoats down the lane,
> Then crossing the fields to emerge again
> Under the trees at the turn of the road,
> And only pausing to fire and load.

So through the night rode Paul Revere;
And so through the night went his cry of alarm
To every Middlesex village and farm
A cry of defiance and not of fear,
A voice in the darkness, a knock at the door,
And a word that shall echo forevermore!
For, borne on the night wind of the past,
Through all our history, to the last,
In the hour of darkness and peril and need,
The people will waken and listen to hear
The hurrying hoofbeats of that steed
And the midnight message of Paul Revere.

JOHN PAUL JONES

Attributed. Aboard the Bonhomme Richard

I have not yet begun to fight.

OLIVER HAZARD PERRY

*Dispatch from U.S. Brig Niagara to General William Henry Harrison,
announcing his victory at the battle of Lake Erie*

We have met the enemy and they are ours: two ships, two brigs, one schooner, and one sloop.

ATTRIBUTED TO CAPTAIN JAMES LAWRENCE,
COMMANDER OF THE AMERICAN FRIGATE, CHESAPEAKE

*Remarks made during her fight with the British ship, Shannon. Fatally wounded early in the action,
he is said to have kept crying these words from the cockpit until the last.*

Keep the guns going! Fight her till she strikes or sinks! Don't give up the ship!

AN ORDINANCE TO DISSOLVE THE UNION BETWEEN THE STATE OF SOUTH CAROLINA
AND OTHER STATES UNITED WITH HER UNDER THE COMPACT ENTITLED
THE CONSTITUTION OF THE UNITED STATES OF AMERICA

We, the people of the State of South Carolina, in Convention assembled, do declare and ordain, and it is hereby declared and ordained, that the ordinance adopted by us in Convention, on the 23rd day of May, in the year of our Lord 1788, whereby the Constitution of the United States of America was ratified, and also all Acts and parts of Acts of the General Assembly of this State ratifying amendments of the said Constitution are hereby repealed; and that the union now subsisting between South Carolina and other States, under the name of the United States of America, is hereby dissolved.

LUCY LARCOM

April 14: This day broke upon our country in gloom; for the sounds of war came up to us from the South,—war between brethren; civil war; well may "all faces gather blackness." And yet the gloom we feel ought to be the result of sorrow for the erring, for the violators of national unity, for those who are in black rebellion against truth, freedom, and peace. The rebels have struck the first blow, and what ruin they are pulling down on their heads may be guessed though not yet fully foretold; but it is plain to see that a dark prospect is before them, since they have no high principle at the heart of their cause.

It will be no pleasure to any American to remember that he lived in this revolution, when brother lifted his hand against brother; and the fear is, that we shall forget that we are brethren still, though some are so unreasonable and wander so far from the true principles of national prosperity. Though the clouds of this morning have cleared away into brightness, it seems as if we could feel the thunder of those deadly echoes passing to and from Fort Sumter. But there is a right, and God always defends it. War is not according to His wish; though it seems one of the permitted evils yet. He will scatter those who delight in it, and it is not too much to hope and expect that He will uphold the government which has so long been trying to avert bloodshed.

April 21. The conflict is deepening; but thanks to God, there is no wavering, no division, now, at the North! All are united, as one man; and from a peaceful, unwarlike people, we are transformed into an army, ready for the battle at a moment's warning.

The few days I have passed in Boston this week are the only days in which I ever carried my heart into a crowd, or hung around a company of soldiers with anything like pleasure. But I felt a soldier-spirit rising within me, when I saw the men of my native town armed and going to risk their lives for their country's sake; and the dear old flag of our Union is a thousand times more dear than ever before. The streets of Boston were almost canopied with the stars and stripes, and the merchants festooned their shops with the richest goods of the national colors.

And now there are rumors of mobs attacking our troops, of bridges burnt, and arsenals exploded, and many lives lost. The floodgates of war are opened, and when the tide of blood will cease, none can tell.

PROVIDE FOR THE COMMON DEFENSE

GENERAL WILLIAM TECUMSEH SHERMAN
His signal to General Corse from the top of Kenesaw Mountain,
when Corse was attacked at Allatoona

Hold the fort, for I am coming!

ETHEL LYNN BEERS
The Picket Guard, printed in Harper's Weekly

"All quiet along the Potomac," they said,
"Except, now and then a stray picket
  Is shot as he walks on his beat to and fro
  By a rifleman hid in the thicket."

CARL SANDBURG
Among the Red Guns

Among the red guns,
In the hearts of soldiers
Running free blood
In the long, long campaign:
    Dreams go on.

Among the leather saddles,
In the heads of soldiers
Heavy in the wracks and kills
Of all straight fighting:
    Dreams go on.

Among the hot muzzles,
In the hands of soldiers
Brought from flesh-folds of women—
Soft amid the blood and crying—
In all your hearts and head
Among the guns and saddles and muzzles:
    Dreams,
Dreams go on,
Out of the dead on their backs,
Broken and no use any more:
Dreams of the way and the end go on.

If Grant Had Been Drinking at Appomattox

JAMES THURBER

The morning of the ninth of April 1865, dawned beautifully. General Meade was up with the first streaks of crimson in the eastern sky. General Hooker and General Burnside were up, and had breakfasted, by a quarter after eight. The day continued beautiful. It drew on toward eleven o'clock. General Ulysses S. Grant was still not up. He was asleep in his famous old navy hammock, swung high above the floor of his headquarters' bedroom. Headquarters was distressingly disarranged: papers were strewn on the floor; confidential notes from spies scurried here and there in the breeze from an open window; the dregs of an overturned bottle of wine flowed pinkly across an important military map.

Corporal Shultz, of the Sixty-fifth Ohio Volunteer Infantry, aide to General Grant, came into the outer room, looked around him, and sighed. He entered the bedroom and shook the General's hammock roughly. General Ulysses S. Grant opened one eye.

"Pardon, sir," said Corporal Shultz, "but this is the day of surrender. You ought to be up, sir."

"Don't swing me," said Grant, sharply, for his aide was making the hammock sway gently. "I feel terrible," he added, and he turned over and closed his eye again.

"General Lee will be here any minute now," said the Corporal firmly, swinging the hammock again.

"Will you cut that out?" roared Grant. "D'ya want to make me sick, or what?" Shultz clicked his heels and saluted. "What's he coming here for?" asked the General.

"This is the day of surrender, sir," said Shultz. Grant grunted bitterly.

"Three hundred and fifty generals in the Northern armies," said Grant, "and he has to come to *me* about this. What time is it?"

"You're the Commander-in-Chief, that's why," said Corporal Shultz. "It's eleven twenty-five, sir."

"Don't be crazy," said Grant. "Lincoln is the Commander-in-Chief. Nobody in the history of the world ever surrendered before lunch. Doesn't he know that any army surrenders on its stomach?" He pulled a blanket up over his head and settled himself again.

"The generals of the Confederacy will be here any minute now," said the Corporal. "You really ought to be up, sir."

Grant stretched his arms above his head and yawned.

"All right, all right," he said. He rose to a sitting position and stared about the room. "This place looks awful," he growled.

"You must have had quite a time of it last night, sir," ventured Shultz.

"Yeh," said General Grant, looking around for his clothes. "I was wrassling some general. Some general with a beard."

Schultz helped the commander of the Northern armies in the field to find his clothes.

"Where's my other sock?" demanded Grant. Schultz began to look around for it. The General walked uncertainly to a table and poured a drink from a bottle.

"I don't think it's wise to drink, sir," said Shultz.

"Nev' mind about me," said Grant, helping himself to a second, "I can take it or let it alone. Didn' ya ever hear the story about the fella went to Lincoln to complain about me drinking too much? 'So-and-So says Grant drinks too much,' this fella said. 'So-and-so is a fool,' said Lincoln. So this fella went to What's-His-Name and told him what Lincoln said and he came roarin' to Lincoln about it. 'Did you tell So-and-So I was a fool?' he said. 'No,' said Lincoln, 'I thought he knew it.'" The General smiled, reminiscently, and had another drink. "*That's* how I stand with Lincoln," he said proudly.

The soft thudding sound of horses' hooves came through the open window. Shultz hurriedly walked over and looked out.

"Hoof steps," said Grant, with a curious chortle.

"It is General Lee and his staff," said Shultz.

"Show him in," said the General, taking another drink. "And see what the boys in the back room will have."

Shultz walked smartly over to the door, opened it, saluted, and stood aside. General Lee, dignified against the blue of the April sky, magnificent in his dress uniform, stood for a moment framed in the doorway. He walked in, followed by his staff. They bowed, and stood silent. General Grant stared at them. He only had one boot on and his jacket was unbuttoned.

"I know who you are," said Grant. "You're Robert Browning, the poet."

"This is General Robert E. Lee," said one of his staff, coldly.

"Oh," said Grant. "I thought he was Robert Browning. He certainly looks like Robert Browning. There was a poet for you, Lee: Browning. Did ja ever read 'How They Brought the Good News from Ghent to Aix'? "'Up Derek, to saddle, up Derek, away; up Dunder, up Blitzen, up Prancer, up Dancer, up Bouncer, up Vixen, up—'"

"Shall we proceed at once to the matter in hand?" asked General Lee, his eyes disdainfully taking in the disordered room.

"Some of the boys was wrassling here last night," explained Grant. "I threw Sherman, or some general a whole lot like Sherman. It was pretty dark." He handed a bottle of Scotch to the commanding officer of the Southern armies, who stood holding it, in amazement and discomfiture. "Get a glass, somebody," said Grant, looking straight at General Longstreet. "Didn't I meet you at Cold Harbor?" he asked. General Longstreet did not answer.

"I should like to have this over with as soon as possible," said Lee. Grant looked vaguely at Shultz, who walked up close to him, frowning.

"The surrender, sir, the surrender," said Corporal Shultz in a whisper.

"Oh sure, sure," said Grant. He took another drink. "All right," he said. "Here we go." Slowly, sadly, he unbuckled his sword. Then he handed it to the astonished Lee. "There you are, General," said Grant. "We dam' near licked you. If I'd been feeling better we *would* of licked you."

ABRAHAM LINCOLN
Response to comments about General Grant's drinking, printed in the New York Herald

Tell me the brand of whiskey that Grant drinks. I would like to send a barrel of it to my other generals.

ULYSSES S. GRANT
Reply to General Simon B. Buckner

No terms except an unconditional and immediate surrender can be accepted. I propose to move immediately upon your work.

FRANCIS MILES FINCH
The Blue and the Gray

No more shall the war-cry sever,
Or the winding rivers be red;
They banish our anger forever,
When they laurel the graves of our dead.
Under the sod and the dew,
Waiting the judgment day;
Love and tears for the Blue;
Tears and love for the Gray.

WOODROW WILSON
Memorial Day address, Arlington National Cemetery

We are constantly thinking of the great war...which saved the Union...but it was a war that did a great deal more than that. It created in this country what had never existed before—a national consciousness. It was not the salvation of the Union, it was the rebirth of the Union.

The Latest Improvements in Artillery

ORPHEUS C. KERR

By invitation of a well-known official, I visited the Navy-yard yesterday, and witnessed the trial of some newly-invented rifled cannon. The trial was of short duration, and the jury brought in a verdict of "innocent of any intent to kill."

The first gun tried was similar to those used in the Revolution, except that it had a larger touch-hole, and the carriage was painted green, instead of blue. This novel and ingenious weapon was pointed at a target about sixty yards distant. It didn't hit it, and as nobody saw any ball, there was much perplexity expressed. A midshipman did say that he thought the ball must have run out of the touch-hole when they loaded up—for which he was instantly expelled from the service. After a long search without finding the ball, there was some thought of summoning the Naval Retiring Board to decide on the matter, when somebody happened to look into the mouth of the cannon, and discovered that the ball hadn't gone out at all. The inventor said this would happen sometimes, especially if you didn't put a brick over the touch-hole when you fired the gun. The Government was so pleased with this explanation, that it ordered forty of the guns on the spot, at two hundred thousand dollars apiece. The guns to be furnished as soon as the war is over.

The next weapon tried was Jink's double back-action, revolving cannon for ferry-boats. It consists of a heavy bronze tube, revolving on a pivot, with both ends open, and a touch-hole in the middle. While one gunner puts a load in at one end, another puts in a load at the other end, and one touch-hole serves for both. Upon applying the match, the gun is whirled swiftly round on a pivot, and both balls fly out in circles, causing great slaughter on both sides. This terrible engine was aimed at the target with great accuracy; but as the gunner has a large family dependent on him for support, he refused to apply the match. The Government was satisfied without firing, and ordered six of the guns at a million dollars apiece. The guns to be furnished in time for our next war.

The last weapon subject to trial was a mountain howitzer of a new pattern. The inventor explained that its great advantage was, that it required no powder. In battle it is placed on the top of a high mountain, and a ball slipped loosely into it. As the enemy passes the foot of the mountain, the gunner in charge tips over the howitzer, and the ball rolls down the side of the mountain into the midst of the doomed foe. The range of this terrible weapon depends greatly on the height of the mountain and the distance to its base. The Government ordered forty of these mountain howitzers at a hundred thousand dollars apiece, to be planted on the first mountains discovered in the enemy's country.

These are great times for gunsmiths, my boy; and if you find any old cannon around the junk-shop, just send them along.

There is much sensation in nautical circles arising from the immoral conduct of the rebel privateers; but public feeling has been somewhat easier since the invention of a craft for capturing the pirates, by an ingenious Connecticut chap. Yesterday he exhibited a small model of it at a cabinet meeting, and explained it thus:

"You will perceive," says he to the President, "that the machine itself will only be four times the size of the Great Easter, and need not cost over a few millions of dollars. I have only got to discover one thing before I can make it perfect. You will observe that it has a steam-engine on board. This engine works a pair of immense iron clamps, which are let down into the water from the extreme end of a very lengthy horizontal spar. Upon approaching the pirate, the captain orders the engineer to put on steam. Instantly the clamps descend from the end of the spar and clutch the privateer athwartships. Then the engine is reversed, the privateer is lifted bodily out of the water, the spar swings around over the deck, and the pirate ship is let down into the hold by the run. Then shut your hatches, and you have ship and pirates safe and sound.

The President's gothic features lighted up beautifully at the words of the great inventor; but in a moment they assumed an expression of doubt, and says he:

"But how are you going to manage, if the privateer fires upon you while you are doing this?"

"My dear sir," says the inventor, "I told you I had only one thing to discover before I could make the machine perfect, and that's it."

So you see, my boy, there's a prospect of our doing something on the ocean next century, and there's only one thing in the way of our taking in pirates by the cargo.

Last evening a new brigadier-general, aged ninety-four years, made a speech to Regiment Five, Mackerel Brigade, and then furnished each man with a lead pencil. He said that, as the Government was disappointed about receiving some provisions it had ordered for the troops, those pencils were intended to enable them to draw their rations as usual. I got a very big pencil, my boy, and have lived on a sheet of paper ever since.

WOODROW WILSON
Declaration of World War I

It is a distressing and oppressive duty, gentlemen of the Congress, which I have performed in thus addressing you. There are, it may be, many months of fiery trial and sacrifice ahead of us. It is a fearful thing to lead this great peaceful people into war, into the most terrible and disastrous of all ways, civilization itself seeming to be in the balance. But the right is more precious than peace, and we shall fight for the things which we have always carried nearest our hearts—for democracy, for the right of those who submit to authority to have a voice in their own governments, for the rights and liberties of small nations, for a universal dominion of right by such a concert of free peoples as shall bring peace and safety to all nations and make the world itself at last free. To such a task we can dedicate our lives and our fortunes, everything that we are and everything that we have with the pride of those who know that the day has come when America is privileged to spend her blood and her might for the principles that gave her birth and happiness and the peace which she has treasured. God helping her, she can do no other.

"A War Against All Nations..."

WOODROW WILSON

It is a war against all nations. American ships have been sunk, American lives taken, in ways which it has stirred us very deeply to learn of, but the ships and people of other neutral and friendly nations have been sunk and overwhelmed in the waters in the same way. There has been no discrimination. The challenge is to all mankind. Each nation must decide for itself how it will meet it. The choice we make for ourselves must be made with a moderation of counsel and a temperatenness of judgment befitting our character and our motives as a nation. We must put excited feeling away. Our motive will not be revenged on the victorious assertion of the physical might of the nation, but only the vindication of right, of human right, of which we are only a single champion.

When I addressed the Congress on the twenty-sixth of February last I thought that it would suffice to assert our neutral rights with arms, our right to use the seas against unlawful interference, our right to keep our people safe against unlawful violence. But armed neutrality, it now appears, is impracticable. Because submarines are in effect outlaws when used as the German submarines have been used against merchant shipping, it is impossible to defend ships against their attacks as the law of nations has assumed that merchantmen would defend themselves against privateers or cruisers, visible craft giving chase upon the open sea. It is common prudence in such circumstances, grim necessity indeed, to endeavor to destroy them before they have shown their own intention. They must be dealt with upon sight, if dealt with at all. The German Government denies the right of neutrals to use arms at all within the areas of the sea which it has proscribed, even in the defense of rights which no modern publicist has ever before questioned their right to defend. The intimidation is conveyed that the armed guards which we have placed on our merchant ships will be treated as beyond the pale of law and subject to be dealt with as pirates would be. Armed neutrality is ineffectual enough at best; in such circumstances and in the face of such pretensions it is worse than ineffectual; it is likely only to produce what it was meant to prevent; it is practically certain to draw us into the war without either the rights or the effectiveness of belligerents. There is one choice we cannot make, we are incapable of making: we will not choose the path of submission and suffer the most sacred rights of our nation and our people to be ignored or violated. The wrongs against which we now array ourselves are no common wrongs: they cut to the very roots of human life.

With a profound sense of the solemn and even tragical character of the step I am taking and of the grave responsibilities which it involves, but in unhesitating obedience to what I deem my constitutional duty, I advise that the Congress declare the recent course of the Imperial German Government to be in fact nothing less than war against the government and people of the United States; that it formally accept the status of belligerent which has thus been thrust upon it; and that it take immediate steps not only to put the country in a more thorough state of defense but also to exert all its power and employ all its resources to bring the Government of the German Empire to terms and end the war.

EDMUND L. GRUBER
The Caisson Song

Over hill, over dale,
We have hit the dusty trail,
And those caissons go rolling along.
"Counter March! Right about!"
Hear those wagon soldiers shout,
While those caissons go rolling along.
For it's Hi! Hi! Hee!
In the Field Artillery,
Call off your numbers loud and strong!
And where e'er we go,
You will always know
That those caissons are rolling along.

To the Front, day and night,
Where the dough-boys dig and fight,
And those caissons go rolling along.
Our barrage will be there,
Fired on the rocket's flare,
Where those caissons go rolling along.
For it's Hi! Hi! Hee!
In the Field Artillery,
Call off your numbers loud and strong!
And where e'er we go,
You will always know
That those caissons are rolling along.

GEORGE M. COHAN
United States song, World War I: Over There

We'll be over, we're coming over,
and we won't come back till it's over over there.

ATTRIBUTED TO GENERAL JOHN J. PERSHING

Hell, Heaven or Hoboken by Christmas.

FRANKLIN D. ROOSEVELT

Hostilities exist. There is no blinking at the fact that our people, our territory, and our interests are in grave danger.

With confidence in our armed forces, with the unbounding determination of our people, we will gain the inevitable triumph. So help us God.

I ask that the Congress declare that since the unprovoked and dastardly attack by Japan on Sunday, December 7, 1941, a state of war has existed between the United States and the Japanese Empire.

LIEUTENANT-COMMANDER FORGY

Praise the Lord and pass the ammunition.

GENERAL DOUGLAS MACARTHUR
Speech in Australia after leaving the Philippines

I shall return.

GENERAL GEORGE CATLETT MARSHALL
Military Review

It is not enough to fight. It is the spirit which we bring to the fight that decides the issue. It is morale that wins the victory.

GENERAL DOUGLAS MACARTHUR
Speech at the Republican National Convention

It is fatal to enter any war without the will to win it.

GENERAL GEORGE S. PATTON
Cavalry Journal

Wars may be fought with weapons, but they are won by men. It is the spirit of the men who follow and of the man who leads that gains the victory.

GENERAL A.C. MCAULIFFE
Reply to German demand to surrender Bastogne

Nuts!

GENERAL DOUGLAS MACARTHUR
Remarks to Colonel George M. Jones and 503rd Regimental Combat Team, who recaptured Corregidor

I see that the old flagpole still stands. Have your troops hoist the colors to its peak, and let no enemy ever haul them down.

GENERAL OMAR BRADLEY
Military Review

In war there is no second prize for the runner-up.

GENERAL DWIGHT D. EISENHOWER
Broadcast on D-Day

People of Western Europe: A landing was made this morning on the coast of France by troops of the Allied Expeditionary Force. This landing is part of the concerted United Nations plan for the liberation of Europe, made in conjunction with our great Russian allies . . . I call upon all who love freedom to stand with us now. Together we shall achieve victory.

GULF OF TONKIN RESOLUTION, PASSED BY CONGRESS

Whereas naval units of the Communist regime in Vietnam, in violation of the principles of the Charter of the United Nations and of international law, have deliberately and repeatedly attacked United States naval vessels . . . and Whereas these attacks are part of a deliberate and systematic campaign of aggression . . . and Whereas the United States is assisting the peoples of southeast Asia to protect their freedom and has no territorial, military or political ambitions in that area . . . Now, therefore, be it Resolved by the Senate and the House of Representatives of the United States of America in Congress assembled, that the Congress approves and supports the determination of the President, as Commander in Chief, to take all necessary measures to repel any armed attack against the forces of the United States and to prevent further aggression.

LYNDON B. JOHNSON
Speech after the Gulf of Tonkin incident

We still seek no wider war.

FRANCES FITZGERALD
Fire in the Lake

[President] Johnson condemned his officials who worked on Vietnam to the excruciating mental task of holding reality and the official version of reality together as they moved farther and farther apart.

NORMAN MAILER
The Armies of the Night

The war in Vietnam was bad for America because it was a bad war, as all wars are bad if they consist of rich boys fighting poor boys when the rich boys have an advantage in the weapons.

MARTIN LUTHER KING, JR.
Where Do We Go From Here? Chaos or Community

The bombs in Vietnam explode at home; they destroy the hopes and possibilities for a decent America.

GEORGE WASHINGTON
Letter to merchants and traders of Philadelphia

The friends of humanity will deprecate war, wheresoever it may appear; and we have experienced enough of its evil in this country to know that it should not be wantonly or unnecessarily entered upon.

RALPH WALDO EMERSON
Journals

The cannon will not suffer any other sound to be heard for miles and for years around it.

ROBERT E. LEE

It is well that war is so terrible—we would grow too fond of it.

GENERAL WILLIAM TECUMSEH SHERMAN
Letter to James Calhoun and others

You cannot qualify war in harsher terms than I will. War is cruelty, and you cannot refine it.

GENERAL WILLIAM TECUMSEH SHERMAN
Address before the Michigan Military Academy graduating class

I am tired and sick of war. Its glory is all moonshine. It is only those who have neither fired a shot nor heard the shrieks and groans of the wounded who cry aloud for more blood, more vengeance, more desolation. War is hell.

CHIEF JOSEPH
To the Nez Perce tribe after surrendering to General Nelson A. Miles

Our chiefs are killed....The old men are all dead....The little children are freezing to death. My people, some of them have run away to the hills and have no blankets, no food. No one knows where they are, perhaps freezing to death. I want to have time to look for my children and see how many of them I can find. Maybe I can find them among the dead. Hear me, my chiefs. My heart is sick and sad. From where the sun now stands I will fight no more forever.

WILLIAM LYON PHELPS
Sermon in Riverside church

The only war I ever approved of was the Trojan War; it was fought over a woman and the men knew what they were fighting for.

GENERAL DWIGHT D. EISENHOWER

Men acquainted with the battlefield will not be found among the members that glibly talk of another war.

ERNEST HEMINGWAY

Never think that war, no matter how necessary nor how justified, is not a crime.

GENERAL DWIGHT D. EISENHOWER
Cited in John Gunther, Eisenhower: The Man and the Symbol

I hate war as only a soldier who has lived it can, only as one who has seen its brutality, its futility, its *stupidity.*

GENERAL DWIGHT D. EISENHOWER
Letter to Mamie Doud Eisenhower

War creates such a strain that all the pettiness, jealousy, ambition, greed, and selfishness begin to leak out the seams of the average character. On top of this are the problems created by the enemy, by weather, by international politics, including age-old racial and nationalistic animosities, by every conceivable kind of difficulty, and, finally, just by the nature of war itself.

GENERAL OMAR BRADLEY
Speech in Washington, D.C.

We are now speeding inexorably towards a day when even the ingenuity of our scientists may be unable to save us from the consequences of a single rash act or a lone reckless hand upon the switch of an uninterceptible missile . . . Have we already gone too far in this search for peace through the accumulation of peril? Is there any way to halt this trend—or must we push on with new devices until we inevitably come to judgment before the atom?

WOODROW WILSON

The war we have just been through, though it was shot through with terror, is not to be compared with the war we would have to face next time.

JOHN F. KENNEDY
Address to the United Nations

[A] nuclear disaster, spread by winds and waters and fears, could well engulf the great and the small, the rich and the poor, the committed and the uncommitted alike. Mankind must put an end to war or war will put an end to mankind.

JEANNETTE RANKIN
Cited in Hannah Josephson, Jeannette Rankin: First Lady in Congress

You can no more win a war than you can win an earthquake.

ERNEST HEMINGWAY
"Notes on the Next War: A Serious Letter," Esquire

We in America should see that no man is ever given, no matter how gradually, or how noble and excellent the man, the power to put this country into a war which is now being prepared and brought closer each day with all the premeditation of a long-planned murder. For when you give power to an executive you do not know who will be filling that position when the time of crisis comes.

Farewell Address

DWIGHT D. EISENHOWER

Now, this conjunction of an immense military establishment and a large arms industry is new in the American experience. The total influence—economic, political, even spiritual—is felt in every city, every state house, every office of the federal government. We recognize the imperative need for this development. Yet we must not fail to comprehend its grave implications. Our toil, resources, and livelihood are all involved; so is the very structure of our society.

In the councils of government, we must guard against the acquisition of unwarranted influence, whether sought or unsought, by the military industrial complex. The potential for the disastrous rise of misplaced power exists and will persist.

We must never let the weight of this combination endanger our liberties or democratic processes. We should take nothing for granted. Only an alert and knowledgeable citizenry can compel the proper meshing of the huge industrial and military machinery of defense with our peaceful methods and goals, so that security and liberty may prosper together.

Akin to and largely responsible for the sweeping changes in our industrial military posture has been the technological revolution during recent decades.

In this revolution research has become central. It also becomes more formalized, complex, and costly. A steadily increasing share is conducted for, by, or at the direction of the federal government.

Today the solitary inventor, tinkering in his shop, has been overshadowed by the task forces of scientists in laboratories and testing fields. In the same fashion, the free university, historically the fountainhead of free ideas and scientific discovery, has experienced a revolution in the conduct of research. Partly because of the huge costs involved, a government contract becomes virtually a substitute for intellectual curiosity.

For every old blackboard there are not hundreds of new electronic computers.

Another factor in maintaining balance involves the element of time. As we peer into society's future, we—you and I, and our government—must avoid the impulse to live only for today, plundering, for our own ease and convenience, the precious resources of tomorrow.

We cannot mortgage the material assets of our grandchildren without risking the loss also of their political and spiritual heritage. We want democracy to survive for all generations to come, not to become the insolvent phantom of tomorrow.

Such a confederation must be one of equals. The weakest must come to the conference table with the same confidence as do we, protected as we are by our moral, economic, and military strength. That table, though scarred by many past frustrations, cannot be abandoned for the certain agony of the battlefield.

Disarmament, with mutual honor and confidence, is a continuing imperative. Together we must learn how to compose differences—not with arms but with intellect and decent purpose. Because this need is so sharp and apparent, I confess that I lay down my official responsibilities in this field with a definite sense of disappointment. As one who has witnessed the horror and the lingering sadness of war, as one who knows that another war could utterly destroy this civilization which has been so slowly and painfully built over thousands of years, I wish I could say tonight that a lasting peace is in sight.

Happily, I can say that war has been avoided. Steady progress toward our ultimate goal has been made. But so much remains to be done. As a private citizen, I shall never cease to do what little I can to help the world advance along that road.

ROBERT M. LaFOLLETTE, Sr.
Speech in the Senate

I maintain that Congress has the right and the duty to declare the object of the war, and the people have the right and the obligation to discuss it.

HENRY STEELE COMMAGER
Freedom and Order

Whether history will judge this war to be different or not, we cannot say. But this we can say with certainty: a government and a society that silences those who dissent is one that has lost its way. This we can say: that what is essential in a free society is that there should be an atmosphere where those who wish to dissent and even to demonstrate can do so without fear of recrimination or vilification.

WALTER LIPPMANN
Column, New York Herald Tribune

The time has come to stop beating our heads against stone walls under the illusion that we have been appointed policemen to the human race.

BENJAMIN FRANKLIN
Letter to Joseph Banks

I join with you most cordially in rejoicing at the return of peace. I hope it will be lasting, and that mankind will at length, as they call themselves reasonable creatures, have reason and sense enough to settle their differences without cutting throats; for, in my opinion, there never was a good war or a bad peace. What vast additions to the conveniences and comforts of living might mankind have acquired, if the money spent in wars had been employed in works of public utility! What an extension of agriculture, even to the tops of our mountains; what rivers rendered navigable or joined by canals; what bridges, aqueducts, new roads and other public works, edifices and improvements . . . might have been obtained by spending those millions in doing good which in the last war have been spent in doing mischief.

GEORGE WASHINGTON
Letter to David Humphrey

My first wish is to see this plague to mankind banished from off the earth, and the sons and daughters of this world employed in more pleasing and innocent amusements, than in preparing implements and exercising them for the destruction of mankind.

THOMAS JEFFERSON
Letter to Noah Worcester

Of my disposition to maintain peace until its condition shall be made less tolerable than that of war itself, the world has had proofs, and more, perhaps, than it has approved. I hope it is practicable, by improving the mind and morals of society, to lessen the disposition to war; but of its abolition I despair.

THOMAS JEFFERSON
Letter to Tench Coxe

I love peace, and I am anxious that we should give the world still another useful lesson, by showing to them other modes of punishing injuries than war, which is as much a punishment to the punisher as to the sufferer.

RALPH WALDO EMERSON
"Worship," *The Conduct of Life*

The real and lasting victories are those of peace, and not of war.

ABRAHAM LINCOLN

The ballot is stronger than the bullet.

WILLIAM JAMES

The Varieties of Religious Experience

What we now need to discover in the social realm is the moral equivalent of war: something heroic that will speak to omen as universally as war does, and yet will be as compatible with their spiritual selves as war has proved to be incompatible.

WOODROW WILSON

The example of America must be the example not merely of peace because it will not fight, but of peace because peace is the healing and elevating influence of the world, and strife is not. There is such a thing as a man being too proud to fight. There is such a thing as a nation being so right that it does not need to convince others by force that it is right.

ALBERT EINSTEIN

The World as I See It

As long as armies exist, any serious conflict will lead to war. A pacifism which does not actively fight against the armament of nations is and must remain impotent.

GENERAL GEORGE CATLETT MARSHALL

Biennial Report of the Chief of Staff, United States Army

If man does find the solution for world peace it will be the most revolutionary reversal of his record we have ever known.

NORMAN THOMAS

Speech to antiwar demonstrators, Washington, D.C.

I'd rather see America save her soul than her face.

MARTIN LUTHER KING, JR.

The Trumpet of Conscience

Somehow this madness must cease. We must stop now. I speak as a child of God and brother to the suffering poor of Vietnam. I speak for those whose land is being destroyed, whose culture is being subverted. I speak for the poor of America who are paying the double price of smashed hopes at home and death and corruption in Vietnam. I speak as a citizen of the world, for the world as it stands aghast at the path we have taken. I speak as an American to the leaders of my own nation. The great initiative in this war is ours. The initiative to stop it must be ours.

MARTIN LUTHER KING, JR.
Address given at Riverside Church

Here is the true meaning and value of compassion and nonviolence when it helps us to see the enemy's point of view, to hear his questions, to know his assessment of ourselves. For from his view we may indeed see the basic weaknesses of our own condition, and if we are mature we may learn and grow and profit from the wisdom of the brothers who are called the opposition.

DICK GREGORY
Dick Gregory's Political Primer

[Peace:] An idea which seems to have originated in Switzerland but has never caught hold in the United States. Supporters of this idea are frequently accused of being unpatriotic and trying to create civil disorder.

BERNARD BARUCH

Peace is never long preserved by weight of metal or by an armament race. Peace can be made tranquil and secure only by understanding and agreement fortified by sanctions. We must embrace international cooperation or international disintegration.

Science has taught us how to put the atom to work. But to make it work for good instead of for evil lies in the domain dealing with the principles of human duty. We are now facing a problem more of ethics than of physics.

The solution will require apparent sacrifice in pride and in position, but better pain as the price of peace than death as the price of war.

E.B. WHITE

I should imagine today would be a discouraging day for the northern France correspondent of Friends of the Land. The organic matter now being added to French soil is of a most embarrassing nature. Until we quit composting our young men we shall not get far with a program of conservation.

Promote the General Welfare

FRANKLIN D. ROOSEVELT
Address to the Federal Council of Churches of Christ

If I were asked to state the great objective which Church and State are both demanding for the sake of every man and woman and child in this country, I would say that that great objective is "a more abundant life."

FRANKLIN D. ROOSEVELT
Second Inaugural Address

The test of our progress is not whether we add more to the abundance of those who have much; it is whether we provide enough for those who have too little.

FRANKLIN D. ROOSEVELT
"Four Freedoms" *speech*

There is nothing mysterious about the foundations of a healthy and strong democracy...They are: equality of opportunity for youth and for others; jobs for those who can work; security for those who need it; the ending of special privilege for the few; the preservation of civil liberties for all; the enjoyment of the fruits of scientific progress in a wider and constantly rising standard of living.

"Great Society" speech

LYNDON B. JOHNSON

I have come today from the turmoil of your Capitol to the tranquillity of your campus to speak about the future of our country. The purpose of protecting the life of our nation and preserving the liberty of our citizens is to pursue the happiness of our people. Our success in that pursuit is the test of our success as a nation. For a century we labored to settle and to subdue a continent. For half a century, we called upon unbounded invention and untiring industry to create an order of plenty for all our people. The challenge of the next half century is whether we have the wisdom to use that wealth to enrich and elevate our national life, and to advance the quality of our American civilization.

Your imagination, your initiative, and your indignation will determine whether we build a society where progress is the servant of our needs, or a society where old values and new visions are buried under unbridled growth. For in your time we have the opportunity to move not only toward the rich society and the powerful society, but upward to the Great Society. The Great Society rests on abundance and liberty for all. It demands an end to poverty and racial injustice, to which we are totally committed in our time. But that is just the beginning.

The Great Society is a place where every child can find knowledge to enrich his mind and to enlarge his talents. It is a place where leisure is a welcome chance to build and reflect, not a feared cause of boredom and restlessness. It is a place where the city of man serves not only the needs of the body and the demands of commerce, but the desire for beauty and the hunger for community.

It is a place where man can renew contact with nature. It is a place which honors creation for its own sake and for what it adds to the understanding of the race. It is a place where men are more concerned with the quality of their goals than the quantity of their goods. But most of all, the Great Society is not a safe harbor, a resting place, a final objective, a finished work. It is a challenge constantly renewed, beckoning us toward a destiny where the meaning of our lives matches the marvelous products of our labor.... So will you join in the battle to give every citizen the full equality which God enjoins and the law requires, whatever his belief, or race, or the color of his skin? Will you join in the battle to give every citizen an escape from the crushing weight of poverty? Will you join in the battle to make it possible for all nations to live in enduring peace as neighbors and not as mortal enemies? Will you join in the battle to build the Great Society, to prove that our material progress is only the foundation on which we will build a richer life of mind and spirit?

There are timid souls who say this battle cannot be won, that we are condemned to a soulless wealth. I do not agree. We have the power to shape the civilization that we want. But we need your will, your labor, your hearts, if we are to build that kind of society.

JOHN KENNETH GALBRAITH
The Good Society

In the good society all of its citizens must have personal liberty, basic well-being, racial and ethnic equality, the opportunity for a rewarding life. Nothing, it must be recognized, so comprehensively denies the liberties of the individual as a total absence of money. Or so impairs it as too little. In the years of Communism it is not clear that one would wisely have exchanged the restraints on freedom of the resident of East Berlin for those imposed by poverty on the poorest citizens of the South Bronx in New York. Meanwhile, nothing so inspires socially useful effort as the prospect of pecuniary reward, both for what it procures and not rarely for the pleasure of pure possession it accords.

ANN MARKUSEN AND JOEL YUDKEN
Dismantling the War Economy

Environment, health, and community stability—these areas must compete with national security as a major national priority. For fifty years, Americans have devoted the lion's share of their surplus to pursuing national security above all else, with disappointing results for the economy and growing environmental, health and community crises. Today, it can be argued that resolving environmental, health, and economic crises is an essential dimension of any meaningful definition of national security. Moreover, unlike expenditures on costly MX or Patriot missiles, gains in these three areas would boost productivity in the economy as a whole.

FRANKLIN D. ROOSEVELT
Second Inaugural Address

We have always known that heedless self-interest was bad morals; we know now that it is bad economics.

Race Matters

CORNEL WEST
Introduction

How do we capture a new spirit and vision to meet the challenges of the post-industrial city, post-modern culture, and post-party politics?

First, we must admit that the most valuable sources for help, hope, and power consist of ourselves and our common history. As in the ages of Lincoln, Roosevelt, and King, we must look to new frameworks and languages to understand our multilayered crisis and overcome our deep malaise.

Second, we must focus our attention on the public square—the common good that undergirds our national and global destinies. The vitality of any public square ultimately depends on how much we *care* about the quality of our lives together. The neglect of our public infrastructure, for example—our water and sewage systems, bridges, tunnels, highways, subways, and streets—reflects not only our myopic economic policies, which impede productivity, but also the low priority we place on our common life.

The tragic plight of our children clearly reveals our deep disregard for public well-being. About one out of every five children in this country lives in poverty, including one out of every two black children and two out of every five Hispanic children. Most of our children—neglected by overburdened parents and bombarded by the market values of profit-hungry corporations—are ill-equipped to live lives of spiritual and cultural quality. Faced with these facts, how do we expect ever to constitute a vibrant society?

One essential step is some form of large-scale public intervention to ensure access to basic social goods—housing, food, health care, education, child care, and jobs. We must invigorate the common good with a mixture of government, business, and labor that does not follow any existing blueprint. After a period in which the private sphere has been sacralized and the public square gutted, the temptation is to make a fetish of the public square. We need to resist such dogmatic swings.

Last, the major challenge is to meet the need to generate new leadership. The paucity of courageous leaders—so apparent in the response to the events in Los Angeles—requires that we look beyond the same elites and voices that recycle the older frameworks. We need leaders —neither saints nor sparkling television personalities—who can situate themselves within a larger historical narrative of this country and our world, who can grasp the complex dynamics of our peoplehood and imagine a future grounded in the best of our past, yet who are attuned to the frightening obstacles that now perplex us. Our ideals of freedom, democracy, and equality must be invoked to invigorate all of us, especially the landless, propertyless, and luckless. Only a visionary leadership that can motivate "the better angels of our nature," as Lincoln said, and activate possibilities for a freer, more efficient and stable America—only that leadership deserves cultivation and support.

This new leadership must be grounded in grass-roots organizing that highlights democratic accountability. Whoever *our* leaders will be as we approach the twenty-first century, their challenge will be to help Americans determine whether a genuine multiracial democracy can be created and sustained in an era of global economy and a moment of xenophobic frenzy.

Let us hope and pray that the vast intelligence, imagination, humor, and courage of Americans will not fail us. Either we learn a new language of empathy and compassion, or the fire this time will consume us all.

LYNDON B. JOHNSON
Speech, signing the Medicare Extension Bill

I want to be remembered as one who spent his whole life trying to get more people more to eat and more to wear, to live longer, to have medicine and have attention, nursing, hospitals, and doctors' care when they need it, and to have their children have a chance to go to school and carry out really what the Declaration of Independence says, "all men are created equal."

JACK NEWFIELD
Robert Kennedy

[Robert] Kennedy identified with people, not data, or institutions, or theories. Poverty was a specific black face for him, not a manila folder full of statistics.

JESSE JACKSON
Speech before the Democratic National Convention

If in my high moments, I have done some good, offered some service, shed some light, healed some wounds, rekindled some hope, or stirred someone from apathy and indifference, or in any way along the way helped somebody, then this campaign has not been in vain...If in my low moments, in word, deed or attitude, through some error of temper, taste or tone, I have caused anyone discomfort, created pain or revived someone's fears, that was not my truest self. I am not a perfect servant. I am a public servant doing my best against the odds. As I develop and serve, be patient. God is not finished with me yet.

The Glory and the Dream
WILLIAM MANCHESTER

In the Connecticut manufacturing city of Winsted his Lebanese immigrant father was the local populist, a familiar American type. Customers at Nadra Nader's Highland Sweet Shop, a restaurant and bakery, complained that the proprietor never let them eat in peace. Nadra was always lecturing them about the wrongs, the inequities, the injustices of the system. Like many immigrants, he was a more ardent Democrat than the natives. He went on about the crimes of the Interests and was forever threatening to sue them. In time nearly everyone there tuned him out, with one exception: his youngest son Ralph.

In 1938, at the age of four, Ralph Nader was a tiny spectator when lawyers harangued juries in the local courthouse. At fourteen he became a daily reader of the *Congressional Record*.

He won a scholarship to Princeton, where he refused to wear white bucks or other symbols of sartorial conformity and staged a protest against the spraying of campus trees with DDT. He was locked so often in the university library after hours that he was given a key. Characteristically he responded by denouncing the administration for callous disregard of other students' legal rights. In 1955 he was elected to Phi Beta Kappa, graduated magna cum laude, and was admitted to Harvard Law School, which he described as a "high-priced tool factory" turning out servants of power.

His reputation as a puritan grew. He foreswore the reading of novels; they were a waste of time. So were movies; he would limit himself to two a year. He scorned plays, tobacco, alcohol, girls, and parties. At Harvard he also quit driving automobiles, but here his motive was different. He had become interested in auto injury cases, and after some research in car technology at nearby MIT he wrote an article for the Harvard Law Record entitled, "American Cars: Designed for Death."

The problem continued to bother him. Throughout his career he was to be concerned with the protection of the human body—from unsafe natural gas pipelines, food additives, tainted meat, pollution, mining health hazards, herbicides, unwholesome poultry, inadequate nursing homes, and radiation emission from color TVs—but the auto threat was basic. He opened a private law practice in Hartford (which rapidly became a source of free legal advice for the poor) and continued to urge stronger car safety regulations on local governments. Early in 1964 he took his campaign to Washington, where Assistant Secretary of Labor Daniel Patrick Moynihan hired him as a fifty-dollar-a-day consultant to the Labor Department.

Working with Connecticut's Senator Abraham Ribicoff, Nader turned out a two-hundred-page brief calling for auto safety legislation with teeth. A General Motors engineer became the first of his many secret contacts in industry by pointing out the Chevrolet Corvair's tendency to flip over. In November 1965 Nader's first book, *Unsafe at Any Speed: The Designed-in Dangers of the American Automobile*, called the Corvair "one of the nastiest-handling cars ever built" and charged that the industry had taken "four years of the model and 1,124,076 Corvairs before they decided to do something."

Unsafe at Any Speed, which sold 450,000 copies in cloth and paper, brought its author before a Ribicoff committee on February 10, 1966, as an expert witness on hazardous autos. Three weeks later Nader became a national figure when he accused General Motors of harassing him with private detectives, abusive telephone calls, and women who tried to entice him into compromising situations. A GM operative admitted under oath that he had been instructed by his superiors "to get something somewhere on this guy...get him out of their hair...shut him up." Nader filed suit for 26 million dollars and collected $280,000. Like his book royalties, the money went to the cause; when the National Traffic and Motor Vehicle Safety Act was passed that summer the *Washington Post* declared that "Most of the credit for making possible this important legislation belongs to one man—Ralph Nader...a one-man lobby for the public prevailed over the nation's most powerful industry."

Nader set himself up as a watchdog of the National Traffic Safety Agency and then went after the meat packers; the result was the Wholesome Meat Act of 1967. He broadened his attack on exploiters of the consumer to include the Food and Drug Administration, Union Carbide smokestacks, think tanks, unsafe trucks, pulp and paper mills, property taxes, bureaucrats, consumer credit, banks, and supermarkets. One observer said, "Ralph is not a consumer champion. He is just plain against consumption."

Unlike the muckrakers of the Lincoln Steffens era, Nader acquired a conservative constituency. At a time of anarchy and disorder he believed in working within the system. He was a linear thinker, an advocate of law and industrial order. Stockbrokers contributed to his causes. Miss Porter's School sent him volunteer workers. He was acquiring lieutenants now—"Nader's Raiders," a reporter dubbed them—and they were mostly white upper-middle-class graduates of the best schools, with names like Pullman cars: Lowell Dodge, William Harrison Wellford, Reuben B. Robertson III, and William Howard Taft IV. One of them, Edward F. Cox, became a son-in-law of President Nixon.

He installed them in cubbyhole offices in the National Press Building furnished with secondhand desks, chairs bought at rummage sales, apple crate files, and shelves made from planks and bricks. He worked them a hundred hours a week and paid them poverty-level salaries. Royalties from the books they turned out went into his campaigns. They didn't complain; he himself was earning $200,000 a year and spending $5,000.

He lived in an $80-a-month furnished room near Dupont Circle, paid $97 a month office rent, and had no secretary. People gave him briefcases; he turned them into files and traveled instead with his papers in a sheaf of manila envelopes. His black shoes were scuffed, the laces broken and knotted. He wore a gray rumpled suit, frayed white shirts, and narrow ties which had been out of style for years. Standing six feet four inches, with wavy black hair and a youthful face, he was compared by Newsweek to a "Jimmy Stewart hero in a Frank Capra movie." His only unusual expense was his telephone bill. It was enormous. He was paying for calls from all his volunteer spies in industry.

Most of his income came from lecture fees. Each week he received fifty invitations to speak; he accepted 150 a year, charging as much as $2,000. He became known as the most long-winded speaker since Walter Reuther, rarely relinquishing the lectern before an hour and forty-five minutes. There was never any flourish at the end. He would simply stop talking and pivot away. College audiences gave him wild ovations, but he never turned back to acknowledge them. If asked to autograph a book he would curtly reply, "No." A friend said, "Ralph is so afraid of being turned into a movie star, of having his private life romanticized, that he has renounced his own private life."

He was an impossible customer. To a waitress he would say when ordering, "Is the ham sliced for each sandwich? Is that genuine or processed cheese? Do *you* eat sugar? You do? Let me tell you something—it's absolutely useless, no food value." To an airline stewardess, he said, "The only thing you should be proud to serve on this whole plane is the little bag of nuts. And you should take the salt off the nuts." When Allegheny Airlines had the temerity to bump him from a flight on which he had a confirmed reservation, he filed suit and was awarded $50,000 in punitive damages, half for him and half for the consumer group he had been unable to address because of the missed flight.

Asked by Robert F. Kennedy why he was "doing all this," he answered, "If I were engaged in activities for the prevention of cruelty to animals, nobody would ask me that question." His ultimate goal, he said, was "nothing less than the qualitative reform of the industrial revolution," and he refused to be lured from it by any bait. Nicholas von Hoffman and Gore Vidal proposed him for the Presidency. He said, "I'm not interested in public office. The biggest job in this country is citizen action. Politics follows that."

Yet for all his evangelism, his devotion to public good, and his monastic life, Nader's impact on society was questionable. At times he seemed to know it. "We always fail," he said once. "The whole thing is limiting the degree of failure." His audiences appeared to regard him as a performer. They applauded him, but it was as though they were applauding an act. Few of them felt compelled to get involved, to follow his example or even his advice. They went right on driving big Detroit cars, eating processed foods, coating themselves with expensive cosmetics and smoking poisonous cigarettes.

In a pensive moment he reflected that "A couple thousand years ago in Athens, a man could get up in the morning, wander around the city, and inquire into matters affecting his well-being and that of his fellow citizens. No one asked him 'Who are you with?'" Americans of the 1970s did not inquire about him; they knew. Yet they themselves remained uncommitted. The painful fact—excruciating for him—was that however loud their cheers for Ralph Nader, however often they said that they were for him, in this Augustan age of materialism they were not really with him.

E. B. WHITE
Letter to Mr. Nadeau

As long as there is one upright man, as long as there is one compassionate woman, the contagion may spread and the scene is not desolate. Hope is the thing that is left us in a bad time.

JANE ADDAMS

A great party has pledged itself to the protection of children, to the care of the aged, to the relief of overworked girls, to the safe-guarding of burdened men. Committed to these human undertakings, it is inevitable that such a party should appeal to women . . . I second the nomination of Theodore Roosevelt because he is one of the few men in our public life who has been responsive to the social appeal and who has caught the significance of the modern movement.

FRANKLIN D. ROOSEVELT

The liberal party is a party which believes that, as new conditions and problems arise beyond the power of men and women to meet as individuals, it becomes the duty of the Government itself to find new remedies with which to meet them. The liberal party insists that the Government has the definite duty to use all its power and resources to meet new social problems with new social controls—to ensure to the average person the right to his own economic and political life, liberty, and the pursuit of happiness.

E.B. WHITE
Liberalism

The liberal holds that he is true to the republic when he is true to himself. (It may not be as cozy an attitude as it sounds.) He greets with enthusiasm the fact of the journey, as a dog greets a man's invitation to take a walk. And he acts in the dog's way, too, swinging wide, racing ahead, doubling back, covering many miles of territory that the man never traverses, all in the spirit of inquiry and the zest for truth. He leaves a crazy trail, but he ranges far beyond the genteel old party he walks with and he is usually in a better position to discover a skunk. The dog often influences the course the man takes, on his long walk; for sometimes a dog runs into something in nature so arresting that not even a man can quite ignore it, and the man deviates—a clear victim of the liberal intent in his dumb companion. When the two of them get home and flop down, it is the liberal—the wide-ranging dog—who is covered with burdocks and with information of a special sort on out-of-the-way places. Often ineffective in direct political action, he is the opposite of the professional revolutionary, for, unlike the latter, he never feels he knows where the truth lies, but is full of rich memories of places he has glimpsed it in. He is, on the whole, more optimistic than the revolutionary, or even than the Republican in a good year.

A Liberal Reaches for her Whip

GARRISON KEILLOR

Liberals are fundamentally democrats with a quick social conscience who carry water for a million good causes from here to 123 Maple Street, Anywhere, U.S.A. They are teachers, boosters, and inveterate instillers of social obligation. Call them schoolmarms, goody two-shoes, busybodies, or bleeding hearts: basically, a liberal is a person who knows you very well and loves you very very much, perhaps more than you deserve.

Who wanted you to be aware of the hungry children in China as you played with the food on your plate?

Who taught you to take turns on the swings and share your cake with other children and made you feel guilty for being such a greedy selfish little child?

Who taught you to be decent to children whom you *despised?*

Who, when you lost the game and incurred the silent wrath and contempt of Dad, took you in her arms and said she loved you?

Who could possibly be more liberal than that?

> M is for Minorities and helpless,
> O is Obligation to the poor,
> T is Taking money from the greedy,
> H is Helping beggars at our door,
> E of course is Eleanor our Mother,
> R is Reagan's mom, the lovely Nell.
> A fine old Christian liberal and a lady—
> He kicks her down the stairs, but what the hell.

The old lady lay face up on the dank cellar floor, stunned and dizzy. A Sunday afternoon and she had been fixing pot roast and potatoes in the kitchen and then—It all happened so fast: the sudden blows from her two sons, the long terrible fall backward down the steps like in a nightmare, her hands grasping for the railing as she slid half sideways and then turned a complete somersault and banged headfirst on the concrete. She couldn't see. Her neck felt like it might be broken, and also her right wrist. She could taste blood. There seemed to be a loose tooth in her mouth. Her head started to pulse with pain. She lifted her left hand and touched her forehead. A dent there, and something wet. A radio was playing upstairs. She could hear loud breathing. Her dress was gathered up above her knees, and as she tried to straighten it she saw, standing in the light at the top of the stairs, arm in arm, Ron and George, laughing.

"Guess we showed you!"

She raised her head. What had she said to make them so angry? She certainly was sorry, whatever it was. Had she been too hard on them about how they ought to attend church? Had she nagged them too often about doing their homework and their Boy Scout projects? She didn't mean to be a scold. She moved her lips, *Ronnie, George,* but no sound came out. She struggled to her knees. George took two steps down and spat at her.

"Ptew. Guess *you* learned a lesson! Guess you won't be buttin' inna *my* bidness, Ma! Huh, Ron? Guess you won't be tellin' *me* what to do for a while, huh!"

The pain in her head was deafening, and the words wouldn't come out. *Oh my dear boys forgive me for provoking you to anger. But no matter what you do—if you kill me and throw my body in a ditch and rip out my heart—remember that with the last beat of my heart I will always love you. A liberal's love can never be less. Never, no matter what you do.*

"Kinda weak on defense, ain't ya, Ma? Ha ha ha." With the last ounce of strength in her battered aching body, she hoisted herself to her feet.

"Mother! Your dress!"

She looked down and saw that her blue knit dress had fallen down in a heap around her ankles, leaving her clad in a black one-piece spandex bodysuit she didn't know she possessed and also a pair of black knee-high steel-toe kangaroo combat boots with white laces and red and blue sequins. Her hair was long and snarly, not in a bun like she usually wore it, and in her right hand she held a long riding crop. Across her bosom were silver-lamé letters two inches high that spelled "One Helluva Woman."

"Mother?"

"Don't say another word," she said, "or I'll bust your heads."

"Mom?"

She placed her right foot on the first stair, keeping her weight nicely balanced, her eyes fastened on the bottom youth as he shrank back whimpering. She shook her head slowly and smiled and licked her lips. She grabbed both banisters and rocked up and down on the balls of her feet. "Liberal," she said. "I'm going to liberate you boys from ignorance or die in the attempt." She took three long deep breaths, and sprang like a tiger, her hairy arms outstretched, her eyes burning bright red, and the sound she made deep in her throat was one they had never ever heard before.

FRANKLIN D. ROOSEVELT

Some people have been saying of late: "We are tired of progress, we want to go back to where we were before..."; to restore "normal" conditions. They are wrong....We can never go back....In this faith I am strengthened by the firm belief that the women of this nation, now about to receive the National franchise, will throw their weight into the scale of progress....We cannot anchor our ship of state in this world tempest....We must go forward or flounder. America's opportunity is at hand. We can lead the world by great example.

The Democratic program . . . is a plan of hope. . . . We oppose money in politics, we oppose the private control of national finances . . . the treatment of human beings as commodities . . . the saloon-bossed city . . . [and] we oppose starvation wages. . . .

LYNDON B. JOHNSON
My Hope for America

A compassionate government keeps faith with the trust of the people and cherishes the future of their children. Through compassion for the plight of one individual, government fulfills its purpose as the servant of all people.

MARIO CUOMO
Keynote address to the Democratic National Convention

The difference between Democrats and Republicans has always been measured in courage and confidence. The Republicans believe the wagon train will not make it to the frontier unless some of our old, some of our young, and some of our weak are left behind by the side of the trail. The strong will inherit the land! We Democrats believe that we can make it all the way with the whole family intact.

BERNARD M. BARUCH
Press conference in New York City

You talk about capitalism and communism and all that sort of thing, but the important thing is the struggle everybody is engaged in to get better living conditions, and they are not interested too much in the form of government.

FRANKLIN D. ROOSEVELT
Radio address

These unhappy times call for the building of plans . . . that build from the bottom up and not from the top down, that put their faith once more in the forgotten man at the bottom of the economic pyramid.

HUEY LONG
Radio speech

"Every Man a King." Every man to eat when there is something to eat; all to wear something when there is something to wear. That makes us all a sovereign.

ADLAI E. STEVENSON

A hungry man is not a free man.

HARRY HOPKINS

Hunger is not debatable.

BENJAMIN FRANKLIN
Poor Richard's Almanack

Necessity never made a good bargain.

FRANKLIN D. ROOSEVELT
Message to Congress

People who are hungry and out of a job are the stuff of which dictatorships are made.

THOMAS JEFFERSON
Letter to James Madison

Whenever there is, in any country, uncultivated land and unemployed poor, it is clear that the laws of property have been so far expended as to violate natural right.

FREDERICK DOUGLASS
Speech on the twenty-fourth anniversary of Emancipation

Where justice is denied, where poverty is enforced, where ignorance prevails, and where any one class is made to feel that society is an organized conspiracy to oppress, rob, and degrade them, neither persons nor property will be safe.

GROVER CLEVELAND
Speech, laying of the cornerstone of the Fitch Institute of Buffalo, New York

The poor are to be relieved. And not only their physical, but their moral and intellectual wants are to be provided for. And all this is to be done for the worthy poor, because they are poor and worthy, and not because they profess any creed, or religious belief. A common humanity is the only necessary credential.

JOHN F. KENNEDY

If a free society cannot help the many who are poor, it cannot save the few who are rich.

The Other America; Poverty in the U.S.

MICHAEL HARRINGTON

The United States in the sixties contains an affluent society within its borders. Millions and tens of millions enjoy the highest standard of life the world has ever known. This blessing is mixed. It is built upon a peculiarly distorted economy, one that often proliferates pseudo-needs rather than satisfying human needs. For some, it has resulted in a sense of spiritual emptiness, of alienation. Yet a man would be a fool to prefer hunger to satiety, and the material gains at least open up the possibility of a rich and full existence.

At the same time, the United States contains an underdeveloped nation, a culture of poverty. Its inhabitants do not suffer the extreme privation of the peasants of Asia or the tribesmen of Africa, yet the mechanism of the misery is similar.

The new nations, however, have one advantage: poverty is so general and so extreme that it is the passion of the entire society to obliterate it. Every resource, every policy, is measured by its effect on the lowest and most impoverished. There is a gigantic mobilization of the spirit of the society: aspiration becomes a national purpose that penetrates to every village and motivates a historic transformation.

But this country seems to be caught in a paradox. Because its poverty is not so deadly, because so many are enjoying a decent standard of life, there are indifference and blindness to the plight of the poor. There are even those who deny that the culture of poverty exists. It is as if Disraeli's famous remark about the two nations of the rich and the poor had become true in a fantastic fashion. At precisely that moment in history where for the first time a people have the material ability to end poverty, they lack the will to do so. They cannot see, they cannot act. The consciences of the well-off are the victims of affluence; the lives of the poor are the victims of a physical and spiritual misery.

The problem, then, it to a great extent one of vision. The nation of the well-off must be able to see through the wall of affluence and recognize the alien citizens on the other side. And there must be vision in the sense of purpose, of aspiration: if the word does not grate upon the ears of gentle America, there must be a passion to end poverty, for nothing less than that will do.

In this summary chapter, I hope I can supply at least some of the material for such a vision. Let us try to understand the other America as a whole, to see its perspective for the future if it is left alone, to realize the responsibility and the potential for ending this nation in our midst.

But, when all is said and done, the decisive moment occurs after all the sociology and the description is in. There is really no such thing as "the material for a vision." After one reads the facts, either there are anger or shame, or there are not. And, as usual, the fate of the poor hangs upon the decision of the better-off. If this anger and shame are not forthcoming, someone can write a book about the other America a generation from now and it will be the same, or worse.

Perhaps the most important analytic point to have emerged in this description of the other America is the fact that poverty in America forms a culture, a way of life and feeling, that it makes a whole. It is crucial to generalize this idea, for it profoundly affects how one moves to destroy poverty.

The most obvious aspect of this interrelatedness is in the way in which the various sub-cultures of the other America feed into one another. This is clearest with the aged. There the poverty of the declining years is, for some millions of human beings, a function of the poverty of the earlier years. If there were adequate medical care for everyone in the United States, there would be less misery for old people. It is as simple as that. Or there is the relation between the poor farmers and the unskilled workers. When a man is driven off the land because of the impoverishment worked by technological progress, he leaves one part of the culture of poverty and joins another. If something were done about the low-income farmer, that would immediately tell in the statistics of urban unemployment and the economic underworld. The same is true of Negroes. Any gain for America's minorities will immediately be translated into an advance for all the unskilled workers. One cannot raise the bottom of a society without benefiting everyone above.

Indeed, there is a curious advantage in the wholeness of poverty. Since the other America forms a distinct system within the United States, effective action to any one decisive point will have a "multiplier" effect; it will ramify through the entire culture of misery and ultimately through the entire society.

Then poverty is a culture in the sense that the mechanism of impoverishment is fundamentally the same in every part of the system. The vicious circle is a basic pattern. It takes different forms for the unskilled workers, for the aged, for the Negroes, for the agricultural workers, but in each case the principle is the same. There are people in the affluent society who are poor because they are poor, and who stay poor because they are poor.

To realize this is to see that there are some tens of millions of Americans who are beyond the welfare state. Some of them are simply not covered by social legislation: they are omitted from Social Security and from minimum wage. Others are covered, but since they are so poor they do not know how to take advantage of the opportunities, or else their coverage is so inadequate as not make a difference.

The welfare state was designed during that great burst of social creativity that took place in the 1930s. As previously noted its structure corresponds to the needs of those who played the most important role in building it: the middle third, the organized workers, the forces of urban liberalism, and so on. At the worst, there is "socialism for the rich and free enterprise for the poor," as when the huge corporation farms are the main beneficiaries of the farm program while the poor farmers get practically nothing; or when public funds are directed to aid in the construction of luxury housing while the slums are left to themselves (or become more dense as space is created for the well-off).

So there is the fundamental paradox of the welfare state: that it is not built for the desperate, but for those who are already capable of helping themselves. As long as the illusion persists that the poor are merrily free-loading on the public dole, so long will the other America continue unthreatened. The truth, it must be understood, is the exact opposite. The poor get less out of the welfare state than any group in America.

This is, of course, related to the most distinguishing mark of the other America: its common sense of hopelessness. For even when there are programs designed to help the other Americans, the poor are held back by their own pessimism.

On one level this fact has been described in this book as a matter of "aspiration." Like the Asian peasant, the impoverished American tends to see life as a fate, an endless cycle from which there is no deliverance. Lacking hope (and he is realistic to feel this way in many cases), that famous solution to all problems—let us educate the poor—becomes less and less meaningful. A person has to feel that education will do something for him if he is to gain from it. Placing a magnificent school with a fine faculty in the middle of a slum is, I suppose, better than having a run-down building staffed by incompetents. But it will not really make a difference so long as the environment of the tenement, the family, and the street counsels the children to leave as soon as they can and to disregard schooling.

On another level, the emotions of the other America are even more profoundly disturbed. Here it is not lack of aspiration and of hope; it is a matter of personal chaos. The drunkenness, the unstable marriages, the violence of the other America are not simply facts about individuals. They are the description of an entire group in the society who react this way because of the conditions under which they live.

In short, being poor is not one aspect of a person's life in this country; it is his life. Taken as a whole, poverty is a culture. Taken on the family level, it has the same quality. These are people who lack education and skill, who have bad health, poor housing, low levels of aspiration and high levels of mental distress. They are, in the language of sociology, "multiproblem" families. Each disability is the more intense because it exists within a web of disabilities. And if one problem is solved, and the others are left constant, there is little gain.

One might translate these facts into the moralistic language so dear to those who would condemn the poor for their faults. The other Americans are those who live at a level of life beneath moral choice, who are so submerged in their poverty that one cannot begin to talk about free choice. The point is not to make them wards of the state. Rather, society must help them before they can help themselves.

LYNDON B. JOHNSON
Telephone remarks, Convention of the Plasterers' Union

Let those who are well-fed, well-clothed, and well-housed never forget and never overlook those who live on the outskirts of hope.

LYNDON B. JOHNSON
State of the union address

The war against poverty will not be won here in Washington. It must be won in the field, in every private home, in every public office, from the courthouse to the White House.

LYNDON B. JOHNSON
Message to Congress

Poverty has many roots, but the tap root is ignorance.

BOOKER T. WASHINGTON

There is no defense or security for any of us except in the highest intelligence and development of all.

HERBERT HOOVER

If we could have but one generation of properly born, trained, educated, and healthy children, a thousand other problems of government would vanish.

THE CHILDREN'S CHARTER
Established by Herbert Hoover's Conference on the Health and Protection of Children

■ For every child a school which is safe from hazards, sanitary, properly equipped, lighted and ventilated.

■ For every child who is in conflict with society the right to be dealt with intelligently as society's charge, not society's outcast.

■ For every child the right to grow up in a family with an adequate standard of living and the security of a stable income as the surest safeguard against social handicaps.

HERBERT HOOVER
Radio broadcast from Egypt

The reconstruction of children is more precious than factories and bridges.

JOHN KENNETH GALBRAITH
The Good Society

Every child must have access to and be required to receive a good elementary and secondary education; he or she must also be subject to the discipline essential thereto. Compulsion and discipline are both necessary; the good society does not allow to the very young liberty of choice as between diligence and juvenile distraction. Thereafter as to higher education there must be full opportunity for achievement so far as aspiration seeks and ability allows. For all this, public resources must be available. There is no test of the good society so clear, so decisive, as its willingness to tax—to forgo private income, expenditure and the expensively cultivated superfluities of private consumption—in order to develop and sustain a strong educational system for all its citizens. The economic rewards of doing so are not in doubt. Nor the political gains. But the true reward is in the larger, deeper, better life for everyone that only education provides.

Private and religious schools, colleges and universities are, of course, encouraged; they are an expression of an essential freedom in the free society. They must not, however, be a design for according a better education and superior educational opportunity to those who are able to pay.

The prestige and the income of the teaching profession must reflect the high importance of education in the modern society. Education must both attract and celebrate the best. On two very practical matters all with a concern for the good society should conscientiously reflect. One is the ease and abundance with which money is available for the television that children now so intensively watch as compared with the money provided for their schools and the pay of their teachers. The other is how readily resources are available for the military as opposed to resources for the educational establishment.

NEWTON MINOW
Speech to the National Association of Broadcasters, Washington

If parents, teachers, and ministers conducted their responsibilities by following the ratings, children would have a steady diet of ice cream, school holidays, and no Sunday School. What about your responsibilities? Is there no room on television to teach, to inform, to uplift, to stretch, to enlarge the capacities of our children? Is there no room for programs deepening their understanding of children in other lands? Is there no room for a children's news show explaining something about the world to them at their level of understanding? Is there no room for reading the great literature of the past, teaching them the great traditions of freedom? There are some fine children's show, but they are drowned out in the massive doses of cartoons, violence, and more violence. Must these be your trademarks? Search your consciences and see if you cannot offer more to your young beneficiaries, whose future you guide so many hours each and every day.

JOHN SILBER

As television has ravenously consumed our attention, it has weakened the formative institutions of church, family and schools, thoroughly eroding the sense of individual obedience to the unenforceable on which manners and morals and ultimately the law depend. Obviously, we need to rebuild our families, our schools, and our churches. But we cannot complete these reforms until something is done about television, for in both its advertising and its programming it has created demands that appeal, not to the best in our natures, but to the worst.

JAMES AGEE
Let Us Now Praise Famous Men

In every child who is born under no matter what circumstances and of no matter what parents, the potentiality of the human race is born again, and in him, too, once more, and each of us, our terrific responsibility toward human life: toward the utmost idea of goodness, of the horror of terrorism, and of God.

MARION WRIGHT EDELMAN
Utne Reader

So much of America's tragic and costly failure to care for all its children stems from our tendency to distinguish between our own children and other people's children—as if justice were divisible. An African proverb reminds us that the rain falls on all the village huts and not just on some. So it is with violence and drugs and family and cultural decay today. All of us are afffected by other people's children, in the fears we harbor, the taxes we pay, the prisons we build, the welfare we love to hate, and in the nagging sense that we are not living up to our professed values of fair opportunity for all.

I hope God will guide our feet as parents—and guide America's feet—to reclaim our nation's soul, and to give back to all of our children their sense of security and their ability to dream about and work toward a future that is hopeful—and attainable.

OLIVER WENDELL HOLMES
Dissent in Hammer v. Dagenhart

If there is any matter upon which civilized countries have agreed...it is the evil of premature and excessive child labor.

JANE ADDAMS
Twenty Years at Hull-House

Our very first Christmas at Hull-House, when we as yet knew nothing of child labor, a number of little girls refused the candy which was offered them as part of the Christmas good cheer, saying simply that they "worked in a candy factory and could not bear the sight of it." We discovered that for six weeks they had worked from seven in the morning until nine at night, and they were exhausted as well as satiated. . . .

During the same winter three boys from a Hull-House club were injured at one machine in a neighboring factory for lack of a guard which would have cost but a few dollars. When the injury of one of these boys resulted in his death, we felt quite sure that the owners of the factory would share our horror and remorse. To our surprise, they did nothing whatever, and I made my first acquaintance then with those pathetic documents signed by the parents of working children, that they will make no claim for damages resulting from "carelessness."

"Human Rights for All People..."
MADELEINE ALBRIGHT
Remarks to the Fourth World Conference on Women, Beijing

We have come here from all over the world to carry forward an age-old struggle: The pursuit of economic and social progress for all people, based on respect for the dignity and value of each. We are here to promote and protect human rights and to stress that women's rights are neither separable nor different from those of men. We are here to stop sexual crimes and other violence against women; to protect refugees, so many of whom are women; and to end the despicable notion—in this era of conflicts—that rape is just another tactic of war.

We are here to empower women by enlarging their role in making economic and political decisions, an idea some find radical, but which my government believes is essential to economic and social progress around the world; because no country can develop if half its human resources are devalued or repressed.

We are here because we want to strengthen families—the heart and soul of any society. We believe that girls must be valued to the same degree as boys. We believe, with Pope John Paul II, in the "equality of spouses with respect to family rights." We think women and men should be able to make informed judgments as they plan their families, and we want to see forces that weaken families—including pornography, domestic violence, and the sexual exploitation of children—condemned and curtailed.

Finally, we have come to this conference to assure for women equal access to education and health care, to help women protect against infection by HIV, to recognize the special needs and strengths of women with disabilities, and to attack the root causes of poverty in which so many women, children, and men are entrapped.

We have come to Beijing to make further progress toward each of these goals. But real progress will depend not on what we say here, but on what we do after we leave here. The Fourth World Conference for Women is not about conversations; it is about commitments.

For decades, my nation has led efforts to promote equal rights for women. Women in their varied roles—as mothers, farm laborers, factory workers, organizers, and community leaders—helped build America. My government is based on principles that recognize the right of every person to equal rights and equal opportunity. Our laws forbid discrimination on the basis of sex, and we work hard to enforce those laws. A rich network of non-governmental organizations has blossomed within our borders, reaching out to women and girls from all segments of society—educating, counseling, and advocating change.

The United States is a leader, but leaders cannot stand still. Barriers to the equal participation of women persist in my country. The Clinton Administration is determined to bring those barriers down. Today, in the spirit of this conference and in the knowledge that concrete steps to advance the status of women are required in every nation, I am pleased to announce the new commitments my government will undertake.

First, President Clinton will establish a White House Council on Women to plan for the effective implementation within the United States of the Platform for Action. That council will build on the commitments made today and will work every day with the non-governmental community.

Second, in accordance with recently approved law, the Department of Justice will launch a six-year, $1.6 billion initiative to fight domestic violence and other crimes against women. Funds will be used for specialized police and prosecution units and to train police, prosecutors, and judicial personnel.

Third, our Department of Health and Human Services will lead a comprehensive assault on threats to the health and security of women—promoting healthy behavior, increasing awareness about AIDS, discouraging the use of cigarettes, and striving to win the battle against breast cancer. As Mrs. Clinton made clear yesterday, the United States remains firmly committed to the reproductive health rights gains made in Cairo.

Fourth, our Department of Labor will conduct a grassroots campaign to improve work conditions for women in the workplace. The campaign will work with employers to develop more equitable pay and promotion policies, and to help employees balance the twin responsibilities of family and work.

Fifth, our Department of the Treasury will take new steps to promote access to financial credit for women. Outstanding U.S. micro-enterprise lending organizations will be honored through special Presidential awards, and we will improve coordination of federal efforts to encourage growth in this field of central importance to the economic empowerment of women.

Sixth, the Agency for International Development will continue to lead in promoting and recognizing the vital role of women in development. Today, we announce important initiatives to increase women's participation in political processes and to promote the enforcement of women's legal rights.

There is a seventh and final commitment my country is making today. We, the people and Government of the United States of America, will continue to speak out openly and without hesitation on behalf of the human rights of all people.

ELEANOR ROOSEVELT
Speech to nominate Al Smith, New York

Democratic women...do not want the economy which refuses to help those who need and deserve the help of the State, nor do we want the kind of economy which saves a little today and loses thereby much opportunity for the future. We do not want a purely Wall Street, Aluminum Trust prosperity, a prosperity of invested capital as against several millions of unemployed. The human values mean more to us than the money values.

WENDELL PHILLIPS
Speech, Boston

Governments exist to protect the rights of minorities. The loved and the rich need no protection: they have many friends and few enemies.

WOODROW WILSON

What I am interested in is having the government of the United States more concerned about human rights than about property rights. Property is an instrument of humanity; humanity isn't an instrument of property.

"The American Promise"
LYNDON B. JOHNSON

I speak tonight for the dignity of man and the destiny of democracy.

I urge every member of both parties, Americans of all religions and of all colors, from every section of this country, to join me in that cause.

At times history and fate meet at a single time in a single place to shape a turning point in man's unending search for freedom. So it was at Lexington and Concord. So it was a century ago at Appomattox. So it was last week in Selma, Alabama.

There, long-suffering men and women peacefully protested the denial of their rights as Americans. Many were brutally assaulted. One good man, a man of God, was killed.

There is no cause for pride in what has happened in Selma. There is no cause for self-satisfaction in the long denial of equal rights of millions of Americans. But there is cause for hope and for faith in our democracy in what is happening here tonight.

For the cries of pain and the hymns and protests of oppressed people have summoned into convocation all the majesty of this great Government—the Government of the greatest Nation on earth.

Our mission is at once the oldest and the most basic of this country; to right wrong, to do justice, to serve man. . . . What happened in Selma is part of a far larger movement with reaches into every section and State of America. It is the effort of American Negroes to secure for themselves the full blessings of American life.

Their cause must be our cause too. Because it is not just Negroes, but really it is all of us, who must overcome the crippling legacy of bigotry and injustice.

And we shall overcome.

As a man whose roots go deeply into Southern soil I know how agonizing racial feelings are. I know how difficult it is to reshape the attitudes and the structure of our society.

But a century has passed, more than a hundred years, since the Negro was freed. And he is not fully free tonight.

It was more than a hundred years ago that Abraham Lincoln, a great President of another party, signed the Emancipation Proclamation, but emancipation is a proclamation and not a face.

A century has passed, more than a hundred years, since equality was promised. And yet the Negro is not equal.

A century has passed since the day of promise. And the promise is unkept.

The time of justice has now come. I tell you that I believe sincerely that no force can hold it back. It is right in the eyes of man and God that it should come. And when it does, I think that day will brighten the lives of every American.

For Negroes are not the only victims. How many white children have gone uneducated, how many white families have lived in stark poverty, how many white lives have been scarred by fear, because we have wasted our energy and our substance to maintain the barriers of hatred and terror?

So I say to all of you here, and to all in the Nation tonight, that those who appeal to you to hold on to the past do so at the cost of denying you your future.

This great, rich, restless country can offer opportunity and education and hope to all: black and white, North and South, sharecropper and city dweller. These are the enemies: poverty, ignorance, disease. They are the enemies and not our fellow man, not our neighbor. And these enemies too, poverty, disease and ignorance, we shall overcome.

LYNDON B. JOHNSON
News conference, LBJ Ranch

We are not interested in black power and we are not interested in white power. But we are interested in American democratic power, with a small "d." We believe that the citizen, regardless of his race or his religion or color, ought to be armed with the right to have a job at decent wages.

ABRAHAM LINCOLN
First annual message to Congress

Inasmuch as most good things are produced by labor, it follows that all such things ought to belong to those whose labor has produced them. But it has happened in all ages of the world that some have labored, and others, without labor, have enjoyed a larger proportion of the fruits. This is wrong, and should not continue. To secure to each laborer the whole product of his labor as nearly as possible is a worthy object of any good government.

ABRAHAM LINCOLN

I am glad to see that a system of labor prevails in New England under which laborers can strike when they want to, where they are not obliged to work under all circumstances and are not tied down and obliged to labor whether you pay them or not.

BENJAMIN HARRISON

We cannot afford in America to have any discontented classes, and if fair wages are paid for fair work we will have none.

THEODORE ROOSEVELT

No man can be a good citizen unless he has a wage more than sufficient to cover the bare cost of living, and hours of labor short enough so that after his day's work is done he will have time and energy to bear his share in the management of the community, to help in carrying the general load. We keep countless men from being good citizens by the conditions of life with which we surround them. We need comprehensive workmen's compensation acts, both State and national laws to regulate child labor and work for women, and especially, we need in our common schools not merely education in book-learning, but also practical training for daily life and work. We need to enforce better sanitary conditions for our workers and to extend the use of safety appliances for our workers in industry and commerce, both within and between the States. Also, friends, in the interest of the working man himself we need to set our faces like flint against mob-violence just as against corporate greed; against violence and injustice and lawlessness by wage-workers just as much as against lawless cunning and greed and selfish arrogance of employers.

FRANKLIN D. ROOSEVELT

No business which depends for its existence on paying less than living wages to its workers has any right to continue in this country.

SAMUEL GOMPERS

To protect the workers in their inalienable rights to a higher and better life; to protect them, not only as equals before the law, but also in their health, their homes, their firesides, their liberties as men, as workers, and as citizens; to overcome and conquer prejudices and antagonism; to secure to them the right to life, and the opportunity to maintain that life; the right to be full sharers in the abundance which is the result of their brain and brawn, and the civilization of which they are the founders and the mainstay. . . . The attainment of these is the glorious mission of the trade unions.

CLARENCE S. DARROW
The Railroad Trainman

With all their faults, trade-unions have done more for humanity than any other organization of men that ever existed. They have done more for decency, for honesty, for education, for the betterment of the race, for the developing of character in man, than any other association of men.

FRANKLIN D. ROOSEVELT
Address before the Teamsters' Union convention

It is one of the characteristics of a free and democratic modern nation that it have free and independent labor unions.

JOHN L. LEWIS

No tin hat brigade of goose-stepping vigilantes or bible-babbling mob of blackguarding and corporation-paid scoundrels will prevent the onward march of labor, or divert its purpose to play its natural and rational part in the development of the economic, political, and social life of our nation.

Unionization, as opposed to communism, presupposes the relation of employment; it is based upon the wage system, and it recognizes fully and unreservedly the institution of private property and the right to investment profits. It is upon the fuller development of collective bargaining, the wider expansion of the labor movement, the increased influence of labor in our national councils, that the perpetuity of our democratic institutions must largely depend.

The organized workers of America, free in their industrial life, conscious partners of production, secure in their homes, and enjoying a decent standard of living will prove the finest bulwark against the intrusion of alien doctrines of government.

EUGENE DEBS

Speech delivered in court before being sentenced for violating the Espionage Act

I am thinking this morning of the men in the mills and factories; of the men in the mines and on the railroads. I am thinking of the women who for a paltry wage are compelled to work out their barren lives; of the little children who in this system are robbed of their childhood and in their tender years are seized in the remorseless grasp of Mammon and forced into the industrial dungeons, there to feed the monster machines while they themselves are being starved and stunted, body and soul. I see them dwarfed and diseased and their little lives broken and blasted because in this high noon of our twentieth-century Christian civilization money is still so much more important than the flesh and blood of childhood. In very truth gold is god today and rules with pitiless sway in the affairs of men.

THEODORE ROOSEVELT

We cannot afford to let any group of citizens, any individual citizens, live or labor under conditions which are injurious to the common welfare. Industry must submit to such public regulation as will make it a means of life and health, not of death of inefficiency.

FRANKLIN D. ROOSEVELT

Gubernatorial Inaugural Address

To secure more of life's pleasures for the farmer; to guard the toilers in the factories and to ensure them a fair wage and protection from the dangers of their trades; to compensate them by adequate insurance for injuries received while working for us; to open the doors of knowledge to their children more widely; to aid those who are crippled and ill; to pursue with strict justice, all evil persons who prey upon their fellow men; and at the same time, by intelligent and helpful sympathy, to lead wrongdoers into right paths—all of these great aims of life are more fully realized here than in any other State of the Union.

THE NATIONAL RECOVERY ACT

A national emergency, productive of widespread unemployment and disorganization of industry, which burdens interstate and foreign commerce, affects the public welfare, and undermines the standards of living of the American people, is hereby declared to exist. It is hereby declared to be the policy of Congress to remove obstructions to the free flow of interstate and foreign commerce which tend to diminish the amount thereof; and to provide for the general welfare by promoting the organization of industry for the purpose of cooperative action among trade groups, to induce and maintain united action of labor and management under adequate governmental sanctions and supervision, to eliminate unfair competitive practices, to promote the fullest possible utilization of the present productive capacity of industries, to avoid undue restriction of production (except as may be temporarily required), to increase the consumption of industrial and agricultural products by increasing purchasing power, to reduce and relieve unemployment, to improve standards of labor, and otherwise to rehabilitate industry and to conserve natural resources.

FRANKLIN D. ROOSEVELT
Speech, Washington, D.C.

True wealth is not a static thing. It is a living thing made out of the disposition of men to create and to distribute the good things of life with rising standards of living.

FRANKLIN D. ROOSEVELT
Remarks made upon signing The Social Security Act

Today a hope of many years standing is in large part fulfilled. The civilization of the past hundred years, with its startling industrial changes, has tended more and more to make life insecure. Young people have come to wonder what would be their lot when they came to old age. The man with a job has wondered how long the job would last.

This Social Security measure gives at least some protection to thirty million of our citizens who will reap direct benefits through unemployment compensation, through old-age pensions, and through increased services for the protection of children and the prevention of ill health.

We can never ensure 100 percent of the population against 100 percent of the hazards and vicissitudes of life, but we have tried to frame a law which will give some measure of protection to the average citizen and to his family against the loss of a job and against poverty-ridden old age.

This law, too, represents a cornerstone in a structure which is being built but is by no means complete—a structure intended to lessen the force of possible future depressions, to act as a protection to future administrations of the government against the necessity of going deeply into debt to furnish relief to the needy—a law to flatten out the peaks and valleys of deflation and of inflation—in other words, a law that will take care of human needs and at the same time provide for the United States an economic structure of vastly greater soundness.

FRANKLIN D. ROOSEVELT
Fireside chat

Not only our future economic soundness but the very soundness of our democratic institutions depends on the determination of our government to give employment to idle men. The people of America are in agreement in defending their liberties at any cost, and the first line of that defense lies in the protection of economic security.

HARRY S TRUMAN
Labor Day address

Today too many Americans in country clubs and fashionable resorts are repeating, like parrots, the phrase "labor must be kept in its place." It is time that all Americans realize that the place of labor is side by side with the businessman and with the farmer, and not one degree lower.

A. PHILIP RANDOLPH
Speech given at Lincoln Memorial

We are gathered here in the largest demonstration in the history of this nation. Let the nation and the world know the meaning of our numbers. We are not pressure groups, we are not an organization or a group of organizations, we are not a mob. We are the advance guard of a massive moral revolution for jobs and freedom.

LYNDON B. JOHNSON

Giving a man a chance to work and feed his family and provide for his children does not destroy his initiative. Hunger destroys initiative. Ignorance destroys initiative. A cold and indifferent government destroys initiative.

FRANKLIN D. ROOSEVELT

Better the occasional faults of a government that lives in a spirit of charity than the constant omissions of a government frozen in the ice of its own indifference.

First Inaugural Address

FRANKLIN D. ROOSEVELT

This is a day of national consecration, and I am certain that my fellow-Americans expect that on my induction into the Presidency I will address them with a candor and a decision which the present situation of our nation impels.

This is pre-eminently the time to speak the truth, the whole truth, frankly and boldly. Nor need we shrink from honestly facing conditions in our country today. This great nation will endure as it has endured, will revive and will prosper.

So first of all let me assert my firm belief that the only thing we have to fear is fear itself —namely, unreasoning, unjustified terror which paralyzes needed efforts to convert retreat into advance.

In every dark hour of our national life a leadership of frankness and vigor has met with that understanding and support of the people themselves which is essential to victory. I am convinced that you will again give that support to leadership in these critical days.

In such a spirit on my part and on yours we face our common difficulties. They concern, thank God, only material things. Values have shrunken to fantastic levels; taxes have risen; our ability to pay has fallen, government of all kinds is faced by serious curtailment of income; the means of exchange are frozen in the currents of trade; the withered leaves of industrial enterprise lie on every side; farmers find no markets for their produce; the savings of many years in thousands of families are gone.

More important, a host of unemployed citizens face the grim problem of existence, and an equally great number toil with little return. Only a foolish optimist can deny the dark realities of the moment.

Yet our distress comes from no failure of substance. We are stricken by no plague of locusts. Compared with the perils which our forefathers conquered because they believed and were not afraid, we have still much to be thankful for. Nature still offers her bounty and human efforts have multiplied it. Plenty is at our doorstep, but a generous use of it languishes in the very sight of the supply.

Primarily, this is because the rulers of the exchange of mankind's goods have failed through their own stubbornness and their own incompetence, have admitted their failure and abdicated. Practices of the unscrupulous money changers stand indicted in the court of public opinion, rejected by the hearts and minds of men.

True, they have tried, but their efforts have been cast in the pattern of an outworn tradition. Faced by failure of credit, they have proposed only the lending of more money.

Stripped of the lure of profit by which to induce our people to follow their false leadership, they have resorted to exhortations, pleading tearfully for restored confidence. They know only the rules of a generation of self-seekers.

They have no vision, and when there is no vision the people perish.

The money changers have fled from their high seats in the temple of our civilization. We may now restore that temple to the ancient truths.

The measure of the restoration lies in the extent to which we apply social values more noble than mere monetary profit.

Happiness lies not in the mere possession of money; it lies in the joy of achievement, in the thrill of creative effort.

The joy and moral stimulation of work no longer must be forgotten in the mad chase of evanescent profits. These dark days will be worth all they cost us if they teach us that our true destiny is not to be ministered unto but to minister to ourselves and to our fellow-men.

Recognition of the falsity of material wealth as the standard of success goes hand in hand with the abandonment of the false belief that public office and high political position are to be valued only by the standards of pride of place and personal profit; and there must be an end to a conduct in banking and in business which too often has given to a sacred trust the likeness of callous and selfish wrongdoing.

Small wonder that confidence languishes, for it thrives only on honesty, on honor, on the sacredness of obligations, on faithful protection, on unselfish performance. Without them it cannot live.

Restoration calls, however, not for changes in ethics alone. This nation asks for action, and action now.

Our greatest primary task is to put people to work. This is no unsolvable problem if we face it wisely and courageously.

It can be accomplished in part by direct recruiting by the government itself, treating the task as we would treat the emergency of a war, but at the same time, through this employment, accomplishing greatly needed projects to stimulate and reorganize the use of our natural resources.

Hand in hand with this, we must frankly recognize the overbalance of population in our industrial centers and, by engaging on a national scale in the redistribution, endeavor to provide a better use of the land for those best fitted for the land.

The task can be helped by definite efforts to raise the values of agricultural products and with this the power to purchase the output of our cities.

It can be helped by preventing realistically the tragedy of the growing loss, through foreclosure, of our small homes and our farms.

It can be helped by insistence that the Federal, State and local governments act forthwith on the demand that their cost be drastically reduced.

It can be helped by the unifying of relief activities which today are often scattered, uneconomical and unequal. It can be helped by national planning for and supervision of all forms of transportation and of communications and other utilities which have a definitely public character.

There are many ways in which it can be helped, but it can never be helped merely by talking about it. We must act, and act quickly.

Finally, in our progress toward a resumption of work we require two safeguards against a return of the evils of the old order; there must be a strict supervision of all banking and credits and investments; there must be an end to speculation with other people's money, and there must be provision for an adequate but sound currency.

These are the lines of attack. I shall presently urge upon a new Congress in special session detailed measures for their fulfillment, and I shall seek the immediate assistance of the several States.

Through this program of action we address ourselves to putting our own national house in order and making income balance outgo....

If I read the temper of our people correctly, we now realize as we have never before, our interdependence on each other; that we cannot merely take, but we must give as well; that if we are to go forward we must move as a trained and loyal army willing to sacrifice for the good of a common discipline, because, without such discipline, no progress is made, no leadership becomes effective.

THEODORE DREISER
Ev'ry Month

It is an ideal so commonplace that it is almost a necessity, and so perfect that, if struggled for, gives rise to almost every other virtue....This is the ideal...of living the spirit of a social Samaritan, of, in short, working for the general good of others.

At first it may seem as if this were not so much of a pleasing ideal, as one difficult and severe, but it seems so only to those who have never had it presented to them in their youth....It is an ideal that is compatible with the teachings of every religion, and much more inspiring than the dogmas of most. It is one that appeals direct to the heart of the child.

HILLARY RODHAM CLINTON
It Takes a Village

One way in which young people have historically come together and expressed their sense of humanity and compassion is by giving their service to a greater cause. This is an American tradition that extends from the YMCAs and YWCAs and the Boy Scouts and Girl Scouts, begun around the turn of the century, to the Civilian Conservation Corps and National Youth Administration of the Great Depression, and the Peace Corps, which was launched in the early 1960s.

As civil rights leader Martin Luther King, Jr., reminded us, "Everybody can be great because everybody can serve."

Throughout our history, American thinkers and philosophers have recognized that public service is crucial to safeguarding democracy and to maintaining national unity in peacetime as well as in war. Harvard professor Robert Putnam observes that people who join the PTA or their local garden clubs or bowling leagues learn lessons that are central to democracy: mutual trust, cooperation, the habit of expressing their opinions openly and listening to those of others. In the words of former senator Harris Wofford, who helped to found the Peace Corps and who now heads the Corporation for National Service, "the service ethic should be to democracy what the work ethic is to capitalism."

BO LOZOFF
Utne Reader

The responsibility of living a conscious life is to always be reflecting on the now, on what we need now. There's a beautiful story of one of the Hasidic Jewish masters of the Middle Ages. After he died, somebody asked one of his disciples, "What was the most important thing to your master?" The disciple thought for a minute and said, "Whatever he happened to be doing at the moment."

I think we are suffering terribly from being really deep, divine people and not acting like it, not structuring our society around it, not leaving time in our day for being deep, reflective people who appreciate the sun coming up and going down, and who cherish each other. The culture is constantly trying to bait people with the idea that time is of the essence, that you have to accomplish more; you need to be at your computer with headphones on learning that extra language, with a broom up your ass so you can sweep the floor at the same time. We have to resist that.

To be *civilized* means to live a life that cherishes others and exudes gratitude and joy. I find that I hardly ever use the word *joy* without the adjective *simple* in front of it. At the same time, I think that the "new simplicity" movement is soon going to take off in a different direction from its current one. People will soon realize that they ought to cut down on their material needs and their work time in order to be part of the community and of all creation, not just to have this little enclosed feeling of selfhood that says, "I'm going to bike down to the bagel shop and get a baguette." Ultimately, that's not much fun.

ABRAHAM LINCOLN

We can succeed only by concert. It is not, "Can any of us imagine better?" but, "Can we all do better?"

CAROLYN FORCHÉ
Utne Reader

We would be much better off if more of us understood ourselves to be workers. I have a white-collar occupation—professor—but I am one paycheck away from poverty like millions of others. If we truly understood ourselves to be workers and wager earners, we would take better care of one another—after all, who is going to look out for common working folk if not for common working folk? We *are* becoming aware, I think, that we are all interrelated. Once we relate in a way that doesn't reduce or dominate either party... with a spouse or a loved one, I think we begin to appreciate the radiance of the larger web of interrelatedness, and we wake up. There is no 'social Beyond.' The division and suffering in Bosnia are neighbor to us, are possible for us. We already have gated communities; we're already taking part in a refeudalization of our community life, in order to realize something called *security*.

It's an illusion. We'll never be secure while life is insecure for millions. The security of anyone is contingent upon the safety of everyone.

MARTIN LUTHER KING, JR.

Everybody can be great. Because anybody can serve. You don't have to have a college degree to serve. You don't have to make your subject and your verb agree to serve. You don't have to know about Plato and Aristotle to serve. You don't have to know Einstein's theory of relativity to serve. You don't have to know the second theory of thermodynamics in physics to serve. You only need a heart full of grace. A soul generated by love.

ROBERT PENN WARREN
All the King's Men

"I have a speech here," he said. "It is a speech about what this state needs. But there's no use telling you what this state needs. You are the state. You know what you need. Look at your pants. Have they got holes at the knee? Listen to your belly. Did it ever rumble for emptiness? Look at your crop. Did it ever rot in the field because the road was so bad you couldn't get it to market? Look at your kids. Are they growing up ignorant as you and dirty because there isn't any school for them?"

Willie paused, and blinked around at the crowd. "No," he said, "I'm not going to read you any speech. You know what you need better'n I could tell you. But I'm going to tell you a story.... It's a funny story.... Get ready to laugh. Get ready to bust your sides for it is sure a funny story. It's about a hick. It's about a red-neck, like you all, if you please. Yeah, like you. He grew up like any other mother's son on the dirty roads and gully washes of a north-state farm. He knew all about being a hick. He knew what it was to get up and milk before breakfast so he could set off by sunup to walk six miles to a one-room, slab-sided schoolhouse. He knew what it was to pay high taxes for that windy shack of a schoolhouse and those gully-washed red-clay roads to walk over to break his wagon axle or string-halt his mules on.

"Oh, he knew what it was to be a hick, summer and winter. He figured if he wanted to do anything he had to do it himself. So he sat up nights and studied books and studied law so maybe he could do something about changing things. He didn't study that law in any man's school or college. He studied it nights after a hard day's work in the field. So he could change things some. For himself and for folks like him. I am not lying to you. He didn't start out thinking about all the other hicks and how he was going to do wonderful things for them. He started out thinking of number one, but something came to him on the way. How he could not do something for himself and not for other folks or for himself without the help of other folks. It was going to be all together or none."

STEPHANIE MILLS
Utne Reader

Compassion is a very scary thing to wish for in yourself, because if you are granted it you have to change what you are doing. Of course joy is part of the package too. If I'm utterly compassionate with all beings—if I'm in perfect sympathy with the chickadees on my farm, those little balls of life, I can partake of their unselfconsciousness, vitality, and animation. Strength comes with that. But at the same time, compassion for the *suffering* around us—if we really felt it—would oblige us to liquidate our holdings, get out on the street with a begging bowl, really dramatically reduce our demands on the rest of the beings on earth. Yes, there is a certain awe at the total set of possibilities that compassion implies.

MARTIN LUTHER KING, JR.

I am convinced that if we are to get on the right side of the world revolution, we as a nation must undergo a radical revolution of values. We must rapidly begin the shift from a "thing-oriented" society to a "person-oriented" society. When machines and computers, profit motives and property rights are considered more important than people, the giant triplets of racism, materialism, and militarism are incapable of being conquered.

MORRIS ROSENFELD
Cited in World of Our Fathers *by Irving Howe*

Over whom shall we weep first?
Over the burned ones?
Over those beyond recognition?
Over those who have been crippled?

Or driven senseless?
Or smashed?
I weep for them all.

PEARL S. BUCK
My Several Worlds

Our society must make it right and possible for old people not to fear the young or be deserted by them, for the test of a civilization is the way that it cares for its helpless members.

MARY CATHERINE BATESON
Composing a Life

Caring can be learned by all human beings, can be worked into the design of every life, meeting an individual need as well as a pervasive need in society.

JAMES KELLER

A candle loses nothing of its light by lighting another candle.

RALPH WALDO EMERSON

To believe your own thought, to believe that what is true for you in your private heart is true for all men—that is genius.

MARTIN LUTHER KING, JR.
Address given at Riverside Church, 1967

True revolution of value will soon cause us to question the fairness and justice of many of our past and present policies. On the one hand we are called to play the Good Samaritan on life's roadside; but that will be only an initial act. One day we come to see that men and women will not be constantly beaten and robbed as they make their journey on Life's highway. True compassion is more than flinging a coin to a beggar; it is not haphazard and superficial. It comes to see that an edifice which produces beggars needs restructuring. A true revolution of values will soon look uneasily on the glaring contrast of poverty and wealth.

WILL ALLEN DROMGOOLE
"The Bridge Builder"

An old man, going a lone highway,
Came, at the evening, cold and gray,
To a chasm, vast, and deep, and wide,
Through which was flowing a sullen tide.
The old man crossed in the twilight dim;
The sullen stream had no fears for him;
but he turned, when safe on the other side,
and built a bridge to span the tide.
"Old man," said a fellow pilgrim, near,
"You are wasting strength with building here;
Your journey will end with the ending day;
You never again must pass this way;
You have crossed the chasm, deep and wise—
Why build you the bridge at the eventide?"

The builder lifted his old gray head:
"Good friend, in the path I have come," he said,
"There followeth after me today
A youth, whose feet must pass this way.
This chasm, that has been naught to me,
To that fair-haired youth may a pitfall be.
He, too, must cross in the twilight dim;
Good friend, I am building the bridge for *him*."

THEODORE ROOSEVELT
Message to Congress

To waste, to destroy, our natural resources, to skin and exhaust the land instead of using it so as to increase its usefulness, will result in undermining in the days of our children the very prosperity which we ought by right to hand down to them amplified and developed.

THEODORE ROOSEVELT

Conservation means development as much as it does protection. I recognize the right and duty of this generation to develop and use the natural resources of our land; but I do not recognize the right to waste them, or to rob, by wasteful use, the generations that come after us. I ask nothing of the nation except that it so behave as each farmer here behaves with reference to his own children. That farmer is a poor creature who skins the land and leaves it worthless to his children. The farmer is a good farmer who, having enabled the land to support himself and to provide for the education of his children, leaves it to them a little better than he found it himself. I believe the same thing of a nation.

Moreover, I believe that the natural resources must be used for the benefit of all our people, and not monopolized for the benefit of the few, and here again is another case in which I am accused of taking a revolutionary attitude. People forget now that one hundred years ago there were public men of good character who advocated the nation selling its public lands in great quantities, so that the nation could get the most money out of it, and giving it to the men who could cultivate it for their own uses. We took the proper democratic ground that the land should be granted in small sections to the men who were actually to till it and live on it. Now, with the water-power, with the forests, with the mines, we are brought face to face with the fact that there are many people who will go with us in conserving the resources only if they are to be allowed to exploit them for their benefit. That is one of the fundamental reasons why the special interests should be driven out of politics. Of all the questions which can come before this nation, short of the actual preservation of its existence in a great way, there is none which compares in importance with the great central task of leaving this land even a better land for our descendants than it is for us, and training them into a better race to inhabit the land and pass it on. Conservation is a great moral issue, for it involves the patriotic duty of ensuring the safety and continuance of the nation. Let me add that the health and vitality of our people are at least as well worth conserving as their forests, waters, lands, and minerals, and in this great work the national government must bear the most important part.

FRANKLIN D. ROOSEVELT
Letter to the governors urging uniform soil conservation laws

The nation that destroys its soil destroys itself.

GIFFORD PINCHOT
Cited in Otis L. Graham, Jr., The Great Campaign

Conservation . . . stands for development. There has been a fundamental misconception that conservation meant nothing but the husbanding of resources for future generations. There could be no more serious mistake. Conservation does mean provision for the future, but it means also and first of all the recognition of the right of the present generation to the fullest necessary use of all the resources . . . now existing. . . . We have a limited supply of coal. There will never be any more of it than there is now. . . . If it can be preserved, if its life can be extended, if by preventing waste there can be more coal in this country when this generation is gone, after we have made every needed use of this source of power, then this country is just so much further ahead. Conservation . . . stands emphatically for the use of substitutes for all the exhaustible natural resources, for the development and use of water power, for the prevention of waste...for the use of foresight, prudence, thrift and intelligence in dealing with public matters for national efficiency.

BOOKER T. WASHINGTON
Speech to the Convention of National Negro Business League

Let us spend less time talking about the part of the city that we cannot live in and more time making the part of the city that we can live in beautiful and attractive.

EDWIN WAY TEALE
Circle of the Seasons

The long fight to save wild beauty represents democracy at its best. It requires citizens to practice the hardest of virtues—self-restraint.

ALDO LEOPOLD
Cited in Stewart L. Udall's The Quiet Crisis

We abuse land because we regard it as a commodity belonging to us. When we see land as a community to which we belong, we may begin to use it with love and respect.

RANDY HAYES
Utne Reader

The basic ideas of what constitutes a sustainable society are known. Now we need every sector of society from the business realm to the citizens' watchdog realm to the government realm to really put the ideas in place and implement them. Hence what I call the 75 percent solution. Let's implement a 75 percent reduction of wood and wood paper use. Then let's assess what's needed after that. But at least in that 10-year period we will have done something of a deep systemic nature. It wouldn't be a drop in the bucket.

Jesse Jackson used to say that people change from either inspiration or desperation. I fear it's going to take a few more spasms, more Chernobyls and Mexican economic crises and Ethiopian droughts, to get people to realize the degree of change necessary to build a sustainable society.

The ecological security of the biosphere is a national security issue. The UN is projecting that the main causes of refugee migration in the upcoming decades will be ecological—floods in Bangladesh, et cetera. If global warming gets to the point where the ocean rises, well, there are plenty of statistics on how much of the world's population lives on coasts. Where are they going to go? What kind of political and national security threat is that going to cause? People are going to have to accept that old cliché from the '70s: Nature bats last.

LEWIS MUMFORD
The Way and The Life

Nothing is unthinkable, nothing impossible to the balanced person, provided it arises out of the needs of life and is dedicated to life's further developments.

JAMES BALDWIN
Just Above My Head

Watching my children grow, old enough to have some sense of where I've been, having suffered enough to be no longer terrified of suffering, and knowing something of joy, too, I know that we must attempt to be responsible for what we know. Only this action moves us, without fear, into what we do not know, and what we do not know is limitless.

EUGENE McCARTHY
Speech denouncing the war in Vietnam

Instead of the language of promise and of hope, we have in politics today a new vocabulary in which the critical word is "war": war on poverty, war on ignorance, war on crime, war on pollution. None of these problems can be solved by war but only by persistent, dedicated, and thoughtful attention. . . .

The scriptural promise of the good life is one in which the old men see visions and the young men dream dreams. In the context of this war and all of its implications, the young men of America do not dream dreams, but many live in the nightmare of moral anxiety, of concern and great apprehension; and the old men, instead of visions which they can offer to the young, are projecting, in the language of the secretary of state, a specter of one billion Chinese threatening the peace and safety of the world—a frightening and intimidating future.

The message from the administration today is a message of apprehension, a message of fear, yes—even a message of fear of fear.

This is not the real spirit of America. I do not believe that it is. This is a time to test the mood and spirit:

To offer in place of doubt—trust.

In place of expediency—right judgment.

In place of ghettos, let us have neighborhoods and communities.

In place of incredibility—integrity.

In place of murmuring, let us have clear speech; let us again hear America singing.

In place of disunity, let us have dedication of purpose.

In place of near despair, let us have hope.

This is the promise of greatness which was seated for us by Adlai Stevenson and which was brought to form and positive action in the words and actions of John F. Kennedy.

Let us pick up again these lost strands and weave them again into the fabric of America. Let us sort out the music from the sounds and again respond to the trumpet and the steady drum.

Benjamin Mays
"What Man Lives By"

However hard the road, however difficult today, tomorrow things will be better. Tomorrow may not be better, but we must believe that it will be. Wars may never cease, but we must continue to strive to eliminate them. We may not abolish poverty, but we must believe that we can provide bread enough and to spare for every living creature and that we can find the means to distribute it. We may not exterminate racism, but we must believe that different racial groups can live together in peace, and we must never cease to try. . . .

Lyndon B. Johnson
Message to Congress

We have never lost sight of our goal: an America in which every citizen shares all the opportunities of his society, in which every man has a chance to advance his welfare to the limit of his capacities. We have come a long way toward this goal. We still have a long way to go.

Martin Luther King, Jr.
Speech on the steps of the Alabama State Capitol after the march from Selma to Montgomery

I know some of you are asking today, "How long will it take?" I come to say to you this afternoon however difficult the moment, however frustrating the hour, it will not be long, because truth pressed to earth will rise again.

How long? Not long, because no lie can live forever.

How long? Not long, because you will reap what you sow.

How long? Not long, because the arm of the moral universe is long, but it bends toward justice.

EUGENE DEBS

I can see the dawn of the better day for humanity. The people are awakening. In due time they will and must come to their own.

RALPH WALDO EMERSON

Every spirit builds itself a house, and beyond its house a world, and beyond its world a heaven.

Freedom is the Right to Choose

ARCHIBALD MACLEISH

We have, and we know we have, the abundant means to bring our boldest dreams to pass—to create for ourselves whatever world we have the courage to desire. We have the metal and the men to take this country down, if we please to take it down, and to build it again as we please to build it. We have the tools and the skill and the intelligence to take our cities apart and to put them together, to lead our roads and rivers where we please to lead them, to build our houses where we want our houses, to brighten the air, to clean the wind, to live as men in this Republic, free men, should be living. We have the power and the courage and the resources of good-will and decency and common understanding—a long experience of decency and common understanding—to enable us to live, not in this continent alone but in the world, as citizens in common of the world, with many others.

We have the power and the courage and the resources of experience to create a nation such as men have never seen. And, more than that, we have the moment of creation in our hands. Our forefathers, when they came to the New England valleys or the Appalachian meadows, girdled the trees and dragged the roots into fences and built themselves shelters and, so roughly housed, farmed the land for their necessities. Then, later, when there were means to do it, when there was time, when the occasion offered, they burned the tangled roots and rebuilt their fences and their houses—but rebuilt them with a difference: rebuilt them as villages, as neighborhoods; rebuilt them with those lovely streets, those schools, those churches which still speak of their conception of the world they wanted. When the means offered, when the time offered, men created, on the clearings of the early useful farms, the town that made New England and the Alleghenies.

Now is the time for the re-creation, the rebuilding, not of the villages and towns but of a nation. Now is the time to consider that the trees are down, that the land has been broken, that the means are available and the continent itself must be rebuilt. Our necessities have been accomplished as men have always accomplished their necessities—with wastefulness, with ugliness, with cruelty, as well as with the food of harvests. Our necessities have been accomplished with the roots of the broken trees along the fences, the rough shelters, the lonely lives. Now is the time to build the continent itself—to take down and to rebuild; and not the houses and the cities only, but the life itself, raising upon the ready land the brotherhood that can employ it and delight in it and use it as people such as ours should use it.

We stand at the moment of the building of great lives. . . . But to seize the moment and the means we must agree, as men in those New England valleys were agreed, upon the world we mean to bring about. We must agree upon the image of that world.

Secure the Blessings of Liberty

GEORGE WASHINGTON
Letter to James Madison

Liberty, when it begins to take root, is a plant of rapid growth.

THOMAS PAINE
"The Liberty Tree"

In a chariot of light from the regions of day,
The Goddess of Liberty came.
Ten thousand celestials directed the way
And hither conducted the dame.
A fair budding branch from the gardens above,
Where millions with millions agree,
She brought in her hand as a pledge of her love,
And the plant she named Liberty Tree.

MARK TWAIN
Letter to the Bartholdi Pedestal Fund Art Loan Exhibition

Another thing: What has liberty done for us? Nothing in particular that I know of. What have we done for her? Everything. We've given her a home, and a good home, too. And if she knows anything, she knows it's the first time she ever struck that novelty. She knows that when we took her in she had been a mere tramp for 6,000 years, Biblical measure. Yes, and we not only ended her troubles and made things soft for her permanently, but we made her respectable—and that she hadn't ever been before.

JAMES OTIS
His personal motto

Ubi libertas ibi patria [Where liberty is, there is my country].

THOMAS JEFFERSON
Summary View of the Rights of British America

The God who gave us life, gave us liberty at the same time.

WOODROW WILSON

Liberty is its own reward.

AMBROSE BIERCE
The Devil's Dictionary

Liberty, n. One of Imagination's most precious possessions.

JAMES B. CONANT
Our Unique Heritage

Liberty like charity must begin at home.

HERMAN MELVILLE
White Jacket

We Americans are the peculiar, chosen people—the Israel of our time; we bear the ark of the liberties of the world.

CARL SANDBURG
"Washington Monument by Night"

The republic is a dream.
Nothing happens unless first a dream.

JAMES RUSSELL LOWELL
New England Two Centuries Ago

Puritanism, believing itself quick with the seed of religious liberty, laid, without knowing it, the egg of democracy.

Massachusetts General Court
Massachusetts Body of Liberties

The free fruition of such liberties Immunities and priviledges as humanite, Civilitie, and Christianitie call for as due to every man in his place and proportion without impeachment and Infringement hath ever bene and ever will be the tranquillitie and Stabilitie of Churches and Commonwealths. And the deniall or deprivall thereof, the disturbance if not the ruine of both.

We hould it therefore our dutie and safetie whilst we are about the further establishing of this Government to collect and expresse all such freedomes as for present we foresee may concern us, and our posteritie after us, and to ratify them with our solemne consent....

No mans life shall be taken away, no mans honour or good name shall be stayned, no mans person shall be arested, restrayned, banished, dismembred, nor any wayes punished, no man shall be deprived of his wife or children, no mans goods or estaite shall be taken away from him, nor any way indammaged under coulor of law or Countenance of Authoritie, unless it be by vertue or equitie of some espresse law of the Country warranting the same, established by a Generall Court and sufficiently published, or in case of the defect of a law in any particular case by the word of God. And in Capitall cases, or in cases concerning the dismembring or banishment, according to that word to be judged by the Generall Court.

Every person within this Jurisdiction, whether Inhabitant or forreiner shall enjoy the same justice and law, that is generall for the plantation, which we constitute and execute one towards another without partialitie or delay....

Every man whether Inhabitant or forreiner, free or not free shall have libertie to come to any lawfull, seasonable, and materiall question, or to present any necessary motion, complaint, petition, Bill or information, whereof that meeting hath proper cognizance, so it be done in convenient time, due order, and respective manner.

John Winthrop
Liberty and Governmental Authority

There is a twofold liberty—natural (I mean as our nature is now corrupt) and civil or federal. The first is common to man with beasts and other creatures. By this, man, as he stands in relation to man simply, hath liberty to do what he lists; it is at liberty to evil as well as to good. This liberty is incompatible and inconsistent with authority, and cannot endure the least restraint of the most just authority. The exercise and maintaining of this liberty makes men grow more evil, and in time to be worse than brute beasts: *omnes sumus licentia deteriores*. This is that great enemy of truth and peace, that wild beast, which all the ordinances of God are bent against, to restrain and subdue it.

The other kind of liberty I call civil or federal; it may also be termed moral, in reference to the covenant between God and man, and the politic covenants and constitutions, amongst men themselves. This liberty is the proper end and object of authority, and cannot subsist without it; and it is a liberty to that only which is good, just, and honest. This liberty you are to stand for, with the hazard (not only of your good, but) of your lives, if need be. Whatsoever crosseth this is not authority but a distemper thereof. This liberty is maintained and exercised in a way of subjection to authority; it is of the same kind of liberty wherewith Christ hath made us free.

SAMUEL ADAMS
"The Rights of Colonists"

Among the natural rights of colonists are these: first, a right to life; secondly, to liberty; thirdly, to property; together with the right to support and defend them as best they can.

SAMUEL ELIOT MORISON
The Oxford History of the American People

Make no mistake; the American Revolution was not fought to obtain freedom, but to preserve liberties that Americans already had as colonials. Independence was no conscious goal, secretly nurtured in cellar or jungle by bearded conspirators, but a reluctant last resort, to preserve "life, liberty and the pursuit of happiness."

The Declaration of Independence
SECOND CONTINENTAL CONGRESS

When in the course of human events, it becomes necessary for one people to dissolve the political bands which have connected them with another, and to assume among the powers of the earth the separate and equal station to which the laws of nature and of nature's God entitle them, a decent respect to the opinions of mankind requires that they should declare the causes which impel them to the separation.

We hold these truths to be self-evident: that all men are created equal, that they are endowed by their Creator with certain unalienable rights, that among these are life, liberty, and the pursuit of happiness. That to secure these rights, governments are instituted among men, deriving their just powers from the consent of the governed; that whenever any form of government becomes destructive of these ends, it is the right of the people to alter or to abolish it, and to institute new government, laying its foundation on such principles and organizing its powers in such form, as to them shall seem most likely to effect their safety and happiness.

Prudence, indeed, will dictate that governments long established should not be changed for light and transient causes; and accordingly all experience hath shown, that mankind are more disposed to suffer, while evils are sufferable, than to right themselves by abolishing the forms to which they are accustomed. But when a long train of abuses and usurpations, pursuing invariably the same object, evinces a design to reduce them under absolute despotism, it is their right, it is their duty, to throw off such government, and to provide new guards for their future security. Such has been the patient sufferance of these colonies; and such is now the necessity which constrains them to alter their former systems of government.

The history of the present king of Great Britain is a history of repeated injuries and usurpations, all having in direct object the establishment of an absolute tyranny over these states. To prove this, let facts be submitted to a candid world.

He has refused his assent to laws, the most wholesome and necessary for the public good.

He has forbidden his governors to pass laws of immediate and pressing importance, unless suspended in their operation till his assent should be obtained; and when so suspended, he has utterly neglected to attend to them.

He has refused to pass other laws for the accommodation of large districts of people, unless those people would relinquish the right of representation in the legislature, a right inestimable to them and formidable to tyrants only.

He has called together legislative bodies at places unusual, uncomfortable, and distant from the depository of their public records, for the sole purpose of fatiguing them into compliance with his measures.

He has dissolved representative houses repeatedly, for opposing with manly firmness his invasions on the rights of people.

He has refused for a long time, after such dissolutions, to cause others to be elected; whereby the legislative powers, incapable of annihilation, have returned to the people at large for their exercise; the state remaining in the meantime exposed to all the dangers of invasion from without, and convulsions within.

He has endeavored to prevent the population of these states; for that purpose obstructing the laws for naturalization of foreigners; refusing to pass others to encourage their migration hither, and raising the conditions of new appropriations of lands.

He has obstructed the administration of justice, by refusing his assent to laws for establishing judiciary powers.

He has made judges dependent on his will alone, for the tenure of their offices, and the amount and payment of their salaries.

He has erected a multitude of new offices, and sent hither swarms of officers to harass our people, and eat out their substance.

He has kept among us, in times of peace, standing armies without the consent of our legislature.

He has affected to render the military independent of and superior to the civil power.

He has combined with others to subject us to a jurisdiction foreign to our constitution, and unacknowledged by our laws; giving his assent to their acts of pretended legislation:

For quartering large bodies of armed troops among us;

For protecting them, by a mock trial, from punishment for any murders which they should commit on the inhabitants of these states;

For cutting off our trade with all parts of the world;

For imposing taxes on us without our consent;

For depriving us, in many cases, of the benefits of trial by jury;

For transporting us beyond seas to be tried for pretended offenses;

For abolishing the free system of English laws in a neighboring province, establishing therein an arbitrary government, and enlarging its boundaries so as to render it at once an example and fit instrument for introducing the same absolute rule into these colonies;

For taking away our charters, abolishing our most valuable laws, and altering fundamentally the forms of our governments;

For suspending our own legislatures, and declaring themselves invested with power to legislate for us in all cases whatsoever.

He has abdicated government here, by declaring us out of his protection and waging war against us.

He has plundered our seas, ravaged our coasts, burnt our towns, and destroyed the lives of our people.

He is at this time transporting large armies of foreign mercenaries to complete the works of death, desolation, and tyranny, already begun with circumstances of cruelty and perfidy scarcely paralleled in the most barbarous ages, and totally unworthy of the head of a civilized nation.

He has constrained our fellow citizens taken captive on the high seas to bear arms against their country, to become the executioners of their friends and brethren, or to gall themselves by their hands.

He has excited domestic insurrections amongst us, and has endeavored to bring on the inhabitants of our frontiers, the merciless Indian savages, whose known rule of warfare is an undistinguished destruction of all ages, sexes, and conditions.

In every stage of these oppressions we have petitioned for redress in the most humble terms; our repeated petitions have been answered only by repeated injury. A prince, whose character is thus marked by every act which may define a tyrant, is unfit to be the ruler of a free people.

Nor have we been wanting in attention to our British brethren. We have warned them from time to time of attempts by their legislature to extend an unwarrantable jurisdiction over us. We have reminded them of the circumstances of our emigration and settlement here. We have appealed to their native justice and magnanimity, and we have conjured them by the ties of our common kindred to disavow these usurpations, which would inevitably interrupt our connections and correspondence. They too have been deaf to the voice of justice and of consanguinity. We must, therefore, acquiesce in the necessity, which denounces our separation, and hold them, as we hold the rest of mankind, enemies in war, in peace friends.

We, therefore, the representatives of the United States of America, in general congress, assembled, appealing to the Supreme Judge of the world for the rectitude of our intentions, do, in the name and authority of the good people of these colonies, solemnly publish and declare, that these united colonies are, and of right ought to be, free and independent states; that they are absolved from all allegiance to the British crown, and that all political connection between them and the state of Great Britain, is and ought to be totally dissolved; and that as free and independent states, they have full power to levy war, conclude peace, contract alliances, establish commerce, and to do all other acts and things which an independent state may of right do. And for the support of this declaration, with a firm reliance on the protection of Divine Providence, we mutually pledge to each other our lives, our fortunes, and our sacred honor.

LEVITICUS 25:10
Words inscribed on the Liberty Bell

Proclaim Liberty throughout the land unto all the inhabitants thereof.

ROBERT TREAT PAINE
Adams and Liberty

Ye sons of Columbia, who bravely have fought
For those rights which unstain'd from your sires you descended,
May you long taste the blessings your valor has brought,
And your sons reap the soil which your fathers defended.
'Mid the reign of mild peace,
May your nation increase,
With the Glory of Rome and the Wisdom of Greece;
And ne'er may the sons of Columbia be slaves,
While the earth bears a plant or the sea rolls its waves.

Let Fame to the world sound America's voice;
No intrigue can her sons from the government sever;
Her pride is her Adams—his laws are her choice,
And shall flourish till Liberty slumber forever!
Then unite heart and hand,
Like Leonidas' band,

And swear to the God of the ocean and land
that ne'er shall the sons of Columbia be slaves,
While the earth bears a plant or the sea rolls its waves.

PATRICK HENRY

Is life so dear or peace so sweet as to be purchased at the price of chains and slavery? Forbid it, Almighty God. I know not what course others take, but as for me, give me liberty or give me death.

BARRY GOLDWATER

I would remind you that extremism in the defense of liberty is no vice. And let me remind you also that moderation in the pursuit of justice is no virtue.

MALCOLM X
Speech at Oxford University

. . . America is one of the best examples when you read its history, about extremism. Old Patrick Henry said, "Liberty or death!" That's extreme, very extreme.

JOHN DICKINSON
"The Liberty Song"

Come join hand in hand, brave Americans all,
And rouse your bold hearts at fair Liberty's call;
No tyrannous acts shall suppress your just claim,
Or stain with dishonor America's name.

In freedom we're born, and in freedom we'll live,
Our purses are ready,
Steady, friends, steady,
Not as slaves, but as freemen our money we'll give.

Our worthy forefathers—let's give them a cheer—
To climates unknown did courageously steer;
Thro' oceans to deserts for freedom they came,
And dying bequeth'd us their freedom and fame.

Their generous bosoms all dangers despis'd
So highly, so wisely, their birthrights they priz'd;

We'll keep what they gave, we will piously keep,
Nor frustrate their toils on the land and the deep.

The tree their own hands had to liberty rear'd
They live to behold growing strong and rever'd;
With transport then cried, "Now our wishes we gain,
For our children shall gather the fruits of our pain."

Swarms of placeman and pensioners soon will appear
Like locusts deforming the charms of the year;
Suns vainly will rise, showers vainly descend,
If we are to drudge for what others shall spend.

Then join in hand, brave Americans all,
By uniting we stand, by dividing we fall;
In so righteous a cause let us hope to succeed,
For heaven approves of each generous deed.

JOHN ADAMS

Strait is the gate and narrow is the way that leads to liberty, and few nations, if any, have found it.

ELLEN ALDERMAN AND CAROLINE KENNEDY
In Our Defense

Considered together, the ten amendments in the Bill of Rights outline the most comprehensive protection of individual freedom ever written.

THOMAS JEFFERSON
Letter to James Madison

A Bill of Rights is what the people are entitled to against every government on earth, general or particular; and what no just government should refuse, or rest on inference.

U.S. Constitution, The Bill of Rights

AMENDMENT I

Congress shall make no law respecting an establishment of religion, or prohibiting the free exercise thereof; or abridging the freedom of speech, or of the press; or the right of the people to peaceably assemble, and to petition the Government for a redress of grievances.

AMENDMENT II

A well-regulated Militia, being necessary to the security of a free State, the right of the people to keep and bear Arms shall not be infringed.

AMENDMENT III

No soldier shall, in time of peace, be quartered in any house, without the consent of the Owner, nor in time of war, but in a manner prescribed by law.

AMENDMENT IV

The right of the people to be secure in their persons, houses, papers, and effects against unreasonable searches and seizures, shall not be violated, and no Warrants shall issue, but upon probable cause, supported by Oath or affirmation, and particularly describing the place to be searched, and the persons or things to be seized.

AMENDMENT V

No person shall be held to answer for a capital, or otherwise infamous crime, unless on a presentment or indictment of a Grand Jury, except in cases arising in the land or naval forces, or in the Militia, when in actual service in time of War or public danger; nor shall any person be subject for the same offence to be twice put in jeopardy of life or limb; nor shall be compelled in any criminal case to be a witness against himself, nor be deprived of life, liberty, or property, without due process of law; nor shall private property be taken for public use, without just compensation.

AMENDMENT VI

In all criminal prosecutions, the accused shall enjoy the right to a speedy and public trial, by an impartial jury of the State and district wherein the crime shall have been committed, which district shall have been previously ascertained by law, and to be informed of the nature and cause of the accusation; to be confronted with the witnesses against him; to have compulsory process for obtaining witnesses in his favor, and to have the Assistance of Counsel for his defence.

AMENDMENT VII

In suits at common law, where the value in controversy shall exceed twenty dollars, the right of trial by jury shall be preserved, and no fact tried by a jury, shall be otherwise reexamined in any Court of the United States, than according to the rules of the common law.

AMENDMENT VIII

Excessive bail shall not be required, nor excessive fines imposed, nor cruel and unusual punishments inflicted.

AMENDMENT IX

The enumeration in the Constitution, of certain rights, shall not be construed to deny or disparage others retained by the people.

AMENDMENT X

The powers not delegated to the United States by the Constitution, nor prohibited by it to the States, are reserved to the States respectively, or to the people.

JAMES MADISON
National Gazette

Every word [of the Constitution] decides a question between power and liberty.

WOODROW WILSON
Speech in New York City

Liberty has never come from the government. Liberty has always come from the subjects of government. The history of liberty is a history of limitation of government power, not the increase of it.

ALEXANDER HAMILTON
Constitutional Convention debates

We are now forming a republican government. Real liberty is neither found in despotism or the extremes of democracy, but in moderate governments.

BENJAMIN FRANKLIN

Nothing brings more Pain than too much Pleasure; nothing more bondage than too much Liberty.

DANIEL WEBSTER
Speech at Charleston Harbor, Massachusetts

Liberty exists in proportion to wholesome restraint.

JAMES MADISON
Letter to Thomas Jefferson

It is a melancholy reflection that liberty should be equally exposed to danger whether the Government have too much or too little power.

The Raising: A New Song for Federal Mechanics
FRANCES HOPKINSON

I.
Come muster, my Lads, your mechanical Tools,
Your Saws and your Axes, your Hammers and Rules;
Bring your Mallets and Planes, your Level and Line,
And Plenty of Pins of American Pine;
For our roof we will raise, and our Song still shall be—
A government firm and our Citizens free.

II.
Come, up with Plates, lay them firm on the Wall,
Like the People at large, they're the Ground-work of;
Examine them well, and see that they're sound,
Let no rotten Parts in our Building be found;
For our Roof we will raise, and our Song still shall be—
Our Government firm, and our Citizens free.

III.
Now hand up the Girders, lay each in his Place,
Between them the Joists must divide all the Space;
Like Assembly-men, these should lye level along,
Like Girders, our Senate prove loyal and strong;
For our Roof we will raise, and our Song still shall be—
A government firm, over Citizens free.

IV.

The Rafters now frame—your King-Posts and Braces,
And drive your Pins home, to keep all in their Places;
Let Wisdom and Strength in the Fabric combine,
And your Pins be all made of American Pine;
For our Roof we will raise, and our Song still shall be—
A government firm, over Citizens free.

V.

Our King-Posts are Judges—How upright they stand,
Supporting the Braces, the Laws of the Land—
The Laws of the Land, which divide Right from Wrong,
And strengthen the Weak, by weak'ning the Strong;
For our Roof we will raise, and our Song still shall be—
Laws equal and just, for a People that's free.

VI.

Up! Up with the Rafters—each Frame is a State!
How nobly they rise! their Span, too, how great!
From the North to the South, o'er the Whole they extend,
And rest on the Walls, while the Walls they defend!
For our Roof we will raise, and our Song still shall be—
Combined in Strength, yet as Citizens free.

VII.

Now enter the Purlins, and drive your Pins through,
And see that your Joints are drawn home, and all true;
The Purlins will bind all the Rafters together,
The strength of the Whole shall defy Wind and Weather;
For our Roof we will raise, and our Song still shall be—
United as States, but as Citizens free.

VIII.

Come, raise up the Turret—our Glory and Pride—
In the Centre it stands, o'er the Whole to preside;
The Sons of Columbia shall view with Delight
Its Pillars, and Arches, and Towering Height;
Our Roof is now rais'd, and our Song still shall be—
A Federal Hearth, o'er a People still free.

IX.
Huzza! my brave Boys, our Work is complete,
The World shall admire Columbia's fair Seat;
It's strength against Tempest and Time shall be Proof,
And Thousands shall come to dwell under our ROOF.
Whilst we drain the deep Bowl, our Toast still shall be—
Our government firm, and our Citizens free.

GEORGE WASHINGTON
First Inaugural Address

The preservation of the sacred fire of liberty and the destiny of the republican model of government, are justly considered as deeply, perhaps as finally staked, on the experiment entrusted to the hands of the American people.

HENRY WARD BEECHER
Proverbs from Plymouth Pulpit

Liberty is the soul's right to breath, and when it can not take a long breath, laws are girdled too tight.

ROBERT G. INGERSOLL
"Progress" lecture

What light is to the eyes—what air is to the lungs—what love is to the heart, liberty is to the soul of man. Without liberty, the brain is a dungeon, where the chained thoughts die with their pinions pressed against the hingeless doors.

JOHN GREENLEAF WHITTIER
"The Moral Warfare"

When Freedom, on her natal day,
Within her war-rocked cradle lay,
An iron race around her stood,
Baptized her infant brow in blood;
And, through the storm which round her swept,
Their constant ward and watching kept.

Then, where our quiet heirs repose
The roar of baleful battle rose,
And brethren of a common tongue

To mortal strife as tigers sprung,
And every gift on Freedom's shrine
Was man for beast, and blood for wine!

Our fathers to their graves have gone;
Their strife is past, their triumph won;
But sterner trials wait the race
Which rises in their honored place;
A moral warfare with the crime
And folly of an evil time.

So let it be. In God's own might
We gird us for the coming fight,
And, strong in Him whose cause is ours
In conflict with unholy powers,
We grasp the weapons He has given,—
The Light, and Truth, and Love of Heaven!

ABRAHAM LINCOLN
Speech in Edwardsville, Illinois

Our reliance is in the love of liberty which God has planted in us. Our defense is in the spirit which primed liberty as the heritage of all men, in all lands everywhere. Destroy this spirit and you have planted the seeds of despotism at your door.

ULYSSES S. GRANT

God gave us Lincoln and Liberty; let us fight for both.

ABRAHAM LINCOLN
The Gettysburg Address

Fourscore and seven years ago our fathers brought forth on this continent a new nation, conceived in Liberty, and dedicated to the proposition that all men are created equal.

Now we are engaged in a great civil war, testing whether that nation or any nation so conceived and so dedicated, can long endure. We are met on a great battle-field of that war. We have come to dedicate a portion of that field, as a final resting place for those who here gave their lives that that nation might live. It is altogether fitting and proper that we should do this.

But, in a larger sense, we can not dedicate—we can not consecrate—we can not hallow —this ground. The brave men, living and dead, who struggled here, have consecrated it, far above our poor power to add or detract. The world will little note nor long remember what we say here, but it can never forget what they did here. It is for us the living, rather, to be dedicated here to the unfinished work which they who fought here have thus far so nobly advanced. It is rather for us to be here dedicated to the great task remaining before us—that from these honored dead we take increased devotion to that cause for which they gave the last full measure of devotion—that we here highly resolve that these dead shall not have died in vain—that this nation, under God, shall have a new birth of freedom—and that government of the people, by the people, for the people, shall not perish from the earth.

AMERICAN CIVIL LIBERTIES UNION

Liberty is always unfinished business.

LEARNED HAND

Speech to the Board of Regents, University of the State of New York

I had rather take my chance that some traitors will escape detection than spread abroad a spirit of general suspicion and disgust, which accepts rumor and gossip in place of undismayed and unintimidated inquiry.…

That community is already in the process of dissolution where each man begins to eye his neighbor as a possible enemy, where nonconformity with the accepted creed, political as well as religious, is a mark of disaffection; where denunciation, without specification or backing, takes the place of evidence; where orthodoxy chokes freedom of dissent; where faith in the eventual supremacy of reason has become so timid that we dare not enter our convictions in the open lists, to win or lose.…

The mutual confidence on which all else depends can be maintained only by an open mind and a brave reliance upon free discussion.

HARRY EMERSON FOSDICK

Liberty is always dangerous—but it is the safest thing we have.

HARRY S TRUMAN

Radio address after the signing of the terms of unconditional surrender by Japan

Liberty does not make all men perfect nor all society secure. But it has provided more solid progress and happiness and decency for more people than any other philosophy of government in history.

DANIEL WEBSTER

God grants liberty only to those who love it, and are always ready to guard and defend it.

JAMES MADISON
National Gazette

Liberty and order will never be perfectly safe, until a trespass on the constitutional provisions for either shall be felt with the same keenness that resents an invasion of the dearest rights, until every citizen shall be an Argus to espy, and an Aegeon to avenge, the unhallowed deed.

HENRY WARD BEECHER
Proverbs from Plymouth Pulpit

Make men large and strong, and tyranny will bankrupt itself in making shackles for them.

THOMAS JEFFERSON
Letter to Dr. Benjamin Rush

I have sworn upon the altar of God, eternal hostility against every form of tyranny over the mind of man.

THOMAS JEFFERSON

Timid men prefer the calm of despotism to the boisterous sea of liberty.

JOHN ADAMS
Comment to Samuel Adams

The numbers of men in all ages have preferred ease, slumber, and good cheer to liberty, when they have been in competition.

ANDREW JACKSON
Comment to a Presbyterian clergyman

No people ever lost their liberties unless they themselves first became corrupt. The people are the safeguards of their own liberties, and I rely wholly on them to guard themselves.

Obituary of Barbara Jordan

By Francis X. Clines, The New York Times

Barbara Jordan, the black Congresswoman and scholar who stirred the nation with her Churchillian denunciations of the Watergate abuses of Richard M. Nixon, died today [January 17, 1996] in her home state of Texas at the age of fifty-nine.

Ms. Jordan, the first black elected to Congress from Texas after Reconstruction, retired from the House in 1979 after three terms to teach political ethics at the university's Lyndon B. Johnson School of Public Affairs, never losing her potent talent for public speaking even from the confines of a wheelchair.

Most recently, her rich, impassioned voice was heard once more in Congress when, as chairwoman of the Commission on Immigration Reform, she spoke out last year against a proposal to deny automatic citizenship to the children of illegal immigrants born in this country. "To deny birthright citizenship would derail this engine of American liberty," she warned with the same eloquence that mesmerized her American audience on July 25, 1974, when Representative Jordan argued for the impeachment of President Nixon.

Ms. Jordan, whom her students recalled as never being without a copy of the Constitution in her purse, rooted that Watergate speech in her faith in the Constitution's promise and in her personal history as a child of the Jim Crow South.

"I felt somehow for many years that George Washington and Alexander Hamilton just left me out by mistake," she declared, catching the nation's attention with measured, sepulchral oratory from her seat on the House Judiciary Committee. "But through the process of amendment, interpretation and court decision I have finally been included in 'We, the people.'"

Then, with a smoldering glance across the proceedings of the historic Constitutional crisis, Ms. Jordan added, "My faith in the Constitution is whole, it is complete, it is total, and I am not going to sit here and be an idle spectator of the diminution, the subversion, the destruction of the Constitution."

Ms. Jordan was one of American politics' pioneer black women. In 1966, she was elected as the first black state Senator in Texas history, and went on to be the first woman and first black elected to Congress from Texas. In 1976, she was the first black woman to deliver a keynote address at the Democratic National Convention, riveting her audience on national television as she spoke magisterially from the stage at New York's Madison Square Garden.

"All blacks are militant in their guts," she told an interviewer during her first Congressional campaign. "But militancy is expressed in different ways."

As a model of the Democratic politician from the New South, Ms. Jordan was less an angry or confrontational liberal than an imposing master of the process and its details. A consummate politician from her earliest days in the Texas Legislature, Ms. Jordan won a seat on the House Judiciary Committee though only a freshman by importuning her political mentor and friend, President Lyndon B. Johnson, to pull some strings.

"She proved that black is beautiful before we knew what it meant," Mr. Johnson said of her. His widow, Lady Bird Johnson, led Texans in mourning their native daughter. "I feel a stabbing sense of loss at the passing of a good friend," Mrs. Johnson said today.

Ms. Jordan's political prowess saw her ascend to the post of Speaker pro tem in the Texas Senate six years after having arrived there as a political oddity and an outcast.

The youngest of three sisters, Barbara Charline Jordan was born on February 21, 1936, into the poverty of Houston's Fourth Ward. She attended Houston's segregated public schools, and graduated magna cum laude with debating honors from the all-black Texas Southern University. Her father, Benjamin, a Baptist minister, moonlighted as a warehouse clerk to help her pay for college, where her scholarship and assertiveness were honed.

As leader of the debating team, Ms. Jordan, known as B.J. to her friends, later proudly recalled maneuvering the Harvard team to a draw. "When an all-black team ties Harvard, it wins," she said.

Ms. Jordan received a law degree in 1959 from Boston University and was soon at practice from her family's dining-room table. Eventually, she had a second-story office above a print shop near her family's simple frame house.

"I never wanted to be run-of-the-mill," she told Molly Ivins, the Texas writer who was a friend since 1969 and likened interviewing Ms. Jordan to "a bit like grilling God" because of the care, scholarship and booming authority of her speech.

"We were poor," Ms. Jordan said of her strict but loving upbringing. "But so was everyone around us, so we did not notice it."

When Ms. Jordan was eleven, she quit her piano lessons—a defiant act that angered her father. He told her that the only good jobs for black women were in teaching music or in performing, and asked her what she intended to do if she could not play the piano. "I don't know," she recalled telling him, "but I'll manage somehow."

As a Congressional newcomer, Ms. Jordan served notice that she had received 80 percent of the vote and would therefore have far broader interests than the Black Caucus agenda, and would hardly be a "female chauvinist."

"You know, Barbara wasn't really that concerned about the guilt or innocence of Nixon," said Representative Charles B. Rangel, the Manhattan Democrat who served with Ms. Jordan on the impeachment hearings. "She was most concerned that the Constitution not be distorted for political reasons."

Some of Ms. Jordan's earliest politicking was as a young lawyer when she directed one of Houston's first voter drives in support of the Kennedy-Johnson ticket in 1960. She lost her first two bids for elective office in rough-and-tumble, racism-tinged bouts. But she succeeded when state legislative districts were finally redrawn and she became the first black of either sex to be elected to the Texas Senate since 1883.

Even amid the political turmoil of 1974, when Congresswoman Jordan contended that the Watergate conspirings had put the nation "on the edge of repression and tyranny," the outspoken Texan still led with her optimism. During that summer of the Watergate crisis, she took care to visit the graduates of Howard University and urge them: "Reaffirm what ought to be. Get back to the truth; that's old, but get back to it. Get back to what's honest; tell government to do that. Affirm the civil liberties of the people of this country. Do that."

JAMES RUSSELL LOWELL
"The Present Crisis"

They have rights who dare maintain them.

ABRAHAM LINCOLN
Letter to Henry Asbury

The fight must go on. The cause of civil liberty must not be surrendered at the end of one or even one hundred defeats.

WENDELL PHILLIPS

Whether in chains or in laurels, Liberty knows nothing but victories.

HENRY WARD BEECHER
Sermon at Plymouth Congregational Church

. . . And wherever this flag comes, and men behold it, they see in its sacred emblazonry no ramping lion, and no fierce eagle; no embattled castles, or insignia of imperial authority; they see the symbols of light. It is the banner of dawn. It means liberty; and the galley-slave, the poor, oppressed conscript, the trodden-down creature of foreign despotism, sees in the American flag the very promise and prediction of God—"The people which sat in darkness and saw a great light; and to them which sat in the region and shadow of death light is sprung up." . . .

If one, then, asks me the meaning of our flag, I say to him, it means just what Concord and Lexington meant, what Bunker Hill meant; it means the whole glorious Revolutionary War, which was, in short, the rising up of a valiant young people against an old tyranny, to establish the most momentous doctrine that the world has ever known, or has since known—the right of men to their own selves and to their liberties.

In solemn conclave our fathers had issued to the world that glorious manifesto, the Declaration of Independence. A little later, that the fundamental principles of liberty might have the best organization, they gave to this land our imperishable Constitution. Our flag means, then, all that our fathers meant in the Revolutionary War; all that the Declaration of Independence meant; it means all that the Constitution of our people, organizing for justice, for liberty, and for happiness, meant. Our flag carries American ideas, American history, and American feelings. Beginning with the colonies, and coming down to our time, in its sacred heraldry, in its glorious insignia, it has gathered and stored chiefly this supreme idea: Divine right of liberty in man. Every color means liberty; every thread means liberty; every form of star and beam or stripe of light means liberty; not lawlessness, not license; but organized, institutional liberty —liberty through law, and laws for liberty!

This American flag was the safeguard of liberty. Not an atom of crown was allowed to go into its insignia. Not a symbol of authority in the ruler was permitted to go into it. It was an ordinance of liberty by the people for the people. That it meant, that it means, and by the blessing of God, that it shall mean to the end of time!

SAMUEL SMITH
"America"

My country 'tis of thee
Sweet land of liberty:
Of thee I sing.
Land where my fathers died
Land of the pilgrims' pride
From every mountainside
Let freedom ring.

My native country—thee
Land of the noble free
Thy name I love;
I love thy rocks and rills
Thy woods and templed hills
My heart with rapture thrills
Like that above.

Let music swell the breeze
And ring from all the trees
Sweet freedom's song
Let all that breathe partake
Let mortal tongues awake
Let rocks their silence break
The sound prolong.

Our fathers' God to thee
Author of liberty
To thee we sing
Long may our land be bright
With freedom's holy light
Protect us by thy might
Great God, our King.

GEORGE WASHINGTON
First Inaugural Address

The preservation of the sacred fire of liberty and the destiny of the republican model of government are justly considered, perhaps, as deeply, as finally, staked on the experiment intrusted to the hands of the American people.

MARY FUTRELL

To secure the blessings of liberty, we must secure the blessings of learning.

JOHN ADAMS
Dissertation on the Canon and the Feudal Law

Liberty cannot be preserved without general knowledge among people, who have a right . . . and a desire to know; but besides this, they have a right, an indisputable, unalienable, indefeasible, divine right to that most dreaded and envied kind of knowledge, I mean of the character and conduct of their rulers. . . . Let us . . . cherish, therefore, the means of knowledge. Let us dare to read, think, speak, and write. . . . Let every sluice of knowledge be opened and set a-flowing.

JAMES MADISON
Second annual message to Congress

It is universally admitted that a well-instructed people alone can be permanently a free people.

THOMAS JEFFERSON
Letter to George Ticknor

Education is the key to unlock the golden door of freedom.

GEORGE WASHINGTON CARVER

Knowledge is power . . . knowledge is safety . . . knowledge is happiness.

DANIEL WEBSTER
Comment on completion of the Bunker Hill Monument, Boston

Knowledge is the only fountain both of the love and principles of human liberty.

JAMES MADISON
Letter to George Thompson

The diffusion of knowledge is the only guardian of true liberty.

JAMES MONROE
Inaugural Address

It is only when the People become ignorant and corrupt, when they degenerate into a populace, that they are incapable of exercising their sovereignty. Let us, by all wise and constitutional measures, promote intelligence among the People, as the best means of preserving our liberties.

ROBERT G. INGERSOLL
"The Liberty of Man, Woman, and Child"

There is no slavery but ignorance. Liberty is the child of intelligence.

FRANKLIN D. ROOSEVELT
Speech in Boston

Knowledge—that is, education in its true sense—is our best protection against unreasoning prejudice and panic-making fear, whether engendered by special interest, illiberal minorities, or panic-stricken leaders.

JOHN F. KENNEDY
Address at Vanderbilt University, Nashville

Liberty without learning is always in peril, and learning without liberty is always in vain.

HENRY WARD BEECHER
Proverbs from Plymouth Pulpit

Ignorance is the womb of monsters.

John Quincy Adams
Letter to James Lloyd

Individual liberty is individual power, and as the power of a community is a mass compounded of individual powers, the nation which enjoys the most freedom must necessarily be in proportion to its numbers the most powerful nation.

Louis D. Brandeis
Olmstead v. United States

They [the makers of the Constitution] conferred, as against the Government, the right to be let alone—the most comprehensive of rights and the right most valued by civilized men.

Woodrow Wilson
Speech in New York City

America is not a mere body of traders; it is a body of free men. Our greatness is built upon our freedom—is moral, not material. We have a great ardor for gain; but we have a deep passion for the rights of man.

Henry Ward Beecher
Proverbs from Plymouth Pulpit

The real democratic American idea is not that every man shall be on a level with every other man, but that every man shall have liberty to be what God made him, without hindrance.

Samuel Adams
"American Independence"

Political right and public happiness are different words for the same idea.

Abraham Lincoln
Speech in Peoria, Illinois

No man is good enough to govern another without that other's consent.

Woodrow Wilson
Speech in Pittsburgh

Just what is it that America stands for? If she stands for one thing more than another, it is for the sovereignty of self-governing people.

DANIEL WEBSTER
Speech at Charleston Bar Dinner

Liberty exists in proportion to wholesome restraint.

BERNARD BARUCH

The greatest blessing of our democracy is freedom. But in the last analysis, our only freedom is the freedom to discipline ourselves.

JOHN F. KENNEDY
Speech in Washington, D.C.

Self-government requires qualities of self-denial and restraint.

WILLIAM JENNINGS BRYAN
"American Mission" speech

Anglo-Saxon civilization has taught the individual to protect his own rights; American civilization will teach him to respect the rights of others.

FRANKLIN D. ROOSEVELT
State of the Union Address

Democracy, the practice of self-government, is a covenant among free men to respect the rights and liberties of their fellows.

WILLIAM ALLEN WHITE
Emporia Gazette

Liberty is the only thing you cannot have unless you are willing to give it to others.

GEORGE C. HOMANS
The Human Group

Liberty is a beloved discipline.

JOHN JAY CHAPMAN

Attack another's rights and you destroy your own.

William Graham Sumner
"The Forgotten Man"

If I want to be free from any other man's dictation, I must understand that I can have no other man under my control.

Adlai E. Stevenson
Speech in New York City

The sound of tireless voices is the price we pay for the right to hear the music of our own opinions.

James Russell Lowell
"A Fable for Critics"

And I honor the man who is willing to sink
Half his present repute for the freedom to think,
And, when he has thought, be his cause strong or weak,
Will risk t'other half for the freedom to speak.

Henry Ward Beecher
Speech in Liverpool, England

The things required for prosperous labor, prosperous manufactures, and prosperous commerce are three. First, liberty; second, liberty; third, liberty.

Herbert Hoover
Speech in New York City

Free speech does not live many hours after free industry and free commerce die.

Walter Lippmann

While the right to talk may be the beginning of freedom, the necessity of listening is what makes the right important.

Max Lerner
"The Muzzling of the Movies"

The problem of freedom in America is that of maintaining a competition of ideas, and you do not achieve that by silencing one brand of idea.

WILLIAM ALLEN WHITE
The Editor and His People

You can have no wise laws nor free enforcement of wise laws unless there is free expression of the wisdom of the people—and, alas, their folly with it. But if there is freedom, folly will die of its own poison, and the wisdom will survive.

OLIVER WENDELL HOLMES

With effervescing opinions, as with the not yet forgotten champagne, the quickest way to let them go flat is to let them get exposed to the air.

HENRY STEELE COMMAGER
Freedom and Order

The justification and the purpose of freedom of speech is not to indulge those who want to speak their minds. It is to prevent error and discover the truth. There may be other ways of detecting error and discovering the truth than that of free discussion, but so far we have not found them.

ALLAN BLOOM
The Closing of the American Mind

Freedom of the mind requires not only, or not even especially, the absence of legal constraints but the presence of alternative thoughts.

OLIVER WENDELL HOLMES, JR.
Abrams v. the United States

When men have realized that time has upset many fighting faiths, they may come to believe even more than they believe the very foundations of their own conduct that the ultimate good desired is reached by the free trade in ideas—that the best test of truth is the power of the thought to get itself accepted in the competition of the market. That at any rate is the theory of our Constitution.

My Day; September 3, 1949

ELEANOR ROOSEVELT

A great deal of feeling has been aroused by the riots that took place in Peekskill, New York, at a meeting sponsored by the Civil Liberties Union. I, myself, cannot understand why anyone goes to a meeting at which Paul Robeson is going to speak unless they are in sympathy with what he is going to say, since by this time everyone must be familiar with his thinking. I have been told that what I once experienced, namely, seeing him turn his concert into a medium for Communist propaganda, is his constant practice, so whoever goes to hear him sing, in spite of knowing that he would sing certain songs that they might not like, or at some point, talk in a way with which they might not agree. If so, in this country, it is their privilege to go to hear him and leave. I think if we care for the preservation of our liberties we must allow all people, whether we disagree with them or not, to hold meetings and express their views unmolested as long as they do not advocate the overthrow of our Government by force.

It seems to me that peaceful picketing of such a meeting is also an unwise gesture. I can well understand why veterans want to show their displeasure, but I think there are other ways of doing it. They can hold a meeting and see to it that their speakers are as well reported as those at any other meeting. They can see that the press carries refutation of whatever arguments are given at any meeting with which they disagree, but I do not think they need fear that the average American is an easy prey to the Paul Robeson type of propaganda.

I believe the average American should realize that rioting and lawlessness—even when we can prove that they were, as some people are trying to prove the case, incited by some Communists—are still not good propaganda for democracy in the world.

We in the United States should, I think, make it very clear that we disagree with and disapprove of many views of Paul Robeson, but it is well also for us to remember that Paul Robeson left this country and took his family to the USSR until the coming of the war. He wanted to find something he did not find here. He was a brilliant law student and could not find a job in any good New York firm, staffed for the most part by men and women of the white race. In other words, he could not be a lawyer, so he became a singer—a gain for art—but perhaps there was some bitterness in his heart, brought about by the fact that there was no equality of opportunity for educated men of his race. He did not want his boy to have the same experiences. Others might feel the same way. In the USSR he was recognized as an educated man, as an artist and as an equal. We disapprove of his speeches, but we must also understand him and above all other things, we must be jealous to preserve the liberties that are inherent in true democracy.

ELLEN ALDERMAN AND CAROLINE KENNEDY
In Our Defense

In guaranteeing the fundamental right of assembly, the Supreme Court has recognized that protecting individual rights in times of stability and social harmony is easy. It becomes more difficult in times of crisis, but that is precisely when the right to assemble, to speak out, and to disagree with the prevailing orthodoxy must be vigilantly protected.

HARRY S TRUMAN
Speech in Chicago

You cannot stop the spread of an idea by passing a law against it.

RONALD REAGAN
Speech in London, England

You can't massacre an idea, you cannot run tanks over them.

SAMUEL GOMPERS

You may not know that the labor movement as represented by the trades unions, stands for right, stands for justice, for liberty. You may not imagine that the issuance of an injunction depriving men of a legal as well as a natural right to protect themselves, their wives, their little ones, must fail of its purpose. Repression or oppression never yet succeeded in crushing the truth or redressing a wrong.

HARRY S TRUMAN
Message to Congress vetoing the McCarran Act

We need not fear the expression of ideas—we do need to fear their suppression.

Declaration of Conscience

MARGARET CHASE SMITH

Mr. President, I speak as a Republican. I speak as a woman. I speak as a United States senator. I speak as an American.

The United States Senate has long enjoyed worldwide respect as the greatest deliberative body in the world. But recently that deliberative character has too often been debased to the level of a forum of hate and character assassination sheltered by the shield of congressional immunity.

It is ironical that we senators can debate in the Senate, directly or indirectly, by any form of words, impute to any American who is not a senator any conduct or motive unworthy or unbecoming an American—and without that nonsenator American having any legal redress against us—yet if we say the same thing in the Senate about our colleagues we can be stopped on the grounds of being out of order.

It is strange that we can verbally attack anyone else without restraint and with full protection, and yet we hold ourselves above the same type of criticism here on the Senate floor. Surely the United States Senate is big enough to take self-criticism and self-appraisal. Surely we should be able to take the same kind of character attacks that we "dish out" to outsiders.

I think it is high time for the United States Senate and its members to do some real soul-searching and to weigh our consciences as to the manner in which we are performing our duty to the people of America and the manner in which we are using or abusing our individual powers and privileges.

I think it is high time that we remembered that we have sworn to uphold and defend the Constitution. I think it is high time that we remembered that the Constitution, as amended, speaks not only of the freedom of speech but also of trial by jury instead of trial by accusation.

Whether it be a criminal prosecution in court or a character prosecution in the Senate, there is little practical distinction when the life of a person has been ruined.

Those of us who shout the loudest about Americanism in making character assassinations are all too frequently those who, by our own words and acts, ignore some of the basic principles of Americanism—the right to criticize; the right to hold unpopular beliefs; the right to protest; the right of independent thought.

The exercise of these rights should not cost one single American citizen his reputation or his right to a livelihood, nor should he be in danger of losing his reputation or livelihood merely because he happens to know someone who holds unpopular beliefs. Who of us does not? Otherwise none of us could call our souls our own. Otherwise thought control would have set in.

The American people are sick and tired of being afraid to speak their minds lest they be politically smeared as Communists or Fascists by their opponents. Freedom of speech is not what it used to be in America. It has been so abused by some that it is not exercised by others.

The American people are sick and tired of seeing innocent people smeared and guilty people whitewashed. But there have been enough proved cases, such as the Amerasia case, the Hiss case, the Coplon case, the Gold case, to cause nationwide distrust and strong suspicion that there may be something to the unproved, sensational accusations.

As a Republican, I say to my colleagues on this side of the aisle that the Republican Party faces a challenge today that is not unlike the challenge it faced back in Lincoln's day. The Republican Party so successfully met that challenge that it emerged from the Civil War as the champion of a united nation—in addition to being a party which unrelentingly fought loose spending and loose programs.

Today our country is being psychologically divided by the confusion and the suspicions that are bred in the United States Senate to spread like cancerous tentacles of "know nothing, suspect everything" attitudes. Today we have a Democratic administration which has developed a mania for loose spending and loose programs. History is repeating itself—and the Republican Party again has the opportunity to emerge as the champion of unity and prudence....

Yet to displace [the Democratic administration] with a Republican regime embracing a philosophy that lacks political integrity or intellectual honesty would prove equally disastrous to the nation. The nation sorely needs a Republican victory. But I do not want to see the Republican Party ride to political victory on the Four Horsemen of Calumny—fear, ignorance, bigotry, and smear.

I doubt if the Republican Party could do so, simply because I do not believe the American people will uphold any political party that puts political exploitation above national interest. Surely we Republicans are not so desperate for victory.

I do not want to see the Republican Party that way. While it might be a fleeting victory for the Republican Party, it would be a more lasting defeat for the American people. Surely it would ultimately be suicide for the Republican Party and the two-party system that has protected our American liberties from the dictatorship of a one-party system.

As members of the minority party, we do not have the primary authority to formulate the policy of our government. But we do have the responsibility of rendering constructive criticism, of clarifying issues, of allaying fears by acting as responsible citizens.

As a woman, I wonder how the mothers, wives, sisters, and daughters feel about the way in which members of their families have been politically maligned in Senate debate—and I use the word "debate" advisedly.

As a United States senator, I am not proud of the way in which the Senate has been made a publicity platform for irresponsible sensationalism. I am not proud of the reckless abandon in which unproved charges have been hurled from this side of the aisle. I am not proud of the obviously staged, undignified countercharges which have been attempted in retaliation from the other side of the aisle.

I do not like the way the Senate has been made a rendezvous for vilification, for selfish political gain at the sacrifice of individual reputations and national unity. I am not proud of the way we smear outsiders from the floor of the Senate and hide behind the cloak of congressional immunity and still place ourselves beyond criticism on the floor of the Senate.

As an American, I am shocked at the way Republicans and Democrats alike are playing directly into the Communist design of "confuse, divide, and conquer." As an American, I do not want a Democratic administration whitewash or coverup any more than I want a Republican smear or witch-hunt.

As an American, I condemn a Republican Fascist just as much as I condemn a Democrat Communist. I condemn a Democrat Fascist just as much as I condemn a Republican Communist. They are equally dangerous to you and me and to our country. As an American, I want to see our nation recapture the strength and unity it once had when we fought the enemy instead of ourselves.

BENJAMIN FRANKLIN

Resistance to tyrants is obedience to God.

JOHN ADAMS
Dissertation on the Canon and the Feudal Law

Let us dare to read, think, speak and write.

SAMUEL GOMPERS
Seventy Years of Life and Labor

I hold a jail more roomy in the expression of my judgment and convictions than would be the whole world if I were to submit to repression and be denied the right to express myself.

HUGO BLACK
New York Times Company v. Sullivan

An unconditional right to say what one pleases about public affairs is what I consider to be the minimum guarantee of the First Amendment.

WILLIAM O. DOUGLAS
The New York Times

The First Amendment makes confidence in the common sense of our people and in the maturity of their judgment the great postulate of our democracy.

Democracy in America: Liberty of the Press in the United States

ALEXIS DE TOCQUEVILLE

The influence of the liberty of the press does not affect political opinions alone, but extends to all the opinions of men, and modifies customs as well as laws.... I confess that I do not entertain the firm and complete attachment to the liberty of the press which is wont to be excited by things that are supremely good in their very nature. I approve of it from a consideration more of the evils it prevents, than of the advantages it insures. If any one could point out an intermediate and yet a tenable position between the complete independence and the entire servitude of opinion, I should, perhaps, be inclined to adopt it; but the difficulty is, to discover this intermediate position. Intending to correct the licentiousness of the press, and to restore the use of orderly language, you first try the offender by a jury; but if the jury acquits him, the opinion which was that of a single individual becomes the opinion of the whole country. Too much and too little has therefore been done; go farther, then. You bring the delinquent before permanent magistrates; but even here, the cause must be heard before it can be decided; and the very principles which no book would have ventured to avow are blazoned forth in the pleadings, and what was obscurely hinted at in a single composition is thus repeated in a multitude of other publications. The language is only the expression, and (if I may so speak) the body, of the thought, but it is not the thought itself. Tribunals may condemn the body, but the sense, the spirit, of the work is too subtle for their authority. Too much has still been done to recede, too little to attain your end; you must go still farther. Establish a censorship of the press. But the tongue of the public speaker will still make itself heard, and your purpose is not yet accomplished; you have only increased the mischief. Thought is not, like physical strength, dependent upon the number of its agents; nor can authors be counted like the troops which compose an army. On the contrary, the authority of a principle is often increased by the small number of men by whom it is expressed. The words of one strong-minded man, addressed to the passions of a listening assembly, have more power than the vociferations of a thousand orators; and if it be allowed to speak freely in any one public place, the consequence is the same as if free speaking was allowed in every village. The liberty of speech must therefore be destroyed, as well as the liberty of the press. And now you have succeeded, everybody is reduced to silence. But your object was to repress the abuses of liberty, and you are brought to the feet of a despot. You have been led from the extreme of independence to the extreme of servitude, without finding a single tenable position on the way at which you could stop....

The small influence of the American journals is attributable to several reasons, amongst which are the following.

The liberty of writing, like all other liberty, is most formidable when it is a novelty; for a people who have never been accustomed to hear state affairs discussed before them, place implicit confidence in the first tribune who presents himself. The Anglo-Americans have enjoyed this liberty ever since the foundation of the Colonies; moreover, the press cannot create human passions, however skillfully it may kindle them where they exist. In America, political life is active, varied, even agitated, but is rarely affected by those deep passions which are excited only when material interests are impaired: and in the United States, these interests are prosperous. A glance at a French and an American newspaper is sufficient to show the difference which exists in this respect between the two nations. In France, the space allotted to commercial advertisements is very limited, and the news-intelligence is not considerable; but the essential part of the journal is the discussion of the politics of the day. In America, three quarters of the enormous sheet are filled with advertisements, and the remainder is frequently occupied by political intelligence or trivial anecdotes; it is only from time to time, that one finds a corner devoted to passionate discussions, like those which the journalists of France every day give to their readers.

It has been demonstrated by observation, and discovered by the sure instinct even of the pettiest despots, that the influence of a power is increased in proportion as its direction is centralized. In France, the press combines a two-fold centralization; almost all its power is centered in the same spot, and, so to speak, in the same hands; for its organs are far from numerous. The influence of a public press thus constituted, upon a sceptical nation, must be almost unbounded. It is an enemy with whom a government may sign an occasional truce, but which it is difficult to resist for any length of time.

Neither of these kinds of centralization exists in America. The United States have no metropolis; the intelligence and the power of the people are disseminated through all the parts of this vast country, and instead of radiating from a common point, they cross each other in every direction; the Americans have nowhere established any central direction of opinion, any more than of the conduct of affairs. The difference arises from local circumstances, and not from human power; but it is owing to the laws of the Union that there are no licenses to be granted to printers, no securities demanded from editors, as in France, and no stamp duty, as in France and England. The consequence is, that nothing is easier than to set up a newspaper, as a small number of subscribers suffices to defray the expenses.

Hence the number of periodical and semi-periodical publications in the United States is almost incredibly large. The most enlightened Americans attribute the little influence of the press to this excessive dissemination of its power; and it is an axiom of political science in that country, that the only way to neutralize the effect of the public journals is to multiply their number. I cannot see how a truth which is so self-evident should not already have been more generally admitted in Europe. I can see why the persons who hope to bring about revolutions by means of the press should be desirous of confining it to a few powerful organs; but it is inconceivable that the official partisans of the existing state of things, and the natural supporters of the laws, should attempt to diminish the influence of the press by concentrating its power. The governments of Europe seem to treat the press with the courtesy which the knights of old showed to their opponents; having found from their own experience that centralization is a powerful weapon, they have furnished their enemies with it, in order doubtless to have more glory for overcoming them.

In America, there is scarcely a hamlet which has not its newspaper. It may readily be imagined, that neither discipline nor unity of action can be established among so many combatants; and each one consequently fights under his own standard. All the political journals of the United States are, indeed, arrayed on the side of the administration or against it; but they attack and defend it in a thousand different ways. They cannot form those great currents of opinion which sweep away the strongest dikes. This division of influence of the press produces other consequences scarcely less remarkable. The facility with which a newspaper can be established produces a multitude of them; but as the competition prevents any considerable profit, persons of much capacity are rarely led to engage in these undertakings. Such is the number of the public prints, that, even if they were a source of wealth, writers of ability could not be found to direct them all. The journalists of the United States are generally in a very humble position, with a scanty education and a vulgar turn of mind. The will of the majority is the most general of laws, and it established certain habits to which every one must then conform; the aggregate of these common habits is what is called the class-spirit of each profession; thus there is the class-spirit of the bar, of the court, etc. The class-spirit of the French journalists consists in a violent, but frequently eloquent and lofty, manner of discussing the great interest of the state: and the exceptions to this mode of writing are only occasional. The characteristics of the American journalist consist in an open and coarse appeal to the passions of his readers; he abandons principles to assail the characters of individuals, to track them into private life, and disclose all their weaknesses and vices....

But, although the press is limited to these resources, its influence in America is immense. It causes political life to circulate through all the parts of that vast territory. Its eye is constantly open to detect the secret springs of political designs, and to summon the leaders of all parties in turn to the bar of public opinion. It rallies the interests of the community round certain principles, and draws up the creed of every party; for it affords a means of intercourse between those who hear and address each other, without ever coming into immediate contact. When many organs of the press adopt the same line of conduct, their influence in the long run becomes irresistible; and public opinion, perpetually assailed from the same side, eventually yields to the attack. In the United States, each separate journal exercises but little authority; but the power of the periodical press is second only to that of the people.

GEORGE MASON
Virginia Bill of Rights

Freedom of the press is one of the great bulwarks of liberty, and can never be restrained but by despotic government.

CHARLES PINCKNEY
Resolution presented to the Constitutional Convention

The legislature of the United States shall pass no law on the subject of religion nor touching or abridging the liberty of the press.

THOMAS JEFFERSON
Letter to Colonel Edward Carrington

Our liberty depends on the freedom of the press, and that cannot be limited without being lost.... Were it left to me to decide whether we should have a government without newspapers, or newspapers without government, I should not hesitate a moment to prefer the latter.

FELIX FRANKFURTER
The New York Times

Freedom of the press is not an end in itself but a means to the end of a free society.

FRANKLIN D. ROOSEVELT
Letter to W.H. Hardy

Freedom of conscience, of education, of speech, of assembly are among the very fundamentals of democracy and all of them would be nullified should freedom of the press ever be successfully challenged.

WALTER LIPPMANN
Address at the International Press Institute, London

A free press is not a privilege but an organic necessity in a great society.... A great society is simply a big and complicated urban society.

GEORGE SUTHERLAND
Crosjean v. American Press Co.

A free press stands as one of the great interpreters between the government and the people. To allow it to be fettered is to fetter ourselves.

MAXWELL PERKINS
Editor to Author: The Letters of Maxwell Perkins

What we publishers think is that our function is to bring everything out into the open, on the theory that we have an adult population that knows values, or can learn them, and let them decide.

HUGO BLACK
Interview before the American Jewish Congress

I am for the First Amendment from the first word to the last. I believe it means what it says.

HARRY S TRUMAN
Message to Congress vetoing the McCarran Act

There is no more fundamental axiom of America than the familiar statement: In a free country we punish men for the crimes they commit but never for the opinions they have.

LYNDON B. JOHNSON
Speech in Washington, D.C.

Our house is large, and it is open. It is open to all, those who agree and those who disagree.

THOMAS JEFFERSON
Virginia Statute of Religious Freedom

The opinions of men are not the object of civil government, nor under its jurisdiction.

LYNDON B. JOHNSON
White House speech

Opinion and protest are the life breath of democracy—even when it blows heavy.

HEYWOOD BROUN
"The Miracle of Debs," *New York World*

Free speech is about as good a cause as the world has ever known.

SAMUEL GOMPERS
Reply before being sentenced for contempt of court

The freedom of speech and the freedom of press have not been granted to the people in order that they may say the things which please, and which are based on accepted thought, but the right to say things which may convey the new and yet unexpected thoughts, the right to say things, even though they do a wrong.

CHARLES F. KETTERING

Where there is an open mind, there will always be a frontier.

THOMAS MERTON

May God prevent us from becoming "right-thinking men"—that is to say men who agree perfectly with their own police.

ROBERT G. INGERSOLL

By physical liberty I mean the right to do anything which does not interfere with the happiness of another. By intellectual liberty I mean the right to think wrong.

ROBERT H. JACKSON
American Communications Association v. Douds

It is not the function of our Government to keep the citizen from falling into error; it is the function of the citizen to keep the Government from falling into error.

E.B. WHITE
Letter to the New York Herald Tribune

I am a member of a party of one, and I live in an age of fear. Nothing lately has unsettled my party and raised my fears so much as your editorial, on Thanksgiving Day, suggesting that employees should be required to state their beliefs in order to hold their jobs. The idea is inconsistent with our constitutional theory and has been stubbornly opposed by watchful men since the early days of the Republic. . . .

Security for me took a tumble not when I read that there were Communists in Hollywood but when I read your editorial in praise of loyalty testing and thought control. If a man is in health, he doesn't need to take anybody else's temperature to know where he is going.

ADLAI E. STEVENSON
Speech in Salt Lake City, Utah

The mind is the expression of the soul, which belongs to God and must be let alone by government.

U.S. SUPREME COURT JUSTICE THURGOOD MARSHALL
Stanley v. Georgia

If the First Amendment means anything, it means that a State has no business telling a man, sitting alone in his own house, what books he may read or what films he may watch. Our whole constitutional heritage rebels at the thought of giving government the power to control men's minds.

JAMES B. CONANT
Education in a Divided World

Diversity of opinion within the framework of loyalty to our free society is not only basic to a university but to the entire nation.

LOUIS D. BRANDEIS
Whitney v. California

Those who won our independence believed that the final end of the State was to make men free to develop their faculties; and that in its government the deliberative forces should prevail over the arbitrary. They valued liberty both as an end and as a means. They believed liberty to be the secret of happiness and courage to be the secret of liberty. . . . Fear of serious injury cannot alone justify suppression of free speech and assembly. Men feared witches and burned women. It is the function of speech to free men from the bondage of irrational fears.

HUGO BLACK
One Man's Stand for Freedom

Freedom of speech means that you shall not do something to people either for the views they have, or the views they express, or the words they speak or write.

FRANKLIN D. ROOSEVELT
Radio address

It is a good thing to demand liberty for ourselves and for those who agree with us, but it is a better thing and a rarer thing to give liberty to others who do not agree with us.

THOMAS PAINE
Dissertation on First Principles of Government

He that would make his own liberty secure must guard even his enemy from oppression.

THOMAS JEFFERSON
Notes on Virginia

It is error alone which needs the support of government. Truth can stand by itself.

WENDELL PHILLIPS
Speech in Boston

Governments exist to protect the rights of minorities. The loved and the rich need no protections; they have many friends and few enemies.

CHARLES EVAN HUGHES
De Jonge v. Oregon

The greater the importance of safeguarding the community from incitements to the overthrow of our institutions by force and violence, the more imperative is the need to preserve inviolate the constitutional rights of free speech, free press and free assembly in order to maintain the opportunity for free discussion, to the end that government may be responsive to the will of the people and that changes, if desired, may be obtained by peaceful means. Therein lies the security of the Republic, the very foundation of constitutional government.

BENJAMIN N. CARDOZO
Palko v. Connecticut

Freedom of expression is the matrix, the indispensable condition, of nearly every other form of freedom.

THOMAS JEFFERSON
Letter to Doctor Benjamin Rush

It behooves every man who values liberty of conscience for himself, to resist invasions of it in the case of others.

ABE FORTAS
Tinker v. Des Moines

... [I]n our system, undifferentiated fear or apprehension of disturbance is not enough to overcome the right of freedom of expression. Any departure from absolute regimentation may cause trouble. Any variation from the majority's opinion may inspire fear. Any word spoken, in class, in the lunchroom, or on the campus, that deviates from views of another person may start an argument or cause a disturbance. But our Constitution says we must take this risk, ... and our history says that it is this sort of hazardous freedom—this kind of openness —that is the basis of our national strength and of the independence and vigor of Americans who grow up and live in this relatively permissive, often disputatious, society.

In order for the State in the person of school officials to justify prohibition of a particular expression of opinion, it must be able to show that its action was caused by something more than a mere desire to avoid the discomfort and unpleasantness that always accompany an unpopular viewpoint. Certainly where there is no finding and no showing that engaging in the forbidden conduct would "materially and substantially interfere with the requirements of appropriate discipline in the operation of the school," the prohibition cannot be sustained.

It is also relevant that the school authorities did not purport to prohibit the wearing of all symbols of political and controversial significance. The record shows that students in some of the schools wore buttons relating to national political campaigns, and some even wore the Iron Cross, traditionally a symbol of Nazism. The order prohibiting the wearing of armbands did not extend to these. Instead, a particular symbol—black armbands worn to exhibit opposition to this Nation's involvement in Vietnam—was singled out for prohibition. Clearly, the prohibition of expression of one particular opinion, at least without evidence that it is necessary to avoid material and substantial interference with schoolwork or discipline, is not constitutionally permissible.

In our system, state-operated schools may not be enclaves of totalitarianism. School officials do not possess absolute authority over their students. Students in schools as well as out of school are "persons" under our Constitution. They are possessed of fundamental rights which the State must respect, just as they themselves must respect their obligations to the State. In our system, students may not be regarded as closed-circuit recipients of only that which the State chooses to communicate. They may not be confined to the expression of those sentiments that are officially approved. In the absence of specific showing of constitutionally valid reasons to regulate their speech, students are entitled to freedom of expression of their views.

ROBERT H. JACKSON
West Virginia Board of Education v. Barnette

...Those who begin coercive elimination of dissent soon find themselves exterminating dissenters. Compulsory unification of opinion achieves only the unanimity of the graveyard.

It seems trite but necessary to say that the First Amendment to our Constitution was designed to avoid these ends by avoiding these beginnings. There is no mysticism in the American concept of the State or of the nature or origin of its authority. We set up government by consent of the governed, and the Bill of Rights denies those in power any legal opportunity to coerce that consent. Authority here is to be controlled by public opinion, not public opinion by authority.

[This] case is made difficult not because the principles of its decision are obscure but because the flag involved is our own. Nevertheless, we apply the limitations of the Constitution with no fear that freedom to be intellectually and spiritually diverse or even contrary will disintegrate the social organization. To believe that patriotism will not flourish if patriotic ceremonies are voluntary and spontaneous instead of compulsory and routine is to make an unflattering estimate of the appeal of our institutions to free minds. We can have intellectual individualism and the rich cultural diversities that we owe to exceptional minds only at the price of occasional eccentricity and abnormal attitudes. When they are so harmless to others or to the State as those we deal with here, the price is not too great. But freedom to differ is not limited to things that do not matter much. That would be a mere shadow of freedom. The test of its substance is the right to differ as to the things that touch the heart of the existing order.

If there is any fixed star in our constitutional constellation, it is that no official, high or petty, can prescribe what shall be orthodox in politics, nationalism, religion, or other matters of opinion, or force citizens to confess by word or act their faith therein. If there are any circumstances which permit an exception, they do not now occur to us.

We think the action of the local authorities in compelling the flag salute and pledge transcends constitutional limitations on their power and invades the sphere of intellect and spirit which it is the purpose of the First Amendment to our Constitution to reserve from all official control.

Love of country must spring from willing hearts and free minds, inspired by a fair administration of wise laws enacted by the people's elected representatives within the bounds of expressed constitutional prohibitions. These laws must, to be consistent with the First Amendment, permit the widest toleration of conflicting viewpoints consistent with a society of free men.

Neither our domestic tranquillity in peace nor our martial effort in war depend on compelling little children to participate in a ceremony which ends in nothing for them but a fear of spiritual condemnation. If, as we think, their fears are groundless, time and reason are the proper antidotes for their errors. The ceremonial, when enforced against conscientious objectors, more likely to defeat than to serve its high purpose, is a handy implement for disguised religious persecution. As such, it is inconsistent with our Constitution's plan and purpose.

OLIVER WENDELL HOLMES, JR.
United States v. Schwimmer

If there is any principle of the Constitution that more imperatively calls for attachment than any other it is the principle of free thought—not free thought for those who agree with us but freedom for the thought that we hate.

"Publicly Burning an American Flag..."
WILLIAM J. BRENNAN, JR.
Texas v. Gregory Lee Johnson

After publicly burning an American flag as a means of political protest, Gregory Lee Johnson was convicted of desecrating a flag in violation of Texas law. This case presents the question whether his conviction is consistent with the First Amendment. We hold that it is not.

While the Republican National Convention was taking place in Dallas in 1984, respondent Johnson participated in a political demonstration dubbed the "Republican War Chest Tour." As explained in literature distributed by the demonstrators and in speeches made by the respondent, the purpose of this event was to protest the policies of the Reagan administration and of certain Dallas-based corporations. The demonstrators marched through the Dallas streets, chanting political slogans and stopping at several corporate locations to stage "die-ins" intended to dramatize the consequences of nuclear war. On several occasions they spray-painted the walls of buildings and overturned potted plants, but Johnson himself took no part in such activities. He did, however, accept an American flag handed to him by a fellow protestor who had taken it from a flag pole outside one of the targeted buildings.

The demonstration ended in front of Dallas City Hall, where Johnson unfurled the American flag, doused it with kerosene, and set it on fire. While the flag burned, the protestors chanted, "America, the red, white, and blue, we spit on you." After the demonstrators dispersed, a witness to the flag burning collected the flag's remains and buried them in his backyard. No one was physically injured or threatened with injury, though several witnesses testified that they had been seriously offended by the flag burning.

Of the approximately one hundred demonstrators, Johnson alone was charged with a crime. The only criminal offense with which he was charged was the desecration of a venerated object in violation of Texas Penal Code Ann. 42.09(a)(3)(1989). After a trial he was convicted, sentenced to one year in prison, and fined two thousand dollars.

The State of Texas conceded for purposes of its oral argument in this case that Johnson's conduct was expressive conduct.... Johnson burned an American flag as part—indeed, as the culmination—of a political demonstration that coincided with the convening of the Republican Party and its renomination of Ronald Reagan for President. The expressive, overtly political nature of this conduct was both intentional and overwhelmingly apparent. At his trial, Johnson explained his reasons for burning the flag as follows: "The American Flag was burned as Ronald Reagan was being renominated as President. And a more powerful statement of symbolic speech, whether you agree with it or not, couldn't have been made at that time. It's quite a juxtaposition. We had new patriotism and no patriotism."... In these circumstances, Johnson's burning of the flag was conduct "sufficiently imbued with elements of communication . . . to implicate the First Amendment."

...The State offers two separate interests to justify this conviction: preventing breaches of peace, and preserving the flag as a symbol of nationhood and national unity. We hold that the first interest is not implicated on this record and that the second is related to the suppression of expression.

Texas claims that its interest in preventing breaches of the peace justifies Johnson's conviction for flag desecration. However, no disturbance of the peace actually occurred or threatened to occur because of Johnson's burning of the flag. Although the State stresses the disruptive behavior of the protestors during their march toward City Hall, . . . it admits that "no actual breach of the peace occurred at the time of the flag burning or in response to the flag burning."...The State's emphasis on the protestors' disorderly actions prior to arriving at City Hall is not only somewhat surprising, given that no charges were brought on the basis of this conduct, but it also fails to show that a disturbance of the peace was a likely reaction to Johnson's conduct. The only evidence offered by the State at trial to show the reaction to Johnson's actions was the testimony of several persons who had been seriously offended by the flag burning.

The State's position, therefore, amounts to a claim that an audience that takes serious offense at particular expression is necessarily likely to disturb peace and that the expression may be prohibited on this basis. Our precedents do not countenance such a presumption. On the contrary, they recognize that a principal "function of free speech under our system of government is to invite dispute. It may indeed best serve its high purpose when it induces a condition of unrest, creates dissatisfaction with conditions as they are, or even stirs people to anger." Terminiello v. Chicago (1949).

Texas' focus on the precise nature of Johnson's expression, moreover, misses the point of our prior decisions: their enduring lesson, that the Government may not prohibit expression simply because it disagrees with its message, is not dependent on the particular mode in which one chooses to express an idea. If we were to hold that a State may forbid flag burning wherever it is likely to endanger the flag's symbolic role, but allow it wherever burning a flag promotes that role—as where, for example, a person ceremoniously burns a dirty flag—we would be saying that when it comes to impairing the flag's physical integrity, the flag itself may be used as a symbol—as a substitute for the written or spoken word or a "short cut from mind to mind"—only in one direction. We would be permitting a State to "prescribe what shall be orthodox" by saying that one may burn the flag to convey one's attitude toward it and its referents only if one does not endanger the flag's representation of nationhood and national unity.

. . . It is not the State's ends, but its means, to which we object. It cannot be gainsaid that there is a special place reserved for the flag in this Nation, and thus we do not doubt that the Government has a legitimate interest in making efforts to "preserve the national flag as an unalloyed symbol of our country.". . . We reject the suggestion, urged at oral argument by counsel for Johnson, that the Government lacks "any state interest whatsoever" in regulating the manner in which the flag may be displayed.

To say that the Government has an interest in encouraging proper treatment of the flag, however, is not to say that it may criminally punish a person for burning a flag as a means of political protest. "National unity as an end which officials may foster by persuasion and example is not in question. The problem is whether under our Constitution compulsion as here employed is a permissible means for its achievement.". . .

The way to preserve the flag's special role is not to punish those who feel differently about these matters. It is to persuade them that they are wrong. . . . And, precisely because it is our flag that is involved, one's response to the flag burner may exploit the uniquely persuasive power of the flag itself. We can imagine no more appropriate response to burning a flag than waving one's own, no better way to counter a flag burner's message than by saluting the flag that burns, no surer means of preserving the dignity even of the flag that burned than by—as one witness here did—according its remains a respectful burial. We do not consecrate the flag by punishing its desecration, for in doing so we dilute the freedom that this cherished emblem represents.

Johnson was convicted for engaging in expressive conduct. The State's interest in preventing breaches of the peace does not support his conviction because Johnson's conduct did not threaten to disturb the peace. Nor does the State's interest in preserving the flag as a symbol of nationhood and national unity justify his criminal conviction for engaging in political expression.

W.E.B. DuBois
"The Legacy of John Brown"

The cost of liberty is less than the price of repression.

WILL ROGERS
There's Not a Bathing Suit in Russia

Liberty don't work as good in practice as it does in Speech.

FELIX FRANKFURTER

It is a fair summary of history to say that the safeguards of liberty have frequently been forged in cases involving not very nice people.

CLARENCE DARROW
Address to a Chicago jury

You can only protect your liberties in this world by protecting the other man's freedom. You can only be free if I am free.

WOODROW WILSON
Speech in Philadelphia

Liberty does not consist in mere general declarations of the rights of men. It consists of those declarations put into definite action.

JOHN ADAMS
Letter to J.H. Tiffany

I would define liberty to be a power to do as we would be done by.

WILLIAM FAULKNER
Harper's Magazine

Systems political or religious or racial or national—will not just respect us because we practice freedom, they will fear us because we do.

JANE ADDAMS
Address to the Union League Club, Chicago

A wise patriotism, which will take hold of these questions by careful legal enactment, by constant and vigorous enforcement, because of the belief that if the meanest man in the Republic is deprived of his rights, then every man in the Republic is deprived of his rights, is the only patriotism by which public-spirited men and women, with a thoroughly aroused conscience can worthily serve this Republic. Let us say again that the lessons of great men are lost unless they reinforce upon our minds the highest demands which we make upon ourselves; that they are lost unless they drive our sluggish wills forward in the direction of their highest ideals.

RALPH WALDO EMERSON
"History," *Essays*

Every revolution was first a thought in one man's mind.

THOMAS JEFFERSON
Letter to Abigail Adams

The spirit of resistance to government is so valuable on certain occasions, that I wish it to be always kept alive. It will often be exercised when wrong but better so than not to be exercised at all. I like a little rebellion now and then. It is like a storm in the atmosphere.

JAMES GARFIELD

I love agitation and investigation and glory in defending unpopular truth against popular error.

HEYWOOD BROUN
New York World Telegram

Show me a community or a country where all the minor vices are discouraged and I will show you one bereft of major virtues.

ELEANOR ROOSEVELT
Lecture at Duke University

We need our radicals.

MRS. OLIVER H.P. BELMONT
Letter to The New York Times

And shall we not protest when men not only continue to refuse to give us our liberty but decide the manner in which we shall demand our liberty?...."Militant?" why all this tenderness and delicacy about "militancy" in the form of banner-bearing when the Governments of all nations are conscripting their men, including our own nation, to be militant? The sentimental ladies and gentlemen who are so afraid lest we fatigue the President are urged to remember that we ourselves are very, very tired, and perhaps the sentimentalists will confer some pity on the faithful women who have struggled for three-quarters of a century for democracy in their own nation.

So Long, Woody, It's Been Good to Know Ya
(Woody Guthrie, 1912–1967)

PETE SEEGER

One of Woody Guthrie's last songs, written a year after he entered the hospital, was titled "I Ain't Dead Yet." The doctors told him he had Huntington's chorea, probably inherited, a progressive degeneration of the nervous system for which there was no cure known. For thirteen more years he hung on, refusing to give up. Finally he could no longer walk nor talk nor focus his eyes nor feed himself, and his great will to live was not enough and his heart stopped beating.

The news reached me while I was on tour in Japan. All I could think of at first was, "Woody will never die, as long as there are people who like to sing songs." Dozens of these are known by guitar pickers across the U.S.A., and one of them has become loved by tens of millions of Americans:

> This land is your land, this land is my land,
> From California to the New York island,
> From the redwood forests to the Gulf Stream waters,
> This land was made for you and me.

He was a short, wiry guy with a mop of curly hair under a cowboy hat, as I first saw him. He'd stand with his guitar slung on his back, spinning out stories like Will Rogers, with a faint, wry grin. Then he'd hitch his guitar around and sing the longest long outlaw ballad you ever heard, or some Rabelaisian fantasy he'd concocted the day before and might never sing again.

His songs are deceptively simple. Only after they have become part of your life do you realize how great they are. Any damn fool can get complicated. It takes genius to attain simplicity. Woody's songs for children are now sung in many languages:

> Why can't a dish break a hammer?
> Why, oh why, oh why?
> Because a hammer's got a pretty hard head.
> Goodbye, goodbye, goodbye.

His music stayed rooted in the blues, ballads and breakdowns he'd been raised on in the Oklahoma Dust Bowl. Like Scotland's Robert Burns and the Ukraine's Tara Shevchenko, Woody was a national folk poet. Like them, he came of a small-town background, knew poverty, had a burning curiosity to learn. Like them, his talent brought him to the city, where he was lionized by the literati but from whom he declared his independence and remained his own profane, radical, ornery self.

This honesty also eventually estranged him from his old Oklahoma cronies. Like many an Oklahoma farmer, he had long taken a dim view of bankers. In the desperate early Depression years he developed a religious view of Christ the Great Revolutionary. In the cities he threw in his lot with the labor movement:

> There once was a Union maid.
> She never was afraid
> Of goons and ginks and company finks
> And the deputy sheriff that made the raids.

He broadened his feeling to include the working people of all the world, and it may come as a surprise to some readers to know that the author of "This Land Is Your Land" was in 1940 a columnist for the small newspaper he euphemistically called *The Sabbath Employee*. It was *The Sunday Worker*, weekend edition of the *Communist Daily Worker*. Woody never argued theory much, but you can be quite sure today he would have poured his fiercest scorn on the criminal fools who sucked America into the Vietnam mess:

> Why do your warships sail on my waters?
> Why do your bombs drop down from the sky?
> Why do you burn my towns and cities?
> I want to know why, yes, I want to know why.

But Woody always did more than condemn. His song "Pastures of Plenty" described the life of the migrant fruit pickers, but ends on a note of shining affirmation:

> It's always we've rambled, that river and I.
> All along your garden valley I'll work till I die.
> My land I'll defend with my life if it be,
> For my Pastures of Plenty must always be free.

A generation of songwriters have learned from him—Bob Dylan, Tom Paxton, Phil Ochs and I guess many more to come.

As we scatter his ashes over the waters I can hear Woody hollering back to us, "Take it easy —but take it!"

HENRY WARD BEECHER
Proverbs from Plymouth Pulpit

The real democratic American idea is, not that every man shall be on a level with every other man, but that every man shall have liberty to be what God made him, without hindrance.

LOUIS KRONENBERGER
Company Manners

True individualists tend to be quite unobservant; it is the snob, the would-be sophisticate, the frightened conformist, who keeps a fascinated or worried eye on what is in the wind.

RALPH WALDO EMERSON
"Self-Reliance," *Essays*

Nothing is at last sacred by the integrity of our own mind. Absolve you to yourself, and you shall have the suffrage of the world

RALPH WALDO EMERSON
"Politics," *Essays*

Every actual State is corrupt. Good men must not obey the laws too well.

ROBERT F. KENNEDY
The Pursuit of Justice

If freedom makes social progress possible, so social progress strengthens and enlarges freedom. The two are inseperable partners in the great adventure of humanity.

HENRY DAVID THOREAU
Civil Disobedience

Under a government which imprisons any unjustly, the true place for a just man is also a prison . . . on that separate, but more free and honorable, ground, where the State places those who are not with her, but against her—the only house in a slave State in which a free man can abide with honor.

MUHAMMAD ALI
Refusal to Serve in Vietnam

I am proud of the title "World Heavyweight Champion," I won in the ring in Miami on February 25, 1964. The holder of it should at all times have the courage of his convictions and carry out those convictions, not only in the ring but throughout all phases of his life. It is in light of my own personal convictions that I take my stand in rejecting the call to be inducted into the armed services. I do so with full realization of its implications and possible consequences. I have searched my conscience, and find I cannot be true to my belief in my religion by accepting such a call. My decision is a private and individual one. In taking it I am dependent solely upon Allah as the final judge of these actions brought about by my own conscience. I strongly object to the fact that so many newspapers have given the American public and the world the impression that I have only two alternatives in taking this stand—either I go to jail or go to the Army. There is another alternative, and that alternative is justice. If justice prevails, if my constitutional rights are upheld, I will be forced to go neither to the Army nor jail. In the end, I am confident that justice will come my way, for the truth must eventually prevail.

DANIEL WEBSTER
Address at Bunker Hill Monument

If the true spark of religious and civil liberty be kindled, it will burn. Human agency cannot extinguish it. Like the earth's central fire, it may be smothered for a time; the ocean may overwhelm it; mountains may press it down; but its inherent and unconquerable force will heave both the ocean and the land, and at some time or other, in some place or other, the volcano will break out and flame up to heaven.

GEORGE SANTAYANA
Character and Opinion in the United States

Religion should be disentangled as much as possible from history and authority and metaphysics, and made to rest honestly on one's fine feelings, on one's indomitable optimism and trust in life.

GEORGE WASHINGTON
Letter to the Jewish congregation of Newport, Rhode Island

Happily the Government of the United States, which gives to bigotry no sanction, to persecution no assistance, requires only that they who live under its protection should demean themselves as good citizens in giving it on all occasions their effectual support.

HENRY CLAY
Speech in the U.S. House of Representatives

All religions united with government are more or less inimical to liberty. All separated from government are compatible with liberty.

MARTIN LUTHER KING, JR.
Strength to Love

The church must be reminded that it is not the master or the servant of the state, but rather the conscience of the state.

Ulysses S. Grant
Speech at Des Moines, Iowa

Leave the matter of religion to the family altar, the church, and the private school, supported entirely by private contributions. Keep the church and State forever Separate.

My Day; July 5, 1962

Eleanor Roosevelt

The nation's governors, in their annual meeting in Hershey, Pennsylvania, had a wordy wrangle regarding the resolution to be submitted to Congress for an amendment to the First Article of the Constitution, which of course deals with freedom of religion and the separation of church and state.

All this, it seems to me, stems from a misunderstanding of what the Supreme Court ruled regarding the New York State Board of Regents-written prayer and the saying of it in the schools of the state under state direction.

The fact is that this is a prayer written and backed by the government of the state and directed to be used in the schools, and which the Supreme Court has declared unconstitutional. The prayer is innocuous, but this procedure would be an injection of state interference in religious education and religious practice.

Under our Constitution no individual can be forced by government to belong to a special religion or to conform to a special religious procedure. But any school, or any group of people, or any individual may say a prayer if he or they so wish if it is not under the order of the government or connected with government direction in any way. This seems to me very clear in the Supreme Court decision and conforms exactly, I think, with the Constitution.

It is my feeling that many of our newspapers put sensational headlines on stories pertaining to this decision, and people have suddenly—without really reading the court ruling themselves—reacted emotionally.

Someone reported to me that he had heard a man on the radio in tears saying that he never thought he would live to see the day when God would be outlawed from our schools. Another told me that a Southern woman wrote to her daughter in New England, saying she was horrified to find that the Supreme Court was controlled by the Communists and, of course, the Communists were controlled by the Eastern European Jews. Such nonsense, such ignorance is really vicious.

One hears it said, of course, that at present in the South the accusation of communisim is rather loosely bandied about and covers whatever you happen not to like. Not knowing, however, that the Jewish communities of Eastern Europe are constantly trying to get away from those Soviet-controlled countries because they do not have security or equality of opportunity makes the accusation of their influence in communism and adherence to it a show of complete ignorance of the situation as it really exists. If any people have a reason for disliking communism, it is the Jews.

When unthinking emotions are aroused, we usually find that whatever prejudices are held are channeled by the emotions into expressions that have nothing to do with reality but simply are an outlet for the prejudices.

Years ago, in the South, I can remember my husband telling me when he took to Warm Springs the first nurse who had been trained in physiotherapy and had worked for the State of New York, that he hardly dared mention the fact that she happened to be a Roman Catholic. He hoped—before anyone discovered this fact—that her kindliness of spirit, her skill and her helpfulness would have won a place among the neighbors where she was going to work.

He was right, but he could not help being amused when an old man came to see him and said: "Miss——is such a good woman. But I thought when I heard she was a Roman Catholic she ought to have horns and a tail!"

This attitude has worn off somewhat, but in certain areas, such as where the author of the letter I have mentioned comes from, one can still find astounding beliefs about the Roman Catholics and the Jews.

There is a general lack of knowledge, too, about what communism is and how much influence it may have in our country. And the emotional reaction to a Supreme Court decision, such as we are witnessing, seems to me to be the product of an unwillingness to read with care what is actually said and an unwillingness to look at the Constitution and reread the First Amendment.

I thought the President's comment was one of the very best. The Constitution does not specify that we are not to be a religious people; it gives us the right to be religious in our own way, and it places upon us the responsibility for the observance of our religion. When the President said that he hoped this decision would make us think more of religion and our observance individually and at home, he emphasized a fact which I think it would be well for all of us to think about.

Real religion is displayed in the way we live in our day-by-day activities at home, in our own communities, and with our own families and neighbors. The Supreme Court emphasized that we must not curtail our freedom as safeguarded under the First Article of the Constitution.

JOHN WITHERSPOON
"The Dominion of Providence over the Passions of Men" *sermon*

True religion is nothing else but an inward temper and outward conduct suited to your state and circumstances in Providence at any time. And as peace with God, and conformity to him, adds to the sweetness of created comforts while we possess them, so in times of difficulty and trial, it is in the man of piety and inward principle that we may expect to find the uncorrupted patriot, the useful citizen, and the invincible soldier. God grant that in America true religion and civil liberty may be inseparable, and that unjust attempts to destroy the one may in the issue tend to the support and establishment of both.

JOHN F. KENNEDY

I am not so much concerned with the right of everyone to say anything he pleases as I am about our need as self-governing people to hear everything relevant.

The Spirit of Liberty
LEARNED HAND
Speech in New York City

We have gathered here to affirm a faith, a faith in a common purpose, a common conviction, a common devotion. Some of us have chosen America as the land of our adoption; the rest have come from those who did the same. For this reason we have some right to consider ourselves a picked group, a group of those who had the courage to break from the past and brave the dangers and the loneliness of a strange land. What was the object that nerved us, or those who went before us, to this choice? We sought liberty—freedom from oppression, freedom from want, freedom to be ourselves. This we then sought; this we now believe that we are by way of winning. What do we mean when we say that first of all we seek liberty? I often wonder whether we do not rest our hopes too much upon constitutions, upon laws, and upon courts. These are false hopes; believe me, these are false hopes. Liberty lies in the hearts of men and women; when it dies there, no constitution, no law, no court can save it; no constitution, no law, no court can even do much to help it. While it lies there, it needs no constitution, no law, no court to save it. And what is this liberty which must lie in the hearts of men and women? It is not the ruthless, the unbridled will; it is not freedom to do as one likes. That is the denial of liberty, and leads straight to its overthrow. A society in which men recognize no check upon their freedom soon becomes a society where freedom is the possession of only a savage few— as we have learned to our sorrow.

What, then, is the spirit of liberty? I cannot define it; I can only tell you my own faith. The spirit of liberty is the spirit which is not too sure it is right; the spirit of liberty is the spirit which seeks to understand the minds of other men and women; the spirit of liberty is the spirit which weighs their interests alongside its own without bias; the spirit of liberty remembers that not even a sparrow falls to earth unheeded; the spirit of liberty is the spirit of him who, near two thousand years ago, taught mankind that lesson it has never learned, but has never quite forgotten—that there may be a kingdom where the least shall be heard and considered side by side with the great. And now in that spirit, that spirit of an America which has never been, and which may never be—nay, which never will be except as the conscience and courage of Americans create it—yet in the spirit of that America which lies hidden in some form in the aspirations of us all; in the spirit of that America for which our young men are at this moment fighting and dying; in that spirit of liberty and of America so prosperous, and safe, and contented, we shall have failed to grasp its meaning, and shall have been truant to its promise, except as we strive to make it a signal, a beacon, a standard, to which the best hopes of mankind will ever turn. In confidence that you share that belief, I now ask you to raise your hands and repeat with me this pledge:

I pledge allegiance to the flag of the United States of America, and to the Republic for which it stands—one nation, indivisible, with liberty and justice for all.

RALPH WALDO EMERSON
"Voluntaries"

Freedom all winged expands,
Nor perches in a narrow place;
Her broad van seeks unplanted lands;
She loves a poor and virtuous race.

E.B. WHITE
Letter from the West

Liberty is never out of bounds or off limits; it spreads wherever it can capture the imagination of men.

BENJAMIN FRANKLIN
Letter from Paris to Samuel Cooper

It is a common observation here that our cause is the cause of all mankind, and that we are fighting for their liberty in defending our own.

JOHN F. KENNEDY
West Berlin, Germany

All free men, wherever they may live, are citizens of Berlin. And therefore, as a free man, I take pride in the words "Ich bin ein Berliner."

MADELEINE ALBRIGHT
United Nations Conference of Women speech in Beijing, China

No woman—whether in Birmingham, Bombay, Beirut or Beijing—should be forcibly sterilized or forced to have an abortion. No mother should feel compelled to abandon her daughter because of a societal preference for males. No woman should be forced to undergo genital mutilation, or to become a prostitute, or to enter into marriage, or to have sex. No one should be forced to remain silent for fear of religious or political persecution, arrest, abuse, or torture. All of us should be able to exercise control over the course of our own lives and be able to help shape the destiny of our communities and countries.

Let us be clear: Freedom to participate in the political process of our countries is the inalienable right of every woman and man. Deny that right, and you deny everything. It is unconscionable, therefore, that the right to free expression has been called into question right here, at a conference conducted under the auspices of the UN, and whose very purpose is the free and open discussion of women's rights.

It is a challenge to us all that so many countries in so many parts of the world—north, south, west, and east—fall far short of the noble objectives outlined in the Platform for Action. Every nation, including my own, must do better and do more to make equal rights a fundamental principle of law; to enforce those rights and to remove barriers to the exercise of those rights.

Can Democracy Prevail?

ADLAI E. STEVENSON

As an ex-politican and a practicing diplomat—although many would doubtless dissent from both these claims—let me say that when it comes to faith in democracy, I refuse to take a back seat even for my distinguished predecessors on this platform. Because I believe in democracy and freedom, and I believe in their ultimate triumph with the fundamentalist fervor of a survivor of Valley Forge or a Presidential Campaign—not to mention two! As Macauley said of Lord Brougham, or vice versa, "I wish I was as sure of anything as he is of everything." Well, the one thing I'm sure of is that constitutional democracy is that form of government which best fulfills the nature of man. Moreover, my faith, I remind you, has survived some rather disillusioning experiences.

That's why I'm so glad to be here among people of like conviction who are trying so hard to make freedom and democracy working realities. And that's why I toil in the tangled vineyards of the United Nations, where the leaders of the whole world are trying to practice parliamentary democracy on a global scale....

[W]hether democracy can prevail in the great upheaval of our time is a valid question. Certainly, after 150 years of uninterrupted expansion of the idea of government by consent of the governed, it has recently met with mounting and formidable challenges all over the world from Fascist, Nazi, Communist authoritarians and a variety of dictatorships. And we have good reason to know how clumsy, slow, inefficient and costly it is compared to the celerity, certainty and secrecy of absolutism.

But the important thing is that it has survived. The important thing is that even the absolutists masquerade as democrats; even the military and quasi-military dictatorships strive in the name of democracy to manage the public business. And all of them say that authoritarianism is only a necessary transition to democracy.

Why? Because it is the most popular form of government yet devised; because it is, as it always has been, not only the prize of the steadfast and the courageous, but the privilege of those who are better off; because, in short, as Jefferson said, it is "the only form of government which is not eternally at open or secret war with the rights of the people."

I have therefore no doubt that, distant as it may be for many people, it will ultimately prevail, that it will regain lost ground, that it will expand its dominion, that it can withstand the wild winds that are blowing through the world—if and I repeat if—we who are its custodians continually re-examine and adapt its principles to the changing needs of our changing times.

Years ago, Reinhold Niebuhr observed that "man's capacity for justice makes democracy possible; but man's inclination to injustice makes democracy necessary."

And I suppose that most of us, if we were asked to name the most profound issues at stake in the world today, would say the issues of freedom and democracy. We would say that the Western world, for all its errors and shortcomings, has for centuries tried to evolve a society in which the individual has enough legal, social and political elbow room to be, not the puppet of the community, but his own autonomous self.

And we would say that the enemies of freedom, whatever the magnificent ends they propose—the brotherhood of man, the kingdom of saints, "from each according to his ability, to each according to his needs"—miss just this essential point: that man is greater than the social purposes to which he can be put. He must not be kicked about even with the most high-minded objectives. He is not a means or an instrument. He is an end in himself.

This, I take it, is the essence of what we mean by democracy—not so much voting systems or parliamentary systems or economic or legal systems (though they all enter in) as an irrevocable and final dedication to the dignity of man. In this sense, democracy is perhaps mankind's most audacious experiment. This dignity and equality of the human person could hardly be further removed from the existential facts of human existence. There is precious little dignity or equality in our natural state.

Most human beings have to spend their lives in utter vulnerability. All are murderable and torturable and survive only through the restraint shown by more powerful neighbors. All are born unequal, in terms of capacity or strength. All are born to the inherent frailty of the human condition, naked and helpless, vulnerable all through life to the will of others, limited by ignorance, limited by physical weakness, limited by fear, limited by the phobias that fear engenders.

For nearly three thousand years now, the political and social genius of what we can permissibly call "Western man" has struggled with these brute facts of our unsatisfactory existence. Ever since the Hebrews discovered personal moral responsibility and the Greeks discovered the autonomy of the citizen, the effort has been made—with setbacks and defeats, with dark ages and interregnums and any number of irrelevant adventures on the side—to create a social order in which weak, fallible, obstinate, magnificent man can maintain his dignity and exercise his free and responsible choice.

The task has never been easy. Each step has been a groping in the dark—the dark of violence and brute power and overweening arrogance. Yet we have learned some of the preconditions and expedients of freedom. And we have incorporated them in societies and institutions. What we seek to defend today against new critics and new adversaries is essentially a great body of experience, not theories or untried ideals, but a solid mass of lived-through facts. First in time came the great medieval discovery that the king must be subject to the law.

Equality before the law has been expanded and safeguarded by consultation and representation—in other words, the vote. This is not simply a device for peacefully changing government, although it is that, too. It is not only a means of allowing the wearer to say where the shoe pinches. It is, in addition, a means of offsetting the natural inequalities which grow up in any society, however organized, as a result of the unequal endowment of people.

The head of, say, General Electric, has more means of influencing society than a small-town electrician. Against the advantages of brains and money, the vote is the only advantage the small man has. His voice, or vote, added to millions of other voices, offsets the accumulated power of society's entrenched positions.

But equality before the law and at the ballot box are only strands in the seamless robe in which all our liberties are woven together. Carelessly unravel one and the robe itself may come apart.

Another is enough social and economic opportunity for each man, even the poorest, to hold his dignity intact. The wildest access to education and training, equal opportunity for talent to find its niche, security of income and work, the chances of health—all these belong to a social order of responsible and respected citizens. We no longer define democracy solely in political terms. The great effort of this century has been to work out its economic and social implications.

If we take these three main strands of democracy—equality before the law, constitutional representative government and social and economic opportunity—it is clear that they face, as evolving free society has always faced, new challenges in our own day. It is profoundly concerned with the extension of the concept of democracy—extension in depth, for we now believe that no human being, however lowly his occupation or poor his resources, can be excluded from the dignity of man—extension in space, for the whole world is now a community and we have to find ways in which the idea of a truly human society can be realized on a planetary scale. The two processes, going forward simultaneously in every part of the globe, make up the vast revolutionary ferment of our duty.

What we have to attempt today is the building of intercontinental forms of free community—certainly the most testing experiment of all those made so far by free men. Yet our past achievements give us the right to hope for future success.

One form of association already exists between virtually all the nations of this globe and, whatever work we may accomplish on a regional basis, progress at the United Nations in the direction of a free society of equals must be part of our effort to extend the principle of liberty as the essential working principle of mankind.

How are we to set about this task? There is one method which, I most profoundly hope, we shall avoid, and that is the method of self-righteous exhortation. We have, I fear, sometimes displayed an unattractive tendency to lecture new governments on their constitutional shortcomings and to point, sometimes openly, sometimes implicitly, to the superior performance of the West.

We can admit that free government is a Western invention—by all odds, its finest political achievement. But there are several things we must remember as well. We must remember that it took about eight centuries to develop these patterns of life in our own culture. We must remember that our form of democracy is the most subtle and sophisticated form of government in the world; other, more primitive, still developing peoples cannot be expected to master it overnight. But move toward it they will, and such institutions as the United Nations help to train their leadership in our ways. Moreover, new states always face appalling problems of readjustment, and we must be smart enough to recognize when and how these alien leaderships move our way.

If now we see in Africa single-party rule dominated by one leader, with changing policies and political choice severely restricted, we should not hold up our hands in horror, but remember that this is not far from our politics of two centuries ago.

Where we have every right to express our alarm is in the breakdown of constitutional protection by the law. The danger lies not so much in parliamentary failure as in judicial failure. Yet, even here, our alarm should be expressed in modest terms. In eighteenth-century England, a man could be hanged for stealing a sheep, and horrible ships took convicts to Australia for no more than petty larceny. Nor was Europe's recent Fascism precisely a law-abiding mode of government.

No—the way ahead does not lie through sermonizing carried on by people whose own eyes are too full of beams to judge clearly the others' motes. It lies rather in a sustained effort to work out, within the United Nations and in partnerships with other nations, the chief lines of advance toward a more coherent and viable world community, with freedom as its working principle and constitutionalism as its political habit. No one is likely to underestimate the appalling complexities of the task. But the outlook must have seemed as daunting to the lawyers struggling against Stuart despotism or the Founding Fathers attempting to turn federalism into a workable system.

The task is indeed "piled high with difficulty." We should attempt it, therefore, with all the more vigor and clarity, and I would suggest that the three criteria I stressed in domestic democracy are relevant, too, to the global democracy we painfully must try to build.

Today, the first of all tasks is to restrain the nation-state from taking law into its own hands —in other words, from using force to assert its will—or, in the final word, from making war.

From domestic society, we know the only way to banish lawless violence and fratricidal strife is by accepting rules of peaceful change and adjustment and building an impartial police force to enforce the peaceful solutions that are agreed. This I take to be a task of the United Nations; however, no world body can yet take on the tasks of global peace. Some of our vast modern states are still, like the medieval barons, too powerful to be controlled in their feudal fastnesses.

But perhaps we have reached a first stage of restraint on arbitrary power. Troubled areas— Palestine, the Congo, Laos—are policed not by rivals whose rivalry would lead to war, but by an external and impartial third force.

Could we not extend the principle? Could we not aim at the policing by the United Nations of more and more areas in which the rival interests of powerful states threaten to clash? Global systems of restraint may still evade us. But history suggests we can start from the particular instance and then extend the principle, and every area withdrawn from the naked arbitrament of force is an area saved for the constitutional working of a sane human society.

Does the second principle I have picked out—the procedure of equal voting—apply to the building of a free world society? The critics say the new states, holding the balance of power by means of their combined vote, drive the United Nations on toward ferocious extremes of anticolonialism and attempt to impose other imprudent policies on the Great Powers which must disrupt the whole organization. Meanwhile, the great foot the bill.

There is much to be said for this score. For the moment, let me only say that in world society, the small nation, like the small man in domestic society, is most likely to be vulnerable. His equal voice, his capacity to unite it with other small voices, is a measure of protection against his inequality. We see the need for this countervailing power inside our states. So let us not be too quick to denounce it in the world at large.

There is a further reason for being cautious and patient about the workings inside the United Nations of the potential ex-colonial majority. If we turn to the third principle of democracy—equality of esteem, equal dignity, equal access to the social and economic possibilities of society—we find that the disproportions which distort true community inside our states are present in world society, too. This Afro-Asian bloc—a misnomer, for, save on the colonial issue, there is no block—represents most of the world's most truly underprivileged peoples. If they cling to their United Nations status, it is because, as citizens of our planet, they have not yet much else to cling to. Pushed to the first outskirts of modernity by Western investment and trade, emancipated before they had received either the training or the powers of wealth—cre-ation needed for a modern society, they are caught between two worlds—the powerful, afflu-ent, expanding world of the developed "North" and the traditional, pretechnological, largely poor world of the underdeveloped "South."

This division in world society is a great obstacle to the expansion of the confidence and community the world needs for a truly human society. And it threatens to become worse if such experiments as the European Common Market or the Atlantic Community prove to be, vis-a-vis the less fortunate parts of the world, a rich man's club, exclusive in its commerce, its investments, its arrangements and its interests. The gap exists. We must not make it worse.

What can we do? I would like to suggest that we, the wealthiest, most fortunate of all the developed states of the "North" have two lines to follow, both of them essential if we in this generation are to make our full contribution to the advance of world democracy.

I know there is much dissatisfaction about aid, much feeling that it is wasted and never achieves a breakthrough, and dribbles away down thousands of unspecified drains and ratholes. Yet just so did the Victorians talk about tax money devoted to lifting the standards of the very poor in early industrial society. There were the "good poor" who said "Please" and "Thank you" and touched their forelocks. Then there were the "bad poor" who kept coal in the bath-tub. But over a couple of generations, it was the raising of all this unfortunate mass of human-ity that turned Western society into the first social order in history in which everyone could expect something of an equal chance.

After ten years, we are only at the beginning of the experiment of international aid. We are learning greatly. We see the relevance of some policies, the supreme obstacles offered by oth-ers. We discriminate more. We are learning to be better givers.

Our second task is harder. It is harder for us than for any other member of the world's wealthy elite. It is to see that the last vestiges of discrimination inside our own society are speed-ily abolished. It is no use talking to ourselves as the vanguard of freedom and democracy while any of our fellow Americans can be treated like a James Meredith at the University of Mississippi.

Must we not, as lovers of freedom and as—too often—self-styled prophets of the free way of life, sometimes lapse into a shamed silence when we even have to talk about social injustice, let alone deal with it—one hundred years after the Emancipation Proclamation?

I must end as I began. The essence of democracy is the dignity of man. We shall create a free world order on no other basis. If we attack communism—as we must—for its contempt for political dignity, we must attack as unrelentingly lapses in social dignity.

It sometimes seems to me today as though, through all the great issues of the day—the anticolonial revulsion, the political contest with communism, the unification of Europe, the clamor of poorer lands for advance—there runs the underlying desire for some lasting realization of the dignity of man; man with a measure of political autonomy, man with the economic elbow room to live above the torturing doubts of food and work, man with the dignity to look his neighbor in the face and see a friend.

"Affirmation of Freedom"

ROBERT F. KENNEDY

Speech at the University of Cape Town, South Africa

I come here this evening because of my deep interest and affection for a land settled by the Dutch in the mid-seventeenth century, then taken over by the British, and at last independent. A land in which the native inhabitants were at first subdued, but relations with whom remain a problem to this day, a land which defined itself on a hostile frontier, a land which has tamed rich natural resources through the energetic application of modern technology, a land which was once the importer of slaves and now must struggle to wipe out the last traces of that former bondage. I refer of course to the United States of America.

This is a day of affirmation—a celebration of liberty. We stand here in the name of freedom. At the heart of that Western freedom and democracy is the belief that the individual man, the child of God, is a touchstone of value and all society, all groups and states exist for that person's benefit. Therefore the enlargement of liberty for individual human beings must be the supreme goal and the abiding practice of any Western society.

The first element of this individual liberty is the freedom of speech, the right to express and communicate ideas, to set ourselves from the dumb beasts of field and forest, the right to recall governments to their duties and to their obligations. Above all the right to affirm one's membership and allegiance to the body politic, to society, to the men with whom we share our land, our heritage, and our children's future.

Hand in hand with freedom of speech goes the power to be heard, to share in the decisions of government which shape men's lives. Everything that makes man's life worthwhile—family, work, education, a place to rear one's children and a place to rest one's head—all this depends on the decisions of government. All can be swept away by a government which does not heed the demands of its people, and I mean all of its people; therefore the essential humanity of man can be protected and preserved only where government must answer not just to the wealthy, not just to those of a particular religion, not just to those of a particular race, but to all of the people.

And even government by the consent of the governed, as in our own Constitution, must be limited in its power to act against its people so that there may be no interference with the right to worship, but also no interference with the security of the home. No arbitrary imposition of pains or penalties on an ordinary citizen by officials high or low, no restriction on the freedom of men to seek education or to seek work or opportunity of any kind so that each man may become all that he is capable of becoming.

These are the sacred rights of Western society. These were the essential differences between us and Nazi Germany, as they were between Athens and Persia. They are the essence of our differences with communism today. I am unalterably opposed to communism because it exalts the state over the individual and over the family, and because the system contains a lack of freedom of speech, of protest, of religion, and of the press which is characteristic of totalitarian regimes. The way of opposition to communism, however, is not to imitate its dictatorship but to enlarge individual human freedom.

There are those in every land who would label as communist every threat to their privilege, but may I say to you, as I have seen on my travels of all sections of the world, reform is not communism, and the denial of freedom in whatever name only strengthens the very communism it claims to oppose.

Many nations have set forth their own definitions and declarations of these principles. There have often been wide and tragic gaps between promise and performance, ideal and reality. Yet the great ideals have constantly recalled us to our own duties. With painful slowness we in the United States have extended and enlarged the meaning and the practice of freedom to all of our people. For two centuries my country has struggled to overcome the self-imposed handicap of prejudice and discrimination based on nationality, on social class, or race, a discrimination profoundly repugnant to the theory and to the command of our own Constitution. Even as my father grew up in Boston, Massachusetts, signs told him, "No Irish need apply."

Two generations later President Kennedy became the first Irish Catholic and the first Catholic to head the nation, but how many men of ability had before 1961 been denied the opportunity to contribute to the nation's progress because they were Catholic or of Irish extraction? How many sons of Italian or Jewish or Polish parents slumbered in the slums untaught, unlearned, their potential lost forever to our nation and to the human race? Even today what price will we pay before we have assured full opportunity to millions of Negro Americans? In the last five years we have done more to assure equality to our Negro citizens and to help the deprived both white and black than in the hundred years before that time. But much, much more remains to be done, for there are millions of Negroes untrained for the simplest of jobs, and thousands denied every day their full and equal rights under the law. And the violence of the disinherited, the insulted, the injured looms over the streets of Harlem and of Watts and of the south side of Chicago. But a Negro American trains now as an astronaut, one of mankind's first explorers into outer space, another is the chief barrister of the United States government and dozens sit on the benches of our courts. And another, Dr. Martin Luther King, is the second man of African descent to win the Nobel Peace Prize for his nonviolent efforts for social justice between all of the races. We have passed laws prohibiting discrimination in education, in employment, in housing, but these laws alone cannot overcome the heritage of centuries of broken families and stunted children and poverty and degradation and pain. For the road toward equality and freedom is not easy and great cost and danger march alongside all of us. We are committed to peaceful and nonviolent change, and that is important for all to understand, though change is unsettling. Still, even in the turbulence of protest and struggle is greater hope for the future as men learn to claim and achieve for themselves the rights formerly petitioned from others.

Most important of all, all of the panoply of government power has been committed to the goal of equality before the law as we are now committing ourselves to the achievement of equal opportunity in fact. We must recognize the full human equality of all of our people before God, before law, and in the councils of government. We must not do this because it is economically advantageous, although it is. Not because the laws of God command it, although they do. Not because people in other lands wish it so. We must do it for the single and fundamental reason that it is the right thing to do. We recognize that there are problems and obstacles before the fulfillment of these ideals in the United States. We recognize that other nations in Latin America, and in Asia and in Africa have their own political and economic problems, their unique barriers to the elimination of injustices. In some there is concern that change will submerge the rights of a minority, particularly where that minority is of a different race than that of the majority. We in the United States believe in the protection of minorities. We recognize the contributions that they can make, and the leadership that they can provide. And we do not believe that any people, whether minority or majority, or individual human beings, are expendable in the cause of theory or policy. We recognize also that justice between men and nations is imperfect, and that humanity sometimes progresses very slowly indeed.

All do not develop in the same manner and at the same pace. Nations, like men, often march to the beat of different drummers. The precise solutions of the United States can neither be dictated nor transplanted to others, and that is not our intention. What is important, however, is that all nations must march forward toward increasing freedom, toward justice for all, toward a society strong and flexible enough to meet the demands of all its people, whatever their race, and the demands of a world of immense and dizzying change that face us all.

In a few hours the plane that brought me to this country crossed over oceans and countries which have been a crucible of human history. In minutes we traced migrations of men over thousands of years, seconds, the briefest glimpse.

We passed battlefields in which millions of men once struggled and died. We could see no national boundaries, no vast gulfs or high walls dividing people from people. Only nature and the works of man, homes and factories and farms, everywhere reflecting man's common effort to enrich his life. Everywhere new technology and communication bring men and nations closer together. The concerns of one inevitably become the concerns of all. And our new closeness is stripping away the false masks, the illusion of differences which is the root of injustice and of hate and of war. Only earthbound man still clings to the dark and poisoning superstition that his world is bounded by the nearest hill, his universe ends at river shore, his common humanity is enclosed in the tight circle of those who share his town or his views and the color of his skin.

It is your job, the task of young people in this world, to strip the last remnants of that ancient cruel belief from the civilization of man. Each nation has different obstacles and different goals shaped by the vagaries of history and of experience. Yet, as I talk to young people around the world, I am impressed not by the diversity but by the closeness of their goals, their desires, and their concerns, and their hopes for the future.

There is discrimination in New York, the racial inequality of apartheid in South Africa and serfdom in the mountains of Peru. People starve to death in the streets of India. A former prime minister is summarily executed in the Congo. Intellectuals go to jail in Russia and thousands are slaughtered in Indonesia. Wealth is lavished on armaments everywhere in the world.

These are different evils but they are the common works of man. They reflect the imperfections of human justice, the inadequacy of human compassion, the defectiveness of our sensibility toward the sufferings of our fellows. They mark the limit of ability to use knowledge for the well-being of our fellow human beings throughout the world. And therefore they call upon common qualities of conscience and indignation and a shared determination to wipe away the unnecessary suffering of our fellow human beings at home and around the world. It is these qualities which make of our youth today the only true international community. More than this I think that we could agree on what kind of world we would all want to build. It would be a world of independent nations moving forward in an international community, each of which protected and respected the basic human freedom. It would be a world which demanded of each government that it accept its responsibility to ensure social justice. It would be a world of constantly accelerating economic progress, not material welfare as an end in of itself but as a means to liberate the capacity of every human being to pursue his talents and to pursue his hopes. It would, in short, be a world that we would all be proud to have built.

Just to the north of here are lands of challenge and of opportunity, rich in natural resources, land and minerals and people, yet they are also lands confronted by the greatest odds: overwhelming ignorance, internal tensions and strife, and great obstacles of climate and geography. Many of these nations as colonies were oppressed and were exploited yet they have not estranged themselves from the broad traditions of the West. They are hoping and they are gambling their progress and their stability on the chance that we will meet our responsibility to them to help them overcome their poverty. In the world we would like to build, South Africa could play an outstanding role of leadership in that effort. This country is without question a pre-eminent repository of the wealth and the knowledge and the skill of this continent. Here are the greater part of Africa's research scientists and steel production, most of its reservoirs of coal and electric power. Many South Africans have made major contributions to African technical development and world science. The names of some are known wherever men seek to eliminate the ravages of tropical disease and of pestilence. In your faculties and councils, here in this very audience are hundreds and thousands of men and women who could transform the lives of millions for all time to come, but the health and the leadership of South Africa, or of the United States, cannot be accepted if we, within our own countries or in our relations with others, deny individual integrity, human dignity, and the common humanity of man.

If we would lead outside our own borders, if we would help those who need our assistance, if we would meet our responsibilities to mankind, we must first all of us demolish the borders which history has erected between men within our own nations, barriers of race and religion, social class and ignorance. Our answer is the world's hope. It is to rely on you. The cruelties of the obstacles of this swiftly changing planet will not yield to obsolete dogmas and outworn slogans. We cannot be moved by those who cling to a present which is already dying, who prefer the illusion of security to the excitement of danger which comes with even the most peaceful progress. This world demands the qualities of youth, not a time of life but a state of the mind, a temper of the will, a quality of the imagination, a predominance of courage over timidity, an appetite for adventure over a life of ease, a man like the chancellor of this university.

It is a revolutionary world that we all live in and thus as I have said in Latin America, and in Asia, and in Europe, and in my own country, the United States, it is the young people who must take the lead. Thus, you and your young compatriots have had thrust upon you a greater burden of responsibility than any generation that has ever lived. There is, said an Italian philosopher, nothing more difficult to take in hand, more perilous to conduct, or more uncertain in its success, than to take the lead in the introduction of a new order of things. Yet this is the measure of the task of your generation and the road is strewn with many dangers.

First is the danger of futility, the belief there is nothing one man or one woman can do against the enormous array of the world's ills, against misery, against ignorance or injustice and violence. Yet many of the world's great movements of thought and action have flowed from the work of a single man. A young monk began the Protestant Reformation, a young general extended an empire from Macedonia to the borders of the earth, and a young woman reclaimed the territory of France. It was a young Italian explorer who discovered the New World. It was thirty-two-year-old Thomas Jefferson who proclaimed that all men are created equal.

"Give me a place to stand," said Archimedes, "and I will move the world." These men moved the world and so can we all. Few will have the greatness to bend history, but each of us can work to change a small portion of the event, and in the total all of these acts will be written in the history of this generation.

Thousands of Peace Corps volunteers are making a difference in the isolated villages and in the city slums of dozens of countries. Thousands of unknown men and women in Europe resisted the occupation of the Nazis and many died, but all added to the ultimate strength and the freedom of their country. It is from numberless, diverse acts of courage such as these that human history is thus shaped. Each time a man stands up for an ideal or acts to improve the lot of others or strikes out against an injustice, he sets out a tiny ripple of hope and, crossing each other from a million different centers of energy and daring, those ripples build a current which can sweep down the mightiest walls of oppression and resistance.

"If Athens shall appear great to you," said Pericles, "consider then that her glories were purchased by valiant men and by men who learned their duty." That is the source of all greatness in all societies and it is the key to progress in our time.

The second danger is that of expediency, of those who say the hopes and beliefs must bend before immediate necessity. Of course if we must act effectively we must deal with the world as it is. We must get things done. But if there was one thing that President Kennedy stood for, that touched the most profound feeling of young people around the world, it was the belief that idealism, high aspirations, and deep convictions are not incompatible with the most practical and efficient of programs, that there is no basic inconsistency between ideals and realistic possibilities, no separation between the deepest desires of heart and of mind, and the rational application of human effort to human problems. It is not realistic or hardheaded to solve problems and take an action unguided by ultimate moral aims and values, although we all know some who claim that it is so. In my judgment it is thoughtless folly for it ignores the realities of human faith and of passion and of belief, forces ultimately more powerful than all the calculations of our economists or of our generals. A course to adhere to standards, to idealism, to vision in the face of immediate dangers takes great courage and takes self-confidence, but we also know that only those who dare to fail greatly can ever achieve greatly. It is this new idealism which is also I believe the common heritage of a generation which has learned that while efficiency can lead to the camps of Auschwitz or the streets of Budapest, only the ideals of humanity or love can climb the hills of the Acropolis.

The third danger is timidity. Few men are willing to brave the disapproval of their fellows, the censure of their colleagues, the wrath of their society. Moral courage is a rarer commodity than bravery in battle or great intelligence. Yet it is the one essential, vital quality for those who seek to change the world which yields most painfully to change. Aristotle tells us, at the Olympic Games it is not the finest or the strongest men who are crowned, but those who enter the list. So too in the life of the honorable and the good, it is they who act rightly who win the prize. I believe that in this generation, those with the courage to enter the conflict will find themselves with companions in every corner of the world.

For the fortunate amongst us, the fourth danger, my friends, is comfort, the temptation to follow the easy and familiar path of personal ambition and financial success so grandly spread before those who have the privilege of an education, but that is not the road history has marked out for us.

There is a Chinese curse which said, "May he live in interesting times." Like it or not, we live in interesting times. They are times of danger and uncertainty, but they are also the most creative of any time in the history of mankind. And every one here will ultimately be judged, will ultimately judge himself on the effort he has contributed to building a new world society and the extent to which his ideal and goals have shaped that effort.

So we part. I to my country and you to remain. We are, if a man of forty can claim the privilege, fellow members of the world's largest younger generation. Each of us have our own work to do. I know at times you must feel very alone with your problems and with your difficulties, but I want to say how impressed I am by what you stand for and for the efforts that you are making. I say this not just for myself, but for men and women all over the world.

I hope you will often take heart in the knowledge that you are joined with your fellow young people in every land, they struggling with their problems and you with yours, but all joined in a common purpose, that like the young people of my own country and in every country that I have visited you are all in many ways more closely united to the brothers of your time than to the older generation in any of these nations. You are determined to build a better future. President Kennedy was speaking to the young people of America, but beyond them to young people everywhere, when he said: "The energy, the faith, the devotion which we bring to this endeavor will light our country and all who serve it, and the glow from that fire can truly light the world." And he added, "With a good conscience our only sure reward, with history the final judge of our deeds, let us go forth to lead the land we love, asking His blessing and His help but knowing that here on earth, God's work must truly be our own."

Let Freedom Ring

DWIGHT D. EISENHOWER
Message to Congress

America is best described by one word, freedom.

ALICE WALKER
Living by the Word

Freedom is like love: the more you give to others, the more you have.

YIP HARBURG
"Bloomer Girl"

We gotta be free
The eagle and me.

JIMMY DURANTE

Don't put no constrictions on da people. Leave 'em ta hell alone.

CLINT EASTWOOD

There's a rebel lying deep in my soul. Anytime anybody tells me the trend is such and such, I go in the opposite direction. I hate the idea of trends. I hate imitation. I have a reverence for individuality.

MARK TWAIN
Seventieth birthday

We can't reach old age by another man's road.

MARK TWAIN

Each man must for himself alone decide what is right and what is wrong, which course is patriotic and which isn't. You cannot shirk this and be a man.

FELIX FRANKFURTER
Felix Frankfurter Reminisces

Anybody who is any good is different from anybody else.

BOB DYLAN
"Blowin' in the Wind"

How many roads must a man walk down
Before you call him a man?

OLIVER WENDELL HOLMES, SR.
The Professor at the Breakfast Table

The very aim and end of our institutions is just this: that we may think what we like and say what we think.

DOROTHY PARKER

I shall stay the way I am
Because I do not give a damn.

POPEYE

I ams what I am.

DR. SEUSS

You have brains in your head.
You have feet in your shoes.
You can steer yourself
Any direction you choose.

ETHEL WATERS

His Eye Is on the Sparrow

I can come when I please
I can go when I please
I can flit, fly, and flutter like the birds in the trees.

ARCHIBALD MACLEISH

"A Declaration of Freedom"

Freedom is the right to one's dignity as a man.

Freedom

E.B. WHITE

I believe in freedom with the same burning delight, the same faith, the same intense abandon that attended its birth on this continent more than a century and a half ago. I am writing my declaration rapidly, much as though I were shaving to catch a train. Events abroad give a man a feeling of being pressed for time. Actually I do not believe I am pressed for time, and I apologize to the reader for a false impression that may be created. I just want to tell, before I get slowed down, that I am in love with freedom and that it is an affair of long standing and that it is a fine state to be in, and that I am deeply suspicious of people who are beginning to adjust to fascism and dictators merely because they are succeeding in war. From such adaptable natures a smell arises. I pinch my nose.

For as long as I can remember I have had a sense of living somewhat freely in a natural world. I don't mean I enjoyed freedom of action, but my existence seemed to have the quality of freeness. I traveled with secret papers pertaining to a divine conspiracy. Intuitively I've always been aware of the vitally important pact that a man has with himself, to be all things to himself, and to be identified with all things, to stand self-reliant, taking advantage of his haphazard connection with a planet, riding his luck, and following his bent with the tenacity of a hound. My first and greatest love affair was with this thing we call freedom, this lady of infinite allure, this dangerous and beautiful and sublime being who restores and supplies us all.

It began with the haunting intimation (which I presume every child receives) of his mystical inner life; of God in man; of nature publishing herself through the "I." This elusive sensation is moving and memorable. It comes early in life: a boy, we'll say, sitting on the front steps on a summer night, thinking of nothing in particular, suddenly hearing as with a new perception and as though for the first time the pulsing sound of crickets, overwhelmed with the novel sense of identification with the natural company of insects and grass and night, conscious of a faint answering cry to the universal perplexing question: "What is 'I'?" Or a little girl, returning from the grave of a pet bird and leaning with her elbows on the windowsill, inhaling the unfamiliar draught of death, suddenly seeing herself as part of the complete story. Or an older you, encountering for the first time a great teacher who by some chance word or mood awakens something and the youth beginning to breathe as an individual and conscious of strength in his vitals. I think the sensation must develop in many men as a feeling of identity with God—an eruption of the spirit caused by allergies and the sense of divine existence as distinct from mere animal existence. This is the beginning of the affair with freedom.

But a man's free condition is of two parts: the instinctive freeness he experiences as an animal dweller on a planet, and the practical liberties he enjoys as a privileged member of human society. The latter is, of the two, more generally understood, more widely admired, more violently challenged and discussed. It is the practical and apparent side of freedom. The United States, almost alone today, offers the liberties and the privileges and the tools of freedom. In this land the citizens are still invited to write their plays and books, to paint their pictures, to meet for discussion, to dissent as well as to agree, to mount soapboxes in the public square, to enjoy education in all subjects without censorship, to hold court and judge one another, to compose music, to talk politics with their neighbors without wondering whether the secret police are listening, to exchange ideas as well as goods, to kid the government when it needs kidding, and to read real news of real events instead of phony news manufactured by a paid agent of the state. This is a fact and should give every person pause.

To be free, in a planetary sense, is to feel that you belong to earth. To be free, in a social sense, is to feel at home in a democratic framework. In Adolf Hitler, although he is a freely flowering individual, we do not detect either type of sensibility. From reading his book I gather that his feeling for the earth is not a sense of communion but a driving urge to prevail. His feeling for men is not that they co-exist, but that they are capable of being arranged and standardized by a superior intellect—that their existence suggests not a fulfillment of their personalities but a submersion of their personalities in common racial destiny. His very great absorption in the destiny of the German people somehow loses some of its effect when you discover, from his writings, in what vast contempt he holds all people. "I learned," he wrote, ". . . to gain an insight into the unbelievably primitive opinions and arguments of the people." To him the ordinary man is a primitive, capable only of being used and led. He speaks continually of people as sheep, halfwits, and impudent fools—the same people from whom he asks the utmost in loyalty, and to whom he promises the ultimate in prizes.

Here in America, where our society is based on belief in the individual, not contempt for him, the free principle of life has a chance of surviving. I believe that it must and will survive. To understand freedom is an accomplishment all men may acquire who set their minds in that direction; and to love freedom is a tendency many Americans are born with. To live in the same room with freedom, or in the same hemisphere, is still a profoundly shaking experience for me.

One of the earliest truths (and to him most valuable) that the author of *Mein Kampf* discovered was that it is not the written word, but the spoken word, that in heated moments moves great masses of people to noble or ignoble action. The written word, unlike the spoken word, is something every person examines privately and judges calmly by his own intellectual standards, not by what the man standing next to him thinks. "I know," wrote Hitler, "that one is able to win people far more by the spoken than by the written word..." Later he adds contemptuously: "For let it be said to all knights of the pen and to all the political dandies, especially of today: the greatest changes in this world have never yet been brought about by a goose quill! No, the pen has always been reserved to motivate these changes theoretically."

Luckily I am not out to change the world—that's being done for me, and at a great clip. But I know that the free spirit of man is persistent in nature; it recurs, and has never successfully been wiped out, by fire or flood. I set down the above remarks merely (in the words of Mr. Hitler) to motivate that spirit, theoretically. Being myself a knight of the goose quill, I am under no misapprehension about "winning people"; but I am inordinately proud these days of the quill, for it has shown itself, historically, to be the hypodermic that inoculates men and keeps germs of freedom always in circulation, so that there are individuals in every time in every land who are the carriers, the Typhoid Marys, capable of infecting others by mere contact and example. These persons are feared by every tyrant—who shows his fear by burning the books and destroying the individuals. A writer goes about his task today with the extra satisfaction that comes from knowing that he will be the first to have his head lopped off—even before the political dandies. In my own case this is a double satisfaction, I am the same as dead and would infinitely prefer to go into fascism without my head than with it, having no use for it any more and not wishing to be saddled with so heavy an encumbrance.

ROBERT A. TAFT
A Foreign Policy for Americans

When I say liberty I do not simply mean what is referred to as "free enterprise." I mean liberty of the individual to think his own thoughts and live his own life as he desires to think and to live; the liberty of the family to decide how they wish to live, what they want to eat for breakfast and for dinner, and how they wish to develop his ideas and get other people to teach those ideas, if he can convince them that they have some value to the world; liberty of every local community to decide how its children shall be educated, how its local services shall be run, and who its local leaders shall be; liberty of a man to run his own business as he thinks it ought to be run, as long as he does not interfere with the right of other people to do the same thing.

ADLAI E. STEVENSON
Speech in Philadelphia

Freedom—effective freedom—does not exist as a formula which can be written out by some and then used by others. The freedom that counts is simply what is in the minds and hearts of millions of free people. It is nothing more than the total of the feelings of people as they are expressed in the way we, the people, deal with our own families and our own neighbors and associates.

WENDELL L. WILLKIE
Creed inscribed on a marker by his grave

I believe in America because in it we are free—
free to choose our government, to speak our minds,
to observe our different religions.
Because we are generous with our freedom, we share
our rights with those who disagree with us.
Because we hate no people and covet no people's lands.
Because we are blessed with a natural and varied abundance.
Because we have great dreams and because we have the
opportunity to make those dreams come true.

For My Brothers and Sisters in the Failure Business
SEYMOUR KRIM

. . . I come from America, which has to be the classic, ultimate, then-they-broke-the-mold incubator of not knowing who you are until you find out. I have never really found out and I expect what remains of my life to be one long search party for the final me. I don't kid myself that I'm alone in this, hardly, and I don't really think that the great day will ever come when I hold a finished me in my fist and say here you are, congratulations. I'm talking primarily about the expression of that me in the world, the shape it takes, the profile it zings out, the "work" it does.

You may sometimes think everyone lives in the crotch of the pleasure principle these days except you, but you have company, friend. I live under the same pressures you do. It is still your work or role that finally gives you your definition in our society, and the thousands upon thousands of people who I believe are like me are those who have never found the professional skin to fit the riot in their souls. Many never will. I think what I have to say here will speak for some of their secret life and for that other sad America you don't hear too much about. This isn't presumption so much as a voice of scars and stars talking. I've lived it and will probably go on living it until they take away my hot dog.

Consider (as the noble Dickens used to say about just such a lad as I) a boy at the turn of the '30s growing up in this land without parents, discipline, any religion to speak of, yet with a famished need that almost unconsciously filled the vacuum where the solid family heart should be, the dizzying spectacle of his senses. America was my carnival at an earlier age than most and I wanted to be everything in it that turned me on, like a youth bouncing around crazed on a boardwalk. I mean literally everything. I was as unanchored a kid as you can conceive of, an open fuse-box of blind yearning, and out of what I now assume was unimaginable loneliness and human hunger I greedily tried on the personalities of every type on the national scene as picked up through newspapers, magazines, movies, radio, and just nosing around.

And what a juicy parade through any inexperienced and wildly applauding mind America was then, what a nonstop variety show of heroes, adventurers, fabulous kinds of human beings to hook on to if you were totally on your own without any guidance and looking for your star in a society that almost drove you batty with desire. In my earnest role-playing the philosophical tramp and the cool millionaire-playboy were second nature to me, as were the style and stance of ballplayers, barnstorming pilots, polar explorers, radio personalities (how can I ever forget you, gorgeous-voiced Ted Husing?), generals, bridge-building engineers, treasure-hunters, crooners, inventors. I wanted to be and actually was Glenn Cunningham, Joe E. Penner, Kid Chocolate, Chandu the Magician, Eugene O'Neill, a Gangbuster. If you're old enough, tick off the names of the rotogravure big-shots of the time and see Seymour impersonating them in his private magic theater. And later on when I had lost my adolescent shame and knew myself to be a freak of the imagination, even wallowed in it, I identified with women like Amelia Earhart and even the hot ripe early pinup girl, Iris Adrian, and transvestited my mind to see the world through their long lashes and tough lace. Democracy means democracy of the fantasy life, too, there are no cops crouching in the corridors of the brain. Dr. Freud's superego hasn't been able to pull its old country rank over here, even though it's tried like a mother, or should I say a father?

But my point is this: what a great fitting-room for experimentation, a huge sci-fi lab for making the self you wanted, America was for those of us who needed models, forms, shapes we could throw ourselves into. Obviously, everyone from my generation didn't chuck caution out the window even if they felt the lure, as I did, of a new make-your-own-lifesize-man era. Some of my more realistic contemporaries narrowed it all down early and became the comparative successes they are today. Whether it's making a lot of money selling scrap in a junkyard (Ed Feinberg) or writing thrillers for connoisseurs of kinkiness (Patricia Highsmith), they all had to focus clearly, work hard. As traps and frustrations of 51 close down around me, with all the small defects and petty hurts that sometimes seem to choke away all thoughts of the unique Homeric journey of the inner person in America, everyone's inner person, I salute them for achieving some of what they wanted. Nobody gets it all. But I salute anyone in this bewildering dreamland of a nation who has managed to cut through the wilderness of tangled trails to some definite cabin of achievement and reward.

Yet those of us who have never really nailed it down, who have charged through life from enthusiasm to enthusiasm, from new project to new project, even from personality-revolution to personality-revolution, have a secret also. I'm sorry to say it isn't the kind that desperate people can use to improve themselves, like those ads in the newspaper. Sadly enough, it is the kind that people in my seven-league but very leaky boots often take to psychiatrists, hoping to simplify their experience because they can't cope with the murderous tangle of it. But for those of us who have lived through each twist and turn, the psychiatry sessions, the occasional abyss, the endless review of our lives to see where we went wrong, and then come to see our natures as strange and special manifestations of a time and place that will never come again, there is a wonder in it that almost makes up for the beating we are beginning to take at the hands of the professional heavyweight world.

Our secret is that we still have an epic longing to be more than what we are, to multiply ourselves, to integrate all the identities and action-fantasies we have experienced, above all to keep experimenting with our lives all the way to Forest Lawn to see how much we can make real out of that prolific American Dream machine within. Let me say it plainly: Our true projects have finally been ourselves. It's as if we had taken literally the old cornball Land of Opportunity slogan and incorporated it into the pit of the being instead of the space around us; and fallen so much in love with the ongoing excitement of becoming, even the illusion of becoming, that our pants often fall down and reveal our dirty skivvies and skinny legs. The laughter hurts, believe me, but it doesn't stop us for very long. We were hooked early.

What it comes down to is that the America of the pioneer has been made subjective by us. The endless rolling back of the frontier goes on within our heads all the time. We are the updated Daniel Boones of American inner-space. Each of our lives, for those of us in this countrywide fraternity, seems to us a novel or a play or a movie in itself, draining our energy but then at other moments lifting us up to spectacular highs, yet always moving, the big wagon-train of great new possibilities always crushing on. The fact that all of this is private doesn't make it any less real. What it does do is make us ache with hopelessness at times as to how to find a vocation for this private super-adventure serial out on the streets of life.

John F. Kennedy

When power leads man toward arrogance, poetry reminds him of his limitations. When power narrows the areas of man's concern, poetry reminds him of the richness and diversity of his experience. When power corrupts, poetry cleanses. For art establishes the basic human truths which must serve as the touchstones of our judgment. The artist...faithful to his personal vision of reality, becomes the last champion of the individual mind and sensibility against an intrusive society and offensive state.

JAMES RUSSELL LOWELL
"To the Memory of Hood"

Freedom needs all her poets: it is they
Who give her aspirations wings,
And to the wiser law of music sway
Her wild imaginings.

BRUCE SPRINGSTEEN
"Born to Run"

In the days we sweat it out in the streets of a runaway American dream
At night we ride through mansions of glory in suicide machines
Sprung from cages out on Highway 9
Chrome wheeled, fuel injected
And steppin' out over the line
Baby this town rips the bones from your back
It's a death trap, it's a suicide rap
We gotta get out while we're young
'Cause tramps like us, baby we were born to run

Wendy, let me in, I wanna be your friend
I want to guard your dreams and visions
Just wrap your legs round these velvet rims
And strap your hands across my engines
Together we could break this trap
We'll run till we drop, baby we'll never go back
Will you walk with me out on the wire
'Cause baby I'm just a scared and lonely rider
But I gotta know how it feels
I want to know if your love is wild
Girl I want to know if love is real

Beyond the Palace hemi-powered drones scream down the boulevard
The girls comb their hair in rear-view mirrors
And the boys try to look so hard

The amusement park rises bold and stark
Kids are huddled on the beach in a mist
I wanna die with you out on the streets tonight
In an everlasting kiss

The highways jammed with broken heroes
On a last chance power drive
Everybody's out on the run tonight
But there's no place left to hide
Together, Wendy, we can live with the sadness
I'll love you with all the madness in my soul
Someday girl, I don't know when, we're gonna get to that place
Where we really want to go
And we'll walk in the sun
But till then tramps like us
Baby we were born to run

CHARLES A. LINDBERGH
Autobiography of Values

Real freedom lies in wildness, not in civilization.

AMERICAN FOLK SONG
Kentucky Moonshiner

I've been a moonshiner for seventeen long years,
I've spent all my money for whiskey and beers.
I'll go to sommer holler, I'll put up my still,
I'll make you one gallon for a two dollar bill.

I'll go to some grocery and drink with my friends,
No women to follow to see what I spends.
God bless those pretty women, I wish they were mine,
Their breath smells as sweet as the dew on the vine.

I'll eat when I'm hungry and drink when I'm dry,
If moonshine don't kill me I'll live till I die.
God bless those moonshiners, I wish they were mine,
Their breath smells as sweet as the good old moonshine.

DEBORAH TALL
From Where We Stand

Individualism and mobility are at the core of American identity.

GEORGE SANTAYANA
Materialism and Idealism

Moral freedom is not an artificial condition, because the ideal is the mother tongue of both the heart and the senses. All that is requisite is that we should pause in living to enjoy life, and should lift up our hearts to things that are pure goods in themselves, so that once to have found and loved them, whatever else may betide, may remain a happiness that nothing can sully. This natural idealism does not imply that we are immaterial, but only that we are animate and truly alive. When the senses are sharp, as they are in the American, they are already half liberated, already a joy in themselves; and when the heart is warm, like his, and eager to be just, its ideal destiny can hardly be doubtful. It will not be always merely pumping and working; time and its own pulses will lend its wings.

HENRY DAVID THOREAU
Journal

What other liberty is there worth having, if we have not freedom and peace in our minds—if our inmost and most private man is but a sour and turbid pool?

An American Childhood

ANNIE DILLARD

Our father taught us the culture into which we were born. American culture was Dixieland above all, Dixieland pure and simple, and next to Dixieland, jazz. It was the pioneers who went West singing "Bang away my Lulu." When someone died on the Oregon Trail, as someone was always doing, the family scratched a shallow grave right by the trail, because the wagon train couldn't wait. Everyone paced on behind the oxen across the empty desert and some families sang "Bang away my Lulu" that night, and some didn't.

Our culture was the stock-market crash—the biggest and best crash to young Amy and me, around the dining-room table. He tried to explain why men on Wall Street had jumped from skyscrapers when the stock market crashed: "They lost everything!"—but of course I thought they lost everything only when they jumped. It was the bread-lines of the Depression, and the Okies fleeing the Dust Bowl, and the proud men begging on city streets, and families on the move seeking work—dusty women, men in black hats pulled over their eyes, haunted, hungry children: what a mystifying spectacle, this almost universal misery, city families living in cars, farm families eating insects, because—why? Because all the businessmen realized at once, on the same morning, that paper money was only paper. What terrible fools. What did they think it was?

American culture was the World's Fair in Chicago, baseball, the Erie Canal, fancy nightclubs in Harlem, silent movies, summer-stock theater, the California forty-niners, the Alaska gold rush, Henry Ford and his bright idea of paying workers enough to buy cars, P.T. Barnum and his traveling circus, Buffalo Bill Cody and his Wild West Show. It was the Chrysler Building in New York and the Golden Gate Bridge in San Francisco; the Concord and the Merrimack, the Alamo, the Little Bighorn, Gettysburg, Shiloh, Bull Run, and "Strike the tent."

It was Pittsburgh's legendary Joe Magarac, the mighty Hungarian steelworker, who took off his shirt to reveal his body made of high-grade steel, and who squeezed out steel rail between his knuckles by the ton. It was the brawling river men on the Ohio River, the sandhogs who dug Hudson River tunnels, silver miners in Idaho, cowboys in Texas, and the innocent American Indian Jim Thorpe, who had to give all his Olympic gold medals back. It was the men of every race who built the railroads, and the boys of every race who went to war.

Above all, it was the man who wandered unencumbered by family ties: Johnny Appleseed in our own home woods, Daniel Boone in Kentucky, Jim Bridger crossing the Rockies. Father described for us the Yankee peddler, the free trapper, the roaming cowhand, the whalerman, roustabout, gandy dancer, tramp. His heroes, and my heroes, were Raymond Chandler's city detective Marlowe going, as a man must, down these mean streets; Huck Finn lighting out for the territories; and Jack Kerouac on the road.

CARL SANDBURG
"Freedom is a Habit"

Freedom is a habit
and a coat worn
some born to wear it
some never to know it.
Freedom is cheap
or again as a garment
is so costly
men pay their lives
rather than not have it.
Freedom is baffling:
men having it often
know not they have it

till it is gone and
they no longer have it.
What does this mean?
Is it a riddle?
Yes, it is first of all
in the primers of riddles.
To be free is so-so:
you can and you can't:
walkers can have freedom
only by never walking
away their freedom
unless they overrun:
eaters have often outeaten
their freedom to eat
and drinkers overdrank
their fine drinking freedom.

Working, "Bud Freeman: Jazz Musician"

STUDS TERKEL

He is sixty-five years old, though his appearance and manner are of William Blake's "golden youth." He has been a tenor saxophone player for forty-seven years. Highly respected among his colleagues, he is a member of "The World's Greatest Jazz Band." It is a cooperative venture, jointly owned by the musicians, established jazz men.

"I'm with the young people because they refuse to be brainwashed by the things you and I were brainwashed by. My father, although he worked hard all his life, was very easy with us. Dad was being brainwashed by the people in the neighborhood. They'd come in every day and say, "Why don't your boys go to work?" So he made the mistake of awakening my brother at seven-thirty. I pretended to be asleep. Dad said, "You're going to get up, go out in the world and get jobs and amount to something." My brother said, "How dare you wake us up before the weekend?" (Laughs.) I don't recall ever having seen my father since. (Laughs.)

I get up about noon. I would only consider myself outside the norm because of the way other people live. They're constantly reminding me I'm abnormal. I could never bear to live the dull lives most people live, locked up in offices. I live in absolute freedom. I do what I do because I want to do it. What's wrong with making a living doing something interesting?

I wouldn't work for anybody. I'm working for me. Oddly enough, jazz is a music that came out of the black man's oppression, yet it allows for great freedom of expression, perhaps more than any other art form. The jazz man is expressing freedom in every note he plays. We can only please the audience doing what we do. We have to please ourselves first.

I know a good musician who worked for Lawrence Welk. The man must be terribly in need of money. It's regimented music. It doesn't swing, it doesn't create, it doesn't tell the story of life. It's just the kind of music that people who don't care for music would buy.

I've had people say to me: "You don't do this for a living, for heaven's sake?" I was so shocked. I said, "What other way am I going to make a living? You want to send me a check?" (Laughs.) People can't understand that there are artists in the world as well as drones.

I only know that as a child I was of a rebellious nature. I saw life as it was planned for most of us. I didn't want any part of that dull life. I worked for Lord and Taylor once, nine to five. It was terribly dull. I lasted six weeks. I couldn't see myself being a nine-to-five man, saving my money, getting married, and having a big family—good God, what a way to live!

I knew when I was eight years old that I wasn't going to amount to anything in the business world. (Laughs.) I wanted my life to have something to do with adventure, something unknown, something involved with free life, something to do with wonder and astonishment. I loved to play—the fact that I could express myself in improvisation, the unplanned.

I love to play now more than ever, because I know a little more about music. I'm interested in developing themes and playing something creative. Life now is not so difficult. We work six months a year. We live around the world. And we don't have to work in night clubs night after night after night.

Playing in night clubs, I used to think, When are we going to get out of here? Most audiences were drunk and you tended to become lazy. And if you were a drinker yourself, there went your music. This is why so many great talents have died or gotten out of it. They hated the music business. I was lucky—now I'm sixty-five—in having played forty-seven years.

If jazz musicians had been given the chance we in this band have today—to think about your work and not have to play all hours of the night, five or six sets—God! Or radio station work or commercial jingle work—the guys must loathe it. I don't think the jazz man has been given a fair chance to do what he really wants to do, to work under conditions where he's not treated like a slave, not subject to the music business, which we've loathed all our lives.

I've come to love my work. It's my way of life. Jazz is a luxurious kind of music. You don't play it all day long. You don't play it all night long. The best way to play it is in concerts. You're on for an hour or two and you give it everything you have, your best. And the audience is sober. And I'm not in a hurry to have the night finish. Playing night clubs, it was endless.

If you're a creative player, something must happen, and it will. Some sort of magic takes place, yet it isn't magic. Hundreds of times I've gone to work thinking, Oh my God, I hate to think of playing tonight. It's going to be awful. But something on a given night takes place and

I'm excited before it's over. Does that make sense? If you have that kind of night, you're not aware of the time, because of this thing that hits you.

There's been a lot of untruths told about improvisation. Men just don't get up on the stage and improvise on things they're not familiar with. True improvisation comes out of hard work. When you're practicing at home, you work on a theme and you work out all the possibilities of that theme. Since it's in your head, it comes out when you play. You don't get out on the stage and just improvise, not knowing what the hell you are doing. It doesn't work out that way. Always just before I play a concert, I get the damn horn out and practice. Not scales, but look for creative things to play. I'll practice tonight when I get home, before I go to work. I can't wait to get at it.

I practice because I want to play better. I've never been terribly interested in technique, but I'm interested in facility. To feel comfortable, so when the idea shoots out of my head I can finger it, manipulate it. Something interesting happens. You'll hear a phrase and all of a sudden you're thrown into a whole new inspiration. It doesn't happen every night. But even if I have a terrible night and say, "Oh, I'm so tired, I'll go to sleep and I'll think of other things," the music'll come back. I wasn't too happy about going to work last night because I was tired. It was a drag. But today I feel good. Gonna go home and blow the horn now for a while.

Practicing is no chore to me. I love it. I really do love to play the horn alone. They call me the narcissistic tenor (laughs), because I practice before the mirror. Actually I've learned a great deal looking in the mirror and playing. The dream of all jazz artists is to have enough time to think about their work and play and to develop.

Was there a time when you were altogether bored with your work?

Absolutely. I quit playing for a year. I met a very rich woman. We went to South America to live. We had a house by the sea. I never realized how one could be so rich, so unhappy, and so bored. It frightened me. But I did need a year off. When I came back, I felt fresh.

The other time was when I had a band of my own. I had a name, so I no longer worked for big bands. I was expected to lead one of my own. But I can't handle other people. If I have a group and the pianist, let's say, doesn't like my playing, I can't play. I don't see how these band leaders do it. I can't stand any kind of responsibility other than the music itself. I have to work as a soloist. I can be the custodian only of my own being and thinking.

I had this band and the guys were late all the time. I didn't want to have to hassle them. I didn't want to mistreat them, so I said, "Fellas, should we quit?" I wouldn't let them go and stay on myself. We were good friends. I'd say I'd quit if they didn't come on time. They started to come on time. But I wasn't a leader. I used to stand by in the band! A bit to the side. (Laughs.) Now we have a cooperative band. So I have a feeling I'm working for myself.

I don't know if I'll make it, but I hope I'll be playing much better five years from now. I oughta, because I know a little bit more of what I'm doing. It takes a lifetime to learn how to play an instrument. We have a lot of sensational young players come up—oh, you hear them for six months, and then they drop out. The kid of the moment, that's right. Real talent takes a long time to mature, to learn how to bring what character you have into sound, into your playing. Not the instrument, but the style of music you're trying to create should be an extension of you. And this takes a whole life.

I want to play for the rest of my life. I don't see any sense in stopping. Were I to live another thirty years—that would make me ninety-five—why not try to play? I can just hear the critics: "Did you hear that wonderful note old man Freeman played last night?" (Laughs.) As Ben Webster says, "I'm going to play this goddamned saxophone until they put it on top of me." It's become dearer to me after having done it for forty-seven years. It's a thing I need to do.

MAX ROACH
"Jazz Men: A Love Supreme," *Ebony*

Jazz is a very democratic musical form. It comes out of a communal experience. We take our respective instruments and collectively create a thing of beauty. Everybody's allowed to be out front and supportive during a composition. Everybody's free.

LANGSTON HUGHES
"The Negro Artist and the Racial Mountain," *The Nation*

Jazz to me is one of the inherent expressions of Negro life in America: the eternal tom-tom beating in the Negro soul—the tom-tom of revolt against weariness in a white world, a world of subway trains, and work, work, work; the tom-tom of joy and laughter, and pain swallowed in a smile.

HENRY DAVID THOREAU
Journals

The Indian stands free and unconstrained in Nature, is her inhabitant and not her guest, and wears her easily and gracefully. But the civilized man has the habits of the house. His house is a prison.

MARK TWAIN
The Adventures of Huckleberry Finn

The Widow Douglas, she took me for her son, and allowed she would sivilize me; but it was rough living in the house all the time, considering how dismal regular and decent the widow was in all her ways; and so when I couldn't stand it no longer, I lit out. I got into my old rags, and my sugar-hogshead again, and was free and satisfied.

THOMAS JEFFERSON

Taste cannot be controlled by law.

WILLIAM FAULKNER
"On Privacy," *Essays, Speeches and Public Letters*

We have no laws against bad taste, perhaps because in a democracy the majority of the people who make the laws don't recognize bad taste when they see it, or perhaps because in our democracy bad taste has been converted into a marketable and therefore taxable and therefore lobbyable commodity.

E.E. CUMMINGS
"Poem, Or Beauty Hurts Mr. Vinal"

take it from me kiddo
believe me
my country, 'tis of

you, land of the Cluett
Shirt Boston Garter and Spearmint
Girl With The Wrigley Eyes (of you
land of the Arrow Ide
and Earl &
Wilson
Collars) of you i
sing: land of Abraham Lincoln and Lydia E. Pinkham,
land above all of Just Add Hot Water And Serve—
from every B.V.D.

let freedom ring

amen.

Learning From Las Vegas

ROBERT VENTURI, DENISE SCOTT BROWN AND STEVEN IZENOUR

The Las Vegas Strip at night, like the Martorama interior, is symbolic images in dark, amorphous space; but, like the Amalienburg, it glitters rather than glows. Any sense of enclosure or direction comes from lighted signs rather than from reflected light. The source of light in the Strip is direct; the signs themselves are the source. They do not reflect the light from external, sometimes hidden, sources as is the case with most billboards and Modern architecture. The mechanical movement is greater to accommodate the greater spaces, greater speeds, and greater impacts that our technology permits and our sensibilities respond to. Also, the tempo of our economy encourages that changeable and disposable environmental decoration known as advertising art. The messages are different now, but despite the differences the methods are the same, and architecture is no longer simply the "skillful, accurate, and magnificent play of masses seen in light."

The Strip by day is a different place, no longer Byzantine. The forms of the buildings are visible but remain secondary to the signs in visual impact and symbolic content. The space of the urban sprawl is not enclosed and directed as in traditional cities. Rather, it is open and indeterminate, identified by points in space and patters on the ground; these are two-dimensional or sculptural symbols in space rather than buildings in space, complex configurations that are graphic or representational. Acting as symbols, the signs and buildings identify the space by their location and direction, and space is further defined and directed by utility poles and street and parking patterns. In residential sprawl the orientation of houses toward the street, their stylistic treatment as decorated sheds, and their landscaping and lawn fixtures—wagon wheels, mailboxes on erect chairs, colonial lamps, and segments of split-rail fence—substitute for the signs of commercial sprawl as the definers of space.

Like the complex architectural accumulations of the Roman Forum, the Strip by day reads as chaos if you perceive only its forms and exclude its symbolic content. The Forum, like the Strip, was a landscape of symbols with layers of meaning evident in the location of roads and buildings, buildings representing earlier buildings, and the sculpture piled all over. Formally the Forum was an awful mess; symbolically it was a rich mix.

The series of triumphal arches in Rome is a prototype of the billboard (mutatis mutandis for scale, speed, and content). The architectural ornament, including pilasters, pediments, and coffers, is a kind of bas-relief that makes only a gesture toward architectural form. It is as symbolic as the bas-reliefs of processions and the inscriptions that compete for the surface. Along with their function as billboards carrying messages, the triumphal arches in the Roman Forum were spatial markers channeling processional paths within a complex urban landscape. On Route 66 the billboards set in a series at a constant angle toward the oncoming traffic, with a standard distance between themselves and from the roadside, perform a similar formal-spatial function. Often the brightest, cleanest, and best-maintained elements in industrial sprawl, the billboards both cover and beautify the landscape. Like the configurations of sepulchral monuments along the Via Appia (again mutatis mutandis for scale), they mark the way through the vast spaces beyond urban sprawl. But these spatial characteristics of form, position, and orientation are secondary to their symbolic function. Along the highway, advertising Tanya via graphics and anatomy, like advertising the victories of Constantine via inscriptions and bas-reliefs, is more important than identifying the space.

Urban Sprawl and the Megastructure

The urban manifestations of ugly and ordinary architecture and the decorated shed are closer to urban sprawl than to the megastructure. We have explained how, for us, commercial vernacular architecture was a vivid initial source for symbolism in architecture. We have described in the Las Vegas study the victory of symbols-in-space over forms-in-space in the brutal automobile landscape of great distances and high speed, where the subtleties of pure architectural space can no longer be savored. But the symbolism of urban sprawl lies also in its residential architecture, not only in the strident, roadside communications of the commercial strip (decorated shed or duck). Although the ranch house, split level or otherwise, conforms in its spatial configuration to several set patterns, it is appliqued with varied though conforming ornament, evoking combinations of Colonial, New Orleans, Regency, Western, French Provincial, Modern, and other styles. Garden apartments—especially those of the Southwest—equally are decorated sheds whose pedestrian courts, like those of motels, are separate from, but close to, the automobile.

Sprawl City's image is a result of process. In this respect it follows the canons of Modern architecture that require form to result from function, structure, and construction methods, that is, from the process of its making. But for our time the megastructure is a distortion of normal city building processes for the sake inter alia of image. Modern architects contradict themselves when they support functionalism and the megastructure. They do not recognize the image of the process city when they see it on the Strip, because it is both too familiar and too different from what they have been trained to accept.

HENRY STEELE COMMAGER
Freedom and Order

If we create an atmosphere in which men fear to think independently, inquire fearlessly, express themselves freely, we will in the end create the kind of society in which men no longer care to think independently or to inquire fearlessly. If we put a premium on conformity we will, in the end, get conformity.

BENJAMIN MAYS
Born to Rebel

I would rather go to hell by choice than to stumble into Heaven by following the crowd.

JOHN KILLENS
Black Man's Burden

What a tiresome place America would be if freedom meant we had to think alike and be the same color and wear the same gray flannel suit. That road leads to the conformity of the graveyard.

Mannahatta

WALT WHITMAN

I was asking for something specific and perfect for my city,
Whereupon, lo! upsprang the aboriginal name!
Now I see what there is in a name, a word, liquid, sane, unruly,
     musical, self-sufficient;
I see that the word of my city is that word up there,
Because I see that word nested in nests of water-bays, superb, with
     tall and wonderful spires,
Rich, hemm'd thick all around with sailships and steamships—an
     island sixteen miles long, solid-founded,
Numberless crowded streets—high growths of iron, slender, strong,
     light, splendidly uprising toward clear skies;
Tide swift and ample, well-loved by me, toward sundown,
The flowing sea-currents, the little islands, larger adjoining islands,
     the heights, the villas,
The countless masts, the white shore steamers, the lighters, the
     ferryboats, the black sea-steamers well model'd
The downtown streets, the jobbers' houses of business, the houses
     of business of the ship-merchants and money-brokers, the
     river-streets,
Immigrants arriving, fifteen or twenty thousand in a week,
The carts hauling goods, the manly race of drivers of horses, the
     brown-faced sailors,

The summer air, the bright sun shining, and the sailing clouds aloft,
The winter snows, the sleigh-bells, the broken ice in the river,
    passing along up or down with the flood-tide or ebb-tide,
The mechanics of the city, the masters, well-form'd, beautiful-faced,
    looking you straight in the eyes,
Trottoirs throng'd, vehicles, Broadway, the women, the shops and
    shows,
The parades, processions, bugles playing, flags flying, drums
    beating;
A million people—manners free and superb—open voices—
    hospitality—the most courageous and friendly young men,
The free city! no slaves! no owners of slaves!
The beautiful city, the city of hurried and sparkling waters! city of
    spires and masts!
City nested in bays! my city!
The city of such women, I am mad to be with them! I will return
    after death to be with them!
The city of such young men, I swear I cannot live happy, without I
    often go talk, walk, eat, drink, sleep with them!

ROBERT FROST

The best things and best people rise out of their separateness; I'm against a homogenized society because I want the cream to rise.

MARK TWAIN
Pudd'nhead Wilson's Calendar, Pudd'nhead Wilson

It were not best that we should all think alike; it is difference of opinion that makes horse races.

WILLIAM JAMES
The Importance of Individuals

An unlearned carpenter of my acquaintance once said in my hearing: "There is very little difference between one man and another; but what little there is, is very important." That distinction seems to go to the root of the matter.

GORE VIDAL
The Second American Revolution and Other Essays

Many human beings enjoy sexual relations with their own sex; many don't; many respond to both. This plurality is part of our nature and not worth fretting about.

HARRY A. BLACKMUN
Dissenting opinion on Supreme Court Case Bowers v. Hardwick
regarding constitutionality of law prohibiting sodomy

We protect the decision whether to have a child because parenthood alters so dramatically an individual's self-definition, not because of demographic considerations or the Bible's command to be fruitful and multiply. And we protect the family because it contributes so powerfully to the happiness of individuals, not because of a preference for stereotypical households.

Only the most willful blindness could obscure the fact that sexual intimacy is "a sensitive, key relationship of human existence, central to family life, community welfare, and the development of human personality." The fact that individuals define themselves in a significant way through their intimate sexual relationships with others suggests, in a Nation as diverse as ours, that there may be many "right" ways of conducting those relationships, and that much of the richness of relationship will come from the freedom an individual has to choose the form and nature of these intensely personal bonds.

EDNA ST. VINCENT MILLAY
From "Poem and Prayer for an Invading Army"

Let us forget such words, and all they mean,
as Hatred, Bitterness and Rancor, Greed.
Intolerance, Bigotry; let us renew
our faith and pledge to Man, his right to be
Himself, and free.

MARGARET SANGER
Parade

No woman can call herself free who does not own and control her body. No woman can call herself free until she can choose consciously whether she will or will not be a mother.

GLORIA STEINEM
Response to question on why she never married

I can't mate in captivity.

HARRY A. BLACKMUN
Majority opinion in Roe v. Wade

The Constitution does not explicitly mention any right of privacy. In a line of decisions, however...the Court has recognized that a right of personal privacy, or a guarantee of certain areas or zones of privacy, does exist under the Constitution....They also make it clear that the right has some extension to activities relating to marriage; procreation; contraception; family relationships; and child rearing and education.

The right of privacy...is broad enough to encompass a woman's decision whether or not to terminate her pregnancy....We need not resolve the difficult question of when life begins. When those trained in the respective disciplines of medicine, philosophy, and theology are unable to arrive at any consensus, the judiciary, at this point in the development of man's knowledge, is not in a position to speculate as to the answer.

ARCHIBALD MACLEISH
"A Declaration of Freedom"

What is freedom? Freedom is the right to choose: the right to create for oneself the alternatives of choice. Without the possibility of choice and the exercise of choice a man is not a man but a member, an instrument, a thing.

DWIGHT D. EISENHOWER
Speech in Pittsburgh, Pennsylvania

The history of free men is never really written by chance but by choice—their choice.

JOHN F. KENNEDY
Speech at University of Maine

Let us resolve to be masters, not the victims, of our history, controlling our own destiny without giving way to blind suspicions and emotions.

MARGARET MEAD
Coming of Age in Samoa

Chief among our gains must be reckoned this possibility of choice, the recognition of many possible ways of life, where other civilizations have recognized only one. Where other civilizations give a satisfactory outlet to only one temperamental type, be he mystic or soldier, businessman or artist, a civilization in which there are many standards offers a possibility of satisfactory adjustment to individuals of many different temperamental types, of diverse gifts and varying interests.

JOHN DEWEY
Human Nature and Conduct

To say that a man is free to choose to walk while the only walk he can take will lead him over a precipice is to strain words as well as facts.

LYNDON B. JOHNSON
State of the Union Address

Our own freedom and growth have never been the final goal of the American dream. We were never meant to be an oasis of liberty and abundance in a worldwide desert of disappointed dreams. Our Nation was created to help strike away the chains of ignorance and misery and tyranny wherever they keep man less than God wants him to be.

PIETER VAN MUSSCHENBROEK
Letter to Benjamin Franklin

Go on making experiments entirely on your own initiative and thereby pursue a path entirely different from that of the Europeans, for then you shall certainly find many things which have been hidden to natural philosophers throughout the space of centuries.

J. ROBERT OPPENHEIMER
Life magazine

As long as men are free to ask what they must, free to say what they think, free to think what they will, freedom can never be lost, and science can never regress.

FRANKLIN D. ROOSEVELT
Speech at Temple University

The truth is found when men are free to pursue it.

ADLAI E. STEVENSON
Speech at University of Wisconsin

If we value the pursuit of knowledge, we must be free to follow wherever that search may lead us. The free mind is no barking dog, to be tethered on a ten-foot chain.

WALT WHITMAN
"Song of the Open Road"

From this hour, freedom!
From this hour I ordain myself loos'd of limits and imaginary lines,
Going where I list, my own master, total and absolute,
Listening to others, and considering well what they say,
Pausing, searching, receiving, contemplating,
Gently, but with undeniable will, divesting myself of the holds that
    would hold me.
I inhale great droughts of space;
The east and the west are mine, and the north and the south are
    mine.

I am larger, better than I thought;
I did not know I held so much goodness.
All seems beautiful to me;
I can repeat over to men and women, You have done such good to
    me, I would do the same to you.

I will recruit myself and you as I go;
I will scatter myself among men and women as I go;
I will toss the new gladness and roughness among them;
Whoever denies me, it shall not trouble me;
Whoever accepts me, he or she shall be blessed, and shall bless me.

WALT WHITMAN
"One's-Self I Sing"

One's-Self I sing—a simple, separate Person;
Yet utter the word Democratic, the word En-masse.

Of Physiology from top to toe I sing;
Not physiognomy alone, nor brain alone, is worthy for the muse—
    I say the Form complete is worthier far;
The Female equally with the male I sing.

Of Life immense in passion, pulse, and power,
Cheerful—for freest action form'd, under the laws divine,
The Modern Man I sing.

Charles A. Lindbergh

It is the greatest shot of adrenaline to be doing what you've most wanted to do so badly. You almost feel like you could fly without the plane.

Richard Wright

Men can starve from a lack of self-realization as much as they can from a lack of bread.

Joan Baez

You don't get to choose how you're going to die. Or when. You can only decide how you're going to live.

Eleanor Roosevelt

Remember always that you have not only the right to be an individual, you have an obligation to be one.

James Fenimore Cooper
The American Democrat

Individuality is the aim of political liberty. By leaving to the citizen as much freedom of action and of being as comports with order and the rights of others, the institutions render him truly a freeman. He is left to pursue his means of happiness in his own manner.

Ralph Ellison
Going to the Territory

Democracy is a collectivity of individuals.

Joseph Campbell
The Power of Myth

The function of the society is to cultivate the individual. It is not the function of the individual to support society.

Theodore Dreiser

[An artist has a freedom that is] not the pseudo-freedom of strong men, financially or physically, but the real, internal, spiritual freedom, where the mind, as it were, stands up and looks at itself, faces Nature unafraid, is aware of its own weaknesses, its strengths; examines its own and the creative impulses of the universe and of men with a kindly and non-dogmatic eye, in fact kicks dogma out of doors, and yet deliberately and of choice holds fast to many, many simple and human things, and rounds out life, or would, in a natural, normal, courageous, healthy way.

ALICE WALKER
Living by the Word

Our beliefs are
our country.
Our hair is
our flag.
Our love of ourselves
is our freedom.

We, too, fucking yes,
sing America.

CHIEF JOSEPH
An Indian's View of Indian Affairs

Let me be a free man—free to travel, free to stop, free to work, free to trade where I choose, free to choose my own teachers, free to follow the religion of my fathers, free to think and talk and act for myself—and I will obey every law, or submit to the penalty.

HENRY DAVID THOREAU
Civil Disobedience

[T]he State never intentionally confronts a man's sense, intellectual or moral, but only his body, his senses. It is not armed with superior wit or honesty, but with superior physical strength. I was not born to be forced. I will breathe after my own fashion. Let us see who is strongest. What force has a multitude? They only can force me who obey a higher law than I. They force me to become like themselves. I do not hear of men being forced to live this way or that by masses of men. What sort of life were that to live? When I meet a government which says to me, "Your money or your life," why should I be in haste to give it my money? It may be in a great strait, and not know what to do: I cannot help that. It must help itself; do as I do. It is not worth the while to snivel about it. I am not responsible for the successful working of the machinery of society. I am not the son of the engineer. I perceive that, when an acorn and a chestnut fall side by side, the one does not remain inert to make way for the other, but both obey their own laws, and spring and grow and flourish as best they can, till one, perchance, overshadows and destroys the other. If a plant cannot live according to its nature, it dies; and so a man.

WILLIAM O. DOUGLAS
The New York Times

My faith is that the only soul a man must save is his own.

JAMES BALDWIN
Notes of a Native Son

When we said that men are endowed with certain inalienable rights, among these are life, liberty, and the pursuit of happiness, we did not pause to define happiness. That is the unexpressed quality in our quest, and we never tried to put it into words. That is why we say, "Let each man serve God in his own fashion."

PAUL ROBESON
Born of the People

Freedom is a precious thing, and the inalienable birthright of all who travel this earth.

JAMES CONE
Black Theology and Black Power

A man is free when he can determine the style of his existence in an absurd world. A man is free when he sees himself for what he is and not as others define him.

ELBERT HUBBARD
The Note Book

Freedom is the supreme good—freedom from self-imposed limitation.

DUKE ELLINGTON
Music Is My Mistress

Freedom from hate unconditionally, freedom from self pity. Freedom from the fear of doing something that would help someone else more than me. Freedom from the kind of pride that makes me feel I am better than my brother.

RICHARD WRIGHT
Native Son

You can make me do nothing but die!

JAMES WELDON JOHNSON
Negro Americans, What Now?

I will not allow one prejudiced person or one million or one hundred million to blight my life. I will not let prejudice or any of its attendant humiliations and injustices bear me down to spiritual defeat. My inner life is mine, and I shall defend and maintain its integrity against all the power of hell.

MAYA ANGELOU
Essence magazine

My grandmother, who was one of the greatest human beings I've ever known, used to say, "I am a child of God and I'm nobody's creature." That to me defined the Black woman through the centuries.

OLIVER WENDELL HOLMES, SR.
Over the Teacups

It is mere childishness to expect men to believe as their fathers did; that is, if they have any minds of their own. The world is a whole generation older and wiser than when the father was his son's age.

THOMAS PAINE
The Rights of Man

Every age and generation must be free to act for itself in all cases as the ages and generations which preceded it. The vanity and presumption of governing beyond the grave is the most ridiculous and insolent of all tyrannies.

HENRY CLAY
Speech to Congress

All oppressed people are authorized, whenever they can, to rise and break their fetters.

BLANCHE K. BRUCE
Speech in Mississippi Senate after fraudulent elections

I have confidence, not only in my country and her institutions, but in the endurance, capacity, and destiny of my people. Whatever our ultimate position in the composite civilization of the Republic and whatever varying fortunes attend our career, we will not forget our instincts for freedom nor our love for country.

FENTON JOHNSON
"The New Day"

For we have been with thee in No Man's Land,
Through lake of fire and down to Hell itself;
And now ask of thee our liberty,
Our freedom in the land of Stars and Stripes.

JOHN LEWIS
Speech at Lincoln Memorial

The revolution is at hand, and we must free ourselves of the chains of political and economic slavery. We cannot be patient, we do not want to be free gradually, we want our freedom, and we want it now.

"I Have A Dream" speech at Lincoln Memorial
MARTIN LUTHER KING, JR.

I am happy to join with you today in what will go down in history as the greatest demonstration for freedom in the history of our nation.

Fivescore years ago, a great American, in whose symbolic shadow we stand today, signed the Emancipation Proclamation. This momentous decree came as a great beacon light of hope to millions of Negro slaves who had been seared in the flames of withering injustice. It came as a joyous daybreak to end the long night of their captivity.

But one hundred years later, the Negro still is not free; one hundred years later, the life of the Negro is still sadly crippled by the manacles of segregation and the chains of discrimination; one hundred years later, the Negro lives on a lonely island of poverty in the midst of a vast ocean of material prosperity; one hundred years later, the Negro is still languished in the corners of American society and finds himself in exile in his own land.

So we've come here today to dramatize a shameful condition. In a sense we've come to our nation's capital to cash a check. When the architects of our republic wrote the magnificent words of the Constitution and the Declaration of Independence, they were signing a promissory note to which every American was to fall heir. This note was the promise that all men, yes, black men as well as white men, would be guaranteed the unalienable rights of life, liberty, and the pursuit of happiness.

It is obvious today that America has defaulted on this promissory note in so far as her citizens of color are concerned. Instead of honoring this sacred obligation, America has given the

Negro people a bad check; a check which has come back marked "insufficient funds." We refuse to believe that there are insufficient funds in the great vaults of opportunity of this nation. And so we've come to cash this check, a check that will give us upon demand the riches of freedom and the security of justice.

We have also come to this hallowed spot to remind America of the fierce urgency of now. This is no time to engage in the luxury of cooling off or to take the tranquilizing drug of gradualism. Now is the time to make real the promises of democracy; now is the time to rise from the dark and desolate valley of segregation to the sunlit path of racial justice; now is the time to lift our nation from the quicksands of racial injustice to the solid rock of brotherhood; now is the time to make justice a reality for God's children. It would be fatal for the nation to overlook the urgency of the moment. This sweltering summer of the Negro's legitimate discontent will not pass until there is an invigorating autumn of freedom and equality.

Nineteen sixty-three is not an end, but a beginning. And those who hope that the Negro needed to blow off steam and will now be content, will have a rude awakening if the nation returns to business as usual.

There will be neither rest nor tranquillity in America until the Negro is granted his citizenship rights. The whirlwinds of revolt will continue to shake the foundations of our nation until the bright day of justice emerges.

But there is something that I must say to my people who stand on the warm threshold which leads into the palace of justice. In the process of gaining our rightful place we must not be guilty of wrongful deeds.

Let us not seek to satisfy our thirst for freedom by drinking from the cup of bitterness and hatred. We must forever conduct our struggle on the high plane of dignity and discipline. We must not allow our creative protest to degenerate into physical violence. Again and again we must rise to the majestic heights of meeting physical force with soul force.

The marvelous new militancy which has engulfed the Negro community must not lead us to a distrust of all white people, for many of our white brothers, as evidenced by their presence here today, have come to realize that their destiny is tied up with our destiny, and they have come to realize that their freedom is inextricably bound to our freedom. This offense we share mounted to storm the battlements of injustice must be carried forth by a biracial army. We cannot walk alone.

And as we walk, we must make the pledge that we shall always march ahead. We cannot turn back. There are those who are asking the devotees of civil rights, "When will you be satisfied?" We can never be satisfied as long as the Negro is the victim of the unspeakable horrors of police brutality.

We can never be satisfied as long as our children are stripped of their selfhood and robbed of their dignity by signs stating "for whites only." We cannot be satisfied as long as a Negro in Mississippi cannot vote and a Negro in New York believes he has nothing for which to vote.

No, we are not satisfied, and we will not be satisfied until justice rolls down like water and righteousness like a mighty stream.

I am not unmindful that some of you have come here out of excessive trials and tribulation. Some of you have come fresh from narrow jail cells. Some of you have come from areas where your quest for freedom left you battered by the storms of persecution and staggered by the winds of police brutality. You have been the veterans of creative suffering. Continue to work with the faith that unearned suffering is redemptive.

Go back to Mississippi; go back to Alabama; go back to South Carolina; go back to Georgia; go back to Louisiana; go back to the slums and ghettos of the northern cities, knowing that somehow this situation can, and will be changed. Let us not wallow in the valley of despair.

So I say to you, my friends, that even though we must face the difficulties of today and tomorrow, I still have a dream. It is a dream deeply rooted in the American dream that one day this nation will rise up and live out the true meaning of its creed—we hold these truths to be self-evident, that all men are created equal.

I have a dream that one day on the red hills of Georgia, sons of former slaves and sons of former slave-owners will be able to sit down together at the table of brotherhood.

I have a dream that one day, even the state of Mississippi, a state sweltering with the heat of injustice, sweltering with the heat of oppression, will be transformed into an oasis of freedom and justice.

I have a dream my four little children will one day live in a nation where they will not be judged by the color of their skin but by the content of their character. I have a dream today!

I have a dream that one day, down in Alabama, with its vicious racists, with its governor having his lips dripping with the words of interposition and nullification, that one day, right there in Alabama, little black boys and black girls will be able to join hands with little white boys and white girls as sisters and brothers. I have a dream today!

I have a dream that one day every valley shall be exalted, every hill and mountain shall be made low, the rough places shall be made plain, and the crooked places shall be made straight and the glory of the Lord will be revealed and all flesh shall see it together.

This is our hope. This is the faith that I go back to the South with.

With this faith we will be able to hear out of the mountain of despair a stone of hope. With this faith we will be able to transform the jangling discords of our nation into a beautiful symphony of brotherhood.

With this faith we will be able to work together, to pray together, to struggle together, to go to jail together, to stand up for freedom together, knowing that we will be free one day. This will be the day when all of God's children will be able to sing with new meaning—"my country 'tis of thee; sweet land of liberty; of thee I sing; land where my fathers died, land of the pilgrim's pride; from every mountain side, let freedom ring"—and if America is to be a great nation, this must become true.

So let freedom ring from the prodigious hilltops of New Hampshire.

Let freedom ring from the mighty mountains of New York.

Let freedom ring from the heightening Alleghenies of Pennsylvania.

Let freedom ring from the snow-capped Rockies of Colorado.

Let freedom ring from the curvaceous slopes of California.

But not only that.

Let freedom ring from Stone Mountain of Georgia.

Let freedom ring from Lookout Mountain of Tennessee.

Let freedom ring from every hill and molehill of Mississippi, from every mountainside, let freedom ring.

And when we allow freedom to ring, when we let it ring from every village and hamlet, from every state and city, we will be able to speed up that day when all of God's children—black men and white men, Jews and Gentiles, Catholics and Protestants—will be able to join hands and to sing in the words of the old Negro spiritual, "Free at last, free at last; thank God Almighty, we are free at last."

FREDERICK DOUGLASS
Address to the British People

I deny the charge that I am saying a word against the institutions and people of America, as such. What I have to say is against slavery and slaveholders. I feel at liberty to speak on this subject. I have on my back the marks of the lash; I have four sisters and one brother now under the galling chain. I feel it is my duty to cry aloud and spare not. I am not averse to being kindly regarded by all men; but I am bound, even at the hazard of making a large class of religionists in this country hate me, oppose me, and malign me as they have done—I am bound by the prayers, and tears, and entreaties of three millions of kneeling bondsmen, to have no compromise with men who are in any shape or form connected with the slaveholders of America. I expose slavery in this country, because to expose it is to kill it. Slavery is one of those monsters of darkness to whom the light of truth is death. Expose slavery, and it dies. Light is to slavery what the heat of the sun is to the root of a tree; it must die under it. All the slaveholder asks of me is silence. He does not ask me to go abroad and preach in favor of slavery; he does not ask any one to do that. He would not say that slavery is a good thing, but the best under the circumstances. The slaveholders want total darkness on the subject. They want the hatchway shut down, that the monster may crawl in his den of darkness, crushing human hopes and happiness, destroying the bondsmen at will, and having no one to reprove or rebuke him. Slavery shrinks from the light; it hateth the light, neither cometh to the light, lest its deeds should be reproved. To tear off the mask from this abominable system, to expose it to the light of heaven, aye, to the heat of the sun, that it may burn and wither it out of existence, is my object in coming to this country. I want the slaveholder surrounded, as by a wall of anti-slavery fire, so that he may see the condemnation of himself and his system glaring down in letters of light. I want him to feel that he has no sympathy in England, Scotland, or Ireland; that he has none in Canada, none in Mexico, none among the poor wild Indians; that the voice of the civilized, aye, and savage world is against him. I would have condemnation blaze down upon him in every direction, till, stunned and overwhelmed with shame and confusion, he is compelled to let go the grasp he holds upon the persons of his victims, and restore them to their long-lost rights.

JOHN BROWN

Speech at his hanging

I believe that to have interfered as I have done, as I have always freely admitted I have done, in behalf of his despised poor, I did not wrong but right. Now, if it is deemed necessary that I should forfeit my life for the furtherance of the ends of justice, and mingle my blood further with the blood of my children and with the blood of millions in this slave country whose rights are disregarded by wicked, cruel and unjust enactments, I say let it be done.

DRED SCOTT

Petition to the Supreme Court

Your petitioner therefore prays your Honorable Court to grant him leave to sue as a poor person, in order to establish his right to freedom.

MARIA STEWART

Speech advocating education for black women

Did the pilgrims, when they first landed on these shores, quietly compose themselves, and say, "The Britons have all the money and all the power, and we must continue their servants forever?" Did they sluggishly sigh and say, "Our lot is hard; the Indians own the soil, and we cannot cultivate it?" No, they first made powerful efforts to raise themselves. And, my brethren, have you made a powerful effort? Have you prayed the legislatures for mercy's sake to grant you all the rights and privileges of free citizens, that your daughters may rise to that degree of respectability which true merit deserves, and your sons above the servile situations which most of them fill?

JAMES BALDWIN

Nobody Knows My Name

Freedom is not something that anybody can be given; freedom is something that people take and people are as free as they want to be.

FRANKLIN D. ROOSEVELT
Speech at Cambridge, Massachusetts

In the truest sense freedom cannot be bestowed, it must be achieved.

MALCOLM X
Malcolm X Speaks

You can't separate peace from freedom because no one can be at peace unless he has his freedom.

CHARLES SUMNER
Speech in New York City

Where slavery is, there liberty cannot be; and where liberty is, there slavery cannot be.

ALICE WALKER
In Search of Our Mothers' Gardens

I could never live happily in Africa—or anywhere else—until I could live freely in Mississippi.

PAUL ROBESON
Testimony before the House Un-American Activities Committee

My father was a slave and my people died to build this country, and I'm going to stay right here and have a part of it, just like you. And no fascist-minded people like you will drive me from it. Is that clear?

"AIN'T GONNA LET NOBODY TURN ME 'ROUND"
American folk song

Ain't gonna let nobody turn me 'round,
I'm gonna keep on a-walkin', Lord,
Keep on a-talkin',
Marching up to freedom land.

MALCOLM X
Speech in New York City

Power in defense of freedom is greater than power in behalf of tyranny and oppression.

ABRAHAM LINCOLN
"Fragment on Slavery"

As I would not be a slave, so I would not be a master. Whatever differs from this, to the extent of the difference, is no democracy.

ABRAHAM LINCOLN
Letter

I intend no modification of my oft-expressed personal wish that all men everywhere could be free.

ABRAHAM LINCOLN
Letter to H.L. Pierce

This is a world of compensation; and he who would be no slave must consent to have no slave. Those who deny freedom to others deserve it not for themselves, and, under a just God, cannot long retain it.

OH, FREEDOM
American folk song

Oh, freedom! Oh, freedom!
Oh, freedom over me!
And before I'd be a slave, I'll be buried in my grave,
And go home to my Lord and be free.

Emancipation Proclamation
ABRAHAM LINCOLN

Whereas, on the 22nd day of September, in the year of our Lord 1862, a proclamation was issued by the President of the United States, containing, among other things, the following, to wit:

That on the 1st day of January, in the year of our Lord 1863, all persons held as slaves within any state or designated part of a state, the people whereof shall then be in rebellion against the United States, shall be then, thenceforward, and forever free; and the executive government of the United States, including the military and naval authority thereof, will recognize and maintain the freedom of such persons and will do no act or acts to repress such person, or any of them, in any efforts they may make for their actual freedom.

Then the executive will, on the 1st day of January aforesaid, by proclamation, designate the states and parts of states, if any, in which the people thereof, respectively, shall then be in rebellion against the United States; and the fact that any state or the people thereof shall on that day be in good faith represented in the Congress of the United States by members chosen thereto at elections wherein a majority of the qualified voters of such states shall have participated shall, in the absence of strong countervailing testimony, be deemed conclusive evidence that such state and the people thereof are not then in rebellion against the United States.

Now, therefore, I, Abraham Lincoln, President of the United States, by virtue of the power in me vested as commander in chief of the Army and Navy of the United States, in time of actual armed rebellion against the authority and government of the United States, and as a fit and necessary war measure for suppressing said rebellion, do, on this 1st day of January, in the year of our Lord 1863, and in accordance with my purpose so to do, publicly proclaimed for the full period of 100 days from the day first above mentioned, order and designate as the states and parts of states wherein the people thereof, respectively, are this day in rebellion against the United States to following, to wit:

Arkansas, Texas, Louisiana (except the parishes of St. Bernard, Plaquemines, Jefferson, St. John, St. Charles, St. James, Ascension, Assumption, Terrebonne, Lafourche, St. Mary, St. Martin, and Orleans, including the city of New Orleans), Mississippi, Alabama, Florida, Georgia, South Carolina, North Carolina, and Virginia (except the forty-eight counties designated as West Virginia, and also the counties of Berkeley, Accomac, Northampton, Elizabeth City, York, Princess Anne, and Norfolk, including the cities of Norfolk and Portsmouth), and which excepted parts are for the present left precisely as if this proclamation were not issued.

And, by virtue of the power and for the purpose aforesaid, I do order and declare that all persons held as slaves within said designated states and parts of state are, and henceforward shall be, free; and that the executive government of the United States, including the military and naval authorities thereof, will recognize and maintain the freedom of said persons.

And I hereby enjoin upon the people so declared to be free to abstain from all violence, unless in necessary self-defense; and I recommend that, in all cases when allowed, they labor faithfully for reasonable wages.

And I further declare and make known that such persons of suitable condition will be received into the armed service of the United States to garrison forts, positions, stations, and other places, and to man vessels of all sorts in said service.

And upon this act, sincerely believed to be an act of justice, warranted by the Constitution upon military necessity, I invoke the considerate judgment of mankind and the gracious favor of Almighty God.

Thirteenth Amendment, U.S. Constitution

Section 1. Neither slavery nor involuntary servitude, except as a punishment for crime whereof the party shall have been duly convicted, shall exist within the United States, or any place subject to their jurisdiction.

Section 2. Congress shall have power to enforce this article by appropriate legislation.

Julia Ward Howe
Battle Hymn of the Republic

Mine eyes have seen the glory of the coming of the Lord;
He is trampling out the vintage where the grapes of wrath are stored;
He hath loosed the fateful lightning of His terrible swift sword:
His truth is marching on.

I have seen Him in the watch-fires of a hundred circling camps;
They have builded Him an altar in the evening dews and damps;
I can read His righteous sentence by the dim and flaring lamps:
His day is marching on.

I have read a fiery gospel writ in burnished rows of steel:
"As ye deal with my condemners, so with you my grace shall deal;
Let the Hero, born of woman, crush the serpent with his heel,
Since God is marching on."

He has sounded forth the trumpet that shall never call retreat;
He is sifting out the hearts of men before His judgment-seat;
Oh, be swift, my soul, to answer Him! be jubilant, my feet!
Our God is marching on.

In the beauty of the lilies Christ was born across the sea,
With a glory in his bosom that transfigures you and me:
As he died to make men holy, let us live to make men free,
While God is marching on.

James Russell Lowell
Stanzas on Freedom

Men! whose boast it is that ye
Come of fathers brave and free,
If there breathe on earth a slave,
Are ye truly free and brave?

If ye do not feel the chain,
When it works a brother's pain,
Are ye not base slaves indeed,
Slaves unworthy to be freed?

Women! who shall one day bear
Sons to breathe New England air,
If ye hear, without a blush,
Deeds to make the roused blood rush
Like red lava through your veins,
For your sisters now in chains,—
Answer! are ye fit to be
Mothers of the brave and free?

Is true Freedom but to break
Fetters for our own dear sake,
And, with leather hearts, forget
That we owe mankind a debt?
No! true freedom is to share
All the chains our brothers wear,
And, with heart and hand, to be
Earnest to make others free!

They are slaves who fear to speak
For the fallen and the weak;
They are slaves who will not choose
Hatred, scoffing, and abuse,
Rather than in silence shrink
From the truths they needs must think;
They are slaves who dare not be
In the right with two or three.

GROVER CLEVELAND
Washington Inauguration Centennial speech

In their cry for freedom, it may truly be said, the voice of the people is the voice of God.

HARRIET TUBMAN
To her biographer Sarah H. Bradford about her becoming free

When I found I had crossed that line, I looked at my hands to see if I was the same person. There was such a glory over everything.

"WE SHALL NOT BE MOVED"
American folk song

We are fighting for our freedom,
We shall not be moved.

"WE'LL SOON BE FREE"
American folk song

We'll soon be free,
When de Lord will call us home
We'll fight for liberty,
When de Lord will call us home.

JOHN F. KENNEDY
Speech on 100th anniversary of Emancipation Proclamation

In giving rights to others which belong to them, we give rights to ourselves and to our country.

LILLIAN HELLMAN
"Watch on the Rhine"

For every man who lives without freedom, the rest of us must face the guilt.

MARK TWAIN
Speech in London, England

Lincoln's proclamation...not only set the black slaves free, but set the white man free also.

The Adventures of Huckleberry Finn

MARK TWAIN

We slept most all day, and started out at night, a little ways behind a monstrous long raft that was as long going by as a procession. She had four long sweeps at each end, so we judged she carried as many as thirty men, likely. She had five big wigwams aboard, wide apart, and an open camp fire in the middle, and a tall flag-pole at each end. There was a power of style about her. It amounted to something being a raftsman on such a craft as that.

We went drifting down into a big bend, and the night clouded up and got hot. The river was very wide, and was walled with solid timber on both sides; you couldn't see a break in it hardly ever, or a light. We talked about Cairo, and wondered whether we would know it when we got to it. I said likely we wouldn't, because I had heard say there warn't but about a dozen houses there, and if they didn't happen to have them lit up, how was we going to know we was passing a town? Jim said if the two big rivers joined together there, that would show. But I said maybe we might think we was passing the foot of an island and coming into the same old river again. That disturbed Jim—an me too. So question was, what to do? I said, paddle ashore the first time a light showed, and tell them pap was behind, coming along with a trading-scow, and was a green hand at the business, and wanted to know how far it was to Cairo. Jim thought it was a good idea, so we took a smoke on it and waited.

There warn't nothing to do now, but to look out sharp for the town, and not pass it without seeing it. He said he'd be mighty sure to see it, because he'd be a free man the minute he seen it, but if he missed it he'd be in the slave country again and no more show for freedom. Every little while he jumps up and says:

"Dah she is!"

But it warn't. It was Jack-o-lanterns, or lightning bugs; so he set down again, and went to watching, same as before. Jim said it made him all over trembly and feverish to be so close to freedom. Well, I can tell you it made me all over trembly and feverish, too, to hear him, because I begun to get it through my head that he was most free—and who was to blame for it? Why, me. I couldn't get that out of my conscience, no how nor no way. It got to troubling me so I couldn't rest; I couldn't stay still in one place. It hadn't ever come home to me before, what this thing was that I was doing. But now it did; and it staid with me, and scorched me more and more. I tried to make out to by myself that I warn't to blame, because I didn't run Jim off from his rightful owner; but it warn't no use, conscience up and says, every time, "But you knowed he was running for his freedom, and you could a paddled ashore and told somebody." That was so—I couldn't get around that, noway. That was where it pinched. Conscience says to me, "What had poor Miss Watson done to you, that you could see her nigger go off right under your eyes and never say one single word? What did that poor old woman do to you, that you could treat her so mean? Why, she tried to learn you your book, she tried to learn you your manners, she tried to be good to you every way she knowed how. That's what she done."

I got to feeling so mean and miserable I most wished I was dead. I fidgeted up and down the raft, abusing myself to myself, and Jim was fidgeting up and down past me. We neither of us could keep still. Every time he danced around and says, "Dah's Cairo!" it went through me like a shot, and I thought if it was Cairo I reckoned I would die of miserableness.

Jim talked out loud all the time while I was talking to myself. He was saying how the first thing he would do when he got to a free State he would go to saving up money and never spend a single cent, and when he got enough he would buy his wife, which was owned on a farm close to where Miss Watson lived; and then they would both work to buy the two children, and if their master wouldn't sell them, they'd get an Ab'litionist to go and steal them.

It most froze me to hear such talk. He wouldn't ever dared to talk such talk in his life before. Just see what a difference it made in him the minute he judged he was about free. It was according to the old saying, "give a nigger an inch and he'll take an ell." Thinks I, this is what comes of my not thinking. Here was this nigger which I had as good as helped to run away, coming right out flat-footed and saying he would steal his children—children that belonged to a man I didn't even know; a man that hadn't ever done me no harm.

I was sorry to hear Jim say that, it was such a lowering of him. My conscience got to stirring me up hotter than ever, until at last I says to it, "Let up on men—it ain't too late, yet—I'll paddle ashore at the first light, and tell. I felt easy, and happy and light as a feather, right off. All my troubles was gone. I went to looking out sharp for a light, and sort of singing to myself. By-and-by one showed. Jim sings out:

"We's safe, Huck, we's safe! Jump up and crack yo' heels, dat's de good ole Cairo at las', I jis know it!"

I says:

"I'll take the canoe and go see, Jim. It mightn't be, you know."

He jumped and got the canoe ready, and put his old coat in the bottom for me to set on, and give me the paddle; and as I shoved off, he says:

"Pooty soon I'll be a shout'n for joy, en I'll say, it's all on accounts o' Huck; I's a free man, en I couldn't ever ben free if it hadn' been for Huck; Huck done it. Jim won't ever forgit you, Huck; you's de bes' fren' Jim's ever had; en you's de only fren' ole Jim's got now."

I was paddling off, all in a sweat to tell on him; but when he says this, it seemed to kind of take the tuck all out of me. I went along slow then, and I warn't right down certain whether I was glad I started or whether I warn't. When I was fifty yards off, Jim says:

"Dah you goes, de ole true Huck; de on'y white genlman dat ever kep' his promise to ole Jim."

Well, I just felt sick. But I says, I got to do it—I can't get out of it. Right then, along comes a skiff with two men on it, with guns, and they stopped and I stopped. One of them says:

"What's that, yonder?"

"A piece of a raft," I says.

"Do you belong on it?"

"Yes, sir."

"Any men on it?"

"Only one, sir."

"Well, there's five niggers run off tonight, up yonder above the head of the bend. Is your man white or black?"

I didn't answer up prompt. I tried to, but the words wouldn't come. I tried, for a second or two, to brace up and out with it, but I warn't man enough—hadn't the spunk of a rabbit. I see I was weakening; so I just give up trying, and up and says—

"He's white."

"I reckon we'll go and see for ourselves."

"I wish you would," says I, "because it's pap that's there, and maybe you'd help me tow the raft ashore where the light is. He's sick—and so is mam and Mary Ann."

"Oh, the devil! we're in a hurry, boy. But I s'pose we've got to. Come—buckle to your paddle, and let's get along."

I buckled to my paddle and they laid to their oars. When we had made a stroke or two, I says:

"Pap'll be mighty much obleeged to you, I can tell you. Everybody goes away when I want them to help me tow the raft ashore, and I can't do it by myself."

"Well, that's infernal mean. Odd, too. Say, boy, what's the matter with your father?"

"It's the—a—the—well, it ain't anything, much."

They stopped pulling. It warn't but a mighty little ways to the raft, now. One says:

"Boy, that's a lie. What is the matter with your pap? Answer up square, now, and it'll be the better for you."

"I will, sir, I will, honest—but don't leave us, please. It's the—the—gentlemen, if you'll only pull ahead, and let me heave the head-line, you won't have to come a-near the raft—please do."

"Set her back, John, set her back!" says one. They backed water. "Keep away, boy—keep to looard. Confound it, I just expect the wind has blowed it to us. Your pap's got the small-pox, and you know it precious well. Why didn't you come out and say so? Do you want to spread it all over?"

"Well," says I, a-blubbering, "I've told everybody before, and then they just went away and left us."

"Poor devil, there's something in that. We are right down sorry for you, but we—well, hand it, we don't want the small-pox, you see. Look here, I'll tell you what to do. Don't you try to land by yourself, or you'll smash everything to pieces. You float along down about twenty miles and you'll come to a town on the left-hand side of the river. It will be long after sun-up, then, and when you ask for help, you tell them your folks are all down with chills and fever. Don't be a fool again, and let people guess what is the matter. Now we're trying to do you a kindness; so you just put twenty miles between us, that's a good boy. It wouldn't do any good to land yonder where the light is—it's only a wood-yard. Say, I reckon your father's poor, and I'm bound to say he's in pretty hard luck. Here, I'll put a twenty dollar gold piece on this board, and you get it when it floats by. I feel mighty mean to leave you, but my kingdom! it won't do to fool with small-pox, don't you see?"

"Hold on, Parker," says the other man, "here's a twenty to put on the board for me. Good-bye, boy, you do as Mr. Parker told you, and you'll be all right."

"That's so, my boy, good-bye, good-bye. If you see any runaway niggers, you get help and nab them, and you can make some money by it."

"Good-bye, sir," says I, "I won't let no runaway niggers get by me if I can help it."

They went off, and I got aboard the raft, feeling bad and low, because I knowed very well I had done wrong, and I see it warn't no use for me to try to learn to do right; a body that don't get started right when he's little, ain't got no show—when the pinch comes there ain't nothing to back him up and keep him to his work, and so he gets beat. Then I thought a minute, and says to myself, hold, s'pose you'd a done right and give Jim up; would you felt better than what you do now? No, says I, I'd feel bad—I'd feel just the same way I do now. Well, then, says I, what's the use you learning to do right, when it's troublesome to do right and ain't no trouble to do wrong, and the wages is just the same? I was stuck. I couldn't answer that. So I reckoned I wouldn't bother no more about it, but after this always do whichever come handiest at the time.

FRANKLIN D. ROOSEVELT

We believe that the only whole man is a free man.

FRANTZ FANON
Black Skins, White Masks

It is by risking life that freedom is obtained.

WILLIAM CULLEN BRYANT
"Freedom"

O Freedom! thou art not, as poets dream,
A fair young girl, with light and delicate limbs,
And wavy tresses gushing from the cap
With which the Roman master crowned his slave
When he took off the gyves. A bearded man,
Armed to the teeth, art thou; one mailed hand
Grasps the broad shield, and one the sword; thy brow,
Glorious in beauty though it be, is scarred
With tokens of old wars; thy missive limbs
Are strong with struggling.

MICHAEL HARRINGTON
The Accidental Century

How can one defend the sober virtues of Protestant individualism by disaffiliating from the world?

JAMES RUSSELL LOWELL

[O]h! fair Freedom, if our choice must be
'Twixt war and craven recreance to thee,
Sooner, dear land, let each manchild of thine
Sleep death's red sleep within the enemy's line...
Sooner than brook, what only slaves hold dear,
A suppliant peace that is not Peace, but Fear!

DWIGHT D. EISENHOWER
Speech in London, England

Freedom has its life in the hearts, the actions, the spirit of men and so it must be daily earned and refreshed—else like a flower cut from its life-giving roots, it will wither and die.

PEARL S. BUCK
Letter to the Cardozo High School, Washington, D.C., class of 1951

In strange ways and for different reasons human freedom is lost, and as we watch the process wherever it takes place, we who are still free must resolve with fresh courage to keep human freedom alive, and first of all in our own beloved country in order that from here it may spread to a beleaguered world.

This courage may cost us much. The time may come, if we are not brave enough in the beginning, when it may cost us everything. What does courage mean? It means the determination to practice our ideals. We cannot keep our freedom unless we practice it. You and I, as individuals, must practice it, wherever we are. We cannot harbor prejudice against other persons. Race prejudice is not the only prejudice in our land. Within any one group there is prejudice. We must not allow it in ourselves for any reason whatsoever, for to the degree we allow it we deny human freedom. We must root out of ourselves the denial of freedom before we can fight for freedom in the world. Only with a pure love for humanity, only with true respect for the human individual, can the struggle for human freedom be won.

CARL SANDBURG
"Is There Any Easy Road to Freedom?"

A relentless man loved France
Long before she came to shame
And the eating of bitter dust,
Loving her as mother and torch,
As bone of his kith and kin
And he spoke passion, warning:
"Rest is not a word for free peoples—
rest is a monarchical word."

A relentless Russian loved Russia
Long before she came to bare agony
And valor amid rivers of blood,
Loving her as mother and torch,
As bone of his kith and kin:
He remembered the old Swedish saying:
"The fireborn are at home in fire."

A Kentucky-born Illinoisan found himself
By journey through shadow and prayer
The Chief Magistrate of the American people
Pleading in words close to low whispers:
"Fellow citizens . . . we cannot escape history.
The fiery trial through which we pass
Will light us down in honor or dishonor
To the latest generation . . .

We shall nobly save or meanly lose
 the last best hope of earth."
Four little words came worth studying over:
"We must disenthrall ourselves."
And what is a thrall? And who are thralls?
Men tied down or men doped, or men drowsy?
He hoped to see them
 shake themselves loose
 and so be disenthralled.

There are freedom shouters.
There are freedom whisperers.
Both may serve.
Have I, have you, been too silent?
Is there an easy crime of silence?
Is there an easy road to freedom?

JOHN ADAMS

If it be the pleasure of Heaven that my country shall require the poor offering of my life, the victim shall be ready, at the appointed hour of sacrifice, come when that hour may. But while I do live, let me have a country, and that a free country.

FELICIA HEMANS
"Landing of the Pilgrim Fathers"

The breaking waves dashed high,
On a stern and rock-bound coast,
And the woods against a stormy sky,
Their giant branches tossed;

And the heavy night hung dark,
The hills and water o'er,
When a band of exiles moored their bark
On the wild New England shore.

Not as the conqueror comes,
They, the true-hearted came;
Not with the roll of the stirring drums,
And the trumpet that sings of fame;

Not as the flying come,
In silence and in fear—
They shook the depths of the desert gloom
With their hymns of lofty cheer.

Amidst the storm they sang,
And the stars heard, and the sea;
And the sounding aisles of the dim woods rang
To the anthem of the free.

The ocean eagle soared
From his nest by the white wave's foam;
And the rocking pines of the forest roared—
This was their welcome home.

There were men with hoary hair
Amidst that pilgrim band:
Why had they come to wither there,
Away from their childhood's land?

There was a woman's fearless eye,
Lit by her deep love's truth;
There was manhood's brow serenely high,
And the fiery heart of youth.

What sought they thus afar?
Bright jewels of the mine?
The wealth of seas, the spoils of war?
They sought a faith's pure shrine!

Aye, call it holy ground,
The soil where first they trod;
They have unstained what there they found—
Freedom to worship God.

W.E.B. DuBois
"Education and Work" *commencement address at Howard University*

To increase abiding satisfaction for the mass of our people, and for all people, someone must sacrifice something of his own happiness. This is a duty only to those who recognize it as a duty. . . . It is silly to tell intelligent human beings: Be good and you will be happy. The truth is today, be good, be decent, be honorable and self-sacrificing and you will not always be happy.

You will often be desperately unhappy. You may even be crucified, dead and buried, and the third day you will be just as dead as the first. But with the death of your happiness may easily come increased happiness and satisfaction and fulfillment for other people—strangers, unborn babies, uncreated worlds. If this is not sufficient incentive, never try it—remain hogs.

WILLIAM J. BRENNAN, JR.
The New York Times

If I have drawn one lesson in ninety years, it is this: To strike a blow for freedom allows a man to walk a little taller and raise his head a little higher. While he can, he must.

STEVEN BARBOZOA
American Visions

The struggle for freedom is part of our common heritage.

FRANKLIN D. ROOSEVELT
On receiving degree from Oxford University

We, too, born to freedom, are willing to fight to maintain freedom. We, and all others who believe as dearly as we do, would rather die on our feet than live on our knees.

JOSIAH QUINCY
Observations on the Boston Port Bill

Blandishments will not fascinate us, nor will threats of a "halter" intimidate. For, under God, we are determined that wheresoever, whensoever, or howsoever we shall be called to make our exit, we will die free men.

RALPH WALDO EMERSON
"Boston"

For what avail the plow or sail,
Or land or life, if freedom fail?

SIDNEY HOOK
Bread and Freedom

Whether our choices are good or bad, wise or foolish, we feel diminished as human beings if we are prevented from making them. Denied freedom to make choices, we are denied responsibility, and to deny our responsibility is to deny our humanity. It is the unique glory of man that although he hopes and works for an abundant life, he is prepared to die in order to prove that he is human.

THOMAS JEFFERSON
Letter to Colonel Charles Yancey

If a nation expects to be ignorant and free, in a state of civilization, it expects what never was and never will be.

JAMES RUSSELL LOWELL
New England Two Centuries Ago

It was in making education not only common to all, but in some sense compulsory on all, that the destiny of the free republics of America was practically settled.

MARTIN LUTHER KING, JR.
Speech in Montgomery, Alabama

Freedom is not free.

HELEN GAHAGAN DOUGLAS
Speech to Congress

It is not easy to be free men, for to be free you must afford freedom to your neighbor, regardless of race, color, creed, or national origin, and that sometimes, for some, is very difficult.

THOMAS PAINE
The American Crisis

Those who expect to reap the blessings of freedom must, like men, undergo the fatigue of supporting it.

ADLAI E. STEVENSON
Putting First Things First

We have confused the free with the free and easy.

LUCIUS D. CLAY

The road to democracy is not a freeway. It is a toll road on which we pay by accepting and carrying out our civic responsibilities.

THOMAS JEFFERSON
Letter to Lafayette

We are not to expect to be translated from despotism to liberty in a featherbed.

BENJAMIN FRANKLIN
An Historical Review of Pennsylvania

They that can give up essential liberty to obtain a little temporary safety deserve neither liberty nor safety.

W.E.B. DUBOIS
"The Legacy of John Brown"

Liberty trains for liberty. Responsibility is the first step in responsibility.

HENRY MILLER
Sunday after the War

The man who looks for security, even in the mind, is like a man who would chop off his limbs in order to have artificial ones which will give him no pain or trouble.

ALICE WALKER
In Search of Our Mothers' Gardens

For in the end, freedom is a personal and lonely battle and one faces down fears of today so that those of tomorrow might be engaged.

EDITH HAMILTON

When the freedom they wished for most was the freedom from responsibility, then Athens ceased to be free and never was free again.

WILLIAM FAULKNER
Harper's Magazine

We cannot choose freedom established on a hierarchy of degrees of freedom, on a caste system of equality like military rank. We must be free not because we claim freedom, but because we practice it.

MILTON AND ROSE FRIEDMAN
Free to Choose

Freedom is a tenable objective only for responsible individuals.

HENRY STEELE COMMAGER
Freedom, Loyalty, Dissent

Freedom is not a luxury that we can indulge in when at last we have security and prosperity and enlightment; it is, rather, antecedent to all of these, for without it we can have neither security nor prosperity nor enlightenment.

FRANKLIN D. ROOSEVELT
Fireside chat

The only sure bulwark of continuing liberty is a government strong enough to protect the interests of the people, and a people strong enough and well enough informed to maintain its sovereign control over its government.

HARRY S TRUMAN
Speech in Washington, D.C.

Freedom is still expensive. It still costs money. It still costs blood. It still calls for courage and endurance, not only in soldiers, but in every man and woman who is free and who is determined to remain free.

Four Freedoms Speech
FRANKLIN D. ROOSEVELT

The Nation takes great satisfaction and much strength from the things which have been done to make its people conscious of their individual stake in the preservation of democratic life in America. Those things have toughened the fiber of our people, have renewed their faith and strengthened their devotion to the institutions we make ready to protect.

Certainly this is no time for any of us to stop thinking about the social and economic problems which are the root cause of the social revolution which is today a supreme factor in the world.

For there is nothing mysterious about the foundations of a healthy and strong democracy. The basic things expected by our people of their political and economic systems are simple. They are:

Equality of opportunity for youth and for others.

Jobs for those who can work.

Security for those who need it.

The ending of special privilege for the few.

The preservation of civil liberties for all.

The enjoyment of the fruits of scientific progress in a wider and constantly rising standard of living.

These are the simple, basic things that must never be lost sight of in the turmoil and unbelievable complexity of our modern world. The inner and abiding strength of our economic and political systems is dependent upon the degree to which they fulfill these expectations.

Many subjects connected with our social economy call for immediate improvement.

As examples:

We should bring more citizens under the coverage of old-age pensions and unemployment insurance.

We should widen the opportunities for adequate medical care.

We should plan a better system by which persons deserving or needing gainful employment may obtain it.

I have called for personal sacrifice. I am assured of the willingness of almost all Americans to respond to that call.

A part of the sacrifice means the payment of more money in taxes. In my Budget Message I shall recommend a greater portion of this great defense program be paid from taxation that we are paying today. No person should try, or be allowed, to get rich out of this program; and the principle of tax payments in accordance with ability to pay should be constantly before our eyes to guide our legislation.

If the Congress maintains these principles, the voters, putting patriotism ahead of pocketbooks, will give you their applause.

In the future days, which we seek to make secure, we look forward to a world founded upon four essential human freedoms.

The first is the freedom of speech and expression—everywhere in the world.

The second is the freedom of every person to worship God in his own way—everywhere in the world.

The third is freedom from want—which, translated into world terms, means economic understandings which will secure to every nation a healthy peacetime life for its inhabitants—everywhere in the world.

The fourth is freedom from fear—which, translated into world terms, means a worldwide reduction of armaments to such a point and in such a thorough fashion that no nation will be in a position to commit an act of physical aggression against any neighbor—anywhere in the world.

That is no vision of a distant millennium. It is a definite basis for a kind of world attainable in our own time and generation. That kind of world is the very antithesis of the so-called new order of tyranny which the dictators seek to create with the crash of a bomb.

To that new order we oppose the greater conception—the moral order. A good society is able to face schemes of world domination and foreign revolutions alike without fear.

Since the beginning of our American history, we have been engaged in change—in perpetual peaceful revolution—a revolution which goes on steadily, quietly adjusting itself to changing conditions—without the concentration camp or the quick-lime in the ditch. The world order which we seek is the cooperation of free countries, working together in a friendly, civilized society.

This nation has placed its destiny in the hands and heads and hearts of its millions of free men and women; and its faith in freedom under the guidance of God. Freedom means the supremacy of human rights everywhere. Our support goes to those who struggle to gain those rights or keep them. Our strength is our unity of purpose.

To that high concept there can be no end save victory.

Harry S Truman
Speech in Independence, Missouri

Freedom has never been an abstract idea to us here in the United States. It is real and concrete. It means not only political and civil rights, it means much more. It means a society in which man has a fair chance. It means an opportunity to do useful work. It means the right to an education. It means protection against economic hardship.

Andrew Johnson
Message to Congress regarding reconstruction and military rule

Personal freedom, property and life, if assailed by the passion, the prejudice, or the rapacity of the ruler, have no security whatever.

Woodrow Wilson
1912 Democratic National Convention

To be free is not necessarily to be wise. Wisdom comes with counsel, with the frank and free conference of untrammeled men united in the common interest.

BOB DYLAN
"Blowin' in the Wind"

Yes, 'n' how many years can some people exist
Before they're allowed to be free?
Yes, 'n' how many times can a man turn his head
Pretending he just doesn't see?
The answer, my friend is blowin' in the wind

WOODROW WILSON
Speech in Mobile, Alabama

I would rather belong to a poor nation that was free than to a rich nation that had ceased to be in love with liberty. We shall not be poor if we love liberty.

GEORGE SANTAYANA
The Irony of Liberalism

I like to walk about amidst the beautiful things that adorn the world; but private wealth I should decline, or any sort of personal possessions, because they would take away my liberty.

Walden

HENRY DAVID THOREAU

I do not propose to write an ode to dejection, but to brag as lustily as changicleer in the morning, standing on his roost, if only to wake my neighbors up.

When I wrote the following pages, or rather the bulk of them, I lived alone, in the woods, a mile from any neighbor, in a house which I had built myself, on the shore of a Walden pond, in Concord, Massachusetts, and earned my living by the labor of my hands only. I lived there two years and two months. At present I am a sojourner in civilized life again....

I would fain say something, not so much concerning the Chinese and Sandwich Islanders as you who read these pages, who are said to live in New England; something about your condition or circumstance in this world, in this town, what it is, whether it is necessary that it be as bad as it is, whether it cannot be improved as well as not. I have traveled a good deal in Concord; and every where, in shops, and offices, and fields, the inhabitants have appeared to me to be doing penance in a thousand remarkable ways. What I have heard of Bramins sitting exposed to four fires and looking in the face of the sun; or hanging suspended, with their heads downward, over flames; or looking at the heavens over their shoulders "until it becomes impossible for them to resume their natural position, while from the twist of the neck nothing but liquids can pass into the stomach;" or dwelling, chained for life, at the foot of a tree; or measuring with their bodies, like caterpillars, the breadth of vast empires; or standing on one leg on the tops of pillars,—even these forms of conscious penance are hardly more incredible and astonishing than the scenes which I daily witness. The twelve labors of Hercules were trifling in comparison with those which my neighbors have undertaken; for they were only twelve, and had an end; but I could never see that these men slew or captured any monster or finished any labor. They have no friend Iolas to burn with a hot iron the root of the hydra's head, but as soon as one head is crushed, two spring up.

I see young men, my townsmen, whose misfortune it is to have inherited farms, houses, barns, cattle, and farming tools; for these are more easily acquired than got rid of. Better if they had been born in the open pasture and suckled by a wolf, that they might have seen with clearer eyes what field they were called to labor in. Who made them serfs of the soil? Why should they eat their sixty acres, when man is condemned to eat only his peck of dirt? Why should they begin digging their graves as soon as they are born? They have got to live a man's life, pushing all these things before them, and get on as well as they can. How many a poor immortal soul have I met well nigh crushed and smothered under its load, creeping down the road of life, pushing before it a barn seventy-five feet by forty, its Augean stables never cleansed, and one hundred acres of land, tillage, mowing, pasture, and wood-lot! The portionless, who struggle with no such unnecessary inherited encumbrances, find it labor enough to subdue and cultivate a few cubic feet of flesh.

But men labor under a mistake. The better part of the man is soon ploughed into the soil for compost. By a seeming fate, commonly called necessity, they are employed, as it says in an old book, laying up treasures which moth and rust will corrupt and thieves break through and steal. It is a fool's life, as they will find when they get to the end of it, if not before. It is said that Deucelion and Pyrrha created men by throwing stones over their heads behind them:—

> Inde genus durum sumus, experiesque laborum,
> Et documenta damus qua simus origine nati.

Or, as Raleigh rhymes it in his sonorous way,—

> "From thence our kind hard-hearted is, enduring pain and care,
> Approving that our bodies of a stony nature are."

So much for a blind obedience to a blundering oracle, throwing the stones over their heads behind them, and not seeing where they fell.

Most men, even in this comparatively free country, through mere ignorance and mistake, are so occupied with the factitious cares and superfluously coarse labors of life that its finer fruits cannot be plucked by them. Their fingers, from excessive toil, are too clumsy and tremble too much for that. Actually, the laboring man has not leisure for a true integrity day by day; he cannot afford to sustain the manliest relations to man; his labor would be depreciated in the market. He has no time to be any thing but a machine. How can he remember well his ignorance —which his growth requires—who has so often used his knowledge? We should feed and clothe him gratuitously sometimes, and recruit him with our cordials, before we judge him. The finest qualities of our nature, like the bloom on fruits, can be preserved only by the most delicate handling. Yet we do not treat ourselves nor one another thus tenderly.

Some of you, we all know, are poor, find it hard to live, are sometimes, as it were, gasping for breath. I have no doubt that some of you who read this book are unable to pay for all the dinners which you have actually eaten, or for the coats and shoes which are fast wearing or are already worn out, and have come to this page to spend borrowed or stolen time, robbing your creditors of an hour. It is very evident what mean and sneaking lives many of you live, for my sight has been whetted by experience; always on the limits, trying to get into business and trying to get out of debt, a very ancient slough, called by the Latins aes alienum, another's brass, for some of their coins were made of brass; still living, and dying, and buried by this other's brass; always promising to pay, promising to pay, tomorrow, and dying today, insolvent; seeking to curry favor, to get custom, by how many modes, only not state-prison offenses; lying, flattering, voting, contracting yourselves into a nutshell of civility, or dilating into an atmosphere of thin and vaporous generosity, that you may persuade your neighbor to let you make his shoes, or his hat, or his coat, or his carriage, or import his groceries for him; making yourselves sick, that you may lay up something against a sick day, something to be tucked away in an old chest, or in a stocking behind the plastering, or, more safely, in the brick bank; no matter how much or how little.

I sometimes wonder that we can be so frivolous, I may almost say, as to attend to the gross but somewhat foreign form of servitude called Negro Slavery, there are so many keen and subtle masters that enslave both north and south. It is hard to have a southern overseer; it is worse to have a northern one; but worst of all when you are the slave-driver of yourself. Talk of a divinity of man! Look at the teamster on the highway, wending to market by day or night; does any divinity stir within him? His highest duty is to fodder and water his horses! What is his destiny compared with the shipping interests? Does not he drive for Squire Make-a-stir? How godlike, how immortal, is he? See how he cowers and sneaks, how vaguely all the day he fears, not being immortal nor divine, but the slave and prisoner of his own deeds. Public opinion is a weak tyrant compared with our own private opinion. What a man thinks of himself, that it is which determines, or rather indicates, his fate. Self-emancipation even in the West Indian provinces of the fancy and imagination,—what Wilberforce is there to bring that about? Think, also, of the ladies of the land weaving toilet cushions against the last day, not to betray too green an interest in their fates! As if you could kill time without injuring eternity.

The mass of men lead lives of quiet desperation. What is called resignation is confirmed desperation. From the desperate city you go into the desperate country, and have to console yourself with the bravery of minks and muskrats. A stereotyped but unconscious despair is concealed even under what are called the games and amusements of mankind. There is no play in them, for this comes after work. But it is a characteristic of wisdom not to do desperate things.

When we consider what, to use the words of the catechism, is the chief end of man, and what are the true necessaries and means of life, it appears as if men had deliberately chosen the common mode of living because they preferred it to any other. Yet they honestly think there is no choice left. But alert and healthy natures remember that the sun rose clear. It is never too late to give up our prejudices. No way of thinking or doing, however ancient, can be trusted without proof. What everybody echoes or in silence passes by as true today may turn out to be falsehood tomorrow, mere smoke of opinion, which some had trusted for a cloud that would sprinkle fertilizing rain on their fields. What old people say you cannot do, you try and find that you can. Old deeds for old people, and new deeds for new. Old people did not know enough once, perchance, to fetch fresh fuel to keep the fire a-going; new people put a little dry wood under a pot, and are whirled round the globe with the speed of birds, in a way to kill old people, as the phrase is. Age is no better, hardly so well, qualified for an instructor as youth, for it has not profited so much as it has lost. One may almost doubt if the wisest man has learned anything of absolute value by living. Practically, the old have no very important advice to give the young, their own experience has been so partial, and their lives have been such miserable failures, for private reasons, as they must believe; and it may be that they have some faith left which belies that experience, and they are only less young than they were. I have lived some thirty years on this planet, and I have yet to hear the first syllable of valuable or even earnest advice from my seniors. They have told me nothing, and probably cannot tell me anything to the purpose. Here is life, an experiment to a great extent untried by me; but it does not avail me that they have tried it. If I have any experience which I think valuable, I am sure that this my Mentors said nothing about.

One farmer says to me, "You cannot live on vegetable food solely, for it furnishes nothing to make bones with;" and so he religiously devotes a part of his day to supplying his system with the raw material of bones; walking all the while he talks behind his oxen, which, with vegetable-made bones, jerk him and his lumbering plow along in spite of every obstacle. Some things are really necessaries of life in some circles, the most helpless and diseased, which in others are luxuries merely, and in others still are entirely unknown.

The whole ground of human life seems to some to have been gone over by their predecessors, both the heights and valleys, and all things to have been cared for. According to Evelyn, "the wise Solomon prescribed ordinances for the very distance of trees; and the Roman praetors have decided how often you may go into your neighbor's land to gather acorns which fall on it without trespass, and what share belongs to that neighbor." Hippocrates has even left directions how we should cut our nails; that is, even with the ends of the fingers neither shorter nor longer. Undoubtedly the very tedium and ennui which presume to have exhausted the variety and the joys of life are as old as Adam. But man's capacities have never been measured; nor are we to judge of what he can do by any precedents, so little has been tried. Whatever have been thy failures hitherto, "be not afflicted, my child, for who shall assign to thee what thou hast left undone?"

We might try our lives by a thousand simple tests; as, for instance, that the same sun that ripens my beans illumines at once a system of earths like ours. If I had remembered this it would have prevented some mistakes. This was not the light in which I hoed them. The stars are the apexes of what wonderful triangles! What distant and different beings in the various mansions of the universe are contemplating the same one at the same moment! Nature and human life are as various as our several constitutions. Who shall say what prospect life offers to another? Could a greater miracle take place than for us to look through each other's eyes for an instant? We should live in all the ages of the world in an hour; nay, in all the worlds of all the ages. History, Poetry, Mythology!—I know of no reading of another's experience so startling and informing as this would be.

The greater part of what my neighbors call good I believe in my soul to be bad, and if I repent of anything, it is very likely to be my good behavior. What demon possessed me that I behaved so well? You may say the wisest thing you can, old man,—you who have lived seventy years, not without honor of a kind,—I hear an irresistible voice which invites me away from all that. One generation abandons the enterprises of another like stranded vessels.

I think that we may safely trust a good deal more than we do. We may waive just so much care of ourselves as we honestly bestow elsewhere. Nature is as well adapted to our weakness as to our strength. The incessant anxiety and strain of some is a well-nigh incurable form of disease. We are made to exaggerate the importance of what work we do; and yet how much is not done by us! or, what if we had been taken sick? How vigilant we are! Determined not to live by faith if we can avoid it; all day long on the alert, at night we unwillingly say our prayers and commit ourselves to uncertainties. So thoroughly and sincerely are we compelled to live, reverencing our life, and denying the possibility of change. This is the only way, we say; but there are as many ways as there can be drawn radii from one center. All change is a miracle to contemplate; but it is a miracle which is taking place every instant. Confucius said, "To know that we know what we know, and that we do not know what we do not know, that is true knowledge." When one man has reduced a fact of the imagination to be a fact of his understanding, I foresee that all men will at length establish their lives on that basis.

All Men Are Created Equal

THOMAS JEFFERSON
Declaration of Independence

We hold these truths to be self-evident, that all men are created equal, that they are endowed with certain unalienable Rights, and among these are Life, Liberty and the pursuit of Happiness.

ABRAHAM LINCOLN
Speech in Springfield, Illinois

I think the authors of that notable instrument [the Declaration of Independence] intended to include all men, but they did not intend to declare all men equal in all respects. They did not mean to say all were equal in color, size, intellect, moral developments, or social capacity. They defined with tolerable distinctness in what respects they did consider all men created equal—equal with "certain inalienable rights, among which are life, liberty, and the pursuit of happiness." This they said, and this they meant.

U.S. SENATOR ALBEN BARKLEY
Democratic Convention

[Thomas Jefferson] did not proclaim that all white, or black, or red, or yellow men are equal; that all Christian or Jewish men are equal; Protestant and Catholic men are equal; that all rich or poor men are equal; that all good or bad men are equal.

What he declared was that all men are created equal; and the equality which he proclaimed was equality in the right to enjoy the blessings of free government in which they may participate and to which they have given their consent.

WALT WHITMAN
Letter

The great country, the greatest country, the richest country is not that which has the most capitalists, monopolists, immense grabbings, vast fortunes, with its sad, sad foil of extreme, degrading, damning poverty, but the land in which there are the most homesteads, freeholds—where wealth does not show such contrasts high and low, where all men have enough—a modest living—and no man is made possessor beyond the sane and beautiful necessities of the simple body and the simple soul. The great country, in fact, is the country of free labor—of free laborers: Negro, white, Chinese, or others.

ALISTAIR COOKE
America Observed: From the 1940s to the 1980s,
"The Coronation of Miss Oklahoma"

Although the Jeffersonian Law ("All men are created equal") is the first article of American faith, the facts of American life have demonstrated for some time now that it is an irksome faith to live by.

BENJAMIN FRANKLIN
Poor Richard's Almanack

The greatest monarch on the proudest throne
is obliged to sit upon his own arse.

THOMAS PAINE
Common Sense

Where there are no distinctions there can be no superiority; perfect equality affords no temptation.

THURGOOD MARSHALL

A goal that is the basis of true democracy above the law: A child born to a black mother in a state like Mississippi—born to the dumbest, poorest, sharecropper—by merely drawing its first breath in the democracy has exactly the same rights as a white baby born to the wealthiest person in the United States. It's not true, but I challenge anyone to say it is not a goal worth working for.

LYNDON B. JOHNSON

White House news conference

The promise of America is a simple promise: Every person shall share in the blessings of this land. And they shall share on the basis of their merits as a person. They shall not be judged by their color or by their beliefs, or by their religion, or by where they were born, or the neighborhood in which they live.

MARK TWAIN

"Does the Race of Man Love a Lord?"

Emperors, kings, artisans, peasants, big people, little people—at bottom we are all alike and all the same; all just alike on the inside, and when our clothes are off, nobody can tell which of us is which.

HUBERT H. HUMPHREY

Beyond Civil Rights—A New Day of Equality

The struggle for equal opportunity in America is the struggle for America's soul. The ugliness of bigotry stands in direct contradiction to the very meaning of America.

HARRY S TRUMAN

You know that being an American is more than a matter of where your parents came from. It is a belief that all men are created free and equal and that everyone deserves an even break. It is a respect for the dignity of men and women without regard to race, creed, or color. That is our creed.

ALEXIS DE TOCQUEVILLE

Democracy in America, Part II

Thus not only does democracy make every man forget his ancestors, but it hides his descendants and separates his contemporaries from him; it throws him back forever upon himself alone and threatens in the end to confine him entirely within the solitude of his own heart.

E.B. WHITE

Letter to Robert M. Hutchins

There is nothing much to be "taught" about equality—you either believe it or you don't. But there is much that can be taught about rights and about liberty, including the basic stuff: that a right derives from a responsibleness, and that men become free as they become willing to accept restrictions on their acts. These are elementary concepts, of course, but an awful lot of youngsters seem to emerge from high school and even from college without acquiring them. Until they are acquired, the more subtle, intricate, and delicate problems of civil rights and freedom of speech are largely incomprehensible.

JOHN UPDIKE

The Englishman is under no constitutional obligation to believe that all men are created equal. The American agony is therefore scarcely intelligible, like a saint's self-flagellation viewed by an atheist.

JAMES CLYMAN

Here lies the bones of Black Harris
who often traveled beyond the far west
and for the freedom of Equal rights
he crossed the snowy mountain Heights
was free and easy kind of soul
Especially with a Belly full.

ELEANOR ROOSEVELT
This Is My Story

No one can make you feel inferior without your consent.

ERICH FROMM
Escape from Freedom

All men are born equal but they are also born different.

JAMES FENIMORE COOPER
The American Democrat

Equality, in a social sense, may be divided into that of condition and that of rights. Equality of condition is incompatible with civilization, and is found only to exist in those communities that are but slightly removed from the savage state. In practice, it can only mean a common misery.

ADAM CLAYTON POWELL
Keep the Faith, Baby!

Unless man is committed to the belief that all of mankind are brothers, then he labors in vain and hypocritically in the vineyards of equality.

BARRY GOLDWATER
Republican Convention speech

Absolute power does corrupt, and those who seek it must be suspect and must be oppressed. Their mistaken course stems from a false notion, ladies and gentlemen, of equality. Equality, rightly understood as our founding fathers understood it, leads to liberty and to the emancipation of creative differences; wrongly understood, as it has been so tragically in our time, it leads first to conformity and then to despotism.

ERICH FROMM
The Art of Loving

Just as modern mass production requires standardization of commodities, so the social process requires standardization of man, and this standardization is called equality.

ALEXIS DE TOCQUEVILLE

Democracy and socialism have nothing in common but one word: equality. But notice the difference: while democracy seeks equality in liberty, socialism seeks equality in restraint.

WENDELL WILLKIE
An American Program

The Constitution does not provide for first and second class citizens.

JOHN F. KENNEDY
Speech in New York City

In America there must be only citizens, not divided by grade, first and second, but citizens, east, west, north and south.

OWEN WISTER

In the United States "First" and "Second" class can't be painted on railroad cars, for all passengers, being Americans, are equal and it would be "unAmerican." But paint "Pullman" on a car and everyone is satisfied.

THOMAS JEFFERSON
Letter to George Washington

The foundation on which all [our constitutions] are built is the natural equality of man, the denial of every preeminence but that annexed to legal office, and particularly the denial of a preeminence by birth.

GERRIT SMITH
Speech to the House of Representatives

Liberty is meek and reasonable. She admits that she belongs to all—to the high and the low, the rich and the poor, the black and the white—and that she belongs to them all equally.

RALPH WALDO EMERSON
"New England Reformers"

As a man is equal to the Church and equal to the State, so he is equal to every other man.

CHIEF JOSEPH
An Indian's View of Indian Affairs

Treat all men alike. Give them all the same law. Give them all an even chance to live and grow. All men were made by the same Great Spirit Chief. They are all brothers. The earth is the mother of all people, and all people should have equal rights upon it....Whenever the white man treats the Indian as they treat each other, then we will have no more wars. We shall all be alike—brothers of one father and one mother, with one sky above us and one country around us, and one government for all.

HENRY GEORGE
Progress and Poverty

The equal right of all men to the use of land is as clear as their equal right to breathe the air—it is a right proclaimed by the fact of their existence. For we cannot suppose that some men have a right to be in this world, and others no right.

CALVIN COOLIDGE
Speech in Philadelphia

The government of the United States is a device for maintaining in perpetuity the rights of people, with the ultimate extinction of all privileged classes.

Harry S Truman
Speech in Madison, Wisconsin

As a nation we are committed to the principle of freedom because we believe that all men are created equal. Freedom is a relationship between equals.

James Madison
Letter to Jacob De La Motta

Equal laws protecting equal rights are . . . the best guarantee of loyalty and love of country.

Alexander Hamilton
Constitutional Convention speech

There can be no truer principle than this—that every individual of the community at large has an equal right to the protection of government.

Independence Day Speech
Abraham Lincoln

Now, it happens that we meet together once every year, sometime about the 4th of July, for some reason or other. These 4th of July gatherings I suppose have their uses. If you will indulge me, I will state what I suppose to be some of them.

We are now a mighty nation, we are thirty—or about thirty millions of people, and we own and inhabit about one-fifteenth part of the dry land of the whole earth. We run our memory back over the pages of history for about eighty-two years and we discover that we were then a very small people in point of numbers, vastly inferior to what we are now, with a vastly less extent of country,—with vastly less of everything we deem desirable among men,—we look upon the change as exceedingly advantageous to us and to our posterity, and we fix upon something that happened away back, as in some way or other being connected with this rise of prosperity. We find a race of men living in that day whom we claim as our fathers and grandfathers; they were iron men, they fought for the principle that they were contending for; and we understood that by what they then did it has followed that the degree of prosperity that we now enjoy has come to us. We hold this annual celebration to remind ourselves of all the good done in this process of time of how it was done and who did it, and how we are historically connected with it; and we go from these meetings in better humor with ourselves—we feel more attached the one to the other, and more firmly bound to the country we inhabit. In every way we are better men in the age, and race, and country in which we live for these celebrations. But after we have done all this we have not yet reached the whole. There is something else connected with it. We have besides these men—descended by blood from our ancestors—among us perhaps half our people who are not descendants at all of these men, they are men who have come from Europe—German, Irish, French and Scandinavian—men that have come from Europe themselves, or whose ancestors have come hither and settled here, finding themselves our equals in all things. If they look back through this history to trace their connection with those days by blood, they find they have none, they cannot carry themselves back into the glorious epoch and make themselves feel that they are part of us, but when they look through that old Declaration of Independence they find that those old men say that "We hold these truths to be self-evident, that all men are created equal," and then they feel that that moral sentiment taught in that day evidences their relation to those men, that it is the father of all moral principle in them, and that they have a right to claim it as though they were blood of the blood, and flesh of the flesh of the men who wrote that Declaration, and so they are. That is the electric cord in that Declaration that links the hearts of patriotic and liberty-loving men together, that will link those patriotic hearts as long as the love of freedom exists in the minds of men throughout the world.

Now, sirs, for the purpose of squaring things with this idea of "don't care if slavery is voted up or voted down," for sustaining the Dred Scott decision, for holding that the Declaration of Independence did not mean anything at all, we have Judge [Stephen] Douglas giving his exposition of what the Declaration of Independence means, and we have him saying that the people of America are equal to the people of England. According to his construction, you Germans are not connected with it. Now I ask you in all soberness, if all these things, if indulged in, if ratified, if confirmed and endorsed, if taught to our children, and repeated to them, do not tend to rub out the sentiment of liberty in the country, and to transform this Government into a government of some other form. Those arguments that are made, that the inferior race are to be treated with as much allowance as they are capable of enjoying; that as much is to be done for them as their condition will allow. What are these arguments? They are the arguments that kings have made for enslaving the people in all ages of the world. You will find that all the arguments in favor of kingcraft were of this class; they always bestrode the necks of the people, not that they wanted to do it, but because the people were better off for being ridden. That is their argument, and this argument of the Judge is the same old serpent that says you work and I eat, you toil and I will enjoy the fruits of it. Turn in whatever way you will—whether it come from the mouth of a King, an excuse for enslaving the people of his country, or from the mouth of men of one race as a reason for enslaving the men of another race, it is all the same old serpent, and I hold if that course of argumentation that is made for the purpose of convincing the public mind that we should not care about this, should be granted, it does not stop with the Negro. I should like to know if taking this old Declaration of Independence, which declares that all men are equal upon principle, and making exceptions to it, where will it stop. If one man says it does not mean a Negro, why not another say it does not mean some other man? If that declaration is not the truth, let us get the Statute book, in which we find it and tear it out! Who is so bold as to do it? If it is not true let us tear it out! [Cries of "no, no" from the audience] Let us stick to it then, let us stand firmly by it then.

JAMES FORTEN
A Series of Letters by a Man of Color

Has the God who made the white man and the black left any record declaring us a different species? Are we not sustained by the same power, supported by the same wrongs, pleased with the same delights, and propagated by the same means? And should we not then enjoy the same liberty; and be protected by the same laws?

ANDREW JACKSON
Veto of the Bank Bill

Equality of talents, of education, or of wealth cannot be produced by human institutions. In the full enjoyment of the gifts of Heaven and the fruits of superior industry, economy, and virtue every man is equally entitled to protection by law; but when the laws undertake to add to these natural and just artificial distinctions, to grant titles, gratuities, and exclusive privileges, to make the rich richer and the potent more powerful, the humble members of society—the farmers, mechanics, and laborers—who have neither the time nor the means of securing like favors to themselves, have a right to complain of the injustice of their government.

There are no necessary evils in government. Its evils exist only in its abuses. If it would confine itself to equal protection, and, as Heaven does its rains, shower its favors alike on the high and low, the rich and the poor, it would be an unqualified blessing.

WILLIAM HENRY SEWARD
Speech at Rochester, N.Y.

It is a party of one idea; but that is a noble one, an idea that fills and expands all generous souls; the idea of equality, the equality of all men before human tribunals and human laws, as they all are equal before the divine tribunal and divine laws.

HAROLD ICKES
On resigning as U.S. Secretary of the Interior

I'm against government by crony.

DAVID DAVIS
Ex Parte Milligan

The Constitution of the United States is a law for rulers and people, equally in war and peace, and covers with the shield of its protection all classes of men, at all times, and under all circumstances.

BOB DYLAN
"It's Alright Ma (I'm Only Bleeding)"

But even the president of the United States
Sometimes must have
To stand naked.

HOUSE JUDICIARY COMMITTEE
Articles of Impeachment of Richard M. Nixon

ARTICLE I

In his conduct of the office of President of the United States, Richard M. Nixon, in violation of his constitutional oath faithfully to execute the office of President of the United States . . . and in violation of his constitutional duty to take care that the laws be faithfully executed, has prevented, obstructed, and impeded the administration of justice. . . . Richard M. Nixon, using the powers of his high office, engaged personally and through his subordinates and agents in a course of conduct or plan designed to delay, impede, and obstruct the investigation of such unlawful entry; to cover up, conceal and protect those responsible; and to conceal the existence and scope of other unlawful covert activities. . . . In all of this, Richard M. Nixon has acted in a manner contrary to his trust as president and subversive of constitutional government, to the great prejudice of the cause of law and justice and to manifest injury of the people of the United States.

Wherefore Richard M. Nixon, by such conduct, warrants impeachment and trial, and removal from office.

ARTICLE II

Using the powers of the office of President of the United States, Richard M. Nixon . . . has repeatedly engaged in conduct violating the constitutional rights of citizens, impairing the due and proper administration of justice in the conduct of lawful inquiries, or contravening the laws governing agencies of the executive branch. . . .

Wherefore, Richard M. Nixon, by such conduct, warrants impeachment and trial, and removal from office.

ARTICLE III

In his conduct of the office of President of the United States, Richard M. Nixon...has failed without lawful cause or excuse to produce papers and things, as directed by duly authorized subpoenas...and willfully disobeyed such subpoenas...thereby assuming for himself functions and judgments necessary to the exercise of the sole power of impeachment vested by the Constitution in the House of Representatives....

Wherefore, Richard M. Nixon, by such conduct, warrants impeachment and trial, and removal from office.

FINLEY PETER DUNNE
Dissertation by Mr. Dooley

This [is the] home iv opporchunity where ivry man is th' equal iv ivry other man before th' law if he isn't careful.

FOURTEENTH AMENDMENT TO THE CONSTITUTION

Section 1. All persons born or naturalized in the United States and subject to the jurisdiction thereof, are citizens of the United States and of the State wherein they reside. No State shall make or enforce any law which shall abridge the privileges or immunities of citizens of the United States; nor shall any State deprive any person of life, liberty, or property, without due process of law; nor deny to any person within its jurisdiction equal protection of the laws.

Section 2. Representatives shall be apportioned among the several States according to their respective numbers, counting the whole number of persons in each State, excluding Indians not taxed. But when the right to vote at any election for the choice of electors for President and Vice President of the United States, Representatives in Congress, the Executive and Judicial officers of a State, or the members of the Legislature thereof, is denied to any of the male inhabitants of such State, being twenty-one years of age, and citizens of the United States, or in any way abridged except for participation in rebellion, or other crime, the basis of representation therein shall be reduced in the proportion which the number of such male citizens shall bear to the whole number of male citizens twenty-one years in such State.

Section 3. No person shall be a Senator or Representative in Congress, or elector of President and Vice President, or hold any office, civil or military, under the United States, or under any State, who, having previously taken an oath as a member of Congress, or as an officer of the United States, or as a member of any State legislature, or as an executive or judicial officer of any State, to support the Constitution of the United States, shall have engaged in insurrection or rebellion against the same, or given aid or comfort to the enemies thereof. But Congress may by a vote of two-thirds of each House, remove such disability.

Section 4. The validity of the public debt of the United States, authorized by law, including debts incurred for payment of pensions and bounties for services in suppressing insurrection or rebellion, shall not be questioned. But neither the United States nor any State shall assume or pay any debt or obligation incurred in aid of insurrection or rebellions against the United States, or any claim for the loss or emancipation of any slave; but all such debts, obligations and claims shall be held illegal and void.

Section 5. The Congress shall have the power to enforce, by appropriate legislation, the provisions of this article.

ROY WILKINS
Standing Fast

We have tried to create a nation where all men would be equal in the eyes of the law, where all citizens would be judged on their own abilities, not their race....We have believed in our Constitution. We have believed that the Declaration of Independence meant what is said. All my life I have believed in these things, and I will die believing them.

FRANKLIN D. ROOSEVELT
Speech at Worcester, Massachusetts

Inside the polling booth every American man and woman stands as the equal of every other American man and woman. There they have no superiors. There they have no masters save their own minds and consciences.

FIFTEENTH AMENDMENT TO THE CONSTITUTION

Section 1. The right of citizens of the United States to vote shall not be denied or abridged by the United States or by any State on account of race, color, or previous condition of servitude.

Section 2. The Congress shall have power to enforce this article by appropriate legislation.

BOOKER T. WASHINGTON

You can't hold a man down without staying down with him.

RALPH WALDO EMERSON
Essays

If you put a chain around the neck of a slave, the other end fastens itself around your own.

Frederick Douglass
Speech at Washington, D.C.

No man can put a chain about the ankle of his fellow man without at last finding the other end fastened about his own neck.

Robert G. Ingersoll
Prose-Poems and Selections

I am the inferior of any man whose rights I trample under foot.

Pearl S. Buck
What America Means to Me

White people who insist on their own superiority because of the color of the skin they were born with—can there be so empty and false a superiority as this? Who is injured the most by that foolish assumption, the colored or the white? In his soul it is the white man.

William Faulkner
Essays, Speeches & Public Letters

To live anywhere in the world today and to be against equality because of race or color, is like living in Alaska and being against snow.

A. Philip Randolph
March on Washington Movement speech

We must have faith that this society divided by race and class, and subject to profound social pressure, can one day become a nation of equals.

Abraham Lincoln
Letter to H.L. Pierce

This is a world of compensations; and he who be no slave, must consent to have no slave. Those who deny freedom to others, deserve it not for themselves; and, under a just God, cannot long retain it.

ABRAHAM LINCOLN
Speech at the Illinois Republican State Convention

"A house divided by itself cannot stand." I believe this government cannot endure permanently half slave and half free. I do not expect the Union to be dissolved; I do not expect the house to fall, but I do expect it will cease to be divided. It will become all one thing, or all the other.

ABRAHAM LINCOLN
Response to Stephen Douglass, Peoria, Illinois

If the Negro is a man, why then my ancient faith teaches me that "all men are created equal," and that there can be no moral right in connection with one man's making a slave of another.

WILL ROGERS
The Autobiography of Will Rogers

The Lord so constituted everybody that no matter what color you are you require the same amount of nourishment.

A. PHILIP RANDOLPH
March on Washington Movement speech

Equality is the heart and the essence of democracy, freedom, and justice, equality of opportunity in industry, in labor unions, schools and colleges, government, politics, and before the law. There must be no dual standards of justice, no dual rights, privileges, duties, or responsibilities of citizenship. No dual forms of freedom.

"Equal..."
SUPREME COURT JUSTICE JOHN MARSHALL HARLAN
Dissent of Plessy v. Ferguson

The white race deems itself to be the dominant race in this country. And so it is, in prestige, in achievements, in education, in wealth, and in power. So, I doubt not, it will continue to be for all time, if it remains true to its great heritage and holds fast to the principles of constitutional liberty. But in view of the Constitution and in the eye of the law, there is in this country no superior, dominant, ruling class of citizens. There is no caste here. Our Constitution is color-blind, and neither knows nor tolerates classes among citizens. In respect to civil rights, all citizens are equal before the law. The humblest is the peer of the most powerful. The law regards man as man, and takes no account of his surroundings or of his color when his civil rights as guaranteed by the supreme law of the land are involved. It is, therefore, to be regretted that this high tribunal, the final expositor of the fundamental law of the land, has reached the conclusion that it is competent for a State to regulate the enjoyment by citizens of their civil rights solely upon the basis of race.

The destinies of the two races, in this country, are indissolubly linked together, and the interests of both require that the common government of all shall not permit the seeds of race hate to be planted under the sanction of law. What can more certainly arouse race hate, what more certainly create and perpetuate a feeling of distrust between these races, than state enactments, which, in fact, proceed on the ground that colored citizens are so inferior and degraded that they cannot be allowed to sit in public coaches occupied by white citizens? That, as all will admit, is the real meaning of such legislation as was enacted in Louisiana.

The arbitrary separation of citizens, on the basis of race, while they are on a public highway, is a badge of servitude wholly inconsistent with the civil freedom and the equality before the law established by the Constitution. It cannot be justified upon any legal grounds.

If evils will result from the commingling of the two races upon public highways established for the benefit of all, they will be infinitely less than those that will surely come from state legislation regulating the enjoyment of civil rights upon the basis of race. We boast of the freedom enjoyed by our people above all other peoples. But it is difficult to reconcile that boast with a state of the law which, practically, puts the brand of servitude and degradation upon a large class of our fellow-citizens, our equals before the law. The thin disguise of "equal" accommodations for passengers in railroad coaches will not mislead any one, nor atone for the wrong this day done.

PRESIDENT'S COMMITTEE ON CIVIL RIGHTS
To Secure These Rights

To strengthen the right to equality of opportunity, the President's Committee recommends:

1. In general:

The elimination of segregation, based on race, color, creed, or national origin, from American life.

The separate but equal doctrine has failed in three important respects. First, it is inconsistent with the fundamental equalitarianism of the American way of life in that it marks groups with the brand of inferior status. Secondly, where it has been followed, the results have been separate and unequal facilities for minority peoples. Finally, it has kept people apart despite incontrovertible evidence that an environment favorable to civil rights is fostered whenever groups are permitted to live and work together. There is no adequate defense of segregation. . . . We believe that federal funds, supplied by taxpayers all over the nation, must not be used to support or perpetuate the pattern of segregation in education, public housing, public health services, or other public services. . . . A federal Fair Employment Practice Act prohibiting discrimination in private employment should provide both educational machinery and legal sanctions for enforcement purposes.

CHIEF JUSTICE EARL WARREN
Brown v. Board of Education of Topeka

We come then to the question presented: Does segregation of children in public schools solely on the basis of race, even though the physical facilities and other "tangible" factors may be equal, deprive the children of the minority group of equal educational opportunities? We believe it does. . . .

To separate them from others of similar age and qualifications solely because of their race generates a feeling of inferiority as to their status in the community that may affect their hearts and minds in a way unlikely ever to be undone. . . .

We conclude that in the field of public education the doctrine of "separate but equal" has no place. Separate educational facilities are inherently unequal.

"Equal Justice Under Law..."
EARL WARREN
Cooper v. Aaron

Law and order are not to be preserved by depriving the Negro children of their constitutional rights.

The controlling legal principles are plain. The command of the Fourteenth Amendment is that no "State" shall deny any person within its jurisdiction the equal protection of the laws. The prohibitions of the Fourteenth Amendment extend to all action of the State denying equal protection of the laws; whatever the agency of the State taking the action or whatever the guise in which it is taken. In short, the constitutional rights of children not to be discriminated against in school admission on grounds of race or color declared by this Court in the Brown case can neither be nullified openly and directly by the state legislators or state executives or judicial officers, nor nullified indirectly by them through evasive schemes for segregation whether attempted "ingeniously or ingenuously." . . .

Article VI of the Constitution makes the Constitution the "supreme Law of the Land." In 1803, Chief Justice Marshall, speaking for a unanimous Court, referring to the Constitution as "the fundamental paramount of law of the nation," declared in the notable case of Marbury v. Madison, that "It is emphatically the province and duty of the judicial department to say what the law is." This decision declared the basic principle that the federal judiciary is supreme in the exposition of the law of the Constitution, and that principle has ever since been respected by this Court and the Country as a permanent and indispensable feature of our constitutional system. It follows that the interpretation of the Fourteenth Amendment enunciated by this Court in the Brown case is the supreme law of the land, and Article VI of the Constitution makes it of binding effect on the States "any Thing in the Constitution or Laws of any State to the Contrary notwithstanding." Every state legislator and executive and judicial officer is solemnly committed by oath taken pursuant to Article VI, clause three, "to support this Constitution."

No state legislator or executive or judicial officer can war against the Constitution without violating his undertaking to support it.

It is, of course, quite true that the responsibility for public education is primarily the concern of the States, but it is equally true that such responsibilities, like all other state activity, must be exercised consistently with federal constitutional requirements as they apply to state action. The Constitution created a government dedicated to equal justice under the law. The Fourteenth Amendment embodied and emphasized that ideal. State support of segregated schools through any arrangement, management, funds, or property cannot be squared with the Amendment's command that no State shall deny to any person within its jurisdiction the equal protection of the laws. The right of a student not to be segregated on racial grounds in schools so maintained is indeed so fundamental and pervasive that it is embraced in the concept of due process of law.

The basic decision in Brown was unanimously reached by this Court only after the case had been briefed and twice argued and the issues had been given the most serious consideration. Since the first Brown opinion three new Justices have come to the Court. They are at one with the Justices still on the Court who participated in that basic decision as to its correctness, and that decision and the obedience of the States to them, according to the command of the Constitution, are indispensable for the protection of the freedoms guaranteed by our fundamental charter for all of us. Our constitutional ideal of equal justice under law is thus made a living truth.

WHITNEY MOORE YOUNG, JR.
Beyond Racism: Building an Open Society

Black is beautiful when it is a slum kid studying to enter college, when it is a man learning new skills for a new job, or a slum mother battling to give her kids a chance for a better life. But white is beautiful, too, when it helps change society to make our system work for black people also. White is ugly when it oppresses blacks—and so is black ugly when black people exploit other blacks. No race has a monopoly on vice or virtue, and the worth of an individual is not related to the color of his skin.

KATHERINE ANNE PORTER

Nannie, born in slavery, was pleased to think she would not die in it. She was wounded not so much by her state of being as by the word describing it. Emancipation was a sweet word to her. It had not changed her way of living in a single particular, but she was proud of having been able to say to her mistress, "I aim to stay wid you as long as you'll have me." Still, Emancipation had seemed to set right a wrong that stuck in her heart like a thorn. She could not understand why God, Whom she loved, had seen fit to be so hard on a whole race because they had got a certain kind of skin. She talked it over with Miss Sophia Jane. Many times. Miss Sophia Jane was always brisk and opinionated about it: "Nonsense! I tell you, God does not know whether a skin is black or white. He sees only souls. Don't be getting notions, Nannie—of course you're going to heaven."

RALPH ELLISON
Invisible Man

I am an invisible man. No, I am not a spook like those who haunted Edgar Allan Poe; nor am I one of your Hollywood-movie ectoplasms. I am a man of substance, of flesh and bone, fiber and liquids—and I might even be said to possess a mind. I am invisible, understand, simply because people refuse to see me. Like the bodiless heads you sometimes see in circus sideshows, it is as though I have been surrounded by mirrors of hard, distorting glass. When they approach me they see only my surroundings, themselves, or figments of their imagination—indeed, everything and anything except me.

COLIN POWELL

What my color is, is somebody else's problem not mine. People will say, "You're a terrific black general." I'm trying to be the best general I can be.

BERNARD SHAW

I refuse to let my nation's fixation with color deter me from fulfilling myself.

JOSHUA HENRY JONES
By Sanction of Law

I have been taught that color counts for nothing. It is what we are—therefore I forget color. Besides what color am I?

ROY WILKINS
Speech in Gary, Indiana

NAACP strategy will continue, regardless of setbacks, to be one of pressing, on all fronts, in every field of endeavor, and by every productive method for the freedom of the individual to win equality under the Constitution and the Declaration of Independence.

MARY MCLEOD BETHUNE
What the Negro Wants

What does the Negro want? His answer is very simple. He wants only what all other Americans want. He wants opportunity to make real what the Declaration of Independence and the Constitution and the Bill of Rights say, what the Four Freedoms establish. While he knows these ideals are open to no man completely, he wants only his chance to obtain them.

MARK TWAIN
Following the Equator

There are many humorous things in the world, among them the white man's notion that he is less savage than the other savages.

HUBERT H. HUMPHREY
Democratic Convention

I do not believe that there can be any compromise of the guarantees of civil rights which I have mentioned.

In spite of my desire for unanimous agreement on the platform, there are some matters which I think must be stated without qualification. There can be no hedging—no watering down.

There are those who say to you—we are rushing this issue of civil rights. I say we are 172 years late.

There are those who say—this issue of civil rights is an infringement on states' rights. The time has arrived for the Democratic party to get out of the shadow of states' rights and walk forthrightly into the bright sunshine of human rights.

People—human beings—this is the issue of the twentieth century. People—all kinds and all sorts of people—look to America for leadership, for help, for guidance.

My friends—my fellow Democrats—I ask you for a calm consideration of our historic opportunity. Let us forget the evil passions, the blindness of the past. In these times of world economic, political, and spiritual—above all, spiritual—crisis, we cannot—we must not—turn from the path so plainly before us.

The path has already led us through many valleys of the shadow of death. Now is the time to recall those who were left on that path of American freedom.

For all of us here, for the millions who have sent us, for the whole two billion members of the human family—our land is now, more than ever, the last best hope on earth. I know that we can—I know that we shall—begin here the fuller and richer realization of that hope—that promise of a land where all men are free and equal, and each man uses his freedom and equality wisely and well.

PAUL ROBESON
"For Freedom and Peace" *speech*

I've never accepted any inferior role because of my race or color. And by God, I never will.

Letter from Birmingham City Jail
MARTIN LUTHER KING, JR.

(Martin Luther King, Jr., was arrested for participating in a civil rights march in Birmingham, Alabama, in 1963. While serving his sentence a group of liberal white clergymen in Birmingham issued a statement supporting integration but condemning the demonstrations as "extreme measures" that would "incite hatred and violence." This was King's response.)

I am in Birmingham because injustice is here. Just as the prophets of the eighth century B.C. left their villages and carried "thus saith the Lord" far beyond the boundaries of their home towns, and just as the Apostle Paul left his village of Tarsus and carried the gospel of Jesus Christ to the far corners of the Greco-Roman world, so am I compelled to carry the gospel of freedom beyond my own home town. Like Paul, I must constantly respond to the Macedonian call for aid.

Moreover, I am cognizant of the interrelatedness of all communities and states. I cannot sit idly by in Atlanta and not be concerned about what happens in Birmingham. Injustice anywhere is a threat to justice everywhere. We are caught in an inescapable network of mutuality, tied in a single garment of destiny. Whatever affects one directly, affects all indirectly. Never again can we afford to live with the narrow, provincial "outsider agitator" idea. Anyone who lives inside the United States can never be considered an outsider anywhere within its bounds.

You deplore the demonstration taking place in Birmingham. But your statement, I am sorry to say, fails to express a similar concern for the conditions that brought about the demonstrations.

Birmingham is probably the most thoroughly segregated city in the United States. Its ugly record of brutality is widely known. Negroes have experienced grossly unjust treatment in the courts. There have been more unsolved bombings of Negro homes and churches in Birming-ham than in any other city in the nation. These are the hard, brutal facts of the case. On the basis of these conditions, Negro leaders sought to negotiate with the city fathers. But the latter consistently refused to engage in good-faith negotiation.

Then, last September, came the opportunity to talk with leaders of Birmingham's economic community. In the course of the negotiations, certain promises were made by the merchants—for example, to remove the stores' humiliating racial signs. . . . [But a] few signs, briefly removed, returned; the others remained.

As in so many past experiences, our hopes had been blasted, and the shadow of deep disappointment settled upon us. We had no alternative except to prepare for direct action, whereby we would present our very bodies as a means of laying our case before the conscience of the local and the national community. Mindful of the difficulties involved, we decided to undertake a process of self-purification. We began a series of workshops on nonviolence, and we repeatedly asked ourselves: "Are you able to accept blows without retaliating?" "Are you able to endure the ordeal of jail?"

You may well ask: "Why direct action? Why sit-ins, marches and so forth? Isn't negotiation a better path?" You are quite right in calling for negotiation. Indeed, this is the very purpose of direct action. Nonviolent direct action seeks to create such a crisis and foster such a tension that a community which has constantly refused to negotiate is forced to confront the issue. It seeks so to dramatize the issue that it can no longer be ignored. My citing the creation of tension as part of the work of the nonviolent-resister may sound rather shocking. But I must confess that I am not afraid of the word "tension." I have earnestly opposed violent tension, but there is a type of constructive, nonviolent tension which is necessary for growth. Just as Socrates felt that it was necessary to create tension in the mind so that individuals could rise from the bondage of myths and half-truths to the unfettered realm of creative analysis and objective appraisal, so must we see the need for nonviolent gadflies to create the tension in society that will help men rise from the dark depths of prejudice and racism to the majestic heights of understanding and brotherhood.

The purpose of our direct-action program is to create a situation so crisis-packed that it will inevitably open the door to negotiation. I therefore concur with you in your call for negotiation. Too long has our beloved Southland been bogged down in a tragic effort to live in monologue rather than dialogue. . . .

We know through painful experience that freedom is never voluntarily given by the oppressor; it must be demanded by the oppressed. Frankly, I have yet to engage in a direct-action campaign that was "well timed" in the view of those who have not suffered unduly from the disease of segregation. For years now I have heard the word "Wait!" It rings in the ear of every Negro with piercing familiarity. This "Wait" has almost always meant "Never." We must come to see, with one of our distinguished jurists, that "justice too long delayed is justice denied."

We have waited for more than 340 years for our constitutional and God-given rights. The nations of Asia and Africa are moving with jet-like speed toward gaining political independence, but we still creep at horse-and-buggy pace toward gaining a cup of coffee at a lunch counter. Perhaps it is easy for those who have never felt the stinging darts of segregation to say, "Wait." But when you have seen the viscous mobs lynch your mothers and fathers at will and drown your sisters and brothers at whim; when you see the vast majority of your twenty million Negro brothers smothering in an airtight cage of poverty in the midst of an affluent society; when you suddenly find your tongue twisted and your speech stammering as you seek to explain to your six-year-old daughter why she can't go to the public amusement park that has just been advertised on television, and see tears welling up in her eyes when she is told that Funtown is closed to colored children, and see ominous clouds of inferiority beginning to form in her little mental sky, and see her beginning to distort her personality by developing an unconscious bitterness toward white people; when you have to concoct an answer for a five-year-old son who is asking: "Daddy, why do white people treat colored people so mean?"; when you take a cross-country drive and find it necessary to sleep night after night in the uncomfortable corners of your automobile because no motel will accept you; when you are humiliated day in and day out by nagging signs reading "white" and "colored"; when your first name becomes "nigger," your middle name becomes "boy" (however old you are) and your last name becomes "John," and your wife and mother are never given the respected title "Mrs."; when you are harried by day and haunted by night by the fact that you are a Negro, living constantly at tiptoe stance, never quite knowing what to expect next, and are plagued with inner fears and outer resentments; when you are forever fighting a degenerating sense of "nobodiness"—then you will understand why we find it difficult to wait. There comes a time when the cup of endurance runs over, and men are no longer willing to be plunged into the abyss of despair. I hope, sirs, you can understand our legitimate and unavoidable impatience. . . .

Oppressed people cannot remain oppressed forever. The yearning for freedom eventually manifests itself, and that is what has happened to the American Negro. Something within has reminded him of his birthright of freedom, and something without has reminded him that it can be gained. Consciously or unconsciously, he has been caught up by the Zeitgeist, and with his black brothers of Africa and his brown and yellow brothers of Asia, South America and the Caribbean, the United States Negro is moving with a sense of great urgency toward the promised land of racial justice. If one recognizes this vital urge that has engulfed the Negro community, one should readily understand why public demonstrations are taking place. The Negro has many pent-up resentments and latent frustrations, and he must release them. So let him march; let him make prayer pilgrimages to the city hall; let him go on freedom rides— and try to understand why he must do so. If his repressed emotions are not released in nonviolent ways, they will seek expression through violence; this is not a threat but a fact of history. So I have not said to my people: "Get rid of your discontent." Rather, I have tried to say that this normal and healthy discontent can be channeled into the creative outlet of nonviolent direct action. And now this approach is being termed extremist.

But though I was initially disappointed at being categorized as an extremist, as I continued to think about the matter I gradually gained a measure of satisfaction from the label. Was not Jesus an extremist for love: "Love your enemies, bless them that curse you, do good to them that hate you, and pray for them which despitefully use you, and persecute you." Was not Amos an extremist for justice: "Let justice roll down like waters and righteousness like an ever-flowing stream." Was not Paul an extremist for the Christian gospel: "I bear in my body the marks of the Lord Jesus." Was not Martin Luther an extremist: "Here I stand; I cannot do otherwise, so help me God." And John Bunyan: "I will stay in jail to the end of my days before I make a butchery of my conscience." And Abraham Lincoln: "This nation cannot survive half slave and half free." And Thomas Jefferson: "We hold these truths to be self-evident, that all men are created equal. . . ." So the question is not whether we will be extremists, but what kind of extremists we will be. Will we be extremists for hate or for love? Will we be extremists for the preservation of injustice? In that dramatic scene on Calvary's hill three men were crucified. We must never forget that all three were crucified for the same crime—the crime of extremism. Two were extremists for immortality, and thus fell below their environment. The other, Jesus Christ, was an extremist for love, truth and goodness, and thereby rose above his environment. Perhaps the South, the nation and the world are in dire need of creative extremists. . . .

I have no fear about the outcome of our struggle in Birmingham, even if our motives are at present misunderstood. We will reach the goal of freedom in Birmingham and all over the nation, because the goal of America is freedom. Abused and scorned though we may be, our destiny is tied up with America's destiny. Before the pilgrims landed at Plymouth, we were here. Before the pen of Jefferson etched the majestic words of the Declaration of Independence across the pages of history, we were here. For more than two centuries our forebears labored in this country without wages; they made cotton king; they built the homes of their masters while suffering gross injustice and shameful humiliation—and yet out of a bottomless vitality they continued to thrive and develop. If the inexpressible cruelties of slavery could not stop us, the opposition we now face will surely fail. We will win our freedom because the sacred heritage of our nation and the eternal will of God are embodied in our echoing demands. . . .

Over the past few years I have consistently preached that nonviolence demands that the means we use must be as pure as the ends we seek. I have tried to make clear that it is wrong to use immoral means to attain moral ends. But now I must affirm that it is just wrong, or perhaps even more so, to use moral means to preserve immoral ends. . . .

I wish you had commended the Negro sit-inners and demonstrators of Birmingham for their sublime courage, their willingness to suffer and their amazing discipline in the midst of great provocation. One day the South will recognize its real heroes. They will be the James

Merediths, with the noble sense of purpose that enables them to face jeering and hostile mobs, and with the agonizing loneliness that characterizes the life of the pioneer. They will be old, oppressed, battered Negro women, symbolized in a seventy-two-year-old woman in Montgomery, Alabama, who rose up with a sense of dignity and with her people decided not to ride segregated buses, and who responded with ungrammatical profundity to one who inquired about her weariness: "My feets is tired, but my soul is at rest." They will be the young high school and college students, the young ministers of the gospel and a host of their elders, courageously and nonviolently sitting in at lunch counters and willingly going to jail for conscience' sake. One day the South will know that when these disinherited children of God sat down at lunch counters, they were in reality standing up for what is best in the American dream and for the most sacred values in our Judeo-Christian heritage, thereby bringing our nation back to those great wells of democracy which were dug deep by the founding fathers in their formulation of the Constitution and the Declaration of Independence.

If I have said anything in this letter that overstates the truth and indicates an unreasonable impatience, I beg you to forgive me. If I have said anything that understates the truth and indicates my having a patience that allows me to settle for anything less than brotherhood, I beg God to forgive me.

I hope this letter finds you strong in the faith. I also hope that circumstances will soon make it possible for me to meet each of you, not as an integrationist or a civil-rights leader but as a fellow clergyman and a Christian brother. Let us all hope that the dark clouds of racial prejudice will soon pass away and the deep fog of misunderstanding will be lifted from our fear-drenched communities, and in some not too distant tomorrow the radiant stars of love and brotherhood will shine over our great nation with all their scintillating beauty.

ARTHUR ASHE
Letter to his daughter shortly before he died of AIDS

Camera, because of the color of your skin and the fact that you are a girl, not a boy, your credibility and competence will constantly be questioned no matter how educated or wealthy you are. At the same time, your brown skin may bring you a few advantages. You should be wary of them. When the Supreme Court Justice Thurgood Marshall was asked if he should be replaced on retirement from the Court by another African American, he replied emphatically: "No, it should go to the best qualified person the president can find!" That is as it should be.

WILLIAM LLOYD GARRISON
W.P. and F. J.T. Garrison, Volume 1, 1885–1889

Wherever I see a human being, I see God-given rights inherent in that being whatever may be the sex or complexion.

JAMES THURBER

The most frightening study of mankind is man. I think he has failed to run the world, and that Woman must take over if the species is to survive. Almost any century now Woman may lose her patience with black politics and red war and let fly. I wish I could be on earth then to witness the saving of our self-destructive species by its greatest creative force. If I have sometimes seemed to make fun of Woman, I assure you it has only been for the purpose of egging her on.

ELIZABETH CADY STANTON
Letter to Thomas Wentworth Higginson

Our "pathway" is straight to the ballot box, with no variableness nor shadow of turning. . . . We demand in the Reconstruction suffrage for all citizens of the Republic. I would not talk of Negroes or women, but of citizens.

WALT WHITMAN
Starting from Paumanok

And I will show of male and female that either is but the equal of the other.

SUSAN B. ANTHONY
The Revolution

Join the union, girls, and together say Equal Pay for Equal Work.

ALICE STONE BLACKWELL
Woman's Journal, "The Revolt against Matrimony"

There is no greater mistake than the idea that freedom, education and an acquaintance with public questions are prejudicial to feminine virtue. . . . There is not, and never will be, any general "revolt against matrimony" on the part of women. The revolt is against the unjust and unequal conditions in matrimony which have been established by one-sided legislation. That is a revolt which is growing irresistibly, and in which the best men are fighting side by side with the best women. The sooner and the more completely it succeeds, the better it will be both for the individual and for the race.

BETTY FRIEDAN
The Feminine Mystique

A girl should not expect special privileges because of her sex, but neither should she "adjust" to prejudice and discrimination. She must learn to compete then, not as a woman, but as a human being.

ELIZABETH CADY STANTON
First Women's Rights Convention, Seneca Falls, New York

We hold these truths to be self-evident, that all men and women are created equal.

ABIGAIL ADAMS
Letter to John Adams

I long to hear that you have declared an independency—and by the way in the New Code of Laws which I suppose it will be necessary for you to make I desire you would Remember the ladies, and be more generous and favorable to them than your ancestors. Do not put such unlimited power into the hands of the Husbands. Remember all Men would be tyrants if they could. If particular care and attention is not paid to the Ladies we are determined to foment a Rebellion, and will not hold ourselves bound by any laws in which we have no voice, or Representation.

That your Sex are Naturally Tyrannical is a Truth so thoroughly established as to admit of no dispute, but such of you as wish to be happy willingly give up the harsh title of Master for the more tender and endearing one of Friend. Why, then, not put it out of the power of the vicious and the Lawless to use us with cruelty and indignity with impunity. Men of Sense in all Ages abhor those customs which treat us only as the vassals of your Sex. Regard us then as Beings placed by providence under your protection and in imitation of the Supreme Being make use of that power only for our happiness.

ABIGAIL ADAMS
Letter to John Adams

Patriotism in the female sex is the most disinterested of virtues. Excluded from honors and from office, we cannot attach ourselves to the State or Government from having held a place of eminence. Even in the freest countries our property is subject to the control and disposal of partners, to whom the laws have given a sovereign authority. Deprived of a voice in legislation, obliged to submit to those laws which are imposed upon us, is it not sufficient to make us indifferent to the public welfare? Yet all history and every age exhibit instances of patriotic virtue in the female sex; which considering our situation equals the most heroic of yours.

Resolutions on Women's Rights

SENECA FALLS 1848 WOMEN'S RIGHTS CONVENTION

Whereas, The great precept of nature is conceded to be that "man shall pursue his own true and substantial happiness." Blackstone in his Commentaries remarks that this law of nature being coeval with mankind, and dictated by God himself, is of course superior in obligation to any other. It is binding over all the globe, in all countries and at all times; no human laws are of any validity if contrary to this, and such of them as are valid, derive all their force, and all their validity, and all their authority, mediately and immediately, from this original; therefore,

Resolved, That all laws which prevent woman from occupying such a station in society as her conscience shall dictate, or which place her in a position inferior to that of man, are contrary to the great precept of nature, and therefore of no force or authority.

Resolved, That woman is man's equal—was intended to be so by the Creator, and the highest good of the race demands that she should be recognized as such.

Resolved, That the women of this country ought to be enlightened in regard to the laws under which they live, that they may no longer publish their degradation by declaring themselves satisfied with their present position, nor their ignorance by asserting that they have all the rights they want.

Resolved, That inasmuch as man, while claiming for himself intellectual superiority, does accord to woman moral superiority, it is preeminently his duty to encourage her to speak and teach, as she has an opportunity, in all religious assemblies.

Resolved, That the same amount of virtue, delicacy, and refinement of behavior that is required of woman in the social state, should also be required of man, and the same transgressions should be visited with equal severity on both man and woman.

Resolved, That the objection of indelicacy and impropriety, which is so often brought against woman when she addresses a public audience, comes with a very ill-grace from those who encourage, by their attendance, her appearance on the stage, in the concert, or in the feats of the circus.

Resolved, That woman has too long rested satisfied in the circumscribed limits which corrupt customs and a perverted application of the Scriptures have marked out for her, and that it is time she should move in the enlarged sphere which her great Creator has assigned her.

Resolved, That it is the duty of the women of this country to secure to themselves their sacred right to the elective franchise.

Resolved, That the speedy success of our cause depends upon the zealous and untiring efforts of both men and women, for the overthrow of the monopoly of the pulpit, and for the securing to women an equal participation with men in the various trades, professions, and commerce.

Resolved, therefore, That, being invested by the Creator with the same capabilities, and the same consciousness of responsibility for their exercise, it is demonstrably the right and duty of woman, equally with man, to promote every righteous cause by every righteous means; and especially in regard to the great subjects of morals and religion, it is self-evidently her right to participate with her brother in teaching them, both in private and in public, by writing and by speaking, by any instrumentalities proper to be used, and in any assemblies proper to be held; and this being a self-evident truth growing out of the divinely implanted principles of human nature, any custom or authority adverse to it, whether modern or wearing the hoary sanction of antiquity, is to be regarded as a self-evident falsehood, and at war with mankind.

SOJOURNER TRUTH

If women want any rights more'n they got, why don't they just take 'em, and not be talkin' about it.

SOJOURNER TRUTH
A Woman's Rights

Well, children, where there is so much racket there must be something out of kilter. I think that 'twixt the Negroes of the South and the women of the North, all talking about rights, the white men will be in a fix pretty soon. But what's all this here talking about?

That man over there says that women need to be helped into carriages, and lifted over ditches, and to have the best place everywhere. Nobody ever helps me into carriages, or over mud puddles, or gives me any best place! And ain't I a woman? Look at me! Look at my arm. I have plowed and planted, and gathered into barns, and no man could head me! And ain't I a woman? I could work as much and eat as much as a man—when I could get it—and bear the lash as well! And ain't I a woman? I have borne thirteen children, and seen them most all sold off to slavery, and when I cried out with my mother's grief, none but Jesus heard me! And ain't I a woman?

Then they talk about this thing in the head; what's this they call it? [Someone tells her, "intellect."] That's it, honey. What's that got to do with women's rights or Negro's rights? If my cup won't hold but a pint, and yours holds a quart, wouldn't you be mean not to let me have my little half-measure full?

Then that little man in black there, he says women can't have as much rights as men, 'cause Christ wasn't a woman! Where did your Christ come from? Where did your Christ come from? From God and a woman!! Man had nothing to do with him.

If the first woman God ever made was strong enough to turn the world upside down all alone, these women together ought to be able to turn it back, and get it right side up again! And now they is asking to do it, the men better let them.

Obliged to you for hearing me, and now old Sojourner ain't got nothing more to say.

SOJOURNER TRUTH
Address to the Fourth National Women's Right Convention, New York

We'll have our rights; see if we don't; and you can't stop us from them; see if you can. You may hiss as much as you like, but it is comin'. Women don't get half as much rights as they ought to; we want more, and we will have it.

Women's Right to Vote

SUSAN B. ANTHONY

Friends and Fellow Citizens: I stand before you tonight under indictment for the alleged crime of having voted at the last presidential election, without having a lawful right to vote. It shall be my work this evening to prove to you that in thus voting, I not only committed no crime, but, instead, simply exercised my citizen's rights, guaranteed to me and all United States citizens by the National Constitution, beyond the power of any State to deny.

The preamble of the Federal Constitution says:

We the people of the United States, in order to form a more perfect union, establish justice, insure domestic tranquillity, provide for the common defense, promote the general welfare, and secure the blessings of liberty to ourselves and our posterity, do ordain and establish this Constitution for the United States of America.

It was we, the people; not we, the white male citizens; nor yet, we, the male citizens; but we, the whole people, who formed the Union. And we formed it, not to give the blessings of liberty, but to secure them; not to the half of ourselves and the half of our posterity, but to the whole people—women as well as men. And it is a downright mockery to talk to women of their enjoyment of the blessings of liberty while they are denied the use of the only means of securing them provided by this democratic-republican government—the ballot.

For any State to make sex a qualification that must ever result in the disenfranchisement of one entire half of the people is to pass a bill of attainder, or an ex post facto law, and is therefore a violation of the supreme law of the land. By it the blessings of liberty are for ever withheld from women and their female posterity. To them this government has no just powers derived from the consent of the governed. To them this government is not a democracy: It is not a republic. It is an odious aristocracy; a hateful oligarchy of sex: the most hateful aristocracy ever established on the face of the globe. An oligarchy of wealth, where the rich govern the poor; an oligarchy of learning, where the educated govern the ignorant; or even an oligarchy of race, where the Saxon rule the African, might be endured; but this oligarchy of sex, which makes father, brother, husband, sons, the oligarchs over the mother and sisters, the wife and daughters of every household—which ordains all men sovereigns, all women subjects, carries dissension, discord and rebellion into every home of the nation.

Webster, Worcester and Bouvier all define a citizen to be a person in the United States, entitled to vote and hold office.

The only question left to be settled now is: Are women persons? And I hardly believe any of our opponents will have the hardihood to say they are not. Being persons, then, women are citizens; and no State has a right to make any law, or to enforce any old law, that shall abridge their privileges or immunities. Hence, every discrimination against women in the constitutions and laws of the several States is today null and void, precisely as is every one against Negroes.

NINETEENTH AMENDMENT TO THE CONSTITUTION

The right of citizens of the United States to vote shall not be denied or abridged by the United States or by any State on account of sex.

Congress shall have the power to enforce this article by appropriate legislation.

SUSAN FALUDI
Backlash

In place of equal respect, the nation offered women the Miss America beauty pageant, established in 1920—the same year women won the vote.

NATIONAL ORGANIZATION FOR WOMEN
NOW Statement of Purpose

We, men and women who hereby constitute ourselves as the National Organization for Women, believe that the time has come for a new movement toward true equality for all women in America, and toward a fully equal partnership of the sexes, as part of the world-wide revolution of human rights now taking place within and beyond our national borders....

WE REJECT the current assumption that a man must carry the sole burden of supporting himself, his wife, and family, and that a woman is automatically entitled to lifelong support by a man upon her marriage, or that marriage, home and family are primarily women's world and responsibility—hers, to dominate—his, to support. We believe that a true partnership between the sexes demands a different concept of marriage, an equitable sharing of the responsibilities of home and children and of the economic burdens of their support....

IN THE INTERESTS OF THE HUMAN DIGNITY OF WOMEN, we will protest, and endeavor to change, the false image of women now prevalent in the mass media, and in the texts, ceremonies, laws, and practices of the major social institutions. Such images perpetuate contempt for women by society and by women for themselves....WE BELIEVE THAT women will do most to create a new image of women by acting now, and by speaking out in behalf of their own equality, freedom, and human dignity—not in pleas for special privilege, nor in enmity toward men, who are also victims of the current, half-equality between the sexes—but in an active, self-respecting partnership with men.

LOUISA MAY ALCOTT
Rose in Bloom

I believe that it is as much a right and duty for women to do something with their lives as for men and we are not going to be satisfied with such frivolous parts as you give us.

BETTY FRIEDAN
The Feminine Mystique

Who knows what women can be when they are finally free to become themselves? Who knows what women's intelligence will contribute when it can be nourished without denying love? The time is at hand when the voices of the feminine mystique can no longer drown out the inner voice that is driving women on to become complete.

ELEANOR ROOSEVELT

It is disagreeable to take stands. It was always easier to compromise, always easier to let things go. To many women, and I am one of them, it is extraordinarily difficult to care about anything enough to cause disagreement or unpleasant feelings, but I have come to the conclusion that this must be done for a time until we can prove our strength and demand respect for our wishes.

We will be enormously strengthened if we can show that we are willing to fight to the very last ditch for what we believe in.

ELEANOR ROOSEVELT

Where, after all, do universal human rights begin? In small places, close to home—so close and so small they cannot be seen on any maps of the world. Yet they are the world of the individual persons; the neighborhood...; the school or college...; the factory, farm or office.... Such are the places where every man, woman and child seeks equal justice, equal opportunity, equal dignity without discrimination. Unless these rights have meaning there, they have little meaning anywhere. Without concerned citizen action to uphold them close to home, we shall look in vain for progress in the larger world.

ELIZABETH CADY STANTON
The Solitude of Self

The point I wish plainly to bring to you on this occasion is the individuality of each human soul; our Protestant idea, the right of individual conscience and judgment; our republican idea, individual citizenship. In discussing the rights of woman, we are to consider, first what belongs to her as an individual, in a world of her own, the arbiter of her own destiny, an imaginary Robinson Crusoe, with her woman Friday on a solitary island. Her rights under such circumstances are to use all her faculties for her own safety and happiness.

Secondly, if we consider her as a citizen, as a member of a great nation, she must have the same rights as all other members, according to the fundamental principles of our government. Thirdly, viewed as a woman, an equal factor in civilization, her duties are still the same; individual happiness and development....

To throw obstacles in the way of a complete education is like putting out the eyes; to deny the rights of property, like cutting off the hands. To deny political equality is to rob the ostracized of a self-respect; of credit in the market place; of recompense in the world of work; of a voice in [the choice of] those who make and administer the law; a choice in the jury before whom they are tried, and in the judge who decides their punishment.

Address to the American Missionary Association
FREDERICK DOUGLASS

In answer to the question as to what shall be done with the Negro, I have sometimes replied, "Do nothing with him, give him fair play and let him alone." But in reporting me, it has been found convenient and agreeable to place the emphasis of my speech on one part of my sentence. They willingly accepted my idea of letting the Negro alone, but not so my idea of giving the Negro fair play. It has always been easier for some of the American people to imitate the priest and the Levite, rather than the example of the good Samaritan; to let the Negro alone rather than to give him fair play. Even here in New England—the most enlightened and benevolent section of our country—the Negro has been excluded from nearly all profitable employments. I speak from experience. I came here from the South fifty-six years ago, with a good trade in my hands, and might have commanded by my trade three dollars a day, but my white brethren, while praying for their daily bread, were not willing that I should obtain mine by the same means open to them. I was compelled to work for one dollar a day, when others working at my trade were receiving three dollars a day.

But to return. When we consider the long years of slavery, the years of enforced ignorance, the years of injustice, of cruel strifes and degradation to which the Negro was doomed, the duty of the nation is not, and cannot be, performed by simply letting him alone.

If Northern benevolence could send a missionary to a very dark corner of the South, if it could place a church on every hilltop in the South, a schoolhouse in every valley, and support a preacher in the one, and a teacher in the other, for fifty years to come, they could not then even compensate the poor freedmen for the long years of wrong and suffering he has been compelled to endure. The people of the North should remember that slavery and the degradation of the Negro were inflicted by the power of the nation, that the North was a consenting party to the wrong, and that a common sin can only be atoned and condoned by a common repentance.

Under the whole heavens, there never was a people emancipated under conditions more unfavorable to mental, moral and physical improvement than were the slaves of our Southern States. They were emancipated not by the moral judgment of the nation as a whole; they were emancipated not as a blessing for themselves, but as a punishment to their master; not to strengthen the emancipated but to weaken the rebels, and, naturally enough, taking the emancipation in this sense, the old master class have resented it and have resolved to make his freedom a curse rather than a blessing to the Negro. In many instances they have been quite successful in accomplishing this purpose. Then the manner of emancipation was against the Negro. He was turned loose to the open sky without a foot of earth on which to stand; without a single farming implement; he was turned loose to the elements, to hunger, to destitution; without money, without friends; and to endure the pitiless storm of the old master's wrath. The old master had in his possession the land and the power to crush the Negro, and the Negro in return had no power of defense. The difference between his past condition and his present condition is that in the past the old master class could say to him, "You shall work for me or I will whip you to death;" in the present condition he can say to him, "You shall work for me or I will starve you to death." And today the Negro is in this latter condition....

With all the discouraging circumstances that now surround what is improperly called the Negro problem, I do not despair of a better day. It is sometimes said that the condition of the colored man today is worse than it was in the time of slavery. To me this is simply extravagance. We now have the organic law of the land on our side. We have thousands of teachers, and hundreds of thousands of pupils attending schools; we can now count our friends by the million. In many of the States we have elective franchise; in some of them we have colored office-holders. It is no small advantage that we are citizens of this Republic by special amendment of the Constitution. The very resistance that we now meet on Southern railroads, steamboats and hotels is evidence of our progress. It is not the Negro in his degradation that is objected to, but the Negro educated, cultivated and refined. The Negro who fails to respect himself, who makes no provision for himself or his family, and is content to live the life of a vagabond, meets no resistance. He is just where he is desired by his enemies. Perhaps you will say that this proves that education, wealth and refinement will do nothing for the Negro; but the answer to this is, "that the hair of the dog will cure the bite" eventually. All people suddenly springing from a lowly condition have to pass through a period of probation. At first they are denounced as "upstarts," but the "upstarts" of one generation are the elite of the next.

The history of the great Anglo-Saxon race should encourage the Negro to hope on and hope ever, and work on and work ever. They were once the slaves of Normans; they were despised and insulted. They were looked upon as the coarser clay than the haughty Norman. Their language was despised and repudiated, but where today is the haughty Norman? What people and what language now rock the world by their power?

My hope for the Negro is largely based upon his enduring qualities. No persecutions, no proscriptions, no hardships are able to extinguish him. He neither dies out, nor goes out. He is here to stay, and while here he will partake of the blessings of your education, your progress, your civilization, and your Christian religion. His appeal to you today is for an equal chance in the race of life, and dark and stormy as the present appears, his appeal will not go unanswered.

LYNDON B. JOHNSON
Howard University commencement address

Freedom is not enough. You do not wipe away the scars of centuries by saying: Now you are free to go where you want, and do as you desire, and choose the leaders you please. You do not take a person who for years has been hobbled by chains and liberate him, bring him to the starting line of a race and then say, "you are free to compete with all the others," and still justly believe that you have been completely fair. Thus it is not enough just to open the gates of opportunity. All citizens must have the ability to walk through those gates. This is the next and most profound stage of the battle for civil rights. We seek not just legal equity but human stability, not just equality as a right and a theory but equality as a fact and equality as a result.

WHITNEY YOUNG, JR.

The core of the civil rights problem is the matter of achieving equal opportunity for Negroes in the labor market. For it stands to reason that all our other civil rights depend on that one for fulfillment. We cannot afford better education for our children, better housing or medical care unless we have jobs.

Dissenting Argument in San Antonio v. Rodriguez
THURGOOD MARSHALL

In my judgment, the right of every American to an equal start in life, so far as the provision of a state service as important as education is concerned, is far too vital to permit state discrimination on grounds as tenuous as those presented by this record. Nor can I accept the notion that it is sufficient to remit these appellees to the vagaries of the political process which, contrary to the majority's suggestion, has proved singularly unsuited to the task of providing a remedy for this discrimination. I, for one, am unsatisfied with the hope of an ultimate "political" solution sometime in the indefinite future while, in the meantime, countless children unjustifiably receive inferior educations that "may affect their hearts and minds in a way unlikely ever to be undone."

The appellants do not deny the disparities in educational funding caused by the variations in taxable district property wealth. They do contend, however, that whatever the differences in per-pupil spending among Texas districts, there are no discriminatory consequences for the children of the disadvantaged districts. In their view, there is simply no denial of equal educational opportunity to any Texas schoolchildren as a result of the widely varying per-pupil spending.

We sit, however, not to resolve dispute over educational theory but to enforce our Constitution. It is an inescapable fact that if one district has more funds available per pupil than another district, the former will have greater choice in educational planning than will the latter. In this regard, I believe the question of discrimination in educational quality must be deemed to be an objective one that looks to what the State provides its children, not to what the children are able to do with what they receive. Indeed, who can ever measure for a child the opportunities lost and the talents wasted for want of a broader, more enriched education? Discrimination in the opportunity to learn that is afforded a child must be our standard.

In my view, then, it is inequality—not some notion of gross inadequacy—of educational opportunity that raises a question of denial of equal protection of the laws. I find any other approach to the issue unintelligible and without directing principle. Here, appellees have made a substantial showing of wide variations in educational funding and the resulting educational opportunity afforded to the schoolchildren of Texas. This discrimination is, in large measure, attributable to significant disparities in the taxable wealth of local Texas school districts. This is a sufficient showing to raise a substantial question of discriminatory state action in violation of the equal protection clause. Texas has chosen to provide free public education for all its citizens, and it has embodied that decision in its constitution. Yet, having established public education for its citizens, the State, as a direct consequence of the variations in local property wealth endemic to Texas' financing scheme, has provided some Texas schoolchildren with substantially less resources for their education than others. Thus, while on its face the Texas scheme may merely discriminate between local school districts, the impact of that discrimination falls directly upon the children whose educational opportunity is dependent upon where they happen to live. Consequently, the District Court correctly concluded that the Texas financing scheme discriminates from a constitutional perspective, between schoolchildren on the basis of the amount of taxable property located within their local districts. . . .

To support the demonstrated discrimination in the provision of educational opportunity the State has offered a justification which, on analysis, takes on at best an ephemeral character. Thus, I believe that the wide disparities in taxable district property wealth inherent in the local property tax element of the Texas financing scheme render that scheme violative of the Equal Protection Clause.

HORACE MANN
Report to the Massachusetts State Board of Education

Education then, beyond all other devices of human origin, is a great equalizer of the conditions of men,—the balance wheel of the social machinery.

FRANKLIN D. ROOSEVELT
Democratic Convention speech

We stand committed to the proposition that freedom is not a half-and-half affair. If the average citizen is guaranteed equal opportunity in the polling place, he must have equal opportunity in the market place.

RALPH ELLISON
Going to the Territory

The American creed of democratic equality encourages the belief in a second chance that is to be achieved by being born again—and not simply the afterlife, but here and now, on earth.

FRANKLIN D. ROOSEVELT
State of the Union Address

We are fighting, as our fathers have fought, to uphold the doctrine that all men are equal in the sight of God. Those on the other side are striving to destroy this deep belief and to create a world in their own image—a world of tyranny and cruelty and serfdom.

Jimmy Carter
Inaugural address as governor of Georgia

No poor, rural, weak, or black person should ever again have to bear the additional burden of being deprived of the opportunity for an education, a job, or simple justice.

Fourth of July Speech in London
Mark Twain

Mr. Chairman and ladies and gentlemen: I thank you for the compliment which has just been tendered me, and to show my appreciation of it I will not afflict you with many words. It is pleasant to celebrate in this peaceful way, upon this old mother soil, the anniversary of an experiment which was born of war with this same land so long ago, and wrought out to a successful issue by the devotion of our ancestors. It has taken nearly a hundred years to bring the English and Americans into kindly and mutually appreciative relations, but I believe it has been accomplished at last. It was a great step when the two last misunderstandings were settled by arbitration instead of cannon. It is another great step when England adopts our sewing machines without claiming the invention—as usual. It was another when they imported one of our sleeping cars the other day. And it warmed my heart more than I can tell, yesterday, when I witnessed the spectacle of an Englishman ordering an American sherry cobbler of his own free will and accord—and not only that, but with a great brain and level head, reminding the barkeeper not to forget the strawberries. With a common origin, a common literature, a common religion and common drinks, what is longer needful to the cementing of the two nations together in a permanent bond of brotherhood?

This is an age of progress, and ours is a progressive land. A great and glorious land, too—a land which has developed a Washington, a Franklin, a William M. Tweed, a Longfellow, a Motley, a Jay Gould, a Samuel C. Pomeroy, a recent Congress which has never had its equal—(in some respects) and a United States Army which conquered sixty Indians in eight months by tiring them out—which is much better than uncivilized slaughter, God knows. We have a criminal jury system which is superior to any in the world; and its efficiency is only marred by the difficulty of finding twelve men every day who don't know anything and can't read. And I may observe that we have an insanity plea that would have saved Cain. I think I can say, and say with pride, that we have some legislatures that bring higher prices than any in the world.

I refer with effusion to our railway system, which consents to let us live, though it might do the opposite, being our owners. It only destroyed 3,700 lives last year by collisions and 27,260 by running over heedless and unnecessary people at crossings. The companies seriously regretted the killing of these 30,000 people, and went so far as to pay for some of them—

voluntarily, of course, for the meanest of us would not claim that we possess a court treacherous enough to enforce a law against a railway company. But thank heaven the railway companies are generally disposed to do the right and kindly thing without compulsion. I know of an instance which greatly touched me at the time. After an accident the company sent home the remains of a dear, distant old relative of mine in a basket, with the remark, "Please state what figure you hold him at—and return the basket." Now there couldn't be anything friendlier than that.

But I must not stand here and brag all night. However, you won't mind a body bragging a little about his country on the Fourth of July. It is a fair and legitimate time to fly the eagle. I will say only one more word of brag—and a hopeful one. It is this. We have a form of government which gives each man a fair chance and no favor. With us no individual is born with a right to look down upon his neighbor and hold him in contempt. Let such of us as are not dukes find our consolation in that. And we may find hope for the future in the fact that as unhappy as is the condition of our political morality today, England has risen up out of a far fouler since the days when Charles II ennobled courtesans and all political place was a matter of bargain and sale. Be sure there is hope for us yet.

ALLEN SANGREE
New York World

A tonic, an exercise, baseball is second only to Death as a leveler. So long as it remains our national game, America will abide no monarchy, and anarchy will be too slow.

Baseball: Our Game, A Model Institution

JOHN THORN

Father Chadwick had been typically prescient when he wrote in 1876, the inaugural year of the National League and the centenary of America's birth:

"What Cricket is to an Englishman, Base-Ball has become to an American. . . . On the Cricket-field—and there only—the Peer and the Peasant meet on equal terms; the possession of courage, nerve, judgment, skill, endurance and activity alone giving the palm of superiority. In face, a more democratic institution does not exist in Europe than this self-same Cricket; and as regards its popularity, the records of the thousands of Commoners, Divines and Lawyers, Legislators and Artisans, and Literateurs, as well as Mechanics and Laborers, show how great a hold it has on the people. If this is the characteristic of Cricket in aristocratic and monarchical England, how much more will the same characteristics mark Base-Ball in democratic and republican America."

Chadwick's vision of baseball as a model democratic institution would have to wait for the turn of the century to be fully articulated, and for Jackie Robinson and Branch Rickey to be fully realized. But Chadwick's belief that baseball could be more than a game, could become a model of and for American life, presaged baseball's golden age of 1903 to 1930....

Baseball mania seized America [after 1901] as new heroes like Christy Mathewson, Honus Wagner, Ty Cobb, Walter Johnson, and Nap Lajoie found a public hungry for knowledge of their every action, their every thought. A fan's affiliation with his team could exceed in vigor his attachment to his church, his trade, his political party—all but family and country, and even these were wrapped up in baseball. The national pastime became the great repository of national ideals, the symbol of all that was good in American life: fair play (sportsmanship); the rule of law (objective arbitration of disputes); equal opportunity (each side has its innings); the brotherhood of man (bleacher harmony); and more.

The baseball boom of the early twentieth century built on the game's simple charms of exercise and communal celebration, adding the psychological and social complexities of vicarious play: civic pride, role models, and hero worship. It became routine for the President to throw out the first ball of the season. Supreme Court Justices had inning-by-inning scores from the World Series relayed to their chamber. Business leaders, perhaps disingenuously, praised baseball as a model of competition and fair play. "Baseball," opined a writer of *American Magazine* in 1913, "has given our public a fine lesson in commercial morals.... Some day all business will be reorganized and conducted by baseball standards."

Leaders of recent immigrant groups advised their peoples to learn the national game if they wanted to become Americans, and foreign-language newspapers devoted space to educating their readers about America's strange and wonderful game. (New York's *Staats-Zeitung*, for example, applauded Kraftiges Schlagen—hard-hitting—and cautioned German fans not to kill the Unparteiischer.) As historian Harold Seymour wrote, "The argot of baseball supplied a common means of communication and strengthened the bond which the game helped to establish among those sorely in need of it—the mass of urban dwellers and immigrants living in the anonymity and impersonal vortex of large industrial cities...With the loss of traditional ties known in a rural society, baseball gave to many the feeling of belonging." And rooting for a baseball team permitted city folk, newcomers and native-born, the sense of pride in community that in former times—when they may have lived in small towns—was commonplace.

Thus baseball offered a model of how to be an American, to be part of the team: Baseball was "second only to death as a leveler," wrote essayist Allan Sangree. Even in those horrifically leveling years of 1941–45, when so many of our bravest and best gave their lives to defend American ideals, baseball's role as a vital enterprise was confirmed by President Franklin Delano Roosevelt's "green light" for continued play. Many of baseball's finest players—Ted Williams, Joe DiMaggio, Hank Greenberg, Bob Feller, to name a few—swapped their baseball gear for Uncle Sam's, and served with military distinction or helped to boost the nation's morale. Even old-timers like Babe Ruth, Walter Johnson, and Ty Cobb donned uniforms, as they staged exhibitions on behalf of war bonds. Servicemen overseas looked to letters from home and the box scores in The Sporting News to keep them in touch with what they had left behind, and what they were fighting for—an American way of life that was a beacon for a world in which the light of freedom had been nearly extinguished.

I was one of the countless immigrants who from the 1960s on saw baseball as the "open sesame" to the door of their adopted land. A Polish Jew born in occupied Germany to Holocaust survivors, I arrived on these shores at age two. After checking in at Ellis Island, I happened to chance to spend the first night in my new land in the no-longer-elegant hotel where in 1876 the National League had been founded. I learned to read by studying the backs of Topps baseball cards, and to be an American by attaching myself passionately to the Brooklyn Dodgers (who also taught me about the fickleness of love).

The Brooklyn Dodgers, in the persons particularly of Rickey and Robinson, also taught America a lesson: that baseball's integrative and democratic models, by the 1940s long held to be verities, were hollow at the core.

David Halberstam has written:

. . . it was part of our folklore, basic to our national democratic myth, that sports was the great American equalizer, that money and social status did not matter upon the playing fields. Elsewhere life was assumed to be unfair: those who had privilege passed it on to their children, who in turn had easier, softer lives. Those without privilege were doomed to accept the essential injustices of daily life. But according to the American myth, in sports the poor but honest kid from across the tracks could gain (often in competition with richer, snottier kids) recognition and acclaim for his talents.

Until October 23, 1945, when Robinson signed a contract to play for the Montreal Royals, Brooklyn's top farm club, the myth as far as African Americans were concerned was not a sustaining legend but a mere falsehood.

Rickey's rectitude and Robinson's courage have become central parables of baseball and America, exemplars of decency and strength that inspire all of us. Their "great experiment" came too late for such heroes of black ball as Josh Gibson and Oscar Charleston and Ray Dandridge, but its success has been complete. Once the integrative or leveling model of baseball —all America playing and working in harmony—was extended to African Americans, the effect on the nation was profound. Eighty years after the Civil War, America had proved itself unable to practice the values for which it was fought; baseball showed the way. This is what Commissioner Ford Frick said to the St. Louis Cardinals, rumored to be planning a strike in May 1947:

If you do this you will be suspended from the league. You will find that the friends you think you have in the press box will not support you, that you will be outcasts. I do not care if half the league strikes. Those who do it will encounter quick retribution. They will be suspended and I don't care if it wrecks the National League for five years. This is the United States of America, and one citizen has as much right to play as another. The National League will go down the line with Robinson whatever the consequence.

As Monte Irvin said, "Baseball has done more to move America in the right direction than all the professional patriots with their billions of cheap words." The Supreme Court decision of Brown v. Topeka Board of Education; civil rights heroes like Martin Luther King, Jr., James Meredith, Thurgood Marshall, and others; the freedom marches and the voting rights act—all were vital to America's progress toward unity, but the title of one of Jackie Robinson's books may not overstate the case: Baseball Has Done It.

A final way in which baseball supplies models for America is one that has been present from the game's beginning: a model for children wishing to be grownups, wrestling with their insecurities and wondering, What does it mean to be a man? What does a man do? (Most of us old boys occasionally wonder this as well.) The answers in baseball, at least, are unequivocal; as Satchel Paige said in his later years, "I loved baseball. There wasn't no 'maybe so' about it."

Baseball gives children a sense of how wide the world is, in its possibilities but also in its geography. Reading the summations of minor-league ball in The Sporting News each week piqued the curiosity of baseball-ma boys like me: where were Kokomo and Mattoon and Thibodeaux and Nogales? How did people behave in Salinas or Rocky Mount? What did they eat in Artesia? How many exciting places, exotic places this enormous country contained! But a note of comfort—they couldn't be all that strange if baseball was played there.

And to that other vast *terra incognita*—the world of adults—baseball also offered a talk with adults, principally their fathers, by nodding wisely at an assessment of a shortstop's range or a pitcher's heart, and mock—confidently venturing an opinion about the hometown team's chances? Our dads are our first heroes (and, decades later, our last); but in between, baseball players are what we want to be. For heroes are larger than life, and when as adults we have taken the measure of ourselves and found we are no more than life-size, and on our bad days seemingly less than that, baseball can puff us up a bit.

Douglass Wallop put it nicely:

"... only yesterday the fan was a kid of nine or ten bolting his breakfast on Saturday morning and hurtling from the house with a glove buttoned over his belt and a bat over his shoulder, rushing to the nearest vacant lot, perhaps the nearest alley, where the other guys were gathering, a place where it would always be spring. For him, baseball would always have the sound and look and smell of that morning or other mornings just like it. Only by an accident of chance would he find himself, in the years to come, up in the grandstand, looking on. But for a quirk of fate, he himself would be down on that field; it would be his likeness on the television screen and his name in the newspaper high on the list of .300 hitters. He was a fan, but a fan only incidentally. He was, first and always, himself a baseball player."

Crown Thy Good With Brotherhood

"To Replace Violence...With an Effort to Understand..."

ROBERT F. KENNEDY

Speech delivered upon the death of Martin Luther King, Jr.

I have bad news for you, for all of our fellow citizens, and people who love peace all over the world, and that is that Martin Luther King was shot and killed tonight.

Martin Luther King dedicated his life to love and to justice for his fellow human beings, and he died because of that effort.

In this difficult day, in this difficult time for the United States, it is perhaps well to ask what kind of nation we are and what direction we want to move in. For those of you who are black —considering the evidence there evidently is that there were white people who were responsible—you can be filled with bitterness, with hatred, and a desire for revenge. We can move in that direction as a country, in great polarization—black people amongst black, white people amongst white, filled with hatred toward one another.

Or we can make an effort, as Martin Luther King did, to understand and to comprehend, and to replace that violence, that stain of bloodshed that has spread across our land, with an effort to understand with compassion and love.

For those of you who are black and are tempted to be filled with hatred and distrust at the injustice of such an act, against all white people, I can only say that I feel in my own heart the same kind of feeling. I had a member of my family killed, but he was killed by a white man. But we have to make an effort in the United States, we have to make an effort to understand, to go beyond these rather difficult times.

My favorite poet was Aeschylus. He wrote, "In our sleep, pain which cannot forget falls drop by drop upon the heart until, in our own despair, against our will, comes wisdom through the awful grace of God."

What we need in the United States is not division; what we need in the United States is not hatred; what we need in the United States is not violence or lawlessness but love and wisdom, and compassion toward one another, and a feeling of justice towards those who still suffer within our country, whether they be white or they be black.

So I shall ask you tonight to return home, to say a prayer for the family of Martin Luther King, that's true, but more importantly to say a prayer for our own country, which all of us love —a prayer for understanding and that compassion of which I spoke.

We can do well in this country. We will have difficult times. We've had difficult times in the past. We will have difficult times in the future. It is not the end of violence; it is not the end of lawlessness; it is not the end of disorder.

But the vast majority of white people and the vast majority of black people in this country want to live together, want to improve the quality of our life, and want justice for all human beings who abide in our land.

Let us dedicate ourselves to what the Greeks wrote so many years ago: to tame the savageness of man, to make gentle the life of this world.

Let us dedicate ourselves to that, and say a prayer for all our country and for our people.

MAX LERNER
"The United States as Exclusive Hotel"

America is a passionate idea or it is nothing. America is a human brotherhood or it is chaos.

MARTIN LUTHER KING, JR.
"The American Dream" *speech at Oxford, Pennsylvania*

America is essentially a dream, a dream as yet unfulfilled. It is a dream of a land where men of all races, of all nationalities and of all creeds can live together as brothers.

MARTIN LUTHER KING, JR.
Strength to Love

The good neighbor looks beyond the external accidents and discerns those inner qualities that make all men human and, therefore, brothers.

LYNDON B. JOHNSON

The world has narrowed to a neighborhood before it has broadened to a brotherhood.

LYNDON B. JOHNSON
News conference in Johnson City, Texas

As man increases his knowledge of the heavens, why should he fear the unknown of earth? As man draws near to the stars, why should he not also draw nearer to his neighbor?

ALBERT SCHWEITZER
On receiving the Nobel Prize

You don't live in the world all alone. Your brothers are here too.

MALCOLM X
Speech in Paris

A man has to act like a brother before you can call him a brother.

BETTY SHABAZZ
Voices of Freedom

What should be remembered about Malcolm [X] is his love of humanity, his willingness to work. He stressed the fact that our young people—all young people, not just blacks—need to accept the responsibility to do what is best to salvage civilization. . . . Surely people of goodwill can come together to salvage the world.

QUINCY JONES
To participants in the song "We Are the World"

Check your ego at the door.

WILL ROGERS

There ain't nothing but one thing wrong with every one of us, and that's selfishness.

BENJAMIN FRANKLIN

A man wrapped up in himself makes a very small bundle.

W.H. AUDEN

There is no such thing as the State
And no one exists alone;
Hunger allows no choice
To the citizen or the police;
We must love one another or die.

HENRY DAVID THOREAU
Letter to Mrs. E. Castleton

Nothing makes the earth seem so spacious as to have friends at a distance; they make the latitudes and longitudes.

HENRY DAVID THOREAU

A man cannot be said to succeed in this life who does not satisfy one friend.

WHOOPI GOLDBERG

If you don't look out for others, who will look out for you?

TENNESSEE WILLIAMS
A Streetcar Named Desire

I have always depended on the kindness of strangers.

CARTER G. WOODSON
The Story of the Negro Retold

History is a record of the progress of mankind rather than of racial or national achievements.

PRINCE HALL

He that despises a black man for the sake of his color, reproacheth his Maker.

WOODROW WILSON
Speech in St. Paul, Minnesota

There are a great many hyphens left in America. For my part, I think the most un-American thing in the world is a hyphen.

GEORGE WASHINGTON
Farewell Address

The name of American, which belongs to you, in your national capacity, must always exalt the just pride of patriotism, more than any appellation derived from local discriminations. . . . You have in a common cause fought and triumphed together. The independence and liberty you possess are the work of joint councils and joint efforts, of common dangers, suffering.

ABRAHAM LINCOLN
Inaugural Address

I am loath to close. We are not enemies but friends. We must not be enemies. Though passion may have strained, it must not break our bonds of affection. The mystic chords of memory, stretching from every battlefield and patriot grave to every living heart and hearthstone all over this broad land, will yet swell the chorus of the Union, when again touched, as surely they will be, by the better angels of our nature.

CARL SANDBURG
Excerpt from "Timesweep"

There is only one horse on the earth
and his name is All Horses.
There is only one bird in the air
and his name is All Wings.
There is only one fish in the sea
and his name is All Fins.
There is only one man in the world
and his name is All Men.
There is only one woman in the world
and her name is All Women.
There is only one child in the world
and the child's name is All Children.

    There is only one maker in the world
    and His children cover the earth
    and they are named All God's Children.

WENDELL WILLKIE
One World

Freedom is an indivisible word. If we want to enjoy it, and fight for it, we must be prepared to extend it to everyone, whether they are rich or poor, whether they agree with us or not, no matter what their race or the color of their skin.

HENRY WADSWORTH LONGFELLOW
"The Great Metropolis"

I have an affection for a great city. I feel safe in the neighborhood of man, and enjoy the sweet security of streets.

HENRY WADSWORTH LONGFELLOW

To say the least, a town life makes one more tolerant and liberal in one's judgment of others.

WALT WHITMAN
Leaves of Grass

A great city is that which has the greatest men and women.

ROBERT FROST
"The Star-Splitter"

To be social is to be forgiving.

GEORGE SANTAYANA
Materialism and Idealism

In his affections the American is seldom passionate, often deep, and always kindly. If it were given to me to look into the depths of a man's heart, and I did not find goodwill at the bottom, I should say without any hesitation, You are not an American. But as the American is an individualist his goodwill is not officious. His instinct is to think well of everybody, and to wish everybody well, but in a spirit of rough comradeship, expecting every man to stand on his own legs and to be helpful in his turn.

HENRY DAVID THOREAU

Between whom there is hearty truth, there is love.

MARGARET MEAD
Sex and Temperament in Three Primitive Societies

If we are to achieve a richer culture, rich in contrasting values, we must recognize the whole gamut of human potentialities, and so weave a less arbitrary social fabric, one in which each diverse human gift will find a fitting place.

OLIVER WENDELL HOLMES
Voyage of the Good Ship Union

One flag, one land, one heart, one hand, One Nation, evermore!

JOHN F. KENNEDY
Speech in Washington, D. C.

Our most basic common link is that we all inhabit this planet. We all breathe the same air. We all cherish our children's future. And we are all mortal.

HERMAN MELVILLE

We cannot live for ourselves alone. Our lives are connected by a thousand invisible threads, and along these sympathetic fibers, our actions run as causes and return to us as results.

CALVIN COOLIDGE
Republican Convention speech

This commonwealth is one. We are all members of one body. The welfare of the weakest and welfare of the most powerful are inseparably bound together. Industry cannot prosper if manufacturers decline. The general welfare cannot be provided for in any one act, but it is well to remember that the benefit of one is the benefit of all, and the neglect of one is the neglect of all. The suspension of one man's dividends is the suspension of another man's pay envelope.

ROBERT FROST
"The Tuft of Flowers"

"Men work together," I told him from the heart,
"Whether they work together or apart."

The American Standard

BOOKER T. WASHINGTON
Harvard alumni dinner

Mr. President and Gentlemen:

It would in some measure relieve my embarrassment if I could, even in a slight degree, feel myself worthy of the great honor which you do me today. Why you have called me from the Black Belt of the South, from among my humble people, to share in the honors of this occasion, is not for me to explain; and yet it may not be inappropriate for me to suggest that it seems to me that one of the most vital questions that touch our American life, is how to bring the strong, wealthy, and learned into helpful touch with the poorest, most ignorant, and humble, and at the same time make the one appreciate the vitalizing, strengthening influence of the other. How shall we make the mansions on yon Beacon Street feel and see the need of the spirits in the lowliest cabin in Alabama cotton fields or Louisiana sugar bottoms? This problem Harvard University is solving, not by bringing itself down, but by bringing the masses up.

If through me, a humble representative, seven millions of my people in the South might be permitted to send a message to Harvard—Harvard that offered up on death's altar, young Shaw, and Russell, and Lowell and scores of others, that we might have a free and united country—that message would be, "Tell them that the sacrifice was not in vain. Tell them that by the way of the shop, the field, the skilled hand, habits of thrift and economy, by way of industrial school and college, we are coming. We are crawling up, working up, yea, bursting up. Often through oppression, unjust discrimination, and prejudice, but through them we are coming up, and with proper habits, intelligence, and property, there is no power on earth that can permanently stay our progress."

If my life in the past has meant anything in the lifting up of my people and the bringing about of better relations between your race and mine, I assure you from this day it will mean doubly more. In the economy of God, there is but one standard by which an individual can succeed—there is but one for a race. This country demands that every race measure itself by the American standard. By it a race must rise or fall, succeed or fail, and in the last analysis mere sentiment counts for little. During the next half century and more, my race must continue passing through the severe American crucible. We are to be tested in our patience, our forbearance, our perseverance, our power to endure wrong, to withstand temptations, to economize, to acquire and use skill; our ability to compete, to succeed in commerce, to disregard the superficial for the real, the appearance for the substance, to be great and yet small, learned and yet simple, high and yet the servant of all. This, this is the passport to all that is best in the life of our Republic, and the Negro must possess it, or be debarred.

While we are thus being tested, I beg of you to remember that wherever our life touches yours, we help or hinder. Wherever your life touches ours, you make us stronger or weaker. No member of your race in any part of our country can harm the meanest member of mine, without the proudest and bluest blood in Massachusets being degraded. When Mississippi commits a crime, New England commits a crime, and in so much lowers the standard of your civilization. There is no escape—man drags man down, or man lifts man up.

In working out our destiny, while the main burden and center of activity must be with us, we shall need in a large measure in the years that are to come as we have in the past, the help, the encouragement, the guidance that the strong can give the weak. Thus helped, we of both races in the South soon shall throw off the shackles of racial and sectional prejudices and rise as Harvard University has risen and as we all should rise, above the clouds of ignorance, narrowness, and selfishness, into that atmosphere, that pure sunshine, where it will be our highest ambition to serve man, our brother regardless of race or previous condition.

MARIO CUOMO
Democratic National Convention speech

We believe we must be the family of America, recognizing that at the heart of the matter we are bound to one another.

LANGSTON HUGHES
Simple Speaks His Mind

Everybody should take each other as they are, white, black, Indians, Creole. Then there would be no prejudice, nations would get along.

JESSE JACKSON
Democratic Convention speech

Our flag is red, white, and blue, but our nation is a rainbow—red, yellow, brown, black, and white—we're all precious in God's sight. America is not like a blanket—one piece of unbroken cloth, the same color, the same texture, the same size, America is more like a quilt—many patches, many pieces, many colors, many sizes, all woven and held together by a common thread.

FRANKLIN D. ROOSEVELT
Campaign speech

We are a nation of many nationalities, many races, many religions—bound together by a single unity, the unity of freedom and equality. Whoever seeks to set one nationality against another, seeks to degrade all nationalities. Whoever seeks to set one race against another seeks to enslave all races. Whoever seeks to set one religion against another seeks to destroy all religions. I am fighting for a free America—for a country in which all men and women have equal rights to liberty and justice. I am fighting, as I always have fought, for the rights of the little man as well as the big man—for the weak as well as the strong, for those who are helpless as well as those who can help themselves.

PEARL BAILEY
Hurry Up, America, and Spit

In America, we have people who are too rich, people who are too poor, people who are hungry, people who are sick, people who are homeless, people who are imprisoned, people who are bored, people who are strung-out, people who are lonely, people who are exploited, people who lose and can't find their way, people who give up on life. America, we better live as sisters and brothers. Let us take care of our land.

HERBERT HOOVER

Modern society cannot survive with the defense of Cain, "Am I my brother's keeper?"

MARTIN LUTHER KING, JR.
Where Do We Go From Here?

All life is interrelated. The agony of the poor impoverishes the rich; the betterment of the poor enriches the rich. We are inevitably our brother's keeper because we are our brother's brother. Whatever affects one directly affects all indirectly.

JAMES BALDWIN
"Why I Left America"

I was the older brother. And when I was growing up I didn't like all those brothers and sisters. No kid likes to be the oldest.... But when they turn to you for help—what can you do?... [T]hey kept me so busy caring for them ... that I had no time ... to become a junkie or an alcoholic.

EUGENE DEBS
Address before being sentenced for his opposition to World War I

Your Honor, years ago I recognized my kinship with all living beings, and I made up my mind that I was not one bit better than the meanest on earth. I said then, and I say now, that while there is a lower class, I am in it; while there is a criminal element, I am of it; and while there is a soul in prison, I am not free.

E.B. WHITE
One Man's Meat

A "fraternity" is the antithesis of fraternity. The first (that is, the order of organization) is predicated on the idea of exclusion; the second (that is, the abstract thing) is based on the feeling of total equality.

ADAM CLAYTON POWELL, JR.
Speech at Liberty Hall, Philadelphia

That crack of hatred, prejudice, and man's inhumanity to man. There is not metal in the world nor skill of an artisan which can weld this bell together so there will be no crack and its tone will be true—the summons to pure freedom. That crack will only be closed by the unity of blacks and whites.

ROBERT PURVIS
Appeal of 40,000 Citizens

It is the safeguard of the strongest that he lives under a government which is obliged to respect the voice of the weakest. When you have taken from an individual his right to vote, you have made the government, in regard to him, a mere despotism; and you have taken a step towards making it a despotism to all....We love our native country, much as it has wronged us: and in the peaceable exercise of our inalienable rights, we will cling to it...Will you starve our patriotism? Will you cast our hearts out of the treasure of the commonwealth? Do you count our enmity better than our friendship?

THOMAS PAINE
The Age of Reason

I believe in one God and no more, and I hope for happiness beyond this life. I believe in the equality of man; and I believe that religious duties consist in doing justice, loving mercy, and endeavoring to make our fellow creatures happy.

JOHN F. KENNEDY
Loyola College speech

Let us not seek the Republican answer or the Democratic answer, but the right answer. Let us not seek to fix the blame for the past. Let us accept our own responsibility for the future.

JOHN F. KENNEDY
Inaugural Address

In the long history of the world, only a few generations have been granted the role of defending freedom in its hour of maximum danger. I do not shrink from this responsibility—I welcome it. I do not believe that any of us would exchange places with any other people or any other generation. The energy, the faith, the devotion which we bring to this endeavor will light our country and all who serve it—and the glow from that fire can truly light the world.

And so, my fellow Americans: Ask not what your country can do for you—ask what you can do for your country.

CARL SAGAN AND ANN DRUYAN
Speech during the 125th anniversary of the Battle of Gettysburg

The real triumph of Gettysburg was not, I think, in 1863 but in 1913, when the surviving veterans, the remnants of the adversary forces, the Blue and the Gray, met in celebration and solemn memorial. It had been the war that set brother against brother, and when the time came to remember, on the fiftieth anniversary of the battle, the survivors fell, sobbing, into one another's arms. They could not help themselves.

It is time now for us to emulate them, NATO and the Warsaw Pact, Israelis and Palestinians, whites and blacks, Americans and Iranians, the developed and the underdeveloped worlds.

We need more than anniversary sentimentalism and holiday piety and patriotism. Where necessary, we must confront and challenge conventional wisdom. It is time to learn from those who fell here. Our challenge is to reconcile, not after the carnage and the mass murder, but instead of the carnage and the mass murder.

It is time to act.

PETER DE VRIES
The Glory of the Hummingbird

We must love one another, yes, yes, that's all true enough, but nothing says we have to like each other.

BOOKER T. WASHINGTON
Atlanta International Exposition address

To those of my race who underestimate the importance of cultivating friendly relations with the Southern white man, who is their next door neighbor, I would say, "Cast down your bucket where you are and cast it down in making friends in every manly way of the people of all races by whom we are surrounded."

MARTIN LUTHER KING, JR.
Strength to Love

Life at its best is a coherent triangle. At one angle is the individual person. At the other angle are other persons. At the tiptop is the Infinite Person, God. Without the development of each part of the triangle, no life can be complete.

JOSEPHINE BAKER

My ideal is so simple, yet so many people view it as a crazy dream. Surely the day will come when color means nothing more than skin tone; when religion is seen uniquely as a way to speak one's soul; when birthplaces have the weight of the dice and all men are born free; when understanding breeds love and brotherhood.

Christmas Message

ALABAMA GOVERNOR JAMES FOLSOM

I am happy to have this opportunity to talk to the people of Alabama on Christmas Day. This is the greatest day, the most revered day, of our entire calendar. It is the birthday of Christ, who was the greatest humanitarian the world has ever known.

This is a day to talk about loving our neighbors, lending help to the less fortunate, and bringing joy to others by good work.

We set aside Thanksgiving Day to honor the Almighty's bountifulness to us; we celebrate the Fourth of July, which marks the freedom of our country; but on Christmas Day we pay tribute for the freedom of our souls.

It is great to live in America, with all of its plenty and bounty—yet it behooves us not to forget that we are the most blessed people on earth. And to remember that with that greatness goes a like share of responsibility.

The world looks to America today for leadership, for physical relief, for spiritual uplifting. These things we must provide if we are to retain our position of greatness. Because, like the foolish and wise virgins, those who have and use not, from their possessions shall be taken away. They will wither away because they are not used.

This nation has prospered in many and magnificent ways, and it has done so under the freedom of a democratic government, a government in which the people retain the final source of power through their exercise of the ballot.

The very foundation of democracy itself rests upon Christianity, upon the principles set forth by Christ himself. And I believe that it is no mere speculation to say that, without a government which guaranteed the freedom of religious worship, this nation would never have become the great America which it is today.

So often in our democracy we have failed to make the most of the very weapons itself—that is, providing a human, decent way of life for all of our people.

Under the extensive freedom of a democratic country, there emerges a pattern of life which creates economic barriers among the people. And as a democracy grows in years and expansiveness, there comes about a controlling minority group. That group controls because through the advantages and opportunities it obtains great portions of wealth. Wealth means power and power influence. And so often that influence becomes an evil thing, in that it is used for a few, and not for the good of all. It is for that reason that we must have laws to establish control over power and authority, control over forces which are based on self-gain and exploitation. And it is necessary that we have laws to establish a measure of assistance and help for those who are not able to grub out a meager, respectable living.

And so we founded in this country great and far-reaching welfare programs. These programs were not created, nor are they operated, as a great leveler, but rather as an obligation of a democracy to its people, in order that the unfortunate may feast on more than crumbs and clothe themselves with more than rags.

What has gone before us in the way of welfare work exemplifies rich rewards of human endeavor. But we are actually just becoming of age, just beginning to scratch the surface in fulfilling the needs which are so widespread. So long as we have a person hungry, ill clothed, or without medical aid, we can take no pride in what has been done.

It is a good Christmas to turn our thoughts to the neglected because Christmas is a time to think of others and not of ourselves. It is a time for us to ask questions of our inner self. . . .

Our Negroes, who constitute 35 percent of our population in Alabama—are they getting 35 percent of the fair share of living? Are they getting adequate medical care to rid them of hookworms, rickets, and social diseases? Are they provided with sufficient professional training which will produce their own doctors, professors, lawyers, clergymen, scientists—men and women who can pave the way for better health, greater earning powers, and a higher standard of living for all of their people? Are the Negroes being given their share of democracy, the same opportunity of having a voice in the government under which we live?

As long as the Negroes are held down by deprivation and lack of opportunity, the other poor people will be held down alongside them.

There are others, too, who should share in our thoughts of the neglected—wounded veterans, the blind, the shut-ins, the crippled and on and on.

The job for us here in Alabama is a positive one. It is time for us to adopt a positive attitude toward our fellow man.

Let's start talking fellowship and brotherly love and doing-unto-others, and let's do more than talk about it—let's start living it.

In the past few years there has been too much negative living, too much stirring up of old hatreds, and prejudices, and false alarms. And the best way in the world to break this down is to lend our ears to the teachings of Christianity and the ways of democracy.

We must all constantly strive to put our democracy to fuller service for our people in order that all may be more richly rewarded with the fullness of the earth.

And certainly that is in keeping with the spirit of Christ, who said, "Do unto others as you would have them do unto you."

I hope the time will soon come when nations are brought together by the spirit of Christmas in much the same manner in which families join in reunion during the Holy Week.

People feel better when they gather together for the sake of love and fellowship. Their hearts are cleansed and kindled by the warm fire of eternal goodness. Nothing but good comes out of people at Christmas time—and that is how it should be at all times....

I believe that the people of all nations, the people of Alabama, the people of China, Africa, Russia, and tiny Luxembourg—I believe that all of them want to see lasting peace and goodness on this earth. And it is that great desire in the hearts of the people that gives me hope for a brighter future, a world without constant warfare, suffering, and distress.

I believe that such a goal is within our grasp—that it can become a force real and wonderful for all people, if we will set our hearts and our minds to that end....

MARTIN LUTHER KING, JR.
New York Journal-American

I want to be the white man's brother, not his brother-in-law.

C. LENOX REMOND
The Mind of the Negro As Reflected in Letters Written During the Crisis, 1800–1860

Shame on the cant and hypocrisy of those who can teach virtue, preach righteousness, and pray blessings for those only with skins colored like their own.

JOHN F. KENNEDY
Message to Congress

There are no "white" or "colored" signs on the foxholes or graveyards of battle.

PEARL S. BUCK

Race prejudice is not only a shadow over the colored—it is a shadow over all of us, and the shadow is darkest over those who feel it least and allow its evil effects to go on.

MELBA P. BEALS (ONE OF NINE CHILDREN WHO DESEGREGATED CENTRAL HIGH SCHOOL IN LITTLE ROCK, IN 1957)
Warriors Don't Cry

If my Central High School experience taught me one lesson, it is that we are not separate. The effort to separate ourselves whether by race, creed, color, religion, or status is as costly to the separator as to those who would be separated....The task that remains is to cope with our interdependence—to see ourselves reflected in every other human being and to respect and honor our differences.

WILLIAM WELLS BROWN
Letter to The Liberator

I will not yield to you in affection for America, but I hate her institution of slavery. I love her, because I am identified with her enslaved millions by every tie that binds man to his fellow-man.

WOODROW WILSON
Speech in Helena, Montana

The rest of the world is necessary to us, if you want to put it on that basis. I do not like to put it on that basis. That is not the American basis. America does not want to feed upon the rest of the world. She wants to feed it and serve it. America...is the only national idealistic force in the world, and idealism is going to save the world....That is the program of civilization.

Black and White in Birmingham
HARRISON E. SALISBURY
Heroes of My Time

I met some remarkable people in Birmingham, none more so than Cecil Roberts and Bessie Estell. For thirty or forty years Cecil Roberts made things happen in Birmingham. By the time of her death in 1991, Birmingham had become a monument to change in the rock-bound racist South. And Bessie Estell's vaulting career had become a symbol of black partnership in the new Birmingham.

Cecil Roberts used to say: "I never went to college. My college was The New York Times." There was a bit of truth to this. But only a bit. What was true was that in her forty years of public life The New York Times had become in her hands an instrument of her ceaseless crusade for a better life for the people of Birmingham, black and white.

Cecil was born in England. On the eve of World War I her parents took their large family (Cecil had six brothers and four sisters) to the south of France. When war came one brother wheeled Cecil to the railroad station in her baby carriage. It was a narrow escape, but Cecil's life would be filled with alarums and triumphs against the odds.

All her life Cecil preserved a light but unmistakable English accent. She was at some pains to retain it, and when she came to Birmingham it instantly set her apart in that land of Tom Heflin drawl. But she was not really English. Her father was a midwestern American named Edward Johnson who had moved to England, where he met Cecil's mother. They had a house in Surrey until Cecil was eight years old. "My father," she once told me, "inherited wall-to-wall mortgages." After World War I they wound up on Long Island "in the potato country playing around with horses." At seventeen she was working at Bonwit Teller, first as a salesgirl, then as a model and fashion consultant. She loved it.

She met David Roberts, III, son of Birmingham's first family, toward the end of World War II. She was engaged at the time, but David swept her off her feet. She had never met anyone so honest, so good, with so much integrity. They met on December 18, 1943, and eloped and were married February 12, 1944. David was a naval lieutenant assigned to the battleship South Dakota. When David was released from the service in 1945, they went straight to Birmingham.

"She turned Birmingham upside down," David remembered nearly fifty years later. This was no exaggeration. The gritty, grim steel-and-coal town had seen nothing like Cecil. Her eyes sparkled, her grin was irrepressible, and she wore her chestnut hair like a crown. Her ruddy skin glowed with energy. Give her a Spanish shawl, and she could pose as a gypsy.

At first her talents turned to the arts, and long before her death she had become the first lady of music and theater in Alabama. She raised money for polio and the March of Dimes, Planned Parenthood, and welfare groups but quickly burst those bonds and was revitalizing and setting up theater groups. As a newspaper editor recalled: "She pressured us all to use our possibilities."

From the beginning Cecil couldn't stand the racial inequality. People called her radical. "I wasn't a radical," she said. "I just wanted blacks to have the rights they paid for with their taxes. I didn't think everyone should integrate. I just thought we couldn't afford to maintain two systems."

Cecil Roberts set about to change the rules. She had no sympathy for words like "segregation" and "integration," and she let everyone know it. David stood by her. He was the third generation of a clan that had made a fortune in coal. Without David she could not have changed this Gibraltar of race, the city where the police commissioner swore he would not permit "blacks and whites to integrate together."

Cecil had flair. After she had raised enough money to put Birmingham's Symphony Orchestra on its feet, she realized that it was not integrated. It played to an all-white audience.

She changed that. Opening night in formal dress she walked down the center aisle, holding the arm of Birmingham's leading black businessman, and took her place with him in the first row, center aisle. Birmingham gasped but took the point.

The hate mail, the threats, the hints of retaliation became an everyday fact of life to Cecil. Sometimes she told the police; more often she didn't bother. She was fearless in her own person, driving her car alone into all-black neighborhoods, crossing every segregated pattern, heedless of the fact that Birmingham possessed a deadly dynamite-wielding Ku Klux Klan which had bombed churches, schools, and the homes of civil rights advocates.

Cecil's telephone line was tapped, her mail was opened, and she was under almost constant surveillance by uniformed and undercover police. She paid no heed to this. Her relations with Bull Connor, whose nightstick-ready officers reinforced segregation with brutality, were equivocal. She often bantered with him and once told me that "I think he has a sneaking admiration for me."

I think Bull was afraid of Cecil. He assured her that he had her followed for her own protection, and this may have been at least partially true. Had anything happened to Birmingham's first citizen, he would have paid a heavy price. He could not cope with Cecil's irrepressible sense of fun. She got a supply of police nightsticks somewhere and put labels on them "Bull Connor Nightstick Award," sending them as Christmas presents to some national correspondents who had been in Birmingham. During the Little Rock school integration fight an editor called her for help in persuading a fiery black orator to postpone a speaking engagement to a less-troubled moment. Cecil pondered the problem, then said: "Perhaps I can get Bull Connor to put him in jail." It was a joke—but just barely.

"Ol' Bull," Cecil once said, "could have arrested me many times for doing decent human things like taking blacks to places where it was against the law. Of course he knew what I was doing but he never arrested me."

In 1955 Birmingham voted Cecil Roberts their Woman of the Year. Not everyone agreed with her, but they had learned to respect her.

Twenty years later, in 1975, Bessie Estell was elected Birmingham's Woman of the Year. She was almost everything Cecil was not—quiet, careful, cautious, low profile, but superb in her profession, which was teaching—and black.

The selection in each case was made by the Junior Chamber of Commerce. Bessie Estell was bowled over. "I remember what I said when I heard the news: 'Birmingham has come a long ways.'"

Cecil Roberts had helped bring the city along. So had Bessie Estell. She had spent her life in education, which she believed must be the cornerstone of the rise of blacks to equal status with whites. Integration served no real purpose unless it meant equal opportunity under the rules, a level playing field. And for that to come about, blacks must be educated and possess the skills they needed to take their place in a black-and-white society.

When I met Bessie Estell she had just been elected to the Birmingham City Council, the first black woman to hold such a post. She joined two other blacks on the council, a certain sign of their rise to a share of political power in a state where most adult blacks could remember not even possessing the right to vote.

Bessie Estell was a trim, handsome woman, perfectly groomed with a quiet but commanding presence. No one could speak with her without knowing that they were confronted with a woman of character, dignity, and knowledge. She spoke with precision, choosing her words carefully with only a light southern accent. She was in her fifties when we met, born in Alabama, a product of the black educational system, segregated schools, and the Tuskegee Institute. She had taught in Birmingham's segregated schools during her professional career, rising to head the number one black high school, which, in the opinion of educators, was not only the leading black school in the city but the best school in Alabama, black or white.

This was the quality of education that Bessie Estell believed would equip the blacks to compete in the new world that she saw opening up. She did not expect miracles. In the twenty years before we met she had brought the adolescents in her school through a period of deep traumas stemming from the seemingly endless violence in Birmingham, the bombings, the assaults, the relentless hatreds.

Bessie Estell had persisted. The worst thing had been the bombing that killed the four black Sunday school children. The worst thing, she thought, was that no one had then been arrested for the crime, although everyone whispered that the perpetrators were known.

But Bessie Estell believed the shock of that bombing had awakened Birmingham, much as Pearl Harbor had awakened America. It had convinced the people that action had to be taken. She had moved out of her chosen field of education to become a player in the new power group that was running Birmingham and heading it into the twentieth century.

She had become one of a small group of political and business leaders who met informally for breakfast every Monday morning with the mission of resolving problems before they boiled over. And, she believed, it was working.

Not long before we talked, she, herself, had organized and overseen arrangements for the largest meeting ever held in Birmingham, a black conference of the Baptist Sunday School Training Conference, 16,000 blacks pouring into the once iron-clad segregationist city, filling every hotel and motel for miles around, eating with the whites in every Birmingham restaurant, shopping and visiting in every Birmingham facility. There was not a single racial incident. That, said Bessie Estell, is evidence of a changed city.

"We still have not arrived," she said. "We have a lot to do before we sleep." She, as expected, put her first priority on education. Its quality for both blacks and whites had to be improved. And crime must be brought under control. That was an economic problem. As the economy of the working class improved, crime would automatically be reduced. There had to be better employment for black males and better income for all. So much crime and so much hatred were generated in the fierce competition of the underclass for jobs and wages.

One thing, she thought, would help Birmingham and Alabama—more conventions, more people coming in from outside. It would help to shake things up. And bring in more income.

Like her friend Cecil Roberts, Bessie Estell was undaunted by every single obstacle she faced in life. She had overcome much. And she would go on fighting for more to the end of her days. She did not possess Cecil's flamboyance. But her work was equally effective, and she possessed equal courage.

Both women died in 1991, a grievous loss for the city they so loved and changed. Bessie Estell died quietly and conventionally. Not Cecil Roberts.

Cecil left special instructions for her burial. She was to be garbed in her favorite red silk dress. She was to wear the special "Yellow Dog Democrat" button she had devised ("I'll vote for a Yellow Dog if it's on the Democratic ticket"), and in her lap rested her reading glasses and a copy of The New York Times.

Once a friend had asked her what was her idea of Heaven. She said daily home delivery of the New York Times. What was her idea of Hell? To be without my reading glasses. Whatever her destination, Cecil Roberts was properly equipped.

ANNA JULIA COOPER
A Voice in the South

The cause of freedom is not the cause of a race or a sect, a party or a class—it is the cause of human kind, the very birthright of humanity.

ROY WILKINS
Standing Fast

[A] man [can] get along if he has faith in the goodness of the people . . . and believes in himself.

SAM WALTER FOSS
"The House by the Side of the Road"

There are hermit souls that live withdrawn
    In the peace of their self-content;
There are souls, like stars, that swell apart,
    In a fellowless firmament;
There are pioneer souls that blaze their paths
    Where highways never ran;
But let me live by the side of the road
    And be a friend to man.

Let me live in a house by the side of the road,
    Where the race of men go by—
The men who are good and the men who are bad,
    As good and as bad as I.
I would not sit in the scorner's seat,
    Or hurl the cynic's ban;
Let me live in a house by the side of the road
    And be a friend to man.

I see from my house by the side of the road,
    By the side of the highway of life,
The men who press with the ardor of hope,
    The men who are faint with the strife.
But I turn not away from their smiles nor their tears—
    Both parts of an infinite plan;
Let me live in my house by the side of the road
    And be a friend to man.

Let me live in my house by the side of the road
    Where the race of men go by—
They are good, they are bad, they are weak,
    they are strong.
    Wise, foolish—so am I.
Then why should I sit in the scorner's seat
    Or hurl the cynic's ban?
Let me live in my house by the side of the road
    And be a friend to man.

ALBERT EINSTEIN

A hundred times every day I remind myself that my inner and outer life depend on the labors of other men, living and dead, and that I must exert myself in order to give in the same measure as I have received.

JACKIE ROBINSON
Baseball Has Done It

The many of us who attain what we may and forget those who help us along the line—we've got to remember that there are so many others to pull along the way. The further they go, the further we all go.

DWIGHT D. EISENHOWER

Humility must always be the portion of any man who receives acclaim earned in the blood of his followers and the sacrifices of his friends.

ANNE MORROW LINDBERGH
"Pilgrim"

This is a road
One walks alone;
Narrow the track
And overgrown.

Dark is the way
And hard to find,
When the last village
Drops behind.

Never a footfall
Light to show
Fellow traveler—
Yet I know

Someone before
Has trudged his load
In the same footsteps—
This is a road.

BOOKER T. WASHINGTON
Fifth Tuskegee Conference

The highest test of the civilization of any race is in its willingness to extend a helping hand to the less fortunate. A race, like an individual, lifts itself up by lifting others up.

JAMES W. JOHNSON
Along This Way

This country can have no more democracy than it accords and guarantees to the humblest and weakest citizen.

THURGOOD MARSHALL
Concurring in the decision to abolish capital punishment, Furman v. Georgia

The measure of a country's greatness is its ability to retain compassion in time of crisis. No nation in the recorded history of man has a greater tradition of revering justice and fair treatment for all its citizens in times of turmoil, confusion, and tension than ours. . . . In striking down capital punishment, this Court does not malign our system of government. On the contrary it pays homage to it. Only in a free society could right triumph in difficult times, and could civilization record its magnificent advancement. In recognizing the humanity of our fellow beings, we pay ourselves the highest tribute. . . . The Eighth Amendment is our insulation from our baser selves.

An argument against capital punishment
CLARENCE S. DARROW

I hope I will not be obliged to spend too much time on my friend's address. I don't think I shall need to.

First, I deny his statement that every man's heart tells him it is wrong to kill. I think every man's heart desires killing. Personally, I never killed anybody that I know of. But I have had a great deal of satisfaction now and then reading the obituary notices, and I used to delight, with the rest of my 100 percent patriotic friends, when I saw ten or fifteen thousand Germans being killed in a day.

Everybody loves killing. Some of them think it is too messy for them. Every human being that believes in capital punishment loves killing, and the only reason they believe in capital punishment is because they get a kick out of it. Nobody kills anyone for love, unless they get over it temporarily or otherwise. But they kill the one they hate. And before you can get a trial to hang somebody or electrocute him, you must first hate him and then get a satisfaction over his death.

There is no emotion in any human being that is not in every single human being. The degree is different, that is all. And the degree is not always different in people. It depends likewise on circumstances, on time, and on place.

I shall not follow my friend into the labyrinth of statistics. Statistics are a pleasant indoor sport—not so good as crossword puzzles—and they prove nothing to any sensible person who is familiar with statistics.

I might just observe, in passing, that in all of these states where the mortality of homicide is great, they have capital punishment and always have had it. A logical man, when he found out that the death rate increased under capital punishment, would suggest some other way of dealing with it.

I undertake to say—and you can look up yourselves, for I haven't time to bother with it (and there is nothing that lies like statistics)—I will guarantee to take any set of statistics and take a little time to it and prove they mean directly the opposite for what is claimed. But I will undertake to say that you can show by statistics that the states in which there was no capital punishment have a very much smaller percentage of homicides.

I know it is true. That doesn't prove anything, because as a rule, they are states with a less diverse population, without as many large cities, without as much mixtures of all sorts of elements which go to add to the general gaiety—and homicide is a product of that. There is no sort of question but what those states in the United States where there is no capital punishment have a lower percentage than the others. But that doesn't prove the question. It is a question that cannot be proven one way or the other by statistics. It rests upon things, upon feelings and emotions and arguments much deeper than statistics.

The death rate in Memphis and in some other southern cities is high from homicide. Why? Well, it is an afternoon's pleasure to kill a Negro—that is about all. Everybody knows it.

The death rate recently in the United States and all over the world has increased. Why? The same thing has happened that has happened in every country in the world since time began. A great war always increases death rates.

We teach people to kill, and the state is the one that teaches them. If a state wishes that its citizens respect human life, then the state should stop killing. It can be done in no other way, and it will perhaps not be fully done that way. There are infinite reasons for killing. There are infinite circumstances under which there are more or less deaths. It never did depend and never can depend upon the severity of the punishment.

He talks about the United States being a lawless country. Well, the people somehow prefer it. There is such a thing as a people being too servile to law. You may take China with her caste system and much of Europe, which has much more caste than we. It may be full of homicides, but there is less bread and there is less fun; there is less opportunity for the poor. In any new country, homicide is more frequent than in an old country, because there is a higher degree of equality. It is always true wherever you go. And in the older countries, as a general rule, there are fewer homicides because nobody ever thinks of getting out of his class; nobody ever dreams of such a thing.

But let's see what there is in this argument. He says, "Everybody who kills, dreads hanging." Well, he has had experiences as a lawyer on both sides. I have had experience on one side. I know that everybody who is taken into court on a murder charge desires to live, and they do not want to be hanged or electrocuted. Even a thing as alluring as being cooked with electricity doesn't appeal to them.

But that hasn't anything to do with it. What was the state of mind when the homicide was committed? The state of mind is one thing when a homicide is committed and another thing weeks or months afterward, when every reason for committing it is gone. There is no comparison between it. There never can be any comparison between it.

We might ask why people kill. I don't want to dispute with him about the right of the state to kill people. Of course, they have got a right to kill them. That is about all we do. The great industry of the world for four long years was killing. They have got a right to kill, of course. That is, they have got the power. And you have a right to do what you get away with. The words "power" and "right," so far as this is concerned mean exactly the same thing. So nobody who has any knowledge of philosophy would pretend to say that the state had not the right to kill.

But why not do a good job of it? If you want to get rid of killings by hanging people or electrocuting them because they are so terrible, why not make a punishment that is terrible? This isn't so much. It lasts but a short time. There is no physical torture in it. Why not boil them in oil, as they used to do? Why not burn them at the stake? Why not sew them into a bag with serpents and throw them out to sea? Why not take them out on the sand and let them be eaten by ants? Why not break every bone in their body on the rack, as has been done for such serious offenses as heresy and witchcraft?

Those were the good old days in which the judge should have held court. Glorious days, when you could kill them by the million because they worshiped God in a different way from that which the state provided, or when you could kill old women for witchcraft! There might be some sense in it if you could kill young ones, but not old ones. Those were the glorious days of capital punishment. And there wasn't a judge or a preacher who didn't think that the life of the state depended upon their right to hang old women for witchcraft and persecute others for worshiping God in the wrong way.

Why, our capital punishment isn't worth talking about, so far as its being a preventive is concerned. It isn't worth discussing. Why not call back from the dead and barbarous past the hundred and sixty or seventy-odd crimes that were punishable by death in England? Why not once more re-enact the blue laws of our own country and kill people right? Why not resort to all the tortures that the world has always resorted to to keep men in the straight and narrow path? Why reduce it to a paltry question of murder?

Everybody in this world has some pet aversion to something, and on account of that pet aversion they would like to hang somebody. If the prohibitionist made the law, they would be in favor of hanging you for taking a drink, or certainly for bootlegging, because to them that is the most heinous crime there is.

Some men slay or murder. Why? As a matter of fact, murder as murder is very rare; and the people who commit it, as a rule, are of a much higher type than others. You may go to any penitentiary and, as a rule, those who have been convicted of murder become the trusties;

whereas, if you are punishing somebody as a sneak thief or a counterfeiter or a confidence man, they never get over it—never.

Now, I don't know how injustice is administered in New York. I just know about Chicago. But I am glad to learn from the gentleman that if a man is so poor in New York that he can't hire a lawyer, that he has a first-class lawyer appointed to defend him. Don't take a chance and go out and kill anybody on the statement made by my friend.

I suppose anybody can go out and kill somebody and ask to have my friend Sam Untermyer appointed. There never was such a thing. Here and there, a good lawyer may have defended people for nothing. But no court ever interferes with a good lawyer's business by calling him in and compelling him to give his time. They have been lawyers too recently themselves to ever work a trick like that on a lawyer. As a rule, it is the poor and the weak and the friendless who furnish the victims of the law.

Let me take another statement of my friend. He said, "Oh, we don't hang anybody if they kill when they are angry; it is only when they act premeditatedly." Yes, I have been in courts and heard judges instruct people on this premeditated act. It is only when they act under their judgment and with due consideration. He would also say that if a man is moved by anger, but if he doesn't strike the deadly blow until such time as reason and judgment has a chance to possess him, even if it is a second—how many times have I heard judges say, "Even if it is a second?" What does any judge know about premeditation? What does anybody know about it? How many people are there in this world that can premeditate on anything? I will strike out the "pre" and say how many people are there that can meditate?

How long does it take the angry man for his passions to cool when he is in the presence of the thing that angers him? There never was a premeditated murder in any sense of psychology or of science. There are planned murders—planned, yes—but back of every murder and back of every human act are sufficient causes that move the human machine beyond their control.

The other view is an outworn, outlawed, unscientific theory of the metaphysicians. Does everybody ever act in this world without a motive? Did they ever act without a sufficient motive? And who am I to say that John Smith premeditated? I might premeditate a good deal quicker than John Smith did. My judgment might have a chance to act quicker than John Smith's judgment had a chance to act.

We have heard talk of justice. Is there anybody who knows what justice is? No one on earth can measure out justice. Can you look at any man and say what he deserves—whether he deserves hanging by the neck until dead or life in prison or thirty days in prison or a medal? The human mind is blind to all who seek to look in at it and to most of us that look out from it. Justice is something that man knows little about. He may know something about charity and understanding and mercy, and he should cling to these as far as he can.

Now, let me see if I am right about my statement that no man believes in hanging, except for a kick or revenge. How about my friend Judge Tally here. He criticizes the state of New York because a prisoner may be shown moving pictures. What do you think about it—those of you who think? What do you feel about it—those of you who have passed the hyena age? I know what they think. What do you think about shutting up a man in a penitentiary for twenty years, in a cell four feet wide and seven feet long—twenty years, mind!—and complaining because of a chance now and then to go out and see a moving picture—go out of his cell?

A body of people who feels that way could never get rid of capital punishment. If you really felt it, you would feel like the Indian who used the tomahawk on his enemy and who burned him and embalmed his face with ashes.

But what is punishment about anyway? I put a man in prison for the purpose of getting rid of him and for such example as there might be. Is it up to you to torture him while he is there? Supposing you provided that every man who went to prison should be compelled to wear a nail half an inch long in his shoe. I suppose some of you would do it. I don't know whether the judge would or not, from what he said.

Is there any reason for torturing someone who happens to be in prison? Is there any reason why an actor or even an actress might not go there and sing? There is no objection to a preacher going there. Why not give him a little pleasure?

And they really get food there—what do you know about that? Now, when I heard him tell about the wonderful food they get—dietary food—did you ever know anybody that liked dietary food? I suppose the constitution of the state of New York contains the ordinary provisions against cruel and inhuman punishment, and yet you send them up there and feed them on dietary food.

And you can take your meals out! Now, some of you might not have noticed that I walked over and asked the warden about it. The reason I did that is because I am stopping over here at the Belmont, and I didn't know but I'd rather go up and board with him.

Now, this is what I find out: that those who have gained consideration by good conduct over a considerable period—one year—they may spend three dollars a week for board. I pay more than that over here. They ought to pass some law in New York to prevent the inmates getting dyspepsia. And for those who attain the second class, they may spend a dollar and a half a week. And for those below second class, nothing can come from outside—nothing. A pure matter of prison discipline!

Why, I wonder if the judge ever took pains to go up there. I will tell you. I have had some experience with people that know them pretty well. I never saw a man who wanted to go to prison, even to see the movies. I never saw a man in my life who didn't want to get out.

I wonder what you would have. Of course, I live in Chicago, where people are fairly human—I don't know, maybe I don't understand New York people. What would you have? Suppose you could tell yourselves how a person was to be treated while in prison—and it doesn't require a great amount of imagination. Most people can think of some relative or some friends who are there. If you can't, most of you can think of a good many that ought to be there. How would you have them treated—something worse than being shut up in a cell, four by seven, and given light work—like being a judge or practicing law—something worse than dietary food?

I will tell you. There is just one thing in all this question. It is a question of how you feel, that is all. It is all inside you. If you love the thought of somebody being killed, why, you are for it. If you hate the thought of somebody being killed, you are against it.

Let me just take a little brief review of what has happened in this world. They used to hang people on the crossways and on a high hill, so that everybody would be awed into goodness by the sight. They have tortured them in every way that the brain of man could conceive. They have provided every torture known or that could be imagined for one who believed differently from his fellowman—and still the belief persisted. They have maimed and scarred and starved and killed human beings since man began penning his fellowman. Why? Because we hate him. And what has added to it is that they have done it under the false ideal of self-righteousness.

I have heard parents punish their children and tell their children it hurt the parent more than it did the child. I don't believe it. I have tried it both ways, and I don't believe it. I know better.

Gradually, the world has been lopping off these punishments. Why? Because we have grown a little more sensitive, a little more imaginative, a little kindlier, that is all.

Why not reenact the code of Blackstone's day? Why, the judges were all for it—every one of them—and the only way we got rid of those laws was because juries were too humane to obey the courts.

That is the only way we got rid of punishing old women, of hanging old women in New England—because, in spite of all the courts, the juries would no longer convict them for a crime that never existed. And in that way they have cut down the crimes in England for punishment by death from one hundred and seventy to two. What is going to happen if we get rid of them? Is the world coming to an end? The earth has been here ages and ages before man came. It will be here ages and ages after he disappears, and the amount of people you hang with it won't make the slightest difference with it.

Now, why am I opposed to capital punishment? It is too horrible a thing for a state to undertake. We are told by my friend, "Oh, the killer does it; why shouldn't the state?" I would hate to live in a state that I didn't think was better than a murderer.

But I told you the real reason. The people of the state kill a man because he killed someone else—that is all—without the slightest logic, without the slightest application to life, simply from anger, nothing else!

I am against it because I believe it is inhuman, because I believe that as the hearts of men have softened they have gradually gotten rid of brutal punishment, because I believe that it will only be a few years until it will be banished forever from every civilized country—even New York—because I believe that it has no effect whatever to stop murder.

Now, let's make that simple and see. Where do the murders come from? I would say the second-largest class of what we call murders grows out of domestic relations. They follow those deep and profound feelings that are at the basis of life—and the feelings which give the greatest joy are susceptible to the greatest pain when they go ariot.

Can you imagine a woman following a man around with a pistol to kill him that would stop if you said, "Oh, you will be hanged!" Nothing doing—not true if the world was coming to an end! Can you imagine a man doing it? Not at all. They think of it afterwards, but not before.

They come from acts of burglary and robbery. A man goes out to rob or to burglarize. Somebody catches him or stops him or recognizes him, and he kills to save himself. Do you suppose there was ever a burglar or robber since the world began who would not kill to save himself? Is there anybody who wouldn't? It doesn't make any difference who. Wouldn't he take a chance shooting? Anyone would do it. Why, my friend himself said he would kill in self-defense. That is what they do. If you are going to stop them, you ought to hang them for robbery—which would be a good plan—and then, of course, if one started out to rob, he would kill the victim before he robbed him.

There isn't, I submit, a single admissible argument in favor of capital punishment. Nature loves life. We believe that life should be protected and preserved. The thing that keeps one from killing is the emotion they have against it; and the greater the sanctity that the state pays to life, the greater the feeling of sanctity the individual has for life.

There is nothing in the history of the world that has ever cheapened human life like our great war; next to that, the indiscriminate killing of men by the states.

My friend says a man must be proven guilty first. Does anybody know whether anybody is guilty? There is a great deal implied in that. For me to do something or for you to do something is one thing; for some other man to do something quite another. To know what one deserves, requires infinite study, which no one can give it. No one can determine the condition of the brain that did the act. It is out of the question.

All people are products of two things, and two things only—their heredity and their environment. And they act in exact accord with the heredity which they took from all the past, and for which they are in no wise responsible, and the environment, which reaches out to the farthest limit of all life that can influence them. We all act from the same way. And it ought to teach us to be charitable and kindly and understanding of our fellowman.

JAMES BALDWIN
Price of the Ticket

It is a terrible and inexorable law that one cannot deny the humanity of another without diminishing one's own. In the face of one's victim one sees oneself.

NICOLA SACCO
Letter to his son

Help the weak ones that cry for help, help the prosecuted and the victim . . . they are the comrades that fight and fall . . . for the conquest of the joy of freedom for all the poor workers. In this struggle for life you will find more love and you will be loved.

HORACE MANN
Commencement Address, Antioch College

Be ashamed to die until you have won some victory for humanity.

MARGARET MEAD
Redbook magazine

I must admit that I personally measure success in terms of the contributions an individual makes to her or his fellow human beings.

RALPH WALDO EMERSON

You cannot do a kindness too soon, for you never know how soon it will be too late.

ALBERT EINSTEIN

A successful man is he who receives a great deal from his fellow men, usually incomparably more than corresponds to his service to them. The value of a man, however, should be seen in what he gives, and not in what he is able to receive.

HENRY WARD BEECHER
Proverbs from Plymouth Pulpit

Rich men are to bear the infirmities of the poor. Wise men are to bear the mistakes of the ignorant.

LANGSTON HUGHES
"Litany"

Gather up
In the arms of your pity
The sick, the depraved,
The desperate, the tired,
All the scum
Of our weary city
Gather up
In the arms of your pity.
Gather up
In the arms of your love—
Those who expect
No love from above.

LEARNED HAND
The Spirit of Liberty

Would we hold liberty, we must have charity—charity to others, charity to ourselves, crawling up from the moist ovens of a steaming world, still carrying the passional equipment of our ferocious ancestors, emerging from black superstition amid carnage and atrocity to our perilous present.

HERMAN MELVILLE
Moby Dick

Man in the ideal, is so noble and so sparkling, such a grand and glowing creature, that over any ignominious blemish in him all his fellows should run to throw their costliest robes.

WILLIAM H. MCGUFFEY
McGuffey's Second Reader

Beautiful hands are they that do
Deeds that are noble good and true;
Beautiful feet are they that go
Swiftly to lighten another's woe.

JIMMY CARTER
Keeping Faith

If the misery of others leaves you indifferent with no feeling of sorrow, then you cannot be called a human being.

EMILY DICKINSON
"If I Can Stop One Heart from Breaking"

If I can stop one heart from breaking,
I shall not live in vain;
If I can ease one life the aching,
Or cool one pain,
Or help one fainting robin
Unto his nest again,
I shall not live in vain.

ELEANOR ROOSEVELT

It is not fair to ask of others what you are not willing to do yourself.

ADLAI E. STEVENSON
Address to the United Nations upon her death

[Eleanor Roosevelt] would rather light candles than curse the darkness, and her glow has warmed the world.

The Gift of the Magi

BY O HENRY

One dollar and eighty-seven cents. That was all. And sixty cents of it was in pennies. Pennies saved one and two at a time by bulldozing the grocer and the vegetable man and the butcher until one's cheeks burned with the silent imputation of parsimony that such close dealing implied. Three times Della counted it. One dollar and eighty-seven cents. And the next day would be Christmas.

There was clearly nothing to do but flop down on the shabby little couch and howl. So Della did it. Which instigates the moral reflection that life is made up of sobs, sniffles, and smiles, with sniffles predominating.

While the mistress of the home is gradually subsiding from the first stage to the second, take a look at the home. A furnished flat at $8 per week. It did not exactly beggar description, but it certainly had that word on the lookout for the mendicancy squad.

In the vestibule below was a letter-box into which no letter would go, and an electric button from which no mortal finger could coax a ring. Also appertaining thereunto was a card bearing the name "Mr. James Dillingham Young."

The "Dillingham" had been flung to the breeze during a former period of prosperity when its possessor was being paid $30 per week. Now, when the income was shrunk to $20, the letters of "Dillingham" looked blurred, as though they were thinking seriously of contracting to a modest and unassuming D. But whenever Mr. James Dillingham Young came home and reached his flat above he was called "Jim" and greatly hugged by Mrs. James Dillingham Young, already introduced to you as Della. Which is all very good.

Della finished her cry and attended to her cheeks with the powder rag. She stood by the window and looked out dully at a gray cat walking a gray fence in a gray backyard. Tomorrow would be Christmas Day, and she had only $1.87 with which to buy Jim a present. She had been saving every penny she could for months, with this result. Twenty dollars a week doesn't go far. Expenses had been greater than she calculated. They always are. Only $1.87 to buy a present for Jim. Her Jim. Many a happy hour she had spent planning for something nice for him. Something fine and rare and sterling—something just a little bit near to being worthy of the honor of being owned by Jim.

There was a pier-glass between the windows of the room. Perhaps you have seen a pier-glass in an $8 flat. A very thin and very agile person may, by observing his reflection in a rapid sequence of longitudinal strips, obtain a fairly accurate conception of his looks. Della, being slender, had mastered the art.

Suddenly she whirled from the window and stood before the glass. Her eyes were shining brilliantly, but her face had lost its color within twenty seconds. Rapidly she pulled down her hair and let it fall to its full length.

Now, there were two possessions of the James Dillingham Youngs in which they both took a mighty pride. One was Jim's gold watch that had been his father's and his grandfather's. The other was Della's hair. Had the Queen of Sheba lived in the flat across the airshaft, Della would have let her hair hang out the window some day to dry just to depreciate Her Majesty's jewels and gifts. Had King Solomon been the janitor, with all his treasures piled up in the basement, Jim would have pulled out his watch every time he passed, just to see him pluck his beard from envy.

So now Della's beautiful hair fell about her, rippling and shining like a cascade of brown waters. It reached below her knee and made itself almost a garment for her. And then she did it up again nervously and quickly. Once she faltered for a minute and stood still while a tear or two splashed on the worn red carpet.

On went her old brown jacket; on went her old brown hat. With a whirl of skirts and with the brilliant sparkle still in her eyes, she fluttered out the door and down the stairs to the street.

Where she stopped the sign read: "Mme. Sofronie. Hair Goods of All Kinds." One flight up Della ran, and collected herself, panting. Madame, large, too, white, chilly, hardly looked the "Sofronie."

"Will you buy my hair?" asked Della.

"I buy hair," said Madame. "Take ye hat off and let's have a sight at the looks of it."

Down rippled the brown cascade.

"Twenty dollars," said Madame, lifting the mass with a practiced hand.

"Give it to me quick," said Della.

Oh, and the next two hours tripped by on rosy wings. Forget the hashed metaphor. She was ransacking the stores for Jim's present.

She found it at last. It surely had been made for Jim and no one else. There was no other like it in any of the stores, and she had turned all of them inside out. It was a platinum fob chain simple and chaste in design, properly proclaiming its value by substance alone and not by meretricious ornamentation—as all good things should do. It was even worthy of The Watch. As soon as she saw it she knew that it must be Jim's. It was like him. Quietness and value— the description applied to both. Twenty-one dollars they took from her for it, and she hurried home with the 87 cents. With that chain on his watch Jim might be properly anxious about the time in any company. Grand as the watch was, he sometimes looked at it on the sly on account of the old leather strap that he used in place of a chain.

When Della reached home her intoxication gave way a little to prudence and reason. She got out her curling iron and lighted the gas and went to work repairing the ravages made by generosity added to love. Which is always a tremendous task, dear friends—a mammoth task.

Within forty minutes her head was covered with tiny, close-lying curls that made her look wonderfully like a truant schoolboy. She looked at her reflection in the mirror long, carefully, and critically.

"If Jim doesn't kill me," she said to herself, "before he takes a second look at me, he'll say I look like a Coney Island chorus girl. But what could I do—oh! what could I do with a dollar and eighty-seven cents?"

At 7 o'clock the coffee was made and the frying-pan was on the back of the stove hot and ready to cook the chops.

Jim was never late. Della doubled the fob chain in her hand and sat on the corner of the table near the door that he always entered. Then she heard his step on the stair away down on the first flight, and she turned white for just a moment. She had a habit of saying little silent prayers about the simplest everyday things, and now she whispered: "Please God, make him think I am still pretty."

The door opened and Jim stepped inside the door, as immovable as a setter at the scent of a quail. His eyes were fixed upon Della, and there was an expression in them that she could not read, and it terrified her. It was not anger, nor surprise, nor disapproval, nor horror, nor any of the sentiments that she had been prepared for. He simply stared at her fixedly with that peculiar expression on his face.

Della wriggled off the table and went for him.

"Jim, darling," she cried, "don't look at me that way. I had my hair cut off and sold it because I couldn't have lived through Christmas without giving you a present. It'll grow out again—you won't mind, will you? I just had to do it. My hair grows awfully fast. Say 'Merry Christmas!' Jim, and let's be happy. You don't know what a nice—what a beautiful, nice gift I've got for you."

"You've cut off your hair?" asked Jim, laboriously, as if he had not arrived at that patent fact yet even after the hardest mental labor.

"Cut it off and sold it," said Della. "Don't you like me just as well, anyhow? I'm me without my hair, ain't I?"

Jim looked about the room curiously.

"You say your hair is gone?" he said, with an air almost of idiocy.

"You needn't look for it," said Della. "It's sold, I tell you—sold and gone, too. It's Christmas Eve, boy. Be good to me, for it went for you. Maybe the hairs of my head were numbered," she went on with a sudden serious sweetness, "but nobody could ever count my love for you. Shall I put the chops on, Jim?"

Out of his trance Jim seemed quickly to wake. He enfolded his Della. For ten seconds let us regard with discreet scrutiny some inconsequential object in the other direction. Eight dollars a week or a million a year—what is the difference? A mathematician or a wit would give you the wrong answer. The magi brought valuable gifts, but that was not among them. This dark assertion will be illuminated later on.

Jim drew a package from his overcoat pocket and threw it upon the table.

"Don't make any mistake, Dell," he said, "about me. I don't think there's anything in the way of a haircut or a shave or a shampoo that could me like my girl any less. But if you'll unwrap that package you may see why you had me going for a while at first."

White fingers and nimble tore at the string and paper. And then an ecstatic scream of joy; and then, alas! a quick feminine change to hysterical tears and wails, necessitating the immediate employments of all the comforting powers of the lord of the flat.

For there lay The Combs—the set of combs, side and back, that Della had worshipped for long in a Broadway window. Beautiful combs, pure tortoise shell, with jeweled rims—just the shade to wear in the beautiful vanished hair. They were expensive combs, she knew, and her heart had simply craved and yearned over them without the least hope of possession. And no, they were hers, but the tresses that should have adorned the coveted adornments were gone.

But she hugged them to her bosom, and at length she was able to look up with dim eyes and a smile and say: "My hair grows so fast, Jim!"

And then Della leaped up like a little singed cat and cried, "Oh, oh!"

Jim had not yet seen his beautiful present. She held it out to him eagerly upon her open palm. The dull precious metal seemed to flash with a reflection of her bright and ardent spirit.

"Isn't it a dandy, Jim? I hunted all over town to find it. You'll have to look at the time a hundred times a day now. Give me your watch. I want to see how it looks on it."

Instead of obeying, Jim tumbled down on the couch and put his hands under the back of his head and smiled.

"Dell," said he, "let's put our Christmas presents away and keep 'em a while. They're too nice to use just at present. I sold the watch to get the money to buy your combs. And now suppose you put the chops on."

The magi, as you know, were wise men—wonderfully wise men—who brought gifts to the Babe in the manger. They invented the art of giving Christmas presents. Being wise, their gifts were no doubt wise ones, possibly bearing the privilege of exchange in case of duplication. And here I have lamely related to you the uneventful chronicle of two foolish children in a flat who most unwisely sacrificed for each other the greatest treasures of their house. But in a last word to the wise of these days let it be said that of all who give gifts these two were the wisest. Of all who give and receive gifts, such as they are wisest. Everywhere they are wisest. They are the magi.

Land of Opportunity

JOHN LOCKE

Thus, in the beginning, all the world was America.

From Ellis Island to the Governor's Mansion

MARIO CUOMO

(diary entry)

How far is it from King's Park in South Jamaica? How far is it from the stickball game in the backyard in shoes because sneakers were a luxury preserved for gym class where they were required? There will be tennis courts and a swimming pool and guards and servants and more luxury than anyone should have where I'm going now. How far is that from Van Dolan Playground in Queens with free showers for everybody and the Van Wyck Pool which was too expensive at a quarter? And Mama's chicken?

(When I was very young, young enough to be forgiven indiscretions, I went to Mama and told her I was hungry. It was Sunday. The store was very busy. This was behind the store with everyone in the store but me helping out. Momma had put a chicken upstairs. She told me to go and take a little bit of the chicken until she had time to set the table. As she describes it today, "He went up and took a little alright, he left us a wing." The next time I was hungry Mama gave me a big piece of bread instead of sending me to the chicken.)

How much from then to where we'll be going?

Well, how far is it from Ellis Island in that imaginary interview with Mama to where we're going to be?

Remember the imaginary interview? Mama arrives at Ellis Island and a reporter says to you, "What is your name?"

"Immaculata Cuomo."

"Where are you from?"

"Salerno, Italy."

"What do you do?"

"What do you mean, 'What do I do'?"

"Well, what do you do? What do you do for a living?"

"Nothing. I'm going to meet my husband in New Jersey. I have a baby."

"What does he do?"

"Nothing. He's looking for work. Now he's digging ditches in Jersey City. They're making a new church, but that job is going to be over soon."

"What kind of work is he looking for?"

"Any kind of work you have."

"But what can he do? What skills does he have?"

"Well, he has no skills. He never went to school and they never taught him how to be a carpenter or how to make wood into furniture. He was never educated."

"Well, do you have any skills?"

"No, I'm not even a seamstress."

"Well, does he have any friends? Do you have any friends here?"

"No."

"Do you have any relatives here?"

"No."

"Do you have any money?"

"Any money? No, no, we don't have any money. We have a little. We paid the rent, we paid the rent. We don't owe any rent. We have no friends. No money. Just a baby."

"Well, with no friends, no money what do you expect of this country, Immaculata Cuomo?"

A pause.

"Not a lot. Only one thing maybe before I die. I want to see my son become the governor of New York State."

They would have locked her up if she said that, that's how far it is. They would have said to her, "You gotta be crazy, Immaculata Cuomo."

How far is it? Not so far that we didn't make the trip. But it's hard to believe that we did, frankly. I feel something that I don't understand it yet the way I'm expected to understand it, maybe later, maybe later when we get used to this place.

MARY ANTIN
The Promised Land

So at last I was going to America! Really, really going, at last! The boundaries burst. The arch of heaven soared. A million suns shone out for every star. The winds rushed in from outer space, roaring in my ears, "America! America!"

HENRY STEELE COMMAGER

The American was good-natured, generous, hospitable and sociable, and he reversed the whole history of language to make the term "stranger" one of welcome.

HERBERT H. LEHMAN
Congressional testimony

We are a nation of immigrants. It is immigrants who brought to this land the skills of their hands and brains to make of it a beacon of opportunity and of hope for all men.

My Fellow Immigrants speech to the Daughters of the American Revolution

FRANKLIN D. ROOSEVELT

Let me just come here without preparation to tell you how glad I am to avail myself of this opportunity, to tell you how proud I am, as a revolutionary descendant, to greet you.

I thought of preaching on a text, but I shall not. I shall only give you the text, and I shall not preach on it. I think I can afford to give you the text because it so happens, through no fault of my own, that I am descended from a number of people who came over in the Mayflower. More than that, every one of my ancestors on both sides—and when you go back four generations or five generations it means thirty-two or sixty-four of them—every single one of them, without exception, was in this land in 1776. And there was only one Tory among them.

The text is this: remember, remember always that all of us, and you and I especially, are descended from immigrants and revolutionists.

I am particularly glad to know that today you are making this fine appeal to the youth of America. To these rising generations, to our sons and grandsons and great-grandsons, we cannot overestimate the importance of what we are doing in this year, in our own generation, to keep alive the spirit of American democracy. The spirit of opportunity is the kind of spirit that has led us as a nation—not as a small group but as a nation—to meet the very great problems of the past.

We look for a younger generation that is going to be more American than we are. We are doing the best we can, and yet we can do better than that, we can do more than that, by inculcating in the boys and girls of this country today some of the underlying fundamentals, the reasons that brought our immigrant ancestors to this country, the reasons that impelled our revolutionary ancestors to throw off a fascist yoke.

HERMAN MELVILLE

We are not so much a nation as a world.

ISRAEL ZANGWILL
The Melting-Pot

America is God's crucible, the great Melting-Pot where all the races of Europe are melting and re-forming.

The Melting-Pot
ISRAEL ZANGWILL

DAVID
Oh, I love going to Ellis Island to watch the ships coming in from Europe, and to think that all those weary, sea-tossed wanderers are feeling what I felt when America first stretched out her great motherhand to me!

VERA
Were you very happy?

DAVID
It was heaven. You must remember that all my life I had heard of America—everybody in our town had friends there or was going there or got money orders from there. The earliest game I played at was selling off my toy furniture and setting up in America. All my life America was waiting, beckoning, shining—the place where God would wipe away tears from off all faces.

MENDEL
Now, now, David, don't get excited.

DAVID

To think that the same great torch of liberty which threw its light across all the broad seas and lands into my little garret in Russia, is shining also for all those other weeping millions of Europe, shining wherever men hunger and are oppressed—

MENDEL [Soothingly]

Yes, yes, David. [Laying hand on his shoulder]
   Now sit down and—

DAVID [Unheeding]

Shining over the starving villages of Italy and Ireland, over the swarming stony cities of Poland and Alicia, over the ruined farms of Rumania, over the shambles of Russia—

MENDEL [Pleadingly]

David!

DAVID

Oh, Miss Revendal, when I look at our Statue of Liberty, I just seem to hear the voice of America crying: "Come unto me all ye that labour and are heavy laden and I will give you rest— rest—"

THOMAS PAINE

Common Sense

O! ye that love mankind! Ye that dare oppose not only the tyranny but the tyrant, stand forth! Every spot of the Old World is overrun with oppression. Freedom hath been hunted round the globe. Asia and Africa have long expelled her. Europe regards her as a stranger and England hath given her warning to depart. O! receive the fugitive and prepare in time an asylum for mankind.

EMMA LAZARUS

The New Colossus (Inscribed on the Statue of Liberty, 1903)

Not like the brazen giant of Greek fame,
With conquering limbs astride from land to land;
Here at our sea-washed, sunset gates shall stand
A mighty woman with a torch, whose flame
Is the imprisoned lightning, and her name
Mother of Exiles. From her beacon-hand
Glows worldwide welcome; her mild eyes command
The air-bridged harbor that twin cities frame.

"Keep, ancient lands, your storied pomp!" cries she
With silent lips. "Give me your tired, your poor,
Your huddled masses yearning to breathe free,
The wretched refuse of your teeming shores.
Send these, the homeless, tempest-tost to me,
I lift my lamp beside the golden door!"

O. HENRY
The Lady Higher Up

[The Statue of Liberty] was made by a Dago . . . on behalf of the French . . . for the purpose of welcomin' Irish immigrants into the Dutch city of New York.

NINETEENTH-CENTURY CAMP-MEETING SONG

Come hungry, come thirsty, come ragged, come bare,
Come filthy, come lousy, come just as you are.

What Is an American?
J. HECTOR ST. JOHN DE CRÈVECOEUR

The next wish of this traveler will be to know whence came all these people. They are a mixture of English, Scottish, Irish, French, Dutch, Germans, and Swedes. From this promiscuous breed, that race now called Americans have arisen. The eastern provinces must indeed be excepted as being the unmixed descendants of Englishmen. I have heard many wish that they had been more intermixed also; for my part, I am no wisher and think it much better as it has happened. They exhibit a most conspicuous figure in this great and variegated picture; they too enter for a great share in the pleasing perspective displayed in these thirteen provinces. I know it is fashionable to reflect on them, but I respect them for what they have done; for the accuracy and wisdom with which they have settled their territory; for the decency of their manners; for their early love of letters; their ancient college, the first in this hemisphere; for their industry, which to me who am but a farmer is the creation of everything. There never was a people, situated as they are, who with so ungrateful a soil have done more in so short a time. Do you think that the monarchical ingredients have purged them from all foul stains? Their histories assert the contrary.

In this great American asylum, the poor of Europe have by some means met together, and in consequence of various causes; to what purpose should they ask one another what countrymen they are? Alas, two thirds of them had no country. Can a wretch who wanders about, who works and starves, whose life is a continual scene of sore affliction or pinching penury—can that man call England or any other kingdom his country? A country that had no bread for him, whose fields procured him no harvest, who met with nothing but the frowns of the rich, the severity of the laws, with jails and punishments, who owned not a single foot of extensive surface of this planet? No! Urged by a variety of motives, here they came. Everything has tended to regenerate them: new laws, a new mode of living, a new social system; here they are become men: in Europe they were as so many useless plants, wanting vegetative mould and refreshing showers; they withered, and were mowed down by want, hunger, and war; but now, by the power of transplantation, like all other plants they have taken root and flourished! Formerly they were not numbered in any civil lists of their country, except in those of the poor; here they rank as citizens. By what invisible power hath this surprising metamorphosis been performed? By that of the laws and that of their industry. The laws, the indulgent laws, protect them as they arrive, stamping on them the symbol of adoption; they receive ample rewards for their labors; these accumulated rewards procure them lands; those land confer on them the title of freemen, and to that title every benefit is affixed which men can possibly acquire. This is the great operation daily performed by our laws. Whence proceed these laws? From our government. Whence that government? It is derived from the original genius and strong desire of the people ratified and confirmed by the crown. This is the great chain which links us all, this is the picture which every province exhibits, Nova Scotia excepted. There the crown has done all; either there were no people who had genius or it was not much attended to; the consequence is that the province is very thinly inhabited indeed; the power of the crown in conjunction with the muskets has prevented men from settling there. Yet some parts of it flourished once, and it contained a mild, harmless set of people. But for the fault of a few leaders, the whole was banished. The greatest political error the crown ever committed in America was to cut off men from a country which wanted nothing but men!

What attachment can a poor European emigrant have for a country where he had nothing? The knowledge of the language, the love of a few kindred as poor as himself, were the only cords that tied him; his country is now which gives him his land, bread, protection, and consequence; *Ubi panis ibi patria* is the motto of all emigrants. What, then, is the American, this new man? He is either a European or the descendant of a European; hence that strange mixture of blood, which you will find in no other country. I could point out to you a family whose grandfather was an Englishman, whose wife was Dutch, whose son married a French woman, and whose present four sons have now four wives of different nations. He is an American, who, leaving behind him all his ancient prejudices and manners, receives new ones from the new mode of life he has embraced, the new government he obeys, and the new rank he holds. He becomes an American by being received in the broad lap of our great Alma Mater. Here individuals of all nations are melted into a new race of men, whose labors and posterity will one day cause great changes in the world. Americans are the western pilgrims who are carrying along with them that great mass of arts, sciences, vigor, and industry which began long since in the East; they will finish the great circle. The Americans were once scattered all over Europe; here they are incorporated into one of the finest systems of population which has ever appeared, and which will hereafter become distinct by the power of the different climates they inhabit. The American ought to love this country much better than that wherein either he or his forefathers were born. Here the rewards of his industry follow with equal steps the progress of his labor; his labor is founded on the basis of nature, self-interest; can it want a stronger allurement? Wives and children, who before in vain demanded of him a morsel of bread, now, fat and frolicsome, gladly help their father to clear those fields whence exuberant crops are to arise to feed and clothe them all, without any part being claimed, either by a despotic prince, a rich abbot, or a mighty lord. Here religion demands but little of him: a small voluntary salary to the minister and gratitude to God; can he refuse these? The American is a new man, who acts upon new principles; he must therefore entertain new ideas and form new opinions. From involuntary idleness, servile dependence, penury, and useless labor, he has passed to toils of a very different nature, rewarded by ample subsistence. This is an American.

JAMES CONE
Martin and Malcolm and America

America is a rainbow.... America is European and African and much more. It is the "much more"—Indians, Asians, Latinos, and others—which makes the country a rainbow.

LANGSTON HUGHES
"My Early Days in Harlem"

Melting pot Harlem—Harlem of honey and chocolate and caramel and rum and vinegar and lemon and lime and gall. Dusky dream Harlem rumbling into a nightmare tunnel where the subway from the Bronx keeps right on downtown, where the money from the nightclubs goes right on back downtown, where the jazz is drained to Broadway, whence Josephine goes to Paris, Robeson to London. Jean Toomer to a Quaker Meeting House.

THE REV. HUGH JONES

If New England be called a Receptacle of Dissenters, and an Amsterdam of Religion, Pennsylvania the Nursery of Quakers, Maryland the Retirement of Roman Catholics, North Carolina the Refuge of Run-aways, and South Carolina the Delight of Buccaneers and Pirates, Virginia may be justly esteemed the happy Retreat of true Britons and true Churchmen for the most Part; neither soaring too high nor drooping too low, consequently should merit the greater Esteem and Encouragement.

JAMES MADISON
National Gazette

Freedom of emigration is favorable to morals.

SAMUEL ADAMS
Philadelphia speech

Driven from every other corner of the earth, freedom of thought and the right of private judgment in matters of conscience direct their course to this happy country as their last asylum.

JAMES MADISON
Letter to Thomas Jefferson on restrictions placed on immigration

The Alien bill proposed in the Senate is a monster that must forever disgrace its parents.

MILLARD FILLMORE
Newburgh, New York, speech

I have no hostility to foreigners. Having witnessed their deplorable condition in the old country, God forbid that I should add to their sufferings by refusing them an asylum in this.

HENRY CABOT LODGE

It is the flag just as much of the man who was naturalized yesterday as of the man whose people have been here many generations.

ANONYMOUS HUNGARIAN IMMIGRANT

The President is Mister and I am Mister, too.

JOHN F. KENNEDY
Washington, D.C., speech

Our Constitution is founded on the principle that all men are equal as citizens, and entitled to the same rights, whether they achieved citizenship by birth, or after coming here as immigrants, seeking to find in America new freedom and new opportunities.

RALPH ELLISON
The Invisible Man

America is woven of many strands; I would recognize them and let it so remain. Our fate is to become one, and yet many.

JIMMY CARTER
New York City speech

We are, of course, a nation of differences. Those differences don't make us weak. They're the source of our strength. The question is not when we came here but why our families came here. And what we did after we arrived.

RALPH WALDO EMERSON
Journals

A nation, like a tree, does not thrive well till it is engraffed with a foreign stock.

WALTER LIPPMANN
A Preface to Politics

The great social adventure of America is no longer the conquest of the wilderness but the absorption of fifty different peoples.

DWIGHT D. EISENHOWER
State of the Union Address

We are—one and all—immigrants or sons and daughters of immigrants.

LYNDON B. JOHNSON
Message to Congress

Over the years the ancestors of all of us—some 42 million human beings—have migrated to these shores. The fundamental, longtime American attitude has been to ask not where a person comes from but what are his personal qualities. On this basis men and women migrated from every quarter of the globe. By their hard work and their enormously varied talents they hewed a great nation out of a wilderness. By their dedication to liberty and equality, they created a society reflecting man's most cherished ideals.

HARRY S TRUMAN
Chicago speech

No nation on this globe should be more internationally minded than America because it was built by all nations.

WILLIAM JENNINGS BRYAN
"America's Mission" speech

Great has been the Greek, the Latin, the Slav, the Celt, the Teuton, and the Anglo-Saxon, but greater than any of these is the American, in which are blended the virtues of them all.

RALPH WALDO EMERSON
Journals

The office of America is to liberate, to abolish kingcraft, priestcraft, caste, monopoly, to pull down the gallows, to burn up the bloody statute-book, to take in the immigrant, to open the doors of the sea and the fields of the earth.

JIMMY CARTER
Pittsburgh, Pennsylvania, speech

We become not a melting pot but a beautiful mosaic. Different people, different beliefs, different yearnings, different hopes, different dreams.

OSCAR HANDLIN
The Uprooted

Once I thought to write a history of immigrants in America. Then I discovered that the immigrants were American history.

MARY MARGARET McBRIDE
America for Me

Yes, we have a good many poor tired people here already, but we have plenty of mountains, rivers, woods, lots of sunshine and air, for tired people to rest in. . . . So give us as many as come —we can take it, and take care of them.

JOHN F. KENNEDY
Television address

This nation was founded by men of many nations and backgrounds. It was founded on the principle that all men are created equal, and that the rights of every man are diminished when the rights of one man are threatened.

"America"

WILLIAM CULLEN BRYANT

Oh, mother of a mighty race,
Yet lovely in thy youthful grace!
The elder dames, thy haughty peers,
Admire and hate thy blooming years.
    With words of shame
And taunts of scorn they join thy name.

For on thy cheeks the glow is spread
That tints the morning hills with red:
Thy step—the wild deer's rustling feet
Within the woods, are not more fleet;
    Thy hopeful eye
Is bright as thine own sunny sky.

Ay, let them rail—those haughty ones—
While safe thou dwellest with thy sons.
They do not know how loved thou art—
How many a fond and fearless heart
    Would rise to throw
Its life between thee and the foe!

They know not, in their hate and pride,
What virtues with thy children bide;
How true, how good, thy graceful maids
Make bright, like flowers, the valley shades;
    What generous men
Spring, like thine oaks, by hill and glen:

What cordial welcomes greet the guest
By the lone rivers of the west;
How faith is kept and truth revered,
And man is loved, and God is feared,
    In woodland homes,
And where the solemn ocean foams!

There's freedom at thy gates, and rest
For earth's down-trodden and oppressed,
A shelter for the hunted head,
For the starved laborer toil and bread,
    Power, at thy bounds,
Stops and calls back his baffled hounds.

Oh, fair young mother; on thy brow
Shall sit a nobler grace than now.
Deep in the brightness of thy skies
The thronging years in glory rise,
    And, as they fleet,
Drop strength and riches at thy feet.

Thine eye, with every coming hour,
Shall brighten, and thy form shall tower;
And when thy sisters, elder born,
Would brand thy name with words of scorn,
    Before thine eye,
Upon their lips the taunt shall die!

WILLIAM RANDOLPH HEARST

Testimony to American Crime Study Commission

What has become of the descendants of the irresponsible adventurers, the scapegrace sons, the bond servants, the redemptionists and the indentured maidens, the undesirables, and even the criminals, which made up, not all, of course, but nevertheless a considerable part of, the earliest emigrants to these virgin countries? They have become the leaders of the thought of the world, the vanguard in the march of progress, the inspirers of liberty, the creators of national prosperity, the sponsors of universal education and enlightenment.

Theodore Roosevelt

This is a new nation, based on a mighty continent, of boundless possibilities. No other nation in the world has such resources. No other nation has ever been so favored. If we dare to rise level to the opportunities offered us, our destiny will be vast beyond the power of imagination. We must master this destiny, and make it our own; and we can thus make it our own only if we, as a vigorous and separate nation, develop a great and wonderful nationality, distinctively different from any other nationality, of either the present or the past. For such a nation all of us can well afford to give up all other allegiances, and high of heart to stand, a mighty and united people, facing a future of glorious promise.

"Uncle Sam's Farm"

The Hutchinson Family

Of all the mighty nations
In the east or west,
Oh, this glorious Yankee nation
Is the greatest and the best;
We have room for all creation,
And our banner is unfurl'd;
Here's a gen'ral invitation
To the people of the world.

Saint Lawrence marks our northern line,
As fast her waters flow;
And the Rio Grande our southern bound,
'Way down to Mexico.
From the great Atlantic Ocean,
Where the sun begins to dawn,
Leap across the Rocky Mountains
Far away to Oregon.

While the South shall raise the cotton,
And the West, the corn and pork,
New England manufactories
Shall do up the finer work;

For the deep and flowing waterfalls
That course along our hills
Are just the thing for washing sheep,
And driving cotton mills.

Our fathers gave us liberty,
But little did they dream
The grand results that pour along
This mighty are of steam;
For our mountains, lakes, and rivers
Are all a blaze of fire,
And we send our news by lightning,
On the telegraphic wires.

Yes, we're bound to beat the nations,
For our motto's "Go ahead,"
And we'll tell the foreign paupers
That our people are well fed;
For the nations must remember
That Uncle Sam is not a fool,
For the people do the voting,
And the children go to school.

Then come along, come along, make no delay;
Come from ev'ry nation,
Come from ev'ry way;
Our lands, they are broad enough,
Don't be alarmed;
For Uncle Sam is rich enough to give us all a farm.

BENJAMIN FRANKLIN

There is, in short, no Bound to the prolific Nature of Plants or Animals [in America], but what is made by their crowding and interfering with each other's means of Subsistence.

HENRY WADSWORTH LONGFELLOW
"A Psalm of Life"

Let us, then, be up and doing,
With a heart for any fate;
Still achieving, still pursuing,
Learn to labor and to wait.

ULYSSES S. GRANT

Labor disgraces no man; unfortunately, you occasionally find men who disgrace labor.

LOUISA MAY ALCOTT
Letter to the Lukens Sisters

Work is such a beautiful and helpful thing and independence so delightful that I wonder there are any lazy people in the world.

LOUISA MAY ALCOTT
Letter to Abigail May Alcott

I am happy, very happy tonight for my five years work is done, and whether it succeeds or not, I shall be the richer and better for it, because the labor, love, disappointment, hope and purpose, that have gone into it, are a useful experience that I shall never forget.

TENNESSEE WILLIAMS

When I stop [working], the rest of the day is posthumous. I'm only really alive when I'm working.

JAMES RUSSELL LOWELL
A Glance Behind the Curtain

No man is born into the world, whose work
Is not born with him; there is always work,
And tools to work withal, for those who will:
And blessed are the horny hands of toil!

LARRY MOREY
Snow White

Heigh ho, heigh ho!
It's off to work we go!

HELEN KELLER

The world is moved not only by the mighty shoves of the heroes, but also by the aggregate of the tiny pushes of each honest worker.

BENJAMIN FRANKLIN
Poor Richard's Almanack

Little strokes fell great oaks.

KURT VONNEGUT
Player Piano

Where men had once howled and hacked at one another, and fought nip-and-tuck with nature as well, the machines hummed and whirred and clicked, and made parts for baby carriages and bottle-caps, motorcycles and refrigerators, television sets and tricycles—the fruits of peace.

RUSSELL BAKER
The Good Times

A man doesn't amount to something because he has been successful at a third-rate career like journalism. It is evidence, that's all: evidence that if he buckled down and worked hard, he might some day do something really worth doing.

MARTIN LUTHER KING, JR.

If a man is called to be a streetsweeper, he should sweep streets even as Michelangelo painted, or Beethoven composed music, or Shakespeare wrote poetry. He should sweep streets so well that all the hosts of heaven and earth will pause to say, here lived a great streetsweeper who did his job well.

WALT WHITMAN
"I Hear America Singing"

I hear America singing, the varied carols I hear,
Those of mechanics, each one singing his as it should be blithe and strong,
The carpenter singing his as he measures his plank or beam,
The mason singing his as he makes ready for work, or leaves off work,
The boatman singing what belongs to him in his boat, the deck-hand
    singing on the steamboat deck,
The shoemaker singing as he sits on his bench, the hatter singing as
    he stands,
The wood-cutter's song, the ploughboy's on his way in the morning,
    or at noon intermission or at sundown,
The delicious singing of the mother, or of the young wife at work, or
    of the girl sewing or washing,
Each singing what belongs to him or her and to none else,
The day what belongs to the day—at night the party of young
    fellows, robust, friendly,
Singing with open mouths their strong melodious songs.

THOMAS McGUANE

After fifty years of living, it occurs to me that the most significant thing that people do is go to work, whether it is to go to work on their novel or at the assembly plant or fixing somebody's teeth.

OLIVER WENDELL HOLMES, JR.

For me, at least, there came moments when faith wavered. But there is the great lesson and the great triumph: keep the fire burning until, by and by, out of the mass of sordid details there comes some result.

WILLIAM SAROYAN

Good people are good because they've come to wisdom through failure.

RALPH WALDO EMERSON
Journals

Be a football to Time and Chance, the more kicks, the better, so that you inspect the whole game and know its utmost law.

HARRY S TRUMAN

I studied the lives of great men and famous women, and I found that the men and women who got to the top were those who did the jobs they had in hand, with everything they had of energy and enthusiasm and hard work.

ABRAHAM LINCOLN

Property is the fruit of labor; Property is desirable, is a positive good in the world. That some should be rich shows that others may become rich, and hence is just encouragement to industry and enterprise. Let not him who is houseless pull down the house of another, but let him work diligently and build one for himself, thus by example assuring that his own shall be safe from violence when built.

OLIVER WENDELL HOLMES, SR.
The Autocrat of the Breakfast-Table

Of course everybody likes and respects self-made men. It is a great deal better to be made in that way than not to be made at all.

HORATIO ALGER
Mark, the Match Boy

He had observed that those young men who out of economy contented themselves with small and cheerless rooms, in which there was no provision for a fire, were driven in the evening to the streets, theaters, and hotels, for the comfort which they could not find at home. Here they felt obliged to spend money to an extent of which they probably were not themselves fully aware, and in the end wasted considerably more than the two or three dollars a week extra which would have provided them with a comfortable home. But this was not all. In the roamings spent outside many laid the foundation of wrong habits, which eventually led to ruin or shortened their lives. They lost all chance of improvement which they might have secured by study at home in the long winter evenings, and which in the end might have qualified them for posts of higher responsibility, and with a larger compensation.

ANDREW CARNEGIE
"Wealth"

The Socialist or Anarchist who seeks to overturn present conditions is to be regarded as attacking the foundation upon which civilization itself rests, for civilization took its start from the day when the capable, industrious workman said to his incompetent lazy fellow, "If thou doest not sow, thou shalt not reap," and thus ended primitive Communism by separating the drones from the bees. One who studies this subject will soon be brought face to face with the conclusion that upon the sacredness of property civilization itself depends—the right of the laborer to his hundred dollars in the savings bank, and equally the legal right of the millionaire to his millions. . . . Not evil, but good, has come to the race from the accumulation of wealth by those who have had the ability and energy to produce it.

ALEXIS DE TOCQUEVILLE
Democracy in America, Part II

The love of wealth is therefore to be traced, as either a principal or accessory motive, at the bottom of all that the Americans do; this gives to all their passions a sort of family likeness. . . . It may be said that it is the vehemence of their desires that makes the Americans so methodical; it perturbs their minds, but it disciplines their lives.

IRA GERSHWIN
A Damsel in Distress

Nice work if you can get it,
and you can get it—if you try.

THOMAS EDISON
Life

Genius is one percent inspiration and ninety-nine percent perspiration.

BENJAMIN FRANKLIN

He that waits upon fortune is never sure of a dinner.

DIANA ROSS
Essence magazine

You can't just sit there and wait for people to give you that golden dream, you've got to get out there and make it happen yourself.

MARIAN WRIGHT EDELMAN
"We Must Convey to Children That We Believe in Them"

Tell our children they're not going to jive their way up the career ladder. They have to work their way up hard. There's no fast elevator to the top.

ABRAHAM LINCOLN

There is no permanent class of hired laborers among us. Twenty-five years ago, I was a hired laborer. The hired laborer of yesterday, labors on his own account today; and will hire others to labor for him tomorrow.

JAMES RUSSELL LOWELL
New England Two Centuries Ago

There is no better ballast for keeping the mind steady on its keel, and saving it from all risk of crankiness, than business.

PETER DRUCKER

Wherever you see a successful business, someone once made a courageous decision.

JOSH BILLINGS [HENRY WHEELER SHAW]
Affurisms

Put an Englishman into the garden of Eden, and he would find fault with the whole blarsted consarn; put a Yankee in, and he would see where he could alter it to advantage.

CALVIN COOLIDGE

The chief business of the American people is business.

LUIGI BARZINI
O America

Who in Europe could have thought of the disappearing bed, a bed during the night, a handsome wardrobe during the day? Where else than in the United States could the rocking chair have been invented, in which a man could move and sit still at the same time?

RALPH WALDO EMERSON
Nature: Addresses and Lectures

Trade is a plant which grows wherever there is peace, as soon as there is peace, and as long as there is peace.

BENJAMIN FRANKLIN
Poor Richard's Almanack

Keep thy shop, and thy shop will keep thee.

EMILY DICKINSON
Poems

'Tis sweet to know that stocks will stand
When we with daisies lie,
That commerce will continue,
And trades as briskly fly.

RALPH WALDO EMERSON
Representative Men

No man acquires property without acquiring with it a little arithmetic also.

THOMAS JEFFERSON
First annual message to Congress

Agriculture, manufactures, commerce, and navigation, the four pillars of our prosperity, are then most thriving when left most free to individual enterprise.

FRANKLIN D. ROOSEVELT

I believe, I have always believed, and I will always believe in private enterprise as the backbone of economic well-being in America.

BOOKER T. WASHINGTON
Selected Speeches of Booker T. Washington

Go with me tonight to the Tuskegee Institute . . . in an old plantation where a few years ago my people were bought and sold, and I will show you an industrial village with nearly eight hundred young men and women working . . . preparing themselves that they may prepare thousands of others of our race that they may contribute their full quota of virtue, of thrift and intelligence to the prosperity of their beloved country.

JAMES BROWN
Statement in Washington, D.C., during riots after the death of Martin Luther King, Jr.

The real answer to race problems in this country is education. Not burning and killing. Be ready. Be qualified. Own something. Be somebody. That's Black Power.

HENRY DAVID THOREAU

What recommends commerce to me is its enterprise and bravery. It does not clasp its hands and pray to Jupiter.

BENJAMIN FRANKLIN

The secret of success is constancy to purpose.

FRANK LLOYD WRIGHT

I know the price of success: dedication, hard work and an unremitting devotion to the things you want to see happen.

HORATIO ALGER
Nothing to Do

In this model republic, this land of the free—
So our orators call it, and why should not we?—
'Tis refreshing to know that without pedigree
A man may still climb to the top of the tree.

H.L. MENCKEN
"Good Business and Good Sense," *The Baltimore Evening Sun*

I have spoken of the desire for profit as the fundamental motive of the actual business man. I believe that it is, and I believe that the fact is fortunate for all of us. In the long run the only way to get a profit is to offer sound goods at fair prices. If the goods are bad customers will not come back; if the prices are too high they will not come back. When a man has a good business, making money year in and year out, it simply means that his customers have learned to trust him—that he is offering something that people want, and at prices they can comfortably pay. This is service with a small s, but it is real; whereas the kind with the capital S is a fake.

But there is more. A man in business is not a mere machine for making money. The same vanities that are in all of us are in him; he likes to do his job a bit better than the next fellow; he likes to be admired, and maybe envied. In other words, he has pride of workmanship. It pleases him to hear people say that what he sells is good, and to see them part with their money willingly and come back for more. The profits, true enough, caress him, but so do the friendly feelings and the general respect. Good will is not only an asset on his books; it is also something that tickles his midriff.

This pride of workmanship is in all men above the rank of earthworms. It is, beyond even the desire for gain, the thing that makes men labor in the heat of the day. No other incentive to industry offers so powerful a stimulus, or brings such satisfying rewards. The man who has done a good job, and knows it, is a man who comes as near to happiness as anyone ever gets on this lugubrious ball. A cataract of molasses runs down his back; his nostrils are enchanted by the sniff of genuine pre-Prohibition stuff; a sweet singing, as of angels well-grounded in solfeggio, is in his ears.

THEODORE ROOSEVELT

Like all Americans, I like big things: big prairies, big forests, and mountains, big wheat fields, railroads...and everything else. But no people ever yet benefited by riches if their prosperity corrupted their virtue.

Advice to a Young Tradesman

BENJAMIN FRANKLIN
Poor Richard's Almanack

To my Friend, A. B.: As you have desired it of me, I write the following hints, which have been of service to me, and may, if observed, be so to you.

Remember that time is money. He that can earn ten shillings a day by his labor and goes abroad or sits idle one-half of that day, though he spends but sixpence during his diversion or idleness, ought not to reckon that the only expense; he has really spent, or rather thrown away, five shillings besides.

Remember that credit is money. If a man lets his money lie in my hands after it is due, he gives me the interest, or so much as I can make of it during that time. This amounts to a considerable sum where a man has good and large credit and makes good use of it.

Remember that money is of the prolific generating nature. Money can beget money, and its offspring can beget more, and so on. Five shillings turned is six; turned again it is seven and threepence, and so on till it becomes a hundred pounds. The more there is of it the more it produces every turning, so that the profits rise quicker and quicker. He that kills a breeding sow destroys all her offspring to the thousandth generation. He that murders a crown destroys all that might have produced even scores of pounds.

Remember that six pounds a year is but a groat a day. For this little sum (which may be daily wasted either in time or expense unperceived) a man of credit may, on his own security, have the constant possession and use of a hundred pounds. So much in stock briskly turned by an industrious man produces great advantage.

Remember this saying, "Thy good paymaster is lord of another man's purse." He that is known to pay punctually and exactly to the time he promises may at any time and on any occasion raise all the money his friends can spare. This is sometimes of great use. After industry and frugality, nothing contributes more to the raising of a young man in the world than punctuality and justice in all his dealings; therefore never keep borrowed money an hour beyond the time you promised, lest a disappointment shut up your friend's purse for ever.

The most trifling actions that affect a man's credit are to be regarded. The sound of your hammer at five in the morning or nine at night heard by a creditor makes him easy six months longer, but if he sees you at a billiard-table or hears your voice at a tavern, when you should be at work, he sends for his money the next day; demands it, before he can receive it, in a lump.

It shows, besides, that you are mindful of what you owe; it makes you appear a careful as well as an honest man, and that still increases your credit.

Beware of thinking all your own that you possess and of living accordingly. It is a mistake that many people who have credit fall into. To prevent this, keep an exact account for some time, both of your expenses and your income. If you take the pains at first to mention particulars, it will have this good effect; you will discover how wonderfully small, trifling expenses mount up to large sums, and will discern what might have been and may for the future be saved without occasionally any great inconvenience.

In short, the way to wealth, if you desire it, is as plain as the way to the market. It depends chiefly on two words, industry and frugality; that is, waste neither time nor money, but make the best use of both. Without industry and frugality nothing will do, and with them everything. He that gets all he can honestly and saves all he gets (necessary expenses excepted), will certainly become rich, if that Being who governs the world, to whom all should look for a blessing on their honest endeavors, doth not, in His wise providence, otherwise determine.

An Old Tradesman

BENJAMIN FRANKLIN

Thirteen virtues necessary for true success: temperance, silence, order, resolution, frugality, industry, sincerity, justice, moderation, cleanliness, tranquility, chastity, and humility.

RALPH WALDO EMERSON

Without ambition one starts nothing. Without work one finishes nothing. The prize will not be sent to you. As to methods there may be a million and then some, but the principles are few. The man who grasps principles can successfully select his own methods. The man who tries methods, ignoring principles, is sure to have trouble.

MARIA STEWART

Oh, do not say you cannot make anything of your children; but say, with the help and assistance of God, we will try. Perhaps you will say that you cannot send them to high schools and academies. You can have them taught in the first rudiments of useful knowledge, and then you can have private teachers, who will instruct them in the higher branches. It is of no use for us to sit with our hands folded, hanging our heads like bulrushes, lamenting our wretched condition but let us make a mighty choice and arise. Let every female heart become united, and let us raise a fund ourselves; and at the end of one year and a half, we might be able to lay the cornerstone for the building of a high school, that the higher branches of knowledge might be enjoyed by us.

Do you ask, what can we do? Unite and build a store of your own. Fill one side with dry goods and the other with groceries. Do you ask, where is the money? We have spent more than enough for nonsense to do what building we should want. We have never had an opportunity of displaying our talents; therefore the world thinks we know nothing.

HENRY FORD

Before everything else, getting ready is the secret of success.

GREER GARSON

Starting out to make money is the greatest mistake in life. Do what you feel you have a flair for doing, and if you are good enough at it, the money will come.

RALPH WALDO EMERSON
"Spiritual Laws," *Essays: First Series*

As a man thinketh so is he, and as a man chooseth so is he.

SOFIA SMITH
Founder of Smith College, from her will

It is my opinion that by the higher and more thorough Christian education of women, what are called their "wrongs" will be redressed, their wages adjusted, their weight of influence in reforming the evils of society will be greatly increased, as teachers, as writers, as mothers, as members of society, their power for good will be incalculably changed.

W.E.B. DuBois
The Souls of Black Folk

The function of the university is not simply to teach bread-winning, or to furnish teachers for the public schools or to be a center of polite society; it is, above all, to be the organ of that fine adjustment between real life and the growing knowledge of life, an adjustment which forms the secret of civilization.

MOTTO OF THE UNITED NEGRO COLLEGE FUND

A mind is a terrible thing to waste.

ELEANOR ROOSEVELT
What Kind of Education Do We Want for Our Girls? The Woman's Journal

I would like to see our schools and our parents cooperate in teaching the younger generation...that the point of real education is an ability to recognize the spirit that is in a real human being, even though it may be obscured for a time by lack of education or opportunity to observe certain social customs.

MANUELITO OF THE NAVAHOS
Speech to Congress

Education is a ladder.

MARK TWAIN

When I was a boy of fourteen, my father was so ignorant I could hardly stand to have the old man around. But when I got to be twenty-one I was astonished at how much the old man had learned in seven years.

OPRAH WINFREY

Luck is a matter of preparation meeting opportunity.

DEAN ACHESON
Address to the Law Club of Chicago

The American dream, I think, was that within this system every man could become an owner. It has been said that every soldier of Napoleon carried in his knapsack a marshal's baton, and in the early days of this century it seems to have been thought that every young American carried in his lunch box a roll of ticker tape.

JOHN KENNETH GALBRAITH
Economic Development

People are the common denominator of progress. So . . . no improvement is possible with unimproved people, and advance is certain when people are liberated and educated. It would be wrong to dismiss the importance of roads, railroads, power plants, mills, and the other familiar furniture of economic development. . . . But we are coming to realize . . . that there is a certain sterility in economic monuments that stand alone in a sea of illiteracy. Conquest of illiteracy comes first.

BARBARA JORDAN

It may not be polished, may not be smooth, and it may not be silky, but it is there. I believe that I get from the soil and the spirit of Texas the feeling that I, as an individual, can accomplish whatever I want to and that there are no limits, that you can just keep going, just keep soaring. I like that spirit.

LYNDON B. JOHNSON
Address, National Urban League Conference

We must open the doors of opportunity. But we also must equip our people to walk though those doors.

JAMES TRUSLOW ADAMS
"The American Dream"

The point is that if we are to have a rich and full life in which all are to share and play their parts, if the American dream is to be a reality, our communal spiritual and intellectual life must be distinctly higher than elsewhere, where classes and groups have their separate interests, habits, markets, arts, and lives. If the dream is not to prove possible of fulfillment, we might as well become stark realists, become once more class-conscious, and struggle as individuals or classes against one another. If it is to come true, those on top, financially, intellectually, or otherwise, have got to devote themselves to the "Great Society," and those who are below in the scale have got to strive to rise, not merely economically, but culturally. We cannot become a great democracy by giving ourselves up as individuals to selfishness, physical comfort, and cheap amusements. The very foundation of the American dream of a better and richer life for all is that all, in varying degrees, shall be capable of wanting to share in it. It can never be wrought into a reality by cheap people or by "keeping up with the Joneses." There is nothing whatever in a fortune merely in itself or in a man merely in himself. It all depends on what is made of each. Lincoln was not great because he was born in a log cabin, but because he got out of it—that is, because he rose above the poverty, ignorance, lack of ambition, shiftlessness of character, contentment with mean things and low aims which kept so many thousands in the huts where they were born.

JOHN D. ROCKEFELLER III

The road to happiness lies in two simple principles: find what it is that interests you and that you can do well, and when you find it, put your whole soul into it—every bit of energy and ambition and natural ability you have.

HORACE GREELEY
Cited in James Parton, Life of Horace Greeley

The best business you can go into you will find on your father's farm or in his workshop. If you have no family or friends to aid you, and no prospect opened to you there, turn your face to the great West, and there build up a home and fortune.

JONATHAN RABAN
Old Glory

I loved the audacity of that American principle which says, When life gets tainted or goes stale, junk it! Leave it behind! Go West!

MOTTO ON MASTHEAD OF THE EMIGRANT AID JOURNAL

"Dost thou know to play the fiddle?"

   "No," answered Themistocles, "but I understand the art of raising a little village into a great city."

"The Kansas Emigrants"

JOHN GREENLEAF WHITTIER

We cross the prairie as of old
the pilgrims crossed the sea,
to make the West, as they the East,
The homestead of the free!

We go to rear a wall of men
On Freedom's southern line,
and plant beside the cotton-tree
the rugged Northern pine!

We're flowing from our native hills
As our free rivers flow:
The blessing of our Mother-land
Is on us as we go.

We go to plant her common schools
On distant prairie swells,
and give the Sabbaths of the wild
The music of her bells.

Upbearing, like the Ark of old,
The Bible in our van,
We go to test the truth of God
Against the fraud of man.

No pause, nor rest, save where the streams
that feed the Kansas run,
Save where our Pilgrim gonfalon
Shall flout the setting sun!

We'll tread the prairie as of old
Our fathers sailed the sea,
and make the West, as they the East,
The homestead of the free!

WILLIAM LARIMER
Excerpts from two letters

I have taken two claims at La Platte, Nebraska Territory... and we are laying out a town. I am elected President, and secured ⅓ of the town.... I like this country very much indeed.... I think I can make a big raise here in a few years....

Now my plan is this: I intend to live in La Platte City. I intend to open up a large farm. I can raise hemp, corn or anything.... I will go on with the farm and if the land is ever wanted for a town it is ready.... I intend not only to farm simply but I will open a Commission House. I expect to supply the Territory with iron nails, lumber of building up the city. If I go there I can build the city if I do not go only to sell lots as the city may never rise.

TASCOSA, TEXAS, PIONEER

Truly this is a world which has no regard for the established order of things, but knocks them sky west and crooked, and lo, the upstart hath the land and its fatness.

ANONYMOUS LETTER
Letter describing Oregon

One Saturday morning father said that he was going... to hear Mr. Burnett talk about Oregon.... Mr. Burnett hauled a box out on to the sidewalk, took his stand upon it, and began to tell us about the land flowing with milk and honey on the shores of the Pacific... he told of the great crops of wheat which it was possible to raise in Oregon, and pictured in glowing terms the richness of the soil and the attractions of the climate, and then with a little twinkle in his eye he said "and they do say, that out in Oregon the pigs are running about under the great acorn trees, round and fat, and already cooked, whenever you are hungry."... Father was so moved by what he heard... that he decided to join the company that was going west to Oregon... father... was the first to sign his name."

FRANK BAUM
The Wonderful Wizard of Oz

The road to the City of Emeralds is paved with yellow brick.

YIP HARBURG
"Over the Rainbow"

Somewhere over the rainbow,
Way up high:
There's a land of
Once in a lullaby

AL JOLSON AND BUDDY DE SYLVA
"California, Here I Come," *Bombo*

When the wintry winds are blowing,
And the snow is starting in to fall,
Then my eyes turn westward, knowing
That's the place I love the best of all.
California, I've been blue,
Since I've been away from you,
I can't wait 'til I get going,
even now I'm starting to call
California, here I come
Right back where I started from
Where bowers of flowers bloom in the sun
Each morning at dawning,
Birdies singin' and ev'rything.
A sunkist miss said, "Don't be late"
That's why I can hardly wait
Open up that Golden Gate
California, here I come.

Grapes of Wrath

JOHN STEINBECK

Once California belonged to Mexico and its land to Mexicans; and a horde of tattered feverish Americans poured in. And such was their hunger for land that they took the land—stole Sutter's land, Guerrero's land, took the grants and broke them up and growled and quarreled over them, those frantic hungry men; and they guarded with guns the land they had stolen.

They put up houses and barns, they turned the earth and planted crops. And these things were possession, and possession was ownership.

The Mexicans were weak and fed. They could not resist, because they wanted nothing in the world as frantically as the Americans wanted land.

Then, with time, the squatters were no longer squatters, but owners; and their children grew up and had children on the land. And the hunger was gone from them, the feral hunger, the gnawing, tearing hunger for land, for water and earth and the good sky over it, for the green thrusting grass, for the swelling roots. They had these things so completely that they did not know about them any more. They had no more the stomach-tearing lust for a rich acre and a shining blade to plow it, for seed and a windmill beating its wings in the air. They arose in the dark no more to hear the sleepy birds' first chittering, and the morning wind around the house while they waited for the first light to go out to the dear acres. These things were lost, and crops were reckoned in dollars, and land was valued by the principal plus interest, and crops were bought and sold before they were planted. Then crop failure, drought, and flood were no longer little deaths within life, but simple losses of money. And all their love was thinned with money, and all their fierceness dribbled away in interest until they were no longer farmers at all, but little shopkeepers of crops, little manufacturers who must sell before they can make. Then those farmers who were not good shopkeepers lost their land to the good shop-keepers. No matter how clever, how loving a man might be with earth and growing things, he could not survive if he was not a good shopkeeper. And as time went on, the business men had the farms, and the farms grew larger, but there were fewer of them....

And then the dispossessed were drawn west—from Kansas, Oklahoma, Texas, New Mexico; from Nevada and Arkansas families, tribes, dusted out, tractored out. Carloads, caravans, homeless and hungry; twenty thousand and fifty thousand and a hundred thousand and two hundred thousand. They streamed over the mountains, hungry and restless—restless as ants, scurrying to find work to do—to lift, to push, to pull, to pick, to cut—anything, any burden to bear, for food. The kids are hungry. We got no place to live. Like ants scurrying for work, for food, and most of all for land.

We ain't foreign. Seven generations back Americans, and beyond that Irish, Scotch, English, German. One of our folks in the Revolution, an' they was lots of our folks in the Civil War —both sides. Americans.

They were hungry and they were fierce. And they had hoped to find a home, and they found only hatred. Okies—the owners hated them because the owners knew they were soft and the Okies strong, that they were fed and the Okies hungry; and perhaps the owners had heard from their grandfathers how easy it is to steal land from a soft man if you are fierce and hungry and armed. The owners hated them because they had no money to spend. There is no shorter path to a storekeeper's contempt, and all his admirations are exactly opposite. The town men, little bankers, hated Okies because there was nothing to gain from them. They had nothing. And the laboring people hated Okies because a hungry man must work, and if he must work, if he has to work, the wage payer automatically gives him less for his work; and then no one can get more.

And the dispossessed, the migrants, flowed into California, two hundred and fifty thousand, and three hundred thousand. Behind them new tractors were going on the land and the tenants were being forced off. And the new waves were on the way, new waves of the dispossessed and the homeless, hardened, intent, and dangerous.

And while the Californians wanted many things, accumulation, social success, amusement, luxury, and a curious banking security, the new barbarians wanted only two things—land and food; and to them the two were one. And whereas the wants of the Californians were nebulous and undefined, the wants of the Okies were beside the roads, lying there to be seen and coveted: the good fields with water to be dug for, the good green fields, earth to crumble experimentally in the hand, grass to smell, oaten stalks to chew until the sharp sweetness was in the throat. A man might look at a fallow field and know, and see in his mind that his own bending back and his own straining arms would bring the cabbages into the light, and the golden eating corn, the turnips and carrots.

And a homeless, hungry man, driving the roads with his wife beside him and his thin children in the back seat, could look at the fallow fields which might produce food but not profit, and that man could know how a fallow field is a sin and the unused land a crime against the thin children. And such a man drove along the roads and knew temptation at every field, and knew the lust to take these fields and make them grow strength for his children and a little comfort for his wife. The temptation was before him always. The fields goaded him, and the company ditches with good water flowing were a goad to him.

And in the south he saw the golden oranges hanging on the trees, the little golden oranges on the dark green trees; and guards with shotguns patrolling the lines so a man might not pick an orange for a thin child, oranges to be dumped if the price was low.

He drove his old car into a town. He scoured the farms for work. Where can we sleep tonight?

Well, there's Hooverville on the edge of the river. There a whole raft of Okies there.

He drove his old car to Hooverville. He never asked again, for there was a Hooverville on the edge of every town.

The rag town lay close to water; and the houses were tents, and the weed-thatched enclosures, paper houses, a great junk pile. The man drove his family in and became a citizen of Hooverville—always they were called Hooverville. The man put up his own tent as near to water as he could get; or if he had no tent, he went to the city dump and brought back cartons and built a house of corrugated paper. And when the rains came the house melted and washed away. He settled in Hooverville and he scoured the countryside for work, and the little money he had went for gasoline to look for work. In the evening the men gathered and talked together. Squatting on their hams they talked of the land they had seen.

GEORGE SANTAYANA

[Americans] have all been uprooted from their several soils and ancestries and plunged together into one vortex, whirling irresistibly in a space otherwise quite empty. To be an American is of itself almost a moral condition, an education, and a career.

JAMES RUSSELL LOWELL

A Fable for Critics

Nature fits all her children with something to do,
He who would write and can't write, can surely review.

JAMES GARFIELD

There is nothing in this world so inspiring as the possibilities that lie locked up in the head and breast of a young man.

TED WILLIAMS

At his induction into the Hall of Fame

Baseball gives every American boy a chance to excel. Not just to be as good as someone else, but to be better. This is the nature of man and the name of the game. I hope that some day Satchel Paige and Josh Gibson will be voted into the Hall of Fame as symbols of the great Negro players who are not here only because they weren't given the chance.

HENRY DAVID THOREAU

Walden

What old people say you cannot do, you try and find that you can. Old deeds for old people, and new deeds for new.

ALEXIS DE TOCQUEVILLE

Democracy in America

Amongst democratic nations, each new generation is a new people.

PEARL S. BUCK

The young do not know enough to be prudent, and therefore they attempt the impossible— and achieve it, generation after generation.

DOUGLAS ADAMS
The Long Dark Tea-Time of the Soul

The impossible often has a kind of integrity which the merely improbable lacks.

JOHN F. KENNEDY
Address, United Negro College Fund Convocation

When written in Chinese, the word "crisis" is composed of two characters—one represents danger and the other represents opportunity.

RALPH WALDO EMERSON

The human mind cannot be enshrined in a person who shall set a barrier on any one side to this unbounded, unboundable empire. It is one central fire, which, flaming now out of the lips of Etna, lightens the capes of Sicily; and now out of the throat of Vesuvius, illuminates the towers and vineyards of Naples. It is one light which beams out of a thousand stars. It is one soul which animates all men.

BOOKER T. WASHINGTON
Speech in Chicago

Character, not circumstances, makes the man.

OLIVER WENDELL HOLMES, SR.

The great thing in this world is not so much where we stand, as in what direction we are moving.

WALT WHITMAN
"The Silent General," *September 28, 1879, diary entry*

So General Grant, after circumambiating the world, has arrived home again—landed in San Francisco yesterday, from the ship City of Tokio from Japan. What a man he is! what a history! what an illustration—his life—of the capacities of that American individuality common to us all. Cynical critics are wondering "what the people can see in Grant" to make such a hubbub about. They aver (and it is no doubt true) that he has hardly the average of our day's literary and scholastic culture, and absolutely no pronounc'd genius or conventional eminence of any sort. Correct: but proves how an average western farmer, mechanic, boatman, carried by tides of circumstances, perhaps caprices, into a position of incredible military or civic responsibilities, (history has presented none more trying, no born monarch's, no more shining for attack or envy,) may steer his way fitly and steadily through them all, carrying the country and himself with credit year after year—command over a million armed men—fight more than fifty pitch'd battles—rule for eight years a land larger than all the kingdoms of Europe combined —and then, retiring, quietly (with a cigar in his mouth) make the promenade of the whole world, through its courts and coteries, and kings and czars and mikados, and splendidest glitters and etiquettes, as phlegmatically as he ever walk'd the portico of a Missouri hotel after dinner. I say all this is what people like—and I am sure I like it. Seems to me it transcends Plutarch. How those old Greeks, indeed, would have seized on him! A mere plain man—no art, no poetry—only practical sense, ability to do, or try his best to do, what devolv'd upon him. A common trader, money-maker, tanner, farmer of Illinois—general for the republic, in its terrific struggle within itself, in the war of attempted secession—President following (a task of peace, more difficult than the war itself)—nothing heroic, as the authorities put it—and yet the greatest hero. The gods, the destinies, seem to have concentrated upon him.

ADLAI E. STEVENSON

In America, any boy may become president, and I suppose it's just one of the risks he takes.

SYLVIA PLATH
The Bell Jar

Look what can happen in this country, they'd say. A girl lives in some out-of-the-way town for nineteen years, so poor she can't afford a magazine, and then she gets a scholarship to college and wins a prize here and a prize there and ends up steering New York like her own private car.

HENRY DAVID THOREAU

If one advances confidently in the direction of his dreams, and endeavors to live the life which he has imagined, he will meet with a success unexpected in common hours.

HENRY DAVID THOREAU
"Where I Lived, and What I Lived For"

I know of no more encouraging fact than the unquestionable ability of man to elevate his life by a conscious endeavor.

RALPH WALDO EMERSON
Letters

America means opportunity, freedom, power.

RALPH WALDO EMERSON

The world is all gates, all opportunities, strings of tension waiting to be struck.

F. SCOTT FITZGERALD

One should . . . be able to see things as hopeless and yet be determined to make them otherwise.

ELEANOR ROOSEVELT

The future belongs to those who believe in the beauty of their dreams.

BENJAMIN HARRISON

Speech at Marion County, Ohio

I believe also in the American opportunity which puts the starry sky above every boy's head, and sets his foot upon a ladder which he may climb until his strength gives out.

MOTTO AT EDWARDS U.S. AIR FORCE TEST BASE

Ad Inexplorate (Toward the Unknown)

JOHN H. GLENN, JR.

People are afraid of the future, of the unknown. If a man faces up to it, and takes the dare of the future, he can have some control over his destiny. That's an exciting idea to me, better than waiting with everybody else to see what's going to happen.

NEIL ARMSTRONG

Comment upon stepping on the moon's surface

That was one small step for a man and a great leap for mankind.

DOUGLAS MACARTHUR

There is no security on this earth; there is only opportunity.

FRANKLIN D. ROOSEVELT

The only limit to our realization of tomorrow will be our doubts of today. Let us move forward with strong and active faith.

HERBERT HOOVER
Inaugural Address

I have no fears for the future of our country. It is bright with hope.

HAL L. BORLAND
Sundial of the Seasons

All our yesterdays are summarized in our now, and all the tomorrows are ours to shape.

HENRY JAMES
Letter to Hugh Walpole

The only way to know is to have lived and loved and cursed and floundered and enjoyed and suffered. I think I don't regret a single "excess" of my responsive youth—I only regret, in my chilled age, certain occasions and possibilities I didn't embrace.

WALT WHITMAN

Darest thou now O soul,
Walk out with me toward the unknown region,
Where neither ground is for the feet nor any
    path to follow?

RALPH WALDO EMERSON
Essays: Second Series

We think our civilization near its meridian, but we are yet only at the cock-crowing and the morning star.

T.S. ELIOT
Four Quartets, Little Gidding, V

We shall not cease from exploration
and the end of all our exploring
will be to arrive where we started
and know the place for the first time.

James Russell Lowell
Ode recited at Harvard Commemoration

She that lifts up the manhood of the poor,
She of the open soul and open door,
With room about her hearth for all mankind!

Mario Cuomo
Democratic Convention speech

I watched a small man with thick calluses on both hands work fifteen and sixteen hours a day. I saw him once literally bleed from the bottoms of his feet, a man who came [to the United States] uneducated, alone, unable to speak the language, who taught me all I needed to know about faith and hard work by the simple eloquence of his example. I learned about our kind of democracy from my father. I learned about our obligation to each other from him and from my mother. They asked only for a chance to work and to make the world better for their children and they asked to be protected in those moments when they would not be able to protect themselves. This nation and this nation's government did that for them.

Pursuit of Happiness

JOHN ADAMS
Thoughts on Government

All sober inquirers after truth, ancient and modern, pagan and Christian, have declared that the happiness of man, as well as his dignity, consists in virtue.

BENJAMIN FRANKLIN
The Thirteen Virtues

1. Temperance: Eat not to dullness. Drink not to elevation.

2. Silence: Speak not but what may benefit others or yourself. Avoid trifling conversation.

3. Order: Let all your things have their places. Let each part of your business have its time.

4. Resolution: Resolve to perform what you ought. Perform without fail what you resolve.

5. Frugality: Make no expense but to do good to others or yourself, i.e., waste nothing.

6. Industry: Lose no time. Be always employed in something useful. Cut off all unnecessary actions.

7. Sincerity: Use no hurtful deceit. Think innocently and justly; if you speak, speak accordingly.

8. Justice: Wrong none by doing injuries or omitting the benefits that are your duty.

9. Moderation: Avoid extremes. Forbear resenting injuries so much as you think they deserve.

10. Cleanliness: Tolerate no uncleanliness in body, clothes, or habitation.

11. Tranquility: Be not disturbed at trifles or at accidents common or unavoidable.

12. Chastity: Rarely use venery but for health or offspring—never to dullness, weakness, or the injury of your own or another's peace or reputation.

---

13. Humility: Imitate Jesus and Socrates.

Let no Pleasure tempt thee, no Profit allure thee, no Ambition corrupt thee, no Example sway thee, no Persuasion move thee, to do anything which thou knowest to be evil; so shalt thou always live jollily; for a good Conscience is a continual Christmas. Adieu.

OGDEN NASH
"I'm a Stranger Here Myself"

There is only one way to achieve happiness
on this terrestrial ball,
and that is to have either a clear conscience,
or none at all.

THOMAS JEFFERSON

Our greatest happiness does not depend on the condition of life in which chance has placed us, but is always the result of a good conscience, good health, occupation and freedom in all just pursuits.

MARK TWAIN

Good friends, good books and a sleepy conscience: this is the ideal life.

ABRAHAM LINCOLN

Do not worry; eat three square meals a day; say your prayers; be courteous to your creditors; keep your digestion good; exercise; go slow and easy. Maybe there are other things your special case requires to make you happy; but, my friend, these I reckon will give you a good lift.

LOUISA MAY ALCOTT
Letter to Maggie Lukens

I will tell you my experience and as it has stood the test of youth and age, health and sickness, joy and sorrow, poverty and wealth I feel that it is genuine, and seems to get more light, warmth and help as I go on learning more of it year by year. My parents never bound us to any church but taught us that the love of goodness was the love of God, the cheerful doing of duty made life happy, and that the love of one's neighbor in its widest sense was the best help for oneself. Their lives showed us how lovely this simple faith was, how much honor, gratitude and affection it brought them, and what a sweet memory they left behind.

GEORGE WASHINGTON

Human happiness and moral duty are inseparably connected.   .

WALT WHITMAN
Preface to the first edition of Leaves of Grass

This is what you shall do: Love the earth and sun and the animals, despise riches, give alms to every one that asks, stand up for the stupid and crazy, devote your income and labor to others, hate tyrants, argue not concerning God.

T.S. ELIOT

To do the useful thing, to say the courageous thing, to contemplate the beautiful thing: that is enough for one man's life.

WILLIAM JAMES

Lives based on having are less free than lives based either on doing or on being.

HELEN KELLER

Many persons have a wrong idea of what constitutes true happiness. It is not attained through self-gratification but through fidelity to a worthy purpose.

ALBERT SCHWEITZER

One thing I know; the only ones among you who will be really happy are those who will have sought and found how to serve.

ELEANOR ROOSEVELT

When you cease to make a contribution you begin to die.

THOMAS JEFFERSON
Letter to his sister, Mrs. Anna Scott Marks

It is neither wealth nor splendor, but tranquility and occupation, which give happiness.

Ralph Waldo Emerson
"Experience," *Essays, Second Series*

To fill the hour—that is happiness; to fill the hour, and leave no crevice for a repentance or an approval.

Ralph Waldo Emerson

The high prize of life, the crowning fortune of man, is to be born with a bias to some pursuit which finds him in employment and happiness.

David Grayson
Adventures in Contentment

Human happiness is the true odour of growth, the sweet exhalation of work.

John Dewey

To find out what one is fitted to do, and to secure an opportunity to do it, is the key to happiness.

Franklin D. Roosevelt
First Inaugural Address

Happiness lies not in the mere possession of money; it lies in the joy of achievement, in the thrill of creative effort.

William Ralph Inge

The happy people are those who are producing something.

Henry Ford

There is no happiness except in the realization that we have accomplished something.

Henry Miller
The Wisdom of the Heart

The moment one is on the side of life "peace and security" drop out of consciousness. The only peace, the only security, is in fulfillment.

WILLIAM JAMES

Action may not always bring happiness, but there is no happiness without action.

MARK TWAIN

To be busy is man's only happiness.

WILLIAM COWPER
Table Talk

Thus happiness depends, as Nature shows,
Less on exterior things than most suppose.

BENJAMIN FRANKLIN
Poor Richard's Almanack

A little house well filled, a little field well tilled, and a little wife well willed, are great riches.

JEROME K. JEROME
Three Men in a Boat

Let your boat of life be light, packed with only what you need—homely home and simple pleasures, one or two friends, worth the name, someone to love and someone to love you, a cat, a dog, and a pipe or two, enough to eat and enough to wear, and a little more than enough to drink, for thirst is a dangerous thing.

ANNE MORROW LINDBERGH
"Gift From the Sea"

One learns first of all in beach living the art of shedding; how little one can get along with, not how much. Physical shedding to begin with, which then mysteriously spreads into other fields. Clothes, first. Of course, one needs less in the sun. But one needs less anyway, one finds suddenly. One does not need a closet-full, only a small suitcase-full. And what a relief it is! Less taking up and down of hems, less mending, and—best of all—less worry about what to wear.

One finds one is shedding not only clothes—but vanity.

Next, shelter. One does not need the airtight shelter one has in winter in the North. Here I live in a bare sea-shell of a cottage. No heat, no telephone, no plumbing to speak of, no hot water, a two-burner oil stove, no gadgets to go wrong. No rugs. There were some, but I rolled them up the first day; it is easier to sweep the sand off a bare floor. But I find I don't bustle about with unnecessary sweeping and cleaning here. I am no longer aware of the dust. I have shed my Puritan conscience about absolute tidiness and cleanliness. Is it possible that, too, is a material burden? No curtains. I do not need them for privacy; the pines around my house are enough protection. I want the windows open all the time, and I don't want to worry about the rain. I begin to shed my Martha-like anxiety about any things. Washable slipcovers, faded and old—I hardly see them; I don't worry about the impression they make on other people. I am shedding pride. As little furniture as possible; I shall not need much. I shall ask into my shell only those friends with whom I can be completely honest. I find I am shedding hypocrisy in human relationships. What a rest that will be! The most exhausting thing in life, I have discovered, is being insincere. That is why so much of social life is exhausting; one is wearing a mask. I have shed my mask.

HENRY DAVID THOREAU
Journals

That man is richest whose pleasures are the cheapest.

HENRY DAVID THOREAU

A man is rich in proportion to the number of things which he can afford to let alone.

HENRY DAVID THOREAU
Walden

I went to the woods because I wished to live deliberately, to front only the essential facts of life, and see if I could not learn what it had to teach, and not, when I came to die, discover that I had not lived. I did not wish to live what was not life, living is so dear; nor did I wish to practice resignation, unless it was quite necessary. I wanted to live deep and suck out all the marrow of life, to live so sturdily and Spartan-like as to put to rout all that was not life, to cut a broad swath and shave close, to drive life into a corner, and reduce it to its lowest terms, and, if it proved to be mean, why then to get the whole and genuine meanness of it, and publish its meanness to the world; or if it were sublime, to know it by experience, and be able to give a true account of it in my next excursion.

OLIVER WENDELL HOLMES, SR.
"Contentment, The Autocrat of the Breakfast-Table"

I care not much for gold or land;—
    Give me a mortgage here and there,—
Some good bank-stock, some note of hand,
    Or trifling railroad share,—

I only ask that Fortune send
A *little* more than I shall spend.

CHARLES FARRAR BROWNE (ARTEMUS WARD)
Natural History

Let us all be happy and live within our means, even if we have to borrow the money to do it with.

WILLIAM ELLERY CHANNING

To live content with small means; to seek elegance rather than luxury, and refinement rather than fashion; to be worthy, not respectable, and wealthy not rich, to study hard, think quietly, talk gently, act frankly; to listen to the stars and birds, to babes and sages, with open heart; to bear on cheerfully, do all bravely, awaiting occasions, worry never; in a work to, like the spiritual, unbidden and unconscious, grow up through the common.

RALPH WALDO EMERSON
The American Scholar

I embrace the common, I explore and sit at the feet of the familiar, the low. Give me insight into to-day, and you may have the antique and future worlds. What would we really know the meaning of? The meal in the firkin; the milk in the pan; the ballad in the street; the news of the boat.

BENJAMIN FRANKLIN
Autobiography

Human felicity is produced not so much by great pieces of good fortune that seldom happen, as by little advantages that occur every day.

MARTHA WASHINGTON

The greater part of our happiness or misery depends on our dispositions, and not our circumstances.

HELEN KELLER

Everything has its wonders, even darkness and silence, and I learn, whatever state I may be in, therein to be content.

RALPH WALDO EMERSON
Journals

It is a happy talent to know how to play.

MARION WRIGHT EDELMAN
Preface to Guide My Feet: Prayers and Meditations
on Loving and Working for Children

Every schoolday morning we got up to the smells of breakfast cooking and came home every afternoon to a hot dinner and discussions about our day. After cleaning up the kitchen, we did our homework and went out in the yard to play marbles, dodgeball, horseshoes, red light, Mama May I, regular jump rope or double-dutch, hide-and-seek, and hopscotch. We had a snack, read or played a game of jacks, Old Maid, Monopoly, Chinese checkers, or pickup sticks, had our sponge baths, said our prayers, and went to bed about nine o'clock to get ready for another day. We had fun without a lot of money.

WILL DURANT

Civilization is a stream with banks. The stream is sometimes filled with blood from people killing, stealing, shouting, and doing the things historians usually record—while, on the banks, unnoticed, people build homes, make love, raise children, sing songs, write poetry, whittle statues. The story of civilization is the story of what happens on the banks.

ROBERT FROST
Birches

Earth's the right place for love: I don't know where it's likely to go better.

RICHARD EBERHART
"The Goal of Intellectual Man," *Song and Idea*

> But it is human love, love
> Concrete, specific, in a natural move
> Gathering goodness, it is free
> In the blood as in the mind's harmony,
> It is love discoverable here
> Difficult, dangerous, pure, clear
> The truth of the positive hour
> Composing all of human power.

EMILY DICKINSON

Eden is that old-fashioned House
We dwell in every day
Without suspecting our abode
Until we drive away.

THORNTON WILDER
Our Town

Good-by, Good-by, world. Good-by, Grover's Corners... Mama and Papa. Good-by to clocks ticking... and Mama's sunflowers. And food and coffee. And new-ironed dresses and hot baths... and sleeping and waking up. Oh, earth, you're too wonderful for anybody to realize you... Do any human beings ever realize life while they live it?—every, every minute?

GEORGE WASHINGTON
Letter to Martha Washington

I should enjoy more real happiness in one month with you at home, than I have the most distant prospect of finding abroad, if my stay were to be seven times seven years.

THOMAS JEFFERSON

The happiest moments of my life have been the few which I have passed at home in the bosom of my family.

WILLIAM JAMES LAMPTON
"June Weddings"

Same old slippers,
Same old rice,
Same old glimpse of Paradise.

JAMES AGEE
Letter to Father Flye

Inevitably barring one's own family, they're the most beautiful and most happy to know and watch, I'd ever seen. Mr. Saunders is something like my grandfather, with the bitterness and unhappiness removed, but with the same calm, beauty and fortitude. I don't know how brilliant a man he might have been, if he'd grimly fought out one of his talents (music most likely, or painting): at any rate, he evidently decided, when he was quite young, not to try it: rather, to work calmly and hard, but with no egoism, on *all* the things he cared most about—and he's resolved his life into the most complete and genuine happiness.

RALPH WALDO EMERSON
"Give All to Love"

Give all to love;
Obey thy heart;
Friends, kindred, days,
Estate, good fame,
Plans, credit and the Muse,
Nothing refuse.

'Tis a brave master;
Let it have scope:
Follow it utterly,
Hope beyond hope:
High and more high
It dives into noon,
With wing unspent,
Untold intent;
But it is a god,
Knows its own path
And the outlets of the sky.

It was never for the mean;
It requireth courage stout.
Souls above doubt,
Valor unbending,
It will reward,—
They shall return
More than they were,
And ever ascending.

SARA DELANO ROOSEVELT
Letter to Franklin and Eleanor

Well, I hope that while I live I may keep my "Old fashioned" theories and that *at least* in my own family I may continue to feel that *home* is the best and happiest place and that my son and daughter and their children will live in peace and keep from the tarnish which seems to affect so many.

JOHN HOWARD PAYNE
Home, Sweet Home

'Mid pleasures and palaces though we may roam,
Be it ever so humble, there's no place like home;
A charm from the sky seems to hallow us there,
Which, seek through the world, is ne'er met with elsewhere.

The Night the Bed Fell

JAMES THURBER

I suppose that the high-water mark of my youth in Columbus, Ohio, was the night the bed fell on my father. It makes a better recitation (unless, as some friends of mine have said, everyone has heard it five or six times) than it does a piece of writing, for it is almost necessary to throw furniture around, shake doors, and bark like a dog, to lend the proper atmosphere and verisimilitude to what is admittedly a somewhat incredible tale. Still, it did take place.

It happened, then, that my father had decided to sleep in the attic one night, to be away where he could think.

My mother opposed the notion strongly, she said, the old wooden bed up there was unsafe: it was wobbly and the heavy headboard would crash down on father's head in case the bed fell, and kill him. There was no dissuading him, however, and at a quarter past ten he closed the attic door behind him and went up the narrow twisting stairs. We later heard ominous creakings as he crawled into bed. Grandfather, who usually slept in the attic bed when he was with us, had disappeared some days before. (On these occasions he was usually gone six or eight days and returned growling and out of temper, with the news that the federal Union was run by a passel of blockheads and that the Army of the Potomac didn't have any more chance than a fiddler's bitch.)

We had visiting us at this time a nervous first cousin of mine named Briggs Beall, who believed that he was likely to cease breathing when he was asleep. It was his feeling that if he were not awakened every hour during the night, he might die of suffocation. He had been accustomed to setting an alarm clock to ring at intervals until morning, but I persuaded him to abandon this. He slept in my room and I told him that I was such a light sleeper that if anybody quit breathing in the same room with me, I would wake instantly. He tested me the first night—which I suspected he would—by holding his breath after my regular breathing had convinced him I was asleep. I was not asleep, however, and called to him. This seemed to allay his fears a little, but he took the precaution of putting a glass of spirits of camphor on a little table at the head of his bed. In case I didn't arouse him until he was almost gone, he said, he would sniff the camphor, a powerful reviver. Briggs was not the only member of the family who had his crotchets. Old Aunt Melissa Beall (who could whistle like a man, with two fingers in her mouth) suffered under the premonition that she was destined to die on South High Street, because she had been born on South High Street and married on South High Street. Then there was Aunt Sarah Shoaf, who never went to bed at night without the fear that a burglar was going to get in and blow chloroform under her door through a tube. To avert this calamity—for she was in greater dread of anesthetics than of losing her household goods—she always piled her money, silverware, and other valuables in a neat stack just outside her bedroom, with a note reading: "This is all I have. Please take it and do not use your chloroform, as this is all I have." Aunt Gracie Shoaf also had a burglar phobia, but she met it with more fortitude. She was confident that burglars were getting into her house every night for forty years. The fact that she never missed anything was to her no proof to the contrary. She always claimed that she scared them off just before they could take anything, by throwing shoes down the hallway. When she went to bed she piled, where she could get at them handily, all the shoes there were about her house. Five minutes after she had turned off the light, she would sit up in bed and say "Hark!" Her husband, who had learned to ignore the whole situation as long ago as 1903, would either be sound asleep or pretend to be sound asleep. In either case, he would not respond to her tugging and pulling, so that presently she would arise, tiptoe to the door, open it slightly and heave a shoe down the hall in one direction and its mate down the hall in the other direction. Some nights she threw them all, some nights only a couple of pair.

But I am straying from the remarkable incidents that took place during the night that the bed fell on father. By midnight we were all in bed. The layout of the rooms and the disposition of their occupants is important to an understanding of what later occurred. In the front room upstairs (just under father's attic bedroom) were my mother and my brother Herman, who sometimes sang in his sleep, usually "Marching Through Georgia" or "Onward, Christian Soldiers." Briggs and myself were in a room adjoining this one. My brother Roy was in a room across the hall from ours. Our bull terrier, Rex, slept in the hall.

My bed was an army cot, one of those affairs which are made wide enough to sleep on comfortably only by putting up, flat with the middle section, the two sides which ordinarily hang down like the sideboards of a drop-leaf table. When these sides are up, it is perilous to roll too far toward the edge, for then the cot is likely to tip completely over, bringing the whole bed down on top of one with a tremendous banging crash. This, in fact, is precisely what happened, about two o'clock in the morning. (It was my mother who, in recalling the scene later, first referred to it as "the night the bed fell on your father.")

Always a deep sleeper, slow to arouse (I had lied to Briggs), I was at first unconscious of what had happened when the iron cot rolled me onto the floor and toppled over on me. It left me still warmly bundled up and unhurt, for the bed rested above me like a canopy. Hence I did not wake up, only reached the edge of consciousness and went back. The racket, however, instantly awakened my mother, in the next room, who came to the immediate conclusion that her worst dread was realized: the big wooden bed upstairs had fallen on father. She therefore screamed, "Let's go to your poor father!" It was this shout, rather than the noise of my cot falling, that awakened my brother Herman, in the same room with her. He thought that my mother had become, for no apparent reason, hysterical. "You're all right, mamma!" he shouted, trying to calm her. They exchanged shout for shout for perhaps ten seconds: "Let's go to your poor father!" and "You're all right!" That woke up Briggs. By this time I was conscious of what was going on, in a vague way, but did not yet realize that I was under my bed instead of on it. Briggs, awakening in the middle of loud shouts of fear and apprehension, came to the quick conclusion that he was suffocating and we were all trying to "bring him out." With a low moan, he grasped the glass of camphor at the head of his bed and instead of sniffing it poured it over himself. The room reeked of camphor. "Ugf, ahgf!" choked Briggs, like a drowning man, for he had almost succeeded in stopping his breath under the deluge of pungent spirits. He leaped out of bed and groped toward the open window, but he came up against one that was closed. With his hand, he beat out the glass, and I could hear it crash and tinkle in the alley-way below. It was at this juncture that I, in trying to get up, had the uncanny sensation of feeling my bed above me! Foggy with sleep, I now suspected, in my turn, that the whole uproar was being made in a frantic endeavor to extricate me from what must be an unheard-of and perilous situation. "Get me out of this!" I bawled. "Get me out!" I think I had the nightmarish belief that I was entombed in a mine. "Gugh!" gasped Briggs, floundering in his camphor.

By this time my mother, still shouting, pursued by Herman, still shouting, was trying to open the door to the attic, in order to go up to get my father's body out of the wreckage. The door was stuck, however, and wouldn't yield. Her frantic pulls on it only added to the general banging and confusion. Roy and the dog were now up, the one shouting questions, the other barking.

Father, farthest away and soundest asleep of all, had by this time been awakened by the battering on the attic door. He decided that the house was on fire. "I'm coming, I'm coming!" he wailed in a slow, sleepy voice—it took him many minutes to regain full consciousness. My mother, still believing he was caught under the bed, detected in his "I'm coming!" the mournful, resigned note of one who is preparing to meet his Maker. "He's dying!" she shouted.

"I'm all right!" Briggs yelled, to reassure her. "I'm all right!" He still believed that it was his own closeness to death that was worrying mother. I found at last the light switch in my room, unlocked the door, and Briggs ad I joined the others at the attic door. The dog, who never did like Briggs, jumped for him—assuming that he was the culprit in whatever was going on—

and Roy had to throw Rex and hold him. We could hear father crawling out of bed upstairs. Roy pulled the attic door open, with a mighty jerk, and father came down the stairs, sleepy and irritable but safe and sound. My mother began to weep when she saw him. Rex began to howl. "What in the name of God is going on here?" asked father.

The situation was finally put together like a gigantic jigsaw puzzle. Father caught a cold from prowling around in his bare feet but there were no other bad results. "I'm glad," said mother, who always looked on the bright side of things, "that your grandfather wasn't there."

HENRY WADSWORTH LONGFELLOW
"Birds of Passage"

Stay, stay at home, my heart, and rest;
Home-keeping hearts are happiest,
For those that wander they know not where
Are full of trouble and full of care;
To stay at home is best.

JEROME K. JEROME
The Passing of the Third Floor Back

"Nothing, so it seems to me," said the stranger, "is more beautiful than the love that has weathered the storms of life....The love of the young for the young, that is the beginning of life. But the love of the old for the old, that is the beginning of—of things longer."

EDGAR LEE MASTERS
Lucinda Matlock, from "Spoon River Anthology"

I went to the dances at Chandlerville,
And played snap-out at Winchester
One time we changed partners,
Driving home in the moonlight in middle June,
And then I found Davis.
We were married and lived together for seventy years,
Enjoying, working, raising the twelve children,
Eight of whom we lost
Ere I had reached the age of sixty.
I spun, I wove, I kept the house, I nursed the sick,
I made the garden, and for holiday
Rambled over the fields where snag the larks,
And by Spoon River gathering many a shell,

And many a flower and medicinal weed—
Shouting to the wooded hills, singing to the green valleys.
At ninety-six I had lived enough, that is all,
and passed to a sweet repose.
What is this I hear of sorrow and weariness,
Anger, discontent and drooping hopes?
Degenerate sons and daughters,
Life is too strong for you—
It takes life to love life.

MAYA ANGELOU
Conversations with Maya Angelou

Life loves the liver of it.

GRANTLAND RICE
"Alumnus Football"

When the One Great Scorer comes to write against your name—
He marks—not that you won or lost—but how you played the game.

JOHN GREENLEAF WHITTIER
"Raphael"

The tissue of Life to be
We weave with colors all our own,
And in the field of Destiny
We reap as we have sown.

JACK KEROUAC
On the Road

But then they danced down the street like dingledodies, and I shambled after as I've been doing all my life after people who interest me, because the only people for me are the mad ones, the ones who are mad to live, mad to talk, mad to be saved, desirous of everything at the same time, the ones who never yawn or say a commonplace thing, but burn, burn, burn like fabulous yellow roman candles exploding like spiders across the stars and in the middle you see the blue centerlight pop and everybody goes "Awww!"

EDNA ST. VINCENT MILLAY
"First Fig"

My candle burns at both ends;
It will not last the night;
But ah, my foes, and oh, my friends—
It gives a lovely light!

HENRY JAMES
The Ambassadors

Live all you can; it's a mistake not to. It doesn't so much matter what you do in particular, so long as you have your life. If you haven't had that, what *have* you had? . . . What one loses one loses; make no mistake about that. . . . The right time is *any* time that one is still so lucky as to have . . . Life!

OLIVER WENDELL HOLMES, SR.
The Autocrat of the Breakfast Table

I find the great thing in this world is not so much where we stand, as in what direction we are moving: To reach the port of heaven, we must sail sometimes with the wind and sometimes against it—but we must sail, and not drift, nor lie at anchor.

HENRY JAMES
Notebooks

To take what there *is*, and use it, without waiting forever in vain for the preconceived—to dig deep into the actual and get something out of *that*—this doubtless is the right way to live.

MAE WEST
Quoted in Joseph Weintraub's The Wit and Wisdom of Mae West

Too much of a good thing can be wonderful.

WILLIAM JAMES
Letter to his wife, Alice Gibbons James

I have often thought that the best way to define a man's character would be to seek out that particular mental or moral attitude in which, when it came upon him, he felt himself most deeply and intensely active and alive. At such moments there is a voice inside which speaks and says, "This is the real me!"

EUGENE O'NEILL

Happiness hates the timid!

W.E.B. DU BOIS

Believe in life! Always human beings will live and progress to greater, broader, and fuller life.

THEODORE DREISER

Every human life is intensely interesting. If a human being has ideals, the struggle and the attempt to realize those ideals, the going back on his own trail, the failure, the success, the reasons for the individual failure, the individual success...—these are the things I want to write about—life as it is, the facts as they exist, the game as it is played!

GARRISON KEILLOR
Leaving Home

Thank you, God, for this good life and forgive us if we do not love it enough.

HENRY MILLER
"Creative Death," *The Wisdom of the Heart*

The aim of life is to live, and to live means to be aware, joyously, drunkenly, serenely, divinely aware.

RALPH WALDO EMERSON
Considerations by the Way, The Conduct of Life

I wish that life should not be cheap, but sacred. I wish the days to be as centuries, loaded, fragrant.

RABBI ABRAHAM HESCHEL
I Asked for Wonder

Just to be is a blessing. Just to live is holy.

EUGENE O'NEILL
"The Fountain"

Life is a flower
Forever blooming.
Life is a fountain
Forever leaping
Upward to catch the golden sunlight,
Striving to reach the azure heaven;
Falling, falling,
Ever returning
To kiss the earth that the flower may live.

HENRY DAVID THOREAU
The Pond in Winter, Walden

Heaven is under our feet as well as over our heads.

HENRY DAVID THOREAU
The Maine Woods, Ktaadn

Talk of mysteries! Think of our life in nature—daily to be shown matter, to come in contact with it—rocks, trees, wind on our cheeks! the *solid* earth! the *actual* world! the *common sense!* *Contact! Contact! Who* are we? *Where* are we?

RALPH WALDO EMERSON
Journal

Crossing a bare common, in snow puddles, at twilight, under a clouded sky, without having in my thoughts any occurrence of special good fortune, I have enjoyed a perfect exhilaration. I am glad to the brink of fear.

HENRY JAMES

Summer afternoon—summer afternoon; to me those have always been the two most beautiful words in the English language.

WALT WHITMAN
A Song for Occupations

The sun and stars that float in the open air,
The apple-shaped earth, and we upon it,
surely the drift of them is something
    grand,
I do not know what it is except that it is
    grand, and that is happiness.

T.S. ELIOT

It is not necessarily those lands which are the most fertile or most favored in climate that seem to me the happiest, but those in which a long struggle of adaptation between man and his environment has brought out the best qualities of both.

EDNA ST. VINCENT MILLAY
From "Renascence"

The world stands out on either side
No wider than the heart is wide;
Above the world is stretched the sky,—
No higher than the soul is high.
The heart can push the sea and land
Farther away on either hand;
The soul can split the sky in two,
And let the face of God shine through.

Black Elk Speaks

AS TOLD THROUGH JOHN G. NEIHARDT

Twenty days passed, and it was time to perform the dog vision with heyokas. But before I tell you how we did it, I will say something about heyokas and the heyoka ceremony, which seems to be foolish, but is not so.

Only those who have had visions of the thunder beings of the west can act as heyokas. They have sacred power and they share some of this with the people, but they do it through funny actions. When a vision comes from the thunder beings of the west, it comes with terror like a thunder storm; but when the storm of vision has passed, the world is greener and happier; for wherever the truth of vision comes upon the world, it is like rain. The world, you see, is happier after the terror of the storm.

But in the heyoka ceremony, everything is backwards, and it is planned that the people shall be made to feel jolly and happy first, so that it may be easier for the power to come to them. You have noticed that the truth comes into this world with two faces. One is sad, and the other laughs; but it is the same face, laughing or weeping. When people are already in despair, maybe the laughing face is better for them; and when they feel good and are too sure of being safe, maybe the weeping face is better for them to see. And so I think that is what the heyoka ceremony is for.

There was a man by the name of Wachpanne (Poor) who took charge of this ceremony for me because he had acted as a heyoka many times and knew all about it. First he told all the poor to gather in a circle on the flat near Pine Ridge, and in the center, near a sacred teepee that was set there, he placed a pot of water which was made to boil by dropping hot stones from a fire into it. First, he had to make an offering of sweet grass to the west. He sat beside the fire with some sweet grass in his hand, and said: "To the Great Spirit's day, to that day grown old and wise, I will make an offering." Then, as he sprinkled the grass upon the fire and the sweet smoke arose, he sang:

> This I burn as an offering.
> Behold it!
> A sacred praise I am making.
> A sacred praise I am making.
> My nation, behold it in kindness!
> The day of the sun has been my strength.
> The path of the moon shall be my robe.
> A sacred praise I am making.
> A sacred praise I am making.

Then the dog had to be killed quickly and without making any scar, as lightning kills, for it is the power of the lightning that the heyokas have.

Over the smoke of the sweet grass a rawhide rope was held to make it sacred. Then two heyokas tied a slip noose in the rope and put this over the neck of the dog. Three times they pulled the rope gently, one at each end of the rope, and the fourth time they jerked it hard, breaking the neck. Then Wachpanne singed the dog and washed it well, and after he cut away everything but the head, the spine and the tail. Now walking six steps away from the pot, one for each of the Powers, he turned to the west, offering the head and spine to the thunder beings, then to the north, the east and the south, then to the Spirit above and to the Mother Earth.

After this, standing where he was, six steps away, he faced the pot and said: "In a sacred manner I thus boil this dog." Three times he swung it, and the fourth time he threw it so that it fell head first into the boiling water. Then he took the heart of the dog and did with it what he had done with the head and the spine.

During all this time, thirty heyokas, one for each day of a moon, were doing foolish tricks among the people to make them feel jolly. They were all dressed and painted in such funny ways that everybody who saw them had to laugh. One Side and I were fellow clowns. We had our bodies painted all over and streaked with black lightning. The right sides of our heads were shaved, and the hair on the left side was left hanging long. This looked very funny, but it had a meaning; for when we looked toward where you are always facing (the south) the bare sides of our heads were toward the west, which showed that we were humble before the thunder beings who had given us power. Each of us carried a very long bow, so long that nobody could use it, and it was very crooked too. The arrows that were carried were very long and very crooked, so that it looked crazy to have them. We were riding sorrels with streaks of black lightning all over them, for we were to represent the two men of my dog vision.

Wachpanne now went into the sacred teepee, where he sang about the heyokas:

> These are sacred,
> These are sacred,
> They have said,
> They have said.
> These are sacred,
> They have said.

Twelve times he sang this, once for each of the moons.

Afterward, while the pot was boiling, One Side and I, sitting on our painted sorrels, faced the west and sang:

> In a sacred manner they have sent voices.
> Half the universe has sent voices.
> In a sacred manner they have sent voices to you.

Even while we were singing thus, the heyokas were doing foolish things and making laughter. For instance, two heyokas with crooked bows and arrows painted in a funny way, would come to a little shallow puddle of water. They would act as though they thought it was a wide, deep river that they had to cross; so, making motions, but saying nothing, they would decide to see how deep the river was. Taking their long crooked arrows, they would thrust these into the water, not downwards, but flat-wise just under the surface. This would make the whole arrow wet. Standing the arrows up beside them, they would show that the water was far over their heads in depth, so they would get ready to swim. One would then plunge into the shallow puddle head first, getting his face in the mud and fighting the water wildly as though he were drowning. Then the other would plunge in to save his comrade, and there would be more fun antics in the water to make the people laugh.

After One Side and I had sung to the west, we faced the pot, where the heart and the head of the dog had been boiling. With sharp pointed arrows, we charged on horseback upon the pot and past it. I had to catch the head upon my arrow and One side had to catch the heart, for we were representing the two men I had seen in the vision. After we had done this, the heyokas all chased us, trying to get a piece of the meat, and the people rushed to the pot, trying to get a piece of the sacred flesh. Ever so little of it would be good for them, for the power of the west was in it now. It was like giving them medicine to make them happier and stronger.

When the ceremony was over, everybody felt a great deal better, for it had been a day of fun. They were better able now to see the greenness of the world, the wideness of the sacred day, the colors of the earth, and to set these in their minds.

The Six Grandfathers have placed in his world many things, all of which should be happy. Every little thing is sent for something, and in that thing there should be happiness and the power to make happy. Like the grasses showing tender faces to each other, thus we should do, for this was the wish of the Grandfathers of the World.

EDNA ST. VINCENT MILLAY
From "Feast"

I drank at every vine.
The last was like the first.
I came upon no wine
So wonderful as thirst.

LOUISA MAY ALCOTT
Letter to Maggie Lukens

This is my idea of immortality. An endless life of helpful change, with the instinct, the longing to rise, to learn, to love, to get nearer the source of all good, & go on from the lowest plane to the highest, rejoicing more & more as we climb into the clearer light, the purer air, the happier life which must exist....

ELEANOR ROOSEVELT
You Learn by Living

Learning and living. But they are really the same thing aren't they? There is no experience from which you can't learn something.... And the purpose of life, after all, is to live it, to taste experience to the utmost, to reach out eagerly and without fear for newer and richer experience. You can do that only if you have curiosity, an unquenchable spirit of adventure. The experience can have meaning only if you understand it. You can understand it only if you have arrived at some knowledge of yourself, a knowledge based on a deliberately and usually painfully acquired self-discipline, which teaches you to cast out fear and frees you for the fullest experience of the adventure of life....I honor the human race. When it faces life head-on, it can almost remake itself.

HENRY DAVID THOREAU
A Week on the Concord and Merrimack Rivers

This world is but canvas to our imaginations.

WASHINGTON IRVING
The Sketch Book of Geoffrey Crayon, Gent.

Some minds seem almost to create themselves, springing up under every disadvantage and working their solitary but irresistible way through a thousand obstacles.

CARL SAGAN
Broca's Brain

We are an intelligent species and the use of our intelligence quite properly gives us pleasure. In this respect the brain is like a muscle. When it is in use we feel very good. Understanding is joyous.

MARK STRAND
Eating Poetry

I romp with joy in the bookish dark.

KENNETH REXROTH
"Further Advantages of Learning"

One day in the Library,
Puzzled and distracted,
Leafing through a dull book,
I came on a picture
Of the vase containing
Buddha's relics. A chill
Passed over me. I was
Haunted by the touch of
A calm I cannot know,
The opening into that
Busy place of a better world.

THOMAS JEFFERSON
Letter to George Wythe, from Paris

I think by far the most important bill in our whole code is that for the diffusion of knowledge among the people. No other sure foundation can be devised for the preservation of freedom, and happiness.

GEORGE SANTAYANA

Knowledge of what is possible is the beginning of happiness.

An American Childhood

ANNIE DILLARD

All that winter I played with the microscope. I prepared slides from things at hand, as the books suggested. I looked at the transparent membrane inside an onion's skin and saw the cells. I looked at a section of cork and saw the cells, and at scrapings from the inside of my cheek, ditto. I looked at my blood and saw not much; I looked at my urine and saw long iridescent crystals, for the drop had dried.

All this was very well, but I wanted to see the wildlife I had read about. I wanted especially to see the famous amoeba, who had eluded me. He was supposed to live in the hay infusion, but I hadn't found him there. He lived outside in warm ponds and streams, too, but I lived in Pittsburgh, and it had been a cold winter.

Finally late that spring I saw an amoeba. The week before, I had gathered puddle water from Frick Park; it had been festering in a jar in the basement. This June night after dinner I figured I had waited long enough. In the basement at my microscope table I spread a scummy drop of Frick Park puddle water on a slide, peeked in, and lo, there was the famous amoeba. He was as blobby and grainy as his picture; I would have known him anywhere.

Before I had watched him at all, I ran upstairs. My parents were still at table, drinking coffee. They, too, could see the famous amoeba. I told them, bursting, that he was all set up, that they should hurry before his water dried. It was the chance of a lifetime.

Father had stretched out his long legs and was tilting back in his chair. Mother sat with her knees crossed, in blue slacks, smoking a Chesterfield. The dessert dishes were still on the table. My sisters were nowhere in evidence. It was a warm evening; the big dining-room windows gave onto blooming rhododendrons.

Mother regarded me warmly. She gave me to understand that she was glad I had found what I had been looking for, but that she and Father were happy to sit with their coffee, and would not be coming down.

She did not say, but I understood at once, that they had their pursuits (coffee?) and I had mine. She did not say, but I began to understand then, that you do what you do out of your private passion for the thing itself.

JOSEPH CAMPBELL
The Power of Myth

Follow your bliss.

JOSEPH SMITH

Man is that he might have joy.

ALBERT EINSTEIN
New Year's Greeting

I feel that you are justified in looking into the future with true assurance, because you have a mode of living in which we find the joy of life and the joy of work harmoniously combined. Added to this is the spirit of ambition which pervades your very being, and seems to make the day's work like a happy child at play.

EMILY DICKINSON

The mere sense of living is joy enough.

EMILY DICKINSON
Letter to Louise and Fannie Norcross

I hear robins a great way off, and wagons a great way off, and rivers a great way off, and all appear to be hurrying somewhere undisclosed to me. Remoteness is the founder of sweetness; could we see all we hope, or hear the whole we fear told tranquil, like another tale, there would be madness near. Each of us gives or takes heaven in corporeal person, for each of us has the skill of life.

WALT WHITMAN
"Joy, Shipmate, Joy!"

Our life is closed, our life begins,
The long, long anchorage we leave,
The ship is clear at last, she leaps!
She swiftly courses from the shore,
Joy, shipmate, joy.

E.B. WHITE
Letter to Judith W. Preusser

We should all do what, in the long run, gives us joy, even if it is only picking grapes or sorting the laundry.

RALPH WALDO EMERSON
Journal

You shall have joy, or you shall have power, said God; you shall not have both.

HERMAN MELVILLE
White Jacket

Oh, give me again the rover's life—the joy, the thrill, the whirl! Let me feel thee again, old sea! Let me leap into thy saddle once more.

HARRIET BEECHER STOWE
The Pearl of Orr's Island: A Story of the Coast of Maine

All that there was developed of him, at present, was a fund of energy, self-esteem, hope, courage, and daring, the love of action, life, and adventure; his life was in the outward and present, not in the inward and reflective.

HELEN KELLER

One can never consent to creep when one feels an impulse to soar.

HENRY WADSWORTH LONGFELLOW

If you would hit the mark, you must aim a little above it:
Every arrow that flies feels the attraction of earth.

H.L. MENCKEN
On Being American

The human soul craves joy. It is necessary to happiness, to health.

MADELEINE L'ENGLE
A Wrinkle in Time

Mr. Murry was running across the lawn, Mrs. Murry running toward him, and they were in each other's arms, and then there was a tremendous happy jumble of arms and legs and hugging, the older Murrys and Meg and Charles Wallace and the twins, and Calvin grinning by them until Meg reached out and pulled him in and Mrs. Murry gave him a special hug all of his own. They were talking and laughing all at once, when they were startled by a crash, and Fortinbras, who could bear being left out of the happiness not one second longer, catapulted his sleek black body right through the screened door to the kitchen. He dashed across the lawn to join in the joy, and almost knocked them all over with the exuberance of his greeting.

Meg knew all at once that Mrs. Whatsit, Mrs. Who, and Mrs. Which must be near, because all through her she felt a flooding of joy and of love that was even greater and deeper than the joy and love which were already there.

She stopped laughing and listened, and Charles listened, too. "Hush."

Then there was a whirring, and Mrs. Whatsit, Mrs. Who, and Mrs. Which were standing in front of them, and the joy and love were so tangible that Meg felt that if she only knew where to reach she could touch it with her bare hands.

HENRY MILLER
The Colossus of Maroussi

It's good to be just plain happy; it's a little better to know that you're happy; but to understand that you're happy and to know why and how . . . and still be happy, be happy in the being and the knowing, well that is beyond happiness, that is bliss.

WILLIAM H. SHELDON

Happiness is essentially a state of going somewhere, wholeheartedly, one-directionally, without regret or reservation.

ROY M. GOODMAN

Remember that happiness is a way of travel—not a destination.

EDNA ST. VINCENT MILLAY
From "Travel"

My heart is warm with the friends I make,
And better friends I'll not be knowing;
Yet there isn't a train I wouldn't take,
No matter where it's going.

MARY BAKER EDDY

To live and let live, without clamor for distinction or recognition; to wait on divine Love; to write truth first on the tablet of one's own heart—this is the sanity and perfection of living, and my human ideal.

WILLIAM WADSWORTH LONGFELLOW
"The Poets"

Not in the clamor of the crowded street,
Not in the shouts and plaudits of the throng,
But in ourselves, are triumph and defeat.

RALPH WALDO EMERSON
Self-Reliance

There is a time in every man's education when he arrives at the conviction that envy is ignorance; that imitation is suicide; that he must take himself for better, for worse, as his portion; that, though the wide universe is full of good, no kernel of nourishing corn can come to him but through his toil bestowed on that plot of ground which is given to him to till. The power which resides in him is new in nature, and none but he knows what that is which he can do, nor does he know until he has tried. Not for nothing one face, one character, one fact makes much impression on him, and another none. This sculpture in the memory is not without preestablished harmony. The eye was placed where one ray should fall that it might testify of that particular ray. We but half express ourselves, and are ashamed of that divine idea which each of us represents. It may be safely trusted as proportionate and of good issues, so it be faithfully imparted, but God will not have his work made manifest by cowards. A man is relieved and gay when he has put his heart into his work and done his best; but what he has said or done otherwise shall give him no peace. It is a deliverance which does not deliver. In the attempt his genius deserts him; no muse befriends; no invention, no hope.

Trust thyself; every heart vibrates to that iron string. Accept the place the divine providence has found for you, the society of your contemporaries, the connection of events. Great men have always done so, and confided themselves childlike to the genius of their age, betraying their perception that the absolutely trustworthy was seated at their heart, working through their hands, predominating in all their being. And we are now men and must accept in the highest mind the same transcendent destiny; and not minors and invalids in a protected corner, not cowards fleeing before a revolution, but guides, redeemers, and benefactors, obeying the Almighty effort, and advancing on Chaos and the Dark.

FELIX FRANKFURTER
Felix Frankfurter Reminisces

Anybody who is any good is different from anybody else.

HENRY DAVID THOREAU
Walden

If a man does not keep pace with his companions, perhaps it is because he hears a different drummer. Let him step to the music which he hears, however measured or far away. It is not important that he should mature as soon as an apple-tree or an oak. Shall he turn his spring into summer? If the condition of things which we were made for is not yet, what were any reality which we can substitute? We will not be shipwrecked on a vain reality.

LOUIS ARMSTRONG

We all do "do, re, mi" but you have got to find the other notes yourself.

HENRY DAVID THOREAU

Man is the artificer of his own happiness.

ABRAHAM LINCOLN

Most folks are about as happy as they make up their minds to be.

THORNTON WILDER
The Skin of Our Teeth

My advice to you is not to inquire why or whither, but just enjoy your ice cream while it's on your plate—that's my philosophy.

GEORGE SANTAYANA
Soliloquies in England and Later Soliloquies

There is no cure for birth and death save to enjoy the interval.

ROBERT G. INGERSOLL
"Creed"

Justice is the only worship.
Love is the only priest.
Ignorance is the only slavery.
Happiness is the only good.
The time to be happy is now.
The place to be happy is here.
The way to be happy is to make others so.

RALPH WALDO EMERSON

What is success?
To laugh often and much;
To win the respect of intelligent people and the affection of
    children;
To earn the appreciation of honest critics and endure the betrayal of
    false friends;
To appreciate beauty;
To find the best in others;
To leave the world a bit better, whether by a healthy child, a garden
    path or a redeemed social condition;
To know even one life has breathed easier because you have lived;
That is to have succeeded.

GEORGE SANTAYANA
The Life of Reason, vol. I, Reason in Common Sense

Happiness is the only sanction of life; where happiness fails, existence remains a mad and lamentable experiment.

REINHOLD NIEBUHR
The Irony of American History

Happiness is desired by all men; and moments of it are probably attained by most men. Only moments of it can be attained because happiness is the inner concomitant of neat harmonies of body, spirit and society; and these neat harmonies are bound to be infrequent.

NATHANIEL HAWTHORNE
Passages from the American Notebooks

Happiness in this world, when it comes, comes incidentally. Make it the object of pursuit, and it leads us a wild-goose chase and is never attained. Follow some other object, and very possibly we may find that we have caught happiness without dreaming of it.

JOSH BILLINGS (HENRY WHEELER SHAW)

If you ever find happiness by hunting for it, you will find it, as the old woman did her lost spectacles, safe on her nose all the time.

William James
The Varieties of Religious Experience

How to gain, how to keep, how to recover happiness is in fact for most men at all times the secret motive of all they do, and of all they are willing to endure.

Edgar Allan Poe

Man's real life is happy, chiefly because he is ever expecting that it soon will be so.

Edith Wharton

If only we'd stop trying to be happy we'd have a pretty good time.

Benjamin Franklin

The U.S. Constitution doesn't guarantee happiness, only the pursuit of it. You have to catch up with it yourself.

Helen Keller
Optimism

No matter how dull, or how mean, or how wise a man is, he feels that happiness is his indisputable right.

Emily Dickinson

I took one Draught of Life—
I'll tell you what I paid—
Precisely an existence—
The market price, they said.
They weighed me, Dust by Dust—
They balanced Film with Film,
Then handed me my Being's worth—
A single Dram of Heaven!

Walt Whitman
"The Sleepers"

I dream in my dream all the dreams of the other
    dreamers,
And I become the other dreamers.

EDGAR ALLAN POE
"A Dream Within a Dream"

All that we see or seem
Is but a dream within a dream.

RAY CHARLES
Brother Ray

Dreams, if they're any good, are always a little crazy.

BENJAMIN MAYS
What Man Lives By

It isn't a calamity to die with dreams unfulfilled, but it is a calamity not to dream.

JOHN BUNYAN
The Pilgrim's Progress

I awoke, and behold it was a dream.

CLARENCE DAY
This Simian World

What fairy story, what talk from the Arabian Nights of the jinns, is a hundredth part as wonderful as this true fairy story of simians! It is so much more heartening, too, than the tales we invent. A universe capable of giving birth to many such accidents is—blind or not—a good world to live in, a promising universe. . . .

WALT WHITMAN
November Boughs

The strongest and sweetest songs yet remain to be sung.

"The Anatomy of Happiness"

Ogden Nash

Lots of truisms don't have to be repeated but there is one
    that has got to be,
Which is that it is much nicer to be happy than it is not
    to be,
And I shall even add to it by stating unequivocally and
    without restraint
That you are much happier when you are happy than when
    you ain't.
Some people are just naturally Pollyanna,
While others call for sugar and cream and strawberries on
    their manna.
Now, I think we all ought to say a fig for the happiness that
    comes of thinking helpful thoughts and searching your
    soul,
The most exciting happiness is the happiness generated by
    forces beyond your control,
Because if you just depend on your helpful thoughts for
    your happiness and would just as soon drink butter-
    milk as champagne, and if mink is no better than lapin
    to you,
Why you don't even deserve to have anything nice and ex-
    citing happen to you.
If you are really Master of your Fate,
It shouldn't make any difference to you whether Cleopatra
    or the Bearded Lady is your mate,
so I hold no brief for the kind of happiness or the kind of
    unhappiness that some people constantly carry around
    in their breast,
Because that kind of happiness simply consists of being re-
    signed to the worst just as that kind of unhappiness
    consists of being resentful of the best.
No, there is only one kind of happiness that I take the
    stump for,

Which is the kind that comes when something so wonder-
    ful falls in your lap that joy is what you jump for,
    something not of your own doing,
When the blue sky opens and out pops a refund from the
    Government or an invitation to a terrapin dinner or an
    unhoped-for Yes from the lovely creature you have been
    disconsolately wooing.
And obviously such miracles don't happen every day,
but here's hoping they may,
Because then everybody would be happy except the people
    who pride themselves on creating their own happiness
    who as soon as they saw everybody who didn't create
    their own happiness happy they would probably grieve
    over sharing their own heretofore private sublimity,
A condition which I could face with equanimity.

The Strenuous Life

The Strenuous Life

THEODORE ROOSEVELT

I wish to preach, not the doctrine of ignoble ease, but the doctrine of the strenuous life, the life of toil and effort, of labor and strife; to preach that highest form of success which comes, not to the man who desires mere easy peace, but to the man who does not shrink from danger, from hardship, or from bitter toil, and who out of these wins the splendid triumph.

A life of slothful ease, a life of that peace which springs merely from lack either of desire or of power to strive after great things, is as little worthy of a nation as of an individual. I ask only that what every self-respecting American demands from himself and from his sons shall be demanded of the American nation as a whole. Who among you would teach your boys that ease, that peace, is to be the first consideration in their eyes—to be the ultimate goal after which they strive? You work yourselves, and you bring up your sons to work. If you are rich and are worth your salt, you will teach your sons that though they may have leisure, it is not to be spent in idleness; for wisely used leisure merely means that those who possess it, being free from the necessity of working for their livelihood, are all the more bound to carry on some kind of nonremunerative work in science, in letters, in art, in exploration, in historical research —work of the type we most need in this country, the successful carrying out of which reflects most honor upon the nation. We do not admire the man of timid peace. We admire the man who embodies victorious effort; the man who never wrongs his neighbor, who is prompt to help a friend, but who has those virile qualities necessary to win in the stern strife of actual life. It is hard to fail, but it is worse never to have tried to succeed.

In the last analysis a healthy state can exist only when the men and women who make it up lead clean, vigorous, healthy lives; when the children are so trained that they shall endeavor, not to shirk difficulties, but to overcome them; not to seek ease, but to know how to wrest triumph from toil and risk. The man must be glad to do a man's work, to dare and endure and to labor; to keep himself, and to keep those dependent on him....

As it is with the individual, so it is with the nation. It is a base untruth to say that happy is the nation that has no history. Thrice happy is the nation that has a glorious history. Far better it is to dare mighty things, to win glorious triumphs, even though checkered by failure, than to take rank with those poor spirits who neither enjoy much nor suffer much, because they live in the gray twilight that knows not victory nor defeat.

Edith Wharton
A Backward Glance

In spite of illness, in spite even of the archenemy sorrow, one can remain alive long past the usual date of disintegration if one is unafraid of change, insatiable in intellectual curiosity, interested in big things, and happy in small ways.

John D. Rockefeller, Jr.
Ten Principles: Address in behalf of U.S. Organizations

I believe that every right implies a responsibility; every opportunity, an obligation; every possession, a duty.

Martin Luther King, Jr.
Speech accepting the Nobel Peace Prize

I refuse to accept the idea that the "isness" of man's present nature makes him morally incapable of reaching up for the "oughtness" that forever confronts him.

Albert Einstein

Try not to become a man of success, but rather a man of value.

Robert Herrick
The New Republic

It is only the weakling who finds nothing worth fighting about. Whoever cares greatly will give all, even life.

ROBERT G. INGERSOLL
The Gods

Give men the storm and tempest of thought and action, rather than the dead calm of ignorance and faith!

JAMES RUSSELL LOWELL
Rousseau and the Sentimentalists

All the beautiful sentiments in the world weigh much less than a single lovely action.

HELEN KELLER
Let Us Have Faith

Life is either a daring adventure or nothing. To keep our faces toward change and behave like free spirits in the presence of fate is strength undefeatable.

SARA TEASDALE

I make the most of all that comes,
And the least of all that goes.

BENJAMIN FRANKLIN

Were the offer made true, I would engage to run again, from beginning to end, the same career of life. All I would ask should be the privilege of an author, to correct, in a second edition, certain errors of the first.

JOE E. LEWIS

You only live once—but if you work it right, once is enough.

F. SCOTT FITZGERALD
The Crack-Up

Life was something you dominated if you were any good. Life yielded easily to intelligence and effort, or to what proportion could be mustered of both.

THEODORE ROOSEVELT

Do what you can, with what you have, where you are.

ADLAI E. STEVENSON

It is not the years in your life but the life in your years that counts.

WILLIAM PENN

Love labor: for if thou dost not want it for food, thou mayest for physic. It is wholesome for thy body and good for thy mind.

BENJAMIN FRANKLIN
Letter on the Stamp Act

Idleness and pride tax with a heavier hand than kings and parliament.

ABIGAIL ADAMS
Letter to John Adams

Luxury, that baneful poison, has unstrung and enfeebled her sons.

DANIEL WEBSTER
U.S. Senate speech

Employment gives health, sobriety, and morals. Constant employment and well-paid labor produce, in a country like ours, general prosperity, content, and cheerfulness.

ULYSSES S. GRANT
Speech at New England Society Dinner

They [the Pilgrim Fathers] fell upon an ungenial climate, where there were nine months of winter and three months of cold weather, and that called out the best energies of the men, and of the women, too, to get a mere subsistence out of the soil, with such a climate. In their efforts to do that they cultivated industry and frugality at the same time—which is the real foundation of the greatness of the Pilgrims.

THEODORE ROOSEVELT

The first requisite of a good citizen in this republic of ours is that he shall be able and willing to pull his own weight.

GROVER CLEVELAND
Letter accepting nomination for President

A truly American sentiment recognizes the dignity of labor and the fact that honor lies in honest toil.

GROVER CLEVELAND

I have tried so hard to do the right.

EMILY DICKINSON

Luck is not chance—
It's Toil—
Fortune's expensive smile
Is earned—.

BENJAMIN FRANKLIN
The Way to Wealth

Diligence is the mother of good luck, and God gives all things to industry. Then plough deep while sluggards sleep, and you shall have corn to sell and to keep.

HENRY WADSWORTH LONGFELLOW
The Ladder of St. Augustine

The heights by great men reached and kept
Were not attained by sudden flight,
But they, while their companions slept,
Were toiling upward in the night.

MARK TWAIN
Letter to Mr. Burrough

The highest pleasure to be got out of freedom, and having nothing to do, is labor.

FRANKLIN D. ROOSEVELT
Radio address

A Liberal is a man who uses his legs and his hands at the behest—at the command—of his head.

Thomas Jefferson
Letter to Martha Jefferson

Determine never to be idle. No person will have occasion to complain of the want of time who never loses any. It is wonderful how much may be done if we are always doing.

Thomas A. Edison

I never did anything worth doing by accident, nor did any of my inventions come by accident; they came by work.

Thomas A. Edison

There is no substitute for hard work.

Ralph Waldo Emerson
"Success"

The sum of wisdom is, that the time is never lost that is devoted to work.

Notes on the Practice of Law

Abraham Lincoln

I am not an accomplished lawyer. I find quite as much material for a lecture, in those points wherein I have failed, as in those wherein I have been moderately successful.

The leading rule for the lawyer, as for the man, of every calling, is diligence. Leave nothing for tomorrow, which can be done today. Never let your correspondence fall behind. Whatever piece of business you have in hand, before stopping, do all the labor pertaining to it which can then be done. When you bring a common-law suit, if you have the facts for doing so, write the declaration at once. If a law point be involved, examine the books, and note the authority you rely on, upon the declaration itself, where you are sure to find it when wanted. The same of defenses and pleas. In business not likely to be litigated—ordinary collection cases, foreclosures, partitions, and the like,—make all examinations of titles, and note them, and even draft orders and decrees in advance. This course has a triple advantage; it avoids omissions and neglect, saves your labor, when once done; performs the labor out of court when you have leisure, rather than in court, when you have not. Extemporaneous speaking should be practiced and cultivated. It is the lawyer's avenue to the public. However able and faithful he may be in other respects, people are slow to bring him business, if he cannot make a speech.

And yet there is not a more fatal error to young lawyers, than relying too much on speech-making. If any one, upon his rare powers of speaking, shall claim exemption from the drudgery of the law, his case is a failure in advance.

Discourage litigation. Persuade your neighbors to compromise whenever you can. Point out to them how the nominal winner is often a real loser—in fees, and expenses, and waste of time. As a peace-maker the lawyer has a superior opportunity of being a good man. There will still be business enough.

Never stir up litigation. A worse man can scarcely be found than one who does this. Who can be more nearly a fiend than he who habitually overhauls the Registers of deeds, in search of defects in titles, whereon to stir up strife, and put money in his pocket? A moral tone ought to be infused into the profession, which should drive such men out of it.

The matter of fees is important far beyond the mere question of bread and butter involved. Properly attended to, fuller justice is done to both lawyer and client. An exorbitant fee should never be claimed. As a general rule, never take your whole fee in advance, nor any more than a small retainer. When fully paid before hand, you are more than a common mortal if you can feel the same interest in the case, the job will very likely lack skill and diligence in the performance. Settle the amount of fee, and take a note in advance. Then you will feel that you are working for something, and you are sure to do your work faithfully and well. Never sell a fee-note—at least, not before the consideration service is performed. It leads to negligence and dishonesty—negligence, by losing interest in the case, and dishonesty in refusing to refund, when you have allowed the consideration to fail.

There is a vague popular belief that lawyers are necessarily dishonest. I say vague, because when we consider to what extent confidence, and honors are reposed in, and conferred upon lawyers by the people, it appears improbable that their impression of dishonesty is very distinct and vivid. Yet the impression, is common—almost universal. Let no young man, choosing the law for a calling, for a moment yield to this popular belief. Resolve to be honest in all events; and if, in your own judgment, you can not be an honest lawyer, resolve to be honest without being a lawyer. Choose some other occupation, rather than the one in the choosing of which you do, in advance, consent to be a knave.

ABRAHAM LINCOLN
Letter to Major D. Ramsey

The lady—bearer of this—says she has two sons who want to work. Set them at it, if possible. Wanting to work is so rare a merit that it should be encouraged.

OLIVER WENDELL HOLMES, JR.
The Class of '61, from Speeches

I learned in the regiment and in the class the conclusion, at least, of what I think the best service that we can do for our country and for ourselves. To see so far as one may, and to feel the great forces that are behind every detail . . . to hammer out as compact and solid a piece of work as one can, to try to make it first rate, and to leave it unadvertised.

ELBERT HUBBARD
The Note Book

Do your work with your whole heart and you will succeed—there is so little competition.

THOMAS PAINE
The American Crisis

What we obtain too cheap, we esteem too lightly; it is dearness only that gives everything its value.

BENJAMIN FRANKLIN
The Way to Wealth

Dost thou love life, then do not squander time, for that's the stuff life is made of.

BOOKER T. WASHINGTON
Speech at Tuskegee

No race of people ever got upon its feet without severe and constant struggle, often in the face of the greatest disappointment.

B.B. KING

I only went through tenth grade, but you'll see all kinds of textbooks around me. The more popular I become, the more I miss education. Whether you play blues or whatever, don't let people keep you like you were.

MAX BEERBOHM
And Even Now

No fine work can be done without concentration and self-sacrifice and toil and doubt.

LOUIS BRANDEIS

No one can really pull you up very high—you lose your grip on the rope. But on your own two feet you can climb mountains.

THOMAS JEFFERSON
Letter to Martha Jefferson

Idleness begets ennui, ennui the hypochondriac, and that a diseased body. No laborious person was ever yet hysterical.

BOOKER T. WASHINGTON
Up from Slavery

Nothing ever comes to one, that is worth having, except as a result of hard work.

HENRY WADSWORTH LONGFELLOW
"The Masque of Pandora"

Taste the joy
That springs from labor.

HENRY DAVID THOREAU
Journal entry

Good for the body is the work of the body, good for the soul the work of the soul, and good for either the work of the other.

CARDINAL SPELLMAN

Pray as if everything depended on God, and work as if everything depended upon man.

THEODORE ROOSEVELT
Labor Day speech in Syracuse, New York

Far and away the best prize that life offers is the chance to work hard at work worth doing.

JESSE OWENS
Blackthink

The battles that count aren't the ones for gold medals. The struggles within yourself—the invisible, inevitable battles inside all of us—that's where it's at.

MARTIN LUTHER KING, JR.

Each of us is two selves, and the great burden of life is to always try to keep that higher self in command. Don't let the lower self take over.

JOHN F. KENNEDY
Speech to the Massachusetts Legislature

Of those to whom much is given, much is required. And when at some future date the high court of history sits in judgment of each one of us—recording whether in our brief span of service we fulfilled our responsibilities to the state—our success or failure, in whatever office we may hold, will be measured by the answers to four questions—were we truly men of courage . . . were we truly men of judgment . . . were we truly men of integrity . . . were we truly men of dedication?

GEORGE WASHINGTON

I shall never ask, never refuse, nor ever resign an office.

JANIS JOPLIN

Don't compromise yourself. You are all you've got.

ANGELA DAVIS
On Becoming a Fugitive

Work. Struggle. Confrontation lay before us like a rock-strewn road. We would walk it. . . . If we saw this moment of triumph as a conclusion and not as a point of departure, we would be ignoring all the others who remained draped in chains.

ABIGAIL ADAMS
Letter to John Quincy Adams

Great necessities call out for great virtues.

MARCUS GARVEY
In Negro World

Let us not try to be the best or the worst of others, but let us make the effort to be the best of ourselves.

HELEN KELLER
Out of the Dark

When we do the best that we can, we never know what miracle is wrought in our life, or in the life of another.

WALTER LIPPMANN
A Preface to Morals

He has honor if he holds himself to an ideal of conduct though it is inconvenient, unprofitable, or dangerous to do so.

ADLAI E. STEVENSON

I have said what I meant and meant what I said. I have not done as well as I should like to have done, but I have done my best, frankly and forthrightly; no man can do more, and you are entitled to no less.

HARRY S TRUMAN
Campaign remarks

The greatest epitaph in the country is here in Arizona. It's in Tombstone, Arizona, and this epitaph says, "Here lies Jack Williams. He done his damnest." I think that is the greatest epitaph a man could have. Whenever a man does the best he can, then that is all he can do.

RALPH WALDO EMERSON

A man is relieved and gay when he has put his heart into his work and done his best.

MARY HARDY MACARTHUR
Advice to her son Douglas MacArthur

You must believe in yourself, my son, or no one else will believe in you. Be self-confident, self-reliant, and even if you don't make it, you will know you have done your best. Now, go to it.

WILLIAM FAULKNER

Don't bother just to be better than your contemporaries or predecessors. Try to be better than yourself.

MOSS HART
Act One

Can success change the human mechanism so completely between one dawn and another? Can it make one feel taller, more alive, handsomer, uncommonly gifted and indominitably secure with the certainty that this is the way life will always be? It can and it does!

OLIVER WENDELL HOLMES, JR.

I confess that altruistic and cynically selfish talk seem to me about equally unreal. With all humility, I think "whatsoever thy hand findeth to do, do it with thy might," infinitely more important than the vain attempt to love one's neighbor as one's self. If you want to hit a bird on the wing you must have all your will in focus, you must not be thinking about yourself, and equally, you must not be thinking about your neighbors; you must be living with your eye on that bird. Every achievement is a bird on the wing.

"KEEP YOUR EYES ON THE PRIZE"
American folk song

The only thing that we did wrong
Stayed in the wilderness a day too long
Keep your Eyes on the Prize, Hold On
But the one thing we did right
Was the day we started to fight
Keep Your Eyes on the Prize, Hold On

BRANCH RICKEY

The greatest single thing in the qualification of a great player, a great team or a great man is a desire to reach the objective that admits of no interference anywhere. That is the greatest thing I know about baseball or anything.

HENRY JAMES
The Middle Years

We work in the dark—we do what we can—we give what we have. Our doubt is our passion, and our passion is our task.

WILLIAM CULLEN BRYANT

Difficulty, my brethren, is the nurse of greatness—a harsh nurse, who roughly rocks her foster children into strength and athletic proportion.

HENRY WADSWORTH LONGFELLOW
"The Village Blacksmith"

Under a spreading chestnut tree
The village smithy stands;
The smith, a mighty man is he,
With large sinewy hands;
And the muscles of his brawny arms
Are strong as iron bands.

His hair is crisp, and black, and long,
His face is like the tan;
His brow is wet with honest sweat,
He earns whate'er he can;
And looks the whole world in the face,
For he owes not any man.

Week in, week out, from morn till night,
You can hear his bellows blow;
You can hear him swing his heavy sledge,
With measured beat and slow;
Like a sexton ringing the village bell,
When the evening sun is low.

And children coming home from school
Look in at the open door;
They love to see the flaming forge,
And hear the bellows roar;
And catch the burning sparks that fly
Like chaff from a threshing floor.

He goes on Sunday to the church,
And sits among his boys;
He hears the parson pray and preach,
He hears his daughter's voice;
Singing in the village choir,
And it makes his heart rejoice.

It sounds to him like her mother's voice,
Singing in Paradise!
He needs must think of her once more,

How in the grave she lies;
And with his hard, rough hand he wipes
A tear out of his eyes.

Toiling—rejoicing—sorrowing
Onward through life he goes;
Each morning sees some task begin,
Each evening sees it close;
Something attempted, something done,
Has earned a night's repose.

Thanks, thanks to thee, my worthy friend,
For the lesson thou has taught!
Thus at the flaming forge of life
Our fortunes must be wrought;
Thus on its sounding anvil shaped
Each burning deed and thought!

A Life on The Road, "Mr. Black"

CHARLES KURALT

George Black was a brickmaker. He turned out to be a pretty good diplomat for the State Department, too, but that part of the story comes later. George Black was a brickmaker, the craft he and his brother chose when their father died in 1889.

"We aren't going to get to go to school," his brother, fourteen, said to George, eleven. "We're going to have to work for a living. If we haul ourselves up and make men out of ourselves, even if we don't know A from B, we'll make somebody call us 'Mr. Black' someday."

Mr. Black quoted his brother with pride more than eighty years later. He was a tall, dignified old man. Everybody called him Mr. Black.

The little boys, George and his brother, setting out on their own in 1889, walked the forty miles from Randleman, North Carolina, to Winston-Salem. They apprenticed themselves to a brickmaster for a while. After they learned the trade, they started their own business while they were still in their teens. Since well before the turn of the century, George Black had been making bricks the way I watched him do it one afternoon in his backyard.

He had a mule hitched to what he called a "mud mill." With his giant, practiced hands, Mr. Black scooped up the mud mixed by the paddles of the mill as the mule plodded in a circle, and packed the mud expertly into six-brick forms ready for the kiln.

"How many bricks do you figure you've made in your life?" I asked him.

"Oh, Lord," he said. "I don't know. I'd be most afraid to know." He handed a finished form to one of the neighborhood youngsters who were serving as stackers that day, and impatiently awaited another stack of empties.

"I made a million bricks in one year," he said. "Mr. R.J. Reynolds rode out here on a white horse. He always rode a white horse, you know. He asked me if I thought I could make a thousand thousand bricks. He said he had in mind to build a tobacco factory. I studied and said yes, I could. I did, too, and you can go downtown and see them if you want to. That building's still there. They're all my bricks. Yes sir."

I found myself filled with admiration for this man standing in a pit before me in mud up to his elbows. He had made a life of the basic elements, water and earth and fire. And he had made the building blocks of a city.

Mr. Black dressed up in his Sunday suit the next day and took me on a stroll about Winston-Salem.

"These bricks we're walking on," he said, as we passed through the restored village of Old Salem, "I made these only about forty years ago. They're holding up nice. Yeah."

He pointed with his cane. "I made the bricks for that building over there." It was a schoolhouse. "I made the bricks for the Old Home Church over there," he said. "I made the bricks for that brick wall yonder." Wherever we walked, he pointed out the work of his own hands.

When we reached the block-long R.J. Reynolds factory, he said, "I believe I told you wrong about this job. It wasn't a million bricks. It ended up being a million and a half." He leaned on his walking stick and looked up at the massive structure. "Made these bricks six at a time," he said. "Put 'em out on the board and put 'em in a kiln and burned 'em for a dollar and a half a day. You don't know it but that was good pay in those days. Yes sir."

We walked on. "Made all these bricks six at a time," Mr. Black said, "and I'm going to make some more yet!"

The morning after our story about Mr. Black went on the air, I was sitting on the edge of my bed in a motel room, rubbing my eyes and trying to figure out where to go next, when the phone rang. It was the CBS News Department Correspondent of the time, Marvin Kalb.

Of course, that made it a red-letter day for me right there. I wasn't used to getting phone calls from Marvin Kalb.

He said, "There's a guy at the Agency for International Development who wants to talk to you. His name is Harvey J. Witherell. He's on the Guyana desk over there. I think he probably is the Guyana desk. I don't know what he wants with you, but he's been calling me all morning. I wish you'd give him a ring and get him off my neck."

"Sure, Marvin," I said.

"If it turns out to be anything I can help you with, let me know," Marvin said generously, and a little wearily. The life of a State Department Correspondent must be hard. He has the whole world to worry about all the time.

When I reached Harvey J. Witherell, his voice was trembling with excitement.

"I hear you had a story about a brickmaker on television last night," he said.

"Yep," I said.

"Oh, gosh, I've been looking all over this country for a brickmaker who still does the job by hand," Harvey J. Witherell said. "I didn't think there were any left. What's he like?"

"He's a nice man," I said.

"You see," Harvey J. Witherell said, "the government of Guyana wants us to send a brickmaker down there. They have a Five Year Plan or something like that to rebuild the whole country in brick. There's no shortage of raw materials, I mean there's plenty of mud in Guyana, but they don't want to build a big brick factory. They want somebody to go village-to-village for a couple of weeks to teach people how to make bricks for themselves."

"Well," I said, "I've got just the man for you, Harvey, but he is ninety-two years old. . . ."

"I don't care how old he is," Harvey said. "I think he's the last brickmaker." I gave him Mr. Black's address and telephone number. "You've made my day!" said Harvey J. Witherell.

When I called Mr. Black to warn him what was coming, he said he had already had a call from Washington.

"Where's Guyana?" Mr. Black asked.

"It's a little country in South America," I said.

Mr. Black said, "My, my."

The very next day, on official government business and carrying his government briefcase, Harvey J. Witherell caught a plane from Washington to Winston-Salem. He and Mr. Black hit it off. They came to an agreement that amounted to one of the best deals in the history of American foreign aid: Mr. Black would go to Guyana for ten days. He would take his granddaughter, Evelyn Abrams, who also knew how to make bricks, and a kid from the neighborhood, Thomas Brabham, and they would go down there and teach those people how to make bricks. Mr. Black would be paid $100 per day. Not much, I thought when I heard about it, but better than the dollar and a half he got from R.J. Reynolds.

Harvey J. Witherell was awash with a feeling of accomplishment.

He said, "This is a wonderful thing you're going to do, Mr. Black. We in Washington very much appreciate it."

There was no false modesty in Mr. Black. He said, "I believe you have picked the best man to do the job for the U.S.A."

Planning commenced.

No government planning is ever done simply, of course. Harvey J. Witherell had to formulate a detailed proposal for his own superiors and for higher-ups in the Department of State.

He filled out reports in triplicate. He mapped the projected journey hour-by-hour and village-by-village. He developed plans and exigency plans. He put in travel orders and meal requisitions. There are forms for these things, and Henry J. Witherell followed the forms.

All this planning had to be coordinated with the U.S. Embassy in Guyana, of course, and with the office of the Guyanese Prime Minister, Forbes Burnham, and the whole thing had to have a name. It was given the name "Operation Black Jack." It became a pretty big deal.

"THE BALLAD OF JOHN HENRY"

John Henry was a little baby boy
You could hold him in the palm of your hand.
He gave a long and lonesome cry,
"Gonna be a steel-drivin' man, Lawd, Lawd,
Gonna be a steel-drivin' man."

They took John Henry to the tunnel,
Put him in the lead to drive,
The rock was so tall, John Henry so small,
That he laid down his hammer and cried, "Lawd, Lawd,"
Laid down his hammer and he cried.

John Henry started on the right hand,
The steam drill started on the left,
"Fo' I'd let that stream drill beat me down,
I'd hammer my fool self to death, Lawd, Lawd,
Hammer my fool self to death."

John Henry told his captain,
"A man ain't nothin' but a man,
Fo' I let your steam drill beat me down
I'll die with this hammer in my hand, Lawd, Lawd,
Die with this hammer in my hand."

Now the captain told John Henry,
"I believe my tunnel's sinkin' in."
"Stand back, Captain, and doncha be afraid,
That's nothin' but my hammer catchin' wind, Lawd, Lawd,
That's nothin' but my hammer catchin' wind."

John Henry told his cap'n,
"Look yonder, boy, what do I see?
Your drill's done broke and your hole's done choke,
And you can't drive steel like me, Lawd, Lawd,
You can't drive steel like me."

John Henry hammerin' in the mountain,
Till the handle of his hammer caught on fire,
He drove so hard till he broke his po' heart,
Then he laid down his hammer and he died, Lawd, Lawd,
He laid down his hammer and he died.

They took John Henry to the tunnel,
And they buried him in the sand,
An' every locomotive come rollin' by
Say, "There lies a steel-drivin' man, Lawd, Lawd,
There lies a steel-drivin' man."

WILLIAM PENN
Some Fruits of Solitude

Patience and diligence, like faith, remove mountains.

ALEX HALEY

The way to succeed is never quit. That's it. But really be humble about it. You start out lowly and humble and you carefully try to learn an accretion of little things that help you get there.

CALVIN COOLIDGE

Nothing in the world can take the place of persistence. Talent will not; nothing is more common than unsuccessful men of talent. Genius will not; unrewarded genius is almost a proverb. Education will not; the world is full of educated derelicts. Persistence and determination alone are omnipotent.

ARTHUR RUBINSTEIN

Don't tell me how talented you are. Tell me how hard you work.

WALTER LIPPMANN

Industry is a better horse to ride than genius.

BENJAMIN FRANKLIN
Poor Richard's Almanack

Early to bed and early to rise, makes a man healthy, wealthy, and wise.

BENJAMIN FRANKLIN

Industry, perseverance, and frugality make fortune yield.

JAMES RUSSELL LOWELL
"A Glance Behind the Curtain"

No man is born into the world, whose work
Is not born with him; there is always work,
And tools to work withal, for those who will:
And blessed are the horny hands of toil!

THOMAS A. EDISON

Everything comes to him who hustles while he waits.

RALPH WALDO EMERSON

The world belongs to the energetic.

JAMES RUSSELL LOWELL
"Columbus"

Endurance is the crowning quality,
And patience all the passion of great hearts.

HENRY L. MENCKEN

I go on working for the same reason that a hen goes on laying eggs.

F. SCOTT FITZGERALD
Last line of The Great Gatsby

So we beat on, boats against the current, borne back ceaselessly into the past.

HUBERT H. HUMPHREY

Some people look upon any setback as the end. They're always looking for the benediction rather than the invocation.... But you can't quit. That isn't the way our country was built.

YOGI BERRA

The game isn't over till it's over.

SATCHEL PAIGE

Never let your head hang down. Never give up and sit and grieve. Find another way. And don't pray when it rains if you don't pray when the sun shines.

JOSEPH P. KENNEDY

When the going gets tough, the tough get going.

GOLD MEDAL TRACK STAR WILMA RUDOLPH

I had a series of childhood illnesses. The first was scarlet fever. Then I had pneumonia. Polio followed. I walked with braces until I was at least nine years old. My life wasn't like the average person who grew up and decided to enter the world of sports.

HAROLD MEDINA

Speech to editors on the First Amendment

Fight like hell every inch of the way.

HENRY WADSWORTH LONGFELLOW

Perseverance is a great element of success. If you only knock long enough and loud enough at the gate, you are sure to wake up somebody.

ROBERT JOHNSON

"Hellhound on My Trail"

I've got to keep moving, got to keep moving,
Blues fallin' down like hail
And the days keep mindin' me
There's a hellhound on my trail.

AMERICAN FOLK POETRY
"Walk Together Children"

Gwineter mourn and never tire,
Mourn and never tire,
Mourn and never tire.
There's a great camp meeting in the Promised Land.

Oh, get you ready children,
Don't you get weary,
Get you ready children,
Don't you get weary.

JAMES W. JOHNSON
"Lift Ev'ry Voice and Sing"

Sing a song full of the faith that the dark past has taught us
Sing a song full of the hope that the present has brought us.
Facing the rising sun of our new day begun,
Let us march on till victory is won.

LANGSTON HUGHES
"Mother to Son"

Well, son, I'll tell you:
Life for me ain't been no crystal stair.
It's had tacks in it,
And splinters,
And boards torn up,
And places with carpet on the floor—
Bare.
But all the time
I'se been a-climbin' on,
And reachin' lanbdin's,
And turnin' corners,
And sometimes goin' in the dark
Where there ain't been no light.
So boy, don't you turn back.
Don't you set down on the steps
Cause you finds it kiner hard.

Don't you fall no—
For I'se still goin', honey,
I's still combin,
And life for me ain't been no crystal stair.

JOHN HOPE

Dissatisfaction with possession and achievement is one of the requisites to further achievement.

JOHN F. KENNEDY
Address to the U.N. General Assembly

Peace is a daily, a weekly, a monthly process, gradually changing opinions, slowly eroding old barriers, quietly building new structures.

ADLAI E. STEVENSON
Address to American Legion Convention

Patriotism is not a short and frenzied outburst of emotion but the tranquil and steady dedication of a lifetime.

CECIL B. DE MILLE
Sunshine and Shadow

The person who makes a success of living is the one who sees his goal steadily and aims for it unswervingly. That is dedication.

JOAQUIN MILLER
"Sail on! Sail on!"

Behind him lay the gray Azores,
Behind the gates of Hercules;
Before him not the ghost of shores,
Before him only shoreless seas.
The good mate said: "Now must we pray,
For lo! the very stars are gone;
Speak, Admiral, what shall I say?"
"Why say, sail on! and on!"

"My men grow mut'nous day by day;
  My men grow ghastly wan and weak."
The stout mate thought of home; a spray
  Of salt wave wash'd his swarthy cheek.
"What shall I say, brave Admiral,
  If we sight naught but seas at dawn?"
"Why, you shall say, at break of day:
  'Sail on! sail on! and on!'"

They sailed and sailed, as winds might blow,
  Until at last the blanch'd mate said:
"Why, now, not even God would know
  Should I and all my men fall dead.
These very winds forget their way,
  For God from these dread seas is gone.
Now speak, brave Admiral, and say—"
He said: "Sail on! and on!"

They sailed, they sailed, then spoke his mate:
"This mad sea shows his teeth tonight,
  He curls his lip, he lies in wait,
  With lifted teeth as if to bite!
Brave Admiral, say but one word;
  What shall we do when hope is gone?"
The words leaped as a leaping sword:
"Sail on! sail on! and on!"

Then, pale and worn, he kept his deck,
  And thro' the darkness peered that night.
Ah, darkest night! and then a speck—
  A light! a light! a light!
It grew—a star—lit flag unfurled!
  It grew to be Time's burst of dawn;
He gained a world! he gave the world
  Its watchword: "On! and on!"

WILLIAM PENN
Some Fruits of Solitude

No pain, no palm; no thorns, no throne; no gall, no glory; no cross, no crown.

JAMES RUSSELL LOWELL
"Democracy" address

Let us be of good cheer, however, remembering that the misfortunes hardest to bare are those which never come.

TENNESSEE WILLIAMS

Make voyages. Attempt them. There's nothing else.

THOMAS JEFFERSON
Letter to John W. Eppes

The earth belongs to the living.

DANIEL H. BURNHAM
Motto of city planners

Make no little plans: they have no magic to stir men's blood.

RALPH WALDO EMERSON
"Self-Reliance"

What I must do is all that concerns me, not what the people think.

ELEANOR ROOSEVELT
You Learn by Living

You gain strength, courage and confidence by every experience in which you really stop to look fear in the face. You are able to say to yourself, "I lived through this horror. I can take the next thing that comes along."...You must do the thing you think you cannot do.

O. HENRY
The Voice of the City

There is a saying that no man has tasted the full flavor of life until he has known poverty, love, and war.

HENRY WADSWORTH LONGFELLOW
Hyperion

Look not mournfully into the Past. It comes back again. Wisely improve the Present. It is thine. Go forth to meet the shadowy Future, without fear, and with a manly heart.

ROBERT FROST
Bravado

Have I not walked without an upward look
Of caution under stars that very well
Might not have missed me when they shot and fell?
It was a risk I had to take—and took

MARIANNE MOORE
"Nevertheless"

you've seen a strawberry
  that's had a struggle; yet
  was, where the fragments met,

a hedgehog or a star-
  fish for the multitude
  of seeds. What better food

than apple-seeds—the fruit
  within the fruit—locked in
  like counter-curved twin

hazel-nuts? Frost that kills
  the little rubber-plant-
  leaves of *kok-saghyz*-stalks, can't

harm the roots; they still grow
  in frozen ground. Once where
  there was a prickly-pear-

leaf clinging to barbed wire,
  a root shot down to grow
  in earth two feet below;

as carrots form mandrakes
  or a ram's-horn root sometimes. Victory won't come

to me unless I go
  to it; a grape-tendril
  ties a knot in knots till

knotted thirty times,—so
  the bound twig that's under-
  gone and over-gone, can't stir.

The weak overcomes its
  menace, the strong overcomes itself. What is there

like fortitude! What sap
  went through that little thread
  to make the cherry red!

OLIVER WENDELL HOLMES, JR.
Memorial Day Address

I think that, as life is action and passion, it is required of a man that he should share the passion and action of his time at peril of being judged not to have lived.

ELEANOR ROOSEVELT
Letter to Isabella Selmes Ferguson

I sometimes think that the lives of many burdens are not really to be pitied for at least they live deeply and from their sorrows spring up flowers but an empty life is really dreadful!

DOROTHY PARKER
"Fair Weather"

They sicken of the calm, who know the storm.

EUGENE O'NEILL
Strange Interlude

Happiness hates the timid!

HENRY WADSWORTH LONGFELLOW
Hyperion

The mind of the scholar, if you would have it large and liberal, should come in contact with other minds. It is better that his armor should be somewhat bruised by rude encounters even, than hang forever rusting on the wall.

WILLIAM FAULKNER
The Wild Palms

Between grief and nothing I will take grief.

BABE RUTH

How to hit home runs: I swing as hard as I can, and I try to swing through the ball. I swing big with everything I've got or I miss big. I like to live as big as I can.

THEODORE ROOSEVELT
The American Boy

In life, as in a football game, the principle to follow is: Hit the line hard.

ANDREW JACKSON

Take time to deliberate; but when the time for action arrives, stop thinking and go in.

RALPH WALDO EMERSON

Nothing great was ever achieved without enthusiasm.

BEVERLY SILLS

You may be disappointed if you fail, but you are doomed if you don't try.

HENRY WARD BEECHER

Do not be afraid of defeat. You are never so near to victory as when defeated in a good cause.

WENDELL PHILLIPS

What is defeat? Nothing but education, nothing but the first step toward something better.

Theodore Roosevelt

It is not the critic who counts, not the one who points out how the strong man stumbled or how the doer of deeds might have done them better. The credit belongs to the man who is actually in the arena, whose face is marred with sweat and dust and blood; who strives valiantly; who errs and comes short again and again; who knows the great enthusiasms, the great devotions, and spends himself in a worthy cause; and who, if he fails, at least fails while daring greatly, so that his place shall never be with those cold and timid souls who know neither victory nor defeat.

Edwin Way Teale
Autumn Across America

Better a thousand times even a swiftly fading, ephemeral moment of life than the epoch-long unconsciousness of the stone.

Eleanor Roosevelt
Autobiography of Eleanor Roosevelt

Life was meant to be lived, and curiosity must be kept alive. One must never, for whatever reason, turn his back on life.

Oliver Wendell Holmes, Jr.
Speech in Boston

Life is an end in itself, and the only question as to whether it is worth living is whether you have had enough of it.

Henry Wadsworth Longfellow
"A Psalm of Life"

Tell me not, in mournful numbers,
    Life is but an empty dream!
For the soul is dead that slumbers,
    And things are not what they seem.

Life is real! Life is earnest!
    And the grave is not its goal;
Dust thou art, to dust returnest,
    Was not spoken of the soul.

Not enjoyment, and not sorrow,
    Is our destined end or way;
But to act, that each to-morrow
    Find us farther than to-day.

Art is long, and Time is fleeting,
    And our hearts, though stout and brave,
Still, like muffled drums, are beating
    Funeral marches to the grave.

In the world's broad field of battle,
    In the bivouac of Life,
Be not like dumb, driven cattle!
    Be a hero in the strife!

Trust no Future, howe'er pleasant!
    Let the dead Past bury its dead!
Act,—act in the living Present!
    Heart within, and God o'erhead!

Lives of great men all remind us
    We can make our lives sublime,
And, departing leave behind us
    Footprints on the sands of time;

Footprints, that perhaps another,
    Sailing o'er life's solemn main,
A forlorn and shipwrecked brother
    Seeing, shall take heart again.

Let us, then, be up and doing,
    With a heart for any fate;
Still achieving, still pursuing,
    Learn to labor and to wait.

WOODROW WILSON
Speech in New York

Life does not consist in thinking, it consists in acting.

WASHINGTON IRVING

Great minds have purposes, others have wishes.

ABRAHAM LINCOLN
Letter to General McClellan

I say "try"; if we never try, we shall never succeed.

VICTORIO, CHIENNE TRIBE

Every struggle, whether won or lost, strengthens us for the next to come. It is not good for people to have an easy life. They become weak and inefficient when they cease to struggle. Some meet a series of defeats before developing the strength and courage to win a victory.

HELEN KELLER

Be of good cheer. Do not think of today's failures, but of the success that may come tomorrow. You have set yourselves a difficult task, but you will succeed if you persevere; and you will find a joy in overcoming obstacles. Remember, no effort that we make to attain something beautiful is ever lost.

MARTIN LUTHER KING, JR.
Strength to Love

The ultimate measure of a man is not where he stands in moments of comfort and convenience, but where he stands at times of challenge and controversy.

MARCUS GARVEY
Speech before entering the Tombs Prison, Atlanta

Now, understand me well, Marcus Garvey has entered the fight for the emancipation of race; Marcus Garvey has entered the fight for the redemption of a country. From the graves of millions of my forebears at this hour I heard the cry, and I am going to answer it even though hell is cut loose before Marcus Garvey. From the silent graves of millions who went down to make me what I am, I shall make for their memory, this fight that shall leave a glaring page in the history of man.

FREDERICK DOUGLASS
Conference in Canadaigua, New York

If there is no struggle, there is no progress. Those who profess to favor freedom and yet deprecate agitation, are men who want crops without plowing up the ground, they want rain without thunder and lightning. They want the ocean without the awful roar, and it may be both moral and physical, but it must be a struggle. Power concedes nothing without a demand. It never did and it never will. Find out just what any people will quietly submit to and you have found out the exact measure of injustice and wrong that will continue till they are resisted with either words or blows or with both. The limits of tyrants are prescribed by the endurance of those whom they oppress. . . . Men may not get all they pay for in this world, but they must certainly pay for all they get.

WILLIAM LLOYD GARRISON
The Liberator, no. 1

I will be harsh as truth and as uncompromising as justice. On this subject I do not wish to think, or speak, or write, with moderation. No! No! Tell a man whose house is on fire to give a moderate alarm; tell him to moderately rescue his wife from the hands of the ravisher; tell the mother to gradually extricate her babe from the fire into which it has fallen; but urge me not to use moderation.

WILLIAM LLOYD GARRISON
The Liberator, no. 1

I am in earnest—I will not equivocate—I will not excuse—I will not retreat a single inch; and I will be heard!

HARRY S TRUMAN

I never did give anybody hell. I just told the truth and they thought it was hell.

EARL WARREN

Everything I did in my life that was worthwhile I caught Hell for.

HENRY DAVID THOREAU

The frontiers are not east or west, north or south, but wherever a man fronts a fact.

F. SCOTT FITZGERALD
The Crack-Up

If you are strong enough, there are no precedents.

"Pioneers! O Pioneers!"

BY WALT WHITMAN

Come my tan-faced children,
Follow well in order, get your weapons ready,
Have you your pistols? have you your sharp-edged axes?
Pioneers! O Pioneers!

For we cannot tarry here,
We must march my darlings, we must bear the brunt of danger,
We the youthful sinewy races, all the rest on us depend,
Pioneers! O Pioneers!

O you youths, Western youths,
So impatient, full of action, full of manly pride and friendship,
Plain I see you Western youths, see you tramping with the foremost,
Pioneers! O Pioneers!

Have the elder races halted?
Do they droop and end their lesson, wearied over there beyond the
        seas?
We take up the task eternal, and the burden and the lesson,
Pioneers! O pioneers!

All the past we leave behind,
We debouch upon a newer mightier world, varied world,
Fresh and strong the world we seize, world of labor and the march,
Pioneers! O pioneers!

We detachments steady throwing,
Down the edges, through the passes, up the mountains steep,
Conquering, holding, daring, venturing as we go the unknown
        ways,
Pioneers! O pioneers!

We primeval forests felling,
We the rivers stemming, vexing we and piercing deep the mines
    within,
We the surface broad surveying, we the virgin soil upheaving,
Pioneers! O pioneers!

Colorado men are we,
From the peaks gigantic, from the great sierras and the high
    plateaus,
From the mine and from the gully, from the hunting trail we come,
Pioneers! O pioneers!

From Nebraska, from Arkansas,
Central inland race are we, from Missouri, with the continental
    blood intervein'd,
All the hands of comrades clasping, all the Southern, all the
    Northern,
Pioneers! O pioneers!

O resistless restless race!
O beloved race in all! O my breast aches with tender love for all!
O I mourn and yet exult, I am rapt with love for all,
Pioneers! O pioneers!

Raise the mighty mother mistress,
Waving high the delicate mistress, over all the starry mistress, (bend
    your heads all,)
Raise the fang'd and warlike mistress, stern, impassive, weapon'd
    mistress,
Pioneers! O pioneers!

See my children, resolute children,
By those swarms upon our rear we must never yield or falter,
Ages back in ghostly millions frowning there behind us urging,
Pioneers! O pioneers!

On and on the compact ranks,
With accessions ever waiting, with the places of the dead quickly
    fill'd,
Through the battle, through defeat, moving yet and never stopping,
Pioneers! O pioneers!

O to die advancing on!
Are there some of us to droop and die? has the hour come?
Then upon the march we fittest die, soon and sure the gap is fill'd,
Pioneers! O pioneers!

All the pulses of the world,
Falling in they beat for us, with the Western movement beat,
Holding single or together, steady moving to the front, all for us,
Pioneers! O pioneers!

Life's involv'd and varied pageants,
All the forms and shows, all the workmen at their work,
All the seamen and the landsmen, all the masters with their slaves,
Pioneers! O pioneers!

All the hapless silent lovers,
All the prisoners in the prisons, all the righteous and the wicked,
All the joyous, all the sorrowing, all the living, all the dying,
Pioneers! O pioneers!

I too with my soul and body,
We, a curious trio, picking, wandering our way,
Through these shores amid the shadows, with the apparitions
        pressing,
Pioneers! O pioneers!

Lo, the darting bowling orb!
Lo, the brother orbs around, all the clustering suns and planets,
All the dazzling days, all the mystic nights with dreams,
Pioneers! O pioneers!

These are of us, they are with us,
All for primal needed work, while the followers there in embryo
        wait behind,
We today's procession heading, we the route for travel clearing,
Pioneers! O pioneers!

O you daughters of the West!
O you young and elder daughters! O you mothers and you wives!
Never must you be divided, in our ranks you move united,
Pioneers! O pioneers!

Minstrels latent on the prairies!
(Shrouded bards of other lands, you may rest, you have done your
    work,)
Soon I hear you coming warbling, soon you rise and tramp amid us,
Pioneers! O pioneers!

Not for delectations sweet,
Not the cushion and the slipper, not the peaceful and the studious,
Not the riches safe and palling, not for us the tame enjoyment,
Pioneers! O pioneers!

Do the feasters gluttonous feast?
Do the corpulent sleepers sleep? have they lock'd and bolted doors?
Still be ours the diet hard, and the blanket on the ground,
Pioneers! O pioneers!

Has the night descended?
Was the road of late so toilsome? did we stop discouraged nodding
    on our way?
Yet a passing hour I yield you in your tracks to pause oblivious,
Pioneers! O pioneers!

Till with sound of trumpet,
Far, far off the daybreak calls—hark! how loud and clear I hear it
    wind,
Swift! to the head of the army!—swift! spring to your places,
Pioneers! O pioneers!

Home of
the Brave

ELMER DAVIS
But We Were Born Free

This will remain the land of the free only so long as it is the home of the brave.

EDNA ST. VINCENT MILLAY
"Not for a Nation"

Not for the flag
Of any land because myself was born there
Will I give up my life.
But I will love that land where man is free,
And that will I defend.

DWIGHT D. EISENHOWER

If all Americans want is security they can go to prison. They'll have enough to eat, a bed and a roof over their heads. But if an American wants to preserve his dignity and his equality as a human being, he must not bow his neck to any dictatorial government.

HARRY S TRUMAN
Special message to Congress

America was not built on fear. America was built on courage, on imagination and an unbeatable determination to do the job at hand.

ADAM CLAYTON POWELL, JR.
Baccalaureate address, Howard University

These are the days for strong men to courageously expose wrong.

MARTIN LUTHER KING, JR.
Speech in Detroit, Michigan

If a man hasn't discovered something that he will die for, he isn't fit to live.

PATRICK HENRY
"Give me liberty, or give me death"

They tell us, Sir, that we are weak,—unable to cope with so formidable an adversary. But when shall we be stronger? Will it be the next week, or the next year? Will it be when we are totally disarmed, and when a British guard shall be stationed in every house? Shall we gather strength by irresolution and inaction? Shall we acquire the means of effectual resistance by lying supinely on our backs, and hugging the delusive phantom of hope, until our enemies shall have bound us hand and foot? Sir, we are not weak, if we make a proper use of those means which the God of nature hath placed in our power.

Three millions of People, armed in the holy cause of liberty, and in such a country as that which we possess, are invincible by any force which our enemy can send against us. Besides, Sir, we shall not fight our battles alone. There is a just god who presides over the destinies of Nations, and who will raise up friends to fight our battles for us. The battle, Sir, is not to the strong alone, it is to the vigilant, the active, the brave. Besides, Sir, we have no election. If we were base enough to desire it, it is now too late to retire from the contest. There is no retreat but in submission and slavery! Our chains are forged! Their clanking may be heard on the plains of Boston! The war is inevitable; and let it come! I repeat it, Sir, let it come!

It is in vain, Sir, to extenuate the matter. Gentlemen may cry, peace, peace!—but there is no peace. The war is actually begun! The next gale that sweeps from the North will bring to our ears the clash of resounding arms! Our brethren are already in the field! Why stand we here idle? What is it that Gentlemen wish? What would they have? Is life so dear, or peace so sweet, as to be purchased at the price of chains and slavery? Forbid it, Almighty God! I know not what course others may take, but as for me, give me liberty, or give me death!

NATHAN HALE
Last words before being hanged by the British as a spy

I only regret that I have but one life to lose for my country.

Thomas Paine
The American Crisis

I love the man that can smile in trouble, that can gather strength from distress and grow brave by reflection. It is the business of little minds to shrink; but he whose heart is firm, and whose conscience approves his conduct, will pursue his principles unto death.

Arna Botemps
"The Day-Breakers"

Yet would we die as some have done,
Beating a way for the rising sun.

Martin Luther King, Jr.
Let the Trumpet Sound

It may get me crucified, I may even die. But I want it said even if I die in the struggle that "He died to make men free."

Marva Collins
"The Most Unforgettable Person in My Family," *Ebony*

Death cannot put the brakes on a good dream.

Ernest Hemingway
The Old Man and the Sea

A man can be destroyed but not defeated.

Bob Moses
Cited in Freedom Summer by Sally Belfrage

No privileged group in history has ever given up anything without some kind of blood sacrifice, something.

Last Line of the Declaration of Independence

And for the support of this declaration, with a firm reliance on the protection of Divine Providence, we mutually pledge to each other our lives, our fortunes, and our sacred honor.

JOHN HANCOCK
Remark upon signing the Declaration of Independence

There, I guess King George will be able to read that.

ARCHIBALD MACLEISH
Freedom is the Right to Choose

The courage of the Declaration of Independence is a far greater courage than the bravery of those who risked their necks to sign it. The courage of the Declaration of Independence is the courage of the act of the imagination. Jefferson's document is not a call to revolution only. Jefferson's document is an image of a life, a dream—indeed a dream. And yet there were men as careful of their own respect, as hardheaded, as practical, as eager to be thought so, as any now in public life, who signed that Declaration for the world to look at.

The *truth* is that the tradition of imagination is behind us as behind no people in the history of the world. But our right to live as we imagine men should live is not a right drawn from tradition only. There are nations of the earth in which the act of the imagination would be an act *in* the imagination only—an action of escape. But not with us.

JOHN ADAMS
Letter to Abigail Adams

Yesterday, the greatest question was decided, which ever was debated in America, and a greater, perhaps, never was nor will be decided among men. A resolution was passed without one dissenting colony, "that these United Colonies are, and of right ought to be, free and independent States, and as such they have, and of right ought to have, full power to make war, conclude peace, establish commerce, and to do all other acts and things which other States may rightfully do." You will see in a few days a Declaration setting forth the causes which have impelled us to this mighty revolution, and the reasons which will justify it in the sight of God and man. A plan of confederation will be taken up in a few days.

You will think me transported with enthusiasm, but I am not. I am well aware of the toil, and blood, and treasure, that it will cost us to maintain this declaration, and support and defend these States. Yet, through all the gloom, I can see the rays of ravishing light and glory. I can see that the end is more than worth all the means, and that posterity will triumph in that day's transaction, even although we should rue it, which I trust in God we shall not.

DANIEL WEBSTER

The Declaration of Independence will inspire the people with increased courage. Instead of a long and bloody war for the restoration of privileges, for redress of grievances, for chartered immunities, held under a British king, set before them the glorious object of entire independence, and it will breathe into them anew the spirit of life. Read this declaration at the head of the army; every sword will be drawn from its scabbard, and the solemn vow uttered to maintain it, or perish on the field of honour. Publish it from the pulpit; religion will approve it, and the love of religious liberty will cling around it, resolved to stand with it, or fall with it. Send it to the public halls; proclaim it there; let them hear it who heard the first roar of the enemy's cannon—let them see it, who saw their brothers and their sons fall on the field of Bunker Hill, and in the streets of Lexington and Concord,—and the very walls will cry out in its support.

THOMAS PAINE
These are the Times that Try Men's Souls

These are the times that try men's souls. The summer soldier and the sunshine patriot will, in this crisis, shrink from the service of their country; but he that stands it *now*, deserves the love and thanks of man and woman. Tyranny, like hell, is not easily conquered; yet we have this consolation with us, that the harder the conflict, the more glorious the triumph. What we obtain too cheap, we esteem too lightly: it is dearness only that gives everything its value. Heaven knows how to put a proper price upon its goods; and it would be strange indeed, if so celestial an article as FREEDOM should not be highly rated. Britain, with an army to enforce her tyranny, has declared that she has a right (*not only to* TAX) but "to bind *us in all cases* whatsoever," and if being *bound in that manner,* is not slavery, then is there not such a thing as slavery upon earth. Even the expression is impious; for so unlimited a power can belong only to God.

FRANCIS SCOTT KEY
"The Star-Spangled Banner"

Oh, say, can you see by the dawn's early light,
What so proudly we hailed at the twilight's last gleaming?
Whose broad stripes and bright stars, through the perilous fight,
O'er the ramparts we watched were so gallantly streaming?
And the rockets' red glare, the bombs bursting in air,
Gave proof through the night that our flag was still there.
Oh, say, does that star-spangled banner yet wave
O'er the land of the free and the home of the brave?

JAMES RUSSELL LOWELL
The Present Crisis

They have rights who dare maintain them.

ELMER DAVIS
But We Were Born Free

With a great price our ancestors obtained this freedom, but we were born free. But that freedom can be retained only by the eternal vigilance which has always been its price.

JANE ADDAMS
George Washington Birthday Address to Union League Club, Chicago

First, as a soldier. What is it that we admire about the soldier? It certainly is not that he goes into battle; what we admire about the soldier is that he has the power of losing his own life for the life of a larger cause; that he holds his personal suffering of no account; that he flings down in the gage of battle his all and says, "I will stand or fall with this cause." That, it seems to me, is the glorious thing we most admire, and if we are going to preserve that same spirit of the soldier, we will have to found a similar spirit in the civil life of the people, the same pride in civil warfare, the spirit of courage, and the spirit of self-surrender which lies back of this.

WALT WHITMAN
Unnamed Remains the Bravest Soldier

Of scenes like these, I say, who writes—whoe'er can write the story? Of many a score—aye, thousands, north and south, of unwrit heroes, unknown heroisms, incredible, impromptu, first-class desperations—who tells? No history ever—no poem sings, no music sounds, those bravest men of all—those deeds. No formal general's report, nor book in the library, nor column in the paper, embalms the bravest, north or south, east or west. Unnamed, unknown, remain, and still remain, the bravest soldiers. Our manliest—our boys—our hardy darlings; no picture gives them. Likely, the typic one of them (standing, no doubt, for hundreds, thousands,) crawls aside to some bush-clump, or ferny tuft, on receiving his death-shot—there sheltering a little while, soaking roots, grass and soil, with red blood—the battle advances, retreats, flits from the scene, sweeps by—and there, haply with pain and suffering (yet less, far less than is supposed), the last lethargy winds like a serpent round him—the eyes glaze in death—none recks—perhaps the burial-squads, in truce, a week afterwards, search not the secluded spot—and there, at last, the Bravest Soldier crumbles in mother earth, unburied and unknown.

HENRY TIMROD
"Ode"

Sleep sweetly in your humble graves,
Sleep, martyrs of a fallen cause;
Though yet no marble column craves
The pilgrim here to pause.

In seeds of laurel in the earth
The blossom of your fame is blown,
And somewhere, waiting for its birth,
The shaft is in the stone!

Meanwhile, behalf the tardy years
Which keep in trust your storied tombs,
Behold! your sisters bring their tears.
And these memorial blooms.

Small tributes! but your shades will smile
More proudly on these wreaths today,
Than when some cannon-molded pile
Shall overlook this bay.

Stoop, angels, hither from the skies!
There is no holier spot of ground
Than where defeated valor lies,
By mourning beauty crowned!

RALPH WALDO EMERSON
Essays, First Series

Beauty will not come at the call of a legislature, nor will it repeat in England or America its history in Greece. It will come, as always, unannounced, and spring up between the feet of brave and earnest men.

WALT WHITMAN
Death of a Hero

I wonder if I could ever convey to another—to you, for instance, reader dear—the tender and terrible realities of such cases, (many, many happen'd,) as the one I am now going to mention. Stewart C. Glover, company E, 5th Wisconsin—was wounded May 5, in one of those fierce tussles of the Wilderness—died May 21—aged about 20. He was a small and beardless young man—a splendid soldier—in fact almost an ideal American, of his age. He had serv'd nearly three years, and would have been entitled to his discharge in a few days. He was in Hancock's corps. The fighting had about ceas'd for the day, when the general commanding the brigade rode by and call'd for volunteers to bring in the wounded. Glover responded among the first —went out gayly—but while in the act of bearing in a wounded sergeant to our lines, was shot in the knee by a rebel sharpshooter; consequence, amputation and death. He had resided with his father, John Glover, an aged and feeble man, in Batavia, Genesee county, N.Y., but was at school in Wisconsin, after the war broke out, and there enlisted—soon took to soldier-life, liked it, was very manly, was beloved by officers and comrades. He kept a little diary, like so many of the soldiers. On the day of his death he wrote the following in it, *to-day the doctor says I must die—all is over with me—ah, so young to die.* On another blank leaf he pencill'd to his brother, *dear brother Thomas, I have been brave but wicked—pray for me.*

H. NORMAN SCHWARZKOPF

It doesn't take a hero to order men into battle. It takes a hero to be one of those men who go into battle.

STEPHEN CRANE
The Red Badge of Courage

At times he regarded the wounded soldiers in an envious way. He conceived persons with torn bodies to be peculiarly happy. He wished that he, too, had a wound, a red badge of courage.

ERNEST HEMINGWAY
For Whom the Bell Tolls

You have had much luck. There are many worse things than this. Everyone has to do this, one day or another. You are not afraid of it once you know you have to do it, are you? No, he said, truly. It was lucky the nerve was crushed, though. I cannot even feel that there is anything below the break. He touched the lower part of his leg and it was as though it were not part of his body.

He looked down the hill slope again and he thought. I hate to leave it, is all. I hate to leave it every much and I hope I have done some good in it. I have tried to with what talent I had. *Have, you mean. All right, have.*

I have fought for what I believed in for a year now. If we win here we will win everywhere. The world is a fine place and worth the fighting for and I hate very much to leave it.

GARRISON KEILLOR
We Are Still Married

What I wanted to talk about was whether the boys of the First Minnesota Brigade, including the one buried here, who made their heroic and brutal counterattack on July 2, 1863, at Gettysburg against Longstreet's army that had found a great vacancy in the Union line and was swinging into position against its flank to roll up Meade and run him straight to Washington and win the war for the Confederacy—whether those boys thought of us in the future and what the country would come to, what they were fighting for and who would keep their memory

—would they have liked us? Or would our America horrify them? And how all two hundred of them jumped up off the grass and ran toward the smoke, because that's where everyone else was running and they were loyal to each other, loved each other, so in some way they loved the nation and us and our life that owes so much to them. Only forty of them came back out of the smoke; the rest were dead or wounded. Young men in the spring of life. A hot day, thick smoke, horses shrieking and men screaming horribly in that unbearable cannon fire around the peach orchard and meadow. But they all ran into the smoke, and how this somehow changes everything. The citizens of death. Our duty to honor them, a *lovely* duty. It's a civic duty to look at death and thus see life clear, and how life—the furtherance of life—is the purpose of the state and community—parenthood—the value of storytelling—our connection to each. . . .

ROBERT E. LEE
Inscription beneath his bust in the Hall of Fame for Great Americans

Duty then is the sublimest word in our language. Do your duty in all things. You cannot do more. You should never wish to do less.

ABRAHAM LINCOLN
Speech, New York City

Let us have faith that right makes might, and in that faith let us to the end do our duty as we understand it.

WILLIAM BARRET TRAVIS,
LIEUTENANT-COLONEL-COMMANDANT OF THE ALAMO

To the People of Texas & all Americans in the world—

Fellow Citizens & Compatriots: I am besieged, by a thousand or more of the Mexicans under Santa Anna—I have sustained a continual Bombardment & cannonade for 24 hours & have not lost a man—The enemy has demanded a surrender at discretion, otherwise the garrison are to be put to the sword, if the fort is taken—I have answered the demand with a cannon shot, & our flag still waves proudly from the walls—*I shall never surrender or retreat. Then,* I call on you in the name of Liberty, of patriotism & everything dear to the American character, to come to our aid, with all dispatch—The enemy is receiving reinforcements daily & will no doubt increase to three or four thousand in four or five days. If this call is neglected, I am determined to sustain myself as long as possible & die like a soldier who never forgets what is due to his own honor & that of his country—

VICTORY OR DEATH

ABRAHAM LINCOLN
Gettysburg Address

We have come to dedicate a portion of that field as a final resting-place for those who here gave their lives that that nation might live. It is altogether fitting and proper that we should do this. But in a larger sense, we cannot dedicate, we cannot consecrate, we cannot hallow this ground. The brave men, living and dead who struggled here have consecrated it far above our poor power to add or detract. The world will little note nor long remember what we say here, but it can never forget what they did here.

ABRAHAM LINCOLN
Letter to Mrs. Bixby

Dear Madam:

I have been shown in the files of the War Department a statement of the Adjutant General of Massachusetts that you are the mother of five sons who have died gloriously on the field of battle. I feel how weak and fruitless must be any words of mine which should attempt to beguile you from the grief of a loss so overwhelming, but I cannot refrain from tendering to you the consolation that may be found in the thanks of the Republic that they died to save. I pray that the Heavenly Father may assuage the anguish of your bereavement, and leave you only the cherished memory of the loved and lost, and the solemn pride that must be yours to have laid so costly a sacrifice upon the altar of freedom.

MARK TWAIN

Each man must for himself alone decide what is right and what is wrong, which course is patriotic and which isn't. You cannot shirk this and be a man. To decide against your conviction is to be an unqualified and inexcusable traitor, both to yourself and to your country, let men label you as they may.

"Barbara Frietchie"

JOHN GREENLEAF WHITTIER

Up from the meadows rich with corn,
Clear in the cool September morn,
The clustered spires of Frederick stand
green-walled by the hills of Maryland.

Round about them orchards sweep,
Apple and peach tree fruited deep,
Fair as the garden of the Lord
To the eyes of the famished rebel horde.

On that pleasant morn of the early fall
When Lee marched over the mountain-wall;
Over the mountains winding down,
Horse and foot, into Frederick town.

Forty flags with their silver stars,
Forty flags with their crimson bars,
Flapped in the morning wind; the sun
Of noon looked down, and saw not one.

Up rose old Barbara Frietchie then,
Bowed with her fourscore years and ten;
Bravest of all in Frederick town,
She took up the flag the men hauled down;

In her attic window the staff she set,
To show that one heart was loyal yet.
Up the street came the rebel tread,
Stonewall Jackson riding ahead.

Under his slouched hat left and right
He glanced; the old flag met his sight.
"Halt!"—the dust-brown ranks stood fast.
"Fire!"—out blazed the rifle-blast.

It shivered the window, pane and sash;
It rent the banner with seam and gash.
Quick, as it fell, from the broken staff
Dame Barbara snatched the silken scarf.

She leaned far out on the windowsill,
And shook it forth with a royal will.
"Shoot, if you must, this old gray head,
But spare your country's flag," she said.

A shade of sadness, a blush of shame,
Over the face of the leader came;
The nobler nature within him stirred
To life at that woman's deed and word;

"Who touches a hair of yon gray head
Dies like a dog! March on!" he said.
All day long through Frederick street
Sounded the tread of marching feet:

All day long that free flag tost
Over the heads of the rebel host.
Ever its torn folds rose and fell
On the loyal winds that loved it well;

And through the hill-gaps sunset light
Shone over it with a warm good night.
Barbara Frietchie's work is o'er,
And the rebel rides on his raids no more.

Honor to her! and let a tear
Fall, for her sake, on Stonewall's bier.
Over Barbara Frietchie's grave,
Flag of freedom and union, wave!

Peace and order and beauty draw
Round thy symbol of light and law;
And ever the stars above look down
On thy stars below in Frederick town!

ULYSSES S. GRANT
Memoirs

When I had left camp that morning I had not expected so soon the result that was then taking place, and consequently was in rough garb. I was without a sword, as I usually was when on horseback on the field, and wore a soldier's blouse for a coat, with the shoulder straps of my rank to indicate to the army who I was. When I went into the house I found General Lee. We greeted each other, and after shaking hands took our seats. I had my staff with me, a good portion of whom were in the room during the whole of the interview.

What General Lee's feelings were I do not know. As he was a man of much dignity, with an impassable face, it was impossible to say whether he felt inwardly glad that the end had finally come, or felt sad over the result, and was too manly to show it. Whatever his feelings, they were entirely concealed from my observation; but my own feelings, which had been quite jubilant on the receipt of his letter, were sad and depressed. I felt like anything rather than rejoicing at the downfall of a foe who had fought so long and valiantly, and had suffered so much for a cause, though that cause was, I believe, one of the worst for which a people ever fought, and one for which there was the least excuse. I do not question, however, the sincerity of the great mass of those who were opposed to us.

ROBERT E. LEE
Farewell to his Army

After four years of arduous service marked by unsurpassed courage and fortitude, the Army of Northern Virginia has been compelled to yield to overwhelming numbers and resources.

I need not tell the survivors of so many hard-fought battles who have remained steadfast to the last that I have consented to this result from no distrust of them; but feeling that valor and devotion could accomplish nothing that would compensate for the loss that must have attended the continuance of the contest, I determined to avoid the useless sacrifice of those whose past services have endeared them to their countrymen. By the terms of the agreement, officers and men can return to their homes and remain until exchanged.

You may take with you the satisfaction that proceeds from the consciousness of duty faithfully performed, and I earnestly pray that a merciful God will extend to you His blessing and protection.

With an unceasing admiration of your constancy and devotion to your country, and a grateful remembrance of your kind and generous consideration of myself, I bid you all an affectionate farewell.

ANNE MORROW LINDBERGH

It takes as much courage to have tried and failed as it does to have tried and succeeded.

HENRY WARD BEECHER

Do not be afraid of defeat. You are never so near to victory as when defeated in a good cause.

WENDELL PHILLIPS

What is defeat? Nothing but education, nothing but the first step toward something better.

WILLIAM TECUMSEH SHERMAN
Memoirs

I would define true courage to be a perfect sensibility of the measure of danger, and a mental willingness to endure it.

CARL SANDBURG

Valor is a gift. Those having it never know for sure whether they have it till the test comes.

A Prayer for Owen Meany

JOHN IRVING

"DOONG SA," Owen Meany told them. "DON'T BE AFRAID," Owen told the children. "DOONG SA, DOONG SA," he said. It was not only because he spoke their language; it was his *voice* that compelled the children to listen to him—it was a voice like *their* voices. That was why they trusted him, why they listened. "DOONG SA," he said, and they stopped crying.

"It's just the place for you to die," Dick said to Owen. "With all these little *gooks*—with these little *dinks*!" Dick said.

"NAM SOON!" Owen told the children. "NAM SOON! LIE DOWN!" Even the littlest boy understood him. "LIE DOWN!" Owen told them. "NAM SOON! NAM SOON!" All the children threw themselves on the floor—they covered their ears, they shut their eyes.

"NOW I KNOW WHY MY VOICE NEVER CHANGES," Owen said to me. "DO YOU SEE WHY?" he asked me.

"Yes," I said.

"WE'LL HAVE JUST FOUR SECONDS," Owen told me calmly. "YOU'LL NEVER GET TO VIETNAM, DICK," Owen told the terrible, tall boy—who ripped the fuse cord and tossed the bottle-shaped grenade, end over end, right to me.

"Think fast—Mister Fuckin' *Intelligence* Man!" Dick said.

I caught the grenade, although it wasn't as easy to handle as a basketball—I was lucky. I looked at Owen, who was already moving toward me.

"READY?" he said; I passed him the Chicom grenade and opened my arms to catch him. He jumped so lightly into my hands; I lifted him up—as easily as I had always lifted him.

After all: I had been practicing lifting up Owen Meany—forever.

The nun who'd been waiting for the children outside the door of the "Men's Temporary Facilities"—she hadn't liked the looks of Dick; she'd run off to get the other soldiers. It was Major Rawls who caught Dick running away from the temporary men's room.

"What have you done, you fuck-face?" the major screamed at Dick.

Dick had drawn the bayonet. Major Rawls seized Dick's machete—Rawls broke Dick's neck with one blow, with the dull edge of the blade. I'd sensed that there was something more bitter than anger in the major's uncommon, lake-green eyes; maybe it was just his contact lenses, but Rawls hadn't won a battlefield commission in Korea for nothing. He may not have been prepared to kill an unfortunate, fifteen-year-old boy; but Major Rawls was even less prepared to be killed *by* such a kid, who—as Rawls had said to Owen—was (at least on this earth) "beyond saving."

When Owen Meany said "READY?" I figured we had about two seconds left to live. But he soared far above my arms—when I lifted him, he soared even higher than usual; he wasn't taking any chances. He went straight up, never turning to face me, and instead of merely dropping the grenade and leaving it on the window ledge, he caught hold of the ledge with both hands, pinning the grenade against the ledge and trapping it there safely with his hands and forearms. He wanted to be sure that the grenade couldn't roll off the ledge and fall back in the room. He could just manage to wriggle his head—his whole head, thank God—below the window ledge. He clung there for less than a second.

Then the grenade detonated; it made a shattering "crack!"—like lightning when it strikes too close to you. There was a high-velocity projection of fragments—the fragmentation is usually distributed in a uniform pattern (this is what Major Rawls explained to me, later), but the cement window ledge prevented any fragments from reaching me or the children. What hit us was all the stuff that ricocheted off the ceiling—there was a sharp, stinging hail that rattled like BBs around the room, and all the chips of cement and tile, and the plaster debris, fell down upon us. The window was blown out, and there was an instant, acrid, burning stink. Major Rawls, who had just killed Dick, flung the door open and jammed a mop handle into the hinge assembly—to keep the door open. We needed the air. The children were holding their ears and crying; some of them were bleeding from their ears—that was when I noted that my ears were bleeding, too, and that I couldn't actually hear anything. I knew—from their faces —that the children were crying, and I knew from looking at Major Rawls that he was trying to tell me to *do* something.

What does he want me to do? I wondered, listening to the pain in my ears. Then the nuns were moving among the children—all the children were moving, thank God; they were *more* than moving, they were grasping each other, they were tugging the habits of the nuns, and they were pointing to the torn-apart ceiling of the coffin-shaped room, and the smoking black hole above the window ledge.

Major Rawls was shaking me by my shoulders; I tried to read the major's lips because I still couldn't hear him.

The children were looking all around; they were pointing up and down and everywhere. I began to look around with them. Now the nuns were also looking. Then my ears cleared; there was a popping or a ripping sound, as if my ears were late in echoing the explosion, and then the children's voices were jabbering, and I heard what Major Rawls was screaming at me while he shook me.

"Where *is* he? Where is Owen?" Major Rawls was screaming.

I looked up at the black hole, where I'd last seen him clinging. One of the children was staring into the vast sink; one of the nuns looked into the sink, too—she crossed herself, and Major Rawls and I moved quickly to assist her.

But the nun didn't need our help; Owen was so light, even the nun could lift him. She picked him up, out of the sink, as she might have picked up one of the children; then she didn't know what to do with him. Another nun kneeled in the bomb litter on the floor; she settled back on her haunches and spread her habit smoothly across her thighs, and the nun who held Owen in her arms rested his head in the lap of the sister who'd thus arranged herself on the floor. The third and fourth nuns tried to calm the children—to make them move away from him—but the children crowded around Owen; they were all crying.

"DOONG SA—DON'T BE AFRAID," he told them, and they stopped crying.

DWIGHT D. EISENHOWER

What counts is not necessarily the size of the dog in the fight, but the size of the fight in the dog.

RALPH WALDO EMERSON
"Heroism," *Essays, First Series*

Heroism feels and never reasons and therefore is always right.

HENRY WADSWORTH LONGFELLOW

The bravest are the tenderest. The loving are the daring.

THEODORE H. WHITE

Quality—in its classic Greek sense—how to live with grace and intelligence, with bravery and mercy.

BENJAMIN FRANKLIN
"The Busy-Body Papers in the American Weekly Mercury"

It is a grand mistake to think of being great without goodness; and I pronounce it as certain that there was never a truly great man that was not at the same time truly virtuous.

JOHN BUNYAN
"Pilgrim's Progress"

He who would valiant be
'Gainst all disaster
Let him in constancy
Follow the Master.
There's no discouragement
Shall make him once relent,
His first avowed intent
To be a pilgrim.

DANIEL J. BOORSTIN
The Image

The hero was distinguished by his achievement; the celebrity by his image or trademark. The hero created himself; the celebrity is created by the media. The hero was a big man; the celebrity is a big name.

NATHANIEL HAWTHORNE
The Blithedale Romance

The greatest obstacle to being heroic is the doubt whether one may not be going to prove one's self a fool; the truest heroism is to resist the doubt—and the profoundest wisdom, to know when it ought to be resisted, and when to be obeyed.

JOSEPH CAMPBELL
The Power of Myth

A hero is someone who has given his or her life to something bigger than oneself.

WALT WHITMAN
"O Captain! My Captain!"

O Captain! my Captain! our fearful trip is done;
The ship has weather'd every rack, the prize we sought is won;
The port is near, the bells I hear, the people all exulting,
While follow eyes the steady keel, the vessel grim and daring:
    But O heart! heart! heart!
      O the bleeding drops of red,
        Where on the deck my captain lies,
          Fallen cold and dead.

O Captain! my Captain! rise up and hear the bells;
Rise up—for you the flag is flung—for you the bugle trills;
For you bouquets and ribbon'd wreaths—for you the shores a-crowding;
For you they call, the swaying mass, their eager faces turning:
    Here Captain! dear father!
      This arm beneath your head!
        It is some dream that on the deck,
          You've fallen cold and dead.

My Captain does not answer, his lips are pale and still;
My father does not feel my arm, he has no pulse nor will;
The ship is anchor'd safe and sound, its voyage closed and done;
From fearful trip, the victor ship comes in with object won:
    Exult, O shores, and ring, O bells!
      But I, with mournful tread,
        Walk the deck my Captain lies,
          Fallen cold and dead.

FREDERICK DOUGLASS
Speech at the dedication of the Freedmen's Monument, Washington, D.C.,

Abraham Lincoln was clear in his duty, and had an oath in heaven. He calmly and bravely heard the voice of doubt and fear all around him; but he had an oath in heaven, and there was not power enough on the earth to make this honest boatman, backwoodsman, and broad-handed splitter of rails evade or violate that sacred oath. He had not been schooled in the ethics of slavery; his plain life had favored his love of truth. He had not been taught that treason and perjury were the proof of honor and honesty. His moral training was against his saying one thing when he meant another. The trust which Abraham Lincoln had in himself and in the people was surprising and grand, but it was also enlightened and well founded. He knew the American people better than they knew themselves, and his truth was based upon this knowledge. . . .

HENRY LEE
Funeral oration in honor of George Washington

First in war—first in peace—and first in the hearts of his countrymen, he was second to none in the humble and endearing scenes of private life; pious, just, humane, temperate and sincere; uniform, dignified and commanding, his example was as edifying to all around him, as were the effects of that example lasting.

To his equals he was condescending, to his inferiors kind and to the dear object of his affections exemplarily tender; correct throughout, vice shuddered in his presence, and virtue always felt his fostering hand; the purity of his private character gave effulgence to his public virtues.

His last scene comported with the whole tenor of his life—although in extreme pain, not a sigh, not a groan escaped him; and with undisturbed serenity he closed his well-spent life. Such was the man America has lost—such was the man for whom our nation mourns.

Methinks I see his august image, and I hear falling from his venerable lips these deep-sinking words:

"Cease, Sons of America, lamenting our separation: go on, and confirm by your wisdom the fruits of our joint councils, joint efforts, and common dangers; reverence religion, diffuse knowledge throughout your land, patronize the arts and sciences; let Liberty and Order be inseparable companions. Control party spirit, the bane of free governments; observe good faith to, and cultivate peace with all nations, shut up every avenue to foreign influence, contract rather than extend national connection, rely on yourselves only: be Americans in thought, word, and deed;—thus will you give immortality to that union which was the constant object of my terrestrial labors; thus will you preserve undisturbed to the latest posterity the felicity of a people to me most dear, and thus will you supply (if my happiness is now aught to you) the only vacancy in the round of pure bliss high Heaven bestows."

BETTY DERAMUS

A hero is simply someone who rises above his own human weaknesses, for an hour, a day, a year, to do something stirring.

RALPH WALDO EMERSON
"Great Men"

Not gold, but only man can make
A people great and strong;
Men who, for truth and honor's sake,
Stand fast and suffer long.

Brave men who work while others sleep,
Who dare while others fly—
They build a nation's pillars deep
And lift them to the sky.

JACKIE ROBINSON

For one wild and rage-crazed minute I thought, "To hell with Mr. Rickey's 'noble experiment.' It's clear it won't succeed....What a glorious, cleansing thing it would be to let go." To hell with the image of the patient black freak I was supposed to create. I could throw down my bat, stride over to the Phillies dugout, grab one of those white sons of bitches and smash his teeth in with my despised black fist. Then I could walk away from it and I'd never become a sports star. But my son could tell his son someday what his daddy could have been if he hadn't been too much of a man.

ALICE WALKER
In Search of Our Mothers' Garden

He was The One, The Hero, The One Fearless Person for whom we had waited. I hadn't even realized before that we *had* been waiting for Martin Luther King, Jr., but we had. And I knew it for sure when my mother added his name to the list of people she prayed for every night.

TONI MORRISON
Eulogy of James Baldwin

Yours was the courage to live life, in and from its belly as well as beyond its edges, to see and say what it was to recognize and identify evil, but never fear or stand in awe of it.

E.B. WHITE
"On John F. Kennedy," *The New Yorker*

When we think of him, he is without a hat, standing in the wind and the weather. He was impatient of topcoats and hats, preferring to be exposed, and he was young enough and tough enough to confront and to enjoy the cold and the wind of these times, whether the winds of nature or the winds of political circumstance and national danger. He died of exposure, but in a way that he would have settled for—in the line of duty, and with his friends and enemies all around, supporting him and shooting at him. It can be said of him, as of few men in a like position, that he did not fear the weather, and did not trim his sails, but instead challenged the wind itself, to improve its direction and to cause it to blow more softly and more kindly over the world and its people.

RON KARENGA
Speech given at Yale University

None of our heroes fail because of progressive perfection. They did as much as they could given the time and the circumstances.

NORMAN MAILER
Presidential Papers, Special Preface

Ultimately a hero is a man who would argue with the Gods, and awakens devils to contest his vision.

JAMES BALDWIN
Nobody Knows My Name

Heroes can be found less in large things than in small ones, less in public than in private.

ROSA PARKS

I'm just an average citizen. Many Black people were arrested for defying the bus laws. They prepared the way.

ROSA PARKS
Cited in Let the Trumpet Sound

I was frightened, but I figured we needed help to get us more jobs and better education.

ROSA PARKS
Workshop at the Highlander Folk School, Tennessee

It was not at all pre-arranged. It just happened that the driver made a demand and I just didn't feel like obeying his demand...I was quite tired after spending a full day working. I handle and work on clothing that white people wear. That didn't come into my mind but this is what I wanted to know: when and how would we ever determine our rights as human beings.

PHILIP K. DICK
I Hope I Shall Arrive Soon

This, to me, is the ultimately heroic trait of ordinary people; they say *no* to the tyrant and they calmly take the consequences of this resistance.

FLYER DISTRIBUTED IN BIRMINGHAM, ALABAMA

Don't ride the bus to work, to town, to school or any place Monday, December 5. Another Negro woman has been arrested and put in jail because she refused to give up her bus seat. Don't ride the buses to work, to town, to school, or anywhere on Monday. If you work, take a cab, or share a ride, or walk. Come to a mass meeting, Monday at 7:00 P.M. at the Hall Street Baptist Church for further instruction.

DAISY BATES
The Long Shadow of Little Rock

The crowd moved in closer and then began to follow me, calling me names. I still wasn't afraid. Just a little bit nervous, whether I could make it to the center entrance a block away. It was the longest block I ever walked in my whole life.

FREDERICK DOUGLASS
Life and Times of Frederick Douglass

Remember Denmark Vesey… remember Nathaniel Turner… remember Shields Green and Copeland, who followed noble John Brown, and fell as glorious martyrs for the cause of the slave. Remember that in a contest with oppression, the Almighty has no attribute which can take sides with oppressors.

WILLIAM JENNINGS BRYAN
Speech at the National Democratic Convention

The humblest citizen of all the land, when clad in the armor of a righteous cause, is stronger than all the hosts of Error.

A. PHILIP RANDOLPH

It is the hour of the common man. May we rise to the challenge to struggle for our rights. Come what will or may and let us never falter.

HENRY DAVID THOREAU
Walden

I am less affected by their heroism who stood up for half an hour in the front line at Buena Vista, than by the steady and cheerful valor of the men who inhabit the snowplow for their winter quarters; who have not merely the three-o'–clock-in-the-morning courage, which Bonaparte thought was the rarest, but whose courage does not go to rest so early, who go to sleep only when the storm sleeps or the sinews of their iron steed are frozen.

FRANKLIN D. ROOSEVELT
Speech on behalf of the March of Dimes

We have been seeing so much in the papers lately of our need for nurses, and sometimes I imagine the nurses have thought we sounded rather critical of them. A few days ago I received a letter from a mother whose daughter is a 2nd Lieutenant in the army Nurse Corps and who has spent her third Christmas in "some cold camp in Europe." At home she made $50 a week and her food. But her brother went into the army, and so in '42 she went in, too, accepting the munificent salary of $80 a month. That has gone up a bit, but she has worked for it! She started in England, went to Africa and Sicily, and since last October has been in France.

"Their unit always arrives first, when they must live in ice-cold tents or barracks, wash out of their helmets and wade through the mud," writes her mother. "Last January she nearly died of pneumonia. This time, when reaching France, she was again in the hospital with a severe cold. When they reached France the enemy had put cement in all water pipes and heating facilities, so it took some time to get organized. But the nurses worked and froze. Now she works 15 hours a day, walks 20 minutes to the hospital in slush and cold.

"She was offered a leave to come home, but once in France she hoped to see her brother and so refused, saying she wanted to stay until the last gun was fired!"

HELEN CARPENTER
DIARY ENTRIES MADE WHILE CROSSING THE OREGON TRAIL IN 1857

Although there is not much to cook, the difficulty and inconvenience in doing it amounts to a great deal—so by the time one has squatted around the fire and cooked bread and bacon, and made several dozen trips to and from the wagon—washed the dishes...and gotten things ready for an early breakfast, some of the others already have their night caps on—at any rate it is time to go to bed. In respect to women's work, the days are all very much the same—except when we stop...then there is washing to be done and light bread to make and all kinds of odd jobs. Some women have very little help about the camp, being obliged to get the wood and water...make camp fires, unpack at night and pack up in the morning—and if they are Missourians they have the milking to do if they are fortunate enough to have cows. I am lucky in having a Yankee for a husband, so am well waited on...When the sun was just peeping over the top of the mountain, there was suddenly heard a shot and a blood curdling yell, and immediately the Indians we saw yesterday were seen riding at full speed directly toward the horses...father put his gun to his shoulder as though to shoot....The Indians kept...circling...and halooing...bullets came whizzing through the camp. None can know the horror of it, who have not been similarly situated...[the Indians] did not come directly toward us, but all the time in a circular way, from one side of the road to the other, each time they passed, getting a little nearer, and occasionally firing a shot....Father and Reel could stand it no longer, they must let those Indians see how far their Sharps rifles would carry. Without aiming to hit them, they made the earth fly....It is now 18 days since we have seen a train...[we] found the body of a nude woman on the bank of the slough....A piece of hair rope was around her neck....From appearances it was thought she had been tortured by being drawn back and forth through the slough, by this rope around her neck. The body was given the best burial that was possible, under the circumstances....

JOHN F. KENNEDY
Profiles in Courage

For without belittling the courage with which men have died, we should not forget those acts of courage with which men...have *lived*....A man does what he must—in spite of personal consequences, in spite of obstacles and dangers and pressures—and that is the basis of all human morality.

ROBERT HUNTER
Poverty

In this community of workers several thousand human beings were struggling fiercely against want....They toiled with marvelous persistency....On cold, rainy mornings, at the dark of dawn, I have been awakened...by the monotonous clatter of hobnailed boots on the plank sidewalks, as the procession to the factory passed....Heavy, brooding men, tired, anxious women, thinly dressed, unkempt little girls, and frail, joyless little lads passed along, half awake, not one uttering a word....From all directions thousands were entering the various gates,— children of every nation of Europe. Hundreds of others—obviously a hungrier, poorer lot... waited in front of a closed gate...until a man came out and selected twenty-three of the strongest....For these the gates were opened, and the others, with down-cast eyes, marched off to seek employment elsewhere. In this community, fully fifty thousand men, women and children were all the time either in poverty or on the verge of poverty. It would not be possible to describe how they worked and starved and ached to rise out of it.

RALPH WALDO EMERSON
Letters and Social Aims

Each man is a hero and an oracle to somebody.

"A Life's Work..."

WILLIAM FAULKNER
Nobel Prize Speech

I feel that this award was not made to me as a man, but to my work—a life's work in the agony and sweat of the human spirit, not for glory and least of all for profit, but to create out of the materials of the human spirit something which did not exist before. So this award is only mine in trust. It will not be difficult to find a dedication for the money part of it commensurate with the purpose and significance of its origin. But I would like to do the same with the acclaim too, by using this moment as a pinnacle from which I might be listened to by the young men and women already dedicated to the same anguish and travail, among whom is already that one who will some day stand where I am standing.

Our tragedy today is a general and universal physical fear so long sustained by now that we can even bear it. There are no longer problems of the spirit. There is only one question: When will I be blown up? Because of this, the young man or woman writing today has forgotten the problems of the human heart in conflict with itself which alone can make good writing because only that is worth writing about, worth the agony and the sweat.

He must learn them again. He must teach himself that the basest of all things is to be afraid: and, teaching himself that, forget it forever, leaving no room in his workshop for anything but the old verities and truths of the heart, the universal truths lacking which any story is ephemeral and doomed—love and honor and pity and pride and compassion and sacrifice. Until he does so, he labors under a curse. He writes not of love but of lust, of defeats in which nobody loses anything of value, of victories without hope and, worst of all, without pity or compassion. His griefs grieve on no universal bones, leaving no scars. He writes not of the heart but of the glands.

Until he learns these things, he will write as though he stood among and watched the end of man. I decline to accept the end of man. It is easy enough to say that man is immortal simply because he will endure: that when the last ding-dong of doom has clanged and faded from the last worthless rock hanging tideless in the last red and dying evening, that even then there will still be one more sound: that of his puny inexhaustible voice, still talking. I refuse to accept this. I believe that man will not merely endure: he will prevail. He is immortal, not because he alone among creatures has an inexhaustible sacrifice and endurance. The poet's, the writer's, duty is to write about these things. It is his privilege to help man endure by lifting his heart, by reminding him of the courage and honor and hope and pride and compassion and pity and sacrifice which have been the glory of his past. The poet's voice need not merely be the record of man, it can be one of the props, the pillars to help him endure and prevail.

MURIEL RUKEYSER
"Poem"

I lived in the first century of world wars.
Most mornings I would be more or less insane,
The newspapers would arrive with their careless stories,
The news would pour out of various devices
Interrupted by attempts to sell products to the unseen.
I would call my friends on other devices;
They would be more or less mad for similar reasons.
Slowly I would get to pen and paper,
Make my poems for others unseen and unborn.
In the day I would be reminded of those men and women
Brave, setting up signals across vast distances,
Considering a nameless way of living, of almost unimagined
    values.
As the lights darkened, as the lights of night brightened,
We would try to imagine them, try to find each other.
To construct peace, to make love, to reconcile
Waking with sleeping, ourselves with each other,
Ourselves with ourselves. We would try by any means
To reach the limits of ourselves, to reach beyond ourselves,
To let go the means, to wake.

I lived in the first century of these wars.

GENERAL OMAR BRADLEY

Bravery is the capacity to perform properly even when scared half to death.

REINHOLD NIEBUHR

If we survive danger, it steels our courage more than anything else.

RALPH WALDO EMERSON

Our greatest glory consists not in never falling, but in rising every time we fall.

HARRIET BEECHER STOWE

When you get into a tight place and everything goes against you, 'til it seems as though you could not hold on a minute longer, never give up then, for that is just the place and time that the tide will turn.

RALPH WALDO EMERSON

A hero is no braver than an ordinary man, but he is brave five minutes longer.

GENERAL GEORGE S. PATTON

Courage is fear holding on a minute longer.

ABRAHAM LINCOLN

Hold on a with a bulldog grip, and chew and choke as much as possible.

HENRY DAVID THOREAU

Gnaw your own bone; gnaw at it, bury it, unearth it, gnaw it still.

TOM WOLFE
The Right Stuff

A man should have the ability to go up in a hurtling piece of machinery and put his hide on the line and then have the moxie, the reflexes, the experience, the coolness, to pull it back in the last yawning moment—and then to go up *the next day*, and the next day, and every next day, even if the series should prove infinite—and, ultimately, in its best expression, do so in a cause that means something to thousands, to a people, a nation, to humanity, to God.

ROBERT LOUIS STEVENSON

Saints are sinners who kept on going.

ROBERT FROST
The New York Times magazine

I'm not the kind of man who thinks the world can be saved by knowledge. It can only be saved by daring, bravery, going ahead. . . .

JOHN BERRYMAN
A Point of Age

We must travel in the direction of our fear.

JACK NEWFIELD
Robert Kennedy

All his life he [Robert Kennedy] had been schooled that nothing was worse than to finish second. But crushing fears are no longer so crushing once they are experienced.

RALPH WALDO EMERSON

Whatever course you decide upon, there is always someone to tell you that you are wrong. There are always difficulties arising which tempt you to believe that your critics are right. To map out a course of action and follow it to an end requires some of the same courage which a soldier needs.

HENRY VAN DYKE
"Doors of Daring"

The mountains that inclose the vale
With walls of granite, steep and high,
Invite the fearless foot to scale
Their stairway toward the sky.

The restless, deep, dividing sea
That flows and foams from shore to shore,
Calls to its sunburned chivalry,
"Push out, set sail, explore!"

The bars of life at which we fret,
That seem to prison and control,
Are but the doors of daring, set
Ajar before the soul.

Say not, "Too poor," but freely give;
Sigh not, "Too weak," but boldly try;
You never can begin to live
Until you dare to die.

FRANCES RODMAN
"For a Six-Year-Old," *The New York Times*

Courage does not always march to airs blown by a bugle; is not always wrought out of the fabric ostentation wears.

ROBERT F. KENNEDY

Moral courage is a more rare commodity than bravery in battle or great intelligence.

ROBERT FROST

You've got to be brave and you've got to be bold. Brave enough to take your chance on your own discrimination—what's right and what's wrong, what's good and what's bad.

ELEANOR ROOSEVELT
You Learn by Living

Courage is the strength to face pain, act under pressure, and maintain one's values in the face of opposition. You gain strength, courage and confidence by every experience in which you really stop to look fear in the face. You are able to say to yourself, "I lived through this horror. I can take the next thing that comes along."...You must do the thing you think you cannot do.

RAYMOND CHANDLER
"The Simple Art of Murder"

Down these mean streets a man must go who is not himself mean.

HARRY S TRUMAN

It takes courage to face a duelist with a pistol, and it takes courage to face a British general with an army. But it takes still greater and far higher courage to face friends with a grievance. The bravest thing Andrew Jackson ever did was to stand up and tell his own people to their own faces that they were wrong.

EDMUND G. ROSS

*Describing that moment during the impeachment trial of Andrew Johnson when,
as the freshman Senator from Kansas, he voted "Not Guilty"*

I almost literally looked down into my open grave. Friendships, position, fortune, everything that makes life desirable to an ambitious man were about to be swept away by the breath of my mouth, perhaps forever. It is not strange that my answer was carried waveringly over the air and failed to reach the limits of the audience, or that repetition was called for by distant Senators on the opposite side of the Chamber.

DANIEL WEBSTER

Discourse in Commemoration of Adams and Jefferson

Sink or swim, live or die, survive or perish, I give my hand and my heart to this vote.

LILLIAN HELLMAN

Scoundrel Time

I cannot and will not cut my conscience to fit this year's fashions.

ANDREW JACKSON

One man with courage makes a majority.

LOUIS BRANDEIS

New State Ice Co. v. Liebmann

If we would guide by the light of reason, we must let our minds be bold.

JAMES RUSSELL LOWELL

The Present Crisis

Once to every man and nation comes the moment to decide,
In the strife of Truth with Falsehood, for the good or evil side.

THOMAS JEFFERSON

Honesty is the first chapter of the book of wisdom.

George Washington and the Cherry Tree

ADAPTED FROM J. BERG ESENWEIN AND MARIETTA STOCKARD

When George Washington was a little boy he lived on a farm in Virginia. His father taught him to ride, and he used to take young George about the farm with him so that his son might learn how to take care of the fields and horses and cattle when he grew older.

Mr. Washington had planted an orchard of fine fruit trees. There were apple trees, peach trees, pear trees, plum trees, and cherry trees. Once, a particularly fine cherry tree was sent to him from across the ocean. Mr. Washington planted it on the edge of the orchard. He told everyone on the farm to watch it carefully to see that it was not broken or hurt in any way.

It grew well and one spring it was covered with white blossoms. Mr. Washington was pleased to think he would soon have cherries from the little tree.

Just about this time, George was given a shiny new hatchet. George took it and went about chopping sticks, hacking into the rails of fences, and cutting whatever else he passed. At last he came to the edge of the orchard, and thinking only of how well his hatchet could cut, he chopped into the little cherry tree. The bark was soft, and it cut so easily that George chopped the tree right down, and then went on with his play.

That evening when Mr. Washington came from inspecting the farm, he sent his horse to the stable and walked down to the orchard to look at his cherry tree. He stood in amazement when he saw how it was cut. Who would have dared do such a thing? He asked everyone, but no one could tell him anything about it.

Just then George passed by.

"George," his father called in an angry voice, "do you know who killed my cherry tree?

This was a tough question, and George staggered under it for a moment, but quickly recovered.

"I cannot tell a lie, father," he said. "I did it with my hatchet."

Mr. Washington looked at George. The boy's face was white, but he looked straight into his father's eyes.

"Go into the house, son," said Mr. Washington sternly.

George went into the library and waited for his father. He was very unhappy and very much ashamed. He knew he had been foolish and thoughtless and that his father was right to be displeased.

Soon, Mr. Washington came into the room. "Come here, my boy," he said.

George went over to his father. Mr. Washington looked at him long and steadily.

"Tell me, son, why did you cut the tree?"

"I was playing and I did not think—" George stammered.

"And now the tree will die. We shall never have any cherries from it. But worse than that, you have failed to take care of the tree when I asked you to do so."

George's head was bent and his cheeks were red from shame.

"I am sorry, father," he said.

Mr. Washington put his hand on the boy's shoulder. "Look at me," he said. "I am sorry to have lost my cherry tree, but I am glad that you were brave enough to tell me the truth. I would rather have you truthful and brave than to have a whole orchard full of the finest cherry trees. Never forget that, my son."

George Washington never did forget. To the end of his life he was just as brave and honorable as he was that day as a little boy.

HENRY DAVID THOREAU
A Week on the Concord and Merrimack Rivers

It takes two to speak the truth,—one to speak and another to hear.

BENJAMIN FRANKLIN
Poor Richard's Almanack

Only the wise and brave man dares own that he was wrong.

E.B. WHITE
Letter to Stanley Hart White

I have occasionally had the exquisite thrill of putting my finger on a little capsule of truth, and heard it give the faint squeak of mortality under my pressure.

PATRICK HENRY

For my part, whatever anguish of spirit it may cost, I am willing to know the whole truth—to know the worst and provide for it.

THOMAS JEFFERSON

The man who fears no truths has nothing to fear from lies.

DANIEL WEBSTER
Argument in an 1830 murder trial

There is nothing so powerful as truth; and often nothing so strange.

JAMES RUSSELL LOWELL
A Glance Behind the Curtain

I do not fear to follow out the truth,
Albeit along the precipice's edge.

THOMAS JEFFERSON
Letter to William Roscoe

We are not afraid to follow truth wherever it may lead, nor to tolerate any error so long as reason is left free to combat it.

MARGARET FULLER
Letter to William Henry Channing

It is astonishing what force, purity, and wisdom it requires for a human being to keep clear of falsehoods.

ELIZABETH TURNER
"Rebecca's Afterthought"

Yesterday, Rebecca Mason,
In the parlor by herself,
Broke a handsome china basin,
Placed upon the mantle shelf.

Quite alarmed, she thought of going
Very quietly away,
Not a single person knowing,
Of her being there that day.

But Rebecca recollected
She was taught deceit to shun;
And the moment she reflected,
Told her mother what was done;

Who commended her behavior,
Loved her better, and forgave her.

OLIVER WENDELL HOLMES, SR.
The Professor at the Breakfast-Table

Truth is tough. It will not break, like a bubble, at a touch; nay, you may kick it about all day, like a foot-ball, and it will be round and full at evening.

ALICE WALKER
Fathers

I recall a scene when I was only three or so in which my father questioned me about a fruit jar I had accidentally broken. I felt he knew I had broken it, at the same time I couldn't be sure. Apparently breaking it was, in any event, the wrong thing to have done. I could say, Yes, I broke the jar, and risk a whipping for breaking something valuable, or No, I did not break it, and perhaps bluff my way through.

I've never forgotten my feeling that he really wanted me to tell the truth. And because he seemed to desire it—and the moments during which he waited for my reply seemed quite out of time, so much so I can still feel them, and, as I said, I was only three—I confessed. I broke the jar, I said. I think he hugged me. He probably didn't, but I still feel as if he did, so embraced did I feel by the happy relief I noted on his face and by the fact that he didn't punish me at all, but seemed, instead, pleased with me. I think it was at that moment that I resolved to take my chances with the truth, although as the years rolled on I was to break more serious things in his scheme of things than fruit jars.

HENRY DAVID THOREAU
Walden

Rather than love, than money, than fame, give me truth.

CHARLES SEYMOUR
Statement made while president of Yale University, 1937–1950

We seek the truth, and will endure the consequences.

Reginald on Besetting Sins

SAKI

There was once (said Reginald) a woman who told the truth. Not all at once, of course, but the habit grew upon her gradually, like lichen on an apparently healthy tree. She had no children—otherwise it might have been different. It began with little things, for no particular reason except that her life was a rather empty one, and it is so easy to slip into the habit of telling the truth in little matters. And then it became difficult to draw the line at more important things, until at last she took to telling the truth about her age; she said she was forty-two and five months—by that time, you see, she was veracious even to months. It may have been pleasing to the angels, but her elder sister was not gratified. On the Woman's birthday, instead of the opera-tickets which she had hoped for, her sister gave her a view of Jerusalem from the Mount of Olives, which is not quite the same thing. The revenge of an elder sister may be long in coming, but, like a South-Eastern express, it arrives in its own good time.

The friends of the Woman tried to dissuade her from overindulgence in the practice, but she said she was wedded to the truth; whereupon it was remarked that it was scarcely logical to be so much together in public. (No really provident woman lunches regularly with her husband if she wishes to burst upon him as a revelation at dinner. He must have time to forget; an afternoon is not enough.) And after a while her friends began to thin out in patches. Her passion for the truth was not compatible with a large visiting-list. For instance, she told Miriam Klopstock *exactly* how she looked at the Ilexes' ball. Certainly Miriam had asked for her candid opinion, but the Woman prayed in church every Sunday for peace in our time, and it was not consistent.

It was unfortunate, every one agreed, that she had no family; with a child or two in the house, there is an unconscious check upon too free an indulgence in the truth. Children are given us to discourage our better emotions. That is why the stage, with all its efforts, can never be as artificial as life; even in an Ibsen drama one must reveal to the audience things that one would suppress before the children or servants.

Fate may have ordained the truth-telling from the commencement and should justly bear some of the blame; but in having no children the Woman was guilty, at least, of contributory negligence.

Little by little she felt she was becoming a slave to what had once been merely an idle propensity; and one day she knew. Every woman tells ninety per cent of the truth to her dressmaker; the other ten per cent is the irreducible minimum of deception beyond which no self-respecting client trespasses. Madame Draga's establishment was a meeting-ground for naked truths and overdressed fictions, and it was here, the Woman felt, that she might make a final effort to recall the artless mendacity of past days. Madame herself was in an inspiring mood, with the air of a sphinx who knew all things and preferred to forget most of them. As a War Minister she might have been celebrated, but she was content to be merely rich.

"If I take it in here, and—Miss Howard, one moment, if you please—and there, and round like this—so—I really think you will find it quite easy."

The Woman hesitated; it seemed to require such a small effort to simply acquiesce in Madame's views. But habit had become too strong. "I'm afraid," she faltered, "it's just the least little bit in the world too—"

And by that least little bit she measured the deeps and eternities of her thraldom to fact. Madame was not best pleased at being contradicted on a professional matter, and when Madame lost her temper you usually found it afterwards in the bill.

And at last the dreadful thing came, as the Woman had foreseen all along that it must; it was one of those paltry little truths with which she harried her waking hours. On a raw Wednesday morning, in a few ill-chosen words, she told the cook that she drank. She remembered the scene afterwards as vividly as though it had been painted in her mind by Abbey. The cook was a good cook, as cooks go; and as cooks go she went.

Miriam Klopstock came to lunch the next day. Women and elephants never forget an injury.

EMILY DICKINSON
"Tell All the Truth"

Tell all the truth but tell it slant.
Success in circuit lies
Too bright for our infirm delight,
The truth's super surprise
As lightning to the children eased
With explanation kind.
The truth must dazzle gradually
Or everyman be blind.

JAMES FENIMORE COOPER
The American Democrat

The ability to discriminate between that which is true and that which is false is one of the last attainments of the human mind.

RALPH WALDO EMERSON
The Conduct of Life

The highest compact we can make with our fellow is—"Let there be truth between us two forevermore."

HEYWOOD BROUN
The Nation

For truth there is no deadline.

BARTOLOMEO VANZETTI
Last Statement in Court

I am not only innocent of these two crimes, but . . . in all my life I have never stole, never killed, never spilled blood, but I have struggled all my life, since I began to reason, to eliminate crime from the earth. . . .

You already know that we were radicals, that we were underdogs. . . . We were tried during a time that has now passed into history. I mean by that, a time when there was hysteria of resentment and hate against the people of our principles, against the foreigner. . . .

I am suffering because I am a radical and indeed I am a radical; I have suffered because I was an Italian, and indeed I am an Italian; I have suffered more for my family and for my beloved than for myself; but I am so convinced to be right that if you could execute me two times, and if I could be reborn two other times, I would live again to do what I have done already.

MARIANNE MOORE
"What Are Years?"

What is our innocence,
what is our guilt? All are
    naked, none is safe. And whence
is courage: the unanswered question,
the resolute doubt—
dumbly calling, deafly listening—that
    encourages others
    and in its defeat, stirs

    soul to be strong? He
sees deep and is glad, who
    accedes to mortality

and in his imprisonment rises
upon himself as
the sea in a chasm, struggling to be
free and unable to be,
     in its surrendering
      finds its continuing.

   So he who strongly feels,
behaves. The very bird,
    grown taller as he sings, steels
his form straight up. Though he is captive,
his mighty singing
says, satisfaction is a lowly
thing, how pure a thing is joy.
     This is mortality,
     this is eternity.

JAMES THURBER

Let us not look back in anger, nor forward in fear, but around us in awareness.

JAMES BALDWIN
The Fire Next Time

To defend oneself against a fear is simply to ensure that one will, one day, be conquered by it: fears must be faced.

FRANKLIN DELANO ROOSEVELT

The only thing we have to fear is fear itself.

WILLIAM JAMES
The Will to Believe

Be not afraid of life. Believe that life *is* worth living, and your belief will help create the fact.

RALPH WALDO EMERSON

Do not be too timid and squeamish about your actions. All life is an experience.

JAMES WILLIAM FULBRIGHT
Speech in the Senate

We must dare to think "unthinkable" thoughts. We must learn to explore all the options and possibilities that confront us in a complex and rapidly changing world. We must learn to welcome and not to fear the voices of dissent. We must dare to think about "unthinkable things" because when things become unthinkable, thinking stops and action becomes mindless.

MAYA ANGELOU

Courage is the most important of all virtues, because without it we can't practice any other virtue with consistency.

HOWARD COSELL
Like It Is

Courage takes many forms. There is physical courage, there is moral courage. Then there is a still higher type of courage—the courage to brave pain, to live with it, to never let others know of it and to still find joy in life; to wake up in the morning with an enthusiasm for the day ahead.

LOU GEHRIG

Fans, for the past two weeks you have been reading about a bad break I got. Yet today I consider myself the luckiest man on the face of the earth. I have been in ballparks for seventeen years and I have never received anything but kindness and encouragement from you fans. Look at these grand men. Which of you wouldn't consider it the highlight of his career just to associate with them for even one day? Sure, I'm lucky. Who wouldn't have considered it an honor to have known Jacob Ruppert? Also, the builder of baseball's greatest empire, Ed Barrow? To have spent six years with that wonderful little fellow Miller Huggins? Then to have spent the next nine years with that outstanding leader, that smart student of psychology, the best manager in baseball today, Joe McCarthy? Sure, I'm lucky. When the New York Giants, a team you would give your right arm to beat and vice versa, sends you a gift, that's something. When everybody down to the groundskeepers and those boys in white coats remember you with trophies, that's something. When you have a father and mother who work all their lives so that you can have an education and build your body, it's a blessing. When you have a wife who has been a tower of strength and shown more courage than you dreamed existed, that's the finest I know. So I close in saying that I might have had a bad break, but I have an awful lot to live for.

ERNEST HEMINGWAY

[Courage is] grace under pressure.

HELEN KELLER

Although the world is full of suffering, it is full also of the overcoming of it.

THEODORE ROOSEVELT

It is impossible to win the great prizes of life without running risks.

HENRY DAVID THOREAU

If one advances confidently in the direction of his dreams, and endeavors to live the life which he has imagined, he will meet with a success unexpected in common hours.

JOHN F. KENNEDY

We should not let our fears hold us back from pursuing our hopes.

EDGAR GUEST
"The Things That Haven't Been Done Before"

The things that haven't been done before,
Those are the things to try;
Columbus dreamed of an unknown shore
At the rim of the far-flung sky,
And his heart was bold and his faith was strong
As he ventured in dangers new,
And he paid no heed to the jeering throng
Or the fears of the doubting crew.

The many will follow the beaten track
With guideposts on the way.
They live and have lived for ages back
With a chart for every day.
Someone has told them it's safe to go
On the road he has traveled o'er,
And all that they ever strive to know
Are the things that were known before.

A few strike out, without map or chart,
Where never a man has been,
From the beaten paths they draw apart
To see what no man has seen.
There are deeds they hunger alone to do;
Though battered and bruised and sore,
They blaze the path for the many, who
Do nothing not done before.

The things that haven't been done before
Are the tasks worthwhile today;
Are you one of the flock that follows, or
Are you one that shall lead the way?
Are you one of the timid souls that quail
At the jeers of a doubting crew,
Or dare you, whether you win or fail,
Strike out for a goal that's new?

CHARLES A. LINDBERGH
"Lindbergh's Own Story," *The New York Times*

We (that's my ship and I) took off rather suddenly. We had a report somewhere around 4 o'clock in the afternoon before that the weather would be fine, so we thought we would try it.

The Right Stuff

TOM WOLFE

Anyone who travels very much on airlines in the United States soon gets to know the voice of *the airline pilot*... coming over the intercom... with a particular drawl, a particular folksiness, a particular down-home calmness that is so exaggerated it begins to parody itself (nevertheless! —it's reassuring)... the voice that tells you, as the airliner is caught in thunderheads and goes bolting up and down a thousand feet at a single gulp, to check your seat belts because "it might get a little choppy"... the voice tells you (on a flight from Phoenix preparing for its final approach into Kennedy Airport, New York, just after dawn): "Now, folks, uh... this is the captain... ummmm... We've got a little ol' red light up here on the control panel that's tryin' to tell us the *lan*din' gears're not... uh... *lock*in' into position when we lower 'em... Now... *I* don't believe that little ol' red light knows what it's *talk*in' about—I believe it's that little ol' red light that iddn' workin' right"... faint chuckle, long pause, as if to say, *I'm not even sure all this is really worth going into—still, it may amuse you*... "But... I guess to play it by the rules, we oughta *hum*or that little ol' light... so we're gonna take her down to about, oh, two or three hundred feet over the runway at Kennedy, and the folks down there on the ground are gonna see if they caint give us a *vis*ual inspection of those ol' landin' gears"—with which he is obviously on intimate ol'-buddy terms, as with every other working part of this mighty ship— "and if I'm right... they're gonna tell us everything is copa*cet*ic all the way aroun' an' we'll jes take her on in"... and, after a couple of low passes over the field, the voice returns: "Well folks, those folks down there on the ground—it must be too early for 'em or somethin'—I 'spect they still got *sleep*ers in their eyes... 'cause they say they caint tell if those ol' landin' gears are all the way down or not.... But, you know, up here in the cockpit we're convinced they're all the way down, so we're jes gonna take her on in... And oh"... (*I almost forgot*)... "while we take a little swing out over the ocean an' empty some of that surplus fuel we're not gonna be needin' anymore—that's what you might be seein' comin' out of the wings—our lovely little ladies... if they'll be so kind... they're gonna go up and down the aisles and show you how we do what we call 'assumin' the position'" another faint chuckle (*We do this so often, and it's so much fun, we even have a funny little name for it*)... and the stewardesses, a bit grimmer, by the looks of them, than *that voice*, start telling the passengers to take their glasses off and take the ballpoint pens out of their pockets, and they show them *the position,* with the head lowered... while down on the field at Kennedy the little yellow emergency trucks start roaring across the field —and even though in your pounding heart and your sweating palms and your boiling brainpan you *know* this is a critical moment in your life, you still can't quite bring yourself to *believe* it, because if it were... how could *the captain,* the man who knows the actual situation most intimately... how could he keep drawlin' and chucklin' and driftin' and lollygaggin' in that particular voice of his—

Well!—who doesn't know that voice! And who can forget it!—even after he is proved right and the emergency is over.

That particular voice may sound vaguely Southern or Southwestern, but it is specifically Appalachian in origin. It originated in the mountains of West Virginia, in the coal country, in Lincoln County, so far up in the hollows that as the saying went, "they had to pipe in daylight." In the late 1940s and early 1950s this up-hollow voice drifted down from on high, from over the high desert of California, down, down, down from the upper reaches of the Brotherhood into all phases of American aviation. It was amazing. It was *Pygmalion* in reverse. Military pilots and then, soon, airline pilots, pilots from Maine and Massachusetts and the Dakotas and Oregon and everywhere else, began to talk in that polker-hollow West Virginia drawl, or as close to it as they could bend their native accents. It was the drawl of the most righteous of all the possessors of the right stuff: Chuck Yeager.

ROBERT FROST
"The Road Not Taken"

Two roads diverged in a wood, and I—
I took the one less traveled by,
And that has made all the difference.

MARK TWAIN
"Pudd'nhead Wilson's Calendar," Pudd'nhead Wilson

Courage is resistance to fear, mastery of fear—not absence of fear. Except a creature be part coward it is not a compliment to say it is brave; it is merely a loose misapplication of the word. Consider the flea!—incomparably the bravest of all the creatures of God, if ignorance of fear were courage. Whether you are asleep or awake he will attack you, caring nothing for the fact that in bulk and strength you are to him as are the massed armies of the earth to a sucking child; he lives both day and night and all days and nights in the very lap of peril and the immediate presence of death, and yet is no more afraid than is the man who walks the streets of a city that was threatened by an earthquake ten centuries before.

EDGAR ALLAN POE
Marginalia

That man is not truly brave who is afraid either to seem to be, or to be, when it suits him, a coward.

WILLIAM SAROYAN
Madness in the Family

Cowards are nice, they're interesting, they're gentle, they wouldn't think of shooting down people in a parade from a tower. They want to live, so they can see their kids. They're very brave.

O. HENRY

My advice to you, if you should ever be in a hold up, is to line up with the cowards and save your bravery for an occasion when it may be of some benefit to you.

EDDIE RICKENBACKER

Courage is doing what you're afraid to do. There can be no courage unless you're scared.

JOE SUGDEN

If you're scared, just holler and you'll find it ain't so lonesome out there.

WILLIAM JAMES

If you want a quality, act as if you already had it.

ACKNOWLEDGEMENTS

Excerpt from "Freedom" from *One Man's Meat* by E.B. White © 1940 by E.B. White, renewed © 1968 by E.B. White, reprinted by permission of HarperCollins Publishers, Inc.

Excerpts from E.B. White's writings in *The New Yorker*, including "Liberalism" and "A Busy Place" are from *E.B. White: Writings from the New Yorker 1925–1976* (HarperCollins). Copyright © E.B. White. Originally in *The New Yorker*. All rights reserved.

Pearl S. Buck speeches and quotes appeared in *Pearl S. Buck: A Biography* by Theodore Harris, published by John Day & Co. in 1971. Reprinted with permission of the Pearl S. Buck Family Trust.

Excerpts from *An American Childhood* by Annie Dillard © 1987 by Annie Dillard and *Pilgrim at Tinker Creek* by Annie Dillard © 1974 by Annie Dillard reprinted by permission of HarperCollins Publishers, Inc.

My Day—"September 3" and "June 4", by Eleanor Roosevelt copyright © 1989 by Pharos Books. Reprinted by permission of United Feature Syndicate, Inc.

Excerpt from *For Whom the Bell Tolls* by Ernest Hemingway copyright © 1940 by Ernest Hemingway, reprinted with permission of Scribner, a division of Simon & Schuster.

Excerpt from *A Wrinkle in Time* by Madeleine L'Engle copyright © 1962 by Crosswicks Ltd. Copyright © renewed 1990 by Madeleine L'Engle Franklin. Reprinted with permission of Farrar, Straus & Giroux, Inc.

Excerpt from *The Right Stuff* by Tom Wolfe copyright © 1979 by Tom Wolfe. Reprinted with permission of Farrar, Straus & Giroux, Inc.

Excerpt from *The Great Gatsby* reprinted with permission of Scribner, a division of Simon & Schuster, from The Great Gatsby (Authorized text) by F. Scott Fitzgerald. Copyright © 1925 Charles Scribner's Sons. Copyright renewed 1953 by Frances Scott Fitzgerald Lanahan. Copyright © 1991, 1992 by Eleanor Lanahan, Matthew J. Bruccoli and Samuel J. Lanahan as Trustees u/a dated 7/3/75 by Frances Scott Fitzgerald Smith.

"Nevertheless" by Marianne Moore reprinted with permission of Simon & Schuster from *The Collected Works of Marianne Moore* copyright © 1944 by Marianne Moore, renewed in 1972 by Marianne Moore.

ACKNOWLEDGEMENTS

"Heyoka Ceremony" reprinted from *Black Elk Speaks* by John G. Neihardt with permission of the University of Nebraska Press. Copyright 1932, 1959, 1972, by John G. Neihardt. Copyright © 1961 by the John G. Neihardt Trust.

Selection from *Wolf Willow* by Wallace Stegner copyright © 1955, 1957, 1958, 1959, 1962 by Wallace Stegner copyright © renewed 1990 by Wallace Stegner, reprinted by permission of Brandt & Brandt Literary Agents, Inc.

Lines from "Poem, Or Beauty Hurts Mr. Vinal", copyright 1926, 1954, 1991 by the Trustees for the E.E. Cummings Trust. Copyright © 1985 by George James Firmage, from Complete Poems: 1904–1962 by E.E. Cummings, Edited by George J. Firmage. Reprinted by permission of Liveright Publishing Corporation.

Excerpt from *On the Road* copyright 1957 by Jack Kerouac, reprinted by permission of Penguin Books USA Inc.

"Renascence", "Travel", "First Fig", "Feast", "Poem and Prayer for an Invading Army" and "Not for a Nation" by Edna St. Vincent Millay from *Collected Poems*, published by HarperCollins. Copyright © 1912, 1940, 1921, 1948, 1922, 1950, 1923, 1951, 1940, 1964, 1954, 1982 by Edna St. Vincent Millay and Norma Millay Ellis. All rights reserved. Reprinted by permission of Elizabeth Barnett, Literary Executor.

Excerpt of *From the Heart, Voice of the American Indian* by Lee Miller published by Alfred A. Knopf in 1995, reprinted with permission of the publisher.

Doonesbury copyright 1974 G.B. Trudeau. Reprinted with permission of Universal Press Syndicate. All rights reserved.

Excerpt from *Capitalism and Freedom* by Milton Friedman, published in 1962 by University of Chicago Press. Reprinted by permission of the publisher.

"Litany" and "Let America Be America Again" from *Collected Poems* by Langston Hughes copyright © 1994 by the Estate of Langston Hughes. Reprinted by permission of Alfred A. Knopf Inc.

"A Talk for Students" by Robert Frost, from a commencement speech address at Sarah Lawrence College, June 7, 1956 was reprinted in *Robert Frost Poetry and Prose* edited by Edward Connery Lathem and Lawrence Thompson. Copyright © 1956 by Robert Frost, © 1972 by Henry Holt and Co., Inc. Reprinted by permission of Henry Holt and Co., Inc.

The Boy Scout Oath reprinted with permission of the Boy Scouts of America.

"Our Game" from *Total Baseball* edited by John Thorn and Peter Palmer with Michael Gershman copyright © 1995 by John Thorn and Peter Palmer with Michael Gershman. Reprinted by permission of Viking Penguin, a division of Penguin Books USA Inc.

Excerpt from *Interview with Robert Frost* by Edward Connery Lathem, copyright © 1966 by Holt Reinhart & Winston. Reprinted by permission of Harcourt Brace and Company.

"The Goal of Intellectual Man" from *Song and Idea* by Richard Eberhardt, copyright © 1942 by Oxford University Press.

Passage reprinted from *Archibald MacLeish: Reflections*, edited by Bernard A. Drabeck and Helen E. Ellis and published by Amherst: University of Massachusetts Press in 1986. Copyright © 1986 by The University of Massachusetts Press. Reprinted by permission of the publisher.

Excerpt of poem by W.H. Auden copyright 1940, 1968 by W. H. Auden. Reprinted by permission of Random House, Inc.

"American Names" by Stephen Vincent Benet first published Holt, Rinehart and Winston, Inc. From *The Selected Works of Stephen Vincent Benet* copyright 1927 by Stephen Vincent Benet, copyright renewed © 1955 by Rosemary Benet. Reprinted by permission of Brandt & Brandt Literary Agents, Inc.

"Blessed is the Man", copyright © 1956 by Marianne Moore, from *The Complete Poems of Marianne Moore* by Marianne Moore. Used by permission of Viking Penguin, a division of Penguin Books USA Inc.

"Guide My Feet" by Marian Wright Edelman copyright © 1995 by Marian Wright Edelman reprinted by permission of Beacon Press, Boston.

"Further Advantages of Learning" by Kenneth Rexroth, from *Collected Shorter Poems*. Copyright © 1949 by Kenneth Rexroth. Reprinted by permission of New Directions Publishing Corp.

Excerpt from "I Am Waiting", *A Coney Island of the Mind* by Lawrence Ferlinghetti, copyright © 1958 by Lawrence Ferlinghetti. Reprinted by permission of New Directions Publishing Corp.

Excerpts from *The Glory and the Dream* by William Manchester. Copyright © 1973, 1974 by William Manchester, reprinted by permission of Little, Brown and Company.

Excerpt from *Blue Highways* by William Least Heat Moon copyright © 1982 by William Least Heat Moon. By permission of Little, Brown and Company.

Excerpt from *Bronx Primitive* by Kate Simon copyright © 1982 by Kate Simon. Used by permission of Viking Penguin, a division of Penguin Books USA Inc.

Excerpt from "The Fountain" by Eugene O'Neill from *The Complete Plays of Eugene O'Neill Volume II: 1920–1931* copyright © 1988 by The Library of America. Reprinted by arrangement with Random House Inc.

Excerpt from *The American Political Tradition* by Richard Hofstadter copyright © 1948 by Alfred A. Knopf Inc., reprinted with permission of the publisher.

Excerpts from *You Learn By Living* by Eleanor Roosevelt published by Westminster, John Knox Press in 1983 reprinted by permission of the publisher.

"So Long Woody, It's Been Good to Know You" (pages vii–ix) from *Bound for Glory* by Woody Guthrie copyright © 1943 by E.P. Dutton, renewed 1971 © by Marjorie M. Guthrie. Used by permission of Dutton Signet, a division of Penguin Books USA Inc.

"American Tolerance", commencement speech given at Northwestern University 1937 by William Allen White, reprinted with permission of Barbara White Walker.

"Obituary: Barbara Jordan Lawmaker of Resonant Voice by Francis X. Clines and "Flag Day" June 14, 1940 Editorial copyright © 1940,96 by The New York Times Co. Reprinted by permission.

"The Girl Scout Law" used by permission of Girl Scouts of the United States of America.

"If Grant Had Been Drinking at Appomattox" copyright © 1935 James Thurber. Copyright © 1963 Rosemary A. Thurber. Reprinted by permission.

"The Night the Bed Fell" by James Thurber copyright © 1933 James Thurber. Copyright © 1961 Rosemary A. Thurber. Reprinted by permission.

Excerpt from *A Prayer for Owen Meany* by John Irving copyright © 1989 by Garp Enterprises, Ltd. Reprinted by permission of William Morrow & Company, Inc.

"Pretty Boy Floyd", by Woody Guthrie copyright © 1958 (renewed) by Fall River Music Inc. All rights reserved. Used by permission.

Quote from *Dismantling the Cold War Economy* by Ann Markusen and Joel Yudkin copyright © 1993 by Ann Markusen and Joel Yudken. Reprinted by permission of Harper-Collins Publishers, Inc.

Quote from *To Kill a Mockingbird* by Harper Lee copyright © 1960 by Harper Lee, copyright © renewed in 1988 by Harper Lee. Reprinted by permission of HarperCollins Publishers, Inc.

INDEX